SPECULUM VITAE: A READING EDITION

EARLY ENGLISH TEXT SOCIETY
No. 332
2008

And es hayde and calde als þe stane
Ryght swa þe þat hase tane
þe state þat es relygyouse calde
þat are in þe lufe of god fulle calde
And hayde aye with outen pite
And deuocyoune þat felle to be
Tharefore þai hafe noght of perfeccioune
Bot þe habyte of relygyoune
þe false ymage als clerkes expounes ryte
And als es fundene in haly write
þir takens write and significacioune
þat mene sulde hafe in perfeccioune
Fore als þe false sauoure synnes
vnto þe mete þat mene with lynnes
And in his sauoure þe mete may sane
Ryght so a manne sulde his þowne hafe
And significacioune als telles vs clerkes
In his wordes and in his werkes
þis false ymage þurghe ryght schewyng
Sulde gyue write and vnderstandyng
And ryght ensaumple als þe boke telles
To mene þat in relygyoune duelles
þat has lefte þe wele haly
Fore þe lufe of gode alle myghty
þat þai noght turne to þat agayne
þat þai hafe lefte als vanytayne
And þarefore gode says in þe gospelle
To his dyscypulls als I zow telle

SPECULUM VITAE:
A READING EDITION

EDITED BY

RALPH HANNA
using materials assembled by Venetia Somerset

VOLUME II

Published for
THE EARLY ENGLISH TEXT SOCIETY
by the
OXFORD UNIVERSITY PRESS

OXFORD

UNIVERSITY PRESS

Great Clarendon Street, Oxford OX2 6DP
United Kingdom

Oxford University Press is a department of the University of Oxford.
It furthers the University's objective of excellence in research, scholarship,
and education by publishing worldwide. Oxford is a registered trade mark of
Oxford University Press in the UK and in certain other countries

Published in the United States of America by Oxford University Press
198 Madison Avenue, New York, NY 10016, United States of America

British Library Cataloguing in Publication Data
Data available

Library of Congress Cataloging in Publication Data
Data available

Original Series, 332

Set ISBN 978-0-19-956401-9

Vol. 1 ISBN 978-0-19-956399-9
Vol. 2 ISBN 978-0-19-956400-2

CONTENTS OF VOLUME II

SPECULUM VITAE
lines 9063–16097

De Misericordia   Donum Intellectus
De Luxuria

fol. 55rb In his kyngdome þar he es kynge,
To whilk Mercy + sal þam brynge.
Thurgh þis vertu men comes lightly   9065
To þe blissedhede of Mercy
And to þe grete mede to haue
þat es Mercy, als Godde vouches saue.
Als Godde sayde, þat alle thing stables,

Beati misericordes etc. 'Blissed er þe mercyables,   9070
For þai sal noght of Mercy faylle'
At þe last for þair trauaylle.
Now may men se þat tentes þarto
What þe Gift of Counsaylle may do

Fiat voluntas tua etc. þat þe thridde askyng wynne vs may   9075
In þe Pater Noster þat we say.
þat gift mas men bouxsom and balde
To do Mercy, als I haf talde,
And þe synne of Auaryce to fle;
Godde graunt þat gift in our hertes to be.   9080
Amen

De dono Intellectus

After þe Gift of Counsaylle falles
Anothir gift þat clerkes calles
þe gastly Gift of Vndirstandyng
þat we wynne thurgh þe secund askyng

Adueniat regnum tuum Of þe principalle askynges seuen   9085
þat we in þe Pater Noster neuen.
þat gift out puttes, þar it wil wirk,
Alle þat mase þe hert myrke.
Right als þe sunne puttes away

9063 þar] whare L   9064 To] To þe L   whilk] swylk R   *sal] `he´ (*later*) sal AL
þam] men W   9065 þis] his W   9066 To] Vnto LR   9067 And to] Vnto L,
And W   9068 als] þat L   9069 sayde] says R   9070 er] be E   *sidenote: om.*
LSW   etc.] *om.* E   9071 þai] 3e L   9072 þe] *om.* L   last] *adds* day S   þair]
youre L   9075 vs] we W   *sidenote: om.* W   tua etc.] *om.* P   etc.] *om.* E, sicut in ⟨celis⟩
LS   9076 þat] whare L   9079 fle] fele (*partly erased*) P   9080 þat] vs þat P
9080a *om.* LSR   9080b *om.* L   De dono] Donum P   intellectus] *adds* Amen W
9081 þe] þat S   counsaylle] *adds* þat S   9085 *sidenote: om.* LW   tuum] *om.* P

þe myrkenes þat lettes þe day   9090
And þe mystes of þe mornynge,
So dose þe Gift of Vnderstandynge.
  It lightens þe hert so of a man
þat he may se appertly þan
Allekyns thynge þat es withinne   9095
And al þe filthe of his synne.
And alle þat es bynethen him lawe
Als in helle, he may it knawe,
And al þat es oboun hym heghe
Als in heuen, thurgh gastly eghe;   9100
And al þat es obout hym here,
Als Goddis awen creatures sere,
Al may he se and knawe wele

Donum Intellectus   De Luxuria
Adueniat regnum tuum

þat þis gift in hert may fele.   fol. 55va
So may it brynge a man bi skille   9105
Til a grete yhernynge and a wille
Godde almyghty for to se
And euermare with hym to be.
þan puttes he out of hym sone
Al þe synne þat he has done   9110
Thurgh Shrift of Mouth and Penaunce smert
And of alle synne clenses þe hert,
So þat he may Godde gastly se,
And wone with Godde, and with him be.
  þis gift puttes out of þe hert namely   9115
Thurgh myght þe synne of Licchery
And in þat stede, als falles to be,
Settes þe vertu of Chastyte.

De peccato Luxurie

  Litchery es an outrageus luf   *De Luxuria*

9090 þe²] *om.* W   9092 gift] gyftes L   9093 so] *om.* P   9094 he] it L
9096 filthe] fylthes E   9097-8 *couplet trs.* W   9098 it] *om.* W   9099 al] þat W
9103 and] *adds* he L   9104 may] *adds* knawe and E   9106 grete] *om.* L   a²] a good
L, *om.* W   9109 he] itt ELS   9112 And] þat E   of] *om.* L   synne] synnes LW
9115 namely] anely P   9117 þat stede] stede of it R   9118a *om.* ESL, *marg.* De
luxuria PW   9119 outrageus] outerage LS   *sidenote: om.* ELW, Luxuria S

In flesshely lykyng, als clerkes can proue,   9120
In whilk þe fende can a man lede
Thurgh four thynges vnto þe dede.
A thinge es fole sight of eghe;
Anothir es speche of wordes sleghe;
þe thridde es fole touchyng with hande;   9125
þe ferthe es kyssyng neste folwand.
And sone þe litcherous dede folwes þan
To whilk þe fende þus ledes a man.

Sicut piscis in aqua capitur For right als þe fisshe with þe hoke
hamo sic homo capitur May be sone tane, als proues þe boke,   9130
tempore malo So may a man be tane bi skille
In ille tyme thurgh litcherous wille.

⟨*E*⟩*xemplum de* ⟨*pi*⟩*scatore* Als þe fissher þat þe fisshe wil wayte
Couers his hoke first with þe bayte
And when þe fisshe þe bayt may se,   9135
At þat mete fayne wald he be.
þe fisshe drawes nere and bi it houes
And of þat bayt first bytes and proues,
And sethen he swelwes it at þe last;
þan es [he] tane with þe hoke fast.   9140
Right so þe fende latches a man
Thurgh sleghtes and wyles þat he can.
First he shewes a thinge of likynge
Thurgh whilk comes a fole bihaldyng;
And of þat bihaldyng specially   9145
Comes a fole speche of litchery;

Donum Intellectus   De Luxuria
Adueniat regnum tuum

fol. 55ᵛᵇ And of þat speche, als I vnderstande,
Comes a fole handelynge of hande;
And of þat handelyng comes alswa

9121 In] In þe P   9123 fole] fuyle E, foule LSR, fele P, foly W   9124 wordes]
mouthe E   9125 fole] foule LSR, foly R   9129 sidenote: om. W   homo] add in EL
malo] non suo P   9130 proues] says ES   9132 In] In ane L   thurgh] adds a L
litcherous] licherours P   9133 sidenote: Nota bene E, Exemplum S, om. LW
9134 Couers] And couers E   hoke] hokes L   þe] his P   9136 þat] þe ELPSR   mete]
bayte L   he] om. S   9138 þat] þe PR   9139 he ... it] it swaloes E   *9140 he] it
AP   9141 latches] lattes E, hintes L, latthes S   9144 whilk] adds þare L   fole] foly
E, om. L, foule SR   9146 fole] foly EP, foule LSRW   speche] spece E   9147 þat]
om. S, þe W   9148 fole] foly P, foule LSRW   of] with LS

A fole kyssynge bitwene twa. 9150
And after þat kyssyng comes tyte
A flesshely dede of fole delyte.
þus can þe fende a man lede
Al sleghely vnto a litcherous dede.
  Bot we suld fra his sleght kepe vs, 9155 *Dauid*
Als kennes þe prophete þat says þus,
'Turne þine eghe away', says he, *Auerte oculos tuos ne*
'þat it bihalde na vanyte'. *videant vanitatem*
þarefore he þat wil na foly do,
Bihalde noght þat þat es lyke þarto, 9160
Forwhy þe eghe þat wysses þe body
Es þe first messangere of foly.
  Litchery, als þe boke says,
Departes itself in twa ways,
And bathe þa ways may Litchery be, 9165
Als þis clerkes in boke can se.
Ane es Litchery of Hert thurgh thoght;
Anothir es Litchery of Body wroght.
  Litchery of Hert þat es vnclene *Luxuria Cordis*
Has four degrees, als I wene. 9170
Ane es Thoght; anothir es Delyte
þat may falle in þe hert tyte;
þe thridde es Consentyng of Skille;
þe ferthe es Yhernyng to do þat ille.
  For þe wicked gast þat ay es bisy 9175
To kyndell þe fyre of Litchery
Withinne þe hert, whareso he may
Entre thurgh sleght by any way.
  A fole Thoght first he puttes þarinne,
And þat es noght yhete bot venyele synne. 9180

9150 fole] foule LSW, fele R   9152 fole] foly E, foule LSRW   9154 vnto a] to P
9155 suld] sall L   his] þis L   sleght] sleghtes R   *sidenote*: *om*. ELPSW   9156 kennes
. . . prophete] *trs. phrs.* W   þat says þus] vs W   9157 says] saide P   9158 it] þai L
9160 þat²] *om*. L   lyke] skyll R   9161 Forwhy] Forþi L   9164 Departes]
Carpes W   9165 þa] þe W   may . . . be] als clerkes can se P   9166 May þe dede of
lichery be P   boke] bokes LS   9167 thurgh] *om*. R   9169 *sidenote*: *om*. W, *add*
habet iiij^{or}. gradus ES   9170 als] sere as R   9171 delyte] delitite P   9172 falle]
spryng L   þe] *om*. W   tyte] full tite L   9173 skille] will P   9174 ille] will R
9175 þat ay es] 'es' ay P   9177 -so] *om*. RW   9179 fole] foule LSRW   first] *om*. L
þar-] *om*. P   *sidenote*: Primus gradus ES   9180 þat es noght] noght es þat S   yhete]
om. L   bot] bot a P

Bot when he has done it think on ille,
He dose it dwelle in þat thoght stille;
And of þat thoght men may fele tyte
þe secund degre—þat es Delyte—
And þat may be dedely synne,   9185
If a man dwelle lange þareinne.
þe thridde degre comes of fole wille
þat es Consentynge of Skille.
þat es when Skille consentes to Litchery,
And þat Consentynge es synne dedely.   9190

De Luxuria

^{fol. 56ra} þe ferthe degre after Consentynge,
þat es to say a brynnand Yhernyng
þat a man has til a litcherous dede,
Es dedely synne þat men suld drede.
Al-if he faylle of þat dede of Litchery,   9195
þe grete Yhernyng es synne dedely.
And thurgh swilk Yhernyng many men may
Synne dedely oftsythes on a day,
Parauenture neghen sithes or ten,
Thurgh þe sight of som wymmen,   9200
Ladys or othir quayntely dight,
þat dightes þam quayntely to mens sight.
Swilk quaynt tyffyng þai oft vse
To do þe foles opon þam muse.
And yhete þai wene þai do noght ille,   9205
For þai assent noght to swilk foles wille.
Bot certes ful greefly synne þai,
Als men may here wyse clerkes say,

9181 it] to ES, om. LR   think] he (int. P) thinkes LP   9182 it] om. R   9184 þat
es] of þat W   sidenote: Secundus gradus ES   9186 If] If þat R   lange] om. L
9187 fole] foly P, foule LSRW   sidenote: Tercius gradus ES   9189 skille] wyll L
9191 sidenote: Quartus gradus ES   9192 brynnand yhernyng] b`r´ynande ȝeryng P
9194 men] a man LS   9195 Al-] And L   9196 þe] A R   9197 swilk] skille E,
om. L   yhernyng many] syn P   9198 -sythes] om. W   a] þe LPS
9199 Parauenture] adds in þe nyght L   9200 þe] om. P   9201 quayntely]
whytely R   9203 tyffyng] atyre L, dightyng P, tyssyng R   þai oft] þat case of E, þat þai
oft LS, trs. P, er oft R   vse] vsed R   9204 do þe] gerre LS, gare þer R   þe] om. EW
opon] on PW   9205 noght] none S   9206 swilk] om. L   foles] foule LSR   wille]
skyll L   9207 greefly] greuosly ELSRW, gretly P   9208 wyse] grete ELS   clerkes]
men R

For thurgh þe enchesoun of þam þan
þe saulles er lorne of many a man   9210
þat yhernes to synne flesshely thurgh sight
With þam þat er so quayntely dight.
For þe womman þat dightes hir quayntely,
Outhir on heued or on body,
To make men oft hir bihalde   9215
þe fendes snare sho may be called;
Many a man in þat snare-bande
Es tane and broght to þe fendes hand.
   And Salamon spekes and says yhete mare   *Salamon*
þat ilk lym of hir es þe fendes snare.   9220
Wharefore at þe last day of dome,
When alle men sal bifor Cryst com,
In grete drede sal sho answer þan
And resoun yhelde of ilka man
Of wham þe saul dampned es   9225
Thurgh hir dightyng and hir gaynesse.
Al-if sho seme of gode condicioun,
If swilk be hire entencioun
þat men þat bihelde hir heued and body
Had yhernynge with hir to foly,   9230
Sho sal noght be excused bi resoun
þat sho ne es of þaire syne enchesoun.

De Luxuria

   Litchery of Body on som wyse   fol. 56rb
Departes it oft in sere partyse,   *Luxuria Corporis*
Als in Litchery of eghen lokande,   9235
Of eres, of mouth, and of hande,
And of alle þe wittes of þe body,
And specially in vilayne Litchery.
To whilk synne may falle alle thinge
þat stirs þe flesshe to haue lykynge,   9240

9209 þe] *om.* ELS   9210 lorne] loste LS   a] *om.* P   9211 sight] soght W
9214 Outhir] *om.* L   heued] hedys R   on²] aboute hyr L   9215 oft] on E, or L   oft
hir] *trs.* S   hir] hyre to R   9217 a] *om.* P   9224 of] for P   9226 dightyng] atyre
ELS   9227 condicioun] deuocioun R   9232 ne] *om.* LS   es] was R   9233 on]
of R   *sidenote: om.* L, *add* habet xiiij^cem. ramos ES   9234 partyse] wise P   9235 of]
in ELS   eghen] eghe W   9236 of²] *om.* R   9237 þe¹] *om.* E   9238 in] es in P
vilayne] *adds* of E, vilayns LS, velany (*later over eras.*) PW   9239 falle] felle L

Als fayre robes þat men yhernes oft
And beddyng þat es fayre and soft
And in alle maner delices of body
Ouer mesure—al þat es Litchery.

xiiij. rami Luxurie Corporis Litchery of Body, als men may here,   9245
It shewes in fourtene braunches sere
After þe state es mare and lesse
Of þam þat dose swilk writchednes.
þa braunches springes and waxes vpward
Fra wicke to wers; þat þe saul feles hard.   9250

j[ᵘˢ]. ramus Luxurie: inter solutum et solutam þe first es þe dede, als I shewe can,
Bytwene sengle man and womman
þat er noght bunden bi lawe to bowe
Thurgh bande of maryage ne of vowe
Ne of order ne of professioun   9255
Ne of na state of religyoun.
þis flesshely dede es synne dedely;
þat es þe first braunche of Litchery.

ij[ᵘˢ]. ramus Luxurie: inter solutum et comunem meretricem þe secund braunche may þe dede be
Bitwene a sengle man þat es fre   9260
And a common womman of bordell
þat bedes hir body oft to selle.
þis es a synne þat es mare greef
And to þe fende of helle mare leef,
For þis 'es' halden mare vyle   9265
And mare it may þe saul fyle.
Forwhy swilk wymmen of lyf vnclene
Parchaunce er wedded, als oft es sene,
Or er wymmen of relygioun
þat has forsaken þair professyoun   9270
And soiournes in gode touns namely.
þar þai vse þe craft of bordelry

9243 maner] adds of L   delices] delite P, delites W   9245 sidenote: om. ESLW   rami] sunt rami P   9246 braunches] degrese RW   9248 þam] whame R   writchednes] wyckednesse LP   9249 þa degrese lyg euene to helleward R   9251 þe] om. L, altered from hye later P   sidenote: om. LW   *jᵘˢ.] j. A   luxurie] om. EP, luxuria S   solutum . . . solutam] trs. E   9254 Thurgh] To W   ne] and P   of²] om. L, of a- R   9256 na] om. L   9259 braunche] adds of lychery E, degre RW   dede] adds of lychery P   sidenote: om. LR, ij. W   *ijᵘˢ.] ij. A   luxurie] est EPS   comunem] om. ES   9260 þat es fre] thynk me R   9264 helle] adds es L   9265 þis] it R   es] int. later A   9269 er] om. L   9271 soiournes] sogenours R   in] in þe P   touns] toune P   9272 vse] haunt L   þe] om. LS   craft] craftes L   of] or EL   bordelry] borderly R

And forsakes nane of al a kyn
þat has wille with þam to synne—
Fader ne sone ne cosyne ne brothir.   9275
þis synne es mare greef þan þe tothir.

Donum Intellectus   De Luxuria
Adueniat regnum tuum

þe thridde es þe dede, als I trowe,   *fol. 56va*
Bytwene a man and a wydow   *iij[^us]. ramus Luxurie:*
                                      inter solutum et viduam
þat has avowed chastyte;   *que vouit castitatem*
A mare greef synne yhete may þis be.   9280
þe ferthe þe dede es, als I wene,   *iiij. Luxuria inter solutum*
Bitwene a man and a mayden clene.   *et virginem*
For to þe state of Maydenhede
þat clene es keped falles mast mede.
þarefore whaso fyles þat state   9285
Synnes greefly, als clerkes wele wate.
þe fift braunche es mykell to drede   *v. Luxuria inter solutum et*
Of Litchery; þat es þe dede   *coniugatam vel e contrario*
Bitwene a man of vnclene lyf
And anothir mans wedded wyf;   9290
Whethir þe man be wedded or noght,
Auoutry es bitwene þam wroght.
And þat es halden a ful greef synne
þat shendes þam þat lifs þarinne.
For wedded man `or´ wyf namely   9295
þat brekes sposaylle on outhir party,
He synnes greefly bi twa ways,
Als þe boke appertly says.
   Ane es Brekyng of þe Fayth so fre   *Per fidei viol⟨ac⟩ionem*
þat falles thurgh law of mariage be   9300

9274 to] *om.* S   9275 ne¹ . . . cosyne] *trs. phrs.* E   ne²] *om.* LP   9277 es þe dede]
es L, dede is P   *sidenote: om.* LW *iij^us.*] iij. A   luxurie] est ES, luxurie est P   9278 a¹]
a syngle R   a²] *om.* PR   9279 chastyte] chasty P   9280 A] And R   greef] grefus EL,
gret P   9281 es] *after* ferthe PR   *sidenote: om.* LW   iiij.] iiij^us. EPS   Luxuria] ramus
est E, est P, ramus S   9285 þare-] Whare- S   whaso] who P   fyles] feyles W
9286 greefly] greuosly ELSRW, gretly P   wele] *om.* LPW   9287 þe] *om.* E   braunche]
degre RW   *sidenote: om.* LW   v.] v^us. EPS   Luxuria] ramus ES, est P   solutum]
hominem s. S   coniugatam] feminam c. S   vel e contrario] *om.* EPS   9289 a] *om.* L
9293 greef] grete ELR, greuews SW   9294 þat] And S   lifs] lygges ELS   9295 or]
of expunged, `or´ *(later)* A   9297 greefly] greuosly ELW, gretly PS   9299 es] es of þe L
þe] *om.* PW   so] -es R, *om.* W   *sidenote: om.* W   9300 be] `to´ be W

Bitwene a man and a wyf thurgh luf
þat þe tane suld kepe to þe tothir bihoue.

Sacrilegium Anothir es Sacrilege to wirke
Agayne þe sacrament of Halykirke
And agayne þe athe of maryage   9305
þat oft es broken thurgh outrage.
By þise twa wayes men synnes greefly
In þe synne of avoutry,
Thurgh whilk synne þat oft es done
Many perilles may falle ful sone.   9310
  For thurgh þat synne, als I vndirstande,
Er made many fals ayres of lande
And þarewith many fole maryage
And right ayre putted fra þe herytage.
Also thurgh þe fendes combraunce,   9315
þat synne a man brynges to myschaunce:
His body to be confounden or slayne,
And his saul dampned to helle-payne.

Luxuria inter vxoratum et   Yhete þis synne þat I last talde
mulierem coniugatam   Es somtyme turned twyfalde   9320
Bitwen a man þat has a wyf

Donum Intellectus   De Luxuria
Adueniat regnum tuum

fol. 56vb And a wedded woman of fole lyf
þat has also anothir husbande.
þan es þis synne wele mare weghand,
For it es þan double auoutry: 9325
þat tittest fordose saul and body.

vj. Luxuria inordinata   þe sext braunche of Litchery es ille;
inter coniugatum et   þat es when a man thurgh fole wille
vxorem suam propriam With his awen wyf a dede wil wirke

9301 a²] his W   9302 to] *int.* P, *om.* W   9303 *sidenote: om.* W, Per sacrilegium ELPS   9307 By . . . wayes] þir twa L   greefly] greuosly EL, gretly P 9309–19 *lines om.* W   9309 oft es] *trs.* P   9310 ful] *om.* LPSR   9313 fole] foly EP   9314 putted] putte ELSR   9315 combraunce] encom- EPSR 9316 brynges] *after* synne ELPS   9319 last] of L   *sidenote: om.* LW   Luxuria] *om.* ES mulierem] *om.* E   9321 a wyf] *om.* S   9322 fole] foly E, foule W   9323 has] *om.* E   9324 þis] þe W   9325 þan] *adds* a P   9327 braunche] degre RW   es] *om.* P   *sidenote om.* LW   Luxuria inordinata] ramus E, *om.* S   9328 fole] foly P, foule LSW   wille] skill L

þat es forboden thurgh Halykirke   9330
Or vnkyndely dose any outrage
Agayne þe order of maryage.
A ful greef synne þan dose he
Thurgh whilk he may dampned be.
For als a man þat hates his lyf   9335 *Exemplum*
May sla himself with his awen knyf,
Right so a man thurgh lust of body
With his awen wyf may synne dedely.
þarefore men suld do nane outrage
Bot folwe þe order of maryage,   9340
And fare noght als a beste thurgh wille
þat knawes nouthir wytte ne skille.
Wharefore a man þat wedded es
Suld kepe hym ay in clennes
And na dede vnordaynely wirke   9345
Agayne þe sacrament of Halykirke
þat þis clerkes Matrimoyne calles,
Bot þat þat to þat order falles.
For in Matrimoyne swilk vertu es
And swilk myght and halynesse   9350
þat kepes a flesshely werk right wroght
Fra dedely synne þat it greue noght.
þe seuend braunche to vndirstande
Es a synne þat es ful chargeande.
þat es a dede on þis manere,   9355
Bitwene a man and his comere
Or bitwene his awen sone fre
Or his doghter, whethir it be,
And þe childer of þam þat þam houe.
þis es a ful greef synne to proue,   9360

vij. Luxuria inter hominem
et mulierem que filium
suum de sacro fonte leuauit
vel e contrario, siue inter
filium eiusdem hominis et
filiam mulieris vel e
contrario congnatis per
ba⟨p⟩tismum

9333 ful] *om.* R   greef] grefus ELR   9335 als] *om.* S   *sidenote: om.* LSW
9336 his awen] hys L, a P   9337 lust] luf RW   9339 suld] sall L   9340 Bot
folwe] Agayns L   *adds couplet* A full greuous synne dose he | þurgh whylk he may
dampned be L   9342 knawes] *adds* noght L   9345 vnordaynely] vndernnely L
9348 þat³] þe RW   9350 and²] and swylk L   9351 þat] þat it LR   werk] dede EL
9352 greue noght] grewys oft R   9353 braunche] degre RW   to] es to L   *sidenote: om.*
LW   vij.] vijᵘˢ. EPS   Luxuria] ramus nota E, ramus S   inter . . . mulierem] *om.* S   vel e
contrarioꜞ] *om.* E, et e. c. P   velꜞ . . . baptismum] *om.* S   vel e contrario²] *om.* E
9354 Es] þat es L   ful] *om.* L, foule W   9355 *line after* 9357 P   a] a synne L
9356 comere] cometre L, commodere R, compere W   9358 it] þat it L   9359 þam]
þai L   houe] haf R   9360 þis] þat P   ful] foule W   ful greef] grete LR

For ilkane of þam er sibbe til othir
Gastly, als sister and brothir.
   þarefore Halykirke has forbedde
þat any of þam othir wedde,
And if þai did, þai did grete synne,   9365
Bot Halykirke bihoued þam twynne.
Swilk sibred thurgh baptym falles

De Luxuria

fol. 57ʳᵃ þat men gastly sibred calles.
Eodem modo inter cognatos þe same sibred es to vndirstande
per confirmacionem Thurgh confermynge of bisshop hande.   9370
viij. Luxuria inter þe aghned braunche, to shew yhou sone,
hominem et consanguineam Es flesshely dede þat may be done
suam Bytwene ane ille man or a gode
And his sibbe-womman of blode.
þat dede men haldes a grete synne,   9375
For þai er bathe of a kynne;
And þat synne may be mare and lesse
Aftir þat þe sibbered es.
ix. Luxuria inter hominem þe neghent braunche a dede may be
vxoratum et consanguineam In þe sibbered of affinyte,   9380
uxoris sue uel e contrario Bitwene a man of wantoun lyf
And a womman þat es sibbe his wyf
Or bitwene a wyf of fole semblande
And a man þat sibbe es hir husbande.
   þis synne es greef and perillous,   9385
Als þe boke openly shewes vs.
For when a man thurgh lust of body
Has knawen a womman flesshely,
þe lawe þan has him forbedde
Any of hir cosynes to wedde   9390

9362 and] or LS   9365 did¹'²] do S   9366 Bot] For S bihoued] behoues LS, bihoued *with* d *later* P   9368 sibred] sibrybe R *sidenote: om.* LW   9369 sibred] reden L, sibrybe R   9371 braunche] degre RW yhou] *om.* L *sidenote: om.* LP, viij. W viij. Luxuria] *om.* E, viijᵘˢ. ramus S   9373 or] and EL   9376 For] Forwhy R 9377 be] be bathe E   9378 þat] *repeats* P   9379 braunche] degre RW a dede] *om.* L *sidenote: om.* L, ixᵘˢ. ramus S, ix. W ix.] ixᵘˢ. ramus EP vxoratum] coniugatum EP vel] et E   9383 fole] foule LW   9384 sibbe es] *trs.* LPR   9385 greef] greuose E, grete LS, gres? P   9386 shewes] sais P   9387 lust] luf R   9389 þan] *after* him P has him] *trs.* ES

þat hir es sibbe, if sho be
Sibbe withinne þe fift degre.
For þe sibbered þat es tane
In þe fift degre es halden als nane,
Bot þe sibbered, als þe lawe settes,   9395
Withinne þat degre sposaylle lettes.
For in þe ferthe degre and withinne
Men may noght wedde withouten synne,
Na in þat sibbered may na bande
Of matrimoyne thurgh þe law stande.   9400
For þe band of sposayll may noght hald,
Bot it be done als þe lawe walde.

    And if a man a womman wedde
To be his fere at borde and bedde,
And he þareaftir knawe in synne   9405
Thurgh flesshely dede hir cosynne,
þan tynes he for al his lyf
þe right þat he has of his wyf,
þat he ne may noght thurgh þe lawe
His awen wyf withouten syn knawe   9410
By way of dette his wil to haue.

De Luxuria

Bot when sho wille hir dette craue,   fol. 57rb
þan bihoues him hir dette fulfille
With dole of hert, als þe lawe wille.

    þe tende braunche es a flesshely werke   9415 *x. Luxuria inter hominem*
Bytwene a womman and a clerke   *infra sacros ordines*
þat þe haly order beres;   *constitutum et mulierem*
þat synne þe saul ful gretly deres.
Bot þat synne may be mare and lesse
After þe degre [of] þe order es,   9420
For deken has lesse degre þan preste
And subdeken lesse þan deken þat es neste.

    9391 hir es] *trs.* P   if] and if P, if þat R   9393 For] Forwhy R   9396 Withinne]
With W   þat] þe P   9397 For] And L and] or P   9400 þe] *om.* LS   9402 Bot] Bot
if L   9403 a²] and a L womman] *adds* be L   9404 fere] felaughe L   9405 he] if he
L, *om.* P   9406 hir] his R   9408 has] had W of] tyll L   9409 þat] And S
9410 withouten] þurgh L   9411 to] wyll L   9412 when sho] *trs.* E   9414 dole]
sorowe ELS   9415 braunche] degre RW *sidenote: om.* L, x. W x.] x. ramus E, *om.* SP
9419 and] or LS   *9420 of] and AELS, þat 'of' P   9422 þan deken] *om.* P

*xj. Luxuria inter hominem
secularem et religiosam vel
e contrario*

þe elleuent braunche, als I haf soght,
Es flesshely dede þat es wroght
Bytwene a seculere mans persoun   9425
And a womman of religyoun
Or bitwene a man of religyous lyf
And a seculere womman, wenche or wyf.
þis synne mast deres in ilka stede
For þe tane onence þe werlde es dede.   9430

*xij. Luxuria inter
religiosum et religiosam vel
e contrario*

þe twelft braunche neste folwand
Es a flesshely dede to vndirstand
Bitwene a man and a womman
þat religious state bathe has tane.
þis synne es greef, als þe boke says,   9435
And to þe fende of helle mast pays.
For þai er als dede fra þe werld namely
And lyf to serue to Godde almyghty.

*xiij. Luxuria inter
prelatum et mulierem*

þe thryttened braunche men may calle
A flesshely dede þat oft may falle   9440
Bytwene a womman and a prelate
þat beres dignyte and grete state.
þat synne es mare þan othir thre
Thurgh þe heghe state and + dignyte,
For he es ensaumplere to othir men   9445
þat he es halden to chasty and kenne.

*xiiij. Lux(ur)ia contra
naturam que dicitur vicium
sodomiticum*

þe fourtened braunche, als falles in mynde,
Es a foul synne, mast agayne kynde,
þe whilk es ful wlatsom to neuen,
þat gretly greues Godde of heuen.   9450
For þat synne Godde had vengeaunce tane
When he did rayne fyre and brunstane

9423 braunche] degre RW   *sidenote: om.* L, xj^{us}. ramus S, xj. W   xj.] *int. later* E
Luxuria] *om.* E   vel] et E   *adds* xj. E   9427 religyous] relygion PR   9428 seculere]
syngler E   9429 þis] þe W   mast deres] *trs.* S   9431 braunche] degre RW, *adds and* P
sidenote: om. L, xij. W   xij. Luxuria] xij. ES, Luxuria P   vel] et E   vel e contrario] *om.* PS
9435 es greef] es grevous L, greues W   9436 to] *om.* LW   9437 als] *om.* L   namely]
anely P   9438 to²] *om.* L   9439 braunche] degre RW   *sidenote: om.* L, xiij. W   xiij.
Luxuria] xiij. E, *om.* P, xiij. ramus S   9440 dede] luf R   9442 and] or P   grete] hegh
LS   9443 þan] and LS   9444 þe] *om.* LW   *dignyte] þe dignyte AS
9445 -mplere] -mple PR   to] of L   9447 braunche] degre RW   *sidenote: om.* L, xiiij. W
xiiij.] *om.* P, *adds* ramus S   contra naturam] *om.* ES, *adds at end* et est contra naturam E
9448 Es] Es of E   9449 þe ... ful] Hyt his foule W   wlatsom] lathsom P   9451 had]
has PRW   9452 did] gart it L, made S   and] as R   brun-] broun- S, bryn- RW

Opon Sodom and on Gomor
þat war brent and fordone þarfore.

Donum Intellectus   De Castitate
Adueniat regnum tuum

And fyue cytees, als clerkes can telle,   9455 fol. 57va
For þat synne sank doun til helle.
þarefore men calles it 'syn sodomyk',
For it es to nane othir synne lyke.

  þat synne þe fende teches and leres
To men and wymmen on sere maners,   9460
Bot for it es so foul and wlatsom
þat þe fende think shame to com
Nere þam þat he puttes þarto—
So foul it es when þai it do.
þarefore for som skille wil I noght   9465
Shewe yhou hou þat syn es wroght,
Bot if any man fele him gilty
Of þat synne þat es so vnkyndely,
I rede he shew it in shrift sone
And telle it right als it was done.   9470
For þe shame he has to telle þat chaunce
Es a grete parte of his penaunce.
  Now haf I spoken of Litchery,
Bathe of Hert and of Body,
Of whilk þe Gift of Vnderstandynge   9475
Delyuers þe hert at his comynge,
And in þat stede, als clerkes can se,
Settes þe vertu of Chastyte,
Als yhe haf herde me bifore telle
And may here mare if yhe wil dwelle.   9480
Now wil I speke, als in boke es sene,
Of Chastyte, þat vertu clene.

9453 Opon] *adds* bath R   on] *om.* EPRW, apon L   9454 brent . . . fordone]
stroyede and brynnede P   9455 can] gan R   9457 sodomyk] sodomyrk R
sidenote: Peccatum sodomiticum W   9458 es] es lyke E   synne] *om.* LP
9461 es] *om.* E   9462 fende] fendys in helle R   think] thinkes LP   9463 þam]
om. W   he] þai R   puttes] brynges P   9465 for] *om.* LW   wil I] *trs.* LP
9466 yhou] *om.* L   9468 Of] In L   so] *om.* L   9471 þat] þe LW
9472 parte] partye ELS   9477 þat] *om.* L   clerkes] lerkes S   can] may L
9480 here mare] *trs.* ('mare' *later*) P

De virtute Castitatis

De Castitate   Chastite may be called right
A tree of grete vertu and myght,
þe whilk has seuen degrees sere   9485
And seuen braunches, als yhe sal here.
þe first degree es þis to bygynne:
Clene Conscience of hert withinne.
þe secund degre falles to be couthe,
þat es Honest Speche of mouthe.   9490
þe thridde es Kepyng of þe Wittes Fyue;
þe ferthe es Hardenes of Strayt Lyue;
þe fift es Fleyng of Fole Company

Donum Intellectus   De Castitate
Adueniat regnum tuum

fol. 57vb And þe enchesouns of foly;
þe sext es Gode Occupacioun;   9495
þe seuent es Prayere of deuocioun.

j. gradus: De puritate   First of þis tree of Chastyte
consciencie   þe rote Clen Conscience may be,
For withouten Conscience Clene
Nathinge payse Godde þat may be sene.   9500
For Clene Conscience þar it es soght
Kepes þe hert fra wicked thoght
And fra ille willes and ille yhernynges
þat out of wycked thoghtes springes,
So þat þe hert thurgh na wicked wille   9505
May be assentand vntil ille.
For he þat assentes to ille thoght,
Albeit þat he þe dede do noght,
For þat ille wille þat he es inne,

9482a *om.* ELPSW   9483 called] talde S   *sidenote om.* L   9486 sal] may L
9487 *sidenote:* Primus gradus R (cf. 9497), j. W   9489 falles] aught L   *sidenote:* ij. W
9490 of] with R   9491 kepyng] spekyng W   wittes] witte S   *sidenote:* iij. W
9492 hardenes] hardynes, *with eras.* P   hardenes . . . strayt] straytnes of herde EL
sidenote: iiij. W   9493 fleyng] plesyng W   fole] foule RW   *sidenote:* v. W
9494 -souns] -son LP   of] of grete L   9495 *sidenote:* vj. W   9496 of] wyth LS,
and P   *sidenote:* vij. W   9497 þis] these E, þe W   *sidenote: om.* W   gradus] *adds* est P
9498 rote] *adds* of L   9501 þar] whare L   9504 of] þereof E, of þe L   thoghtes]
thoght LP, tonges R   springes] spryngynge E   9506 vntil] to L   9507 to] vntill S
9508 Albeit þat] All-iff P   þe] *om.* E

He may dampned be als for dedely synne. 9510

   Bot thre thinges, als men may fele,
Kepes Clene Conscience of hert wele:
Ane es Gode Wille oft to here
Goddis worde and sarmouns sere;
Anothir es Shrift and Contricioun; 9515
þe thridde es Mynde of Cristes Passioun.
þise thre thinges, als in boke es sene,
Kepes Conscience of hert clene.
   Gode Wille to here Goddis worde be talde
In alle gode mas a man balde, 9520
And argh and dredefull oght to wirk
þat Godde forbedes and Halykirke.
Forwhy God says þus in þe godspell
Til his discyples, als I yhow telle,
'Yhe er', he says, 'clene made nowe 9525
Thurgh wordes þat I haf shewed yhow.'
Goddis worde of þe mouth of prechour
Es als it war a clere mirour,
In þe whilk men may wele se
þe spottes of þe hert þat er priue. 9530
   þe secund thinge þat clenses þe hert
Es verray Shrift and Penaunce smert;
þat mas Conscience clere and bright,
For Shrift of Mouth may be called right

De Castitate

Als a lavour þat hynges or standes, 9535 fol. 58ʳᵃ
At whilk men wasshes oft þair handes.
   In þe *Boke of Kynges* es wryten þus
þat þe prophete Helyseus

Nota: Tria conseruant conscienciam puram et mundam

j. Voluntas bona audiendi verbum Dei

ij. Confessio vera cum contricione cordis

9510 als] *om.* ELS for] to L 9511 Bot] For S *sidenote: om.* W Nota] *om.* ELSP conseruant] obseruant E, sunt que servant L 9513 gode wille] clene conscience R *sidenote:* j. W 9514 sarmouns sere] servyce clere R 9515 es] *om.* W *sidenote:* ij. W 9516 Cristes] goddes L *sidenote:* iij. W 9517 boke] bokes EL 9518 Kepes] *adds* þe L 9519 *sidenote om.* W 9520 alle] alkyn L 9522 and] in S 9525 he says] all L *sidenote:* j. W 9526 haf] *om.* P shewed] sayde to L 9527 worde] wordes L of²] of þe P 9528 als] at W clere] *om.* P 9530 spottes] spouttes E 9531 *sidenote:* ij. W 9532 and] of R 9533 mas] makes þe L clere] clene S 9534 may] *om.* P 9536 At] At þe P wasshes oft] *trs.* P 9537 es wryten] *trs.* P 9538 þe] þe haly P *sidenote:* Helyseus E, Elyseus and Naaman W

Commanded, als I yhow telle,
Vnto Naaman þat was meselle   9540
þat he suld wende and wasshe ʽhim swytheʼ
In þe flum Iordan seuen sythe
To clense hym of þat malady
þat he hadde on his body.
He wesshe hym, als þe prophete badde,   9545
And when he hym so wasshen hadde,
þan was he made al hale and clene
Of þat euell þat bifore was sene.
        þe flumme Iordan, als I shewe yhou may,
Es here þus mykell for to say   9550
Right als a ryuere of iugement—
Als yhe sal here if yhe gif tent—
And bitokens Shrift, whaso tase yheme.
þare a man suld himself right deme
With grete sorow in hert and thoght   9555
For his synnes þat he has wroght
So þat a ryuere of teres bigynne
And thurgh þe cundite of þe eghen ryn.
And also in þat þat þe prophete hight
þat þe mesell, so foulle in sight,   9560
Suld be hale and clene hym fele,
If he wesshe him seuen sithes wele,
þat es to say of alle synne bidene
With Shrift he suld be wasshen clene.

Bernardus   þarfore says Saynt Bernard þus,   9565
Whase wordes er leryng vntil vs:
'Luf Shrift', he says, 'þat may þe saue,
If þou wil fayred in þe haue;
For verray Shrift may noght be
Withouten clennes and bewte.'   9570

9539 Commanded] Commandes W   9540 *sidenote*: Naaman E   9541 wende]
wynd W   and] *repeated, first use expunged* A   him swythe] *added in intercolumnar space,*
possibly original A   9542 flum] *adds* of R   9547 made] *om.* P   al] bathe E, als P
9548 euell] iwell S, ill R   9550 here] *om.* W   9552 if] and L   9553 tase] con W
9554 þare] Whare W   himself right] *trs.* P   9555 in] of E   9557 a] þere L
9558 þe¹] *om.* W   cundite] condetes P   þe²] *om.* E, his PRW   eghen] egh L
9559 in] *om.* P   þat²] *om.* E   9560 so] *om.* P   9561 be] all P   9562 he] he
hym L   9563 alle] *om.* E, all hys L   synne] synnes LPR   9564 With] Thurghe RW
9565 Bernard] Bernande/Bernaude P   *sidenote om.* L   9566 vntil] to LPSW
9568 fayred] fayrnnes L   9569 may] na may LR

þe thridde thinge es Mynde certayne
Of Crystes Passyoun and his payne.
þat es þe wepen, als clerkes redes,
þat þe fende of helle mast dredes,
Thurgh whilk he was ouercommen sone   9575
And his mast powere here fordone.

De Castitate

And of þat haf we in Haly Wrytte
Ensaumple, whaso wil here itte,
Of þe nedder of brasse wroght
þat Moyses on a rodde broght   9580
Agayne whilk nedders þat þan ware,
þat venymed þe folk and stynged sare.
He helde vp heghe þe nedder of brasse,
Als our Louerd commandment wasse,
þat al þe cuntre myght it se;   9585
þe venemous nedders þan gun fle,
And alle war waryst þat it bihelde
þat styngyng of þe nedders felde.

þe nedder þat was made of brasse
þat on þe rodde hynged was   9590
Bytokens þe blissed body
Of Ihesu Cryst, Godde almyghty,
þat was hinged on þe croyce hey
And for vs vouched saaf to dye.
He was þe neddir withouten venym;   9595
Alle treacle of hele come of hym.
þarefore whaso feles hym biten
Or venymde or with tange smyten
Of þe nedders of helle þat sare stynges,
Als fendes þat smytes men with fondynges,   9600
Bihalde he þan þe nedder of brasse,

iij. Memoria passionis Cristi

fol. 58rb
Exemplum de serpente enneo

9571 *sidenote*: iij. W   iij.] 'Nota' E, *om.* LPS   Cristi] Ihesu Cristi ELS, *om.* P (*perhaps in gutter*)   9577 of . . . we] þarefore haue I L   9578 *sidenote*: *om.* W   Exemplum] *om.* S   9581 whilk] *adds* þe L, quyck R   9582 stynged] stangede ELS   9583 He] Be- L   helde] helpde P   9586 gun] con W   9587 war] þat W   9588 styngyng] stangynge ELS   9589–90 *trs. couplet* R   9589 þe] þat R   9591 þe] þat L, wele þe R   9593 was hinged] *trs.* L   9594 to] for to S   9599 stynges] stanges LSW   9601 Bihalde he] Behaldes L, Behalde S   nedder] neddres W

With verray trouthe how he hynged was.
þat es þat he of þe payne haf mynde
þat Cryst tholed for mankynde,
And als-tyte þe fendes sal fle,   9605
And þan sal he delyuerd be
Of alle fondynges þat he feles byte;
So may he best þe fende skomfyte.

ij[ᵘˢ]. gradus Castitatis: þe secund degree of Chastyte,
De refrenacione oris a   Als þe boke says, falles þis to be: 9610
verbis inhone⟨stis⟩   Kepyng of mouth and tunge withinne
Fra vilayne speche þat kyndels syn.
For swilk manere of wynde namely
Oft stirs þe synne of Litchery.

Wharefore þus says Haly Writte,   9615
Als þis clerkes vnderstandes it,
þat þe worde of a fole womman

Donum Intellectus   De Castitate
Adueniat Regnum Tuum

fol. 58ᵛᵃ   Brynnes als fire, whaso fele can.
Paulus   And Saynt Paul in a boke shewes
þat vilayne speche appayres gode thewes.   9620
And þarefore whaso wil chast be
And þe synne of Litchery fle
And spende his tyme in Goddis worshepe,
Fra vilaynes wordes he suld him kepe.
For he þat wil speke blethely   9625
Wordes þat falles to herlotry
Or any wordes wil blethely here
þat es shewed on vilayne manere,
And in swilk speche þe tyme wil wast,
It semes wele þat he es noght chast.   9630

9602 trouthe] tonge W   9603 he] ȝee L   of] on R   haf] of R   9604 þat] *adds*
Ihesu R   man-] mans L   9606 sal he] ȝe sall L   9607 Of] For W   fondynges]
fandes S   he feles] ȝe fele L   9608 may he] may ȝe L, may `he′ (*later*) P, *trs.* S
9609 *sidenote*: Secundus gradus R, ij. W   *ij*ᵘˢ.] ij. A   9611 mouth . . . tunge] *trs.*
nouns E   9612 vilayne] vilayns LPS, vylany RW   9616 þis] *om.* L   9617 fole]
foule RW   9618 als] als a L   9619 *sidenote om.* W   9620 vilayne] vilayns LPS,
vylany RW   appayres] enpayres PR   thewes] twe thewes L   9621 chast] cast W
9624 vilaynes] vilayne E   9625 speke] here L   9626 herlotry] lichery L (*the original
reading, corr.* P).   9628 vilayne] vylanye EP, vilayns LSRW   9629 swilk] whilk R
speche] spece E   wil] *om.* L   9630 þat] *om.* P

For out of þe tunne may noght rynne
Bot swilk likour als es þareinne.

   For if þe speche be foul þat es spoken,
þan semes it wele appert token
þat in þe hert vilany es   9635
And likyng of swilk wrechednes.
For of þe gaderynge þat es in þe hert   *Ex habundancia cordis os*
þe mouth spekes oft ouerthwert.   *loquitur*

   þe thridde degre of chast lyf   *iij. gradus: De obseruacione*
Es Kepynge of þe Wyttes Fyue,   9640   *quinque sensuum*
Als sight of eghe þat opens and speres,
Smellyng of nese, heryng with eres,
Tastyng of mouth, touchyng of hande.
þise er fyue wyttes to vnderstande
Thurgh whilk our lyf es reweld mast;   9645
þa suld he kepe þat wille be chast.

   First bihoued him with al his myght
Kepe þe eghe fra fole sight
Of thinge þat noght es bot vanyte
þat to his flesshe likand may be.   9650
And þe eres kepe fra fole herynge
Of foule wordes and backebytyng;
þe mouthe fra ille speche and tast
Of mete and drynk þat lykes him mast;
þe neese fra swete sauours to fele   9655
þat þe flesshe lykes oft wele;
þe handes and alle þe lyms of þe body
Fra alle ille touchynges of foly.

   þise er fyue wyttes to kepe right
þat er þe yhates of þe hert dight,   9660

9631 þe] *om.* E   9633 þat es] -gates R   9634 semes] schewes S
9636 wrechednes] vnkyndnes R   9637 þat es in] of P   *sidenote om.* W
9638 spekes oft] *trs.* P   oft] full oft L   9639 of] es L   *sidenote*: Quinque sensus
S, iij. W   iij.] ij. E   9640 Es] þat es L   þe] þi P   9641 of eghe] *om.* S
9642 with] of LPRW   9643 touchyng] felyng W   of²] wyth ES   9644 er] er þe P
9646 þa] þat W   wille] wald R   9647 bihoued] behoues LW   9648 þe . . . fole]
trs. phrs. E   þe] hys L   eghe] eghen LS   fole] folye E, foule RW   9649 noght] *om.*
LPR   9651 fole] folye E, foule LSRW   9652 foule] fole P   9653 fra] for P
9654 mete, drynk] metes, drynkes L   him] *om.* SW   9656 þat] And L   lykes oft] þat
ofte lykes sa L, *trs.* R   9658 touchynges] -yng L   9659 er] er þe LPR
9660 þat] And L   þe¹] *om.* R

Donum Intellectus   De Castitate
Adueniat regnum tuum

fol. 58ᵛᵇ   Thurgh whilk þe fende has entree
Into þe hert þar he wald be.
þise er þe fyue wyndous of þe hous
Thurgh whilk þe dede þat es perillous
Withinne þe hert entren may,   9665
Als men may here þe prophete say.
Forwhy many men has oft bene
Ouercommen and tane, als has bene sene,
Forþi þat þai sperred noght als wyse
þe yhates agayne þair enemys.   9670

Exemplum   And if yhe wille ensaumple se,
I sal shewe yhow twa or thre.
Wha was strongar þan was Sampson?
Wha was wyser þan was Salamon?
Wha was halyar þan Dauid was,   9675
Al-if he didde somtyme trespas?
Yhete war þai alle on sere wyse
Ouercommen thurgh wymmens quayntyse.
Bot certes, had þai keped right
þe yhates of þair hert thurgh myght   9680
And þam agayne þair enemys stoken,
Swa strange haldes had þai noght broken.

Ieronimus   For Saynt Ierom says þat þe tour
Of þe hert þat has gode sokour
May noght be wonnen ne tane lightly,   9685
Nouthir thurgh strengthe ne thurgh mayst⟨ry⟩,
Bot if þe yhates war on som wyse
Opend wyde agayne þe enmyse.
Wharefore I fynde, als I haf redde,
þat þis alde philosofres fledde   9690
Fer into wildernes to dwelle

9661 whilk] þe whylk LW   9663 þe¹] *om.* W   9664 þe] þat E, *om.* L
9665 Withinne] Inwith W   9666 *sidenote*: Propheta L   9668 als] *om.* L
9669 Forþi þat] For L, Forwhy PS, Forwhy þat W   als] als þe LW   9671 wille
ensaumple] *trs.* W   *sidenote om.* W   9672 shewe yhow] *adds* outher L, *trs.* P
9673 was²] *om.* PR   9674 was¹] *om.* EL   was²] *om.* P   9680 hert] hertes EL
9681 þam] *om.* L   9684 gode] *om.* L   9686 thurgh¹] by P   thurgh²] *om.* LSR
9687 on] of L   9688 wyde] *om.* L   þe] hys L

þar nouthir toun was ne castelle.
In swilk wildernes som wald be
Whare þai myght nouthir here na se
Nathynge þat war delytable   9695
þat myght make þair hert vnstable
And turne þam to swilk vanytese,
Wharethurgh þai myght þair chastite lese.

   And som philosophirs, als I fynde,
Fordidde þair sight and made þam blynde,   9700
Forthy þat þai suld nathinge knawe
Ne se þat myght þair hertes withdraw⟨e⟩
Fra þair grete contemplacioun.
Swilk was þair entencioun.

De Castitate

   þe wittes of a man þat es idell   9705   fol. 59ra
Fares als a horse withouten brydell
þat rynnes ay on-heued fast
And castes his mayster at þe last.
Bot þe chaste hert of gode wille
Restreynes þe wittes with þe brydell of skille.   9710

   þe ferthe degre of Chastyte es   *iiij[us]. gradus De*
Hardenes of Lyf and straytenes.   *asperitate vite*
For he þat wille fra Litchery drawe
Suld halde his flesshe vndirfote lawe.
þat es ay rebelle vnto þe saul,   9715
Als þe apostell says, Saynt Paul.
Forwhy he þat wille thurgh maystry
Abate þe fyre of Litchery
Bihoues withdrawe alle thinge away
þat þe fyre oght norisshe may.   9720
þat ere eses and delyces of body
þat kyndels þe fyre of Litchery
And fordose Chastyte of hert

9692 toun was] *trs.* R   ne] þe R   9693 swilk] whilk R   som wald] *trs.* P
9694 na] ny W   9695 delytable] dilectabyll R   9696 hert] hertes LSR
9697 to] vnto L   9699 -phirs] -pher W   9701 nathinge] noȝt P   9702 hertes]
hert W   withdrawe] *runs into gutter* A   9708 þe] *om.* LS   9710 with] þurgh S
9711 *sidenote: om.* L, iiijus. W   *iiijus.] iiij. AP   gradus] *om.* P   9714 Suld] And E
9715 es ay] *trs.* LPR   ay] *om.* W   9716 *sidenote:* Paulus ELS   9719 with-] *om.* E,
int. later P   9720 þe] þat L   oght] *om.* L, oft R   9721 delyces] delittes PW

And elles es noght þe saul in quert.

Bernardus For Bernarde says in a tretyce   9725
þat Chastyte perisshes in delyces.
    And þarefore whaso will haally
Hym kepe fra brynnynge of Litchery,
Hym bihoues withdrawe and abate
Alle thinge þat makes þe fyre brynne hate   9730
And slocken it at þe bigynnynge
Thurgh Abstynence and Harde Lyuynge;
þan sal he noght be brent of itte.
Forwhy we fynde in Haly Wrytte
þat þe childer þat harde war ledde   9735
And with grete metes norisshed and fedde
And na delycious mete wald haue
War in þe fyre of Babiloyne saue.
    By Babiloyne I vnderstande
þe fyre of Litchery brennande   9740
þat may be slekkend with short strif
Thurgh Abstinence and Harde Lyf.
Bot metes of delicious sauour
And stalwarde wynes of fayre colour
Mase Litchery to brynne hate and light,   9745
Als grese dose þe fyre brynne bright.

v. gradus: De euitacione   þe fift degre þat chast men kepes
praue societatis et   Es Fleynge of Fole Felawshepes
occasionum peccati

De Castitate

fol. 59rb And of alle ille enchesounes of synne,
Thurgh whilk Litchery may bigynne.   9750
For many men falles in Litchery
By resoun of fole company;
Elles suld þai noght falle so sare,

9725 For] *adds* saynt L   9726 delyces] delites W   9728 brynnynge] þe synne L
9729 abate] debate S   9730 Alle] A W   þat] brynn þat P   brynne] *om.* LS, ay to
bren W   9731 slocken] slecken W   it] þe fyre P   9732 abstynence] *adds* at þe P
9736 metes] mete P   9737 And] þat P   mete] metes LSR   9739 I] I noght elles S
9740 þe] Bot þe S   9741 slekkend] slockend LPSR   with] thurgh E   9742 harde]
herdnes of R   9744 wynes] wyne L   9745 to] *int. later* P, *om.* R   9746 dose]
garres L   brynne] to brenne ESR, *int. later* P   9747 *sidenote: om.* W   gradus] *adds* est P
occasionum] -em L   9748 fole] foly P, foule RW   9751 men] a man L, mane PSRW
9752 of] and R   fole] ille E, foly P, foule RW

Warne wicked company ware.
For als þe leuayne þat es sour   9755
Drawes therf-daghe to þat sauour,
And als an appill þat roten es
Rotes othir thurgh 'þat' moystnesse,
And als a quicke cole þat fyre es inne
May make an heepe of coles to brenne,   9760
Right so may a fole company
Drawe a man vnto Litchery.

   þarefore þe sauter says þus þarby,   *Dauid Cum sancto sanctus*
'þou sal be haly with þe haly'.   *eris*
þat es to say, if þou wil be   9765
Gode and haly and luf Chastyte,
þou sal gif þe, als I þe kenne,
Vnto þe company of gode men.
For if þou luf or folow wille
Mens company þat er ille   9770
And wil noght leue when þou may,
Als ille saltow be als er þai.

   For he þat lufs þe company
Of foles þat gifs þam to foly,
Hym bihoues nedely be a fole   9775
After þe manere of þair skole.
And þat says þe wyse man in his boke,
Als þis clerkes may fynde and loke.

   Also þe man þat wil chast be
Bihoues þe enchesouns of synne fle,   9780
Als pryue speche of man with womman
In suspecious stede by þam ane.
For þat gifs enchesoun synne to do,
When þai haf tyme and stede þarto.

   9754 ware] ne ware R   9755 *sidenote* (repeated at 9757, 9759): Exemplum (*later*) E
9756 therf-] soure- L   to þat] vnto L   þat] þe P   9757 an] þe L   9758 othir]
vnder L   þat] *int.* (*later?*) A, his ELS   9761 fole] foly P, foule RW   9762 vnto] to
PW   9763 *sidenote*: Dauid] *om.* PS   eris] *adds* etc. P   9764 sal] *om.* W   þe] *om.* L
9765 if] and L   9766 chastyte] chaste R   9768 Vnto] To PW   9769 luf . . .
folow] will folow or lufe P   folow] felaugh be S   9770 Mens] Mans W   9772 er]
om. L   9774 to] vnto L   9775 nedely] nedelyng LS, nede P, nedly to W
9777 his] a P   9778 þis] þe wise LP   clerkes] clerk L   may] cane E   9779 wil
chast] *trs.* LS   9780 þe] *om.* ES   9782 suspecious] suspecyoune ES   suspecious
stede] stedes (stede P) of suspecyon LP   stede] stedes W

Wharefore we rede in þe *Boke of Kynges*   9785
þat accordes to many sayinges
þat + Amon þat was Dauid sone
þat with his awen sister wald wone,
Als þai in chaumbre by þam ane ware,
þai synned togider flesshely þare.   9790
And þe lauedy þat Ioseph fande
In hir chaumbre alane standande,
Wald haf done him with hir synne,

Donum Intellectus   De Castitate
Adueniat regnum tuum

fol. 59ᵛᵃ Bot he wald noght þat foly bigynne.
He agaynesayde hir als þe wyse;   9795
þarefore gun sho hym dispyse.
     Wharefore Saynt Paul biddes vs be boun
To fle ay fornycacioun,
þat es to say þe enchesoun of foly
þat tilles a man vnto Litchery.   9800
Forwhy men may na bettir bigynne
To ouercom þat flesshely synne
Ne to kepe rightly Chastyte
In clennes, als it falles to be,
þan to flee fole companyse   9805
And þe enchesouns of folyse.
     Wharefore þe aungell to Loth come
And badde him wende out of Sodome
And out of alle þe marches about
For þe grete vengeaunce þat was to dout.   9810
By Sodom may we vndirstande
Synne of Litchery þat es likande.
þe marches of Sodom we may calle

9785 -fore] *om.* L   Kynges] kyndes L   *sidenote*: In libro Regum E   9786 many]
my PW   *9787 Amon] Damon A, a man L   9789 in] in a ELP
9792 standande] stande W   9793 done] gert LS   9796 gun] con W
9797 Whare-] þare- E   be] *om.* E   *sidenote*: Paulus ELSW   9798 ay] ay faste LS
9800 tilles] *corr. from* telles (*later*) P, telles S   vnto] to W   9802 þat] *om.* L
9803 rightly] ryghtwysly L (*this word and next app. later* E)   9804 falles] aght L
9805 to] for to R   fole] foly P, foule RW   9806 enchesouns] -soun LW
9807 *sidenote*: Angelus ait ad Loth ELS   9809 marches] markethes W   9810 to
dout] done L   9811 may we] *trs.* PRW   9812 Synne] þe synne LR
9813 marches] markethes W

Enchesouns of synne þat mas men falle.
For it es noght inoghe to kepe   9815
A man fra synne ne fole felawshepe,
Bot he flee alle enchesouns of synne
þat mase a man þe synne to bigynne.

    For men says on alde Inglisshe
A comon worde opon þis wyse: 9820
'Swa lang þe potte to þe water gase
þat at þe last it es broken in case.'
And so lange fleghes þe buttirfleghe
About þe fyre, lawe and heghe,
þat at þe last it falles þarinne,   9825
And þan bihoues it nedely brynne.
Right so a man sekes so lange
þe enchesouns of synne amange
þat at þe last hym bihoues falle
In þat synne and be brent withalle.   9830
þarefore whaso dredes fallyng
And wil kepe him fra swilk brennyng,
He suld fra þat fyre withdrawe him fer
So þat þe fyre may him noght dere.

Donum Intellectus   De Castitate
Adueniat regnum tuum

    þe sext degre, als says þis clerkes,   9835 fol. 59vb
Es Occupacioun of Gode Werkes.   *vj[^{us}]. gradus: De*
For þe fende of helle þat wakes ay   *occupacione bonorum*
And neuer slepes nyght ne day,   *operum*
Bot on ilka syde es ay waytande
Wham he may wynne vnto his hande.   9840
And when he fyndes a man idelle
And slawe, he puttes on him a bridell

9814 Enchesouns] Enchesoun L, þe e. W   mas men] may be- L   9816 fra] to W
ne] and LSR, in W   fole] foule R   9817 alle] *add* þe LSW   enchesouns] encheson L
sidenote: Nota E   9818 þe] *om.* L   to] *om.* RW   9819 on] oft on R   alde] a wylde
L, *om.* R   9820 opon] on PRW   *sidenote*: Exemplum (*later?*) E   9822 þe] *om.* LS
in] thurgh RW   9824 lawe] lang L, bath laghe R   9825 þe] *om.* L   9826 þan]
om. E   nedely] nede L, nedelynges S   9828 enchesouns] -son P   9829 þe] *om.* LS
9830 be] *om.* L   9833 suld] sall L   þat] þe RW   9834 him noght] *trs.* EW, nathing
hym L   9836 -acioun] -aciouns S   *sidenote*: *om.* L, vj^{us}. gradus W   *vj^{us}.] vj. A
gradus] *adds* est P   9837 þat] he R   9838 neuer] *adds* mare L   slepes] *adds* by R
9839 es ay] *trs.* P   9840 vnto] to EW   9841 fyndes] fendes S   9842 a] hys L

And occupyes him in his nedes—
þat er wicked thoghtes and ille dedes—
And ledes him so with þe brydel of synne   9845
þat vnnethes may he fra him wynne.
þus may a man þat idell es
Be putted lightly to wickednes.
      Idelnes, als Haly Writte says,
Es Reckelesnes þat þe fende payse,   9850
And Slawnes of hert wele to do
Es maystresce of alle ille þarto.

Paulus þarefore Saynt Paul says wysely,
'Gif na rowme', he says, 'to þe enemy'.
þat es þus mykell for to say   9855
'Ne bees noght idell, nyght ne day',
So þat þe fende may na tyme fynde
To skulk on yhow, byfore na bihynde,
For to fande yhow with dedely synne.
For þarto he wald yhou fayne wynne.   9860
      Forwhy in boke þus redes þis clerkes
þat he þat idell es of gode werkes
Vnto þe fende gyfs rowme and stede
To fanden hym thurgh wycked rede.

Ieronimus þarefore Saynt Ierom biddes vs wirke   9865
Gode werkes ay and be noght irke
So þat þe fende fynde vs ay
Bysy in gode werkes, nyght and day.
For þe idell man þat list do noght
Thurgh Heuynes of hert and thoght,   9870
He may noght wele halde him lange
þat he ne sal falle in synne þat es strange.
      Forwhy þe prophete says in a stede
þat grete Pryde and plente of brede
And Idelnes also was þe synne   9875
Of Sodom; þat men vsed þarinne.
þat es to say, þai wald noght swynk

9844 þat] þa P   9848 putted] putt W   to] vnto LS   9852 ille] *om.* W   9853 *sidenote*
om. W   9854 he says] *om.* EL   þe] þi R, *om.* W   enemy] enuye W   9857 na] noght na E
9858 skulk] luk R   9859 For to] To E   fande] shende R   9860 he wald] *trs.* LR
9861 *line om.* R   boke] bokes S, þe boke W   þis] *om.* LS   9862 werkes] *adds* dede R
9863 Vnto] To W   9865 *sidenote om.* W   9867 fynde] *om.* S   9869 þe] *om.* L
9872 ne] *om.* LS   sal falle] falles W   þat es] *om.* PW   9875 also] *om.* LPR

De Castitate

Ne noght elles do bot ete and drynk.   fol. 60ra

Ne noght elles do bot ete and drynk.   fol. 60ra

Wharefore ful greefly þai sone felle

In þat synne þat es noght to telle.   9880

  On þis wyse many men dose

þat spendes þair tyme in wicked vse,

For alle þe tyme forsothe þai lese

þat þai spende in vanyteese

Or in + outrage thurgh hert-lykynge   9885

Of metes and drynkes or othir thynge,

Or in playes of fole continaunce

Or in iolytees of sanges and daunce.

Swilk outrages and reueryse

Puttes men oft here to folyse   9890

Thurgh lykynge þat þai haf withalle,

And þarefore oft lightly þai falle

In many foull synnes to telle

And aftirwarde in þe pitte of helle.

For Iob in a boke þus says   9895

'þai leden þair lifs in myrthes and plays

And in solaces and in sere delyces

þat stirs men oft to foul vyces.

And at a poynt þai sal wende

To þe fyre of helle withouten ende'.   9900

And þat es in þe poynt of þe dede,

Whare na man may þam wisse na rede.

  þe seuent and þe last degre   *vij.[^{us}] gradus: De*

þat falles vnto Chastyte   *deuota oracione*

Es deuout Prayere of hert bouxsom   9905

9877 es] *om.* W   9879 Whare-] þer- P   full . . . sone] *trs. phrs.* E   greefly] gretely ELS, greuesly W   þai sone] *trs.* LW   9880 to] *om.* E   9881 þis] *om.* E   men] man R   9883 þe] þaire L   *9885 outrage] outrages A   9886 and] or EPRW 9887 playes] place R   of] or E, or in L   fole] foule RW   continaunce] continuaunce SR 9888 iolytees] iolyte W   of] or in L, or S   and] or in L, or PW   9889 outrages] outrage LS   and] and other L, of W   9890 men oft] *trs.* E   to] vnto L, in S 9892 oft] *om.* L   9893 synnes] syn P   9894 -warde] *om.* P   in] into LP 9895 þus says] *trs.* R   *sidenote*: Iob ELPS   9896 þai] þai þat E, þase þat L, þai þai S þair] þai P   lifs] lyfe LP   myrthes] myrthe LS, myr⟨g⟩ht P   9897 delyces] delice P 9898 þat] And R   9899 at] in LS   9900 withouten] þat haues nane S 9901 poynt] poute/ponte S   þe²] *om.* SR   9903 *sidenote*: vij. W   vij^{m}.] vij. A gradus] *adds* est P   De] *om.* L   oracione] oracio L

þat mykill auaylles synne to ouercom,
And namely þe synne of Litchery
þat wastes bathe saul and body.

Ambrosius   Wharefore Saynt Ambros says þis skille
þat Prayere þat comes of gode wille   9910
Es a siker shelde in hande
+ Agayne þe fendes dartes brynnand.

Isidorus   And Isider also says wysely
þat it es a grete remedy
To rynne to þe Prayere of custom.   9915
þat may þe fende sone ouercom,
For ay when he þe hert assaylles,
Agayne him Prayere mast auaylles.
For Prayere, whaso it hauntes thurgh vse,

De Castitate

fol. 60ʳᵇ   Alle þe assautes of synne fordose.   9920
Prayere þat es made right hertly
Onence Godde es ful myghty,
If it be sette on four pileres
þat er four thynges þat it vp beres.

j. Fides Dominus   þe first es stedfast Trouth to telle.   9925
in euangelio   For Godde says þus in þe godspelle:
'In alle þat yhe aske or craue
In yhour prayere, loke þat ye haue
Trouth in Godde and in his myght,
And yhe sal haue þat yhe aske right.'   9930

Iacobus   þus biddes Saynt Iame þat we sal do,
For he says þis þat acordes þarto:
'Men suld Godde aske when þai haf nede
In Trouth, withouten dout to spede.
For he þat doutes may lickend be   9935

9907 þe] of S   9909 Whare-] þare- LP   *sidenote om.* W   9911 Es] It es L   a] a
full R   9912 *Agayne] And agayne AESW   dartes] darte E   9913 also says] *trs.*
SW   also . . . wysely] s. w. a. E   *sidenote om.* W   9914 a] a full L   remedy] *adds*
þareto E   9916 sone] full sone R   9917 he] *int. later* P, *om.* S   þe hert] here E
9918 him] *int. later* P, *om.* R   9919 prayere] *after* hauntes P   it] *om.* P   9920 Alle]
It all L   assautes] assentes W   9922 es] *om.* W   9923 it] he W   on] of W
9925 *sidenote: om.* W   j.] *om.* EL, jᵐ. S   9926 For] Als E   þus] *om.* E   *sidenote: om.*
W, Euangelium ELS   Dominus] Vnde D. P   9927 alle] *adds* thyng R   or] and ELS
9932 þis] þus PR   þat] *om.* L, and R   9933 Godde aske] *trs.* LR   9935 may
lickend] þaim likened sal W

Til a flote þat fletes in þe see
þat þe wynde and þe water togider
Ledes aboute hider and þider.
þarefore he þat askes Godde a thinge
And doutes to spede of his askynge,   9940
He sal noght spede', als þe boke says,
Onence Godde of þat þat he prays.

þe secund thinge þat sal vphald   *ij. Spes*
Prayere, certayne Hope es called
To haue þat es asked bi skille,   9945
If it be asked with gode wille.
Wharefore þe sautere says þus þarby,   *Dauid: Spera in domino et*
'Haf gode hope in Godde almyghty,   *ipse facie⟨t⟩*
And he sal þan do to þe
þat þou askes with herte fre'.   9950
And þarefore says yhete þe sautere
In anothir stede on þis manere,
'Louerd Godde, haf mercy on me,   *Dauid Miserere mei Deus,*
For my hert traystes al in þe'.   *quoniam in te confidit*
                                                        anima mea
    He gifs vs Hope to aske him oght   9955
þat hetes wele and desceyues vs noght,
When oure Lorde says in þe godspell
On þis manere, als I yhow telle: *Qui petit accipit; qui querit*
'He þat askes, tase ar he ga;   *inuenit, et pulsanti*
                                                        aperietur
And he þat sekes, he fyndes alswa;   9960
And he þat rynges and calles fast,

Donum Intellectus   De oracione
De Castitate   Adueniat regnum tuum

Godde opens and lates hym in at þe last.'   fol. 60va
þat es to say to þe vndirstandynge,
He þat askes wysely a thinge
And sekes bisily, als falles,   9965

9936 flote] flode R   9938 and] *om.* E (*corr. later?*)   9943 *sidenote:* ij. W   ij.] *om.*
L, ij². S   9944 Prayere] *adds* of W   9947 -fore] -thurghe E   sautere] pauter S
sidenote: Dauid] *om.* LPSW   Domino] deo W   faciet] *continues with the gloss elsewhere at*
9953 E   9949 he . . . do] þan sall he do all R   to] *repeated and expunged* A
9950 þat] All þat L   askes] *adds* hym L   9951 sautere] pauter S   9953 *sidenote:*
Dauid E   9954 For] Forwhy R   al in] on S   9957 When] And L   9958 als I] I
þus E   I] I sall P   *sidenote: om.* L   qui] qui et S   et²] *om.* P   9960 he²] *om.* EPR
9962 þe] *om.* L   9963 to²] in R

And dwellandely rynges and calles,
When þise thre thinges er rightly soght
In þe prayere with stedfast thoght—
Wytte, Bisines, and Dwellandnes—
Als-tyte Godde heres what þe prayere es.   9970
   Bot many men askes commonly
þat er noght herde of Godde almyghty,
Al-if þai pray neuer so lange,
Forwhy þai fourme þair askyng wrang.

Iacobus apostolus Wharefore Saynt Iame þe apostel says   9975
To þam þat vnwysely prays,
'Yhe aske', he says, 'Godde oft somthing
And wynnes noght by þat askynge,
Forþi þat yhe can noght wele
Aske þat fel to yhow to fele'.   9980
   Som askes hegher thinge to haue
þan felle to þam to aske or craue,
Als didde Iohans moder and Iame.
Scho asked of Godde in þair name
þat bathe hir sones myght sitte euen   9985
On aythir syde by him in heuen.
þis askynge wanted discrecioun,
Bot it semed a presumpcioun,
þat es noght elles bot wrange wenynge
þat men has of þamself in demynge.   9990
And þarefore our Lorde was noght payed;
'Ye wate noght what yhe ask', he sayde.
   Wharefore he þat wil wysely pray
Suld kepe him fra presumpcioun ay,
þat he noght wene of himself anely   9995
þat he war mykell thinge worthy.
Als Godde telles by þe Pharysene

9965 als] as hym R   9967 thre] th'r'e (*corr. later*) P, ther (*corr. later*) R   er rightly]
ryght hertly es L   rightly] right P   9969 Wytte] With W   dwelland-] rightwis- P
9970 þe] thy P   9974 fourme] enforme R   askyng] prayer W   9975 *sidenote: om.* L
apostolus] *om.* EPS   9976 þam] whayme S   9977 he says] *om.* L   he . . . Godde]
trs. phrs. S   he . . . oft] *trs. phrs.* P   Godde oft] *trs.* W   oft] of ESR, oft of L
9981 hegher] othir R   9988 Bot] For LS   9989 bot] bote a E   9990 has] *om.* W
of] *om.* P   9991 And] *om.* P   9992 noght] neuer L   ask] asked R
9993 Whare-] þare- E   he] ȝe P   wil wysely] *trs.* PW (*later corr.* P)   9994 him] *om.* E,
ȝou P   fra] *adds* wrang L

þat helde himself gode and clene
And himself in his prayere rosed
And othir dispysed and accused.   10000
  Bot he þat prayes suld pray mekely
Bifore oure Lorde Godde almyghty
þat sees our hertes and knawes þat greues
And our defautes wate and myscheues

Donum Intellectus   De oracione
De Castitate   Adueniat regnum tuum

And wate what es nedeful to our state   10005 fol. 60ᵛᵇ
Better þan we ourseluen wate.
    þarefore take kepe, he þat sal pray,
To seke men þat sittes bi þe way
How þai in sight shewes þair sare
And alle þair defautes, lesse and mare,   10010
To stir þe men þat þam may se
To haue rewith of þam and pyte.
Swa suld a man with al his myght
Do to Godde, if he didde right,
And mekely shew his defautes withinne   10015
And recorde þare wele al his synne
To purchace hym forgifnes
Of Godde, þat ful of mercy es.
    Som men er þat þe werlde counsaylles
þat can noght aske þat mast auaylles,   10020
Bot thinges þat er lytell and vyle,
Als werldely godes þam to bigyle.
Bot Godde þat es large and curtays
Gifs þat thinge þat es mare to prayse;
He wil gif yhow, als he es right wyse,   10025
þe thinge þat es of mast pryse
þat lastes ay withouten fayllyng.
Bot he wil noght with a lytell thing

9996 þat] om. P   10001 Bot] For L   10002 oure Lorde] om. L
10004 and²] and oure L   10005 wate] om. R   nedeful . . . our] our nedefull L   to]
for P   10007 he þat] whoso R   10009 shewes] schewed S   10010 alle] om. L
10011 þe] om. S   10014 to] vnto LR   if] and L   10015 shew] schewes P
10016 wele] om. L   10017 hym] of hym P   10019 þe] om. E   10021 er] er
bote E   10024 þat] þaim W   es mare] maste es L   10025 yhow] om. E, vs L
10026 of mast] trs. EP

Pay yhow, als men lightly may
With an appil a chylde pay.   10030
  Godde wil ye aske with hert stable
Grete thinges þat er profytable
To saul-hele pryncipally,
And noght anely vnto þe body.
þat es his grace and his blisse,   10035
þe whilk þai sal haue þat er hisse.
For he þat askes of Godde ritchesce
Or any werldely thinge to gesce
Or honours or dede of enemy
To be herde he es noght worthy.   10040
For swilk prayers er wrange soght,
And þarefore Godde ne heres þam noght.

Augustinus Forthy says þus Saynt Austyn,
Als clerkes fyndes in Latyn:
He says, 'He haldes noght grete thinges   10045
þe godes on whilk som mens hertes hing⟨es⟩,

De oracione De Castitate

fol. 61ʳᵃ þat Godde als wele to wicked men gifs
Als to gode men þat clenely lifs'.
He wil say þat men suld noght
Halde ne gesce in þair thoght   10050
For grete thinges þat er ay-lastand
þe godes of þe werlde þat er passand,
þat Godde gifs oft, when he wille,
Als wele and mare to men þat er ille
þan to men þat er gode and clene   10055
þat in gode lyf lange has bene.
  Bot for þis skille, als I yhow kenne,
Godde gifs þam mast to wicked men.

10029 yhow] vs L 10031 þe] þat we L, ȝe S 10033–4 *trs. couplet* L
10033 To] But to þe L 10034 vnto] to ELSRW 10035 es] *om.* W
10038 any] ane S 10039 honours or] honoure (-res R) of LR of] or L
10040 To] For to R herde] *adds* of god S 10041 prayers] prayer R
10042 ne] *om.* LSR 10043 Austyn] Augustyne S *sidenote om.* W
10045 noght] *adds* þes P 10046 on] þe E mens] *om.* L hertes] hert
LPRW, *adds* on S 10048 to] vnto L 10049 He wil say] Wharfor he says R
10051 ay-] *om.* S 10052 er] er is R 10053 Godde] *om.* SW oft] oftsithes R
10056 þat] And L 10057 als] þat L

For gode men suld dispyse in wille
þat þat he gifs to men þat er ille,   10060
And swilk godes er noght mast to prayse,
Als Saynt Austyn openly says.   *Augustinus*
Also Saynt Ambros says þarby,   *Ambrosius*
'When þou prays', he says, 'God almyghty,
Aske grete thinges + with hert stedfast   10065
þat may withouten ende last,
And noght swilk thinges þat passes tyte,
For of swilk prayere God think dispyte'.

  Bot our gode mayster, Godde almyghty,
Teches vs wele to aske wysely   10070
And fourmes our askyng right to vs,
When he says in þe godspelle þus: *Dominus in euangelio*
'If yhe wil ask anythinge free
Of my Fader in þe name of me,
Whethir yhe aske loude or stille,   10075
He sal graunt yhow it bi skille.'

  And he askes in þe name to neuen
Of Ihesu Cryst, Goddis Sone of heuen,
þat askes with gode hert and leel
Thinge þat falles to saul-hele.   10080
For Ihesu es þus mykell to say
Als 'Hele' or 'Helar' þa[t] helen vs may,
And what we sal ask he teches vs
In þe godspell when he says þus: *Dominus in euangelio:*
'Sekes first', he says, 'Goddis kyngdom   10085   *Primo querite regnum dei*
And his rightwisnes, whareso yhe com,   *et eius iusticiam et omnia*
And alle thinge yhe sal haue redy   *adicientur vobis*

10058 þam] ay W   10060 he gifs] es gyfen L   10061–2 *couplet trs.* S
10061 And] þat S   10062 *sidenote om.* LW   10063 Also] And L   *sidenote om.* L
10064 he says] *om.* L   10065 Aske] Aske a L   *thinges] *adds* he says A, thing L
10067 noght] *om.* W   þat] as R   10070 aske] *adds* and   10071 askyng] prayer L
10072 says] sayd R   *sidenote: om.* LW, Euangelium S   Dominus] *om.* E   10073 wil]
om. S   10074 Of] *om.* L   10075–6 *couplet trs.* P   10076 yhow . . . bi] if itt be
EL, ȝou if it be P, it if it be S   10077 And] Forwhy R   he] he þat LP   in] *om.* R   þe]
om. W   10079–80 *couplet om.* P   10079 gode] *om.* L   and] *om.* L   10080 to] to
þe L   10081–2 *couplet om.* L   10081 For] *om.* S   to] for to ER, at S
*10082 þat] þa A   10084 when] whare S   *sidenote:* Dominus in euangelio] *om.*
ELPSW   et . . . iusticiam] *om.* W   eius iusticiam] *trs.* LPS

De oracione   De Castitate

fol. 61rb þat nedefull es to saul and body.'
For als men says, men suld þam spede
Ay first to þat þat war mast nede.   10090
   Twa thinges er nedefull to our fode,
Gastly gode and bodyly gode.
Bot of gastly gode we haf mast nede;
þarefore we suld, if we wil spede,
Aske first þat gode principally.   10095
And our Lorde þat es almyghty
Sal gif vs it and auauntage do
And gif vs bodily godes þarto
þat our bodys may here sustayne.
Bot þat gode es noght so certayne   10100
Als gastly gode þat lastes ay,
For al werldely gode passes away.
   We suld noght make godes principall
Of swilk secund godes so smale,
Als som men dose þat lifs mysse   10105
þat sekes nane othir lyf bot þis.
þe whilke to ende may sone be broght
And faylles þam, whethir þai wil or noght.
   Bot þe kyngdom of Godde so sothfast,
þat es þe lyf þat ay sal last,   10110
We suld first seke, als teches þis clerkes,
Thurgh prayere and thurgh gode werkes.
And þat es þat Godde biddes vs
þar he says in þe godspell þus:
'First sekes þe kyngdom of Godde wele   10115
And his rightwysnes to fele.'
þat es to say we suld wirke right

10088 to] to þe R   and] and to þe R   10089 als] om. PW   þam] men L
10093 haf] repeats P   10094 suld] sall L   if we wil] and we wald R   10095 þat] ate
ESW, of L, þe R   -pally] -pale W   10096 þat es] god W   es] adds god L   al-] om. P
10097 it] tite L   10098 gif vs] gyfes L   godes] good RW   10099 may] after þat E
here] euyr (over eras.) S   10101 gode] goodes R   10102 passes] sall passe P
10103 -pall] -pallye E   10104 smale] smalye E, male W   10105 mysse] omysse LP
10107 may sone] trs. P   10108 wil] repeats P   10110 ay] euer L   10111 suld]
sall L   seke] adds it L   10112 thurgh²] other L   10114 says] sayde S
10115 sidenote: In euangelio ES, Primo querite etc. P   10117 suld] sall L   wirke] adds
wele L

Gode werkes ay with al our myght,
Wharethurgh we may com thurgh trauaylle
Vnto þe kyngdom þat neuer sal faylle.   10120
    Whaso þus askes and sekes þarto,
Godde wille hym mare auauntage do.
For he wil gif hym suffissauntly
þat falles to sustynaunce of body.
Forwhy nathinge þat may auaylle   10125
To lyf or saul sal hym defaylle
þat in hert Godde dredes and lufs,
Als Haly Wrytte says and proues.

Donum Intellectus   De oracione
De Castitate   Adueniat regnum tuum

Bot couatous men of þis lyue   fol. 61ᵛᵃ
þat with þe werlde wil ay stryue,   10130
Euer þe mare þai haue at wille,
þe mare nede þai haue bi þis skille:
For þe mare a man has of meyne,
þe mare nede of fode to þam has he;
And he þat mast of hors haues   10135
Mast has nede of stables and knaues.
And Saynt Ierom says on þis wyse   *Ieronimus*
þat he þat ful es of Couatyse
Has grete defaut al vnsoght
Of þat he has and þat he has noght.   10140
    And þarefore he þat wil Godde pray
And aske oght þat auaylle him may,
He suld aske wysely, if he pray right,
And bisily with al his myght
And lastandly, withouten faylyng.   10145
þan sal he spede of his askynge,

10119 may] myght R   thurgh] with P   10120 Vnto] To PW   10121 Whaso]
Wha E   þus] *om.* R   10123 wil] salle E   10124 falles] *after* sustynaunce P   to] to
þe L   sustynaunce of] saul and to R   of] of his P   10125 nathinge] no tong W   þat]
om. S   10126 or] oure W   saul] *adds* þan R   sal] may L   hym] noght L; *add* noght ES
defaylle] fayle LPSRW   10127 and] or P   10128 says] both says R   10130 þe]
þis EPS   10131 þai] þat þai W   10132 þis] *om.* P   10133 meyne] meȝe R
10134 to þam] *om.* LP   has] had W   10135 þat] *om.* P   10136 stables] stable P
10137 *sidenote om.* S   10138 þat] *om.* P   10139 grete defaut] defautes grete P
10140 þat²] of þat P, *om.* W   10141 And] *om.* P   þare-] whare- L   pray] pay R
10142 auaylle him] *trs.* E   10143 if] and L   pray] prayd R

And Godde sal gif him on þis manere
Al þat es nedeful to haue here
For hele of saul soueraynely
And for sustinaunce of his body.   10150

iij. Deuocio þe thridde thing þat suld vphalde
Prayere es Deuocioun called.
þat liftes a mans hert vp euen
Vnto our Lorde, Godde of heuen,
Withouten thoght of anythinge   10155
þat to Deuocioun war lettynge.

Dominus dicit in euangelio: For Godde says þus, als I yhou say,
Tu cum oraueris intra 'When þou', he says, 'sal Godde pray,
cubiculum ⟨t⟩uum clauso
hostio ora patrem Wende into þi hous in quert
(þat es to say withinne þi hert)   10160
And sperre þe dore opon þe fast.'
þat es to say þou sal out cast
Alle willes and thoghtes of vanyte
þat werldely or flesshely may be.
And þan pray þe Fader of heuen   10165
In priuyte with a mylde steuen.

Ciprianus And Saynt Cipriane says þarby
þat alle werldely thoghtes and flesshely
Suld departe fra þe hert sone
Of hym þat prays Godde of a bone,   10170

Donum Intellectus   De oracione
De Castitate   Adueniat regnum tuum

fol. 61vb So þat þe hert nathinge thinke may
Bot on þat thinge þat he sal pray.
'Wenestow þat Godde heres þe', he says,
'When þou heres noght þiself þat prays?'

Isiderus And Isider says, þe wyse man,   10175

10148 to] for to R   10149 soueraynely] souerlaly L   10150 for] for þe L   his]
þe L   10151 þat] þat vs L   sidenote: De oracione S, iij. W   iij.] om. EP
10152 Prayere] Of prayere LW   Prayere es] trs. W   10155 of] on L   10156 to]
vnto L   10157 sidenote: Dominus dicit] Dominus ES, trs. L   in euangelio] om. SW
Tu] om. L   Tu cum] trs. S   intra] add in EPLW   tuum] add et ELPS   patrem] add
tuum ELPS   10158 þou] þe R   10161 And] A   R   opon] on PW
10163 thoghtes] thoght L   10165 þe Fader] repeats L, `þi´ fader (int. later) P
10166 a] om. ELS   10170 Of . . . Godde] If þou pray God oght L   a] om. E
10172 þat he] þou L   he] it S   10173 þe] þu R

þat we pray sothfastly þan
When we think on nane othir thinge
Bot anely on our askynge.
And Saynt Austyn says, als clerkes proues,   *Augustinus*
'What auaylles', he says, 'þat þe lippe[s] moues   10180
And betes togider ay of custom,
When þe hert of þe man es al dom?'
    Swilk difference als es sene
Bitwene þe caffe and þe corne clene,
And þe branne þat es smal or grete   10185
And þe clene flour of þe whete,
And þe beste and þe bestes hyde—
Swilk difference es on þe tothir syde
Bitwene þe prayere made ouerthwert
And þe Deuocioun of þe hert.   10190
    Godde es na hare þar he dwelles
To be fedde with leeues and noght elles.
Godde weryed þe tree growand
þar he nathinge bot leeues fande.
Right so þe prayere es vnmyghty   10195
þat es in leeues of wordes anely
Withouten hertly Deuocioun;
It payes noght Godde þat orysoun.
Bot he turnes þe ere þarefra away
And wil noght here it, nyght na day;   10200
He vndirstandes noght swilk langage.
Forþi þareof comes nane auauntage.
    He þat withouten Deuocioun prayse,
He prayse als he þat spekes and says
Half Inglisshe and half Frankisshe;   10205
A nyce manere of speche es þis.
He prayse with mouth by vsage—
Bot þe herte spekes anothir langage—
When he thinkes on othir thinges
þat hym to vayne lykynge bringes.   10210

10178 on] of L   our] our awn R   10179 als] *om.* R   *sidenote om.* W   10180 he
says] *om.* L   þat] if L   *lippes] lippe A   10182 dom] doun L   10187 hyde] hede
hyde P   10190 þe deuocioun] *trs.* E   þe²] *om.* P   10191 þar] whare L
10193 growand] grofande P   10196 es] *after* wordes P   in] in þe P, *om.* R
10202 -of] *om.* L   10205 Frankisshe] fra(v)nces, *corr. to* fraynce S, franche R
10207 by] wyth L   10210 lykynge] lygyng E

Wharefore it semes, als þe boke says,
þat swilk men þat Godde so prays
Walde hym skorne al þat whyle,

De oracione   De Castitate

fol. 62ra Als he þat wil a man bigyle
þat es deef and doumbe alswa,   10215
þat stirs his lippes to and fra
And mas anely of speche semblaund
And nathinge says to vnderstande.
To swilk maner of mens prayere
Our Louerd turnes þe deef ere.   10220
    Bot þat prayere þat comes anely
Of þe hert heres Godde almyghty,
For als he says in þe godspelle right,
'Godde es a gaste of mykell myght.
And þarefore whaso herde wil be   10225
Of Godde þat es ful of pyte,
Hym bihoues pray als best es
In gaste and in Sothfastnes'.
    Wharefore þe prophete þat was wytty
Vs teches to pray Godde deuoutely   10230
Dauid: Intret oracio In þe sauter, als yhe may here,
mea sicut incensum in þare he says þus on þis manere:
conspectu tuo 'Louerd, my prayere in þi sight
Als ensense mot ga vpright.'
For when þe ensense, als men may fele,   10235
Es in þe fyre, it flayres wele.
So dose Prayere to vnderstande
þat comes of þe hert brynnande
Of þe luf of Godde almyghty—
Flayres ful swete to Godde namely.   10240
And bot it flayre on þis manere,
Godde wil noght þe prayer here.

10214 wil] walde L   10216 þat] And S   10217 anely of] any W
10220 deef] defer S   10229 Whare-] þer- W   10230 deuoutely] allmyghty L
10231 *sidenote*: Dauid] Propheta ES, *om.* LW   sicut incensum] *om.* P, sicud W   tuo] *adds*
domine W   10232 þare] Whare L   þus] *om.* LS   10233 in] entre into L
10234 Als] Als dose L   ga] gang L   10235 men] 3he W   10236 in] to R   flayres]
sauours EL, smelles R, flauors W   10237 dose] dus þe W   10240 Flayres] Sauours
L, Smelles S, Flauors W   10241 And] *om.* S   flayre] sauoure L, smell R, flauor W

A messangere þat to court wendes
And has þare na knawyng of frendes,
Ne wille na lettres with him brynge,   10245
He may noght com bifor þe kynge.
Right so Prayere and orysoun
Withouten Luf and Deuocioun,
Als clerkes says, es na bettir
þan messanger withouten lettre.   10250
   Prayere es þat men here mase
Als a messangere þat to þe court gase.
Deuocioun es als lettre with seele
þat Prayere beres als messanger leele.
And whaso sendes swilk messangere   10255
Vnto þe court on wrange manere,
Withouten lettre pryue to rede,

De oracione   De Castitate

He sal noght wele his [nedes] spede.   fol. 62ʳᵇ
For men says þus, als oft bytydes,
'He þat fole sendes, he fole habydes';   10260
And fole wendes and fole comes hame,
Bot he þat sendes es mast to blame.
þus falles by Prayere þat men mas
þat na Deuocioun with it has.
   Bot whaso wille pray sothfastly   10265
With hert suld pray þus God almyghty,
Als Dauid did þat þus sayde
In þe sauter when he prayde:
'Lorde, þou here þe voyce of me;   *Dauid*
With al my hert I crye to þe.'   10270
Crye of hert es brynnand luf,
Als clerkes may here Saynt Austyn proue:
'Swilk crye and swilk voyce namely

10243 court] courtes E   10250 þan] þen a P   10251–2 *couplet om.* W
10252 a] *om.* PR   þe] *om.* R   10253 als] als a EL   *sidenote*: Deuocio E
10254 beres] hit beres W   10255 swilk] *add* a EL   10256 Vnto] To P
10257 lettre] letters LR   pryue] *om.* L   10258 wele] *after* nedes S   *nedes] erand
AELS   10260 he²] *om.* E   10261 And¹'²] A R   10262 he] *om.* P
10263 falles] fares it L   10264 it] in L   10266 þus] *adds* to L, *om.* S
10268 sauter] *adds* þat þus P   10269 *sidenote: om.* LP   *adds* Domine exaude vocem
meam qua clamaui ad te E   10271 Crye] Krying L   10272 *sidenote*: Augustinus W

Es lykand vnto Godde almyghty,
And noght þe noyse of wordes soght,   10275
To whilk þe hert acordes noght.'
Gregorius Wharefore Saynt Gregor says right wele,
Als clerkes may rede in boke and fele,
þat sothfastly to pray and fast
Es bitter sighynges to Godde to cast,   10280
With compunccioun ay ouerthwert
(þat es repentaunce with dole of hert),
And thurgh sadde wordes to pray mekely
And na polist wordes to multyply.
Swilk crye chaces helle-theues away,   10285
Fendes þat waytes vs nyght and day
For to robbe vs of alle godenes
And to lede vs to al þat ille es.
þarefore we suld oft to Godde calle
þat we noght in þa theues handes falle,   10290
And crye to hym withouten fayntyse
Agayne þe fyre of Couatyse
And agayne þe fyre of Litchery
þat brynnes bathe saul and body,
þat he vs graunt þe water of teres   10295
To sleken swilk fyre þat vs deres,
þat it noght our hertes vmlappe,
Ne of our saulles fordo þe shappe.
Also we suld crye fast and calle

Donum Intellectus   De oracione
De Castitate   Adueniat regnum tuum

fol. 62ᵛᵃ To Godde, þat louerd es ouer-alle,   10300
Agayne þe grete flowand flode
Of idell thoghtes þat er noght gode

10275 þe] of þe L, in þe W   noyse] voyce LS   wordes] þe worde (*over eras.*) P
10277 right] full P   10278 boke] bokes LPS   10279 and] *om.* R   *sidenote om.* PW
10280 bitter] better LSR   sighynges] syghing LP   cast] tast R   10281 com-
punccioun] comp⟨assio⟩un (*over eras., later; probably originally correct*) P   ay] *om.* L
10283 And] Ad W   10284 polist] polesche L   10285 *line om.* L   crye] wordes P
10288 And brynges vs to all maner of wyckednes S   to¹] *om.* P   lede] bede W   al] helle L
10289 þare-] Whare- LS   Godde] -gyder W   10290 þa] no PR   theues] fendes L
10291 to] on P   10292 Agayne] And agayne L   10296 sleken] slokene ELS, slayk R
þat] als LR   10298 of] *om.* W   our] *om.* P   10300 ouer] of ELSR
10301 flowand] folowand W

þat in þe hert springes on sere wyse,
þat thurgh consentyng we noght perise.

  þarefore cryed Dauid when he prayde 10305
To Godde in þe sauter and þus sayde:
'Saue me, Godde, fra perils smert,
For waters has entred vnto my hert.'
And our Lorde disciples with him pryue,
When þai war inmyddes þe see 10310
And sawe þe tempestes fast ryse
And war in poynt þan to peryse,
þai cryed for-fered and sayd þus:
'Lorde, in þis perill saue vs.'

  For þise thynges þat I tolde last 10315
Suld we ay to Godde crye fast,
To saue vs fra þis perils pryue
þat we thurgh þam noght perisshed be.
þat es to say of þe theues of helle
þat er vgly fendes and felle, 10320
And of þe fyre of Couatyse
And of Litchery þat oft wil ryse,
And of þe flode of ille thoghtes amange
And of alle corrupcions so strange.

  Now vnderstandes, als I yhow say, 10325
þat men suld to Godde ay pray
In alle tymes and in alle stedes
þar men has wille to say þair bedes.
Bot specially, if yhe did right,
Yhe suld pray with al yhour myght 10330
And mare deuoutly, als þe boke telles,
In Halykirke þan + ouwhare elles.
For þat es called 'hous of prayere'
þar þe fende has leste powere,
Whare our Deuocioun suld be ay. 10335
þarefore we suld þare mast pray,

*Dauid: Saluum me fac,
Deus; quoniam intrauerunt
aque vsque ad animam
meam*

10304 we] will P   10306 *sidenote*: Dauid L   Deus] *adds* meus W
10307 Godde] lorde S   10308 vnto] into LS, to PW   10309 Lorde] goddys
R, *om.* W   10310 war] stode R   10311 tempestes] tempest LPSR   10314 saue]
þou saue LR   10316 ay] *after* Godde P   10319 þe] *om.* P   10320 er] ar bath R
10322 of] *om.* P   oft] of þe W   10323 of²] þat W   10328 þar] Whare S
10329 if] and L   10330 al] *om.* ES   *10332 ou-] ouer- ALR, outher- ES, aur- P,
oure- W   10334 þar] For L, Whare S   has] *adds* þe E   10335 Whare] þare S

And namely on Sonendays so dere
And on othir haly days sere
þat er ordayned thurgh Halykirk
Haly werkes þan for to wirke.   10340
Als to serue Godde and loue and pray
And to worshepe hym al þat we may.

Donum Intellectus   De oracione
De Castitate   Adueniat regnum tuum

fol. 62ᵛᵇ þarefore men seses of werldely werkes
On swilk dere days, als teches þis clerkes,
And tentes þan for al þe woke   10345
To gastly werkes, als biddes þe boke.
þat es to loue Godde and honour
And to pray hym ay of sokour.
Sen Godde commanded þat es myghty
In þe Alde Lawe so straytly   10350
To kepe þe Sabate and to halde—
þat ilkan haly day may be called—
And sethen, als þe peple myght se,
Godde did a man to staned be
For he gaderd by þe way   10355
A fone stickes on þe Sabat day,
What sal he do on þam namely
þat dose grete synnes and vilany
On Sonendays and othir festes?
Forwhy þai folow þair wille als bestes   10360
And wastes þe tyme, als men may se,
In folys and in vanyte,
And on swilke days mare ille duse
þan þai on þe werkedays vse.

10337 Sonendays] þe Sononnday L   10338 haly] *om.* L   10340 þan] þare L, *om.* P   10341 Als] And L, Also P   10342 worshepe . . . al] godde do seruice P
10343 seses] *adds* þan L   10344 *line om.* L   þis] *om.* P   10345 þan] *adds* als L
10346 biddes] teches W   10349 commanded] -ndes LSW   10351 sabate] sabotes P
10352 day] *om.* W   10354–5 *lines trs., corr. later* P   10354 did] gart L, made S   to
staned] *trs.* PSR   to] *om.* LW   staned] saued W   10355 For] For þat L   he] he hadde
PRW   10356 on] apon L   þe] a P   10357 on] þan of L   10359 Sonenday and]
þe Sononnday and on L   10361 þe] þat L   men] 3he E   10362 in²] in other LS
vanyte] vanitese S   10364 on] opon R   þe] *om.* W   werke-] werkes S   -days] day L,
-day's' P   vse] dose (*canc.?*) vse P, vses S

Certaynely þan may yhe se 10365
þat þai sal mare punyst be
In þe tothir werlde þat lastes ay
þan Iewes þat brekes þair Sabbat day.
For þe Sonenday mare haly es
þan þe Sabbat day þat es lesse. 10370
    Pryncipall festes of þe yhere
Er ordayned heghe days and dere
Thurgh Halykirke to halugh and kepe,
Godde to loue and to worshepe
And to thanke him of his godenes 10375
þat he has done vs, mare and lesse,
Als Halykirke recordes namely
Of þe festes thurgh sere story.
    First at Yhole of Goddis birthe,
With grete solempnyte and myrthe, 10380
Es mencioun made, euen and morne,
How he was of a mayden borne.
At Paskes also þat comes and gase
How he fra dede to lyue rase.
At Haly Thursday es redde right 10385

De Castitate   De obseruacione dierum festiuorum

How Godde steghe vp to heuen bright,   fol. 63ra
And at Wytsonenday es made mynde mast
How Godde sent doun þe Haly Gast
Til his apostels þat he lufd,
Als es thurgh Halykirke proued. 10390
    Also es ordayned thurgh þe lawe
In Halykirk þat we suld knawe
Festes of halughs þat er in heuen,
Als men may here in kirk oft neuen.
þa festes suld men halugh and kepe 10395

10366 mare] wele mare R   10369 Sonen-] seuent W   10371 festes] *adds* dayes L
10375 to] *om.* R   his] *adds* gret R   10379 at] ate þe ER   *sidenote*: Nota E, j. W
10380 and] and mekyll R   10381 made] *om.* P   10383 *sidenote*: ij. W
10384 lyue] lyffyng R   10385 At] On L   redde] *adds* full L   *sidenote*: iij. W
10386 Godde] he R   10387 And] *om.* L   *sidenote*: iiij. W   10389 Til his] Vnto þe L
10391 es] he P, it is R   10394 kirk] kyrkes LS

And in þair name Godde worshepe
And loue hym, bathe lered and lewed,
Of myrakils þat he has shewed
In þam thurgh myght of þe Haly Gast
For to conferme our trouthe mast.   10400
þarefore þair festes we suld kepe clene
þat in Halykirke ordayned bene
And pray þam þat þai be our sokour
Onence Godde þat dose þam honour,
Bathe in erthe and in heuen bright,   10405
Als Halykirke wytteneses right.
Wharefore he dose grete synne to fele
þat kepes noght þa festes wele,
For he agayne þe commandement wirkes
Of Godde and agayne Halykirkes.   10410
   Bot som may answer þus and say,
'Sir, we may noght alday pray,
Ne ilka day bene at þe kirke;
We most somtyme othir thinge wirk.
What ille or foly suld þis be,   10415
If I yhede somtyme to play me
For som solace and myrth to make?
Why suld Godde þat to ille take?
For whyles I bourde and play in skille,
I do na synne, ne think nane ille'.   10420
   To þat wil I now answer þe
Shortly, als þou sal here and se.
Alle þe tymes and alle þe dayse
þat þou despendes in idell playse,
In reuerys or in + vanytes   10425
þat to Godde es noght ordayned, þou leses.
For I wil þou vnderstande and wytte

10399 myght] þe myght P   10400 conferme] comforth P   10401 þair ... suld]
trs. phrs. S   þair] þase L, þer R   we suld] trs. P   10406 wytteneses] witte῾ne῾s P, adds
hit W   10409 he] after commandement R   commandement] -mentz L, adds dos W
wirkes] wyrk W   10410 agayne] of LR   -kirkes] -kyrk LW   10411 may] om. E
10416 yhede] wente LS   to] at L   10417 For] Or L   and] or LP   10419 and] or P
10420 think] thynkes ELPS   nane] om. L   10421 now] om. L, after þat SW, nown R
10424 despendes] spendes LPS, dyspendyd R   *10425 vanytes] vanyteses A
10426 þou] 3e L

De Castitate   De obseruacione dierum
festiuorum

þat whethir þou gange, stande, or sytte,   fol. 63rb

Alle þe tyme þat þou thinkes noght   *Omne tempus in quo de*
On Godde þat þou suld haf in thoght,   10430   *Deo non cogitas perdere*
                                                       computa
Al sal be reckend als tynt for ay,

Als men may here þis clerkes say.

þat may þus vnderstanden be   *Augustinus: Omne tempus*
                                               impensum requiretur a te
When þou thinkes noght bot on vanyte   *qualiter fuerit expensum*

And on nathynge þat ordayned es   10435

To Godde and to his rightwisnes.

    Certes, a grete thinge he leses

þat spendes his tyme in + vanytes.

And þat says Senek on þis manere: *Seneca*

þat he tynes in þis werlde here   10440

Alle þe godes þat he suld do

And al þe mede þat falles þarto

Of al þe tyme so spended in vayne,

Whilk he sal neuer wynne agayne.

Bot grete syn als methink he dose   10445

þat spendes þe tyme in ille vse.

    Wharefore Godde at þe day of dome,

When alle men sal bifor hym come,

Sal aske of vs resouns certayne

Of al þe tyme we spende in vayne,   10450

Als Saynt Anselyne says in a boke   *Anselmus*

þar clerkes may þis mater loke.

þarefore we suld þe tyme wele spende

Whyle we lif here til our lyues ende.

For þe tyme es short of our lyf-days   10455

And vncertayne, als þe boke says.

For it es na man þat can se

10428 þat] *om.* P   þou] þe L   gange stande] *trs.* S   10429 *sidenote: om.* W   non]
after quo S   computa] compota E   10431 als] and L   tynt] tytte E
10433 *sidenote: om.* W   Augustinus] *om.* ELPS   tempus] *adds* tibi L   inpesum]
impesum E   10434 noght] *om.* PS   10436 and] *repeats* E   to] do S
*10438 vanytes] vanyteses A   10439 þat] *om.* S   says Senek] *trs.* S   *sidenote:* Senek
SW   10442 mede] medes L   10444 Whilk] þe whilk R   10445 als] *om.* LPS
10446 þe] hys LPR   10448 men] *om.* L   10449 of] *om.* L   10451 Anselyne]
Anselme ELPSRW   10453 þare-] Whare- L   10455 lyf-] lyfes S

How lange hys tyme here sal be,
Na so wys es nane ne so sleghe
þat wate whenne ne whare he sal diegh.   10460

De bona occupacione
temporis
And þarefore he þat wil right kepe
þe haly days to Goddis worshepe,
His wille he suld to nathinge gif
þat Godde or his halughs myght greue,
Bot do alle thinge þat es Goddis wille   10465
And in gode werkes þe tyme fulfille
And loue Godde ay in ilka place
And thank hym oft of his grace,
And of alle othir gode namely.

And pray oft Godde of his mercy   10470
And sarmons here with gode talent
And þat tyme to alle gode werkes tent.

Donum Intellectus   De Castitate
Adueniat regnum tuum

fol. 63va
De deuocione in ecclesia et
reuerencia Deo
Also when men es at þe kirke,
Of gode Prayer men suld noght irke.
Bot men suld kepe þam þare fra dyn   10475
Honestly while þai er þarinne
And do Godde honour and reuerence
And his halughs in his presence.
For þe stede es clene and haly
And ordayned to serue God almyghty,   10480
And noght to iangle, als men oft dose,
Ne lagh ne bourde ne trofles vse.
Forwhy Godde says on þis manere,

Domus mea domus
oracionis vocabitur
'Mi hous es cald hous of prayere'.
þarefore men suld in kirke noght do   10485
Bot thynge þat it es ordayned to,

10461 -fore] *om.* S   þat] *om.* P   wil right] ryght sall L   *sidenote: om.* W   temporis]
om. S   10462 to] of W   Goddis] god S   10463 to] *om.* L   10465 þat] to þat P
10466 werkes] werk L   fulfille] fulle E   10467 ilka] all L   10468 oft] *om.* L
10469 gode] godenes L, godes S   10470 oft Godde] *trs.* P   10472 gode] hys L
10473 Also] And swa L   *sidenote: om.* W   in . . . Deo] et reuerencia in ecclesia Dei (*om.* L)
EL   Deo] *om.* S   10474 prayer] prayers LRW, werkes P   noght] *adds* be S
10475 þare] *om.* E, *int.* P   10476 er] ware L   10480 to] for to L, *phrs. int.* P
10481 als] *repeats* E, all S   10484 cald] *add* þe LS, *om.* W   *sidenote: partly cut away* W
domus²] *adds* mea L   10485 kirke] halykirke E   10486 thynge] thynk R   it] *om.*
ELP   to] þareto EP

Als haly Prayere and Goddis seruyse,
Als says Saynt Austyn, þe doctour wyse.   *Augustinus*
   Whaso come, als I vnderstande,
Byfore þe kynge of Ingelande   10490
In his chaumbre to purchace
A thinge þat es of special grace,
He wald hym kepe þat he sayd nathing
þat lightly myght displese þe kynge.

   With mare skille he suld kepe him ay   10495
þat comes in Goddis chaumbre to pray
þat es heghe kynge ouer alle kynges
And cheef gouernour of alle thinges.
þat es to say in Halykirke,
Whare men suld haly werkes wirke,   10500
þe whilk es Goddis chaumbre priue
And his awen hous, als says he
þar he says þus, 'Mi hous es
Hous of prayere and of clennes'.
So þat he þare do ne say nathinge   10505
þat myght displese þat almyghty kynge.

   Godde wil noght þat men make ne sette
Of his hous bothe ne markette.
þarefore Godde alle þa dryue walde
Out of þe temple þat boght and salde,   10510
For he wald noght þat men made dyn
Ne did na werldely dedes þarinne.
He wald men tented til hym anely
To pray hym of helpe and of mercy
And to loue him ay with gode wille   10515
And thank him, bathe loude and stille,

10488 says] *int.* P, *om.* W   *sidenote om.* PW   14089 -so] -some E   come]
comes P   come als] war sted R   *sidenote*: Exemplum E   10490 þe] a R   of Inge-]
in any R   10491 In] Withinne R   10492 es of] warr o LS, fell to R
10493 þat] hym þat L, *om.* P   10494 þe] his P   10497 ouer] of LR
10498 cheef] *om.* W   10499 es] he W   10500 Whare] þer W   10501 priue]
fre RW   10504 prayere] prayeres ES   *sidenote*: Domus vt supra E   10505 he]
ȝhe EL   þare] *om.* L   ne say] *om.* S   10506 myght] mˈaˈy P   þat²] þe S   al-]
om. L   10507 þat] *om.* P   10508 bothe] boche E, borghe P   10509 þa] þen P
10510 and] or LW   10511 þat] ne *canc.* P   10512 did] do LR   dedes] nedes L,
thynges S   10513 wald] *adds* þat L   tented] tended W   10513 of²] *om.* R
10515 to] *om.* LP

Donum Intellectus   De Castitate
Adueniat regnum tuum

fol. 63ᵛᵇ Of alle gode þat he has þam done.
      þan wil Godde here þair prayer sone.
        þare suld a man putte out of his hert
      Alle idell thoghtes þat comes ouerthwert   10520
      And sette stedfastly al his thoght
      On Godde anely, þat hym made of noght
      And fra helle boght with his blode,
      And think wele on alle othir gode
      þat he has done of his curtaysy   10525
      And ilk day dose contynuelly
      And recorde his synnes þat he has done
      And bifore Godde þare meke hym sone
      And pray hym oft of forgifnes
      Of alle his synnes, mare and lesse,   10530
      And þat he gif hym grace forwarde
      To kepe hym fra synne þat byndes harde
      And gif hym wille to do alle thynge
      þat es mast to Goddis likynge
      And mast shendship vnto þe fende   10535
      And wele to lyf and wele to ende.
        þare suld þis grete lordes and ladys
      Forgete þair noblay, if þai war wys,
      And þair dignyte and þair heghenes
      And þair powere þat so grete es,   10540
      And thynk anely þat þai er þan
      Byfore þair lorde and þair domesman
      þat at þe dredeful day of dome,
      When alle men sal bifore hym come,
      Sal resounes ask of þam sone   10545
      Of al þe gode þat he has þam done
      Of þair heghenes and of þair state,

10517 gode] þe (*om.* S) godes LS   10518 þair prayer] þaime L   10523 boght]
add hym LR   his] *adds* precious S   10524 on] *om.* E   10525 done] *add* hym PR
10527 he] *om.* P   10528 hym] -ly P   10529 oft] *om.* PRW   10532 byndes]
bytys R   10535 vnto] to ELPR   10537 þis] 'þe' P   and] and þir L   10538 if . . .
wys] and þaire ryches L   10541 þai] þae P   10543 dredeful] *om.* L   of] of þe
grete L   10545 Sal . . . of] He sall acounte aske L   þam] *adds* full R   10546 gode]
dedes L   he has] þai haue L   þam] *om.* LP   10547 of²] *om.* LW

How þai it vsed, arely and late.
And þan sal he yhelde rightwysly
To ille and gode als þai er worthy.   10550
þarefore þai suld at þe kirke þam lawe
To Godde, bathe thurgh luf and awe,
And noght þam enpryde for þair heghnes
Of þair apparaylle and þair ritchesce.

   Bot take ensaumple of þe lifynge   10555 *Exemplum*
Of Dauid þat was a riche kynge,
þat had forgeten his dignyte
When he prayde to Godde with hert fre
And dispysed himself when he prayde
And bifor Godde on þis wyse sayde: 10560
'I am na man þat men worshepes,   *Dauid*

De Castitate

Bot a worme þat naked crepes.'   fol. 64ra
In þis al his feblesce knewe he,
His pouert and his vanyte.
For als a worme es of na prys   10565
And lytell and vyle to dispyse
And comes crepand naked and bare
Out of þe erth and es bredde þare,
Right so a man es a vyle thinge
And lytell and pouer at his bigynnynge.   10570
For when he comes with sorowful chere
Into þe exile of þis werlde here,
He brynges noght with hym þat day,
And noght sal he bere with him away.
Al naked he comes hider and bare,   10575
And al naked sal he hethen fare.

   Wharefore Saynt Bernard sayde sumtyme   *Bernardus Homo est*
þat man es noght bot a foul slyme,   *sperma fetidum, saccus*
                                                     stercorum, et esca vermium

10548 How] *add* þat LR   it] þai R   10549 sal he] *trs.* P   he] be L   10553 for]
þurgh L   10554 Of] Na for L and] na L þair²] *om.* W   10555 Bot] And L of] at L
sidenote om. P   10557 *line om.* W   10560 bifor] for P   10561 *sidenote: om.* P   Dauid]
adds Nota E   10563 feblesce] febylnesse ELPSR   10565 als] *om.* L   10566 vyle]
wylle S   10568 es bredde] bredes L   10570 and²] 'of' P   10571 *sidenote:* Miseria
hominis E   10574 with him] *om.* L   10575 Al] And R   10576 al] *om.* LP, als S
hethen] hyns R   10577 -fore Saynt] þat L sayde] sais PRW *sidenote: partly cut away* PW
sperma] spina S, ?opus W fetidum] *adds* et L   10578 a] *om.* R noght] *om.* L

And a secke þat es ful of fen
þat stynkes foul vnto alle men,   10580
And wormes mete þam to fede
þat thurgh kynde of þe erth may brede.
   When man es geten thurgh kynde of man,
He es noght bot a foul slyme þan;
And als lange als he es here lifand,   10585
He es a secke ful of fen stynkande;
And when he es dede and layde in graue,
þan es he fode þat wormes wald haue.
   Also þis grete ladys of myght
þat comes so apparaylled and dight   10590
With siluer and perels and golde rede
And precious stanes opon þair hede,
With riche robes to þe kirke namely,
Bifore our Lorde Godde almyghty
Suld take ensaumple, als was sene   10595
By Hester þat was so ryche a quene.
þat did hir riche apparaylle away,
When sho bifore Godde come to pray,
And ful mekely lawed hir in hert
And knewe bifore Godde hir pouert   10600
And sayde to hym þus, 'Lorde, þou wate
þat þe tokenyng of Pryde I hate
Agayne þis wreched werldes consaylle,
For I haf na lykynge in riche apparaylle

De Castitate

fol. 64ʳᵇ Of precious stanes ne of gold rede,   10605
Nouthir on body ne on hede.
Bot it es to me abhomynable,
For it may make mens hertes vnstable'.
   Certes, right so to Godde may be

10581 to] with to R   10583 man] a man L   10584 slyme] skyn R
10590 apparaylled] appayred S   10591 siluer and perels] perry L   perels] perle P
rede] sa rede L   10592 stanes] stane W   opon] on P, in RW   10593 þe] om. P
10594 our . . . Godde] trs. phrs. P   10595 was] es S   10596 so . . . a] a ryche ESR
sidenote: Hester Exemplum EL, Exemplum P, Hester regina (later) W   10597 did]
before away P   apparaylle] robes L   10598 come] befor P, after sho S   10603 þis
wreched] þe wycked L   10604 in] of P   apparaylle] parayle W   10605–6 couplet
trs. L   10605 stanes] stane W   10606 line om. S   on'] of P   on²] of R
10609 right . . . Godde] trs. phrs. LS

Grete abhominacioun to se 10610
Of þam þat has in swilk thinge
Grete pryde and grete lykynge
And dightes þam quayntly to be sene
Vnto þair sight þat foles bene.
Of swilk apparaylle Godde tase na kepe, 10615
Al-if þai it vse for worshepe
In þe kirk in his presence.
Bot of þe meke hert and clene conscience
Godde almyghty mast after þat lokes,
Als clerkes may fynde in sere bokes. 10620
    Saynt Paul þe apostell teches right *Paulus*
How gode wymmen suld þam dight,
When þai suld to þe kirke wende
To pray to Godde, our sikerest frende.
'þai suld haue', he says, 'thurgh skille 10625
Habyte after þair state wille
þat war honest, withouten outrage,
þat war noght of ouermykell costage.'
þat es to vndirstande namely
After þai er of state worthy, 10630
For þat þat es mesure till ane
Til anothir may be at outrage tane.
    Wele mare falles vntill a quene
þan til a countays, als I wene,
And mare til a countay`s´ body 10635
þan to anothir symple lady,
And mare til hir þat men lady calles
þan to a symple woman falles.
    Also Saynt Paul teches þam right *Paulus*
How þai suld be symple of sight, 10640
þat es to say shameful and meke

10611 Of þam] To haue S   in] of E   thinge] thinges L   10612 Grete] Any kynne L   grete lykynge] lykinges L   10614 Vnto] To PW   10615 na] *om*. P 10616 Al-if] Of-all L   it vse] *trs*. S, vsed R   for] to hys L   10618 of þe] of LRW, 'of' P   þe] clene S   hert] hertes L   10621 *sidenote*: De orname(n)to mulierum R, *om*. W   10622 suld] sall L   suld þam] *trs*. S   10623 suld] sall R   suld . . . kirke] vnto þe kyrk sall L   10624 to] *om*. S   our] on P, *om*. RW   10627 withouten] þurgh L   10631 till] vnto R   10632 at] *om*. LSW   tane] be tane L 10633 vntill] to P   10634 countays] *adds* body E   10635 til] vnto LR   countays] s *int., original hand* A   10637 þat] þen W   10638 woman] lady L   10639 Also] As W   *sidenote om*. LW

And na quayntyse to þair hedes seke,
Als tressurs and bilets þai suld nane vse,
Als fole wymmen commonly duse,
þat strekes þe neckes out als þe hert   10645
A[nd a]ls a hors of prys lokes ouerthwert.
Paulus   And yhete Saynt Paul, als teches he,
Wil noght þat þai ouerbisy be

Donum Intellectus   De oracione
De Castitate   Adueniat regnum tuum

fol. 64va Ne ouercuryous þair heuedes to dight,
Nouthir with siluer ne with gold bright.   10650
He wil þai haue, als he counsaylles,
þair heuedes couerd with clene vaylles
And when þai er at þe kirke namely,
Bifor our Lorde Godde almyghty,
So þat na man þare tempted be   10655
Thurgh sight of þam when þai þam se.
Als gode wymmen þai suld þam dight
þat godenes of þair hert shewes right.
Ambrosius Saynt Ambros says þus: 'He þat wille
þat Godde his prayere fulfille,   10660
He suld do away and hyde
Alle manere of tokenynge of Pryde
And bowe to Godde thurgh Mekenes namly
For to stir hym to haue mercy.
For proude apparaylle quayntly wroght   10665
Onence Godde may purchace noght
Bot gifs enchesoun to deme ille
Of hym or hir þat it vse wille.'
Now haf I shewed thinges thre
þat specially in Prayere suld be,   10670

10642 hedes] heued LSR, bodis P   10643 Als] And na (*canc.*?) L, And W
tressurs] trisses P   bilets] bilyetes E, byllyhes L   10644 fole] foule W
10645 strekes] streke LP   neckes] neke RW   þe] a LW   *10646 And als] Als
als A   10647 yhete] *after* als L, als S   als] alsswa L, *om.* S, as RW   *sidenote om.* LPSW
10648 Wil] He will R   10649 to] þai P   10651 He] Na L   he²] *om.* W
10652 heuedes] heued LS   10653 þe] *om.* E   10654 our] þaire L   10655 man]
mene ES   þare] *om.* P   10657 þai] *om.* W   10658 shewes] *adds* in þair P
10659 þus] *om.* L   he þat] *trs.* S   *sidenote om.* LW   10660 prayere] *adds here* R
10661 do] do sone R   10662 tokenynge] takyns R   10663 bowe] vow W   namly]
anely P   10667 gifs] gyf L   10668 it vse] *trs.* EP

Trouth, Hope, and Deuocioun,
Of whilk I haf made mencioun.
Bot to Prayere, als I vnderstande,
If it suld be to Godde lykande
And worthy to be herde sone,   10675
þe ferthe thing bihoued be done.
þat es to þe prayere men suld do
Twa wenges þat falles þarto,
Thurgh whilk it may fleghe vp euen
Byfore our Louerd, Godde of heuen.   10680
þat es Fastynge and Almusdede;
þise twa þe prayere may euen vp lede.
    Wharefore þe aungel spake to Toby
And sayd hym þus appertly,
'Prayere es a siker thynge   10685
With Almusdede and Fastynge'.
Withouten þise twa it may noght flegh
To Godde þat sittes in heuen so heghe.
    Forwhy als an haly man says,
Gode lyf þat es mykell to prayse   10690

Donum Intellectus	De oracione
De Castitate	Adueniat regnum tuum

Makes prayere to fleghe ful swiftly   fol. 64vb
To Godde with þise twa wenges þarby.
Bot synne, als þis clerkes knawes,
When it wald fleghe, agayne it drawes.
For men may wele wyte, whaso wil loke,   10695
Als Isidere says in a boke,   *Isidorus*
þat on twa maners for to neuen
Prayere es letted to fleghe to heuen:
Outhir forthy þat a man for drede
Wil noght [ses]e of synneful dede,   10700

10672 made] *om.* E, had W   10673 Bot] For L   *sidenote:* 'De' (*later*) oracione E
10677 þe] *om.* LP   men] þat men L   10678 wenges] thynges E   þat] þan L
10679 it] þe prayer L   *sidenote*: De duabus alis ES   10680 Louerd Godde] god kyng L
10682 þe] *om.* R   prayere may] *trs.* R   euen] *om.* E   10683 Whare-] Yhare- ELS
-fore] *om.* P   to] vnto L   10685 a] a full R   *sidenote:* Nota E   10686 and] and
with R   10688 so] *om.* L   10689 -why] *om.* R   10690 þat] *om.* E
10691 ful] *om.* L   swiftly] swithly P   10692 þise] hys W   10695 wele] *om.* L
10696 Als] þat W   *sidenote om.* LW   10697 maners] maner S   10698 to] for to L
10700 *sese] lette AELS   of] of his R

Or forthi þat he wil noght þe trespase
Forgif, to þam þat greued hym hase.

    For als nathinge may hele a wounde
þare þar iren ligges in þe grounde,
Nouthir oynement ne medycyne,   10705
Als lange als iren ligges withinne,
Right so his prayere helpes him noght
þat haldes ille wille in hert or thoght.
It es noght herde, als þe boke telles,
Als lange als ille wille in þe hert dwelles.   10710
And þarefore says þus þe prophete,
Whase wordes to rede and here er swete:
'Lift we', he says, 'our hertes vp euen
And our handes to Godde of heuen.'

    He liftes his hert rightwysly   10715
And his handes to Godde almyghty
þat Prayer lifts heghe to be sene
Thurgh Gode Werkes and Conscience Clene.
Also þe apostoyll vs biddes and teches,
Als þis prechours says þat oft preches,   10720
þat we clene handes lift vp ay
In alle our prayers, when we sal pray.

    Clene handes er called here Clene Werkes
Of Clene Conscience, als says þis clerkes.
For Godde wille noght here, als I wene,   10725
Prayer þat comes of hert vnclene
þat has þe conscience withinne
Foul and ful of filthe of synne.

    Wharefore our Lorde Godde spekes to vs
Propheta Thurgh þe prophete þat says þus: 10730
'When yhe make many prayers sere,
I wil nane of þam blethely here,

10701 -thi] *om.* L   noght þe] na R   10704 þare] þat W   þar] *om.* L, whar R   in] at P, wythin S   10707 him] *om.* P   10708–9 *lines trs.* P   10709 noght] *om.* L 10710 þe] *om.* PL   10711 þe] a L   *sidenote*: Propheta E   10712 rede and here] here and se L, here and rede R   here] *om.* S   10713 he . . . hertes] *trs. phrs.* LSRW 10717 heghe] *om.* L, clene hygh S   10719 apostoyll] gospell P   biddes] bides P *sidenote*: Apostolus ES   10720 *after* 10722, *marked for corr.* P   þis] *om.* P   prechours] prechoure W   10721 handes] hand W   10722 prayers] prayer L   when] þat ELS we] 'ȝhe' P   sal] *om.* L   10726 Prayer] Prayers L   10728 of²] and PR 10729 spekes] sais P   10730 þat] þare he L   *sidenote*: *om.* PW

Forwhy yhour handes er al blody'.

De Castitate   De oracione

þus es wryten in þe prophecy.   fol. 65ra
Blody handes þa men has   10735
þat þe pouer men pilles and flaas
þat vndir þam bene, and with maystry
Reues þam þat þat þai suld lif by.
Swilk men has blody handes and rede
Of þe blode of pouer men þat þai shede,   10740
For þai wald þam lyfles make
When [þai] þair lyflade wald fra þam take
Thurgh Couatyse and Rauyne.
þis methynk es ful grete synne.
    Swilk men mykill outrage duse   10745
For þai so blody morsels vse.
Wharefore þai sal make an harde pay
When þai passe fra þis lyf away,
If Haly Writte þat þe boke shewes vs
Be sothe þat telles and says þus: 10750
þat our Lorde, Godde almyghty,
At domesday sal aske straytely
þe blode of men þat pouerly gaase
Of þam þat þe handes blody has.
    Wharefore whaso wrange wil oght take,   10755
Of þat bihoues hym amendes make
And yhelde agayne al wrange-tane thing
To þam þat awe it or in helle hynge.
And þarefore our Lorde God wil noght
þair prayer here þat þus has wroght;   10760
Bot þai þam amende of þat foly,
To be herde þai er noght worthy.
    Whaso wil comme in Goddis sight
Hym to pray and wald be herde right,

10733 Forwhy] Forþi R   10736 men] man S   and] or W   10737 þam] om. P
10738 þat²] om. LPW   10741 þai] int. P, -þi R   wald þam] trs. P   10742 *þai] om.
AS   wald] after þam L, om. W   10744 ful] om. E, a full L   10746 blody] body L
vse] vses W   10747 an] a full L   10748 þai] adds sall S   10749 þat] after boke
L, as S   boke] be P   10750 and] ans E   10752 At] On LS   10754 þe . . . blody]
blody handes L   has] mase S   10755 -so] om. W   10758 awe] aght LSRW
10760 prayer] prayers L   10761 Bot] To 'bot' P   10762 To] For to R   þai] om. R

With drawen swerde he suld noght com,   10765
Ne with blody handes ne handes tome.
þat es to say, in wille to synne
Ne vnclensed of foly withinne
Ne tome-hande of gode dede,
And if he do, he sal noght spede.   10770

Dominus dicit: Non For Godde says þus in Haly Wrytte,
apparebis vacuus in Als þe boke witteneses it:
conspectu meo
'þou sal noght', als he says, 'come
In my sight with handes tome.'
Bifore Godde comes he tome-hande   10775
þat askes hym any bone prayande
Withouten present of Gode Werkes;

De Castitate   De oracione

fol. 65rb He sal noght spede, als says þis clerkes.
Agayne hym sperres Godde þe yhate,
Als þis clerkes wele it wate,   10780
þat prays hym here of anythinge
And wil na presente with him brynge.
Exemplum de virginibus   Of þat we haf ensaumple to telle,
Als es wryten in þe godspelle,
How þe yhates war sperred fast   10785
Agayne þe fole maydens þat come last,
þat þair laumpes tome with þam broght;
þarefore Godde sayde, 'I knaw yhou noght'.
Wharefore Godde wil knaw na man
Bot þam þat serues him als þai can,   10790
And in þair laumpes has oylle of prys,
Als had þe maydens þat war wys.
þat er, als vnderstanded may be,
þa þat þe hertes has ful of Pyte
And shewes it outwith thurgh Gode Werkes;   10795

10766 ne] ne with PRW   10770 do he] *repeats* P   10771 *sidenote:* *om.* AW, at
10779 ES   Dominus dicit] *adds* in euangelio P, *om.* S   10773 als] *om.* LR, allon W
10774 In] Into P   10776 any] of any L   10781 of] to W   10783 *sidenote om.*
LW   10784 es] it is P   10785 How] How þat L   10786 þe] *om.* P   fole] foul
RW   come] *adds* at L, *om.* P   10788 Godde sayde] *trs.* P   10789 knaw] kawe E
10790 þam] þaa L   10793 þat] þase L   vnderstanded] -standen ELPSRW
10794 hertes] hert S   has] *after* þat P   ful] *om.* L   10795 outwith] with P   thurgh]
om. L, with S

Swilk men Godde heres, þus says þis clerkes.
To swilk men Godde opens þe yhate
þat comes noght tome-hand ne ouerlate.
When þai pray and aske a bone,
He resayues þair prayer sone.   10800
    Now haf I shewed how þe prayere
þat þise four pilers suld vp bere—
Trouth, Deuocioun, Hope to spede,
And Fastynge with Almusdede,
þe whilk yhe herde me byfore neuen—   10805
Es myghty onence Godde of heuen.
Forwhy it wynnes of him lightly
Alle þat es nedeful vnto þe body
And to þe saul þat sikirrest es,
Als Haly Wrytte beres wyttenes.   10810

    Wharefore Saynt Iame says in a boke,   *Iacobus*
Als clerkes may se + þat wil it loke,
þat rightwis mans prayer in skille
Es mykell worth þat Godde here wille.
For it helpes and warisshes wele   10815
Alle euels þat a man may fele
Of body and saul þat gretly greues
And þat þai mast drede þat here leues.
Wharefore Godde says, als in boke es sene,

Donum Intellectus   De Castitate
Adueniat regnum tuum

þat þe prayere þat comes of hert clene   10820 fol. 65va
Heles men withouten and withinne
And purchaces forgifnes of alle synne.
    We fynde wryten in þe Alde Lawe
In a boke þat clerkes suld knawe

10796 Godde heres] *trs.* LS   þus] als LS, *om.* R   þis] þe P   10797 To] Vnto L
swilk] whilk PR   10799 and . . . a] hym of rightwyse R   aske] askes L   10801 how]
ȝow W   10802 *sidenote:* Nota E   10803 hope] and hope L   10804 with] as
with R   10806 Es myghty] Als es L   10807 it] he R   of] *om.* L   10808 vnto] to
LSRW   10811 *sidenote:* Sanctus Iacobus L, *om.* P   10812 *se] se it A   þat] whasa L
it] *om.* PS   10814 worth] worthy W   10818 þai] þai may L   10819 says] *om.* L
in] in a LR   10820 þat²] *om.* P   comes of hert] of þe hert comes P   of] of a L
10821–2 *om., and in their place* 10402–14, *the extra lines cancelled with* va . . . cat *and the
couplet added at the page foot* P

þat Moyses ouercome appertly   10825
Amalech, Goddis enemy,
And al his oste þat come on were
Noght thurgh bataylle, bot thurgh prayer.
And also an haly man þus says
þat a rightwis man, when he prayse,   10830
May mare auaylle, to Godde prayande,
þan may ten thousant men fightande.

Breuis oracio penetrat   þe prayere here of a gode man
celum   Thirles heuen and entres þan.
Suld it noght þan ouercom clene   10835
þe enemys þat in erthe er sene?
A gode man prayand mare wynne may
Of heuen in ane hour of þe day
þan a thousant knyghtes suld wyn of lande
In lange tyme thurgh dynt of hande.   10840
  þarefore war gode, als I yhou kenne,
To purchace þe prayers of gode men
þat gifs þam to deuocioun,
And namely of men of religyoun
þat wone togider in company   10845
For to serue Godde specially
And to pray for alle þat dose þam gode,
þat helpes þam to þair lyfs fode.
Forwhy if a gode mans beede
Onence Godde may stande in stede,   10850
Wele mare auaylles, als es oft sene,
Prayere of many gode men and clene.
For als þe haly man namely says,
When many gode men togider prayse,
It may noght faylle on na manere   10855
þat ne Godde wille þair prayer here.

10825 ouercome appertly] *om. (a blank)* R   *sidenote:* Exemplum E   10826 A *only,
rest of line om.* R   Amalech] *adds* þat wasse L   10827 al] *om.* W   þat . . . were] with
hym in fere L   on] of P   10829 And] *om.* L   also] als P   10832 ten] a P   men]
om. L   10833 *sidenote om.* W   10835 þan] *om.* L   10836 er sene] bene P
10838 þe] a LPSRW   10840 In] In full L   thurgh] with P   10841 þare-]
Whare- L   *sidenote:* Nota bene E   10842 prayers] prayer LR   10843 to] vnto LS
10845 wone] wonnes ELPSW   10846 specially] allmyghty LR   10847 alle] *adds*
hom W   10848 þat] And R   þam] *om.* R   lyfs] lyfe W   10850 in] mykell in S
10851 es oft] *trs.* LPR   10852 men] man S   10855 faylle] falle L

And if ane war a fole or twa
Of a company, alle er noght swa,
Als in case may falle ful lightly.
And so felle in Goddis cumpany: 10860
Of his apostels Iudas was ane

Donum Intellectus   De Castitate
Adueniat regnum tuum

þat him bytrayst and made be tane.   fol. 65vb
Bot þe tothir war gode and wele did,
Al-if he war a shrewe kidde.
   þe prayere of al a couent   10865
þat es haally of ane assent
Sal be of þe abbot herde mare
þan sal a munk, whilk-so he ware.
Right so Godde heres tittar þair bede
þat dwelles togider in haly stede   10870
To serue Godde and hym to worshepe
þan of ane of þe felawshepe.
Wharefore Godde says in þe godspelle
In þis manere als I now telle: *Dominus dicit in*
'If twa of yhow with hert fre   10875 *euangelio*
Accorden togider with me,
Whatso yhe of my Fader craue,
Withouten dout yhe sal it haue.'
   Here now haf yhe herde me neuen
In þis boke þe degrees seuen   10880
þat falles proprely vnto þe tre
Of þe vertu of Chastyte.
Now wille I shewe aftir my wytte
þe seuen braunches þat comes of it,
þat seuen manere of states er sere   10885
Of men þat lifs in þis werlde here.

10856 ne] *om.* LS   10859 in] in a PW   10860 in] it in L   10861 apostels] s²
int. P, discipils R   10862 bytrayst] betrayed LPSR, betresend W   made] gert L
10863 þe tothir] other W   10864 Al . . . war] Of-al warr Iudas L   10868 whilk-]
what L, swhilk W   10869 þair] þe P   10871 *line om. (blank)* R   to²] *om.* PW
10872 *line om.* L   10874 In] On PR   now] ȝowe ELR   *sidenote*: Euangelium S, *om.* W
dicit] *om.* EL   10876 Accorden] Be acordande S   10877 yhe] *after* Fader E
10878 it] *om.* W   10879 now] *om.* P   10880 þe] of þe R   10883 shewe] say P
10885–6 *couplet trs.* R   10885 *line om.* W   þat] þe L   manere] maners LP   er] *om.* L

Ane es of maydens þat wil fle
Flesshely dede til þay maryed be;
Anothir es of anelepy
þat has bene fyled and leues þair foly;　　　　　　10890
Þe thridde es of þa þat wedded ben⟨e⟩;
Þe ferthe state es of widous clene;
Þe fift state es of maydens sly
þat thinkes be chast vntil þai dy;
Þe sext state of clerkes may be　　　　　　　　10895
þat er ordayned in haly degre;
Þe seuent, als þe boke mas mencioun,
Es of men of religyoun.

j^{us}. status: De statu
virginum quibus licet
nubere si velint
Þe first state es of maydens namly
þat kepes þam clene of body　　　　　　　　10900
And saues wele þair Maydenhede
Fra alle filth of litcherous dede,

De Castitate

fol. 66ra　Bot so vnbounden er þai and fre
þat þai may leeffully wedded be.
In swilk a state men suld kepe　　　　　　　10905
Chastyte to Goddis worshepe,
þat es clennes of þe body
And of þe hert withouten foly.

ij. De statu corruptorum
penitencium et continere
volencium
Þe secund state to kepe clene
Es of þam þat fyled has bene　　　　　　　　10910
Thurgh þe filth of litcherous dede
And has lost þair maydenhede,
Als man and womman anelepy
þat neuer was wedded—swilk er many—
Na neuer so bounden to Chastyte　　　　　　10915

10887 sidenote: j. W (and further numeration through this verse paragraph)
10888 dede] dedys R　　　　10890 fyled] fylled R　　leues] leued LS　　　10891 þe]
þat P　þa] þam R　　　10892 state] om. S　　state es] es þe state L　　　10893 state es] trs. P
10894 be] to be L　vntil] to L　　　10898 of¹] om. L　　　10899 es] om. R　　namly]
anely P　　sidenote: as in-column heading R　　j^{us}. status] om. R　　De statu] om. W　　De . . .
virginum] virginibus　virginum] virginitatis S　　quibus . . . velint] om. S　　　10900 þam]
þam ay R　　　10902 alle] alkyn L　litcherous] lecchours W　　　10905 suld] schuld ay R
10906 to] vnto R　　　10907 clennes] clene W　þe] om. W　　10908 And] om. S　þe]
om. W　　　10909 to] is to W　　sidenote: as in-column heading R　　ij.] ij^{us}. status EPSW,
Secundo status L, om. R　　statu] adds religioso L　　et] om. L　　　10911 þe] om. W
10915 so] warr L, ys R

þat þai ne may maryed be,
And has bene shryuen and dose penaunce
And in þair hertes has repentaunce
Of alle þair synnes, mare and lesse,
And kepes þam forwarde in clennes.   10920

    In swilk state men suld kepe ryght
Chastyte with al þair myght.
For he þat es here in þat state,
He suld be bisy, arely and late,
Alle þe enchesouns of synne to fle;   10925
In swilke purpos he suld ay be,
And so may he kepe his body chast
And on þat manere plese Godde mast.
To saue he may for certayne skille
Mary hym what tyme so he wille.   10930

    Bot whaso wille kepe hym for mede
Clene and chast of litcherous dede,
Hym bihoues his flesshe chasty
With harde penaunce of body.
For hym bihoues fast and wake   10935
And þat his flesshe lykes forsake,
And þus he may his flesshe doun halde
Fra foly ay when it ryse walde.

    þe thridde state es of þam to knawe   *iij^{us}. De statu*
þat wedded ere thurgh Goddis lawe.   10940   *coniugatorum*
In þat state men suld thurgh right
Kepe C[h]astyte bathe day and nyght.
To saue men suld for certayne skille
þe werke of sposaylle fulfille.
For a man and his wedded wyf   10945

De Castitate

Suld luf togider withouten stryf.   fol. 66rb
And aythir of þam suld þam kepe

10916 þai] *om.* P   ne] *om.* LS   may] may wele R   maryed] weddede P   10917 dose]
done L   10918 And] *om.* P   hertes] herte ES   10919 and] *om.* L   10926 swilke]
whilke P   10927 may he] he sulde L   10928 Godde] hys god L   10930 Mary] To
mary L   10932 of] fro R   10934 of] of his R   10938 ryse] rysche E
10939 *sidenote: as in-column heading* R   iij^{us}.] iij. P, *om.* R, *add* status ELSW   De statu] yd
est W   10940 wedded] wede E   10941 In] *om.* E   *10942 Chastyte] Castyte A
10943 for] þurgh L   10944 werke] werkes L   10947 þam] other S

Leel til othir for Goddis worshepe,
And nouthir of þam do othir wrange
Bot þat þat right es do ay amange;   10950
þis es Halykirkes counsaylle.
And þus wille þe lawe of sposaylle,
Thurgh whilk aythir has othir tane,
And als a body er bathe ane.
For þai er bathe togider knytte   10955
In Goddis yhock, als says Haly Writte.
    And þarefore aythir suld othir luf
Leelly for þair saulles bihoue.
For als þai er bathe a body by skille,
So suld þai be a hert thurgh wille   10960
In certayne fayth and luf stedefast
þat to þair lyues ende suld last,
And na twynnyng make Godde to greue
Of body ne hert whyles þai lif.

Quod Deus coniunxit   For þus es wryten in Haly Wrytte,   10965
homo non separet   Men suld noght l[ou]se þat Godde has knytte'.
Wharefore þai suld kepe þam fra synne
After þe state þat þai lif inne,
Saue þat þai may þe werke wirke
Of sposaylle thurgh þe lawe of Halykirke.   10970

Paulus   þarefore Saynt Paul says þus to proue
þat wymmen suld þair lordes luf
And vnder Godde þam worshepe mast
And ay amange be sobre and chast:
Chast to kepe þam clene of body   10975
Fra alle othir bot þair lordes anely;
Sobre in mete and in drynk,
And on þair state þai suld ay thinke.
For grete outrage, als þe boke shewes,
Of mete and drynk appayres gode thewes   10980

10948 til] vnto L   10949 þam] other L   10950 þat²] *om.* L   10954 And] *om.* S   a] in L   er] er made P   10957 aythir suld] *trs.* PR   10958 þair] ayther W bihoue] behoues S   10959 bathe] *om.* L   10960 thurgh] wyth L   10962 to] *om.* E   lyues] lyf R   10964 ne] na of L, and S   10965 *sidenote: om.* W   homo ... separet] nemo seperabit P   *10966 louse] lese AP, loyse R   10968 lif] er S   10970 þe] *om.* LRW   10971 Paul] Ione W   *sidenote om.* PW   10974 ay] *om.* L be] þaim P   10975 to] for to P   10976 lordes] *adds* body P   10977 in¹] bath in R in²] *om.* R   10978 on] of W   ay] þay S   10980 mete and drynk] metes and drynkes L   appayres] enpayres LR

And kyndels þe fyre of Litchery
And stirs men oft to grete foly.
    Also a man suld kepe hym right
Chast and clene with al his myght
Fra alle wymmen bot fra his wyf   10985
þat hym byhoues halde to terme of lyf.
    Sposaylle es a state to worshepe
þat men suld ay clenely kepe
And halyly after Goddis lawe
For many skils þat men suld knawe.   10990

Donum Intellectus   De Castitate
Adueniat regnum tuum

For Sposaylle es, als men may se,   fol. 66ᵛᵃ
A state of grete auctorite,
Of dignyte, and of halynesse;
Thurgh þise thre Sposaylle stabled es.
    Of grete auctoryte es it,   10995
Als beres wittenes Haly Writte.
Forwhy our Lorde Godde rightwys
It stabled first in Paradyse
In þe state of obedyence,
Ar euer man synned thurgh neclygence.   11000
þarefore men suld with al þair myght
þat state clene kepe, bathe day and nyght,
Als teches and biddes Haly Wrytte,
By resoun of Godde þat first stabled it,
And bi resoune of þe stede clene   11005
þare it was first stabled and sene.
    Also Sposaylle es a heghe state
Of grete dignyte, als clerkes wate.
Forwhy our Lorde wald borne be
Of a wedded womman þat was fre.   11010
þat was blisseful Mary, mayden clene,
þat Ioseph wedded hir to mayntene.

10982 grete] *om.* S   10986 to] *om.* LR   of] of hys L   10987 a] *int.* P, *om.* S
to] of W   10988 ay] allway R   clenely] clene L   10989 halyly] haly L, halaly S,
halely W   10993 Of¹] And of L   10994 stabled] stable LR   10997 Godde] *after*
Forwhy S   11001 men] þai ES   11002 clene kepe] *trs.* LPR   bathe] *om.* L
11005 stede] *adds* so R   11006 first] *om.* W   11007 a] of a L   11008 Of] And
of L

Goddis sone bifore þe heghe message
Made hir þe mantell of Maryage
And wald be vndir þat mantell hemme   11015
Conceyued and borne withouten wemme.
Vndir þat mantell, als clerkes can telle,
Was hidde fra þe deuell of helle
þe counsaylle of our saluacioun
And þe pryuyte of our raunsoun.   11020
þarefore men suld þat state worshepe
And honestly and clene it kepe.
    It es also, þar it es wemmeles,
A state of grete halynes.
For it es ane of þe sacramentes   11025
þat Halykirke mykell to tentes,
And bytokens þe sposaylle
þat es knytte and neuer sal faylle
Bytwene Ihesu Cryst and Halykirke
(Thurgh whase counsaylle vs bihoues wirke)   11030
And bitwene Godde on þe same manere
And mans saul þat he boght dere.
    Wharefore þe state of Maryage
þat clene es keped fra outrage

Donum Intellectus   De Castitate
Adueniat regnum tuum

fol. 66ᵛᵇ Es so haly and so myghty   11035
þat a flesshely dede wroght rightly
In Sposaylle, als it falles to be,
Withouten dedely synne es fre;
And noght anely withouten synne,
Bot it may of Godde grete mede wynne.   11040
þat es to say if it be wroght
Als Goddis lawe wald, and elles noght.
Tres sunt casus in quibus Wharefore yhe sal vnderstande þarby
vir et vxor eius in opere þat in thre case specially
carnali non peccant

11015 þat] þe E   hemme] euen hemme P   11018 þe] *repeats* P, þai R
11020 pryuyte] prynte L   11021 þare-] Whare- L   11023 þar] whare L
11025 þe] þo E   11026 to] *om.* PRW   11027 And] And it R   11030 bihoues]
behoue S   11031 Godde] ged W   11032 he] ys R   boght] *adds* sa L
11034 fra] fra all R   11037 falles] aght L   to] at P   11040 Godde] *om.* P
11041 if] and L   11042 and] or W   11043 *sidenote om.* W   11044 case] causes R

Men may þe dede of Sposaylle saue   11045
Fra synne, and mede for þat dede haue.
   þe first case here to shewe yhou sone   *j. casus*
Es þar þe dede es anely done
In þis entent: for childer-getynge
To serue Godde, and for nane othir thinge.   11050
For swilke entent mast to auaylle
Was ordayned þe dede of Sposaylle.
   þe secund case es þis to witte   *ij.ᵘˢ. casus*
þat when twa er togider knytte
In Weddelayke, if nathinge it lette,   11055
þe tane sal yhelde þe tothir his dette.
When þe tane askes leeffully,
þe tothir to yhelde suld be redy,
For þareto stirs þam Rightwysnes
þat yheldes to ilk man þat his right es.   11060
   Wharefore if þe tane als þe lawe wille
Askes þe dette, outhir loude or stille,
By mouthe appertly or parchaunce
Thurgh som tokenynge of cuntynaunce—
Als shamefull wymmen þat wald fayne haue   11065
þair dette and dar noght for shame + craue
By mouthe, als it asked suld be,
Bot thurgh som continaunce priue—,
Whethir of þam so wil forsake
þe dette to yhelde vnto his make,   11070
He gifs þe tothir enchesoun
To be of ille condycioun
And synnes agayne Rightwisnes
For he dose noght þat þat right es.
He synnes agayne his wedded fere,   11075
For he dose hir wrange on þis manere,
Forwhy þe tane has lawefully

11045 Men] þir R   þe] þis R   11046 dede] *om.* R   11047 here to] I sall L, to R
yhou] þe L   *sidenote: om.* LW   11048 Es¹] *om.* L   þar] ware R   es²] *om.* W
11050 and] *om.* P   for] to L   11053 case] cause R   *sidenote om.* PW   11056 his]
om. ESW   11059 stirs þam] *trs.* P   þam] *om.* S   11060 þat yheldes] To ȝelde P
his] *om.* LS   11061 Whare-] þare- L   11062 Askes] Aske LW   11064 of] or R
*11066 shame] *adds* it AR   11068 Bot] *adds* mon P   som] *om.* W   11069 so] þat
ELS   11070 vnto] to W   his] þaire LR   11071 Vnto þat other gyfes enchesoun L
He gifs] þai gyf R   11072 ille] wycked L   11074 þat²] *om.* L

Powere of þe tothirs body.
Bot he dose wele after Goddis lawe

De Castitate

fol. 67ra þat yheldes þe tothir þat he awe   11080
And if he so do trewely in dede,
In þat entent he es worthy mede,
For Rightwysnes him stirs þarto
And noght his Litchery so to do.

iij. þe thridde case after of þa thre   11085
Es when a man in pryuyte
Bedes his wyf to hir lykynge
þat derne dede withouten askynge,
So þat his entent be swilk wythinne
Anely to kepe hir fra synne.   11090
And namely if sho be in thoght
So shameful þat sho dar noght
Aske hir louerd swilk a thinge
By mouth ne by na takenynge;
And he hoped þat sho wald lightly   11095
Falle in synne and in foly,
If he bedde hir noght þat dede.
þan synnes he noght bot serues mede.
In þis case men suld þus do
For Pyte suld stir men þarto.   11100
In þise thre case men may wirke
Leeffully thurgh þe lawe of Halykirke
þe werke of Weddelayk withouten synne
After þe entent þat men er inne.

Tres sunt casus in quibus vir et vxor eius peccant in opere carnali mortaliter vel venialiter Bot in som case men may synne sone   11105
þar þe dede of Sposaylle suld be done,
Outhir dedely after þe dede es
Or venyally þat es yhete lesse,

11078 of] ouer LR   tothirs] tother ELS   11081 if] *om.* R   so do] *trs.* W
11083 For] And L   11084 his] *om.* L   11085 after] *om.* P   þa] þe ES, þis L
sidenote: Tercius casus ESW, *om.* PL   11088 þat] þe LS   11089 þat] þat þat W
swilk] skille E   11090 fra] out of P, so fro R   11092 sho] *adds* ne R   11094 na]
om. L   11095 hoped] hepede P, hoppe R   11097 If] If þat LR   noght] *om.* L
11098 he] *om.* P   11099 case] cause R   þus] it L   11100 stir men] *trs.* P
11101 case] causes R   11102 þe] *om.* LP   11104 men] þai LP   11105 *sidenote:*
om. LW   in] *om.* ? P   venialiter] *adds* primus casus E   11107 dede] syn P
11108 es yhete] *trs.* P

And specially in thre caase
Men may in þat dede trespase. 11110
   þe first case es, als þe boke telles, *j^us. casus*
When a man sekes noght elles
In þat dede bot to fulfille
His lust and his litcherous wille.
He synnes þus thurgh Litchery 11115
Outhir dedely or venyally.
   Venially, als when þe delyte *Venialiter sic*
(þat may ouercom a mans skille tyte)
Passes noght thurgh grete outrage
þe right boundes of maryage. 11120
þat es when þe delyte with wille
Es bouxsom and sogette vnto skille
So þat he þat es in þat state,
If he dedely synne right hate,

De Castitate

For nathyng wald swilk a dede do 11125 fol. 67rb
Bot with his wyf, ne assent þarto.
   Bot when his delyte and lust amange *Mortaliter sic*
Es to his wyf so grete and strange
And so blynded es þan his skille
þat he wald als wele his lust fulfille 11130
With hir and neuer þe mare hir spare,
Al-if sho noght his wyf ware.
In þis case I halde þat dede
Dedely synne þat men suld drede,
For his delyte has ouergrete rayke 11135
And passes þe boundes of Weddelayke.
   Wharefore our Lorde Godde es oft wrathe
To swilk men and wymmen bathe

11110 in] on W   11111 case] dede L es] *om.* LS *sidenote: om.* LW; hereafter W ceases to offer extensive annotation, and is only noted when a *sidenote* is present 11112 When] When þat L, As when R   11114 litcherous] lichery S 11116 or] or elles L   11117 þe] *om.* E *sidenote:* sic] *om.* LP 11120 boundes] bandes E   11121 es] *om.* L   11122 vnto] to PW   11125 For] And for P a] *om.* W dede] thyng S   11126 with] *om.* E   11127 lust] his loue W *sidenote: om.* L sic] *om.* P   11128 and] and so E   11129 blynded] blynde P   11130 lust] loue W 11132 Al-if] Als if L, If-all P noght] *om.* P wyf] *om.* R   11136 boundes] bandes R 11137 -fore] *om.* P our Lorde] *om.* R   11138 swilk] whilk P

And to þe fende gifs grete powere
To trauaylle þam and noy þam here.   11140
Als men may fynde wryten and knawe

Exemplum de Sarra filia
Raguelis et Thobia filio
Thobie In a boke of þe Alde Lawe
Of Raguell doghter þat ight Sare
þat Toby wyf was—þus fynde I þare—
þat had somtyme seuen husbandes.   11145
Alle war þai slayne thurgh þe fendes handes
þe first nyght, when þai wald ly
By hir thurgh lust of Litchery.
Wharefore þe aungell to Thoby spake
þat he suld hir to wyf take.   11150
    þan sayde Toby þus to þe aungell,
'I ne dar noght for þe case þat felle
Of hir seuen husbandes þat war slayne'.
þan þe aungell answerd agayne;
'I sal', quod þe aungell, 'telle þe   11155
In whilk men þe fende has pouste.
In swilk men he has mast powere
To trauaylle þam and greue þam here
þat puttes Godde out of þair thoght
When þe werke of Weddelayk suld be wroght   11160
And tentes to nane othir thinge
Bot to þair litcherous lykynge
And þair foul lust for to fulfille,
Als dose a beste þat has na skille.'
þarefore somtyme Godde vouches noght saue   11165
þat swilk men fruyt of engendrure haue.
    Alsso a man with his wedded fere
May synne dedely on othir manere.

11139 fende] fendes P   11140 To] And to W   noy] ney W   11141 may fynde]
trs. E   11142 *sidenote*: et] et de P   11144 wyf was] *trs.* E, 'wyf' was P
11145 -tyme] *om.* P   11148 lust of] luf and R   11151 *sidenote*: Thoby E
11152 ne] *om.* S   case] cause R, *om.* W   11154 answerd] *adds* hym L, *adds* þare S
11155 þe] *om.* L   11156 whilk] swilke ERW   11157 *line om.* LW (*supplied at page
foot* L)   swilk] whilk L   he . . . mast] þe fende has P   11161 to] vnto LR
11162 to] vnto L   11163 foul] f'o'ule P, full S   for to] *om.* E, to PW   11164 dose
a beste] *trs. phrs.* P   11165 somtyme] *om.* L   vouches] vouched RW   11166 men]
om. RW   engendrure] engendurr ne E, gendrure PS, *adds* noȝt R, engendryng W
11167 wedded] *after* a S   11168 othir] anothir R

Donum Intellectus   De Castitate
Adueniat regnum tuum

þat es to say when he oght dose   fol. 67ᵛᵃ
With his wyf agayne kyndely vse,   11170
His wille othirwyse to fulfille
þan þe lawe of Weddelayke and Kynde wille.
Swilk men yhete may synne mare
þan othir þat I spake of are.
Bot þai þat in þe state of Sposaylle   11175
Wirkes thurgh Halykirkes counsaylle
And dredes ay Godde almyghty
And kepes þat state here clenely,
Als ordayned es and als þe boke says;
Swilk men our Louerd mykell payse.   11180

    þe secund case þar men synne may   ijᵘˢ. casus
Dedely in Wedlayke es þis to say:
Als when a man has na drede
With his wyf to do þe dede
Thurgh delyte and lust þat may falle sone   11185
In tyme when it suld noght be done.
þat es when sho has a malady
þat som wymmen has comonly.
He þat his wyf þat tyme noght spares,
If he knaw first hou sho fares   11190
And in what state sho es of body,
Forsothe he synnes þan dedely.

    Forwhy our Lorde Godde forbedes
þat any man þat perille dredes
With his ʼwyfʼ dele when he wate   11195
þat sho es proprely in swilk + state
For perils þat er þan to drede
þat myght falle to þe fruyt of þe dede.
For Saynt Ierom shewes and telles   Ieronimus
In swilk tyme er geten meselles   11200

11171 wille] adds on L, likyng R   11173 yhete may] trs. SR   11175 þat] om. L
11178 þat] þaire L   11179 and] om. L   11180 Louerd] adds full L   payse] prays W
11181 þar] þat L   11184 þe] þat EP   11188 comonly] an extra minim L
11189 He þat] And he R   11190 If] And R   11191 And] om. L   es] be W   of] in
o L   11195 wyf] original hand corr. A, wyfe to L   when] adds þat L   *11196 state]
astate A   11198 of þe] for þat L, of R   11199 For] For als PRW   11200 tyme]
om. E, cases L   geten] gotyn R

And som þat has na shappe of man
And foles þat neuermare witte can,
And halt and lame, croked and blynde,
And domb and deef: swilk may men fynde.
   Wharefore þe womman þat wedded es   11205
And feles hir in swilk sekenes
Suld noght fra hir lorde it hele,
If he þat tyme wald with hir dele.
Bot if sho layne and haldes hir stille
And lates him with hir do his wille,   11210
If he knawe noght þat priuyte,
Sho synnes dedely and noght he.

Donum Intellectus   De Castitate
Adueniat regnum tuum

fol. 67ᵛᵇ   Also þai bathe suld kepe þam clene
And fra swilk dede þam abstene
In haly tymes þat er dere,   11215
Als at þe heghe festes of þe yhere;
And do noght elles þa tymes namely
Bot tente to our Lorde, Godde almyghty,
His seruyse þat tyme to fulfille.
For þe tyme es ordayned for þat skille.   11220
   Also þai suld in tyme of fastynge
Abstene þam fra swilke lykynge,
Noght anely for þat it es synne
Bot forþi þat þai myght titter wynne
Thinge þat þai aske of Godde þan,   11225
Als says Saynt Austyn, þe haly man.
   Also þai suld abstene þam right
Fra þat dede with al þair myght
Al þe tyme, if þai be wyse,
When þe womman in gisyne lyse,   11230

11201 has na shappe] schappe has nane P   na] *om.* S   11202 -mare] *om.* P
11203 lame] *add* and LW   11204 men] we P   11206 And] þat L   hir] hirself R
11207 it] *after* noght P   11208 wald] *after* hir R   11209 Bot] For L   haldes] halde
LPSW   11210 do] *after* him R, to W   11212 Sho synnes] þan synnes sho R
11213 þai] *om.* S   11216 Als at] And L, As in R   at þe] *om.* E   11217 þa] þat L, in þa
RW   tymes] tyme L   11218 Bot] And W   11219 to] for to P   11222 þam] *om.* E,
adds ay R   swilke] þat L   11223 þat] þat at R   11224 forþi...myght] for þai may þe L
þai] we S   11226 þe] þat L   *sidenote*: Augustinus L   11230 in] in þe L

Or when þai haf certayne knawynge
þat hir tyme es nere of chyldynge.
þai suld na tyme, arely ne late,
Dele togider in þat state,
Bot abstene þam for honeste   11235
And for drede of perils þat myght be.
And also fra þe dede þam spare
Fra tyme þat sho with quyck childe ware,
[For] if þe dede in þat state be wroght,
Withouten synne es it noght.   11240
    We fynde wryten in a boke
Of kynde of bestes, als men may loke,
þat þe olyfaunt wil forsake
þe felawship of his awen make
Alle tyme while sho with fole es,   11245
And of þis beres þe boke wyttenes.
þan think me þat a man suld be
Mare ledde with skille and attempre
þan a beste þat can na skille
þat folwes after kynde his wille.   11250
þarefore a man suld him abstene
When his wyf in þat state es sene.
    Bot always I wil noght say
þat he synnes in þat dede ay,
If he swilk tyme þe dede wil do   11255

De Castitate

With his wyf þat assentes þarto   fol. 68ra
By gode cause and entencion right.
þat can Godde deme þat es ful of myght.
    þe thridde case þar dedely syn may be   *iij. casus*
In þe dede of Sposaylle so pryue   11260
Es when a man thurgh his awen rede
Deles with his wyf in haly stede,

11231 þai haf] *repeats* L   11232 hir] þe W   nere] negh W   11236 myght] may L, mote P   11237 þe] þat L, *om.* R   11238 Fra] Fra þe R   *11239 For] And AELS   11240 es] na es LPR   es it] *trs.* W   11242 als men may] whasa wyll L   *sidenote*: De elephante exemplum (*trs. phrs.* S) ES   11245 Alle] *add* þe LPSW   while] þat L   11247 me] *om.* E, *adds* wele R   11248 attempre] tempre LP   11250 his] of his PW   11255 If] Of ELS   þe] þat LW   11258 þat es] *om.* W   11259 case] cause R   þar] þat L, whare R   *sidenote: om.* P   iij.] iij^{us}. W   11261 when] *repeats* P

Als kirke halwed and kirke-yharde,
Of whilk men suld take gode rewarde.
For it es appropred anely   11265
To serue our Lorde, Godde almyghty.
þare suld na man swilk dede do
With his wyf, þogh scho assent þarto;
Bot abstene hym, if he haf grace,
For reuerence of þe haly place.   11270
And whoso wil noght hym abstene
Ne kepe þat haly stede clene,
He synnes and dose grete vylany
Vnto þe stede þat es so haly.
For þe werk of Weddelayke þat es fre   11275
In haly stede grete synne may be
And in haly tyme when it es wroght—
þat in othir stede or tyme deres noght.

iiij. De statu viduetatis   þe ferthe state þat suld be clene
Es of þam þat wedded has bene,   11280
þar þe dede þat spares right nane
Has twynned twa and hent þe tane.
Bot whethir of þam þat leues olyue,
Be it þe man or be it þe wyue,
Suld his lyf chastly lede   11285
While he es in state of Wydouhede.
þat es a state mykell to prayse,
Als Saynt Paul þe apostell says.
He counsaylles þam þat wydous er called
þat þai þam in þat state halde,   11290
Paulus: Melius est nubere And if þat state þam noght pay,
quam vri He biddes þam wedde þam when þay may.
'For better it es', als says he,
'A man hym wedde þan brent to be.'

11263 and] or LR   11264 gode] *om.* R   11265 appropred] *after* For P   anely]
namely L   11268 þogh] if LR, all-if S   assent] consent L   11270 þe] þat W
11271 noght hym] *trs.* W   11272 Ne] And L   stede] place EL   11274 Vnto] To
PW   11275 es] es sa LR   11277 es] *om.* E   11279 *sidenote: as in-column
heading* R   iiij.] *om.* ESR, iiij^{us}. status LP   11281 þar] Whar R   11282 hent] tane
ELS   11283 þat] so R   leues] lyfes LR   o-] of S, þat R   11284 or] *om.* ELS   be
it] 3it P   11285 his] þaire LR   chastly] chaste P   lede] hede R   11286 he . . . of]
þai er in L, þai war in þe state of R   in] in þe PSW   11290 þat²] þe   11291 þam
noght] no3t may þam R   11292 He] Hed W   þam] *om.* E   11294 wedde] *adds*
hym S   brent to] brynt L, brynede PW

þat man hym brynnes thurgh foly   11295
þat assentes vnto Litchery.
For he puttes his hert in þe fyre
Of Litchery thurgh fole desyre,

De Castitate

And better it war hym to wedde   fol. 68rb
þan to þat fyre to brynne be ledde.   11300
þis es to vnderstande anely,
Als yhe haf herde in þis party,
Of þam þat suld þair lyf lede
In þe state of symple Wydouhede.
Bot noght of þa, als I wele trowe,   11305
þat to þat state er bounden thurgh vowe
So þat þai may noght þam mary
Withouten synne þat es dedely
After þe vowe es made to last—
For þat byndes þam vnto Godde fast.   11310
And if þai it breke agayne Goddis wille,
þai departe þamself fra Godde thurgh skille.
Bot if þe vowe al pryuy be
And symple withouten solempnyte,
Albeit þat he synne dedely   11315
If he þareafter hym mary,
When he es wedded, al do he ille,
In þat state he may dwelle stille.
Bot þe man or womman þat so dose
For þat vow broken suld penaunce vse.   11320
Bot when þe vowe es made lastande,
Solempnely thurgh prelates hande,
Or thurgh þe makynge of professyoun
þat falles vnto relygioun,

11295 man] *om.* W   11297 his] þe R   þe] *om.* R   11298 fole] foule R, foly W
11299 it] hym L, *om.* W   to] *om.* E, for to L, to be W   11300 þan] þat L   þat] þe L
11301 anely] namely LP   11303 lyf] leiffynge R   11305 I] *om.* PR   I wele] *trs.* W
wele] we R   11306 to] þurgh L   thurgh] *adds* a L   vowe] awe W   11307 noght
þam] *trs.* LP   11310 vnto] to EL   11311 agayne] þurgh S   11315 Albeit . . .
synne] And if it be þat he synnes L   11317 al] all-iff LS (*a corr. of the correct text* S) do
he] *trs.* S (*a corr. of the correct text*)   11318 stille] ill R   11319 Bot] For L
11320 vow broken] wo vowbrekyng L   11322 -pnely] -pny LSR   prelates] prelate L
11323 þe] *om.* ELPSRW   11324 vnto] to men of L

Or thurgh haly order þat men taas 11325
þat suddeken, deken, or prest has,
In þis case es þe maryage noght,
For agayne þe lawe it es wroght.
Bot þam bihoues departed be
þat marys þam in swilk degre, 11330
For þai be noght saue, als says þe boke,
Bot þai kepe þat state þat þai first toke.
  Bot 'to' þe state of Wydowhede
I fynde swilk ensaumple to rede
In a boke of bestes kynde— 11335
þat wydous suld oft haf in mynde—
Of þe turtell þat tynes hir make
þat neuer after wil othir take
Bot flees alle othir company
And dwelles in wildernes anely. 11340

Donum Intellectus   De Castitate
Adueniat regnum tuum

fol. 68ᵛᵃ

Tria pertinent ad statum viduetatis j[ᵘˢ].

Bot thre thinges falles, als I wene,
To þam þat in þat state er sene.
þe first es, als clerkes wate,
þat whaso es in wydow state
Suld hald him priuyly in his inne 11345
And vse scilence withouten dyn
And noght folow straunge company,
Ne obout þe werlde be ouerbysy.
  Of þat ensaumple fynde I can
Of Iudith, þe noble womman 11350
þat was fayre of hide and hewe
And a clene widow was and a trewe.
Of wham þan spekes Haly Wrytte,

11325 order] oder P   11326 suddeken] *adds* or L   prest] presthede R
11327 case] cause R   11332 þat²] *om.* L   11333 to] *original hand corr.* A, *om.* P,
for R   11334 ensaumple] ane sampill R   11335 bestes] *adds* of L   *sidenote:*
Exemplum nota E, Exempla de columba turturis L   11336 oft] *om.* S   in] *om.* P
11337 turtell] *adds* doufe L   11339 flees] lefs R   11340 in] in þe P   11342 þat²]
om. W   11343 *sidenote: om.* LS   jᵘˢ.] j. A, Primus status P   11345 Suld] Sall L
priuyly] priue L   inne] hyne E   11346 vse] haunte L   11347 straunge] strang
LSW   11350 þe] þat L   noble] haly P   *sidenote:* Iudyth E, Exemplum de Iudyth L
11351 was] was so L   11352 was] *om.* P   a²] *om.* PW   11353 þan] *om.* E

Als says þis clerkes þat knawes it,
þat fra hir chaumbre sho wald noght passe 11355
Ne fra hir maydens þat with hir was,
Bot helde hir priuyly in cloose
Fra sight of men and werldes loose.

Wharefore Saynt Paul mykell reproues
þis wydous þat idelnes loues 11360
And yhunge wymmen quayntly dyght
þat shewes þam mykell to mens sight
And er ouermykell iangelande—
þis es to wydous noght semande.
Bot þa þat wydous right er called 11365
Withinne þair cloos suld þam halde
And kepe þam fra mens speche and fle
Alle werldely sightes of vanyte
And þam occupye in godedede.
þis falles to þe state of Wydouhede. 11370

þe secund thinge es oft to pray   ij[ᵘˢ].
And to serue Godde, bathe nyght and day,
And blethely to be at þe kirke
And werkes of deuocioun to wirke.
Als we fynde wryten in boke   11375 *Exemplum in euangelio*
In þe godspelle of Saynt Luke,   *Sancti Luce*
þat spekes of a noble womman
þat was wydow and 'h'ight Anne.
þat wald noght fra þe temple passe
Bot dwelled ay þare, als hir wille was, 11380
And payned hir with al hir myght
To serue Godde bathe day and nyght
In devoute prayers and fastynges
And blethely didde his bidynges.

þe thridde thinge es, als methinke, 11385 *iiij*[ᵘˢ].

11357 priuyly] priue L   in] in þe P   11358 and] of W   werldes] werldely L
11359 Whare-] þare- L   *sidenote*: Paulus LS   11360 loues] lufe E, vse P
11362 mens] mans R   11365 right] rightwys R   11366 cloos] closes L, *add* þai LR
11367 speche] speches S   11368 Alle] *om.* L   sightes] syght PW   of] and L
11370 þis] þir L   11371 *sidenote*: ijᵘˢ.] ij. A, ijᵘˢ. status P   11374 And] *om.* L   to]
for to L, at S, *om.* W   11375 in] in þe LW, in a SR   *sidenote*: *om.* L   Exemplum in]
om. S   euangelio] euangelium S   Sancti] sciencie P   Luce] Luci E   11378 was] *add* a
LP   and] þat L   hight] h *int. later* (cf. 11143) A   11379 þat] And LS   11381 hir²]
om. P   11383 fastynges] fastyng LS   11384 didde] keped S   his] god L
bidynges] byddyng LS   11385 es] *om.* LS   *sidenote*: iijᵘˢ.] iij. AE, iijᵘˢ. status P

Donum Intellectus   De Castitate
Adueniat regnum tuum

fol. 68vb To vse ay strayte mete and drynke.
    For whaso wil halde þam chast
    Bihoues vse grete metes mast
    And noght delicyous dayntees;
    þat makes many Chastyte lees.   11390

Paulus For Saynt Paul says and beres witnes
    þat a womman þat widow es
    þat in delyces hir lyf ledes
    Es dede thurgh synne þat men dredes.

Bernardus: Castitas perit And Bernarde says þat spekes of vyces   11395
in delicijs þat Chastyte perisshes in delyces.
    þat es als he þat perisshes sone
    In þe water and es fordone;
    þat vnder þe water haldes his hede,
    He may so drunken and be dede.   11400
    Wharefore na man may ouerlange halde
    His heued (þat es his hert called)
    In þe water of werldely delyces.
    þat stirs many men to vyces
    And brynges many to helle pyne   11405
    þat he ne sal þe lyf tyne.
    þat es grace of þe Haly Gast
    Thurgh whilk þe lyf lyues in God mast.
    Also to wydous þat er trewe
    Falles meke clethynge of symple hewe   11410
    And noght of gay colours starande,
    Ne of quaynt shappe þat es gay semande.
    Bot wydous suld ensaumple take
    Of Iudith, þat left for Goddis sake

11388 vse] *after* metes P, to vse R   vse grete] haunte strayte L   11390 lees] to lese L
11392 þat²] þat a L   11393 þat] And W   lyf] lyke L   11395 þat] and L
11397 es] *om.* P   11399–400 *couplet om.* L (*at a page-boundary*)   11400 drunken]
droune R, drenchen W   11401 may] *om.* W   -lange] *om.* S   11402 hert] *om.* L
11404 stirs] *adds* full R   men] man PW   to vyces] vnto vice P   11405 And] *om.* R
many] *adds* man P   11406 he] þai P   ne] *om.* LPS   sal] sal þarefore L   11409 to]
þe PW   *sidenote*: iiij. De statu viduitatis ES   11410 clethynge] clothyng R,
clothynges W   11412 quaynt] gay PS   gay] *om.* L, quaynt P   11414 Of] At LS
sidenote: Exemplum (*adds* de L) Iudyth EL, Iudith W

Hir riche robes þat syde gun traylle   11415
And alle hir othir gay apparaylle
þat felle bathe to body and hede.
Sho left alle when hir lorde was dede
And toke þe habite of Wydouhede,
And in þat meke habite sho yhede.   11420
þat was taken mare of dole namely
þan of ioy or of vayneglory.

    And forþi þat sho lufd Chastyte
And wald þe enchesouns of syn fle,
Sho left þe apparaylle þat was fayre   11425
And al hir lyf wered þe hayre
And fasted alle þe days of þe yhere
Bot þa þat war haly and dere.
And yhete sho was ryche, fayre, and yhung,
And wyse of dede and of speche of tung.   11430
Bot þe godenes of hir hert and thoght

De Castitate

And luf of Chastyte þat sho soght,   fol. 69ra
þat sho oft shewed and noght hidde,
Made hir to do al þat sho didde.
    Right so suld wydous þair lyf lede   11435
And kepe þe state of Wydowhede
In Chastyte and in clennes
Fra filth of synne þat cleuand es,
Namely þa þat er bounden to be
Chast thurgh vowe of chastyte.   11440
Othir þat er noght bunden þartille
May maryen þam if þat þai wille.

    þe fift state es of clene virgyns   *v. De statu virginitatis*
þat þe victory of þair flesshe wynnes.
þe whilk er chast and ay has bene   11445

11415 riche] ryches S   gun] con W   11416 hir] *om.* L   gay] ryche L
11423 -þi] *om.* L   11424 enchesouns] encheson LW   11425 was] wasse sa L
11426 lyf] *adds* scho L   þe] he S   11428 *line om.* S   11429 ryche] ryght LSRW
11430 and^2] *om.* PW   of^2] *om.* R   of^3] and of L, and P   11431 and] and þe L
11432 And luf of] þat lufed L   11433 and . . . hidde] þat scho didde P   11434 All
openly and noght hidde P   11435 suld] *om.* R   11437 in^2] *om.* W   11442 þat]
om. PW   11443 fift] furst R   *sidenote: as in-column heading* R, Status virginum W   v.]
v^{us}. ELW, *om.* PSR   De statu] status L   11444 þair] þe R   11445 ay has] *trs.* R

And thynkes ay forward kepe þam clene
Fra alle corrupciouns of body
For þe luf of Godde almyghty.

Propter tria specialiter laudanda virginitas

þis state es mykell for to prayse
For thre thynges, als þe boke says.   11450
þat es to say for þe dygnyte,
For þe bewete, and for þe bounte.

Primo propter dignitatem eius

First men suld kepe þat state
For þe dignyte, als þis clerkes wate.
Forwhy þat state es of swilk myght   11455
þat it mas þam þat kepes it right
Euen lyke vnto Goddis aungels,
Als þe haly man in boke telles.
Bot a clene virgyne þat es leel
Has yhete mare þan has an aungell.   11460
Forwhy þe aungell lyfs gastly
Als gaste withouten flesshe of body,
And virgynes þair flesshe about beres
þat temptes þam oft here and deres.

Bot virgyns has þe victory   11465
Of þair bodys, and þat es ferly
þat þai may kepe so febell castelle
Als þair bodys er to telle
Agayne so stalward enemy
Als þe fende es þat es so wyly,   11470
þat sekes ay alle maner of gynne
Wharethurgh he may þat castell wynne.
For right fayne dispoylle it wald he
Of þe tresour of Virginyte.

þat tresore es mykell to prayse,   11475
Of whilk Godde in þe godspell says

11446 forward] *add* to ELS   11449 for] *om.* W *sidenote:* specialiter] vij^tem. P laudanda] *add* est ELPS 11451 to] for to S þe] *om.* W 11453 *sidenote:* Primo] *om.* P eius] *om.* S 11454 þis] *om.* LP 11457 vnto] to LPW aungels] aungell R 11458 man] men S in] in hys L boke] bokes S, þe boke W telles] cane tell R 11459 *sidenote:* Nota E 11460 yhete] *om.* S has] *om.* LPSR 11461 þe] ane R þe aungell] aungels L 11462 of] and PR 11463 about] *after* virgynes P 11464 þam] *om.* L here] hyr L 11465 Bot] And P 11466 bodys] flesche ELS 11467 febell] *add* a ELPSR 11469 stalward] *add* ane LPSR 11470 es'] *om.* L 11471 gynne] syn W 11473 right] righ P dispoylle] dispeyle W 11474 Of'] For L 11475 *sidenote:* In (Dominus in L) euangelio ELS

De Castitate

þat þe heghe kyngedome of heuen   fol. 69rb

To þat tresour es lickened euen

þat priuyly in þe felde es hidde

þat precious and riche es kydde.   11480

þis tresour hidde in felde namely

Es Maydenhede hidde in body.

þat es als a felde thurgh skille

þat men suld thurgh penaunce tille,

Als þe boundes lys and þe merkes,   11485

And sawe it with + trauaylle and gode werkes.

þis ryche tresour may be lyke

By gode skille vntill heuenryke.

For þe lyf of virgynes es lyke right

Vnto þe kyngedome of heuen bright,   11490

þat es vntill aungels lyf

In heuen whare alle ioy es ryf.

Wharefore Godde says in þe godspelle,

Als yhe may here þis clerkes telle,

þat at þe vprysynge generale   11495

When alle men in flesshe vpryse sal,

þan sal noght be swilk maryage

Als men mas here thurgh vsage.

Bot þai sal be als aungels þan,

Alle þat bees saue, man and womman;   11500

And þair bodys þat now has dymnes

Sal shyne als bright als now þe son es.

Also þis state falles to be   *Secundo propter eius*

Gretly praysed for þe beawte.   *pulcritudinem*

For Maydenhede þat keped es clene   11505

Es þe fayrest state in erthe sene.

Wharefore Salamon says þe wyse

11478 þat] þe PR   11479 þe] *om.* PRW   11480 riche] right R   *sidenote*: De
castitate S   11482 in] in þe S   11484 men] ilk man *after* penaunce P   11486 with]
thurgh P   *trauaylle] trauaylles AE   11489–90 *couplet trs.* W   11490 Vnto] To PW
11491 vntill] anto L   11492 alle] *om.* S   es] es full S   11493 Whare-] þare- L
11495 þat] And L   11499 als] all R   11500 þat] *om.* L   bees] be S   saue] swa L
11502 als . . . als] bryghter þan RW   11503 þis] þat P   to] for to R   *sidenote*: eius] *om.* P
11505 mayden-] mon- W   11506 in erthe] þat in erthe es LR   11507 Whare-] And
þare- L   Salamon says] *trs.* LP   *sidenote*: Salamon ELS

In þe *Boke of Wysdome* þar clergy lyse,
'Haa', he says, 'how fayre it es
Chast engendrure with clerenes'.   11510
    Ful fayre it es, als says he,
Clerenes namely with Chastyte.
Forwhy þan es Chastyte bright
And Maydenhede vnto Goddis sight,
When it 'es' thurgh gode lyf + fayre   11515
And clere, if nathinge it appayre.
Right als þe clerenes of þe sonne
Makes fayre day here þar we wonne,
Right so þe clerenes of clere lyfynge
And of grace þat es þe bigynnynge   11520
Makes Maydenhede fayre and bright

Donum Intellectus   De Castitate
Adueniat regnum tuum

fol. 69ᵛᵃ And plesaunt vnto Goddis sight.
Ieronimus   Wharefore Saynt Ierom says þus,
þat bifore alle othir vertus
Maydenhede es clere and fayre,   11525
If na spotte of synne it appayre,
So þat þe body ne þe hert withinne
Be nanewyse corrumped with synne.
For he þat chast es ay of body
And corrumped es in hert anely,   11530
He, als þe boke beres wyttenes,
Es als a graue þat paynted es.
þat es whyte withouten and fayre
And withinne foul als roten layre
And roten erthe, bathe wate and drye,   11535
With þe carayne of þe body.

11508 þar] whar R   11509 Haa] þar R, Ha ha W   *sidenote*: eya (?) E
11510 Chast] chastite L   -drure] -dure R   clerenes] clennes R   11514 vnto] to PRW
11515 es] *original hand corr.* A   *lyf] lyf and AES   11516 if] and E   appayre]
enpayre L   11517 Right] *adds* so P   þe¹] *om.* L   11518 fayre] *adds* þe L, *repeats* P
here þar] whare L   11519 so] alsso E   þe clerenes] if clennes R   clere] 'clene' P
11522 plesaunt] pleseand LPSW   11524 bifore] he for S   11525 clere] clene LPR
11526 appayre] enpayre L   11527 ne] and LS   11528 Be] Be on ELS
11529 ay] *after* þat LS, *om.* R   11530 anely] namely PW   11531 He] He es E
11532 graue] man ES   11533 þat] And L   whyte withouten] *trs.* LP   11534 als]
and E, *om.* P

Maydenhede, if men clene it halde,
May be bi skille þe whyte robe called
þar foul spottes may be mare sene
þan on any othir robe + clene.   11540
þis whyte robe suld keped be
Fra fylynge of þise thinges thre:
þat es mudde of erthe, and blode,
And fyre þat may do skathe and gode.
þise thre thinges may gretly fyle   11545
þe whyte robe and make it vyle.
     þe mudde of þe erthe þat fyles som wyse
May be called werldely Couatyse,
Fra whilk þai suld kepe þam ay
þat in virgyne state wil Godde pay.   11550
Forwhy na man may kyndely
Pay bathe Godde and his enemy;
þe tane of þam hym bihoues dispyse,
Als Ierom says, þe doctour wyse.   *Ieronimus*
And he semes noght Goddis frende   11555
þat pleses þe Werlde and þe fende,
For þe Werlde es halden Goddis enmy.
Wharefore Saynt Ione says appertly   *Iohannes*
þat he sal enemy to Godde be
þat to þe Werlde es frende priue.   11560
     And Saynt Paul says þus, 'If I wald   *Paulus*
Plese þam þat of þe Werld er called,
I ne suld noght be leel seruand
To Ihesu Cryst, Godde alweldande'.
A tok⟨e⟩n þat men þe Werlde wil plese   11565
(þat puttes men oft fra rest and ese),

11537 if] and L   11538 be] *om.* LPSRW   bi] wyth L   robe] *add* be EL
11539 þar] Whare R   11540 on] *om.* R   any] ane L   *robe] *adds* þat es AELSR
11541 þis] þe L   suld keped] *trs.* S   11542 þise] *om.* SR   thinges] synnes R
11543 mudde of erthe] mode of hert W   *sidenote:* j^{us}. ij. E   11544 do] *om.* P   *sidenote:*
iij. E   11546 robe] *repeats* W   11547 þe²] *om.* LPR   erthe] hert W   11549 Fra]
Fra þe E   11550 wil Godde] *trs.* ER, god walde L   11552 bathe] *om.* W
11553 hym] *om.* R   11554 says] sayd W   11557–8 *couplet trs.* W   11557 For]
om. L, þat W   halden] *om.* W   11558 Ione] Ierome R   *sidenote om.* S   11559 þat]
And W   to] vnto L   11561 þus] *om.* R   if] if þat L   11562 of] *om.* P
11563 ne] *om.* LPSR   be] þan be L   11565 token] *scraped* A?   wil] *after* men E
11566 men oft] *trs.* E   ese] pese L

Donum Intellectus   De Castitate
Adueniat Regnum Tuum

fol. 69vb When þe hert on Godde es noght sette alle,
To wham we suld crye mast and calle,
Es þe curyouste namely
Of gay attyre obout þe body.   11570
For a man wald noght so bisy be
To seke ay swilk curyouste
Of fayre robes and apparaylle clene,
Warne he wald of men be sene.

    Bot whaso mast es aboute   11575
To make þe body fayre withoute
May tittest tyne thurgh filth of synne
þe fayrenes of þe saul wythinne.
þat beaute suld plese Godde mast,
Bot beaute withouten es in wast.   11580

Bernardus   Wharefore Saynt Bernard þat oft sayde
Wordes of whilk Godde was payde
Spekes namely to wymmen þus
þat sekes ay robes precious
And othir noble apparaylle   11585
To plese þe Werlde þat sal faylle
And to shewe þam in mens sight
To lat men se hou fayre þai er dight.
'þe doghters of Babyloyne' he þam calles,
þat es shenship in whilk som falles.   11590
For þair lyf es als a wynde-blast
þat sal turne þam at þe last
To shame and endeles shenshepe,
Bot if þai of þair lyf take kepe.

    þai clethe þam rychely on sere wyse   11595
With ryche clathynge and pelour of pryse,

11567 When] Es when L   11568 crye mast] *trs.* LP   11569 Es þe] Bot es sett in L, Is to W   11570 attyre] tyre W   11571 wald] will R   11572 To] For to R   11574 men] þe folk R   11575 mast es] ys ay mast R   11579 þat] þe R   11580 Bot] For R   -outen] -in R   in] bot S   11581 *sidenote om.* P   11582 whilk] skill R   was] *add* noght LR   11584 robes] clething L   11586 þat] wyth þat L   11587 And] *om.* R   11588 To] And R   11590 in] to R   som] *om.* L   11591 þair lyf es] þai lyf R   wynde-] wyndes LRW   11592 þe] *om.* L   11593 and] and to P   11594 lyf] saul R   11595 þai] And P   clethe] clathe ER   11596 clathynge] clething L

And vnder þa robes with pelure
þai er in saull nakede and pouer.
þai shyne without, als men may se,
With gold and siluer and ryche perre,   11600
Als falles vnto Werldes blisse
þat þam bihoues at þe last mysse.
Bot þai er foul in saull withinne,
For þai er mykell fyled with synne
Thurgh þair maners vnconable   11605
þat er to Godde abhomynable.
    Bot Saynt Bernarde spekes openly   *Bernardus*
Of wymmen þat er so bisy
To apparaylle þam fra fote to croun
In swilk a fole entencioun.   11610
þat es to say for to be sene
And yherned of þam þat foles bene.

De Castitate

And yhete do þai mare þan þair state wille;   fol. 70ra
þa wymmen methinke dose ille,
For bifore Godde þai sal yhelde resoun   11615
Of ilk man þat þai gif enchesoun
To yherne with þam to do foly
Thurgh swilk continance of body.
    Bot alle þe likynge withouten þis
þat þe kynges doghter has of blisse,   11620
Als Dauid says, es wythinne
In gode vertus withouten synne,
And in conscience þat es clene
þar na synne may þan be sene
Ne na poynt of Couatyse,   11625
Bot plese Godde withouten fayntyse.
And þus þe filth of mudde so vyle

11597 with] and ES, and þaire L, of R   11598 nakede] *after* er S   11599 shyne]
schen W   may] *om.* P   11601 werldes] werldely L, þe worldys R   11602 þat] It R
11603 Bot] For R   11604 With pryd and fylth of dedely synne R   11606 to] vnto L
11610 swilk a fole] a fule swilk P   fole] foul RW   11611 to say] *om.* S   for] *om.* L
11612 And] And be L   11613 yhete do þai] duse R   11614 ille] full yll R
11616 þat] *om.* L   gif] haue R   11617 do foly] synne anely L   11618 Thurgh]
Wyth LS   11621 says] sayde L   es] es þat E   *sidenote:* Dauid P   11624 þan]
þere W   11626 withouten] *adds* any S

þe whyte robe ne may noght fyle.
　　Also men suld kepe þat robe clene
Fra spottes of blode þat sone er sene.　　　　　　11630
þat es fra ille thoghtes and lykynges
And fra fole flesshely yhernynges.
Wharefore we may þis in boke rede,
Ieronimus Als Ierom says, þat Maydenhede
Es sacrafyse and offerande　　　　　　　　　11635
To our Lorde, Godde alweldande.
þat es noght fyled in hert thurgh thoght,
Ne in body thurgh Litchery wroght.
Forwhy he says þus, certaynely,
þat þe Maydenhede of body　　　　　　　　　11640
Es noght worth and es medelesse
þar corrupcioun of hert es.
Als þe fruyt ne es noght gode
And es noght worth to mans fode
þat semes hale when it es goten　　　　　　　11645
Withouten, and es withinne roten.
Right so es Maydenhede þat es sene
Hale withouten, and withinne noght clene.
　　Also men suld in þat state
Kepe þe robe clene fra fyre hate.　　　　　　11650
þe fyre þat brynnes þat whyte wede
Of Chastyte and of Maydenhede
Es to here or say with lykande wille
Wordes þat may stir men to ille.
Paulus For Saynt Paul says þat Godde wele payde,　　11655
And als I haf herebifore sayde,

De Castitate

fol. 70ʳᵇ þat vilayne wordes þat men shewes
May sone corrumpn gode thewes.

11628 ne] *om.* RW　　　11631 lykynges] lykyng S　　　11632 fole] foule LSW, foly PR
yhernynges] yernyng S　　　　11633 -fore] *om.* P　　　þis in] *trs.* S　　　rede] dede L
11637 thurgh] *om.* E　　　11639 *sidenote*: Nota E　　　11640 þe] *om.* S　　　11641 mede-]
ned- P　　　11643 ne] *om.* LR　　　11644 es] *om.* LP　　　worth] gude E　　　11645 hale]
holy W　　　goten] geten LS　　　11646 es withinne] *trs.* LP　　　11647 es¹] *om.* P
11648 noght] es noght L　　　11651 þat²] þe P　　　11652 of²] *om.* P　　　11653 Es] *om.* R
or] or to W　　　lykande] gude E　　　11655 Godde] *adds* es L　　*sidenote: add* Corrumpunt
bonos (*om.* L) mores colloquia praua ELS　　　11656 herebifore] before here PR, byfore W
11657 vilayne] vylans ELPS, vilany RW

And þarefore says Senek right,   *Seneca*
'Kepe þe', he says, 'with al þi myght   11660
Fra foul wordes, bathe nyght and day,
þat er noght gode to here ne say'.
For if he bigynne to speke or here
Foul wordes and vses þat manere,
He waxes sone balde þareinne   11665
And falles þe lightlyer in synne.
  And þarefore whaaso clene wil kepe
Fra vylany and fra shendshepe
þe whyte robe of Maydenhede,
To whilk falles right mykell mede,   11670
Hym bihoues hym kepe, nyght and day,
þat he nouthir here ne say
Wordes þat may sone kyndell synne
Thurgh whilk he may be brent withinne.
  For als þe catte þat es pryue   11675
Brynnes hir hippes, als men may se,
Bot þe wylde catte dose noght swa
þat rynnes in þe wode to and fra.
Right so a man may be brent lightly
þat vses to speke or here vylany.   11680
Bot he þat swilk speche wil ay fle
In saul thar hym neuer brenned be.
  Maydenhede and Chastyte
May to þe lily lickened be.
þat es a flour whyte and fayre   11685
þat growes on heght thurgh kynd of þe ayre.
Wharefore Godde says in Haly Wrytte
Thurgh Salamon, þe wyse of witte,   *Salamon*
'My lief es als þe lyly sene
Amange þe thornes þat er kene'.   11690
  Goddis derlynge, als clerkes may rede,

11660 þe] *om.* L   al] *canc.* P   11661 Fra] þe fra L   bathe] *om.* SR
11663 For] Or S   he] þou L   11666 lightlyer] lighter W   11667 whaaso] *adds* wyll
L, who P   11670 right] *om.* LS   11671 hym kepe] *trs.* ES, *adds* and (*canc.?*) P, *adds*
both R   11672 nouthir here] *trs.* S   11674 Thurgh] *adds* þe S   brent] broght R
11675 For þe catte þat nere þe fyre will be R   11676 als] þat W   11680 vses]
hauntes L   11681 he] þai L   wil ay] *after* þat R   ay] *om.* LP   11682 thar . . .
neuer] þanne thar noght L   11684 þe] *om.* E   11686 heght] heghe RW   thurgh]
by P   kynd of] *om.* S   þe] *om.* R   11688 þe] þat wasse L   of] of þe E   11689 lief]
lyfe ELSRW   11691 -lynge] -lynges LS (*corr. out* P)

Es þe saul þat kepes Maydenhede.
For þat es swilk a vertu to prayse
Thurgh whilk þe saul, als clerkes says,
May purchace mast specially   11695
þe luf of Godde almyghty.
Wharefore Saynt Ione þe wangelist
Amange alle þe apostels of Cryst

Donum Intellectus   De Castitate
Adueniat regnum tuum

fol. 70va To Cryst mast hamely was and es,
And Cryst hym shewed mast hamelynes   11700
And mast verray tokenynges of luf,
Als men may in þe godspell proue.
And so was he amange þe tothir called
Crystes disciple þat he luf walde.
And neuerþelesse yhete lufd he þe tothir,   11705
For he made ilkane othir brothir.
Bot hym mast specially lufd he
For his Maydenhede and Chastyte.
    þis lily flour, als clerkes wele wate,
Kepes hir beawte and hir state   11710
Amange sharpe thornes þat springes
Of diuerse flesshely fondynges.
For þe Flesshe es als a middynge
þat of itself forthe bringes nathinge
Bot sharpe thornes and netles kene   11715
And breres and thistels, als es oft sene.
þat er fole styrynges of delyte
þat oft prickes sare þe spiryte.
    Bot þe flour of Maydenhede
Of swilk thornes thar haf na drede   11720

11692 Es þe saul] Er þase saules L   þe] a E   kepes] adds þair L   11694 whilk]
om. W   þe saul] om. S   11697 þe] e- ELPS, þe e- R   sidenote: Iohannes euangelista ES
11699 was and] om. R   11700 hamelynes] halynes W   11701 tokenynges] -nyng
LS, tokynnes R   11702 may] after godspell E   þe] om. E   11703 þe] repeats R
þe tothir] þase other L, þe other W   11705 he] om. EP   þe tothir] þase other L
11706 he] he had W   11708 and] and hys L   11709 þis] Als E   lily] haly P
clerkes wele] þe clerkes P   11710 hir²] adds flour P   11711 Amange] And mange P
11714 forthe] om. L   forthe bringes] trs. P   11716 breres . . . thistels] trs. sbs. P   es
oft] trs. LR, of is W   11717 fole] foule LPSW, foly R   11720 swilk] whylk L

When it es roted sikerly
In þe luf of Godde almyghty
þat ay defendes it and weres
Fra thornes of fondynges þat deres.
   To þis flour þat clerkes calles
'Flour of Maydenhede' sex leues falles
And thre greyns endored withinne.
þis flour falles to ilka virgynne.
   þe first leef of þis flour es
Halenes of Body þat es wemmeles.
þat es to say þat þe body be
Hale and clene thurgh Chastyte,
Withouten wemme of Litchery
þat þe Flesshe yhernes specially.
For if a mayden þat men suld spare
Agayne hir wille corrumped ware,
Sho shuld noght þarefore tyne þe mede
þat falles to clene Maydenhede.
Wharefore Saynt Lucy sayd þus
Vnto þe tyraunt so malicious,
'Al-if I now', sho sayde, 'thurgh þe

Donum Intellectus   De Castitate
Adueniat regnum tuum

Agayne my wille corrumpud be,
My chastnes bees doubled thurgh þis
Onence þe ryche coroun of blisse'.
   þe secund leef als it es soght
Es Clennes of Hert and of Thoght.
For als Saynt Ierom, þe haly man,
Says þus, als I shewe yhow can,
'It es noght worth to haue anely
Clene Maydenhede of body

Side notes:
11725 *Lilium vir⟨gi⟩nitatis ⟨habe⟩t vj. folia èt tria grana deaurata*

⟨j⟩ᵐ. *folium est ⟨int⟩egritas corporis* 11730

11735

Lucia 11740

fol. 70ᵛᵇ

11745 *ijᵐ. folium est puritas cordis*

Ieronimus

11750

11721 es] *om.* L   roted] roten W   11724 of] and S   fondynges] *corr. from* fondyng P, fondynge R   þat] þat it P   11725 *sidenote: om.* L   grana] *om.* (*?in the gutter*) P 11727 with-] þer- L   11729 *sidenote: om.* L (*marked for corr.*) est] *repeats* P 11730 Hale-] Haly- LPSRW   11737 Sho] So W   Sho shuld] *trs.* P   noght þarefore] *trs.* P   ye] hir S   11738 falles] felle L   11739 *sidenote: adds* virgo E 11743 chastnes] chastyte ES   11744 ryche] ryght L   11746 of²] *om.* EP 11747 Saynt Ierom] Ierome says R   *sidenote om.* S   11748 Says þus] Now R   shewe yhow] *trs.* S   yhow] *om.* LP   11749 It] For it P   worth] worthy S

To þam þat to wedde þam has wille
And thinkes þair purpos to fulfille'.
Bot he spekes of þam, whatso þai be,
þat has avowed Chastyte.
For whaso vowes to kepe for mede   11755
Chastyte or Maydenhede,
He suld kepe chastly his hert
Fra fole willes þat comes ouerthwert.

iij^m. folium est humilitas   þe thridde leef es Mekenes called
þat ilka mayden in hert suld halde.   11760
For proude mayden in hert namely
May noght pay Godde almyghty.

Bernardus   And þarefore says Saynt Bernard wele
þat a fayre thinge it es to fele
Maydenhede with Mekenes right   11765
þat mykell pleses Godde ful of myght.
þam lufs Godde of wham gifs Mekenes
Loos to Maydenhede þat clene es.
And Maydenhede þat es clene
Mekenes mas fayre to be sene,   11770
And þus proues he aftirwarde.

Bernardus   'I dar wele say', says Saynt Bernarde,
'þat our Leuedy Mary, mayden clene,
Warne hir grete Mekenes had bene,
Ne had noght payed Godde almyghty   11775
Thurgh hir Maydenhede anely.'

iiij. folium est timor Dei   þe ferthe leef of þat flour es
et verecundia   Drede of Godde and Shamefulnes,
For þa þat verray maydens bene
Dredefull and shamefull er oft sene.   11780
And þat es lytell wonder to se,
If þai dredefull and shameful be,
For þai bere ful precious tresore
In a febill vessaylle þarfore.

11752 þair] þat L   11753 of] to P   -so] -som L, *om.* R   11754 *sidenote*: Nota E
11755 vowes] avowes R   11756 or] or yitt L   11757 chastly] chaste LS, chastite P
his] in P   11758 fole] foule LSRW   11759 *sidenote*: est . . . humilitas] *om.* LW
humilitas] *adds* cordis E   11760 suld] es halden to L   11767 þam] þai L   Godde]
goddes P   of wham] þat L   gifs] begynnes P, commes R   11768 Loos] And lose L
11770 fayre] *om.* E   11773 þat] And W   11775 Ne] Scho L   noght] *om.* S
11777 es] *om.* S   *sidenote*: est . . . verecundia] *om.* W (*mostly in gutter*)   11780 oft] *om.* R

Wharefore our Leuedy Mayden Mary   11785
Was in priue place anely

De Castitate

And dredeful was and sympely lete   fol. 71ʳᵃ
When þe aungell come hir to grete.
Bot Drede of Godde, als yhe may here,
May be called þe tresorere   11790
þat kepes ay, als es grete nede,
þe ryche tresore of Maydenhede
þat þe fende of helle on nane wyse
May it stele thurgh his quayntyse.
For Drede of Godde, als clerkes can telle,   11795
Kepes þe yhates of þe castelle
þar closed es þe ryche tresore
þat es ful siker warnistore.
    þe right yhates of þe castelle
Of þe hert, þar þat tresore suld dwelle,   11800
Of clene Maydenhede namely,
Er þe fyue wyttes of þe body
þat þe Drede of Godde kepes ay
So þat þe enemy noght entre may
Thurgh vayne curyouste to se   11805
Or to here or to speke vanyte.
Forwhy vayne curyouste to here
Or to se on som manere
Vanytees of þe werlde namely
Es way to þe synne of Litchery.   11810
    For sight es first enchesoun of it.
Wharefore men redes in Haly Writte
þat Iacob doghter þat Dyna hight
Was corrumpud thurgh curyous sight.
For when sho went for to se   11815
Vnkouthe wymmen of þe cuntre

11785 -fore] *om.* R   Mayden] Saynt L   11787 was] *om.* R   sympely] symple L
11793 on] of L, in R   11794 quayntyse] couytyse R   11797 þe] þis L, þat RW
11800 þat] þe ELS   suld] wyll L   11802 Er] Of L   11804 noght entre] enter na
LS   11805 to] fore to ELS   11806 to²] *om.* P   11807 to] fore to ELS
11808 to] for to L   11809 Vanytees] Dayntes R   11810 þe] *om.* LPW
11811 *sidenote*: Nota E   11812 Wharefore] Als L   *sidenote*: Exemplum de Dyna filia
Iacob L   11816 þe] þat P

(And yhete sho went þan for nane ille),
Sho was rauyst agayne hir wille
Thurgh þe prynces sone of þe cyte
þat did hir at his wille to be.   11820
And so tynt sho hir maydenhede
For sho to se þe wymmen yhede.

   And þarefore mayden þat clene wil kepe
Hir Maydenhede to Goddis worshepe,
Hir bihoues kepe hir wittes right   11825
And withdrawe þam fra vayne curious sight.
And þat dose men principally
Thurgh haly Drede of Godde almyghty.

De Castitate

fol. 71rb þat er þa þat haues ay drede
To wreth Godde in worde or dede.   11830
And þat es þe wytte and þe quayntyse
Of þe fyue maydens þat war wyse,
Of whilke spekes þe godspelle
On þis wyse, als I wille yhow telle.
þar our Lorde says þat heuenryke   11835
To ten maydens with laumpes es lyke,
Of whilk þe fyue war wys to prayse
And fyue war foles, als þe boke says.

   He calles þe kyngedome of heuen bright,
Als þis clerkes vnderstandes right,   11840
Halykirke thurgh þe trouth ane
þat it has in baptyme tane.
þe fyue wyse maydens bitokens right
þai þat kepes with al þair myght
þe fyue wyttes of þe body,   11845
Of whilk I spake bifore a party.

11817 þan] om. ELS, noȝt R   11819 þe] þat L   11820 þat assented to hys wyll at be L   þat] And W   did] gerte S   11822 se] om. R   þe] how L   11823 And þarefore] þerfore þe P   mayden] maydens L   11824 Hir] Yhoure L   11825 Hir] þaime L   11826 with-] om. L   vayne] om. LW   curious] om. R   11827 And] om. L   11830 wreth] wrath ES   or] and S   11831 quayntyse] couytyse R   11832 fyue] om. R   11833 Of] Of þe EL   whilke] swylk W   11834 als] om. R   wille] om. LS   wille yhow] trs. E   11835 þar] þat LW   our Lorde] Gode R   þat] in R   11837 þe] om. PS   11841 ane] tane S   11844 þai] þaim P   11846 Of] Of þe R   I] I of EP   spake] adds of S   spake bifore] trs. W   a party] of apertly W

þe fyue foles bitokens thurgh skille
þai þat kepes þe fyue wyttes ille.
   þe fift leef es Sharpnes of Lyf
þat with þe Flesshe byhoues stryf.

v[^m]. folium est
11850 asperitas vite

For whoso kepe wille Maydenhede
His flesshe hym bihoues sharply lede
And ay it chasty and halde in awe
And putte it oft vnderfote lawe
Thurgh fastynge, wakyng, and prayere,   11855
And harde liggynge þat may it dere
And grete trauaylle with lytell rest.
þus may men kepe þat state best.
And whaso folwes his flesshe-wille,
þe state of Maydenhede sal he spille.   11860

   Sharpnes of Lyf þat es right soght
Es als ane hegge stalwardely wroght
For to kepe þe yharde of þe hert
þat nane ille beste com in ouerthwert.
þat er called þe fendes of helle,   11865
Our enemys þat er false and felle,
þat eghtles ay, if þai may spede,
To stele þe tresore of Maydenhede.
And þarefore þat tresore so ryche kidde
Suld be sikerly closed and hidde   11870

Donum Intellectus   De Castitate
Adueniat regnum tuum

And wele keped nyght and day
So þat it be noght tynt for ay.
For whaso tynes it, for certayne
He recouers it neuer agayne,
Na mare þan þe laumpe of glasse   11875
When it es broken þat first hale was,
May be made on any wyse

fol. 71va

11847 thurgh] þe LP   11848 þai] þaim P   11849 fift] *om.* S   *sidenote:* 5.
folium W, *at 11843* P   v^m.] v. A   11851 -so] *om.* P   kepe wille] *trs.* LP   11853 ay]
om. E   chasty] chaste L   halde] a halde it L   11857 lytell] -outen SW
11858 kepe] meke P   11860 sal he] *trs.* PRW   11862 -ly] *om.* L   11863 For]
om. L   11864 beste] beestes R   11867 þat eghtles] þai attelen W   11869 so
ryche] þat ryche es L   11870 hidde] kydd S   11872 for ay] away L
11877 May] May noght L   any] nane LPSW

Hale agayne thurgh mans quayntyse.

vj[ᵐ]. folium est   þe sext leef bi vnderstandynge
perseuerancia Es Lastandnes withouten fayllyng.   11880

þat es fast purpos to kepe right
þat þat men has to Godde hight.

Augustinus Wharefore Saynt Austyn þat we of rede
Says in þe *Boke of Maydenhede*
And spekes to maydens þat Godde pays: 11885
'Folow yhe ay þe Lambe', he says,
'þat es Cryst; bees fast kepande
þat yhe haf hight to Godde alweldande.
And do yhe', he says, 'so hardily ay
And bere yhow so ay whyle yhe may 11890
þat þe tresore of Maydenhede soght
In + nane of yhow ne perisshe noght.
For if yhe it tyne, yhe may noght do
Wharethurgh yhe myght com þarto,
Ne thurgh na sleght agayne it gette', 11895
Als I ensaumple by þe laumpe sette.

Bernardus And Saynt Bernard says þus þarby,
'In Lastandnes yhe suld study,
For þat anely thurgh helpe of grace
þe coroun of blisse may purchace'. 11900
þise sex leues bifore sayde,
Of whilk Godde almyghty es payde,
þe lyly of Maydenhede mas fayre,
If na corrupcioun it appayre.

Bot þat flour suld haf inmyddes right 11905
Thre graynes endored, fayre to þe sight,
þe whilke bytokens specially
Thre maners to luf Godde almyghty.
For Maydenhede withouten luf
þat falles to Godde, als I may proue, 11910
Es als a laumpe of glasse clene

11879 *sidenote: om.* L, *in gutter* W vjᵐ.] vj. A 11882 has] *om.* L 11883 -fore]
om. R *sidenote om.* L 11888 to] *om.* PR 11889 he] *om.* R 11890 so ay] *trs.* W
ay] *om.* L 11892 *nane] þe name AELPS ne] *om.* LP 11893 it] *om.* R may]
om. R 11894 -thurgh] -fore P myght com] may com agayne L 11896 þe] *om.* E
11897 Saynt] *om.* P says þus] *trs.* RW *sidenote: om.* P, *in* W 11901 bifore] afor R
11904 appayre] enpayre LPR 11905 Bot] *om.* R þat] þat þe L 11906 to þe] in R
11911 of] with P

Withouten oyle, als es oft sene.
Wharefore þe maydens þat foles ware

Donum Intellectus   De Castitate
Adueniat regnum tuum

þe whilke þair laumpes tome bare,   fol. 71ᵛᵇ
And forthy þat þai filled noght   11915
þair laumpes þat þai with þam broght
With clene oylle bot gaf neuer tale,
þai war sperred out fra þe bridale.
And þe wyse maydens with gode wille
Of þat oylle þair laumpes gun fille,   11920
With þair spouse þai in went
Vnto þe brydale, als was þair entent.

  Thre maners sothfastly to neuen   *Tria grana lilij virginitatis*
To luf and serue Godde of heuen   *significant tres modos*
Er bitokend to telle þarby   *diligendi Deum*
                                                     11925
Thurgh þe thre graynes of þe lily.
þe whilk Saynt Austyne teches vs   *Augustinus*
When he says, 'þou sal luf þus
Godde with al þine Vnderstandynge
Withouten errour of knawynge.   11930
þou sal luf hym with al þi Wille
Withouten gaynsayinge, loud or stille.
þou sal hym luf with al þi Mynde
Withouten forgetynge; þan ertow kynde'.

  In þis manere, als clerkes shewe can,   11935
Es Goddis image sette in man
After þe grete dignytees thre
þat falles in þe saul to be.
þat es to say Mynde thurgh skille
And Vnderstandynge [and] Wille.   11940
When þise thre thinges specially
Ere wele ordayned to Godde almyghty
In þe thre maners þat er to prayse,

11912 als] þat L   es oft] *trs.* EL   11920 gun] con W   11922 Vnto] To PRW
entent] tente P   11923 *sidenote*: at 11905 E, at 11908 S   grana] genera? P
11925 bitokend] lyckned ELS   11926 graynes] grayne W   11927 teches] teche E,
telles S   *sidenote*: *later* E, *om.* LPS (cf. 11944)   11931 hym] god L   11933 hym luf]
trs. S   *11940 and²] with AELS   11941 When] Whe (*canc.*) P   11943 þe] þir
L, *om.* PS

Als Saynt Austyne teches and says,
þan er þe graynes of þe lily alle thre   11945
Endored with þe gold of Charyte.
þat gifs ay vnto vertu
Beaute, bounte, and valu.
For withouten þat gold so bright
Na vertu es fayre in Goddis sight.   11950

Bernardus   Als Saynt Bernarde spekes wysely
Of þe manere to luf Godde almyghty
And says on þis wyse openly þan,
'þou þat es kidde Crysten man
And in Goddis name es baptyst,   11955

De Castitate

fol. 72ʳᵃ Lere hou þou sal luf Cryst.
Lere to luf Godde almyghty
Wysely, swetely, and fastly.
Wysely so þat þou noght be
Deceyued thurgh na vanyte;   11960
Swetely so þat þou neuer þe mare
Be stirde thurgh welth and welefare;
Fastly so þat þou ouercommen be noght
Thurgh nane angre of hert ne thoght'.
þus es þe lyly of Maydenhede   11965
Right fayre þar þat flour wil sprede.
When it es swilk als I haf sayde,
þan es Godde þareof wele payde.
For þat flour es þan semely,
And þis es þe secund skille why   11970
þat Maydenhede þus suld mare be
Praysed for þe grete beaute.

Tercio laudandus est status   þe thridde skille why men suld it prayse,
virginitatis propter eius   Als þe boke proues and says,
bonitatem et vtilitatem   Es for þe bounte and þe profyte   11975

11944 teches] preches P   *sidenote*: Augustinus ELS   11945 þe'] thyr L
11946 þe] *om.* L   charyte] chastite P   11949 þat] þe W   11951 Als] And LS
sidenote: *in* W   11952 þe] þis L   11954 kidde] kynd R, *adds* a L, *adds* for a S
11960 Deceyued] Dedenyd R   11961 þe] *om.* W   11962 and] na L
11964 nane] *om.* R   11965 þe] *om.* W   11966 þat] þe S   11970 þis] þus E
þe] *om.* S (cf. es þe *int.* P) skille] skilk P   11971 þus] *om.* W   11972 Praysed]
Parfyte L   11973 *sidenote*: propter] *cut off* S   11975 þe'] *om.* R

þat worthyly may come of it.
For Maydenhede þat es wemmeles
Of so grete a valu it es
þat it ne may on nane wyse
Be praysed vnto certayne pryse.   11980
Wharefore Haly Wrytte says þus
þat nathinge es so precius
Ne so worthy þat men may tast
þat may be weghed agayne hert chast.
Forwhy it es ay mast worthy   11985
And es to vnderstande namely
Of þe Chastnes of Maydenhede
þat falles in heuen to haf mast mede.
For Maydenhede þat es clene
Ouer alle othir states þat bene   11990
Beres, als I vnderstande,
Mast fruyt vnto þe saul lykande.
    For þai þat lif in maryage
And kepes it clene fra + outrage,
Als I haf here bifore talde,   11995
Sal þare haf fruyte thrittyfalde.
And þai þat kepes clene Widowhede
Sal haue sextyfalde fruyte to mede.

De Castitate

Bot þai þat kepe Maydenhede wele   fo. 72ʳᵇ
Ane hundrethfalde fruyte sal fele.   12000
Wharefore our Louerd ful of myght
In þe godspelle says þus right
To þam þat he til hym calles,
þat þe sede þat in erthe falles
Sal gif fruyte at þe right tyde: 12005
Thrittyfalde on som a syde,
And on anothir syde sexty,

11978 a] om. LS   it] om. W   11979 ne] om. LS   ne may] may noȝt R   on] of P
nane] nanekyn L   11983 Ne] Na nane L   þat] þan P   men] mane ES   11984 sidenote:
Nota castitatis E   11987 þe] om. P   chastnes] chastynes S   11988 mast] grete R
mede] nede LS (corr. later S)   11990 þat bene] es als I wene L   11991 Beres] And
beres L   11992 vnto] to PRW   *11994 fra] fra alle AES   11995 sidenote: Nota
mercedem E   11996 þare haf] haue þaire LS   11997 þai] om. P   widow-] wedded- W
11099 Bot] And L   kepe] kepes LPRW   12000 -falde] om. R   sal] adds þai R
12003 þam] þos W   12004 in] in þe P   12006 a] om. LP

And ane hundreth of þe thridde party.
  þise thre partis þat I þus neuen,
Thritty, sexty, ane hundreth euen,   12010
To þise thre states falles to rede,
Sposaylle, Widouhede, and Maydenhede.
  þe tale of thritty thrys ten I halde,
þat es of ten and of thre called;
For thrys ten of thritty may noght faylle.   12015
þat falles to þe state of Sposaylle.
For in þat state Godde to worshepe
Men suld þe Ten Commandements kepe
Trewely, als þam felle to be
In þe trouth of þe Trynyte.   12020
  þe tale of sexty mare amountes.
Of ten and sex þus men acountes,
For sex sithes ten mas sexty to rede.
þat falles to þe state of Wydowhede.
For in þat state men suld kepe right   12025
þe Ten Commandements with al þair myght,
And þarewith men suld bisily
Do þe sex Werkes of Mercy.
  Bot þe noumbre of a hundreth hale,
þat of þe tothir es mast tale,   12030
O For it representes a lytell figure
þat es rounde aboute in mesure,
þe whilk es mast fayre and semely
Amange alle othir figures þarby,
þat falles to þe state of Maydenhed.   12035
þar men suld yheme in worde and dede
þe Ten Commandements with hert fre
In þe trouthe of þe Trynyte,
And ouer þat, als falles þarto,
þe sex Werkes of Mercy do.   12040

12008 of] on LPR   party] parte W   12009 þus] now L   12010 ane] and an W
12013 I halde] talde R   *sidenote*: xxx. W   12014 of²] *om.* LR   12015 For] *om.* R
faylle] fale P   12017 in] *om.* L   12021 *sidenote*: ⟨l⟩x. W   12022 and] ‘and’ of P
12023 sithes] and P   12024 þe] *om.* P   12025 kepe] *om.* L   12026 ten] sex P   with]
kepe wyth L   al þair] *om.* R   12028 Do] Kepe L   sex] seuen LPS   12029 *sidenote*:
C. W   12030 þe] *om.* R   tothir] oþer PW   12031 *sidenote*: *om.* E, C. PS, *in* W
12032 rounde] arounde E   in] in þe L, ane R   12033 þe] þat þe P   12036 þar] þat
EPLSW   yheme] kepe L   12039 als] *om.* L   12040 sex] seuen LP   do] to do L

Donum Intellectus   De Castitate
Adueniat regnum tuum

For als þe rounde figure es   fo. 72va
þar men sees þe roundnes—   O
þe last ende with agayne-crokynge
Turnes agayne vnto þe bigynnynge
And mas þat figure to seme right   12045
Als a coroun to mans sight.
Right so þe noumbre and þe tale
Of ane hundreth þat es hale   C
Kyndely with his cours may brynge
þe last ende vnto þe bigynnynge.   12050
For ten sithe ten an hundreth mas,
Als þat noumbre in course gas;
þat bitokens þe ryche coroun
þat þe wyse maydens had to warysoun.

  Bot albeit so, þat thurgh trauaylle   12055
In þe state of clene Sposaylle
And in þe state of Wydowhede,
Men may wynne þat serues mede
þe coroun of blisse, als Godde vouches saue;
And onence Godde mare meryte haue   12060
þan ma[n]y maydens þat chast has bene
And kepes þair Maydenhede clene.

  For many er in Paradyse
þat has lifd clene on þis wyse,
In Weddelayke and in Widouhede clene,   12065
And er nerre Godde þan som virgyns bene.
Bot always has þis maydens chast
A speciall coroun to prayse mast
Oboun þe comon coroun of blisse
þat Godde has graunted til alle his.   12070

12041 þe rounde] rounde als þe L   *sidenote*: C. LP, *om.* S, *in* W   12042 þar] þat L
12044 agayne] *om.* R   vnto] to ELSRW   12045 þat] þe W   12048 *sidenote om.*
ELP   12050 vnto] to ELSRW   12051 ten²] *with int. gloss* x. A   hundreth] *with int.*
gloss C. A   12052 þat] þe P   12053 ryche] ryght W   12055 Bot] *om.* R   albeit]
al be E, if al be L   þat] *int.* P, *om.* R   12056 clene] *om.* L   12057 þe] *om.* L
12058 þat] in þat P   serues] seruice LR   *sidenote*: wynne? E   12060 meryte] myrth W
12061 *many] may AELS, ‘many’ P   has] *om.* R   12062 kepes] keped L
12064 has] haued S   12065 in²] *om.* W   12066 þan] þat R   12067 þis] þe P

Forthy þat maydens specially
Has wonnen here þe victory
Of þair flesshe þat þam oft assaylles
Thurgh harde lifynge and gode trauaylles.
    Wharefore þai folow þe Lambes pase,   12075
Whiderwarde so euer he gase,
To wham þai er wedded als fere
And has left flesshely brydals here
For to be with Godde rotefast
At þe brydale þat euer sal last.   12080
þai sal þare apparaylled be
With grete worshepe and solempnyte
In riche apparaylle, fayre and clene;

Donum Intellectus   De Castitate
Adueniat regnum tuum

fo. 72ᵛᵇ So riche apparaylle was neuer sene
Ne so fayre to any mans sight.   12085
Couthe neuer yhete man discryue it right.
Wharefore I wil now na mare say
Bot þat þat Haly Wrytte proue may,
þat spekes of swilk fayre apparaylle
þat maydens has for þair trauaylle.   12090
þat es mare speciele, als clerkes wate,
þan þat any has of othir state.
    Yhete says Haly Writte þis thinge,
þat þai sal a newe sange synge
Withouten trauaylle and study   12095
And make þareinne grete melody.
So delytable þai sal synge þan
þat so swete noyse herde neuer man;
þat nane othir sal synge, I wene,
Bot þai þat kepes þat state clene.   12100
þis newe sange þat þai sal synge

12071 Forthy] Forwhy W   12072 þe] in W   12073 þam oft] *trs.* LW
12075 pase] trace E   12076 -warde] *om.* R   12077 er] *om.* W   12078 has] *om.* R
12079 rote-] rotyd R   12080 þe] *om.* L   euer] ay L   12086 yhete] *om.* R   yhete
man] *trs.* LS   man] any man W   descryue it] discry R   right] *om.* L   12088 þat²]
om. L   12089 swilk] *adds* a L   12092 þat] *om.* R   any] any other LS
12093 Yhete] þis S   12097 delytable] delytablely P, dilectabilly R   þai sal] *trs.* PR
12101 þai] I E

Bytokens a newe ioy of lykynge
And a speciall mede to haue
þat Ihesu Cryst in þam vouches saue,
Forþi þat þai with Luf and Drede   12105
Keped wele þair state of Maydenhede.
þis es þe fift braunche of þe tre
Of þe vertu of Chastyte.

    þe sext state þan es of clerkes   *vj. De statu clericorum in*
þat er ordayned to haly werkes,   12110   *sac⟨ris⟩ ordinibus*
Als suddeken þat beres haly state,   *constitutorum et prelatorum*
And deken and preste, and prelate
þat has heghe order and dignyte.
Alle suld þai kepe wele Chastyte
For many skils þat I can say;   12115
Whaso wil þam here, he may.

    First for þe Order þat haly es,
þat askes noght bot halynes.
Forwhy þe sacrament es so haly
And so heghe and so worthy   12120
þat þai þat has þat state so fre
Er oblyst to kepe Chastyte,
þat þai may mary þam to nane
After þai þat office haf tane.

De Castitate

    For þai er appropred thurgh myght   12125 fo. 73ra
To serue Godde in his temple right
And at his haly auter to stande
And haly thinges to handell with hande,
Als chalyce, corporals, and vestymentes
And othir haly ornamentes,   12130

12104 in] on SR   12105 Forþi] For R   þat] *om.* S   12106 Keped] Kepe P,
Kepes W   þair] þe R   state of] *om.* L   12107 fift] fyrst LSR   12109 þan] þat R
sidenote: as in-column heading R, vj. status clericorum W   vj.] *om.* EPSR, vj^us. status L   et]
et eciam de R   12111–12 *trs. couplet* E, Als subdeken preste and prelate | `þat god sulde
serue arly and late' L   (*the second line in the lower margin, perhaps original hand*)
12113 has] *om.* ES, *after* order L   12114 Alle] As W   wele] *om.* L   12116 þam]
om. L   12117 First] *after* order R   12119 -why þe] þat R, -why þat W   es] *om.* E
12121 *line om. at page boundary* L   þat²] *om.* P   12123 þat] *blank* P, For L   may] *int.*
P, *om.* W   12124 haf] *after* þai LP   12125 *sidenote*: In principio erat verbum et verb
W (*much later*)   12129 Als] *om.* R   chalyce] *blank* P   -mentes] -ment R
12130 -mentes] -ment R

And yhete þat thinge þat es mast worþi.
þat es Ihesu Crystes awen body
þat þe preste in haly stede
At þe messe sacres in fourme of brede
And hymself oft receyues it　　　　　　12135
And gifs til othir þat haly bitte.
　þan suld þai be haly and chast
Bi resoun of þair Louerd mast
To wham þai serue, þat knawes alle states
And clennes lufs and alle filthe hates.　　12140
þarefore Godde says þus appertly,
'Be yhe haly, for haly am I'.
Forwhy swilke als þe lorde wil be,
Swilk suld be alle his menyhe.
　Also þay suld kepe, thurgh wyse men rede,　12145
Chastyte by resoun of þe stede
þar þai serue, þat so haly es
And halde it in allekyns clennes.
þat es þe kirke þat es haly
And halwed to serue Godde almyghty.　　12150
　I haf sene wryten, als me menes,
þat prestes amange þe paens
þat in þair temples serues and singes
Kepes Chastyte in alle fondynges
And fra othir þam twynnes, als men sese,　12155
For þai þair Chastyte suld noght lese.
Wele mare bi skille þai suld chast be
þat er prestes of Cristyante,
þat falles to serue and singe messe
In Goddis temple þat halwed es　　　　　12160
And apropried to his seruyse.
Bot þai be chast þai er noght wyse.

12131 yhete] om. SR　　12132 Crystes] goddys R　　12133 þat] þat es at L, þat es S　in] in þe R　　12134 þe] om. P　　12138 þair] þat R　Louerd] mayster L　12139 alle] om. R　　12140 alle] om. ER　　12141 sidenote: Estote sancti quia ego sanctus sum dicit Dominus ES　　12143 Forwhy] For W　Forwhy swilke] om. L　wil] couaytes to L　　12144 his] þe house L, þe R　　12145 Also þay] And R　12147 þar þai] þat þai in L　so] om. R　　12148 in allekyns] trs. R　allekyns] all PRW　12149 es²] es so EL　　12150 And] And es S　　12152 paens] paryshenes E, sarazenes L, pharysenes S　　12153 temples] temple ELSR　　12158 of] in R　　12159 serue and] serue god and to L

Yhete suld þai þe mare clene be
And þe mare kepe Chastyte

De Castitate

And be mare haly in dede and worde,   12165 fo. 73rb
Forþi þat þai serue at Goddis borde,
Of his coupe and of his brede
And also of his wyne so rede.
þat es his awen flesshe and blode,
þe whilk es our gastly fode.   12170
  Mikill halynes suld þai vse
þat swilk seruyse vnto Godde duse.
For Saynt Paul says, als clerkes can se,   *Paulus*
þat bisshops thurgh þair dignite
And othir þat haly werkes suld wirke,   12175
Als mynystres of Halykirke,
Suld be chast and Chastite kepe,
For þan þai do þair state worshepe.
  þis Chastyte þat þai suld knawe
Es assigned in þe New Lawe,   12180
þar Godde commanded, als þe law es sette,
To þam þat of þe Lambe suld ette—
þe whilk bytokens specyally
Ihesu Crystes awen body—
þat þai suld belt þair lendes wele,   12185
When þai flesshely fondynges fele.
þe belt þat Goddis mynistres fre
Suld belten þam with es Chastyte
þat Litchery of flesshe restreynes
And þair state to Godde ordaynes.   12190
  Wharefore our Lorde Aaron badde
þat preste state and dignyte hadde
þat he and alle his childer bathe

12161 apropried] aproperde LSRW   to] ʼvnʼto S   12162 wyse] wyste E
12163 þe] *om.* SR   12164 þe mare] mare sulde S   kepe] *after* And W   12165 be]
om. S   12166 Forþi] For PSR   12168 And] *om.* R   so] þat es sa L
12169–70 *couplet om.* ES   12172 vnto] to L   duse] vse W   12173 can] may R
sidenote om. S   12174 þat] þe P   bisshops] bishope R   12175 suld wirke] wyrkes R
12178 þan] þai m W   12179 þat] *om.* P   12180 in] to E   12181 commanded]
comaundes W   12182 of] *om.* L   12187 mynistres] minister L   12189 rest-]
const- S   12191 Whare-] þer- W   Lorde] *adds* god L   *sidenote*: Aaron exemplum E,
Aaron W   12192 preste] prestes LP

Suld be cladde in lynnen clathe
And belted þareafter oboun tyte   12195
With a lynnen belt þat war whyte.
Aaron and his childer dere,
For to telle yhow shortly here,
Bytokens clene werkes to wirke
And þe minystres of Halykyrke   12200
þat suld ay clennely cledde be
With þe lynne cote of Chastyte.
þat þai suld fast halde and noght tyne
þat es bytokened by þe whyte lyne.
    For als þe lynne webbe, narow or brade,   12205
When it sal clene and whyte be made,

Donum Intellectus   De Castitate
Adueniat regnum tuum

fo. 73ᵛᵃ Men suld bete and wasshe oft
Til it war made whyte and soft.
Right so þai suld þair flesshe dynge
With discyplynes and harde lyuynge,   12210
þat þe Flesshe may þarewith smert
And also oftsythe wasshe þe hert
Of alle fole thoghtes and yhernynges
And wicked willes and lykynges
Thurgh verray shrift and repentaunce.   12215
þis war a siker ordynaunce
For to haue of Goddis lyuere
þe whyte cote of Chastyte.
    Bot þis cote suld obout it haue
A whyte belt þe cote to saue.   12220
þat es to say þat Chastyte
Suld wele and straytely keped be
And thurgh Abstinence right restreyned
And thurgh Resoun wele ordayned,
þe whilk it suld mast vphalde: 12225

12199 werkes] werk S   12200 þe] om. P   12203 fast] om. S   halde] om. R
12206 and] or LSW   12207 suld] sall L   bete] bete itt ES, it bete LPW   oft] full oft
L, it ofte S   12208 war] be L   12209 suld] sall L   12211 may] may bye S
12212 -sythe] om. R   12213 fole] foule LSRW   yhernynges] -nynge P
12214 lykynges] -kynge P   12216 siker] nobell L   12217 Goddis] god L
12219 Bot] For P, om. R   12223 restr-] str- R   12225 suld ... vp-] vp maste may L

þat es þe bocle of þe belt cald.
  On othir wyse yhete shewe I may
What þe cote and þe belt es to say.
First þe lynne cote bitokens wele
Chastyte of Herte to fele.   12230
þe belt oboun, to telle shortly,
Bytokens Chastyte of Body
þat may restreyne þe Flesshe fra syn
And kepe Chastite of þe Saul within.
  þe same es bytokend to do   12235
By þe aube and þe belt þarto
þat þe minysters of Halykirke
Er cledde inne, haly werkes to wirke,
When þai sal serue at þe autere
Thurgh þe Order þat þai bere.   12240
For þai suld be chast within namely
In hert, and withouten in body.
  Litchery es so foule a synne
þat it fyles body and saul withinne
And þe hertes of men makes ful myrke   12245
And namely of men of Halykirke.

Donum Intellectus   De Castitate
Adueniat regnum tuum

For þai er called þe eghe bright   fo. 73vb
Of Halykirke þat suld loke right.
For als þe eghe wisses þe body
And shewes it þe way kyndely   12250
To what stede so it wil ga,
Whethir it wil wende to or fra,
Right so suld þis prelates wirke
And othir mynystres of Halykyrke.
þai suld shewe, if þai war lele,   12255
Til othir men þe way of hele.

12226 þe^1] om. W   12227 yhete] om. LS   12230 of] of þe P   12234 þe]
om. L   12235 to] for to R   12236 By þè aube] Bot þe webbe L   12240 þe] þat P
12241 within] int. P, om. S, after suld RW   12242 in^2] foly in L, and in P
12243 so] om. P   12245 men] men it L   12248 right] bryght L   12249 þe eghe]
ye E, it L   12250 it] in W   12251 stede] stat W   12252 wil wende] trs. R
12253 sidenote: Nota de prelatis E   12254 mynystres] minores L   12255 if] and L

Wharefore als a spotte þat es blacke,
þat commonly men will lacke,
Semes mare foulle in þe eghe namely
þan in anothir lym of þe body,   12260
Right so methink, in gode faythe,
þe spotte of Litchery es mare laythe
And mare perillous ay to kenne
In clerkes þan in lewed men.
　　　Also þai er by skille called 'mirour   12265
Of Halykirke', þat es our sokour,
Whare þe lewed men þat na clergy hase
Byhaldes and ensaumple tase.
Bot when þe mirour es spotty,
A man may se þan appertly   12270
þe filthe [þat] in þat mirour es
Bot noght his awen lickenes.
þe spottes of filthe may he noght se
On hymself, if þare any be,
For þe mirour es þan so dym   12275
þat he may noght se þe filth on hym.
Bot when þe mirour es made bright,
þan may he knawe his filthe bi sight.
　　　Forsothe methinke it fares right swa
By prelates and bi othir ma   12280
þat minystres bene of Halykirke
Als fares bi þe mirour þat es myrke.
When þai thurgh syn er foul and spotty,
And namely thurgh þe synne of Litchery,
Ful ille ensaumple þan þai gif   12285
Til othir men wele for to lif.

De Castitate

fo. 74ra Bot som tas swilk ensaumple þarby
þat þai to synne er mare hardy.

12257 Whare-] *om.* R　　12260 an-] any LW　　12263 ay] *om.* LS　　12265 Also]
om. R　called] *after* er PR　　12267 men] *om.* PRW　þat] *om.* P　　12271 *þat¹] om.*
AE　þat²] þe `P´RW　　12274 On] Of L　　12276 þe] *om.* S　on] of LPW
12277 þe] *om.* P　　12280 bi] *om.* R　　12281 of] in LS　　12282 es] is so P
12283 foul and] *om.* RW　　12284 þe] þis P　þe . . . of] fals R　　12285 þai] may þai R
12286 for] *om.* LRW　　12287 Bot] *om.* R

þarefore says þe boke þus wele
þat þai er worthy for to fele 12290
Als many specyel paynes thurgh skille
Als þai gif ensaumple of ille.

*Tot mortalia digni sunt
quot mala exempla prebent*

Bot when þai kepe þam clene and chast
And lifs to Goddis lykynge mast,
þan may men by þair lyf thurgh sight 12295
Take ensaumple to lyf right.
þan er þai worthy to haue mede
þat gode ensaumple shewes in dede.
Also methinke þai suld be clene
So þat na synne war in þam sene. 12300
For whaso es foul in conscience,
He may noght othir men wele clense,
þat es to say to haue meryte.
þus men sal vnderstande it.
Forwhy þe haly sacrament 12305
þat es made thurgh right entent
Or mynysterd, als I vnderstande,
Thurgh ane ille ministers hande
Es neuer þe wers of valu
Na neuer þe lesse of vertu 12310
To halow and to gif þam right
þat receyues þat sacrament dight
þan to þam þat it tase knelande
At a gode mynystre hande.
For þe wickednes of an ille man 12315
May noght appayre þe sacrament þan,
Ne godenes of hym þat gode es
May noght amende it to worthynes.
Bot ay þe wickednes of wille
Of a ministre þat es ille 12320

12289 þare-] And þare- L   þus] *om.* L   12291 specyel] specyally E   thurgh] by R
sidenote: Tot mortalia] Gregorius tot mortibus P   digni sunt] *trs.* LS   exempla] exemplo P
12292 of] to P   12294 lifs] byses R   12295 men] *om.* W   thurgh] be R
12296 Take] *add* godde PRW   12298 shewes] gyfes L   12299 Also] Als L
12300 war] *after* þam R   in] on ES   12302 men] *om.* R   wele] *after* noght EL
12304 men sal] *trs.* LP   12307 mynysterd] mynystres ES   12308 ille] *adds* a L
12309 wers] lesse P   12310 lesse] vers ELS   12313 it tase] *trs.* P   tase] has tane R
12316 appayre] enpare PRW   12317 Ne] Na þe LPSRW   12318 it] *om.* LR   to]
to þe R   12320 Of] Bot L

May othir enpayre, als es oft sene,
Thurgh ille ensaumple of lyf vnclene.
  Bot als men may se a candel stand
To othir mens profyte brynnand,
And to harme of itself brynnes ay   12325

De Castitate

fo. 74rb (For it wastes itself away),
Right so þe wicked ministre mas
þe sacrament þat þe office has
And til othir men mynistres it
To þair saul-hele and grete profyte,   12330
And to othir mens saluacioun
And to þair awen dampnacioun.
  þarefore sen þam falles þat office
To halwe othir and clense of vice,
þar þai mynystre thurgh right entent   12335
þis Halykirke sacrament,
þai suld be mare haly and clene
þan othir þat er in lesse state sene.
For if þai be ille, þai sal mare be
Punyst þan othir of lesse degre.   12340
þis es þe sext state right called
Of Chastyte þat clerkes suld halde,
And þe sext braunche of þe seuen
þat springes out of þat tre euen.

vij. De statu religiosorum   þe seuent state es of religioun   12345
þat es stabled thurgh professioun.
For þai þat er in swilk astate
Has hight Godde þat alle thing wate
And made a vowe to hym þarby
þat þai sal lif here chastly.   12350
Wharefore þai er, als I say yhow,

12321 enpayre] payer E   es oft] *trs.* R   12323 *sidenote:* Nota E   12325 to] to
þe S   12328 þe²] he of E   12329 it] he it E, tite L   12330 grete] þaire S
12331 mens] men SR   12333 þat] of RW   12334 halwe] hele R   12335 þar]
þat right] goddes R   12337 þai] þis W   12338 lesse] lawelese E   lesse state] noȝt
haly P   12340 of] in L   12344 *adds line* þarefore say we louyng to God of heuen L
12345 of] of men of L   *sidenote: as in-column heading* R, vij. W   vij.] vij^{us}. (Sextus L)
status ELS, *om.* PR   12346 stabled] stabel ES   12349 made] *after* hym P
12350 þai sal] þi R   lif here] *trs.* LW   12351 say] sayde E

Obliged thurgh swilk a vowe
So þat þai mai neuer þam mary,
After þai er profest namely.
And if þai after mary þam walde,   12355
þat mariage ne suld noght halde.
    And þarefore þai suld with al þair myght
Kepe Chastyte als þai haf hight
For resoun of þair state þat es
Haly and parfyte in Halynes.   12360
For ay þe halyer þat þai suld be,
þe fouller es þair synne to se.
Als a spotte es, whaso right demes:
Til ilk mans sight mare foul semes
On a whyte robe þat es newe   12365
þan on anothir of othir hewe.
And þe ferrer fra heght falles a man,
þe sarer es his falle þan.

Donum Intellectus   De Castitate
Adueniat regnum tuum

    Also þai suld kepe Chastyte right   fo. 74va
For to ouercom þe fendes myght   12370
þat thurgh grete temptacioun
Assayles men of religioun,
And has mare ioy when he may
To wynne ane of þam vnto his pray
þan to wynne, als þis clerkes wate,   12375
Many othir of othir state.
    For als þe aungels of heuen has
Mikell ioy and grete myrth mas
Of a synfull þat hym repentes
And to verray penaunce tentes,   12380
Right so þe fende has grete ioy þan
When he ouercomes a gode man
þat of heghe and haly state es

12353 þat] om. R   mai] adds þanne L   12354 þai] þat þai L   12355 if] om. P
þai after] trs. R   12356 ne] om. ELPSRW   suld] sall P   12357 And] om. P
12364 ilk] a LP   12366 othir] another E   12367 fra] on R   heght] heghe L
12373 when] when þat L   12374 wynne] twynne E   vnto] to EPLSRW
12375 þis] om. P   12377 aungels] aungell P   12379 a] om. S   synfull] adds man L
12380 to] vnto L   12381 fende] fendes P   grete] om. R   12383 and] and of E

And mast parfyte in Halynes.
And als þe fissher has in hert hale   12385
Mare ioy to take grete fisshes þan smale,
Right so þe fende thurgh his wyle
Has mare ioy a man to bygyle
þat es haly, of parfyte lyf,
þan of othir twenty and fyue.   12390

Exemplum Narracio   Men fyndes wryyten in a boke
Of *Vitis Patrum*, þat wil it loke,
þat a munk þat lifd parfytely
Talde how he bicome munk and why,
And wharefore he walde þe werld shone.   12395
And sayde he was a paem sone
þat was þe preste of mawmetryse
And kepar of alle þair sacrafyse.
He talde when he was in chyldehede,
Into þe temple a tyme he yhede   12400
With his fader priuely.
He sawe þan a grete company
Of foul fendes þat war þare;
So grisly a sight sawe he neuer are.
He saw a fende site in a sete   12405
þat was vgly, huge, and grete,
And many fendes hym aboute;
And ane come and bigan him to loute.
      þan at first spake he þat
      þat on þe sete so grysly satte,   12410

Donum Intellectus   De Castitate
Adueniat regnum tuum

fo. 74vb And asked hym whethen he come
And what he didde sen he went fro home.

12385 And] *om.* R   12386 grete fisshes] grete (þe g. P) fisshe LP   þan] þen þe P
12388 a man] *om.* L   to] for to R   12389 haly] *om.* E   12391 *sidenote: om.* LP, *trs.*
S, vitis patrum de monacho (*later*) W   12392 Of] In L   Vitis] vitas LS   þat . . . it]
whasa (who P) wyll LP   12393 þat¹] Of L   þat²] *om.* R   12394 how] why S
12395 þe werld] *om.* R   shone] sone W   12396 paem] payens W   12398 þair] þe L
12399 He] And R   12400 Into] To L   a] on a LS   a tyme] anes R   12401 fader]
adds full P   12402 He] þare he L   þan] *om.* L, þare S   12403 war þare] *trs.* P
12405 saw] se P   in] *om.* S   12408 And] And at P, *om.* S   to] *om.* W   12409 þan]
þat, *with* t *expunged and* `n' A   þan at] And at þe W   12410 þe] þat P   grysly] greifly R
12411 whethen] when L

þe tothir answerde 'in' his degre
And sayde he come fra a cuntre
Whare he had raysed grete were   12415
Amange alle þa þat he myght dere,
And swilk cunteck made and stryf
So þat many þare had tynt þe lyf.

    þan asked þe mayster wham he gan loute
How lange he hadde bene þareaboute.   12420
þan answerd he to hym þat satte
þat in thritty days he had done þat.
þan sayd þe mayster to hym sone,
'So lange tyme hasstow lytel done?'
þan commanded he to bete hym fast   12425
With harde babils whyle þai myght last.

    þan come anothir þat offyce bare
And louted to þe mayster þare.
þe mayster, when he hym had sene,
Asked hym whare he had bene.   12430
þe tothir sayde he come fra þe se
Whare he had fordone grete naue,
Sunken shippes and ryuen in sunder
Thurgh wynde-stormes and dyntes of thunder
And drunkened men þat war þarinne   12435
þat war combred in dedely synne.

    þe mayster hym asked þat loude yhelled
How lange he had about þat dwelled.
þe tothir answerde and sayde sone
þat in twenty days al þat was done.   12440
þan badde þe mayster þam bete him sare
For he so lange tyme didde na mare.

    12413 in] *int., possibly later* A   12414 he] I R   12415 he] I L   grete] *om.* L
12416 he] I L   12417 swilk] *adds* a P   12418 þat þurgh me many loste þaire lyfe L
So] *om.* R   þare] *om.* P   þe] þair PR   12419 gan] gune ELR, con W   12420 he
hadde] haues þou L   þare-] here- L   12423 to] vnto L   12424 So] In swa L
hasstow] þou has P   12426 whyle . . . myght] walde L   12427 *sidenote:* ij. W
12429 when] *precs.* þe R   he] *om.* L   12430 Asked hym] He hym asked L
12431 þe²] *om.* E   12432 fordone] drounde a L, fordo a P   12433 ryuen] dryuen L
12434 wynde] *adds* and L, wyndes P   and] *om.* R   thunder] *partly in gutter* A
12435 drunkened] drounked L, drounede P, drunken W   12437 hym] *om.* R   hym . . .
þat] asked hym (*om.* S) and LS   12438 about þat] þeraboute L   12440 þat¹] *om.* L
al] *om.* R   þat²] þis P, *om.* S   þat was] *trs.* R   12441 þam] *om.* SR   12442 so] in
so S

After hym þan come þe thridde;
þe mayster asked how he had spedde
And whare he was and whethen he come   12445
And what he didde sen he went fro home.
þe tothir answerde als best myght be
And sayde he come fra a cyte
Whare he was at a brydale,
And þare he wroght mykill bale.   12450
He made swilk conteck in þat stede
þat many men was þare dede,

De Castitate

fo. 75ʳᵃ And yhete þe brydegome þan was slayne.
And þareof he sayde he was ful fayne.
       þan asked þe mayster, half on hethynge,   12455
'How lange tyme was þat in spedynge?'
þe tothir answerd and sayde þus þan,
þat in ten days fra he bygan.
þe mayster commanded his menyhe
þat he suld smertly beted be,   12460
And þat nane of þam suld hym spare
For he so lange tyme did na mare.
       þare come þe ferthe at þe last
þat day and nyght had trauaylled fast
About a man of religyoun   12465
To brynge hym vnto his bandoun,
And 'þe' mayster honourde he
þare he sat heghe in his see.
       þe mayster hym asked wheþen he come
And how lange he had bene fro home   12470
And al þat tyme what he had done.
þe tothir spake and answerde sone,

12445 and] om. R   whethen] when S   12446 And] om. R   12449 Whare . . . at]
And sayde he come fra L   12450 wroght] adds full L   12452 men] man L   þare]
done to þe L   12453 þe] om. S   -gome] -grome LPSRW   þan] þer L, om. R
12454 he sayde] om. E   ful] om. SR   12456 þat] þis LPR, þat thyng S
12459 commanded] comandes W   12461 And] om. P   hym] om. R   12462 so] in
sa LS   did] tyd R   12463 þare] þan LS   12464 þat] om. L   had] he had L   had
trauaylled] trs. P   12466 vnto] to ELR   12467 þe] int. later? A   12468 heghe]
om. EP   see] sete fre P, cyte R   12469 hym] om. R   hym asked] trs. LS   wheþen]
when L   12470 he had] trs. R   12471–2 couplet trs. L   12471 And . . . what]
And talde hym how L

þat he come fra an hermytage
þar he had dwelled for auauntage
Fourty yhere contynuelly   12475
To fonde a munke with Litchery,
And he myght hym neuer are wynne
Til þat nyght to do þat synne.
And now, he sayde, he had so wroght
þat he vnto þat synne was broght.   12480
    þan vp stirte þe mayster swythe,
For þat dede made hym mast blythe.
And in his armes he hym hent
And kissed hym with grete talent
And hight hym for þat a warysoun   12485
And of his heued he toke his coroun
And on tothirs heued he sette itte
And didde [hym bi] hymseluen sitte
And sayde he war worthy grete mede
For he did swilk a dughty dede.   12490
    þe haly man sayde þat when he had herd
And sene how þis fendes ferde,
He thoght it was an heghe thinge
þe state of munk in clene lyuynge.
And þarefore he had deuocioun   12495
To bicom man of relygyoun,

De Castitate

And þat state of munk he þan toke,   fo. 75ʳᵇ
Als it es funden wryten in þe boke.
    Bi þis tale þus men may se
þat þe fende has ioy, so fayne es he,   12500

12473 þat] And sayde L   12474 dwelled . . . auauntage] full grete outerage L
12476 To fonde] He hadd fanded L   a] *om*. R   12477 hym . . . are] neuer mare L
12478 Til] Are L   12479 he sayde] *om*. P   sayde] says W   had] has W
12480 vnto] hym to L, was to P, to RW   was] had L, *om*. P   12481 þan] And LW
12482 For] And for L, *om*. R   mast] *om*. P   12485 hym] *after* þat P   a] hys L
12486 his] þe LSR   12487 on] on þe ELSW, on þat P   he] sone L   sette] dyd R
12488 didde] gart LP, made S   *hym . . . hymseluen] W, hymseluen A, hym soyne for
(*om*. S) to ES, hym bysyde hym L, hymselfen by hym P, hym ryse and by R   12489 he]
þat he L   war] was ELPS   12491 haly] hethene ES   sayde] *om*. R   þat] *om*. SR
had] *om*. L, *int*. S   12492 sene] saugh L   þis] þe R   12493 heghe] hight W
12495 And] *om*. P   had] did W   12496 bicom] be ordaynde a L, become a S
12497 þat] þe L   he þan] *trs*. S, þer he R   12498 funden] *om*. W   þe] a L, *om*. S
12499 þus] *int*. P, 'þan' L   men may] *trs*. S   12500 has] *adds* grete L   so] and LP

When he may thurgh sleght wynne
A man of religyoun vnto synne,
And namely vnto Litchery
þat wastes bathe saul and body.
For when a man thurgh deuocioun   12505
Entres into religyoun,
He es als he þat men sees wende
Into þe felde to fight with þe fende.

Wharefore our Lorde, blissed be he,
When he of þe fende fanded wald be,   12510
He went into þe desert to dwell,
Als es wryten in þe godspelle.
For þe dishert of relygyoun
Es a felde of temptacioun.

Religioun þat gode men suld halde   12515
May bi skille 'diserte' be cald.
For als diserte es comonly sene
In sharpe stede þar na delyces bene,
And yhete fer fra men diserte es;
þarefore men calles it wildernes.   12520
Right so þe state of relygioun
þat falles to lyf of Perfeccioun
Suld be sharpe and strayte in alle thing
Thurgh sharpnes of strayte lyuynge.
þat es a thorne-heghe to telle   12525
Agayne þe wicked bestes of helle,
With whilk þe hert es closed about
To halde þa wicked bestes out.
It es a wapen stalwarde and light
Agayne þe enemy for to fight,   12530
Thurgh whilk men may hym skonfyte

12502 vnto] to RW   12505 For] om. R   thurgh] of E   12506 into] adds order of L, adds þe haly order of S, vnto R   12507–698 lines om. (missing folios) W   12507 he] om. L   12508 þe¹] a L   12509 sidenote: Ductus est Ihesus in desertum vt temptaretur a diabolo (om. phrs. LS) ELS   12511 þe] om. ELSR   12514 of] of grete S   12515 men] om. R   12516 bi] be gode L   skille] slyk R   be] om. LR   12518 stede] stedes LS   delyces] dilites P   bene] er sene L   12519 yhete] after men P   12520 -fore] om. E   it] om. L   12522 to] to be þe E, to þe L   of] om. R   12523 sharpe and strayte] trs. adjs. E   12524 sharpnes of strayte] straytenes of scharpe P   12525 es a] es als L, as a R   thorne-] thorne-ȝherde ES, thornne-garthe L   heghe] heght L   12526 bestes] gaste L   12527 With] Wyth þe L   12528 þa] þe P   12529 It] þat S   12530 for] wyth L

And do hym fle away ful tyte.
þat es a siker remedy
Agayne þe fyre of Litchery.
   For he þat wil slecken wele   12535
þat fyre of Litchery ilka dele,
He suld slecken with sleght of witte
Alle þe sparkes þat comes of it,

Donum Intellectus   De Castitate
Adueniat regnum tuum

þat er called flesshely delyces   fo. 75va
þat bringes forthe oft grete vyces.   12540
þe whilk þe gode religious man
Suld putte fra his flesshe ay þan
Thurgh wakynge, fastyng, and discyplyns
And hard werynge þat þe flesshe pynes.
   Whaso wil wynne a cyte   12545
Or a castelle, whethir it be,
He suld in al þat he may lette
þat þai þat haldes it suld noght gette
Vitaylles ne water on nane wyse.
And so myght he þam sone enfamyse,   12550
And þan may þai noght halde lange
þe castelle, war it neuer so strange.
For þan haf þai na langar powere
To halde it agayne þair aduersere.
   Right so þe castelle of þe body,   12555
þat es þe strengthe of þe flesshe þarby,
May noght thurgh na flesshely delyte
Be halden agayne þe spiryte,
When it es famyst with penaunce
Thurgh abstynence of sustynaunce.   12560
   Also þe state of religyoun

12532 do] garr L, make S   fle] to fle E   ful] *om.* LPR   12535 For] *om.* R
slecken] slokene ELSR   12536 þat] þe LR   12537 slecken] slokkene EPSR, it
sloken L   12538 þe] *om.* L   12539–40 *couplet trs.* R   12539 delyces] desires L,
delites SR   12540 forthe oft] *trs.* LP   12541 þe¹] *om.* R þe²] *om.* S religious]
religion R   12543 discyplyns] disciplys R   12545 wil] *om.* S   12546 it] sa it L,
þat it P   12547 al] all thing L   12549 nane] nanekyn L   12550 myght he] *trs.* P
þam sone] *trs.* R   sone] *om.* LS   enfamyse] famyse P   12552 war] be L
12556 flesshe] sleshe R   12559 es] *om.* R famyst] enfameste L

Suld be thurgh right entencioun
Ferre fra þe werlde, als þe boke telles,
Als in diserte þar na man dwelles,
So þat he þat þis state kepes wele   12565
þe maners of þe werlde noght fele.
Forwhy he þat es in þat state,
He es, als þis clerkes wele wate,
Dede als onence þe Werlde namly
And lifs in Godde almyghty,   12570
Paulus Als says Saynt Paul in a stede.
For als a man þat es dede
Bodily thurgh dedes dynt,
Has alle his body-wittes tynt,
þat es to say sight and smellyng,   12575
Herynge, speche, and felynge.
Right so `suld´ þe religious man,
Als to þe Werlde, be dede þan
þat he fele nathinge withinne
þat suld falle til any synne,   12580

Donum Intellectus   De Castitate
Adueniat regnum tuum

fo. 75vb Bot [b]e als dede in þat party
So þat he myght say sothfastly
þis worde þat es mykell to prayse,
þe whilk Saynt Paul þe apostell þus sayse:
Paulus 'þe Werlde es vylly hynged to me,   12585
And I to þe Werlde', þus says he.
þat es, he helde þe Werlde dispysable
And hym to it abhomynable,
Als men dose an hinged man
þat es a thief or a lurdan.   12590
Right so he helde þe Werlde for vyle,

12564 þar] whare L   12565 kepes] *after* þat² LS   12566 þe²] þis R   noght]
sulde noght ELS   12568 þis] *om.* P   12569 namly] anely R   12571 Als] And L
says] *om.* E, *after* Paul LP (*int.* P)   *sidenote*: *adds* Nota (*later*) E, *om.* L   12574 body]
bodely LPR   12577 suld] *int. later?* A   þe] *om.* P   12579 nathinge] *adds* hym R
12581 *be] he AEW, he is P   12582 myght] may E   12583 worde] world R   to]
for to L   12584 þe²] *om.* P   þe apostell] *after* whilk L, *om.* R   þus] *om.* LP
12585 vylly] willy ELS, vile P   *sidenote om.* L   12586 þus] þusgate L   12587 es]
as R   he] he he P   12590 or] and L   12591 he] a S   for] *om.* L, so R

þat es ful of falsed and of gyle,
Als men dose hym þat hynged es
For his trespase and his wickednes.
   Right so he suld thurgh right entencioun   12595
þat es in þe state of relygioun
þe Werlde for ay hate and fle
þat es so ful of vanyte.
þat es to say þe Couatyse
Of þe Werlde and othir folyse,   12600
þat he þareof fele nathinge,
Nouthir thurgh luf na thurgh yhernynge,
So þat his conuersacioun be
In heuen bifore þe Trynyte.
   Als Saynt Paul of hymseluen telles   12605 *Paulus*
And of þam þat in þat state dwelles,
'Our conuersacioun', he says,
'Es in heuen', Goddis palays.
For al-if þe body in erthe be right,
þe hert es heghe in heuen bright   12610
Thurgh hertly yhernynge and thurgh luf,
Als men may by skilles proue.
   þe gode religyous suld nathinge haue   *Monachus habens obolum*
Propre in erthe for hymself to saue,   *non val⟨et⟩ obolum*
Bot he suld do al his tresore   12615
In heuen; þat es sikerest þarfore.
Als says Saynt Ione þe ewangelyst,   *Iohannes euangelista*
'If þou wil be parfyte in Cryst',
He says, 'Ga selle al þat þou has
And gif it to pouer þat obout gase'.   12620
Swa may þou þan þi tresour saue
And in heuen it fynde and haue.

12592 of gyle] begyle R   12594 his²] *om.* P   12595 right] gude P, his R
12596 þe] *om.* ES   12597 þe] Ay þe L   for ay] to L, `for´ ay S   12598 so] *om.* PS
of] *om.* E   12599 þe] of fals S, of R   12600 and] and of PS   folyse] fayntyse P
12601–2 *couplet trs.* P   12604 þe] þe haly E   12605 Als] And L   of] *om.* R
sidenote: om. L, Item Paulus P   12606 And] þat S   þat²] *om.* ER   12608 palays]
place L   12609 al-if] if all L   þe . . . erthe] *trs. phrs.* R   be] *after* body S
12610 heghe] *om.* L   12611 thurgh²] *om.* R   12612 may] *after* skilles R   skilles]
skyll L   12613 religyous] *adds* mane E   *sidenote om.* LP   12615 al] *om.* PR
12616 es sikerest] *trs.* L, ys mast sekir R   12617 says] *after* Ione E, *om.* L   þe] *om.* S
sidenote: euangelista] in euangelio P   12618 If] Says if L   12619 ga] *om.* L
12620 it] *om.* P   to] to þe PR   12621–2 *couplet om.* R

þe tresour of a man religious
Es clene Pouert; þat es precious,

De Castitate

<table>
<tr><td>fo. 76ra</td><td>If it com of a gode wille</td><td>12625</td></tr>
</table>

fo. 76ʳᵃ If it com of a gode wille   12625
And withouten grochyng, loude or stille.
Als says þe haly man þarby
In *Vitis Patrum* specially,
For Pouert to þe mone es like,
Thurgh whilk men may bye heuenryke.   12630
Wharefore Godde says þus, 'Blissed er þai
þat pouer er in gast, nyght and day,
For þairs es, als falles thurgh right,
þe kyngedome of heuen bright'.

Forsothe whaso es pouer in gast,   12635
þat es of wille thurgh grace to tast,
He sekes noght in þis werlde here
Nouthir grete worsheps, ne powere,
Ne ritches, ne delyces to proue,
Bot forgetes al þat for Goddis luf.   12640
Right so suld do þe man of religyoun
þat clymb wil on þe hille of Perfeccioun.

Als þe aungell sayd þat 'to' Loth come,
When he was went out of Sodome:
'Stande noght', he sayde, 'ouernere þat stede   12645
þat þou has left, thurgh my rede;
Bot saue þiself in þe heghe mountayne.
þan may þou be siker and certayne.'

For he þat es went thurgh deuocioun
Out of þe Werldes conuersacioun,   12650
He sal noght nere þe Werlde him halde
Thurgh yhernynge þat werldely es calde.

12623 man] man of L	12627 says] *after* man P	12628 *Vitis*] vitas ELS
sidenote: Vitas patrum E	12629 mone] mene R	12630 may] *om.* P
12631 Whare-] þer- R	þus] *om.* LPR	12633 thurgh] *om.* P, by R	12634 heuen]
adds sa L	12636 es of] his R	thurgh] or þurgh L	to] of R	12638 grete
worsheps] worshippe L	12639 delyces] dilites P	12640 al] he all R	12641 do]
after man L, *om.* PS	12642 on] to P	hille] 'h'ille LS	12643 aungell] aungels L
to] *int. later?* A	*sidenote*: Nota Exemplum E	12644 was] *om.* R	12645 -nere]
om. S	*sidenote*: Dixit angelus ad Loth ES	12647 heghe] *om.* E	12651 sal] salde L
noght] *om.* R	12652 yhernynge] gernynges L	þat] of S	es] er L, þat es S

Bot he suld drawe hym fer away
Fra þe Werlde in al þat he may,
Til he be with right entencioun   12655
On þe hille of Perfeccioun.
þare suld he tent to his hele souerayne
And noght bihynde hym loke agayne.

  For Loth wyf, when sho with him come
Out of þe cyte of Sodome,   12660
Byhynde hir agayne sho lokede
To þe cyte þat brynned and smoked,
And þarefore sho was for þat outrage
Turned into a salte image.
  + Loth wyf m[a]y wele bitaken   12665
þa þat, after þai haf forsaken

De Castitate

þe Werlde withouten condicioun   fo. 76rb
And er entred into religyoun,
And lokes agayn to þe Werld thurgh wille.
Methink þai kepe þair state ful ille   12670
þat in þe cloystre has þe body
And þe hert to þe Werlde haally.

  þai er lyke þe salt image þan
þat has noght bot a fourme of man,
And es harde and calde als þe stane;   12675
Right swa er þai þat has tane
þe state þat es religyous talde.
þai er in þe luf of Godde calde
And harde, ay withouten pyte
And deuocioun þat felle to be.   12680
Wharefore þai haf noght of Perfeccioun
Bot þe habite of religyoun.

12653 suld] om. R   12655 right] om. L   12656 On] And on P   of] of grete S
12657 to] vntyll L   12659 him] om. R   sidenote: Quia vxor Loth respexit ad ciuitatem
(retro S) conuersa est in statuam salis ES   12660 þe cyte] trs. E   12661 hir] om. R
12662 To] Vnto L   12663 And] om. P   12664 into a] vnto þe L   12665 *Loth]
By Loth AELPSRW   *may] my A   wele] we R   bitaken] be taken ELPSRW
12666 þa] þat E   12668 into] vnto L   12669 to] into LS   þe] om. R   thurgh]
be R   12670 þair] þat P   ful] om. R   12671 þe^1] om. ESR   12672 to] in LR
12674 a] om. LS   of] of a P   12675 þe] om. PR   12677 talde] cald R
12678 þai] þat R   Godde] adds fulle E   calde] tald R   12679 ay] er ay P
12681 -fore] om. L   haf] er P   12682 þe] om. L

þe salt image, als clerkes expounes it
And als es founden in Haly Writte,
Bytokens Witte and Discrecioun   12685
þat men suld haue in Perfeccioun.
For als þe salt sauour gyues
Vnto þe mete þat men with lyues
And in his sauour þe mete may saue,
Right so a man suld Wisdome haue   12690
And Discrescioun, als telles þis clerkes,
In his wordes and in his werkes.

þis salt image thurgh right shewyng
Suld gif witte and vnderstandynge
And right ensaumple, als þe boke telles,   12695
To men þat in relygyoun dwelles.
þat has left þe werlde haally
For þe luf of Godde almyghty,
þat þai noght turne to þat agayne
þat þai haf left als vncertayne.   12700

    And þarefore Godde says in þe godspelle
To his disciples, als I yhow telle,
'Thinkes ay', he says, 'I yhow bidde
Of Loth wyf what hir bitidde'.
þat es to say, als says þe boke,   12705
'Yhe sal noght', he says 'Agayne loke,
Namely to þe thinge of vanyte,
þat yhe haf left for þe luf of me'.
So þat yhe thurgh þat tyne noght
Grace and blisse þat yhe haf soght,   12710
Als did somtyme Lothes wyf

Donum Intellectus   De Castitate
Adueniat regnum tuum

fo. 76ᵛᵃ   þat of hir body tynt þe lyf,
Forþi þat sho wald agayne loke

12683 als] _om._ L. expounes] expoundes LPSR   12684 And] _om._ S   es] it es L,
int. P   12685 and] of L   12688 Vnto] To PR   12689 may] _om._ R
12690 Right . . . suld] Swa þan and L   12691 þise] _om._ R   12693 þis] þe P
thurgh] be L   12699 _couplet apparently trs. (and line 12700 om. on lost folio)_ W   þat]
And L   noght turne] _trs._ S   12701 says] says þus R   _sidenote_: Euangelium ES
12703 I] as I R   12704 Loth] Luke W   what] how L   12705 to say] _om._ L
12706 he says] _om._ LS   12707 þe] _om._ W   12708 þe] _om._ ESRW   12712 hir]
_om._ R   12713 -þi] _om._ LR

Til þat þat sho first left and forsoke.
   Wharefore þe godspelle says to vndirstand
þat whaso to þe plogh lays hande
And bihynde lokes agayne langely,
þe kyngedome of Godde he es noght worthi.
Forwhy als he þat þe plogh ledes
Lokes bifore ay how he spedes
And paynes hym with al his myght
To lede þe plogh in þe fur right,
Right so he suld do for alle chaunce
þat ledes þe lyf of penaunce
Or haldes þe state of relygioun
To clymb on þe hille of Perfeccioun.
   For in þat state þai suld haue ay
þe eghen of þe hert, þat es to say
Wille and Vndirstandynge right,
To þat þat es bifore in sight,
And noght to þat þat es bihynde
þat passes away sone als þe wynde.
þat es to say, to godes ay-lastande
þat ay bifore þe hert suld stande.
+ þa er þe grete ritches of heuen
þat er mare worth þan man may neuen;
And noght werldely godes þat we here se
þat bihynde falles ay to be.
For þa suld fra þe hert be hidde,
Als Saynt Paul þe apostell didde,
þat þus sayde, þat forgeten had he
þat þat bihynde hym felle to be.
þat was þe Werlde, ful of fayntyse,
And al þe Werldes Couatyse,

12715 *Qui mittit manum ad*
aratrum respiciens retro
non est aptus regno Dei

12720

12725

12730

12735

12740
Paulus

   12714 first] *om.* PRW   left and] *om.* L   12715 *sidenote:* respiciens] prospiciens ELS
Dei] cel' L   12716 lays] lys R   12717 langely] laughly L   12718 he] *om.* R
12719 -why] *om.* R   als] *om.* P   þe] *om.* P   12720 how] how þat L   12722 þe^2]
om. W   12723 Right] *om.* R   he suld] *trs.* LR   12725 haldes] elles ES, elles at L
12726 on þe] to P   12727 For] *om.* R   12728 hert] erth W   12729 and] *om.* E,
int. P   12730 *line followed by 12727 again, dotted and cancelled* A   12732 away] *om.* R
als] as doys R   12733 godes] god W   12734 þat ay] þase þat L   *12735 þa] þat
AELPS   12736 worth] worthy EW   may] can LPR   12738 ay] *om.* S   to] fore to
ESR   12739 For] *om.* R   fra] ay fra S   12741 þat^2] *om.* LR   *sidenote om.* LW
12742 hym] *om.* P   to] for to S   12744 al] *om.* P   werldes] worlde full of W

þe whilk he wald on nane wyse prayse 12745
Bot dispyse, als þe boke says.
For he had ay þe entencioun right
And his yhernynge to heuen bright.
    Bot many men of religioun
Thurgh a wrange entencioun 12750
Puttes þe plugh, bathe heghe and laghe,
Bifore þe oxen þat it suld draghe.
For whaso sekes thurgh yhernynge
Mare werldely gode þan gastly thing,
þai sette bifore als dose þe blynde 12755
þat þat suld be ay bihynde:

Donum Intellectus   De Castitate
Adueniat regnum tuum

fo. 76ᵛᵇ Bodily gode þat passes away
Bifore gastly gode þat lastes ay.
    Swilk men of religioun
Er in þe way of dampnacioun. 12760
For of þat state þat es parfyte,
þai haue right noght bot þe habyte
þat to religioun falles bi skille,
And þat state þai kepe right ille.

Habitus non facit Men says þat habyte munk mas noght, 12765
monachum Bot haly lyf þat right es soght.
    Bot þe religious þat lufs his saul
Suld take ensaumple at Saynt Paul,
And als he did, þe Werlde forgette
And al þat may religioun lette 12770
And leue haally bihynde hym ay
Alle werldely godes þat wytes away.
And endeles godes þat er heghe

12745 þe] om. R   12746 dispyse] dyspysed R   12747 he] he þat E
12748 And] And in P, Als S   12751 bathe] om. PR   12753 For] om. R
12755 dose] om. L   12756 suld be ay] ay sulde be L, suld ay be P   12757 Bodily]
Worldely S   gode] godes LR   12758 gode] godes LR   lastes ay] passe oway L
12760 þe] om. LPR   12762 noght . . . þe] nathing bot L   12763 to] to þe W
12764 þat] þe L   right] full R   12765 þat] þat þe W   12766 soght] wroght SW
12767 þe] om. E   12769 And] God W   *sidenote*: Paulus E   12770 And] And þat W
þat] þa E   may religioun] *trs.* W   religioun] religious P   12771 haally] om. L
12772 werldely] þe werldes L

He suld haue ay bifore his eghe
And leue þa noght bihynde hym   12775
Bot ay fra vertu to vertu clym,
Til he com on þat mountayne
þar endeles ioy es souerayne.
þare sal he se ay clerely
Our Louerd Cryst, Godde almyghty;   12780
And he sal loue parfytely þare
And haf hym þan for euermare.
  þis es þe blissedhede of lyfynge
þat þe Gift of Vnderstandynge
þam ledes to þat kepes bisily   12785
Clennes of herte and of body,
Of whilk Godde es ay wele payed,
Als I haf herebyfore sayde.
And þarefore Godde says, 'Blissed er þai
þat kepes þam clene of hert ay,   12790
For þai sal se þat blissedhede'
þat here es bigunnen for grete mede.
For þai er clensed of þe mirkenes
Of allekyns thinge þat errour es,
Als to þe vndirstandynge withinne   12795
And to þe wille of filthe of synne.
  By þat þat þai se Godde what he es
Thurgh þe trouthe of þe light of brightnes,
þat comes thurgh gracious shynynge
Of þe Gift of Vnderstandynge,   12800

De Castitate

Thurgh whilk a man knawes gastly   fo. 77ra
His creature, Godde almyghty;
And alle þat specially falles

12775 þa] þai me LS   12777 on] to L, at P   þat] þat heghe EL, þe PS
12778 þar] þat R   12780 Cryst] om. LR   12781 sal loue] shuld R   12782 þan]
þare L   12783 þis] þat L   12784 þat] þat is PW   þe] om. W   12785 þam
ledes] trs. PRW   to] om. P   þat] þat þat L   kepes] adds þam R   12789 And] om. R
says] saide P   þai] ay S   12790 clene] om. L   of] in R   12791 þat] þe P
12793 For] om. R   þe] þat L, om. PW   12794 -kyns] om. RW   12795 Als] And L
12796 filthe] silht R   of²] and P   12797 what] om. L   12798 þe²] om. RW   light
of brightnes] lyghtnes W   brightnes] blys R   12799 comes] come LS
12801 whilk] þe whylk L, swilk W   gastly] þerby R

To þat þat men saul-hele calles,
Withouten doute or varyinge   12805
In þe trouthe of Cryst heuenkynge.
Whare þai er so ioyned at þe last
And so grunded and rotefast
þat þai may noght thurgh skille certayne
Departed be thurgh dede ne payne.   12810
    And þarefore þai er, als I wene,
Blissed þat er of herte clene,
For þai haue þe eghen of þe hert
Clere and hale and in gode quert,
And þe Wille and þe Vndirstandynge   12815
So clere and so clene to right knawynge
þat þai may se Godde, mast souerayne,
And trowe thurgh trouthe þat es mast certayne.
    Wharefore our Lorde sayde, als es proued,
[To] Saynt Thomas þat he wele luued,   12820
'Forþi', he sayde, 'þat þou thurgh sight
Has me sene, þou has trowed right'.
And yhete sayde Godde þise wordes alswa,
'Blissed', he sayde, 'Be alle þa
þat has noght sene me in body   12825
And has trowed wele and stedefastly'.
    Bot þis blissedhede þat here es
Sal be fulfilled in þe lyf endeles.
þar þe clene men of herte clere
Thurgh stedefast trouth may se him here—   12830
And yhete al dym þat sight bihoues be—
Bot þare sal þai hym appertly se
Face to face, thurgh right clere sight,

12805 or] of PW   12806 Cryst] cristes W   heuen-] our R   12807 so ioyned]
trs. R   12808 and²] and swa LRSR   12809 þat] om. E   may] int. after noght P
thurgh skille] be slyk R   12810 dede ne] dedely W   ne] in P   12813 þe¹] om. P
12814 Clere] Fere W   12816 and] om. L   so²] om. RW   so clene] hale P   to right]
of R   12817 mast] our R   12818 trowe] om. L   thurgh] by R   mast] om. RW
12819 Whare-] om. R   sayde] says W   es] it es LR   sidenote: Euangelium EL
12820 *To] þat AEPS   wele] mekill P, om. R   12821 Forþi] Forwhy L, þerfor R
12822 þou has] and þat L   sidenote: Quia vidisti me Thoma crededisti (add etc. LS) ELS
12823 wordes] worde ELPSR   12824 be] er P   12825 sene me] trs. P   me in]
my W   12826 has trowed] trowes L, trowes it R   stede-] suth- W   12828 þe]
om. W   12830 stedefast] om. R   12831 yhete al] om. R   12832 Bot] For L   sal
þai] trs. W   hym] om. L   12833 right] om. LR

Als says Saynt Paul þe apostell right.
   þis es þe blissedhede of aungels   12835
And of halwes þat in heuen dwelles
þat ay may Godde in hys face se
And a Godde knawe in persones thre.
And bihalde clerely thurgh grete lykynge
In þe mirour þat brightes alle thinge,   12840
þar þe aungels and þe halwes haally
þam lokes and meruaylles þam þarby
And may neuermare filled be
Of bihaldynge of þe Trynyte.

De Castitate

For þare es alle bountees ay newe   12845 fo. 77rb
And alle beautes of allekyn hewe,
þe welle of lyf þat lastes ay,
And alle delyces þat herte think may.
Forwhy men fyndes in Haly Writte,
Als clerkes may se þat lokes it,   12850
þat eghe of man, war it neuer so clere,
Might neuer se, na eres here,
Ne herte think, ne tunge telle right
þat Godde to þam þat him lufs has dight.
   Wharefore Saynt Anselyne to þe saul says,   12855 *Anselmus*
'þou saul', he says, 'lift vp and rayse
Obouen þe al þine vnderstandynge
And whyles þou may, think on þis thing.
How mykell and how profytable
And how fayre and how delytable   12860

12834 Als] And L   says] *after* apostell L, *int. after* Paul P   *sidenote*: Paulus ESW
12837 hys] *later, over eras.* A, *om.* L, *int.* P   12839 clerely] *om.* R   thurgh] with P
grete] *om.* W   12840 þat brightes] brightest of R   12841 aungels . . . halwes]
sayntes all R   þe²] *om.* L   12842 þam¹] *om.* R   þam²] þan R   12843 may
neuermare] neuer may R   12844 Of¹] Of þe R   12845 For] *om.* R   alle]
alkynne L, *corr. from* ay P, ay W   bountees] bounte L, beutees W   12846 allekyn]
ilka P   12848 delyces] dilites PW   12849 Forwhy] þerfor R   12850 þat
lokes] whasa wyll loke L   12851 þat] þat þe L, War R   war it] *om.* R
12852 se] hyt se W   eres] ere PW, hegher R   12854 þam] þai R, *om.* W
12855 Wharefore] *om.* R   Anselyne] Anselme ELSRW, *corr. from* Anselyne P
12856 saul] sall L   he says] *om.* L   says] biddes P   vp] vp þe hert L
12857–8 *couplet om.* W   12857 al] *om.* P   12858 And] *om.* R
12860 And¹] *om.* R   delytable] delectable P

þe godes bene þat may contene
Ioy and delyte of alle godes here sene.
And noght swilk ioy þat short whyle dures,
Als men may fynde in creatures,
Bot als mykell mare þar it es soght   12865
Als þe maker es þat þam wroght.
    'Haa, man! How es þi herte sette?
Wharto gastow dotande to gette
Dyuerse godes vnto þi body?
Luf a Godde specially,   12870
þat alle manere of gode contenes.
þat Godde es mare þan any man wenes,
þat neuermare faylles na endes
And þat has Godde dight to his frendes.
þat es hymself to vnderstande,   12875
And þat es souerayne gode ay-lastande,
Of wham alle othir godes to telle
Comes als strandes dose of a welle.'

Augustinus   'Certes', says Saynt Austyne right,
'He sal be blissed þat thurgh clere sight,   12880
Withouten couerd face, [sal] se
þe blisse of Godde in his maieste,
And be shaped als ane of hisse
Into þe image of his blisse.
þar he sal se Godde als he es;   12885
þat sight es coroun þat es endeles.'
    'And alle þe mede þat men may neuen
þat þe halwes has in heuen,
þis sal be', als þe haly man says,
'Alle þe mast blisse of man to prayse,   12890

12861 contene] maynteine P   12862 delyte] delices L, blys R, delites W   of] ouer R
here] þat here L   sene] bene ELS   12863 whyle] *om.* R   dures] endures L
12865–6 *couplet om.* W   12865 mare] mare ioy L   þar] als S   12866 þam] þai L
12867 *sidenote*: Nota L   12868 dotande] deande P, doutand R   12869 vnto] to LR,
into W   12870 a] aye EPW (*after* godde P), euer a L   12872 man] *om.* R
12874 has Godde] *trs.* S   dight] hyght E, vn- L   12875–6 *couplet om.* W
12876 souerayne] souerage R   gode] *int.* P, *om.* R   12877 godes] gode S   12878 a]
þe P   12879 *sidenote om.* EL   12880 clere] *om.* R   *12881 sal] to AELS
12884 Into] Vnto S   12886 coroun] coround W   12887 alle] *om.* P   men] man L
12888 halwes] halynes R   12890 Alle þe] Aller- S

De dono Sapiencie pars Peccati Oris

De Gula que est vna Sanctificetur nomen tuum

To se þe man þat alle men made fo. 77va
And heuen and erthe þat es so brade'.
For þarefore Godde almyghty walde
Bycom man and our manhede halde,
þat made alle men in hym anely 12895
Blissed in saul and in body.
For þat þat man has sene him right
In his manhede thurgh bodily sight,
And his saul has sene in his godhede
Thurgh gastly eghe þat þe saul can lede, 12900
Swa þat he fande swetenes and sauour
And grete delyte in his creatour,
Bathe withinne and without—
þat es certayne withouten dout:
Withinne als in his godhede 12905
And withouten in his manhede.
þis sal be þe blisse of man,
þe whilk na clerke discryue wele can.
þis sal be his ioye parfyte
In heuenryke and his delyte 12910
And his lyf withouten ende right,
And þat sal be þat blissed sight.
    þat blissedhede þai bide namely
þat kepes clennes of herte and body,
To whilk þe vertu of Chastyte 12915
Brynges a man þat wil chast be,
And to þe mede þat Godde hight
þat es of Godde þe verray sight.
Als Godde says, 'Blissed er alle þa *Beati mundo corde,*
þat of hert er clene, whareso þai ga, 12920 *quoniam ipsi Deum videbunt*

12891 men] haues L   12892 And¹] *om.* L, In W   12893 For] *om.* EPSR, And L
12895 anely] (*blank*) amely L, namely P, haly W   12897 þat²] *om.* L   man] men S
12900 Thurgh] Be R   12902 creatour] creaturure E   12903 Bathe] Bot W
12904 þat] þis R   12906 in] als in S   12907 sal be] saule by P   12908 wele] *om.*
LP   12909 his] þis R   12911 ende] *om.* R   12912 þat²] a P   blissed] blysfull L
12913 -hede] he (*followed by erasure*) W   þai] þat R   bide] abyde L   12914 clennes]
om. E, þai me in c. L   and] and of LS   12916 wil chast] *trs.* LS   12918 þe] *om.* L
12919 er] be S   alle] *om.* L   *sidenote*: videbunt] *om.* L   12920 whareso] whar R

For þai sal Godde appertly se',
þar he sittes in Trynyte.
　　Now may yhe se and haf knawyng
What þe Gift dose of Vndirstandynge,
Adueniat regnum tuum þat þe secund askynge wynne vs may　　　12925
In þe Pater Noster when we pray,
Als I bifore haf talde yhow right;
þe whilk Godde graunt in our hertes to light.
Amen

De dono Sapiencie

　　Anothir gift of þe Haly Gast
Es neste abouen; þat es mast.　　　12930
þe whilk men calles þe Gift of Wisdom
þat specially may to vs com

De dono Sapiencie　　　De Gula que est
vna pars Peccati Oris　　　Sanctificetur
nomen tuum

fo. 77vb Thurgh þe first askynge þat we say
Sanctificetur nomen tuum In þe Pater Noster when we pray.
þis es þe heghest gift and þe mast　　　12935
þat mas a man to fele and tast
þe grete swetenes and þe sauour
Of Godde almyghty, his creatour,
So þat hym think þat nathing erthely
Es so swete na yhete so sauory.　　　12940
þan he settes alle his lykynge
Anely in Godde ouer alle thinge.
　　þis Gift of Wisdome specially
Drawes þe synne of Glotony
Out of þe herte þar it wrotes,　　　12945
With alle þe braunches and þe rotes,
And instede of þat synne settes right
A vertu þat es of grete myght.

12922 in] in hys L, in þe P　　Trynyte] mageste L　　12925 þat] And S　　vs] we W
sidenote: as in-column heading R　　tuum] *om.* L　　12926 pray] say W　　12927 yhow]
om. L　　12928 hertes] hert W　　to] *om.* P　　Amen] *om.* LPSR　　12928a *marg.* ELSW
12931–2 *couplet trs.* L　　12931 whilk] whik P　　12933 þat we] ate E　　say] *om.* W
12937 þe²] *om.* W　　12939 nathing] na L, thyng S, *om.* W　　12940 na yhete] na
LRW, and P　　12947 in-] in þe E

þat es þe vertu of Sobrenesse
And of Mesure þat haalsom es.   12950

  First þis gift byhoues bygynne
To drawe out of þe hert þat synne,
Forwhy þat vertu may noght elles
Com in þe hert þar þat synne dwelles.
þat synne has many man bygyled   12955
And many saulles it has fyled.

  To þe body þat synne es couthe,
For it es called a synne of þe mouthe.   *Peccatum oris*
Forwhy þe mouth has twa offyces,
Of whilk comes right many vyces: 12960
Ane offyce falles to þe throte mast,
Als in etynge and drynkynge thurgh tast;
Anothir falles to þe tung by skille,
Als in spekynge of gode or ille.
If synne in outhir of þise twa falle,   12965
'Synne of mouth' men may it calle
þat it departes in twa partyse,
Als I sal shewe yhow on sere wyse.

  Ane es in þe synne of Glotony
þat falles to þe throte and þe bely,   12970
Als in etynge and drynkynge mare
Agayne mesure þan mystre ware.
Anothir es also in þe synne
Of þe Ille Tung of þe mouth withinne,
Als in ille speche þat oft es shewed,   12975
Bathe amange lered and lewed.

De Gula

First I wille speke of Glotony   fo. 78ra
þat corrumpus bathe saul and body,

12949 þe] a P   12950 of] þe R   12951 þis] þe LR   12952 of] *om.* P
12955 many] many a L, many (*over eras.*) P   12956 saulles] a saule L, *after* has P   it
has] *trs.* R   12958 *sidenote om.* LS   12960 right] *om.* LSRW   many] many a L
12961 þe throte] tethe R   *sidenote*: j. W   12962 Als] *om.* R   and] *om.* R   thurgh]
to W   12963 þe] þi R   by] thurgh ELS   *sidenote*: ij. W   12964 Als] And R   of]
om. LPR   12967 it departes] *trs.* LS   12968 yhow] *om.* R   sere] twa L
12969 in] *om.* L   *sidenote*: j. W   12970 to þe throte] in troth P, to þe teth R   and] and
to L, and in P, of R   bely] body R   12971 Als] *om.* R   and] and in R
12973 *sidenote*: ij. W   12974 ille tung] tonge and W   þe²] *om.* R   12975 Als] *om.* R
oft es] *trs.* S   12976 lered] *add* men LP   12978 bathe] *om.* R

And to nane othir harme dose
Bot to þam anely þat it wille vse.   12980
I wille þareafter, als I can,
Speke of þe Wycked Tunge of man
þat othir men mykill mare deres
þan hymself þat it about beres.
For þe Wicked Tunge, als clerkes wate,   12985
May appayre many mens state.

De peccato Gule

Glotony, als þis clerkes proues,
Es a synne þat þe bely luues,
þe whilke thre thinges of a man wastes
þat mete and drynk in outrage tastes.   12990
First it wastes þe saul withinne,
For it es a dedely synne.
It wastes þe body and forduse
Thurgh vnkynde outrageous vse.
It wastes his godes thurgh outrage   12995
Of ouergrete dispens and costage.
Here men may bi skille wele se
How Glotony wastes þise thre.
Glotony es swilk a synne to telle
þat mykill payse þe fende of helle   13000
And myspayse gretly Godde of heuen
By many skils þat I can neuen.
Thurgh þis synne, als I fynde can,
þe fende has grete powere in man.
For men fyndes wryten in þe godspelle   13005
þat Godde gaf leue to þe fendes of helle
To entre namely into swyne
To tourment þam and do þam pyne.
And when þai entred, þe swyne ran wode

12980 anely] om. ER   it] ill W   it wille] trs. E   12982 þe] om. P
12983 mykill] om. R   12984 -self] om. R   12985 For] om. R   þe] om. P
12986 appayre] enpayre L   mens] mans R   12986a om. EL, De (om. W) gula marg.
PW, marg. S, De gula que est vna pars peccati oris as in-column heading before 12993 R
12989 of] om. P   a] om. R   12992 a] a foul R   12994 outrageous] outrage LPR
12995 godes] gode W   12996 ouer-] oþer R   12997 skille] slyk R   wele] om. L
13000 þe] it þe L   13001 gretly] mykell L   13003 als] þat L   13004 has] after
powere L   grete powere] trs. E   13005 For] om. R   sidenote: Euangelium EL

And drunkend þam in þe sees flode, 13010
In tokenynge of þam namely
þat glotouns bene of þair bely,
þat ledes þair lyf als swyne vnclene,
And swilk er many in þis werlde sene.
In þam þe fendes has leue to dwelle 13015
And to drunken þam in þe see of helle
And to do þam so mykill ete

De Gula

þat þai brest nere of þat mete, fo. 78rb
And so mykill to drynke and so fast
þat þai drunken þamself at þe last. 13020
When a champyoun þat es strange
Has foghten with his felaw lange
And has had hym doun at þe last
And haldes hym by þe throte fast,
It es to hym grete noy and payne 13025
To couer vp and ryse agayne.
Right swa it es of a man withinne
þat þe fende haldes in þis synne.
For þe fende sekes blethely
Vnto þe throte of a mans body 13030
Als to þe shepe sekes wolf or hounde,
It to wirghe and to confounde.
And als he dyd thurgh quayntyse
To Adam and Eue in Paradyse;
He hente þam þare bi þe throte, 13035
When þai bathe on þe appell bote.
þis es þe fissher of helle lake
þat bi þe throte þa fisshes can take
And brynges þam hame vnto his inne,

13006 to] vnto LS   fendes] fende PR   13009 And] *om.* R   13010 drunkend] drouncked EW, drounned LSR   sees] see PR, *om.* W   13012 bely] body LPS 13014 þis] þe R   13015 fendes] fende LP   13016 drunken] downe SR   see] *om.* E, pitt L   13017 to] *om.* R   do] gerre L, make S   ete] to ette ESR   13018 of] for P 13020 þai] þai er S   drunken] drynken W   13023 had] *om.* P   doun] *om.* L   þe] *om.* L   13024 haldes] halde P   13027 Right] *om.* R   13028 þis] his ESR, þe L 13029 fende] fendes L   blethely] lecchery W   13030 Vnto] To RW   13031 to] vnto L   sekes] duse R   13032 It] *om.* RW   wirghe] wreygh L   and to] or to L, hir and PRW   13033 And] *om.* L   13034 To] Of W   13036 on] of LW 13038 þa fisshes] þe fisshe W   can] gune R   13039 þam] hym W   vnto] to RW

þat es saulles to helle thurgh þat synne.   13040
   þis synne myspayse Godde almyghty,
For glotouns hym dose grete vilany,
When þai make þair godde thurgh hande
Of a sekke ful of fen stynkande.
þat es of þe foulle bely   13045
þat þai luf mare þan Godde almyghty,
In þat som trowes and traystes ay
And worshepes it, bathe nyght and day.
   Godde biddes a man fast for mede;
þe bely says, 'Nay! þat war na nede,   13050
Bot þou sal ete and drynk saddely
And fede þe wele to strengthe þi body'.
   Godde biddes hym arely out of bedde ryse
And ga to þe kirke to Goddis seruyse.
þe bely answers þan alsone   13055
And says þus, 'þat bees noght done.
I am so fulle', he says, 'of mete
Me bihoues slepe and take a swete.
þe kirke', he says, 'es nane hare;
It habydes til I com þare.'   13060
   And when he ryses, he bygynnes

Donum Sapiencie   De Gula
Sanctificetur nomen tuum

fo. 78va His prayers or his Matyns.
þan bygynnes he to aske and say,
'Lorde! what sal we ete today?
Whethir we may fynde today or gete   13065
Any gode thynge þat we may ete?'
   After Matyns, als falles to be,
Comes þe Laudes and þan says he,
'Lorde! what we hadde yhistereuen gode wyne

13040 saulles] om. S, saule W   to] of W   þat] om. P   13041 þis] þat R   mys-]
om. L   13042 hym dose] trs. LS   13043 godde] goddes L   13045 þe] a R
bely] body L, gluton bely R   13048 it] om. L   bathe] om. R   13049 sidenote:
Disputacio (Litigacio R) inter deum et ventrem hominis gulosi (phrs. om. SR) ESR
13052 þi] my P   13056 bees noght] es noght to L   13057 he says] after am
EL   13058 a] om. R   13060 habydes] wyll abyde me L   13062 or] and L, on S
13063 sidenote: He sunt (clause om. LS) matutine gulosorum ELS   13065 today] om. SR
13066 gode] om. L   13069 we] he W   yhister-] efter P   -euen] daye euen E, day R
sidenote: Ad laudes E, Laudes gul' S

And gode mete þarewith in pleuyne'.   13070
   Afterwarde he gretes sone
For his synnes þat he has done
And says, 'I am als heuy als lede;
I haf bene tonyght nere dede.
þe wyne of yhistereuen was [so] strange   13075
My heued es disy and has werked lange.
I be noght at ese to ryde ne ga
Til I haf drunken a draght or twa'.
þis man lifs ful perillously
þat maas his godde of his bely.   13080
   þis synne brynges a man to shame
And reues a man his gode name.
For first bicomes he tauernere
And afterwarde a dyce-playere
And þareafter bycomes harlote   13085
And vses many vilaynes note;
And aftir þat he bicomes litchour
And sethen a theef and a robbour.
And at þe last for theft he es tane
And es hanged by þe neckebane.   13090
þis es þe skotte þat he þus payse
þat es ledde by þise sex wayse.
   Glotony departes it euen
In fyue braunches þat I wil neuen.
For Saynt Gregor says, als men heres,   13095   *Gregorius*
þat men may synne in fyue maneres
In etynge and in drynkynge namely,
Als in fyue maners of glotony.
And if ye wille þam lere and knawe,
I sal yhou recken þam here on rawe.   13100

13070 þare-] *om.* R   pleuyne] playn R   13074 to-] þis R   13075 yhister-] efter P   -euen] day R   was] it wasse L   so] ful AW   13076 es] *om.* R   and] *om.* R   werked] bene L   13077 noght] neuer wele L   ne] or E   13078 Til] Or L   13079 ful] *om.* R   13080 maas] *int. after* godde P   his'] *om.* LR   bely] body LS, body *corr. later* P   13083 he] *om.* L   13084 -warde] þat P   13085 þareafter] aftir þer R   bycomes] *adds* he E, *adds* he a L, *add* a PS   13086 vses] hauntes L   13087 aftir þat] þerefter L   þat] *om.* W   bicomes] *adds* a S   13088 and] or W   a²] *om.* E, *after* a P   13089 þe] *om.* L   he] *om.* LSR   es] *om.* S   13090 es] *om.* L   13091-2 *couplet om.* L   13091 skotte] stot W   13093 it] it in R   *sidenote:* Gula W   13094 fyue] seuen R   13095 *sidenote om.* P   13097 in²] *om.* PSRW   13098 maners] maner W   13100 here] all S   on] on a P

v. rami Gule: Prore,   þus may men synne in Glotony:
properelante, nimis,
ardenter, studiose   Outhir to ete or drynk ouertymely
                Or oueroutrageously thurgh wille
                Or ouerhastyly agayne skille
                Or ouerdaynteously thurgh talent   13105
                Or ouerbisily oboute mete tent.

Donum Sapiencie   De Gula
Sanctificetur nomen tuum

fo. 78vb   þe first braunche es, als men may se,
j[ᵘˢ]. *ramus*   To ete and drynk ar right tyme be.
                A foul manere it es to a man
                þat has elde and his wytte can,   13110
                When he may on nane wyse habyde
                þe tyme of etynge and þe tyde.
                Of grete lust and Litchery
                Comes þis braunche of Glotony,
                þat a man þat es hale and fere   13115
                And stalwarde and of lightsom chere
                Byfore tyme besekes to þe mete,
                Als dose an hors or elles a nete
                Withouten nedeful enchesoun.
                Methynke þat man folwes na resoun.   13120
                  þarefore many synnes may com
                Of swilk vncomly coustom.
                For som men says he may noght wele
                Fast ne nane othir penaunce fele,
                Ne haunt þe kirke ne bidde na bede,   13125
                For he says he has ane ille hede.
                Bot methink ful sothe says he,
                For he has made it so to be.
                And þarewith he has an ille hert

13101–2 *couplet trs.* EL   13101 synne] se W   *sidenote:* ⟨ ⟩ sunt ra⟨m⟩i gule P, *om.* S
v. rami gule] *om.* EL   Priore] Pre EL   properelante] pre ampulante L   13102 to]
om. L   or] other to W   13103 ouer-] *om.* ELS   -outrageously] -outragely LR
13106 -bisily] -besy L   mete] *adds* to L   13108 and] or LSRW   right] *om.* R
sidenote: om. L   **jᵘˢ.*] j. A   ramus] *add* gule ES   13109 a²] *om.* P   13110 elde]
hele P   13114 þis] þe ES   braunche] braunches S   13115 þat²] *om.* LW
13117 Byfore] *adds* þe P   be-] he EP, *om.* LR   to þe] vnto L   13118 does] *after*
hors W   elles] *om.* PRW   13120 folwes] feles R   13122 swilk] *adds* ane L
13123 men] mane EPW   says] *adds* on (*canc.?*) P   13128 made] *int. after* it P

þat haldes þe heued out of quert   13130
And dose hym oft breke his fast;
þat sal he bye dere at þe last.
   And yhete he wille haue company
þat dose als he dose comonly,
þe whilk he drawes fra gode dedes   13135
And intil helle with hym þam ledes.
For he mas þam oft to breke þair fast
And to do Glotony at þe last,
Fra whilk þai myght þam kepe euermare,
Warne swilk wicked felawship ware.   13140
   For þis glotouns and þise litchours,
þis drynkers and þis ryotours
þat lufs ryots and tentes þarto
Amange alle þe folys þat þai do,
þai do a synne, als I gesce,   13145
þat es called 'þe fendes maystresce'.
þat es when þai withdrawe away
Alle þa fra godenes þat þai may.
þai say þai may fast on nane wyse;
þai leghe: þat es noght bot fayntyse,   13150
For defaut of luf of Godde of heuen

De Gula

Mas þam oft swilk wordes neuen.   fo. 79ra
   For if þai lufd with hert stedfast
Als mykell þe blisse þat ay sal last
Als þai luf here þis Werldes blisse,   13155
þat þam bihoues at þe last mysse,
þai wald fast þan als blethely
For þe luf of Godde almyghty,
And also for þe saul bihuf,

13131 dose] gerres L, *int.* P, makes S   oft] oft to S, *om.* R   his] it R   13132 þe] *om.* LS   13136 intil] to LS   þam] *om.* LP, *adds* he S   13139 whilk] swilk W   þai] men L   þai myght] *om.* R   þam kepe] *trs.* EL   13140 wicked] *om.* W   felawship] company L, felous R   13141 þise] *om.* P   litchours] lycherous R   13142 drynkers] drynkes R   13143 lufs ryots] *trs.* E   ryots] ryot R   13144 folys] foyles R   13145 als] þat LS   13146 maystresce] maysters S   13147 with-] *om.* R   13148 -nes] dedes P   13149 þai say] *om.* R   may] *adds* noȝt   13150 noght] *om.* LR   13151 of^1] of þe L   13152 neuen] to neuen ELS   13153 lufd] luf R, leued W   13154 *sidenote:* Nota (*later*) E   13155 luf] do ELS   13156 þe] *om.* L

Als þai wald for þe Werldes luf.   13160
    Bot som men may til euen fast
For werldely godes þat faylles at þe last,
Bot þai may noght til none of þe day
Fast for þe godes þat lastes ay.
Som men er als childer vnconande   13165
þat wil haf brede ay in þe hande,
And yhe sal wele vndirstande þis,
þat als a man þat tempres hym mysse
May synne in ouerarely dyneres,
So may he synne in ouerlate soperes.   13170
    Wharefore þis men þat lifs noght right,
þat lufs mykell to wake on þe nyght
And dispendes þe tyme in nycetees,
In idelnes and in vanytees,
And late to bedde gase and late ryses,   13175
Swilk men synnes on many wyses.
    First in þat þat þai þe tyme waste
In grete ryots þat þai luf mast,
And thurgh ryots and herlotry
Misturnes þe tyme vnkyndely.   13180
For when þai make þe day of þe nyght
And þe nyght of þe day, þai do noght right.
Swilk men aght make dole and grete,
For Godde þam waryes thurgh þe prophete.
    Bot men suld do wele on þe day   13185
And on þe nyght loue Godde and pray.
And he þat in þe bedde þan lys,
When tyme ware þat he suld ryse,
And wil slepe, when he suld wake
And his prayers to Godde make   13190
And loue Godde and here his seruyse,

13160 for] do for PRW   13161 euen] none R, heuen W   13162 werldely]
werldes LR   godes] om. R   þe] om. L   13163 Bot] om. R   of] on E   13164 þe]
om. L   13165 als] repeats E   childer] barnnes L   13166 þe] þaire L
13167 wele] wele ay P   13168 als] has R   13171 Whare-] þer- R   þis] þase L
noght] om. W   13172 mykell] after wake LS   þe] om. ERW   13173 þe] þare LPR
13174 in²] om. RW   13175 gase] om. R   13179 ryots] ryote ES   13181 For]
om. R   þe¹] om. PR   of] on E   þe²] om. W   13182 þe¹] om. R   þai do] þat ys R
13183 aght] adds to L   dole] dele W   and] om. E   13185 on] all P, of W
13186 on] of W   13187 þe] his PRW   13188 þat] om. L   13189 he] int. P,
þai W   13191 And¹] om. R

Methink þat þat man es noght wyse.
For he tynes here al þe tyme right,
Bathe of þe day and of þe nyght.
    Also in swilk wakynges men dose   13195
Many vanytees thurgh vse,
Als in plays of chesse and tables

De Gula

And in tellynge of trewfles and fables   fo. 79rb
And leghes and lesynges ay amange.
And þus he spendes his tyme wrange,   13200
And alle his godes þus may he waste,
And wrethes Godde þat charges maste
And greues noght yhete Godde anely,
Bot he greues his saul and his body.
   þe secund braunche of Glotony   13205 ij[us]. ramus
Es to ete or drynk outrageously,
þat es to say withouten mesure;
He þat dose so shewes foul nurture.
Bi skille þai may be proprely called
Glotouns þat swilk maners wil halde.   13210
   Bot it es a grete wytte to fele,
To halde and kepe ay Mesure wele
In etynge and drynkynge namely;
þat es a grete hele vnto þe body.
For many a man thurgh swilk custom   13215
Hastes his dede ar his tyme com,
þat es to say thurgh outrageusnes
Of etynge and + drynkynge nedeles.
And þat a man vnto his dede hyes,

13192 þat²] *om.* LSR   13193 al þe] his R   tyme] tymes L   13194 of¹] on W
of²] *om.* S, on W   13195 Also] *om.* R   wakynges] wakyng LS, wakyng`s´ (*later*) P
13196 *line om.* R   vse] ille vse ELS   13197 Als] And LS, *om.* R   tables] table W
13198 And¹] *om.* R   fables] fable W   13199 ay] all S   amange] in mange W
13200 And] *om.* R   he] þai W   his] þe E, her W   13202 And] þat R   wrethes] wreth
hys L   13203 greues] greued L   yhete] þe E, *om.* L, his S   yhete Godde] *trs.* R
13204 he] *om.* RW   greues] greued L   13205 *sidenote*: *om.* LS   *ij*[us].] ij. A   ramus]
adds gule E   13206 or] and EPSRW   outrageously] oureoutragely LP, outragely R
13208 shewes] *adds* a L   nurture] myrroure ES, mesoure L   13209–10 *couplet om.* W
13209 skille] slyk R   13210 maners] maner S   13212 and] and to P   ay] þe W
13214 vnto] to LP, of RW   13215 a] *om.* P   13217 outrageusnes] outeragenes LPR
*13218 and] and of A   13219 And] *om.* L   vnto] to PRW

For þareof comes sere maladyse.   13220
   Bot whaso Mesure lere wille,
He sal vnderstande thurgh skille
þat it er many maners sere
Of lifynge in þis werlde here.
Som lyfs after þair flesshe es,   13225
And som after þair iolyfnes,
And som after þair ipocrysy—
þat I halde a couert foly.
Som lifs after þair Auaryce,
þe whilk men haldes a grete vyce.   13230
And som lyfs after þair fysyke,
þat to nane othir lyuynge es lyke;
And som lyfs after honestee—
A skilfull lyfynge semes þat to be.
And som lyfs þat has done ille   13235
After þat þat þair synne wille,
And som lyfs after þair gaste
And after þe luf of Godde maste.
   First þa þat lyfs after þair flesshe—
þat es ay freill, tender, and nesshe—   13240
þai sla þair awen saul gastly,
For þai make þair godde of þair bely.

Donum Sapiencie   De Gula
Sanctificetur nomen tuum

fo. 79ᵛᵃ þai halde nouthir Mesure na skille
   Bot folwes þair awen flesshely wille.
þarefore þai sal haf endeles payne   13245
Withouten ʻanyʼ mesure certayne.
   þa þat lifs after þair iolyfte,
þat lufs riots and vanyte
And hauntes oft fole felawshepe,

13221 -so] om. P   lere] here R   13222 thurgh] by EL   13223 it] ȝit S, þair R
13225 þair] þe L   13226 som] adds men L   iolyf-] ioly- LSRW   13227 som] adds
men L   13228 couert] cowerde L, couerd R   13229 Som] adds men L
13232 nane othir] nouther W   lyuynge] ʻlyfeʼ (marg.) L   13233 after] in P
13234 A] And L   lyfynge] lyfe P   semes] semand W   to] int. P, for to W
13236 þat²] om. LR   13237 som] ʻsomeʼ men P, some men W   þair] þe haly L
13242 bely] body PW   13243 nouthir] noghter E   13244 Bot folwes] þai folowe R
flesshely] flesshe R   13246 any] int. A   13247 iolyf-] ioli- LSRW   13248 and]
of R   13249 fole] foly R, foles W

Nouthir þai can ne wille Mesure kepe.   13250
  þai þat thurgh sleght couertly
Lifs after þair ipocrosy,
þat bene þe fendes maysters cald.
Twa maners of mesures þai halde.
Forwhy þe twa wicked spirytes   13255
þat tourmentes þise ipocrytes
Er ayther to othir contrary,
And þat methink es grete ferly.
þe tane says þus, 'Ete fast', says he,
'So þat þou may fayre and fatte be'.   13260
þe tothir says þus þat spekes last,
'þou sal noght do so; þou sal fast
Til þou be lene and pale and wan.
þan saltow seme a gastly man'.
  Now þam bihoues þat wil lif swa   13265
Halde and haunt þise mesures twa.
þe tane es lytell and skars to kenne
þat wil he vse in sight of men;
þe tothir es large and better to chese
þat wil he vse when nane hym sese.   13270
Swilk men haldes noght, als I se,
Right Mesure þat best suld be.
  þa þat lifs here in body
After þair Auaryce anely
Haldes na Mesure after skille,   13275
Bot vses it als þe purs wille,
þat lauedy es þar it sal dwelle
And commaundresce of þe hostelle.
Bot bitwene þe bely of þe glotoun
And þe purs es grete disputysoun.   13280
þar þe glotoun es skars and nyce

13250 wille] om. E, þai wyll L   kepe] om. R   13251 þat] þat will W
13253 þat] þai LW   maysters] maistries P   13256 þise] þe P   13258 es] a P
13259 says] biddes P   sidenote: j. W   13261 sidenote: ij. W   13262 do so] trs. PR
13263 be lene] trs. R   and'] om. ELPR   13265 Now] Nore R   13266 mesures]
mesoure L, man'ers P   13268 vse] haunte L   13270 he vse] haunte L   nane hym]
na men LW   13273 þa] þat W   13276 purs] illeg. P, pure RW   13277 þar]
repeats L   it sal] repeats P   sal] wyll L   13278 commaundresce] commaund ys R   þe]
þat P   hostelle] corr. from hospetell R, castell W   13279 of] and of P   sidenote:
Disputacio inter loculum et ventrem (trs. nouns LS) ELS   13280 disputysoun]
disposyon L, disputasoun? P, dispu'ta'cyoun S, destruccion W

Thurgh commandement of Auaryce,
þe bely says als it can think,
'I wald be full of mete and drynke'.
þe purs says þareagayne,   13285
'Nay! þou sal noght spende in vayne,
Bot I wil þat þou restreyne þe ay

Donum Sapiencie   De Gula
Sanctificetur nomen tuum

fo. 79vb And spare and kepe al þat þou may'.
        þus er þise twa ay at stryf.
    What saltou do þan, caytyf,   13290
    þat es thralle and vnderloute
    To swilk twa lordes þat er so stout,
    þat biddes þe hald als þai commande
    Twa mesures of weght fayllande?
    þe mesure of þe bely to charge   13295
    In othir mens house es gode and large,
    And þe mesure of þe purs es skars
    In his awen hous, and droupes and dares.
        þa þat lifs after fysyke
    And hauntes mykell þat practyke,   13300
    þe Mesure 'of' Ipocrase þai halde
    þat es lytell and strayte calde.
    And oft men has sene with eghe
    þat he þat haldes him wyse and sleghe
    þat thurgh fysyke his lyf can cast,   13305
    Thurgh fysyke dyes at þe last.
        þa þat wille with herte fre
    Lif after þair honeste,
    þai halde mast Mesure of resoun;
    þat methinke es mast in sesoun.   13310
    þai lyf honurabilly ay
    þat bydes þe tyme of þe day

13282 Thurgh] *add* þe LS   13285 þe] þan þe L   13287 Bot] *om.* R   wil] walde P
13288 And] *om.* R   þat] *om.* L   13289 þise] þai R   at] in W   13292 swilk] whilk P
13294 weght] wegh noght W   fayllande] fallande P   13295 þe bely] *trs.* S, þe body W
13297 And] Bot L, *om.* R   13298 and¹] *om.* LS, he R   13300 And] þat L   þat] to
þat E   13301 of] *int. later* A, *om.* PRW   13304 þat] *om.* R   13306 at] he at LPR
þe] *om.* L   13307 with] thurgh P   13309 mast] *om.* R   mast mesure] *trs.* P
13310 þat] *om.* W   13311 þai] þai men R   13312 þat] þai PW

And taas with gode wille and gode chere
Curtaysly whatso þai haf here.
   þai þat lifs in manere of skille   13315
After þat þe charge of þair syn wille,
Haldes swilk mesure thurgh Contynaunce
Als þai er charged in penaunce.
   þa þat lifs after þair spirite
Er þai þat etes with grete delyte   13320
In þe luf of Godde, of myghtes mast,
And þam teches þe Haly Gast
To halde order, Mesure, and resoun,
For þise thre er mykill in sesoun.
   þa men has þe right lordeshepe   13325
Of þair body þat þai suld kepe.
þat es so taght thurgh right vsage
So þat it askes here nane outrage
And dose þat es þe spirites bidynge
Withouten gaynsaying or grochynge.   13330
   Now may yhe bathe se and lere
Thurgh þat þat I haue sayd yhow here

De Gula

þat þe fende has ay many wyles,   fo. 80ra
Thurgh whilk he many men bygyles
And hentes þam in þe wirgh at þe last   13335
And by þe throte haldes þam fast.
   First shewes he to bygyle þe þus
þe gode wyne and þe metes delicius,
Als he þe appell didde to Eue
þat sho toke withouten leue.   13340
And if þat hym noght auaylles,
He biddes þe þan and counsaylles
To ete and drynk als othir dose,

13313–14 trs. couplet P   13313 And] þai P   gode²] om. R   13316 þat] om. SR
þe] om. L   of] þat R   13317 thurgh] with P, be R   contynaunce] countenaunce W
13318 in] thurgh P   13319 spirite] spirites L   13320 etes] lyfes LS   with]
thurgh P   13321 myghtes] myght ERW   13324 þise] þa R   13329 spirites]
spiret L   13330 Withouten] adds any L   or] and ES   13331 lere] here L
13332 þat² . . . here] befor I gune you lere R   13333 ay] om. LS   wyles] whyles E
13334 Thurgh] With P   men] man W   13335 wirgh] throte E, wregh LS   þe²] om. R
13336 þe] om. R   throte] wyrghe E, adds he W   13338 þe¹] Wyth L   þe²] om. LPRW
13341 if] if at P   hym noght] trs. LR   13342 þan] om. L

For þe bihoues felawship vse.
   'Wiltow', he says, 'fra now forwarde   13345
þat men halde þe a papillarde,
And wonder on þe and speke ouerthwert
And say þou has a narow hert?
And es so harde and so skars
þat þou noght spendes, bot spars   13350
And dar noght inoghe ete ne drynk?
þus wil men say of þe and think.'
   Or he says, 'þou suld be bysy
To kepe þe hele of þi body
þat it noght out of quert be broght,   13355
For he þat has na hele has noght.
Be noght', he says, 'manslaer
Of þiself, ne man-murtherere,
For þou may so fast þi purs spare
þat þou may sone þi body forfare.   13360
þou awe thurgh right purueaunce
To þi body þe sustynaunce.'
   Or he says þus, 'Bithink þe sone
And take kepe what gode þou has done,
And dose, and may do þat es mare   13365
þan mete or drynk fra þe spare'.
Or he says þus, 'þou etes noght anely
For þe grete delyte of þi body
Bot for to make þe on þe best wyse
Stalwarde to last in Goddis seruyse'.   13370
He says, 'þou awe þi strengthe to kepe
Anely to Godde for his worshepe'.
   þus þe fende a man oft tilles
To Glotony thurgh swilk skilles.
For his skilles to vnderstande   13375

13344 þe] he E   13345 he . . . now] now fra hethen LS   13346 þat] þan R
papillarde] babillard R   13347 on] of P   13349 so²] so sar R   13350 bot] bot all
LR, bot ay P   13351 inoghe ete] trs. R   13352 of] on LPRW   13357 man-] a
man- L, a mans S   13358 ne] ne a L   13360 þou] om. E   body] self R
13361 þou] þe L   awe] aght LS   thurgh] noght (expunged and cancelled) thurgh A
13362 To] To gyf L, Vnto P, To fynd R   þe] þe ryght L, gyf þe S, om. R, þi W
13363 Or] om. R   bi-] vmbe- L   13364 kepe] heyd R   þou has] ys R
13365 and²] om. R   13366 or] and PS   þe] þe to LR   13367 Or] om. R
13368 þi] þe R   13369 þe¹] om. E   þe²] om. RW   13370 Goddis] god R
13371 þou] þe LP   awe] aght LS

Er ay so sutille semande

De Gula

þat it ne es nane so haly man,   fo. 80rb
Ne so wyse þat wisdom can,
þat he ne hym somtyme bigyles
Thurgh swilk skilles and swilk wyles.   13380
    þe thridde braunche of Glotony   *iij[^{us}]. ramus*
Es to ete ouerhastyly.
A foul manere methink es it
Til a man þat has right witte
To ete his mete thurgh a foul vse   13385
Ouerhastyly, als an hound dose
When he es on a caryoun.
He þat so dose semes a glotoun.
And þe mare gredily þat he etes,
þe mare he synnes and Godde f⟨or⟩getes.   13390
    For als I fynde þat it na synne es
To haue godes here and ritches,
Bot it es grete synne to proue
Ritches ouermykell for to luf,
Right so it es na synne to ete   13395
Gode mete, whaso it may gete,
Bot for to ete ouerhastyly,
þat es synne and vilany.
    Alle maner of mete þat es mans fode
Es gode to þam þat er gode,   13400
And specially to þam þat wille
Vse þam with Mesure and with skille
And ete þam with þe saus namely
Of þe Drede of Godde almyghty.
For men suld ay haf Drede in thoght   13405
þat þai in outrage vse þam noght,

13377 it] þer R   ne] *om.* LR   13378 Ne] Na nane L   13379 ne] *om.* S
13380 swilk²] *om.* R   13381 *sidenote: in* W   **iij^{us}.*] iij. AE   ramus] *adds* gule L
13383 foul manere] foly R   13384 right] his P   13385 a] *om.* R   13387 es]
etes W   on] at P, of RW   13389 þat] *om.* S   13390 forgetes] *in a crease* A
13391 I fynde] *om.* L   it] *om.* RW   13394 for] *om.* LRW   13395 *line om.* W
13396 whaso it may] wha may so itt E   it may] *trs.* LPS   13398 es] is both P
13402 Vse] Kepe L   with²] *om.* SR   13403 þam] þan L   saus] saule L
13405 For] *om.* R

And loue Godde with gode talent
And thank hym of al þat he has sent.
　　And by þat mete þat filles right,
Men suld think, bathe day and nyght,　　　　　13410
þe swetenes of Godde so gode to fele
And þe fode þat filles þe hert wele.
And þarefore men vses of custom
þis manere thurgh alle Crystendom
In houses of religyoun　　　　　　　　　　　13415
To rede at þe mete a lessoun.
Wharefore when þe body þat tyde
Receyues þe fode on þe ta syde,
þe hert on þe tothir syde may fele

Donum Sapiencie　　　　De Gula
Sanctificetur nomen tuum

　þe fode þat to it sauours wele.　　　　　　13420
　　þe ferthe braunche es a synne of body
Of þam þat etes ouerdaynteously.
For þai spende on a day and spille
Mare þan men myght with fille
Ane hundreth pouer men and fede　　　　　　13425
Suffisauntly þat has nede.
Swilk men synnes on many maneres,
Als þe boke says on whilk men leres.
　　First þai synne in þe grete outrage
Of grete dispense and grete costage.　　　　　13430
Also þai synne in þe mete vsynge
Thurgh ouergrete lust and lykynge.
þai synne also in Vayneglory
þat þai þareof haf specially.
　　Forwhy it es noght anely synne　　　　　　13435

13408 al] þat R　　has] om. R　　13410 think bathe] thank L　　13411 þe] Of þe L
13412 þe'] of þe L　　wele] sa wele L　　13413 line om. S　　And] om. R　　of] þis R
13414 alle] -oute L　　13415 In] In þe S　　houses] vses L　　of] of parfite S
13416 þe] om. LR　　lessoun] leccioune P　　13419 may] after hert P　　13421 of] of þe
LW　　sidenote: in W　　*iiijᵘˢ.] iiij. A　　ramus] adds gule L　　13422 þam] mene EL
-dayn-] -day- L　　-teously] -teuously R　　13424 men] om. L　　13425 and] wyth L
13426 has] hade ELS　　13427 maneres] manere W　　13428 on . . . men] þat men
on R　　whilk] swilk W　　leres] here W　　13429 þe] om. P　　13430 grete²] om. RW
13431 þai] þai may E　　13433 in] in þe W　　13434 þareof haf] trs. EL
13435 -why] om. R

þe Litchery of þe throte withinne,
Bot it es oft for pompe here
þat þai seke mete of dayntees dere
And so many courses multyplyes,
Of whilk may falle many folyse.   13440

    þe fift braunche es þe curyouste $v[^{us}]$. ramus
Of glotouns þat wil bisy be
To seke gode mete and it to taste,
In whilk þai þam delyte maste.
þise men þat er ay so bisy   13445
May be called litchours proprely,
þat thinkes on nane othir notes
Bot on þair belys and on þair throtes.

    In thre thinges, als I yhow kenne,
Lys þe synne of swilk men: 13450
First in bysynes at þe bigynnynge
In getynge of mete and in dightynge;
Afterwarde in þe delyte grete
In þe vsynge of þat mete;
And sethen in Vayneglory to fele   13455
When þai recorde how þai er fedde wele
And wha may telle, als felle þarto,
What bisynes þai in þat do,
þat þair metes be wele dight
And ilk mete in his sauour right.   13460
And how þai of a thinge of prys
May make sere metes on dyuerse gyse,
Anely for þair awen delyte
And noght for þair mast profyte.

Donum Sapiencie   De Gula
Sanctificetur nomen tuum

    And when þa metes þat er so dight   13465 fo. 80vb
Comes ilkane after othir right,

13438 mete] metes LW   13439 courses] curses LS   13440 whilk] swylk L
13441 þe²] of SW   sidenote: om. P, in W *v^{us}.] v. A ramus] adds gule L   13443 it]
om. E   13444 þai] þai may P   13447 notes] note P   13448 on þair²] om. R
throtes] throte P   13450 synne] synnes R   13452 mete] metes L in²] om. EPRW,
in þe L   13456 er] ware ELS   13458 þai] after þat L, þai had S do] to do S
13459 þat] Bot L   13461 þai] þat W   13462 make] be W on] of LPSR
13465 þa] þaire L   13466 Comes ilkane] trs. P

In sere courses and on sere wyse
After þe manere of seruyse,
þan wil þai haue when þai er at eese
Troefles and bourdes to þe entremees.   13470
And so þe tyme he ouersettes,
And þe caytyf himself forgettes.

   þe resoun slepes þat suld wake;
þan cryes and says þus þe stomake,
'Throte, þou slaas me thurgh maystry;   13475
I brest nerehande, so ful am I'.
þe throte þat es ay litcherous
Answers agayne and says þus,
'And al-if þou sal brest in twa,
þis mees sal noght fra me ga'.   13480

   After swilk Litchery in þat mete,
Comes Vayneglory and likyng grete.
þat es to recorde and to thynk
How þai war serued of mete and drynke.

   Now haf yhe herde specially   13485
þe synnes þat comes of Glotony.
And forþi þat oft alle swilk synnes
In tauerne comonly bigynnes,
þat es of Glotony called þe welle,
þarefore I wille a party telle   13490
Of þe synnes þat som men duse
In þe tauerne when þai it vse.

   þe tauerne norisshes many a fole,
þe whilk may be called þe fendes skole
þar his discyples in his sight   13495
Studys, bathe day and nyght.
Also bi skils þat I can telle,
It may be called his awen chapelle

13467 on] in ELS   13468 of] of þaire L   13470 þe] *om.* LS   entre-] aftur- W
13471 -settes] -sittes L   13472 þe] þat L   13473 slepes] sleples L   *sidenote:*
Disputacio inter guttur et stomachum gulosorum (*om.* LS) ESL   13474 þan] And þus L
þus] *om.* R   13479 And] *om.* R   al-if] if-all L   sal] *om.* L   13480 þis mees] þir
meeses R   fra] for- L   me] *om.* L, þe S   13483 recorde] say R   to²] *om.* L
13485 haf yhe] *trs.* LS   13486 synnes] synne S   13487 And forþi] þarfor R   -þi]
-why ES   oft] *om.* L   alle] *om.* W   13490 a party] apertly S   13491 synnes]
synne L   13492 þe] *om.* PRW   13493 -es] *om.* LS   a fole] foles R   *sidenote:*
Taberna vocatur scola diaboli ES, Taberna W   13494 skole] scoles R   13496 bathe]
in bathe S   13498 his awen] þe fende (-des LP) ELPS

þar men hym serues thurgh ille thewes
And þar he his myrakils shewes,   13500
Swilk als to þe fende may falle.
Som sal I shewe yhow, bot noght alle.
    In kirke Godde shewes his vertus
And his myracles þare he duse,
þat mas þe blynde to haue þe sight   13505
And þe croked to gange right.
He gifs to þam þair right wytte
þat er wode and wantes it;
He mas þe domb haf graythe spekynge
And þe deef men þair right herynge.   13510

De Gula

    Bot þe fende dose comonly   fo. 81ra
In þe tauerne þe contrary.
For when þe glotoun þider gase,
He gaas right euen with fayr paas,
Bot hym wantes, bi he wende agayne,   13515
His fete to bere hym and to sustayne.
When he gaas þider he has sight,
Spekynge with tunge, and heryng right
And vnderstandyng and right mynde
And witte and bodily strengthe of kynde.   13520
    Bot when he comes agayne þarefra,
He has haally tynt alle þa,
Als he þat wantes his eghen-sight,
þat es blynde and sees na light,
And wantes his speche and his herynge   13525
And witte and mynde and vndirstandynge.
Swilk myracles als I yhow telle
In tauerne dose þe fende of helle.
    Bot what lessoun in skole redes he

13499 hym serues] *trs.* R   13500 And] *om.* R   13501 may] *om.* L
13502 yhow] *om.* LR   13503 In] In þe L   13504 And] In L   13505 þat] He
LPSRW   þe²] *om.* L   13506 gange] go PRW   13509 haf] to haue LR
13510 men] *om.* R   13513 *sidenote*: Mirabilia (Miracula L) diaboli in taberna ELS
13514 with] with a P   13515 hym] he W   bi] be þat L   wende] ga R, wynd W
13516 to²] *om.* E   13520 and²...of] o...and L   13523 he] *om.* W   eghen-] *om.* R
13525 his¹·²] *om.* R   13526 And] *om.* R   witte and] wantes W   13529 lessoun]
lessouns S   *sidenote*: Lecciones que (*om.* L, quas S) diabolus legitur (quas legit L, legit S)
scolaribus suis (*phrs. om.* S) in taberna (*phrs. om.* L) ELS

To þam þat wille his skolers be?   13530
þai lere of hym to do vilany:
Glotony and Litchery,
To swere and forswere and leghe ay,
To sklaunder and backebyte and myssay,
To skorne and flyte and to dispyse,   13535
To be ay fals and wrangewyse,
To manace and to make barette,
To mayntenc wrange and right to lette,
To controue gyle and trechery,
To renay Godde almyghty,   13540
And many maners of othir synnes
þat in þe tauerne first bigynnes:
Als contekes, stryfs, and melles withalle,
And manslaghters þat oft may falle.
To stele and reue þai lere fast   13545
And by þe necke to hynge at þe last.
    þise er þe fendes propre lessouns
þe whilk he teches his glotouns
þat hauntes þe tauerne comonly;
þat es called þe skole of Glotony.   13550
    Here haf I shewed yhow, als I couthe,
On þe ta syde þe synne of þe mouthe
þat men þe synne of Glotony calles,

De Mala Lingua

fo. 81rb   þe whilke to þe throte mast falles.

De Mala Lingua

Now wille I shewe and noght hyde   13555
þe synne opon þe tothir syde,
þat synne of þe mouthe es called bi skille
And falles to þe tunge þat es ille.

13530 *line om.* R   13533 To] And P   swere and] *om.* R   13535 and¹] *om.* LR
to²] *om.* R   13537 and] or L   13538 To . . . wrange] Ill mayntene R
13539 controue] countare? R   trechery] lichery LW   13541–2 *couplet trs.* P
13541 many] *om.* E   13542 þat in þe] In þat P   þe] *om.* L   13543 Als] *om.* R
contekes] conteck L   melles] mels R   13544 And] *om.* R   manslaghters] mannes
slaghter LSR   13546 þe²] *om.* SR   13548 þe] *om.* R   13551 Here] *om.* R   haf
I] *trs.* RW   13552 þe²] *om.* R   synne] synnes LPS   þe³] *om.* P   13553 þe] *om.* E
13554 þe¹] *om.* R   mast] *om.* L   13554a *marg.* EPSW, *om.* L   13555 shewe] *adds*
ȝhow W   13556 opon] on PR, of W   13557 þe] *om.* R

Bot whoso wille auyse hym wele
And knawe þe synne of þe tunge and fele,   13560
He suld weghe and counterpayse
With skille ilka worde þat he says.
What 'it' es and whethen comes it
And what ille it duse he suld witte.
For þe worde may be synne bi skille   13565
In itself for þat it es ille;
It may be synne for it comes namely
Of þe wicked hert in þe body;
And at þe last, it may so be
þat þe worde, als men may se,   13570
Es grete synne for þe wicked vse,
Forþi þat it grete ille dose,
þe whilk may greue sone and appayre,
Al-if it seme polyst and fayre.

Bot yhe sal vnderstande and se   13575
þat þe Wicked Tung es þe tre
þat our Lorde, Godde al-weldande,
Weryed, als I vnderstande
Forþi þat þat he fonde noght elles
Bot leefs, als þe boke telles.   13580
By leefs in Haly Writte thurgh skille
Er vnderstanded wordes ille.
And stronge it es to telle bi tale
Alle leefs of þe tre, grete and smale,
So es it stronge to telle þe synnes   13585
þat of þe Ille Tunge first bigynnes.

Bot men may ten braunches knawe
þat on þis tre growes, heghe and lawe,   *x. sunt rami Male Lingue*
And þa ten may be called bi skille
þise ten synnes þat I neuen wille: 13590
Idell Speche and vayne Vauntyng,

13559 Bot] *om.* R   13562 þat] *om.* L   13563 it¹] *int.* A   and] *om.* R   comes]
come ELS   13564 duse] wyll do L   13565–6 *couplet om.* W   13565 bi] thurgh
ELS, with P   13566 þat] *om.* R   13567 namely] anely P   13568 Of] Oute of L
13569 þe] *om.* L   13571 wicked] ill R   13572 ille] ele W   13573 appayre]
payre W   13574 Al-if] Of-all L   seme] semed L   13576 es] of P   13579 -þi]
-why R   þat²] *om.* LPSW   13582 -standed] -stande E, -standen LPSRW
13583 bi] *corr. from* þe P, in R   13584 Alle] Alle þe LW, And P   13588 þis] þe L
sidenote: *in* R   13589 And] þat W   called] tald W

Losengery and Bakkebytynge,
Leghinge and Forsweryng thurgh athe,
Stryuyng also and Grochyng bathe,
Frawardnes and Sclaundre to neuen   13595

Donum Sapiencie   De Mala Lingua
Sanctificetur nomen tuum

fo. 81ᵛᵃ To Godde and to his halwes in heuen.
j[ᵘˢ]. ramus est Vana   First he þat wille ouermykill vse
Locucio Idell Speche, als iangelars duse,
May hent grete harme and losse þarby,
And þat persayues he noght lightly.   13600
Forwhy he synnes and leses þarto
þe godes þat he myght + or suld do,
And þe tresour of þe hert he lese
And agayne filles it with vanytese.

Idell Speche þat oftsithes falles   13605
Idell wordes men proprely calles.
Bot alle idell yhete er þai noght,
For thurgh þam mykill ille es wroght.
For idell wordes þat comes ouerthwert
Of alle godenes voydes þe hert   13610
And filles it agayne of vanyte,
Wharefore þai sal aresoned be
And yhelde resouns on domesday
Of ilkan idel worde þat þai say.
And so says Godde in þe godspelle;   13615
þis es noght idell thinge to telle
Wharefore þai sal for certayne chesouns
In so heghe court yhelde resouns,
Als bifore Godde, first to neuen,
And alle þe barnage of heuen.   13620

13591 vauntyng] avaunesyng L   13593 Leghinge] Hethyng E   and] om. R
forsweryng] florysching L, sweryng W   13594 also] om. R   13595 to] om. R
13596 to²] om. R   in] of PRW   13597 sidenote: in R   *jᵘˢ.] j. AE   est . . . locucio]
om. P   13599 losse þarby] losyngery W   13602 godes] gode P   he] om. E   *or]
'gete' (later) or A   do] ydo L   13603 And] om. R   he] to W   13605 -sithes]
sythe⟨eras.⟩ P, syght W   13606 men proprely] trs. R   13608 ille] om. L
13611 of] wyth ELS   13612 sal] sulde P   13613 yhelde resouns] trs. E
13614 idel] om. E   þat] om. S   13617 sal] say W   chesouns] enchesouns L
13618 heghe] adds a L   yhelde] 3heldes W

In swilk Idell Speche to say
On fyue maners synne men may.
Forwhy it er som mens wordes in vayn
þat er outrage and vncertayne,
Of whilk þair tunges so ful I fynde   13625
þat þai speke bathe bifore and byhynde.
Als þe milne-clappe þai er bi skille
þat may noght bi itseluen be stille.
    It er som mens wordes curyous to here,
Als of men þat bene of [bal]de chere   13630
þat ouerblethely telles tythynges,
þe whilk mens hertes to diseese bringes.
þat manere mas þis iangeleres
Be halden fals and leghers.
    It er som wordes quaynt and sutill   13635
Of men þat has fayre speche at wille.
þai can shewe wordes sutilly,
Bot þare es mykell Vayneglory

Donum Sapiencie   De Mala Lingua
Sanctificetur nomen tuum

To plese þe herars at þe last   fo. 81ᵛᵇ
And to make þam lagh fast.   13640
    It er som wordes þat of tung springes
þat er ful of filthe and of lesynges,
Als bourdes and troefles þat oft falles,
And alle þa idell wordes men calles.
Bot alle idelle er þai noght semande,   13645
For þai oft dere and er stynkande.
    Also of þe tunge som word`es´ skapes

13621 *sidenote*: Quinque modis possunt homines peccare per linguam ES
13622 On] In L   13623 -why] *om.* R   mens] *om.* W   13624 vn-] *om.* W
13625 so . . . I] I (so W) fully LW   13628 þat] þat þai W   bi] bid W   13629 It er]
om. R   13630 þat] þat balde P   *balde] gode AELS, *om.* P   13631 -blethely]
-lyghtly W   *sidenote*: Nota P   13632 hertes] hert L   diseese] nycetes L, dise as R
13635 It] þit S   It er] *om.* R   wordes] *adds* er R   13636 speche] wordes L   at] and R
13638 þare es] þai vse W   13639 herars] eres and L   13640 make] gerre L   þam]
þam to EPSRW   13641 It] þare L, þit S   It er] *om.* R   of] of þe LPW   tung]
tonnges (-es *later*) S   13642 of²] *om.* W   13643 Als] And L   oft] *om.* R
13644 men] *after* þa E   13645-6 *couplet om.* W   13645 Bot] *om.* R   alle] *om.* E
noght] *om.* R   13647 of] *om.* P   þe . . . wordes] *trs. phrs.* P   wordes] -es *int., probably
later* A   skapes] eschapes L, schapes SW

þat er ful of skornes and iapes,
þe whilk skorners þat er vncurtays
To þam þat er gode men oft says   13650
And to alle men þat wele dose,
For þai wald drawe þam fra þat vse.
  Alle swilk er idell wordes called,
Bot I wil noght þam idell halde.
Forwhy þat man es a manslaer   13655
þat thurgh his tunge a man wil dere
Or drawe hym fra gode to ille
And fra gode purpos turne his wille.
Na mare thank cunnes Godde him þan
þan þe kynge wald cun a man   13660
þat had his sone slayne and lorne
And stolne his tresour and away borne.

ij[us]. est Iactancia   After þat of þe tunge may springe
Anothir synne; þat es Vauntyng.
þat synne es bathe grete and vilayns   13665
After þat þe tunge it sustayns.
  For whoso vauntes him openly,
He es a theef to Godde almyghty
And withdrawes fra him þat es his,
þat es to say worshepe and blisse   13670
þat hym awe yhelde ay to Godde sone
For þe gode þat he has hym done,
Als I herebifore haf talde.
þarefore þis vaunters er ouerbalde.
  A greef synne methink þis es,   13675
And þat hauntes it es witteles.
  Forwhy þe godes wharethurgh he myght

13648 skornes] scorne ELPS   13649 skorners] scornes PSW   13650 men] *om.* L
13652 drawe] *om.* E   13653 Alle] And L, As R   13655 -why] -þi S, *om.* R   a] als
PRW   13656 wil] wald W   13658 turne] draw L   13659 mare] noþer R
13660 wald] will P   cun] nyme E   13661 lorne] forlornne L   13662 And¹] Or L
13663 *sidenote*: *om.* L   *ij^m.] ij. AS   est] *om.* S   13664 synne] thing L   vauntyng]
avauntyng LS   13666 þat] *om.* RW   13667 For] *om.* R, Bot W   vauntes] avauntes
L, wayntes R   13669 þat] þat at R   13670 worshepe] worschippes L
13671 awe] *adds* to L   ay] *om.* RW   Godde] goddes LW   13672 gode] godenes S
13673 I herebifore] *trs.* LS   herebifore] *trs.* P   13674 vaunters] avaunters L
13675 greef] grefous ELW, grete S   þis] it LRW   13676 þat] he þat EPW, þase þat L,
þai þat R   es] er full L, `he/ (*later*) es S   13677 -why] -þi L, *om.* R   godes] gode W
-thurgh] -with L

Wynne heuenryke þat es so bright,
He gifs ay for a lytell wynde
Of Vayneglory; þat sal he fynde.   13680
    In þis braunche fyue leefs hynges
þat er fyue maners of vauntynges.
Ane es of thinge þat has bene;

De Mala Lingua

Anothir of thing þat es now sene;   fo. 82ra
þe thridde of thing þat sal be thurgh wille;   13685
þe ferthe es couert, þe fift sutill.

    þe first es þis, to shewe yhou sone,
Vauntynge of thing þat has bene done.
And þat es of þam þat shones noght
To reherce dedes þat þai haf wroght   13690
And says, 'Swilk dedes and þus we didde'.
For þai wald fayne be dughty kydde
And þat men þair pruesce knewe
For werldely loos to haue ay newe.

    Anothir maner of Vauntyng es   13695
Of thinge þat men duse thurgh Lithernes.
þat es þe synne of þam to fele
þat wille noght payne þam to do wele
Ne say wele, als felle to be,
Bot when men may þam here or se.   13700
Swilk men vses mykell Vauntynge
Bathe in saying and in doinge
And in othir thinges þat falles þarto
And selles for noght al þat þai do.

    Hereto falles, als I vnderstande,   13705
þe synne of þam appert semande
þat of þair godes þam vauntes ay

    13680 he] þai R   13681 sidenote: Quinque modi iactancie ES, Super hunc ramum
pendet quinque folia R   13682 vauntynges] avaunsynges L   13683 es] after thinge R
13684 of] es of L   es now] trs. LR   13685 thing] thynges R   þat] om. E
13686 fift] add es LR   13687 shewe] adds 'to' W   13688 Vauntynge] Avaunseyng L
13689 And] om. RW   þam] þai R   shones] semes W   13691 line repeated L   didde]
wroght L (first version of line only)   13692 fayne] om. R   13693 pruesce] prowest
LS (later, marg. S), prufes R   knewe] knawe W   13694 loos] looues R
13695 vauntyng] avaunsyng L   sidenote: ij. E   13696 thurgh lithernes] by lychernes R
13697 þe] om. E, of P   13699–700 couplet om. W   13701 vauntynge] avaunseyng L
13704 al þat] þat at R   13706 þam] man R   13707 vauntes] avaunces L

þat þai haue, þat es to say
Of þair ritchesce and þair nobillesce
Or of þair strengthe or þair pruesce.   13710
þai fare als þe cukkuk bi lickenyng
þat can noght bot of himseluen synge.
    þe thridde es, whaso knawes it,
Of thinge þat may be and es noght yhit.
þat es a synne, als I wene,   13715
Of þam þat surquidrous er sene.
Som says, 'I sal make þis and þat'
For men suld bi hym þe mare lat.
He says he sal make touns and palays,
Bot he wille noght do alle als he says.   13720
    þe ferthe also, to telle on rawe,
Es couert Vauntynge to knawe.
þat es of þam þat couertly duse
And dar noght for shame þamself ruse,
Bot al þat þat othir dose or says   13725
þai wil dispyse and mysprayse,
Right als þai couthe do and say
Mikell better þan euer couthe þai.

De Mala Lingua

fo. 82ʳᵇ   þe fift manere of Vauntynge
        Es sutill to mens vnderstandynge.   13730
    þat es of þam þat blethely walde
    þat men þam praysed and gode men cald
    And dar noght vaunt þam appertly
    For perceyuynge of Surquidery.
    Bot als þai meke ware, þai sutilly say   13735
    þat þare er nane so ille als þay,

13710 Or¹] *om.* W   or²] or of L, and of W   13711 fare] ferre L   lickenyng] lykynge R   13712 him-] þai m- P   *sidenote:* Sunt sicut cuculus qui nescit cantare nisi de ipso (seipso LS) ELS   13713 thridde] *adds* thing L   *sidenote:* iij^us. E   13714 *line om., added later vertically in gutter* P   13715-16 *couplet trs.* P   13715 þat] þis PR   13716 er sene] bene R   13717 and] or LS   13718 hym] bym R   þe] *om.* L   13719 palays] palaces L   13720 Bot] And L   als] þat LR   13721 also] es allswa L, als P   *sidenote:* iiij^us. E   13722 vauntynge] avaunsyng L   13724 þam-] hym- L, þer- R   13725 þat²] *om.* ELPSW   13726 *line om.* L   13727 als] so P   and] or ELPSR   13729 vauntynge] avaunsyng L, avauntyng S   *sidenote:* v^us. E   13732 cald] halde L   13733 vaunt] avaunce L, avaunte S   13735-6 *couplet om.* W   13735 þai sutilly] *trs.* R   sutilly] sotill P

Forþi þat men suld þam meke halde
And prayse þam wele aftir þai walde.

'Allas, allas', says Saynt Bernarde,   *Bernardus*
'þis es a doleful Vauntyng outwarde;   13740
þai make þam deuels and noght elles
For men suld hald þam als aungels;
þai make þam ille als men þat er wode
Forþi þat men suld halde þam gode.'
Bot I trowe þat þai wald be ille payde,   13745
If men answerd þam and sayde
On þis manere, 'Certes, sothe say yhe;
Wers þan yhe er may nane be'.

Hereto þe synne of þam falles
þat seken othir þat men calles   13750
Als auokettes, þam for to prayse
And þair pomp and loos heghe to rayse.
þat es þair nobillesce for to cry,
Thurgh wham þai speke mare hardyly.

þe thridde braunche es Losengery   13755 *iij[us]. est Adulacio*
þat som men hauntes ouercomonly.
þe whilk losengers men may halde,
þat þe fendes noryces er called,
þe whilk his childer at souke gifs
And with glosynge þam fedes þat greues   13760
And mas þam in þair synne ly lange
Thurgh þair fikell flaterand sange.

þai enoynt with swete hony
þe way to helle for þam namely,
Forþi þat þai suld hardylyer ga   13765
By þat way þat enoynte es swa,
Als men dose þat þe beere taas.

13737 -þi] þai L   13739 *sidenote om.* P   13740 þat es a dolefull avaunceyng afterward L, For to þai mseluen þai do full harde P   doleful] delfull W   13741 þam] *om.* L   13742 þam] *om.* L   13743-4 *couplet om.* L   13743 ille] *om.* R   13744 -þi] *om.* R   13745 Bot] *om.* R   þat] *om.* LS   13746 þam and] *trs.* P   13747 certes] *om.* R   yhe] the E   13751 auokettes] aduokes LP   þam . . . praysel for þaim prayes W   13752 and] *adds* þaire L   rayse] prays R   13753 nobillesce] nobilnes R   for] here W   13754 þai . . . mare] þam speche R   13755 es] is of P   *sidenote: om.* L   *iij[us].*] iij. A, vj[us]. ramus ES   est adulacio] *om.* S   13758 noryces] norysce ELSW   er] es L   13760 fedes] fede W   þat] and RW   13761 ly] to lyg L, life P   13762 fikell] *om.* L   13765 -þi] *om.* R   hardylyer] þe h. L, baldlyer R   13766 enoynte es] *trs.* R, þai anoynte W   13767 beere] beres L

þai enoynt his way þar he gaas
With hony to tillen hym to a pitte
þar he falles in ar euer he witte,   13770
And swa he es sleghely tane
Thurgh þat way þat he has gane.

Donum Sapiencie   De Mala Lingua
Sanctificetur nomen tuum

fo. 82ᵛᵃ Right so þis losengeours duse
þat Losengery wille comonly vse;
þai lede men thurgh þair Losengery   13775
Into þe way of Vayneglory,
þe whilk may euen a man lede
To helle-pit; þat es mast to drede.

   þis synne þat þus in þe tung lyse
Departes it in fyue partys   13780
þat out of þis thridde braunche springes,
Als fyue leefs þat on it hinges.

   þe first party es a synne þat deres.
þat es þe synne of þis flateres
þat when þai se wham þai wil glose   13785
þat specially yhernes to haue loose,
If he haue wele sayde or wele done,
þai telle it to hymseluen sone,
Forþi þat he suld haue Vayneglory,
Bot þai wille noght telle hym his foly.   13790

   þe secund es, als I vnderstande,
þe synne of þam þat gloses leghande,
þat when a man dose or says
Litell gode þat es lytell to prayse,
þai make it mare and dose þarto   13795
Swilk twa als he can say or do.
So þat lesynges make þai ma

13768 þar] wharso R   13769 hym] in- E, hym in- LS   13771 es] falles R
13775 men] om. W   þair] om. LS   13776 way] heghway S   way of] repeats R
13777 euen] after man LS   13779 þus] after tung SR   13781 þis] þe LP   thridde]
?threido P   13783 party] synne L   sidenote: jᵘˢ. ES (S at 13773)   13784 þe] a LS
flateres] flatereres LPRW   13785 þat] þat es L   wham] a man L   13786 loose]
glose S   13787 or] and S   wele] om. R   13788 it to] om. L   hymseluen] adds full L
13789 -þi] om. PR   þat] om. R   13790 þai] he L   hym] om. R   13791 secund]
adds synne L   sidenote: ij. ES   13792 gloses leghande] lyeghes glosand L   13795 it]
om. S

þan sothe saynges—yha, swilk twa.
And þarefore þai er in Haly Writte
Called fals wyttenes þat spekes of it.   13800
  þe thridde þe synne of þam es,
Als þe boke here beres wittenes,
þat makes a man to vnderstande
Thurgh sleghe sayinge and fayr semblande
þat he has in hymself alane   13805
Vertus and grace of whilk he has nane.
And þarefore Haly Writte þam calles
Charmers; þat name to þam falles
For þai charme so sleghely a man,
Thurgh sleghe wordes þat þai 'speke' can,   13810
So þat he trowes mare þair sawes
þan himself þat he best knawes;
And better trowes þat a thinge may be
þat he heres þan þat he may se;
And þat þai say of hym so wele   13815
þan þat þat he may se or fele.
  þe ferthe es þe synne of þam also

Donum Sapiencie   De Mala Lingua
Sanctificetur nomen tuum

þat synges commonly *Placebo*.   fo. 82vb
þat es to say, 'Sir, sothe say yhe'
Or 'Yhe do wele, als falles to be',   13820
And turnes to þe gode and wil prayse
Alle þat a man dose or sayse;
Whethir þat it be gode or ille,
þai say it es gode to folow his wille.
  And þarefore þai þat pleses men so   13825
Er called in Haly Writte 'eccho'.

13798 yha] þa L, ʒe PW   13799 And] *om.* P   þai er in] says here L
13800 Called] þat þai called L   of] *om.* LW   13801 þe²] *om.* LW   *sidenote*: iij. ES
13802 here beres] *trs.* PR   13805 in] of L   13806 Vertus] Wertu W   whilk]
swylk L   13807 And] *om.* L   -fore] *om.* EL   13808 Charmers] *corr. from* Charmes
P, Charmes S   name] nane P   to] vnto L   13810 speke] *int.* A, *om.* ER
13813–14 *couplet om.* W   13813 þat] *om.* S   13815 of] on W   13816 þat²] *om.*
LSW   he] þai S   13817 þe²] þis W   *sidenote*: iiij^{us}. Placebo E, iiij. S   13821 þe]
om. L   wil] wyll it L, wele R   13822 a man] men euer L   13823 þat] *om.* S   it]
he R   13824 his] þaire S   13826 eccho] ocko LS, ectho P   *sidenote*: Ocko S,
Eccho W

þat es þe soune þat reboundes agayne
When men spekes at a heghe mountayne,
þat says after þe same worde ay,
Als oft als men wil oght say.   13830
Whethir it be gode or ille to knawe,
Be it lesynge or sothe sawe,
It acordes ay wele to itte,
Als men may vnderstande thurgh witte.
    þe fift es a synne þat charge beres,   13835
þe whilk þai haunt þat er flaterers
þat oft defendes and excuses
And couers þe vyces þat som men vses,
And þe synnes of þam namely
þat þai wil flater thurgh losengery.   13840
And þarefore er þai 'taylles' called
In Haly Writte þat we sothe halde.
For þai couer þe filthe of synne
Of riche men þat þai lif inne,
Outhir for luf or for drede,   13845
Or for werldely profyte or mede.
And þai may be lickened namely
Vnto þe fox-taylle for þair trechery.

iiij[ᵘˢ]. est Detractio   þe ferthe braunche þat may springe
Of þe ille tunge es Backebytynge   13850
þat many men thurgh Envye
Hauntes here ouercommonly.
Bot losengers and backebyters
Er of a skole, þe fendes skolers.
Of whilk þe tane may lickened be   13855
To a meruayllous beste in þe see,
And þe tothir, als I vnderstande,
Til a venymous beste on þe lande.
    þise twa men may fynde in a boke
Of kynde of bestes, whaso wil loke.   13860
þe tane es þe mermayden called.

13827 þe soune] to seme W   13828 at] on R   a] *int.* P, *om.* R   13832 or] be it L
13833 to] vnto L, wyth S   13834 thurgh] be R   13835 *sidenote*: vᵘˢ. ES
13838 þe] *om.* L   13846 or²] or for SR   13848 Vnto] To LPSRW   trechery]
trythery S   13849 *sidenote*: *om.* L, 4. W   *iiijᵘˢ.] iiij. A, *add* ramus ES   13850 þe
ille tunge] ille tonnges L   13855 þe tane] ane L   13858 on] of R   13859 may
fynde] fyndes L   13860 wil] can R   13861 þe] a R   *sidenote*: j. W

þat es a meruayllous beste to bihalde
þat has þe body als a woman

De Mala Lingua

And þe taylle of fysshe þat swym can.   fo. 83ra
And naylles als þe [e]ren sho has redy   13865
And synges in þe see so myryly
þat makes þe shipmen sone slepe
And drunkens þam in þe see so depe.
    þis meruayllous beste on þe see
Methink þis losengers may be,   13870
þat thurgh þair sange þat Losengery es
Makes men slepe in þair wickednes
And haldes þam so lange þarinne
Til þai be drunkened in þair synne.
    þe tothir beste on þe lande es sene   13875
And es a nedder þat es ful kene,
þat rynnes bi [k]ynde and thurgh vse
Swifter on erthe þan a horse duse,
And to rynne lange he may wele dreghe
And somtyme wil it with wenges fleghe   13880
And has venyme so strange to say
þat na treacle ouercom it may.
For þe dede may are com of it,
Ar a man may right fele þe bitte.
    þis nedder þat es so felle and kene   13885
Er backebyters þat bytand bene.
For Salamon says þat þai byte
And als þe nedder with tange `þai´ smyte
And venymes þa þat þai ouertake
And strykes and slaas thre at a strake.   13890

13863 þe] a P   als] of L   13864 of] of a LP   þat] *om.* R, and W   13865 als þe]
of L   *eren] iren AELS   sho has] all R   13867 þe] þir L   -men] -man R   sone] to L
13868 drunkens] drunkes P, drownes SR, drenches W   so] *om.* R   13871 þair] þat W
þair sange] *trs.* E   -gery es] -g`er'ey is P, -gers R   13872 men] men to L
13874 drunkened] dounked L, drouned SR   13875 on] þat on L   þe] *om.* W
sidenote: ij. animal W   13876 And] *om.* L, þat P   þat es ful] and þat es L, and ys full R
13877 þat] And E   *kynde] -hynde AEL   13878 on] on þe L   13879 he] it R
13880 it] he LS   wenges] wengaunce R   13882 na] *om.* W   13884 fele] wele
fele W   13885 þis] þe S   *sidenote*: Serpens W   13887 *sidenote*: Salamon E
13888 And] *om.* W   þe nedder] *om.* L   þai] *int.* A, *om.* PRW   13889 þa] þaim PW

Ane es hymself þat es backebytar;
Anothir es he þat es þe herer;
þe thridde es he wham he backebytes.
þise thre to dede at anes he smytes.

On þis braunche fyue leefs may hynge   13895
þat es fyue manere of Backebytyng.
þe first es, als þe boke proues,
When þe backebytar controues
Any wickednes or lesynges
þat othir men in blame brynges.   13900

þe secund leef es þis to lere:
When þai ille of othir men here,
þai telle it forthe in many a stede
And says mare ay on þair awen hede.

þe thridde es when þai sette at noght   13905
þe gode þat a man has wroght

De Mala Lingua

fo. 83ʳᵇ And mas hym ille be halden þan;
þus ete þai al hale a man.

þe ferthe leef es, als may falle,
When þai a man ete noght alle   13910
Bot bytes a pece of hym away
Thurgh som worde þat þai can say
And if þai durst byte mare, þai walde.
Backebytyng þis es proprely called.

For als men may appertly knawe,   13915
þai of smyte and away drawe
Of othir mens godenes a party
þat þai here spoken of þam namely.
For when a man any gode says

13891 es²] ys þe R   13892 þe] om. LW   13893 he¹] om. LS   13894 smytes]
strykes L   13895 On] Of L   hynge] spryng L   sidenote: De quinque modis
detraccionis ES, 5. folia W   13896 manere] maners L, manerers P   13897 sidenote:
j. E, j. folium W   13898 backebytar] backbiters L   13901 sidenote: ij. E, 2. folium W
13902 þai] þaim P   of] on P   13903-4 couplet trs. P   13903 þai telle] And telles P
many a] may P, many R   13904 mare ay] trs. LR   13905 sidenote: iij. E, 3. folium W
13906 gode] godes L   13908 hale a] a dede R   13909 sidenote: iiij. E, 4. folium W
13910 þai] om. L   ete] etes L   13912 can] om. R   13914 -bytyng] bytynges P   þis
es] trs. LS   13915 als] alle ES   appertly] aperly R   13917 godenes] gudes PW
13918 spoken of] of þam spoken L, trs. S, speke of W   namely] anely P

Of anothir þat he wil prayse,   13920
þe backebyter afferme it wille,
Bot he says a 'botte' þat es ille.
    'Certaynely', þus says he þan,
'Sothe it es, he es a gode man.
And I luf hym right faythfully,   13925
Bathe in saul and in body.
Bot a defaut methynk has he
þat es þis, and þat forthinkes me.'
And thurgh a priue Enuye shewes it,
And þus bytes he of hym a bit.   13930
    He es þe scorpyoun venemous
þat with þe face fawens þus
And venymes with þe taylle bihynde,
Als I in boke wryten fynde.
    þe fift leef of þe braunche es þis,   13935
When he turnes anything mysse—
þat es to say to þe wers party—
Alle þat he heres or sees namely,
þe whilk men may thurgh kyndely skille
Turne bathe to gode and vnto ille.   13940
And þarefore he es called by resoun
A fals domesman for þat enchesoun.
    þe fift braunche es, als shewes þe tung,   *v[ᵘˢ]. est Mendacium*
Leghyng; þat hauntes bath alde and yhung.
Leghyng falses a man þat es leel,   13945
Als men may falsen þe kynges seel,
Or þe kynges monee þat es wroght,
Or þe papes bulle thurgh falsed soght.

13920 *sidenote*: Nota bene E   13922 he] a S   says] mase PRW   botte] bowt S,
buke? W   13924 he] þat he L   13925 right faythfully] f. wele (*canc.*) P
13927 *sidenote*: Nota P   13928 and þat] þareof S, þat R, and W ·   13929 And]
om. R   it] he it R   13930 bytes he] *trs.* LW (*and after* hym W)   he] *om.* SR
13932 þat] *om.* P   þe] his P   face] *adds* vs L   fawens] flakyns R   13933 venymes]
venemous LPR   13934 I in] in a L   boke] *adds* we L   13935 fift] first W
sidenote: vᵘˢ. E, j. folium W   13936 When] Then W   he turnes] *trs.* E   any-] a P
mysse] to mys W   13937 þe] *om.* W   13938 heres or sees] *trs.*
verbs LS   13939 þe] *om.* R   men may] *trs.* P   thurgh] be R   13940 vnto] to
ELPS, *om.* R   13942 for] by ELSRW   13943 es] *om.* LW   *sidenote*: *om.* L
*vᵘˢ.] v. A, *add* ramus ES (*after* est S)   13944 Leghyng] Hethyng E   þat] and W
bath] *om.* R   13945 falses a] may make fals L   a man] hym R   13946 kynges]
kenge E   13948 bulle] bill W

Donum Sapiencie   De Mala Lingua
Sanctificetur nomen tuum

fo. 83ᵛᵃ And right als he þat falses þe mone
Or þe kynges sele, whethir it be,   13950
Sal be demed thurgh þe lawe here
To bere iewes als falsere,
Right so a man þat thurgh Lesynge
Falses hymself in anythinge
þat es Goddis prente and his licknes,   13955
And says agayne sothfastnes,
He sal be demed on domesday
Als falsere, to payne þat lastes ay.
  þe legher es amange othir men
Als es þe fals peny to kenne   13960
Amange othir þat es gode and trewe,
Whethir it be alde monee or newe;
And als es þe caffe þat es oft sene
Amange þe corne þat es gode and clene.
  þe legher es lyke thurgh lickenes   13965
Vnto þe fende þat his fader es.
And so says Godde in þe godspelle,
Als men may here þis clerkes telle.
For þe fende þe chief legher es
And fader of leghes and of wickednes,   13970
Als he þat first forged Lesynge
And yhete foorges thurgh controuyng.
  þe fende þat lettes ay gode thewes
In many shappes he hym shewes
And transfigures hym in many gyses   13975
To deceyue men on sere wyses.
And right so he þat es a legher

13949 And] om. W   right] om. R   þat] om. LW   13950 it] þat it L
13951 thurgh] be R   13952 bere] hafe PRW   als] or L   falsere] fals were E, falshere
S, falles here R   13953 þat] om. L   13955–6 couplet om. W   13955 prente]
priuyte R   his] goddes L   13959 sidenote: Mendax E   13963 es¹] om. LPSW
13964 þat] om. W   13966 Vnto] To PRW   13967 sidenote: Euangelium E
13969 þe²] om. LS   13970 And] And þe L   of²] om. R   13971–2 couplet om. W
13971 lesynge] lyeghing L   13972 foorges] forgege R   13973 þe fende] Yhe
fynde E   13975 -figures] -figure S   in] int. P, on R   many] sere R   13976 To
deceyue] And deceyfes L, To deten R   on] in LW   sere] many P   13977 And] om. R

Deceyues men on þe same maner.
   Wharefore he may right lickened be
To a fowell in som cuntre,   13980
þe whilk men gamalyon calles
þat lifs of þe ayre, als his kynde falles,
And has nathinge in his entraylles
Bot wynde anely þat sone faylles,
And to ilka manere of colour knawen   13985
þat he sees he moues his awen.
   On þis braunche, als I vnderstande,
Thre specyall leefs er hyngande
þat er thre maners of lesynges
þe whilk fra þe ille tunge springes.   13990
For a maner of Leghe es brynnande;
Anothir manere es plesande;

Donum Sapiencie   De Mala Lingua
Sanctificetur nomen tuum

þe thridde es noyande, als yhe may se,   fo. 83vb
And synne es in ilkane of þise thre.
   For Saynt Austyne, þe haly man,   13995 *Augustinus*
Says þus, als I shew yhow can,
þat howsoeuer a man gode dose
To othir thurgh leghes þat he can vse,
Always his awen harme dose he.
Wharefore brynnand Leghes synne may be.   14000
   Bot þe Leghes of þis losengers,
Of þis truffeurs and þis leghers,
þat bourdes and lesynges oft telles
For mans solace and for noght elles
Er proprely synne thurgh þe likynge,   14005

13978 Deceyues] Deteines R   þe same] sere L   13979 right] wele L, *om.* R
13981 *sidenote*: Gamalioun auis W   13982 of] on R   13983 And] þat L
13985 of] *om.* R   colour] *adds* þat es L   13986 he²] *om.* R   13988 *sidenote*: Tria
folia mendacij (*trs.* L) ELS   13989 maners] maner EPSRW   13990 þe²] *om.* L,
þis W   tunge] tonnges L   13993 thridde] *adds* maner P   es] *om.* R   yhe] men L
13995 þe] þat LR   *sidenote*: in W   13996 yhow] *om.* LR   13997 a] any W
sidenote: Nota E   13998 othir] stir R   leghes] leghe W   can] *om.* R
13999–14000 *couplet om.* W   14001 þe] þise ELS, *om.* R   leghes] lyeghers L   þis
losengers] lossyngers garres R   14002 þis truffeurs] þir troffellours LR, trwfuls P
and] and of P   þis²] *om.* R   leghers] lechers W   14004 mans] mene EPSR, mens LW
for²] *om.* LPSRW   14005 þe] *om.* P

Bathe in sayinge and in herynge.
   Bot Leghes þat noyes er synne dedely,
When a man þam shewes namely
Thurgh wytynge and thurgh wille bathe,
To greue othir men and to skathe.   14010
Out of þis braunche springes and spredes
Alle fallaces and alle falsedes,
And alle þe gyles þat men can
For to deceyue or greue a man,
Outhir in saul or in body,   14015
Or in godes or in loos falsely.

vj. est Periurium   þe sext braunche es a perillous thing;
þat es þe synne of Forsweryng.
Ille it es to be a legher,
Bot wers it es a man him forswere;   14020
And perillous and dredefull bathe
Es to swere and to haunt athe.
   And þarefore I fynde, als clerkes redes,
þat our Lorde swerynge forbedes,
Noght for þat þat men may noght swere   14025
Withouten synne þat þe saul may dere;
Bot forþi þat he þat oft sweres
And seldom vayne athes forberes,
To forswere hym oft hym wil falle,
And synnes oftsythe þarewithalle.   14030
   For thurgh athe þat men sweres and heres,
Men may synne in seuen maneres,
þe wilk þis clerkes seuen leefs calles
þat to þis braunche specially falles.
   þe first to shewe in þis party   14035
Es when a man sweres right hertly

14006 Bathe] And L   14008 When] When þat L   14009 thurgh²] om. ER
14010 To greue othir] Outhir to greif R   and] or R   to²] do LSR   14011 springes and
spredes] *trs. verbs* S   14012 alle²] om. L falsedes] false dedes R   14013 alle] om. W
þe] þa E   14014 deceyue] detene R a] om. L, any S   14017 *sidenote*: om. L *vj*ᵘˢ.] vj.
A, *add* ramus ES   14020 a man him] to be a R   14022 to²] om. LS   14023 And] om.
PR   14024 Lorde] *adds* gode R   14025 for þat] om. R may] shuld R noght] om. LS
14026 may] om. R   14027 -þi] om. R þat he] þai L, he R þat²] om. W   14029 hym¹]
om. E oft hym] *adter* wil P hym²] om. LSR wil] may be- L, will he R, *hole* W
14030 synnes] synne L -sythe] -sythes ELPSW, om. R   14031 and heres] om. R
14032 may synne] synnes R *sidenote*: De vij. folijs periurij ES   14033 þis] om. PR
14035 *sidenote*: j. E   14036 right] om. R right hertly] wightwisly P

De Mala Lingua

And right blethely; þis es Despyte,   fo. 84ra
For it semes he has þareinne delyte.
þarefore swerynge forbedes Saynt Iame,   *Iacobus*
Als Godde duse þat forbedes þe same—   14040
Noght to swere when it es nede,
Bot likynge to swere þai forbede.

    Anothir es when men swere wille
Lightly for noght withouten skille.
þat es defended, als men may knawe,   14045
In þe commandementes of þe + lawe
þat Godde first with his fynger wrate
In tables of stane, als clerkes wele wate.

    þe thridde es when men sweres thurgh vse
Coustomabilly, als som men duse,   14050
Als at ilka worde þat þai speke,
And how þai swere þai neuer reck.

    For it er som so vylaynes ay
þat withouten athe can noght say.
þa men er gretly to wyte,   14055
And Godde has þam in dispyte,
When þai coustomabely for noght
Calles hym to wyttenes þat þam wroght.
Ful grete bihoued be þat querele
And skilful and sothfast and right leel   14060
þar men dar calle to wyttenes
So heghe a lorde als our Lorde es,
Or his moder þat we oft neuen
Or any of 'his' halughs in heuen.

14037–8 *couplet om.* W   14037 right] *om.* R   14039 *sidenote: om.* P
14040 Als . . . þat] And (*om.* S) god LS   þat] *om.* R   14041 Noght] Bot R
14042 likynge] lykynges E   14043 *sidenote:* ij. E   14046 -mentes] -ment L   *þe²]
þe olde ('olde' *later, marg.* A) AL, new S   14047 first] *om.* L, *after* fynger S   fynger]
fyngers LW   wrate] wate W   14048 tables] þe (*om.* E) table ES, þe tabels L   wele]
om. PLR   14049 men sweres] þai swer ?R   thurgh] by PR   *sidenote:* iij. E, iijus S
14050 som] *om.* L   14051 Als] *om.* R   at] athe L, *om.* P   14052 And how] How
þat L   swere] speke R   neuer] ne R   14053 it] ȝit S   14054 þat] *om.* R   can] þai
canne LR   14055 to] fore to ELS   14056 in] in grete P   14057 When] When
þat L   14058 þam] hym haues L, hym W   14059 bihoued] behoues W   þat]
þaire L   14060 and¹·²] *om.* LR   right] wonnder L   14061 dar] may P   to] vnto L
14062 our Lorde] godde P   14064 his] *int. later* AP, þe ES   in] of EL

Bot men suld na grete athe swere   14065
Bot when nede ware wyttenes to bere,
For Godde in þe godspell biddes vs
þat we swere nane athe bot þus.
When we sal swere, he biddes vs say
Noght elles bot 'Yha, yha; nay, nay'.   14070
    þe ferthe manere þat grete charge beres
þat es when a man folyly sweres,
Appertly or in pryuyte,
And þat may in many maners be.
Als when men sweres thurgh ire ouersone   14075
And repentes þam when þai haf done.
Or when men sweres oght to bigynne
þat men may noght hald withouten syn.

De Mala Lingua

fo. 84rb For if men it helde, it wald do skathe;
þarefore men suld breke swilk an athe.   14080
Bot þair penaunce bihoued þam take
þat swilk a fole athe wil make.
    Or when men certaynely swere wille
For anythinge, be it gode or ille,
Of whilk men has na certaynte;   14085
Yhete synne þai, al-if it sothe be.
Or when men hetes anythinge
Certaynely, withouten fayllynge,
þat þai ne wate ne knawes noght right
If þai may halde þat þai haf hight.   14090
    Or when men sweres for oght or noght
Bi þe creatures þat Godde has wroght,

14065 Bot] For L, *om.* R   14066 when] *om.* R   nede] mene ES   to] *om.* S
14067 *sidenote*: Euangelium E   14068 swere . . . athe] sall noght swere L
14069-70 *couplet trs.* L   14069 swere] *om.* R   14070 yha yha] ȝe ȝe PW
nay¹] and nay W   14071 þat grete] of R   *sidenote*: iiij. E, iiij^{us}. S   14072 es] *om.* W
a man] *adds* swa L, men PRW   14073 or] or elles E   14074 And] *om.* R
14075 Als] *om.* R   men] a man S   thurgh] be R, in W   14076 þam] *om.* R   haf]
bene L   14077 oght] *om.* R, och? W   14079 For] *om.* R   helde] heuend W   do]
om. R   14080 breke] *om.* R   14081 Bot] *om.* R   14082 fole] foule LS, foly R,
still W   wil] gunn L, couthe W   14083 Or] For L   14084 be it] *om.* P
14086 synne þai] *trs.* S   al-if] if-all L, if R   14087 hetes] hestes L   any-] a L
14088 withouten] *adds* any R   14089 ne¹] *om.* L   noght] *om.* RW   14091 Or]
om. R   or noght] *om.* R

Als som men sweres and says þus right:
'By þe sonne þat shynes bright'
Or 'Bi þis fyre' or 'Bi my hede'   14095
Or 'By my fader saul þat es dede'
Or 'By my moder saul alswa'
Or by swilk othir creatures ma.
Swilk athes our Lorde Godde forbedes,
Als þis clerkes in þe godspelle redes.   14100
  þarefore to þat þat thurgh worde or thoght
Men wil conferme, men suld noght
Drawe to wittenes by na party
Bot souerayne Sothfastnes anely.
þat es our Louerd, Godde al-weldande,   14105
þat made alle thing on water and lande.
Forwhy it es agayne Goddis lawe
þat any man to wittenes drawe
Pouer creatures þat er noght elles
Bot vanyte, als þe boke telles.   14110
And when a man has talent
To swere by þam thurgh auysement,
He dose to þam þat er vnworthy
þe honour þat falles to Godde anely.
  Bot when men sweres by þe boke   14115
Or bi þe godspelle þat men may loke,
þai swere by Godde þat dyed for synne
Whase wordes er wryten withinne.
And when men sweres bi thing worthy,
Als by þe relikes þat er so haly   14120
Or by þe halughs þat er in heuen

Donum Sapiencie   De Mala Lingua
Sanctificetur nomen tuum

þat Halykirke bihoues oft neuen,   fo. 84va

14093 men] *om.* R   þus] *om.* R   14094 þe] þone LS   14098 othir] *om.* LW
14099 Godde] *om.* LR   14100 þis] *om.* R   þe] *om.* SW   14101 þarefore to] *om.* R
(to *int.* P)   14102 men] þat men L, þai R   14103 to] to na SW   14104 anely]
say anly W   14106 on] *om.* LSR   14107 -why] *om.* R   14108 drawe] shuld
drawe R   14111 And] *om.* R   14112 by] to R   þam] name W   14115 Bot]
om. R   14116 Or] And ES, Sythen L   bi] ybe S   men] ȝe R   14117 swere] sweres
after Godde R   14118 Whase] Whar P   wryten] *add* þe boke ESL   14119 And]
om. R   thing] *om.* R   14120 Als] *om.* R   þe] *om.* LR   14121 *line om. at page
bound* L

þai swere by þam and bi Godde bathe
þat wones in þam; þis es þair athe.
   þe fift yhete greues Godde almyghty.   14125
þat es when men sweres vylaynesly,
Outhir bi Godde or by his myght
Or bi his halughs in heuen bright
Or bi his saul or by his hert
Or by his payne þat sare gun smert   14130
Or by his flesshe or by his blode
Or by his dede þat he tholed on rode,
By his fete or by his handes twa,
Or by his naylles of fynger or ta
Or by his body or by his banes   14135
Or by alle his lyms neuend at anes.
   Here es many a vylayne athe.
þe leste + of alle mas Godde ful wrathe;
Grete vilany to Godde men duse
þat swilk vilaynes athes wil vse.   14140
And if Godde be wrathe, it es na wonder,
For þai hym ryue with athes i[n] sunder.
þai er wers and mare vnkynde
þan þe Ieus þat hym a day pynede
And beted hym, bathe body and hede,   14145
And didde hym noght bot anes to dede.
   And þa þat sweres swilk maner of athe
It semes þai do Godde mare skathe,
For ilk day þai do hym on rode,
And ilka day þay shede his blode   14150
With sharp athes in body and hede;
And ilka day þai newe his dede,

14122 -kirke bihoues] buk will R   14124 þam þis] heuen þat L, þam þat R
14125 fift] furst R   yhete] it L, *om.* SR   14126 vylaynesly] vilany R   14130 his]
om. R   payne] paynes LS   gun] con W   14133 By'] By by E, Or by P   or] and L
by his²] *om.* R, by W   14134 Or'] *om.* RW his] *om.* LW of] or L, *canc. (restored in
post-medieval hand)* P, *om.* R   fynger or] fyngers and W   14135 by²] *om.* R
14136 by] *om.* R   alle] *om.* PW   14137-8 *couplet trs.* R   14137 a] *om.* LPR
vylayne] vylans ELSPW   14138 *leste] leste athe ARW   of alle] *om.* R   alle] þai me
LW, all þai m P   ful] *om.* L   14140 vilaynes] *om.* R   wil] men wyll L, will þus R
14141-2 *couplet trs.* W   14141 And] *om.* R   *14142 in] i- A   14144 hym a day]
trs. LS   a day] sare ELS   14145 beted] beten W   hym] *add* ille ELS   bathe] *om.* L
and] *om.* L   14146 hym] *int. after* noght P   noght bot] *om.* R   to] to þe R
14147 athe] athez LS   14148 þai do] þat þai dyde L   þai . . . Godde] to godde þai do P
14149 For] *om.* R   on] on þe R   14151-2 *couplet om.* W   14151 With] And S

In als mykell als in þam es,
Thurgh þair athes and þair wickednes.
   In þis synne er Crysten men   14155
Wers þan er Sarzynes to kenne,
þat wil noght swere on na manere
Ne sweryng of nane othir here
By Ihesu Cryst so vylaynesly,
Als Crysten men duse þat er mare worþi.   14160
   Cristend men er mare felle kidde
þan þe Ieus þat hym on croyce didde.
For yhete þai brake na bane of hym,

Donum Sapiencie   De Mala Lingua
Sanctificetur nomen tuum

Bot Crysten men brekes ilka lym   fo. 84ᵛᵇ
And br⟨e⟩ttens hym, bathe backe and body,   14165
Als a swyne es in þe bouchery.
   Swilk men suld nathing aske here
Of Godde, ne of his moder dere.
For þai þam so vylaynesly dispyse
And alle his halughes on þis wyse   14170
þat it es wonder to mans wytte
How Crystyante may suffre it.
   þe sext es thurgh vnderstandynge
When men sweres falsely for a thinge
Or when men fals wyttenes beres   14175
Or at þair wytyng falsely sweres.
   Swilk men, als methink, dose ille,
Howso þai swere þus, agayne skille,
Be it appertly or couertly,
Thurgh fallace or thurgh sophestry.   14180
For als Haly Writte says and proues,

14156 er] any L, *om.* R, þe W   14159 vylaynesly] vilany R   14160 duse] *om.* L
mare] *om.* R   14161 Cristend] cristene EPSRW, Bote crysten L   er] er now L
14162 þe] *om.* LR   croyce] rode ES, þe rode L   14163 brake] breke L
14165 brettens] eⁱ *over eras.* A, brekes W   bathe] *om.* R   14166 es] *om.* LR   þe] a L
14167 nathing aske] *trs.* LPS   aske] haue W   14169 For] Bot R   vylaynesly] vilany R
14170 his] *om.* R   þis] his R   14171 it] *om.* L   es] es a L   14173 thurgh] to R
sidenote: Sextum (vj. W) folium ESW   14174 falsely for] fals be L   a] any- W
14178 -so] *om.* P   þus] *om.* L   14180 fallace] *altered to* falced S   thurgh] *om.* E
14181 For] *om.* R   als] *om.* L

Symplesce and Sothfastnes God luues.
In swilk witte Godde receyues þe athe
And vnderstandes þe worde bathe,
Als he þat persayues na gilery   14185
Bot vnderstandes þe athe sympilly.
   Mikell methink es þe godenes
Of Godde þat ay so curtays es—
When swilk men sweres thurgh cautele,
þat es noght sothe, als he wate wele;   14190
Or hetes a thing of þair awen wille
þat þai wil noght halde ne fulfille—
þat þe fende of helle for þat dispyte
Ne strangles þam noght als-tyte.
   For when a man sweres, whatso he be,   14195
And says þus, 'Als Godde saue me'
Or 'Als Godde helpe me in my nede',
And he leghe þan, hym aght haf drede.
For he puttes hym thurgh swilk leghyng
Fra Goddis helpe and his kepynge.   14200
þan es he worthy to tyne þarfore
By right his witte and his memore,
His godes, his saul, and his body
And al þat he has of Godde anely.

De Mala Lingua

fo. 85ʳᵃ   þe seuent leef and þe last   14205
þat hynges on þis braunche fast
Es when a man thurgh his fole wille
Brekes his trouth or kepes it ille,
For þat he hetes and grauntes bathe
Thurgh trouthe, als wele als thurgh athe.   14210
Bot he fulfille it, he es forsworne

14182 Symplesce] Sympilnes R, Sympleste W   *sidenote*: Nota bene E
14183 receyues] retenes R   14184 -standes] -standynge R   14185 persayues]
receyfes L   14186 -standes] -stand L   14188 þat] 'þat' þat R   14189 swilk]
om. L   thurgh] be R   14190 he] 3e R   14193-4 *couplet om*. W   14193 þat²]
þe R   14194 þam noght] *trs*. P   noght] *om*. L   14196 als] sa L   14197 in] at L
nede] mede R   14198 þan] *om*. LR   hym aght] he myght P   haf] to haue L
14199 For] Or S   thurgh] be R   leghyng] lesynge W   14201 worthy] worthe L
14203 godes] gode W   14205 *sidenote*: vijᵐ. (7. W) folium ESW   14207 Es] Or S
thurgh his] be R   fole] foly PR, foule W   14210 als wele] *om*. R   als] and L
14211 -sworne] -swere L

And his saul in poynt to be lorne,
For trouthe vnkeped þat es tane
And athe broken er bathe ane.
   þe seuent braunche also men calles   14215 *vij[^{um}]. est Contentio*
Stryuyng þat amange som men falles,
Als when men flytes and myssays;
þis es a synne þat þe fende pays.

   For Saynt Austyn says þat nathinge   *Augustinus*
Payse mare þe fende þan Stryuynge;   14220
By þis we may knawe and fele
þat nane othir synne hym pays so wele.
And þis synne may Godde mast displese,
For he lufs best acorde and peese.

   þis braunche it shewes in seuen thinges,   14225
And er seuen leefs þat of it springes.
þe first es Stryf, anothir Flytynge,
þe thridde Dedeyne, þe ferthe Myssayinge;
þe fift es Reproue, of grete wille;
þe sext es Manace of þat þat es ille.   14230
Bot þe seuent mast greues our Lorde:
þat es raysyng of grete Discorde.

   When þe fende sees luf and pees
Amange gode men þat wald Godde pleese,
Ful mykill sorow has he þan   14235
And dose alle þat he may and can
To make þam at Discorde to be
And makes þam stryue, for þat lufs he.
With þe fyre of Ire he þam enbraces
And stirs þair hertes to Ire and chaces.   14240

   Wharefore after Stryf comonly
Comes Flytyng with noys and cry.
And right als fyre reke vp kestes

14213 es] es þe W   14214 er bathe] *trs.* ESL   14215 also] *om.* S, as W   calles]
called L   *sidenote*: Contencionem L   *vij^{us}.] in gutter* A   vij^{us}. est] *om.* ES
14216 men] *om.* R   14219 For] *om.* R   *sidenote: in* W   14222 so] *om.* E, hym sa L
14223 And] *om.* R   synne] *om.* RW   may] *om.* L   Godde mast] *trs.* LR   14224 best]
om. L   14225 in] it in LS   14228 ferthe] toþer L   14230 manace] malace R
of þat¹] and L   þat²] *om.* W   14232 grete] *om.* L   14234 wald Godde] *trs.* EL
14236 alle] *om.* R   and²] or L   14238 makes þam] to P   makes] gerres L   þam] þan
R, men W   for] and ELS, *om.* R   14239 þe] *om.* R   14242 noys] neye W   and]
with R   14243–4 *couplet om.* R   14243 als] als þe LPW

And after þe reke lowe out brestes,

De Mala Lingua

fo. 85rb Right so after Ire and ille wille,   14245
 Comes Stryf and Contek by þat skille.
 And when ane til anothir says,
 Whethir he lacke a thynge or prayse,
 'It es', he says, 'Swa als I say',
 þe tothir says agayne hym, 'Nay'.   14250
 þe tane says, 'I say, swa was it';
 þe tothir says, 'It was noght yhit'.
 þis es Stryf at þe bygynnynge,
 And after Stryf comes Flytynge.
 For when twa sal bigynne to flyte,   14255
 þe tane leghes þe tothir als-tyte.
 After Flytyng commes Dedeyne
 þat es a lynke of þe fendes cheyne.
 Als when þe tane þe tothir wil pricke
 With felounes wordes þat er wycke,   14260
 Whase tunges er mare sharpe bytande
 þan any rasour in barbours hande,
 And mare sharpe and swift thurgh strengthe
 þan ane arowe þat fleghes on lengthe,
 And mare percheand thurgh felnes   14265
 þan an elsyne poynt þat sharp es.
 Swilk men, whaso þam wil bihalde,
 Er lyke til a beste þat es called
 Porke-de-spyne, þat in Ynde es bredde
 þat es with sharpe hornen pynnes cledde.   14270
 þat beste es felle and sone es wrathe,
 And when he es greued, he wil do skathe.
 For when hym tenes, he launces out felly

14244 lowe] þe lowe E   out] vp LW   14245 Right] om. R   14246 stryf] om. R
14247 And] om. R   14249 swa] om. L   14251 I say] adds þat L, om. P
14255 twa] þai E   sal bigynne] begynnes P   14258 lynke] lynge P   cheyne] shyne R
14260 felounes] felle L   14262 rasour] rasours R   14263 swift] swyfter W
thurgh] þe R   14264 ane] any LSR   arowe] wharow L   14265 percheand]
persande ELS, perteand W   14266 an] any ELPSW   elsyne] helsyne E
14268 sidenote: De porco spinato ES   14269 Ynde] þe wode P   14270 hornen]
hornne LPR, thornne S   14271 es²] om. SR   14272 And] om. R   es] om. P
14273 For] om. R   when] whem S   hym tenes] he es tene L

þa sharp pynnes on his body
And strykes fast with al his myght,   14275
Bathe on þe left syde and on þe right.
Also vnto a felle dogge lyke er þai
þat berkes and bytes ay when he may.

    After Dedeyne þat es oft sene
Comes Missayinge, felle and kene,   14280
Als when þe tane with noys and dyn
Missays þe tothir; þat es grete synne.
For Haly Wrytte says, if men it loke,
Als it es wryten in som boke,
þat whaso wille his neghþur banne,   14285
Of Godde weryed es þat man.

Donum Sapiencie   De Mala Lingua
Sanctificetur nomen tuum

And Saynt Paul says þai may noght haue   fo. 85ᵛᵃ
þe kyngryke of Godde and be saue;   *Paulus*
And Salamon says to vndirstande   *Salamon*
þair mouthes er als a potte wellande   14290
þar som hate dropes sprentes out
And skaldes þam þat er aboute.

    After Missayinge comes Reprouynge.
þat es mare synne þan es Bannynge,
Als when men reproues vilaynesly   14295
A man of any defaute of body
Or of any foly or of synne
Or of pouert þat he es inne
Or of þe state of his pouer frendes.
þis es noght Goddis wille bot þe fendes.   14300

    After Reproues commes Manaces
þat mens hertes to grete Ire chaces
So þat mellees bigynnes and were

14274 þa] þe LS, þat R   on] of EL, fra S   14276 Bathe] *om.* R   14277 vnto] to LPRW   14278 ay] *om.* R   14281 Als] And P   14283 For] *om.* R 14285 þat] *om.* R   14286 weryed] wered R   es] is he W   14287 And] *om.* R may] *om.* W   *sidenote om.* L   14288 -ryke] -dom L   Godde] heuene E   14289 to] þus to L   *sidenote om.* L   14291 sprentes] sprynges W   14295 vilaynesly] vilany L 14297 Or] *om.* P   of¹] *om.* R   or²] *om.* LR   of²] of any R   14299 þe] *om.* L 14301 reproues] reproueyng L   manaces] manaunce S, malices R, manace W 14302 chaces] chace W   14303 þat] þase þat L   mellees] chaudemell P   were] weres R

Amange þamself after þair powere.
And þai seese noght in swilk melle   14305
Til þe tane on þe tothir venged be.
    Bot ouer alle þe synnes þat er neuend
Passes a synne þat es þe seuend,
Of whilk þis boke spekes a party.
þat es þe synne of þam namely   14310
þat Discorde rayses and moues
Bytwene twa frendes þat togider luues,
And fordose pees and rayses were
Thurgh þair ille tunges þat þai bere.
And þareof may com mykell skathe   14315
Vnto þamself, and to othir bathe.
Swilk men þat makes swilk debates,
Als Haly Wrytte says, Godde hates.

viij[us]. est Murmur   þe aghtned braunche of þe tung men calles
þe synne of Grochyng þat oft falles   14320
Thurgh som men and wymmen bathe
þat noght dar answer when þai er wrathe.
For oft it falles þat when a man
Es greued, he dar noght answer þan;
Whethir he thurgh Godde or man be   14325
Greued, he hym beres als pryue.
Bot he groches ay pryuely
And momels with þe tethe a party.
    And þarefore þe synne of Grochyng

Donum Sapiencie   De Mala Lingua
Sanctificetur nomen tuum

fo. 85vb   Es sette after þe synne of Stryuyng,   14330
þe whilk es grete and gretly greuande
To þam þat er commonly grochande.

14304 þam-] þer- R   powere] powers R   14305 þai] *om.* R   14306 þe¹] *om.* R
on] of LP   14307 ouer] of L   þe] *om.* R   *sidenote*: Nota E   14309 a party] apertely
ELS   14312 togider] *om.* R   14314 þair] *om.* R   14315 may com] commes P
14316 Vnto] To PRW   to] *om.* R   14317 *sidenote*: Qui seminat discordias inter fratres
ELS   14318 Godde] *adds* gretely L   14319 men calles] is callid R   *sidenote*: 8. W
*viij^{us}.] viij. AE, *adds* ramus L   est] *om.* ES   14320 falles] befalles L, has fallid R
14321 som] *om.* R   men . . . wymmen] *trs. sbs.* S   14322 þat] And S   14323 falles]
falle E   þat] *om.* S   14324 he] *om.* R   14325 or] be or L   14326 als] alle ELS
14327 ay] all L   14331 þe] *om.* R

Godde for þat synne vengeaunce toke
On sere manere, als says þe boke.
   First Godde for þat syn thurgh his myght   14335
Didde þe erthe here open right
To swelghe Abiron and Dathan
þat doun to helle al quyck felle þan.
Also for þis synne þat I neuen
Godde sent a fyre doun fra heuen   14340
þat brynned Chore and of his company
With hym, twa hundreth and fyfty
Of þe grettest þat in Goddis oste was
In wildernes for þat trespas.
   For þis synne þe Iewes had tynt right   14345
þe Lande of Heste þat [Godde] þam hight,
Swa þat of sex hundreth thousand
þat our Lorde, Godde al-weldande,
Had casten fra þe seruage haally
Of þe kyng of Egipt so myghty   14350
And þat he sustayned in wildernes
Fourty wynter and na lesse
With mete of heuen so swete and gode,
þe whilk men calles 'aungels fode',
Nane entred into þe haly lande   14355
Bot twa, als I vnderstande,
þat Caleph and Iosue hight,
Bot dyed for sorow ilka wight.
And alle was for þis synne alane
þat swilk a vengeaunce was tane.   14360
   þis braunche þat þe tung sustaynes,
þat es Grochyng, has twa graynes,
þe whilk in twa partys springes
þat er twa maners of grochinges.

14335 his] om. R   14336 Didde] Gerte L, Made S   here] to P   here open] trs. S
14337 sidenote: Datan et Abyron absorti sunt in inferno ELS   14338 doun] om. R
felle] after helle R   14339 Also] As W   14340 doun] om. R   14341 Chore] om.
(a blank left) ES   of] om. P   14342 hym] in W   14343 Goddis] goddest S
14344 þat] þer R   14345 had] om. R, ar W   14346 Heste] byeste E, beheste LS
*Godde þam] þam was AELS, god has þaim W   hight] beheght L   14349 þe] om. L
14353 and] so R   14357 Caleph] Caleth ES   14359 And] om. R   for] of W   þis]
þat P   14360 a] om. PRW   was] þar wasse LS   14361 þis] þat R
14363 partys] partes SR

Ane es agayne Godde almyghty;   14365
þe tothir es agayne man namely.
    First agayne Godde al-weldande
For many skils men er grochand.
For a man þat es of ille conscience
And has tynt Grace and Pacience,   14370
He wil always thurgh maystry
Be oboun Godde almyghty.

De Mala Lingua

fo. 86ra So þat whatso Godde wil fulfille,
If he it do noght after his wille,
He groches and thinkes Godde dose wrange,   14375
And þan he synges þe fendes sange.
    For als þe Haly Gaste thurgh techynge
Makes haly men in þair hertes synge
þe delytable sange of heuen,
þat es *Deo Gracias* to neuen,   14380
Of al þat Godde dose thurgh his myght
Or whatso he sendes day or nyght;
Right so þe ille gaste, shortly to telle,
Mas his men synge þe sange of helle.
þat es þe hidous sange of Grochyng   14385
þat þe synfull sal ay in helle synge.
þat sange sal last euermare
Amange þam þat dwelles þare.
    Certes, methink swilk men er wode
And proprely foles þat can na gode   14390
þat wil þat Godde þam resouns yhelde
Of þat he dose, in þair yhouthe or elde.
For if he þam sende angre in herte
Or any sekenes or any pouert,

14366 þe tothir] Another W es] *om.* L namely] sothly LP 14368 men er] man is W 14371 -ways] was E, -way R 14373 whatso] *om.* L, what S 14374 it] *om.* W do] *om.* R his] es S 14375 thinkes] *adds* þat LS 14377 For] *om.* R 14378 þair] *om.* R synge] to syng L 14379 delytable] delectabill R 14381 his] *om.* R 14382 þaim þynke in hert þat `itt′ cordes right P -so] *om.* SR 14383 Right] *om.* R ille] wycked L 14384 Mas] Gerres L þe] a L 14385 hidous] *om.* R 14386 ay] *after* helle P, *om.* R 14390 And] Arn W proprely] proper LPS þat] and L 14391 þam] þai R resouns] resoun W 14392 in þair] to þai me in L, in R or] and L 14393 For] *om.* R þam] nane W þam sende] *trs.* LP angre] any anger L 14394 any²] *om.* PRW

Stormes or weders wate or drye,   14395
Fayllyng of fruyt þat men lifs by,
Dere yheres, als falles thurgh chaunce,
Skarsenes of mans sustynaunce;
And if he wille a man riche make
And fra anothir his godes take,   14400
Bot al be done at þaire deuys,
þai say Godde es noght rightwys.

  þan groche þai agayne hym sone
And blames hym for þat he has done;
And what wonder war it þan to se   14405
If Godde of swilk wald venged be
þat fra hym wald take his worshepe,
His wisdome, and his lordeshepe?
þus groches bathe yhung and alde
Agayne Godde, als I haf talde,   14410
And synges þe sange of Grochyng,
When Godde duse oght agayne þair lykyng.

  Agayn man alsswa yhete groches som
And vses þat synne of custom,

De Mala Lingua

Als seruaunts agayne þair lordes duse   14415 fo. 86rb
Or agayne þair maysters thurgh ille vse;
Als maydens agayne þair ladys;
Als childer, þat er noght ay wys,
Agayne þair faders or moders dere;
Als pouer men agayne ryche men here;   14420
Als cherles þat falles in thraldom be
Agayne knyghtes or lordes of fe;
Als lewed men of diuerse states
Agayne clerkes and prelates;
Als men of religyoun,   14425

14395 weders] wordes E   14397 thurgh] þe R   14398 Skarsenes] Skarnes S
14400 godes] gode L   14401 at] after W   14404 he] int. P, om. R   14405 And]
Na L, om. R   what] om. ELS   it] if it L   14406 If] Of L   wald] after Godde P
14407 his] om. R   14412 duse oght] trs. E   oght] om. R   14413 alsswa] om. E
yhete] om. L   14415 lordes] lorde ER   14416 agayne] om. R   ille] all W
14419 þair] þe L   faders or moders] fader or moder L   14420 men^2] om. R
14421 cherles] carles L, clerkes SR   thral-] ?charl- E   be] to be L   14424 and] and
grete P   14425 Als] And W

Bathe frere, munk, and chanoun,
Agayne þair abbottes or priours
Or othir þat er þair gouernours.
In alle þise states, bathe mare and lesse,
þe synne of Grochyng vsed es,   14430
Outhir thurgh wille þat es frawarde—
Forþi þat þam think ful harde
To do þat men biddes þam do,
When þai haf na wille þarto;
Or thurgh Slawenes of hert anely,   14435
Forþi þat þai er dulle and heuy;
Or thurgh Vnsuffraunce agayne skille,
Forþi þat men dose noght þair wille;
Or thurgh Envye and Felony,
For þat men auaunces specially   14440
Som mare þan othir of þe menyhe
þat er of þe same state and degree;
And thurgh many othir resounes
þat of þat synne er ille enchesouns.
ix. est Rebellio   þe neghent braunche of þe ille tung es   14445
Proprely þe synne of Frawardnes.
Ille es þe Grochyng of þis grochers,
Bot yhete es Frawardnes wele wers.
Frawardnes first comes of þe hert,
Bot þe tung it shewes thurgh speche ouerthwert, 14450
For whaso es frawarde thurgh ille wille,
He folwes nouthir resoun ne skille,
Bot he wald þat allekyns thinge
War ay done at his lykynge.
He wald alle men plesed hym þan,   14455

And he wille pay nane othir man.

Donum Sapiencie   De Mala Lingua
Sanctificetur nomen t⟨uum⟩

His hert es harde and contrarius,   fo. 86va
Of whilk Salamon spekes þus
And says þat he ne may for nathinge   *Salamon*
Faylle at þe last of ille endynge.   14460
And als Grochyng of þam þat witte can
Es agayne Godde and agayne man,
Right so swilk hertes þat er harde
Agayne Godde and man er frawarde.

þis synne þat þe tung so sustaynes,   14465
Als I fynde, has four graynes
And departes it in four partys
And ilka party on sere wyse.
þe first es when þe hertes er sturdy
And frawarde and ille-willy   14470
And harde and styf and wil noght bowe
To Goddes counsaylle for to trowe.
Anothir es when þam wantes wille
Goddis commaundements to fulfille.
þe thridde es when þai wille noght ʿmekelyʾ   14475
Thole chastying, als þai er worthy.
þe ferthe es when þai resoun forsake
And wille noght lerynge mekely take.

If any frende þam wille counsaylle
In anythinge þat may þam vaylle   14480
Or shewe þam oght for þair profyte,
þai take it alle in grete dispyte
And wille nathinge do þarby
Bot mare blethely dose þe contrary.

14456 the following running title: tuum] *partly in gutter* A (*similarly following* 14499)
14458 whilk] swylk L   spekes] says W   14459 þat] *om.* R   ne] *om.* LSRW   na-]
om. R   *sidenote: om.* L   14460 þe] *om.* L   14461 als] *om.* R   14462 agayne[2]]
also R   14463 Right] *om.* R   swilk] þe E   14464 and] and agayne P
14467 And . . . it] As I fynd W   partys] partes R   14469 hertes er] hert es LW
sidenote: j. E   14470 And[1]] *om.* R   willy] wyle L, wyly W   14471 and[1, 2]] *om.* R
14472 *line om.* L   To[1]] *om.* R   14473 þam] men P   *sidenote*: ij. E   14475 mekely]
int. A   *sidenote*: iij. E   14477 *sidenote*: iiij. E   14479 þam wille] *trs.* LPSW
14480 þam] *om.* R   vaylle] avayle LPR   14482 it] þat L   alle in] to R
14483–4 *couplet trs.* L   14483 do] do do R   14484 dose] do S

To Goddis counsaylle er þai rebelle;   14485
If men þam counsaylle to saul-hele,
þai wil þarefore do nathinge
Bot make skorne and hethynge.
    Also þai er fraward of hert
And contraryous, of wille ouerthwert   14490
Goddis commaundementes to do,
þe whilk þai er mast halden to.
And swilk assoynes þe fende þam settes,
Outhir of feblenes þat þam lettes,
Or of elde or elles of yhouthe   14495
Or of othir resouns vncouthe.
þarefore þair saul-hele þai do noght,
And þus may þai to helle be broght.
    Also when a man þam wille chasty

Donum Sapiencie   De Mala Lingua
Sanctificetur nomen t⟨uum⟩

fo. 86ᵛᵇ Or snybbe þam wele of þayr foly,   14500
þai it defend and excuse þam þan
With alle þe skilles þat þai can,
So þat þai wille on nane wyse
þair synnes knawe ne þair folyse.
And ay þe mare þat þai excuse   14505
þair folys þat þai oft vse,
þe mare þai encrese here þair synne,
And þe faster þai er bunden þarinne.
    Also when our Lorde Godde almyghty
þam wille bete or chasty,   14510
To þat þai wille noght bousom be,
Bot cunnes hym þarefore grete maugre
And says, 'Maugre haue he or sho
þat me wille greue or elles mysdo!

14486 þam counsaylle] trs. LS   14488 Bot] Bot þareat L   14489 Also] And so S
of] in P   14493 And] om. R   assoynes] asseynes W   14494 of] corr. from in P, þer R
14495–6 couplet trs. L   14495 elles] om. LS   14497 þai do] trs. W
14499–509 lines om. W   14499 Also] And R   þam wille] trs. LS   14500 wele] om.
LR, wyll S   14501 þam] om. R   14502 þe] om. R   14503 nane] nakyn L
14504 ne] and P   14505 ay] om. E   14506 oft] mykell L   14507 encrese]
egrege P   here] om. R   14508 þe] om. R   14509 Also] And swa L   14510 or]
adds þai me wyll L, and R   14511 þat] þat þat W   14514–15 lines trs. L
14514 me wille] trs. W   elles] om. LPRW

Dere Godde', he says, 'what haf I wroght   14515
þat I em þus angred for noght?'
    þis es a grete Frawardenes,
Bot þus duse a fole þat es witteles
So þat þat treacle war to hym
Turnes hym alle to pure venym,   14520
And medecyne þat suld for hele be done
Hastes hym + to þe dede sone.
    Alswa it er som maner of men
þat er of sere wyttes to kenne
þat wille noght knawe gode techinge   14525
Bot ay defendes þair vnderstandynge
And mayntenes a wrange þarewithalle
So þat þai sone in errour falle,
And in fals opynyouns many
And in mysbileue and heresy.   14530
    þe tende braunche of þe ille tung to neuen   *x*[*us*]*. est Blasfemia*
Es Sclaunder of Godde of heuen
Or of his halwes þat men to calles
Or of oght elles þat to þam falles.
    Sclaunderyng of Godde þat hym myspays   14535
Es þis, als Saynt Austyn says:
When men trowes thurgh wrange trowyng
And says of Godde a wrange thinge
þat men suld nouthir trowe ne halde,
Blasfem in clergy þat es called.   14540
þat es Sclaundryng of Godde in Inglys,
þat may be done on many wyse.

De Mala Lingua

    Sclaunderyng of Godde es specially   fo. 87ra

14515 he says] *om.* L   14516 þus angred] *trs.* LW   angred] anger S
14517 þis] þat R   14518 witteles] noght wyse L   14519 þat²] *om.* L
14520 Turnes] Tornned L   alle] *om.* L   pure] pore LSR   14522 *to] vnto A   þe]
om. W   dede] *adds* full R   14523 it] ȝit R   14524 of sere] *trs.* E   14525 gode]
godes SR, for no W   14527 a] ay P, *om.* R   14528 sone] *om.* W   14530 And¹]
om. R   in] to W   -bileue] -beleues L   and²] and in LPS   14531 þe²] *om.* RW
sidenote: De blasphemia ELS, x. W   *x^us.] x. A   14532 sclaunder] slaunderynge PRW
14533 Or] *om.* RW   14534 elles] *om.* L   þam] godde P   14535 Sclaunderyng]
Sclaunder L   hym myspays] he mysprays W   14536 *sidenote*: Augustinus ES
14537 thurgh] *int.* P, be R   trowyng] *partly in gutter* A   14541 sclaundryng] sclaunder
LP   14542 many] many sere S   14543 Sclaunderyng] Sclaunder LP

When wrange es sayde of God almyghty
Or of any halwes in heuen
þat men suld in Goddis worshep neuen,   14545
Or spekes by wrange auysement
Agayne Halykirkes sacrament,
Als dose men of mysbyleue
For thing þat may auaylle or greue.   14550
Whethir it be for Couatyse
Of wynnynge þat es vnskilwyse,
Als som dose þat er charmers
And witches, þat er als ille or wers;
Or when þai say oght thurgh Despyte   14555
Or thurgh Ire þat kyndels in hert tyte,
Als þis swerers duse þat vylaynesly
Dispyses Ihesu Crystes body
And so vilaynesly thurgh athe-swerand
Missays of Godde al-weldande   14560
And of his blissed moder dere
þat it es an hidous thinge to here.
þai er als wode hundes þat gnawes
And bytes and þair lorde noght knawes.
    þis es a synne þat Godde almyghty   14565
Punyst somtyme al openly,
Als I haf spoken byfore and sayde
Of þe wicked Iues þat Godde myspayd.
    Of þis synne says Godde in þe godspell
On þis manere, als I wille telle,   14570
þat it sal neuer forgyuen be
In þis werlde þat we here se
Ne in þe tothir þat es comande.
þat es þus to vnderstande
þat vnnethes sal it so bifalle   14575
þat it sal be forgyuen alle,

14545 halwes] halow P   14546 worshep] name R   14547 spekes] speke L
14550 thing] þat R   þat may] int. P, þat þai m may W   14551 for] thurgh ELS
14552 Of] Or ELS, On W   14553 som] some mene E   14554 als] om. L   als . . .
or] wele P   14555 thurgh] be R   sidenote: Nota bene E   14557 þis] om. L, þe P
vylaynesly] vilany L, vylanly W   14559 vilaynesly] vylanly W   thurgh] be R
14560 of] om. LPS   14561 of] om. LS   14562 an] om. RW   14563 als] as þe W
gnawes] knawes S   14566 al] fore all L, om. RW   14568 Iues] om. L
14573 comande] comavnde S   14575 so] om. S   bifalle] fall PRW

For it es agayne þe Haly Gast,
And swilk a synne men suld drede 'mast'.
And Godde says, 'Whaso thurgh ille wille
Agayne þe Haly Gast dose ille,   14580
þat synne sal neuer forgyuen be
Here, ne in þe tothir werlde to se'.

   Bot yhete it es na synne þat es done
þat ne Godde wille forgif it sone,

De Sobrietate et Temperancia

If a man hym wille repent   14585 fo. 87rb
And mekely com til amendement.
Bot vnnethes any man bigynnes
To repent hym þat swa synnes,
Namely agayne þe Haly Gast;
þarefore men aght to charge þat syn mast.   14590
   Now haf I talde yhow, als I couthe,
Specially of þe synne of þe mouthe,
And first of þe synne þat men calles
Glotony þat to þe throte falles
And sethen, on þe tothir party,   14595
Of þe Wyck Tung þat es þarby,
And of ten braunches þat of it springes
And of þe leefs þat on þam hynges.
þat es þe vyces and þe synnes
þat of þe Ille Tung first bygynnes.   14600
   Bot bathe Glotony and Wicked Sawes
þe Gift of Wisdom haly drawes
Out of þe hert and þareinne settes
A vertu þat swilk synne ay lettes.
þat es þe vertu of Sobrenes   14605
And of Temperaunce þat nedefull es.

14576 *line om.* L   14578 mast] *int.* A   *sidenote*: Peccatum contra spiritum sanctum ES   14579–82 *lines om.* W   14579 And] *om.* R   14582 in] *om.* S   þe] *om.* R 14583 yhete] *om.* LW   14584 ne] *om.* LS   ne Godde] *trs.* PRW   14585 If] If þat L hym wille] *trs.* R   wille] *adds* hym L   14587 any] a PRW   14590 men aght] *trs.* P þat syn] it R   14592 þe²] *om.* R   14593 of] *om.* P   þe] *om.* R   14595 on] of SW 14596 wyck] wyckede ELSRW   14597 And of] Of þe R   it] þai m E   14598 And of] þat on R   on] of R   14599 þat es] þase er L, þat er R   þe¹] *om.* R 14600 tung] *add* þat (*int.* S) ES   14601 Bot bathe] Bathe of L   bathe] *om.* R 14602 haly] *adds* oute L   *sidenote*: Donum consilij L   14604 ay] *om.* R 14606 -full] *om.* R

De Sobrietate et Temperancia

Sobrenes and Attemperaunce
Es a vertu agayne alle chaunce
Of outrage, namely in alle thing
þat falles vnto a mans lifynge.   14610
þe whilk may noght in þe hert com
Withouten þe Gift of Wisdom.
   þis Gift of Wisdome es þe mast
And þe heghest of þe Haly Gast
And þe heghest to purchace,   14615
And þat es a speciall grace
þat þe Haly Gast to þam gifs
þat in Contemplacioun lifs,
Thurgh whilk þe hert es fulfilled namly
Of þe brynnand luf of God almyghty.   14620
So þat it sekes noght thurgh langyng
Ne desyres here nane othir thinge

Donum Sapiencie   De Sobrietate et
Temperancia   Sanctificetur nomen tuum

fo. 87ᵛᵃ Bot anely Godde to taste and se
And hym to haue and with hym be.
þis es þe heght of Perfeccioun   14625
And þe ende of Contemplacioun.
   þe haly Gift of Vnderstandyng,
Of whilk I haf sayde byfore sumthyng,
Makes þe hert to knawe Godde right
And gastly thinges thurgh gastly sight.   14630
Bot þe Gift of Wisdom, þat es mast,
Mas it to knawe and to fele and tast.
For Wisdom es nane othir thinge
Bot a swete sauory knawynge,

14606a *marg.* ESL, *om.* PW, *as in-column heading* R   14607 at-] *om.* LPRW
14609 in] of R   14610 vnto] to PRW   a] *om.* W   14611 þe²] *om.* RW
14613 þis] þe L   *sidenote:* Donum sapiencie L   14616 And] *om.* L   14617 gifs]
gyfe S   14618 lifs] lyffnes R   14619 ful-] *om.* R   14620 brynnand] *om.* R
14621 sekes] seke L   thurgh] no W   14622 desyres] desyre L   14623 anely
Godde] *trs.* P   14624 And] *om.* R   be] to be PRW   14625 heght] heigh L
14626 þe] *om.* L   14627 gift] gaste LS   14628 sayde byfore] *trs.* P   sayde] *om.* W
14629 Makes] Mekes, þat makes L   14632 knawe . . . fele] fele knaw L, knawe fele R
to²] *om.* PS   and²] and to W   14634 sauory] sauoure E

þat es to say þat sauoures wele 14635
þat þe hert with grete delyte may fele.
Forwhy a man knawes better þe wyne,
If it be right gode and fyne,
When he it drynkes and tastes right,
þan he þat noght knawes it bot by sight. 14640
   Many philosophers couthe knawe
Godde thurgh þe creatures þat þai sawe,
Als it war thurgh a mirour;
Bot of hym þai had na right sauour.
þai sawe þare thurgh Vnderstandyng 14645
And thurgh Resoun, withouten fayllyng,
His beaute, his bounte, and his myght
And his wisdom thurgh þair sight
Of þe creatures þat Godde wroght,
So fayre and so gode, þat first war noght, 14650
And so wele war ordayned thurgh skille
To our bihoue after his wille.
   Wharefore þai knewe wele his myght
Thurgh kyndely way and symple sight
Of Resoun and Vnderstandynge, 14655
Thurgh whilk þai hadde anely knawyng.
Bot of þe luf of Godde ne feled þai noght
Thurgh taste ne thurgh deuocioun soght.
   Right so it er som Crystend men,
Als wele lered als lawed to kenne, 14660
þat knawes Godde wele thurgh Haly Writte
And thurgh Trouth, als þai vnderstand it.
Bot forþi þat þai haue withinne
þe taste al englaymed thurgh synne,

14636 grete] om. PR   14637 better] om. E þe] om. R   14638 right] om. R
14639 it] om. P   14640 it] adds noght, om. SR   14642 þe] om. LW þai] þai
neuer L   14643 war] om. W   14645 thurgh] adds ryght L   14647 his[2,3]] om. R
14648 þair] þat R   14649 þe] þaa L   14650 so[2]] om. R   14651 And] om. R
thurgh] phrs. added later P, om. R   14653 wele] om. R   14655 Of] Or P and] and
of LSR   14656 anely] any W   14657 Bot] om. R ne] om. LPR   14658 thurgh]
om. R soght] wroght W   14659 Right] om. R it] ȝit SR Crystend] cristene
ELPSRW   14661 wele] om. ELSR thurgh] þe R   14662 thurgh] om. R
14663 þat] om. R   14664 al] of W thurgh] wyth S

Donum Sapiencie   De Sobrietate et
Temperancia   Sanctificetur nomen tuum

fo. 87vb þai may na mare of Godde fele,   14665
Na of his luf þat sauours so wele,
þan þe seke man may fele sauour
In gode mete or in gode lycour.

þis Gift of Wisdom so gracius
þat þe Haly Gaste gyues vs   14670
Parfytely clenses þe hert withinne
And mas it clene of alle filth of synne
And liftes þe spirite so of a man
þat he it ioynes fast to Godde þan
Thurgh a luf þat es hertely tane   14675
So þat with Godde it es al ane.

þare he hym fedes wele and greses;
þare he hym sustaynes and eses;
þare he delytes hym and hym kepes;
And þare he ligges, restes, and slepes.   14680
þare forgetes he alle werldely thynges
And his trauaylles and his yhernynges
þat er flesshely and also erthely,
And alle hymself onence his body.
So þat he thinkes on nathing elles   14685
Bot on thinge on whilk his luf dwelles,
þat es anely on Godde of heuen
þat es his maste comforte to neuen.

þe last degree and þe heghest þis es
Of þe steghe of Parfytenes   14690
þat Iacob sawe with gastly eghe,
þe whilk reched to heuen so heghe,
þar aungels vppe and doun went,
Als Godde almyghty had þam sent.
þe degrees of þis steghe to heuen   14695

14666 so] *om.* R   14667 man] *om.* P   may fele] feles R   14668 or] *om.* R
14671 Parfytely] Parfytnes W   14672 filth of] *om.* R   of²] and PS   14674 it
ioynes] *trs.* R   fast] *after* Godde P   14676 þat with] *trs.* E   14679 delytes hym]
trs. R   hym] *om.* P   14682 And] *om.* R   trauaylles] trauayle W   14684 alle] *om.* W
his] þe L   14686 on²] *om.* L, of R   luf] ?lend W   14687 on] of LPR
14688 his] *om.* S   14690 *sidenote*: Vidit Iacob scalam ELS, Iacob W   14692 þe]
om. R   14694 sent] doun sent L

Er þe Giftes of þe Haly Gast seuen,
þat mas þe bandes of synne be broken,
Of whilk I haf bifore spoken.
By seuen degrees, als þe boke telles,
Clymbes vppe þe gode aungels.   14700
þat er þa, als clerkes redes,
þat aungels lyf in erthe ledes,
In clennes and thurgh gode lifynge
And has þe hertes in heuen thurgh yhernyng,
When þai wende here ay profytande,   14705
Fra vertu to vertu vp clymmande
Vntill þai Godde appertly se

De Sobrietate et Temperancia

Thurgh luf in parfyte Charyte.   fo. 88ra
  Bot when þai er clommen so heghe
Vntill þe heghest degre of þe steghe,   14710
þan suld þai in þat Perfeccioun
Somtyme thurgh Mekenes cum doun.
For þe mare þat a man parfyte es,
þe mare he has of Mekenes;
And þe mare þat he es in Charyte,   14715
þe lesse prys by hymseluen settes he.
Wharefore men says þat prouerbes knawes
þat 'He þat best es, mast hym lawes'.
  Wharefore he þat es parfyte and clene
Suld be als a tree þat es grene   14720
þat on ilk syde es charged wele
With fayre fruyte and gode to fele.
And þe mare þat 'it' es, als men trowes,
Charged with fruyt, þe mare it bowes.
  On othir wyse men may vnderstande   14725
þat þe aungels er doun comande.

14697 bandes] band R   be] *om.* L   14698 haf] haue of L   14701 als] als 'þes' P 14703 thurgh] in PR   14704 þe] þair PS   hertes] hert L   thurgh] *om.* R   yhernyng] *partly in gutter* A   14705 wende] went L, wynd W   ay] *om.* W   14707 Godde] *om.* L   14708 in] and ES   14709 er clommen] clymbe R   14712 cum doun] *trs.* R   14713 For] *om.* R   a] *om.* W   parfyte] *after* mare P   *sidenote:* Nota bene (*om.* S) ES   14714 has] nede (*canc. later*) P   14715 þat] *om.* SR   es] has W 14716 þe] *om.* S   prys] *om.* R   14717 þat] þe W   knawes] kennes R   *sidenote:* Prouerbium E   14720 grene] sene L   14723 þat] þat þat P   it] *int.* A   als] *om.* P 14724 þe] and þe P, *om.* R

Forwhy men þat aungels lyf ledes
Here in erthe thurgh haly dedes,
When þai er clommen thurgh deuocioun
In þe heghe degre of Contemplacioun   14730
þar þe Gift of Wisdom wones right,
þat es ioynt to Godde ful of myght
So þat þay forgete here clene
Al þat vnder Godde es sene,
For þat swetenes þat sauours wele,   14735
þat þe hert may tast and fele
þat es so rauyst in Godde almyghty
þat passes alle othir delyces haally.
Fra þat heghe Contemplacioun
Byhoues oftsythe com doun,   14740
And fra þat swetenes and þat rest
And þat delyte þat þam think best—
þe whilk þai fele of þe pappes swete
Of comfort, when þai with þam mete,
þat Godde to þam luflily bedes   14745
And þam gifs at souke and fedes
In swilk a Lyf Contemplatyf—
Vntill þe werkes of Actyue Lyf,

De Sobrietate et Temperancia

fo. 88rb   Of whilk I haue spoken bifore,
þat parfyte men of gode memor   14750
Suld haue vnderstandyng þarby
For þair awen profyte gastly.
    Anothir resoun yhete þare es,
Als þe boke beres wyttenes,
Thurgh whilk þam bihoues cum doun   14755
Of þat degre of Contemplacioun,
þar þe Gast of Wisdom dwelles,

14727 -why] om. R   lyf] lyf here R   14728 Here] Er LW   14729 er] om. R
clommen] commen L   thurgh] adds holy S   14730 heghe] heghest L   14732 ful]
om. R   14734 es] in W   14737 so] om. S   14738 delyces] delites LPW
14740 oftsythe] oftesythes L, hym oftsithes P   14741 And¹] om. R   14743 þe¹]
om. R   pappes] pappe L   14744 Of] For W   14745 luflily] lufly ELSR, luffully W
14746 And¹] om. R   at] a P   14747 swilk] whilk R   14748 þe] om. R   werkes]
life P   14749 haue] adds of L   14750 þat] þare ELPSW   14751–2 couplet
om. W   14751 Suld] Sall L   14755 Thurgh] adds þe L

Als þe boke bifore right telles.
For þe corrupcioun of þe flesche
þat es so tender and so nesshe   14760
So freyll es, þat þe spiryte
þat yhernes after gastly delyte
Ne may noght, als þis clerkes can telle,
In þis dedely lyf lange dwelle
In so heghe state and degree,   14765
Als of Contemplacioun may be,
And þare fele so grete swetenes.
þat passes alle þe delyte þat es
In þis werlde þat men may fele,
Als men wate þat has proued wele.   14770
    Forwhy þe flesshe of þe body
Es so contraryus and so heuy
þat it drawes þe gast oft to ille,
Whethir it wille or it noght wille.
And þarefore þis grete swetenes   14775
þat so gode and so delicious es,
þe whilk þe hert contemplatyf
Feles here in þis dedely lyf
Thurgh þe haly Gift of Wisdom
þat mas men gode, meke, and bouxsom,   14780
Ne es nathinge bot a lytell tast
Thurgh whilk men feles þe sauour mast
Of Godde þat es so swete and soft.
Als men dose þat tastes oft
þe gode wyne by þe sauour   14785
Ar þai ful draght drynk of þat likour.
    Bot when men comes in þe grete tauerne
þat men heres þis haly men yherne,
þar þe tunnes er ful of blissed drynk

14758 right] *om.* R   14759 For þe] Fra L   14761 freyll] frely W   þe] *om.* SW
14763 Ne] *om.* R   14768 þe] *om.* SRW   delyte] delytes E, delices LS   14770 has]
is W   has proued] *trs.* P   14771 þe¹] *om.* R   *sidenote:* Nota E   14772 so¹] *om.* W
14773 ille] telle W   14774 it²] *om.* RW   wille] well W   14776 so²] *om.* LSRW
14778 þis] þe P   14779 haly] *om.* P   gift] gaste EW   14780 men] *om.* L   men
gode] *trs.* S   meke] *om.* LR, and meke W   14781 Ne] þat L, It SR   na-] *om.* W
14782 þe sauour] *om.* R   14783-4 *couplet om.* W   14783 so] *om.* EP   14786 ful
draght] forthe draghe L   þat] þe RW   14787 Bot] *om.* R   þe] *om.* L   grete] *om.* W
14788 þis] *om.* PRW   14789 of] of þe P

Donum Sapiencie Temperancia   De Sobrietate et Sanctificetur nomen tuum

fo. 88ᵛᵃ þat es mare swete þan herte may think.   14790
þat es þe blisse withouten ende
To whilk we hope þat we sal wende,
þar þe Godde of luf, of ioy, and peese
And of solace þat neuer sal seese
So redy sal be til alle his   14795
þat þai sal alle be filled with blisse,
When alle þair yhernynges, mare and lesse,
Sal be fulfilled with swetenes.
Als men may fynde in þe sauter boke
In som stede wryten, whaso wil loke,   14800
When Godde sal do com on his frendes
A floode of pees þat neuer endes.
þus þe prophete appertely says,
Whase wordes er mykell to prayse.
    Wharefore þai sal drynk so fast   14805
Of þat pees þat euer sal last
þat þai sal drunken be of þat flode
þat es so delycious and so gode.
Of þis blissefull drunkennes
þat ful of peese and of ioy es,   14810
Dauid Spekes Dauid on þis wyse
Of þe blisse of Paradyse
And says, 'Lorde, alle sal þai be
Drunken of þe grete plente
þat in þi hous es so gode   14815
And þa þat filled er of þe flode
Of þi delyte þat swete bihoues be,
For þe welle of lyf es with þe'.

14790 mare swete] swetter R may] cane ELS 14792 þat] om. L þat we sal] to P, for to R 14793 þe] om. PR of¹] om. S of¹ . . . ioy] trs. phrs. R of²] and E 14794 seese] lese L 14795 be] he R til] vnto LS 14796 filled] fullfylled L with] of S 14797–8 couplet om. W 14797 alle] om. R -nynges] -nyng LSR 14798 with] of E 14799 Als] For als L fynde] se L 14800 In . . . stede] Fynde L wryten] om. PR wil] will it R 14801 do] gar P 14807 flode] blode EL 14808 so²] om. LPRW then repeats 14805–6 W 14810 ful] sa full L peese] peces W of²] om. ELR 14811 on] in W sidenote: om. L, in W 14814 Drunken] Dronnkende L of] on S 14816 þe] þat L, thy P 14817 þi] þe LS, þis R 14818 welle] whele E

þis es þe welle of lyf endeles
þat euermare springand es.   14820
þar neuer es nyght, bot euer day
þat es Godde hymself þat lastes ay
And þat es þe welle of lyf so heghe
þat neuermare may faylle ne dieghe,
Of whilk springes and rynnes clene   14825
On alle þe halwes þat er sene
In Paradyse and þat sal be
A blisseful flode of grete plente,
Of ioy and delyte and pees
And of rest þat neuer sal sees,   14830
So grete þat al þat drynkes of þis
Sal be drunken of ioy and blisse.

Donum Sapiencie   De Sobrietate et
Temperancia   Sanctificetur nomen tuum

þis es þe pees and þe blissedhede   fo. 88vb
þat parfyte men sal haf to mede
In þe werlde þat es to com   14835
Thurgh þe heghe Gift of Wisdom.
For whilk pees to haue and fele
Men suld sobrely lif and wele
In þis werlde, whoso witte can,
Als Saynt Austyn says, þe haly man.   14840
For nane may drynk þat has threst
Of þis ryuere of pees and rest
Ne nathynge þareof taste ne fele,
Bot þa þat kepes Sobrenes wele.
þis es þe vertu þat synne lettes   14845
þe whilk þe Gift of Wisdom settes
In þe herte agayne Glotony
þat som men vses ouercomonly.

14819 þis] þat S   14821 þar] þat LS   euer] euer is W   14823 And] om. R
of] of þe P   14824 -mare] om. LSR   ne dieghe] bote aye (euer L) dreghe ELS, ne
seghe W   14825 Of] om. R   14826 halwes] halfs L, halues R   14832 drunken]
drunkenede P   and] of R   14833 pees] blys R   14836 heghe] þe (om. R) hegh after
of LR   14837 and] to R   14838 and] om. R   14840 þe] þat L   sidenote:
Augustinus ELPS   14841 nane may] may man R   14843 Ne¹] om. R   ne²] and R
14845 synne] synnes P   14846 þe¹] om. SR   14848 men] om. R   vses] hauntes L
ouer-] om. W

For Wisdome teches vs Sobrenes,
Als Salamon says and als proued es.   14850
    Sobrenes may be a tree called
þat ful precious es to bihalde,
For it kepes þe hele specially
Bathe of þe saul and of þe body,
Als men may fynde in Haly Writte,   14855
Whoso rightly lokes it.
    Of Glotony and of outrage
In etyng and drynkyng thurgh vsage
Comes many manere of sekenes
And oft þe dede þat harder es.   14860
Forwhy thurgh ouermykell etyng
Or thurgh ouermykell drynkynge
Many dyes al sodaynely tane,
And so þai er þair awen bane,
Right als þe fisshe þat es vncouthe   14865
Es tane with þe morsell in þe mouthe.
    þis vertu men suld kepe right
Ouer alle thinge, bathe day and nyght,
For þe godes þat it ay dose
To hym þat wille it kepe and vse.   14870
    First Sobrenes at þe bigynnyng
Kepes, to Skille and Vnderstandyng,
þair fraunchis thurgh skilful vse
þat drunkennes oftsythe forduse.
For he þat es drunken es so tane   14875

De Sobrietate et Temperancia

fo. 89ra With wyne or ale þat skille has he nane,
Bot leses thurgh outrage of drynkyng
Bathe Resoun and Vnderstandyng;

14849 teches vs] *trs.* P, *adds* to kepe L   14850 and] þat R   als²] *om.* LSR
14851 *sidenote:* Salamon ELS   14852 bi-] *om.* L   14853 For] Bot R   *sidenote:*
Sobrietas ES   14854 þe¹] *om.* R   þe²] *om.* SR   14856 rightly] *om.* L, rightwisly P,
right R   14858 In] And L   and drynkyng] drynken R   14859 manere] maners L
14861 Forwhy] *om.* R   14862 thurgh] *om.* R   14863 al] *om.* LR   14864 And]
om. R   14865 Right] *om.* R   fisshe] flesshe W   14866 þe¹,²] *om.* R
14868 bathe] *om.* R   14869 godes] gode L   14871 *sidenote:* j. bonum E, jᵐ. S
14872 to] þe LS   14873 vse] -nes L   14874 -sythe] -sythes LS, *adds* and P, oft R
14875 For] *om.* R   es²] he es EL   14876 þat] *om.* R   has he] *trs.* PW (he *int.* P)
14877 leses] loses ELPS   of] *om.* PR   14878 Bathe] *om.* R

And alle his wittes hym bihoues tyne,
Als he þat es drunkend in wyne.   14880
And when he wenes, als he thinkes,
Drynk þe wyne, þe wyne hym drynkes.
    þe secund gode þat Sobrenes
Dose til a man namely þis es:
It helpes and delyuers hym haally   14885
Of þe vyle thralledom of þe bely.
For þise glotouns þat outrage taas
Of þair bely þair godde maas
þat þai honure, and na godde elles,
Als Saynt Paull þe apostell telles.   14890
Certes, þat man gretly reuyles
Hymself, and foully his saul fyles
þat serues with grete bisynes
Swilk a lorde als his bely es,
Fra whilk lorde nathing may com   14895
Bot stynk and filth þat es wlatsom.
    Bot Sobrenes a man may kepe
In right state and in his lordeshepe.
For þe gast suld ay haue maystry
And be lorde and sire of þe body,   14900
And þe body suld serue þe gast.
þis order kepes Sobrenes mast.
    þe thridde gode þat Sobrenes dose
Es þis, whoso wille it vse:
It kepes wele þe yhate of þe castelle   14905
Agayne þe oste of þe fende of helle.
þat es þe mouthe þat standes ouerthwert,
þe whilk es mayster-yhate of þe hert

14879 And] om. R   wittes] wytte ELPS (over eras. P)   14880 drunkend] drunken
LPSRW   14881 And] om. R   14882 þe'] of þe L   14883 þat] of R   sidenote: ij.
(ij^m. S) bonum ES   14885 and] hym and L   hym] om. S   haally] namely PW
14886 þe²] om. R   bely] body PSRW   14887 For] om. R   sidenote: De (Ve S) illis
quorum deus venter est ES   14888 bely] belyes L   godde] goddes L   14889 and]
þai and L   14890 sidenote: Paulus ELS   14892 foully] foule PW   his] þe W
14895 lorde nathing] na good R   14896 wlatsom] fulsome R   14897 may] adds
bryng and L   14898 and] om. R   his] om. EL   14899 For] om. R   haue] adds þe W
14900 and sire] om. R   of] abouen L   þe] his P   14901–2 couplet om. W
14902 order] vndir R   14903 sidenote: iij. (iij^m. S) bonum ESW   14905 wele] om. R
yhate] yhates L   14906 þe fende] om. R   þe² ... helle] fendes fell P   14907 ouer-]
om. R   14908 þe'] om. R

þat þe fende, þat ay trauaylles
With al his myght, ful oft assaylles.   14910
   Bot Sobrenes so weres þe yhate
þat he may noght entre by na gate.
And when þe yhate of þe mouthe of man
Es wyde open and vnkeped, þan
þe oste of synnes by þat party   14915
Entres withinne þan ful lightly
And fightes þare with othir synnes.

De Sobrietate et Temperancia

fo. 89rb þan gase þe tung and noght blynnes.
   Bot whaso has þis vertu haally,
He has lordeshepe of his body   14920
And may it mayster at his wille
And lede, bathe with Resoun and Skille.
Als men may an horse maystry
With a brydell in þe mouthe namely.
   Sobrenes at þe first bataylle   14925
In þe oste of vertus thurgh trauaylle
Othir vertus kepes and weres
Agayne synnes þat þe saul deres.
Wharefore þe fende þat first ille couthe
First tempted Godde onence þe mouthe.   14930
He badde hym make brede of a stane,
If he war Goddis Sone alane.
He assaylled also þe first man
Onence þe mouthe and ouercome him þan,
For he opend hym sone þe yhate   14935
Of þe castelle and gaf hym gate.
For he assented to þat fondynge
Withouten any agaynestandynge.

14910 ful] om. PRW   14911 weres] ʒhemes E   14912 na] þe P   14913 And
when] When þat R   þe²] om. R   of²] of a L, of þe W   14914 wyde] om. R   open]
oppende LR   sidenote: Nota ES   14915 synnes] synne L   14916 ful] om. R
14918 and] it R   14919 has] om. R   14920 He has] Haue L, adds þe W
14921 at] all at L   his] om. R   14922 lede] add itt ELPS   bathe] om. R   and²] and
wyth LS   14923–4 couplet om. W   14924 namely] anely P   14926 thurgh] be R
14929 first ille] all synne S   sidenote: Nota E   14930 First tempted] Spired R
14931 a] om. LW   14934 þe] om. P   14935 opend] opens E   14936 gate]
state W   14938 agayne-] gayne- LP

Thre thinges namely and na lesse
Teches vs to kepe wele Sobrenes.   14940
Ane es kynde to lede with skille;
Anothir es Haly Writte to fulfille;
þe thridde es ilka creature right
þat Godde has made thurgh his myght.

First kynde vs teches wele to kepe   14945
Sobrenes to Goddis worshepe.
For amange alle bestes man kyndely
Has leste mouthe after his body.
Also man has in comon sight
Othir lyms þat er doubled right,   14950
Als twa eres for to here
And twa eghen of sight clere
þat ledes þe wittes þat he has tane,
Bot he has na mouthe bot ane.
Yhete teches kynde vs, als methink,   14955
þat we suld in mesure ete and drynk,
For kynde has so lytell vphaldyng
þat outrage may it sone doun bryng.
Haly Wrytte þat ay certayne es

Donum Sapiencie   De Sobrietate et
Temperancia   Sanctificetur nomen tuum

Teches vs to kepe Sobrenes   14960 fo. 89va
In many maners, als falles to be,
And thurgh ensaumples, als men may se
þat can it vnderstande in bokes
And oft þe lyues of haly men lokes.

Alsswa vs teches ilka creature   14965
To kepe Sobrenes and Mesure,
For in ilka creature Godde luues

14939 namely] anely P   *sidenote*: iiij. E   14940 Teches] Kennes L   wele] *om*. R
14942 Writte] *om*. E   14944 his] *om*. R   14945 *sidenote*: j. E   14947 For] *om*. R
14948 leste] hys L, left? W   14949 man] mene ELS   14950 þat] þan R   doubled]
dobbell SW   14951 for] wythall L   14952 of] to P   14955 me-] we R
14956 in] with P   *sidenote*: ij. E   14957 For] *om*. R   14959 ay] *om*. R   certayne]
sothe L   *sidenote*: Sacra scriptura ELS   14960 Teches] Kennes L   14962 And]
om. P   ensaumples] ensample PW   men may] we R   14963 it] *om*. E   14964 oft
þe] *om*. R   lyues] lyfe ELSW, lyfe (*corr later*) P   14967–8 *couplet om*. W
14967 For] *om*. R

Right Mesure, als Salamon proues;
For Sobrenes es noght elles
Bot to kepe right Mesure, als he telles.   14970
þat es þe mydward bitwene
Ouermykell and ouerlyttell sene
After þat þat Resoun and Skille
Lightes thurgh grace and teches þe wille.
Forwhy oft þus falles on som party   14975
Onence þe godes þat er werldely
þat thinge þat ouermykell semes
To ane es ouerlytell, als men demes
Til anothir, swilk may he be.
þus falles oft, als we may se,   14980
þat þat to a p'o´ure es outrage
To a ryche war ouerlytell wage.
Bot Sobrenes and Attemperaunce
Settes Mesure agayne ilka chaunce.
    Also on anothir party   14985
In þe godes þat er gastly,
Als in fastyng and in wakyng
And in harde disciplynes takynge,
And in othir werkes of vertus
þat for God and for þe saul men duse   14990
Settes Temperaunce and Sobrenes
Right Mesure als resoun es.
    þis vertu þat es profytable
Haldes Mesure ay resonable,
Noght anely in etyng and drynking   14995
Bot in vsyng of alle othir thing,
And namely of alle gode vertus
þat parfyte men here wille vse,
Als Saynt Bernard in som stede says,
þat we here þis clerkes oft prays.   15000

14968 Right] adds so R   sidenote: Salamon ELS   14970 to] om. LR   right] om.
RW   14973 þat²] om. L   14974 and] om. R   þe] om. E   14975 -why] om. R
þus] so W   14977 thinge] om. R   14979 Til] And to L   14980 oft] it oft L
14981 poure] o int. A   14982 war] is R   14983 at-] om. LPRW   14986 godes]
dedes L   14987 in²] om. R   14989 werkes] maner L   14990 for²] om. RW   þe]
þair W   14991–2 couplet om. W   14994 resonable] conable P   14995 and] and
in W   14997 And] om. R   gode] other W   14998 þat] Of L   men] men þat L
here wille] trs. E   14999 Als] And S   som] a R   sidenote: Bernardus ELS
15000 we] we may L   þis clerkes oft] clerkys R, oft þis werkes W   15001 For] om. R

For þis vertu settes ilka thoght
And ilka wille þat es soght

Donum Sapiencie   De Sobrietate et
Temperancia   Sanctificetur nomen tuum

And alle þe wittes of þe body   fo. 89vb
And alle stirynges of þe hert namely
Vnder þe lordeshepe of Resoun right,   15005
Als þe wyse man says þat Tullus hight.
So þat Resoun þat es lightend wele
Thurgh þe Gift of Wisdom for to fele
Haldes in pees and in quert
His lordeshepe of body and hert.   15010
    þis es þe ende and þe intencioun
Of alle vertus thurgh deuocioun:
So þat þe hert and þe body
Be wele ordayned to Godde almyghty;
So þat Godde þat al can ordayne   15015
Anely be louerd and souerayne
On swilk wyse thurgh his dignyte
þat alle in his obedyence be,
Als to þe right kyngedom haally
Of þe saul and of þe body.   15020
And þat mas anely sobre luf
Of Godde, als þis clerkes can pruf,
þat settes þe hert with right Skille
Alle haally in Goddes awen wille.
    Wharefore Saynt Austyn, als men may here,   15025   *Augustinus*
Spekes and says on þis manere,
þat þe vertu of Sobrenes
And of Attemperaunce proprely es
A luf þat kepes itself wele
And haly to Godde, als men may fele,   15030
Withouten any corrupcioun

15002 soght] wroght R   15004 alle] *add* þe ELP   þe] *om.* R   15005 þe
lordeshepe] lordshippes R   15006 *sidenote*: Tullius ELSW   15007 lightend] light W
15008 þe] *om.* R   for] *om.* R   15010 of] in ELS   15017 swilk] whilk P
15018 be] may be L   15019 *line om.* R   Als to] And to L, Also P   þe] *om.* W
15022 þis] *om.* L   15023 hert] hertes W   15024 haally] anely LS   awen] *om.* PR
15025 Whare-] *om.* R   men may] we R   *sidenote*: *in* W   15027 þe] *om.* L
15028 at-] *om.* LPRW   15030 men] we R

And vs drawes fra luf of here doun.
þat es of luf þat comes ouerthwert
Of þis werlde þat trobles þe hert
Of ilka man þat here werldely es.   15035
þat puttes hym to vayne bisynes
And fordose þe knawyng right
Of hymself, and of Godde þe sight,
Right als men sees noght clerely
In trobled water þat es drouy.   15040
   Bot þe luf of Godde þat es clene
Of werldely luf þat here es sene
And of flesshely affeccioun
Wynnes a gastly warysoun

De Sobrietate et Temperancia

fo. 90ra And maas þe hert here wele at eese   15045
And settes it in gode rest and pees.
For it settes þe hert in his awen stede—
þat es in Godde, our alderhede—
þar it may rest and wele fare,
For na rest na pees es bot þare.   15050
Dominus in euangelio   Wharefore our Lorde swete Ihesus
In þe haly godspelle says þus:
'Yhe sal in þis werlde be thrungen fast,
Bot in me yhe sal fynde pees stedefast.'
Augustinus   And Saynt Austyn says, 'Lorde, my hert   15055
Ne may noght be in pees and quert
Til þat it may rest in þe,
þar pees and rest anely bihoues be'.
   Na swilk luf fra erthely thinges
Out of þe myres of þis werlde springes,   15060
Bot out of þe heghe roche of stane—

15032 luf of] þe luf L, luf ofte S, luf R   15033 of] a W   15034 trobles] drobles
E, drofes L   15035 here werldely] *trs.* S   15036 to] in L   vayne] payne W
15039 Right] *om.* R   *sidenote:* Nota S   15040 trobled] drobled EP, drobell L
15044 a gastly] *trs.* W   15046 it] *om.* PW   15047 awen] *om.* R   15048 alder-]
aller- ELRW   15050 na²] ne na L   es] is nott R   15051 swete] *om.* R   *sidenote:*
Euangelium LS   Dominus] *om.* E   15053 thrungen] thurgh'gyn' R   15054 Bot]
om. R   15055 And] *om.* R   *sidenote: in* W, *om.* LP   15056 and] na LPW, in R
15057 Til] Vnto L   þat] *om.* PS   it] I L   in] wyth L   15058 anely bihoues] sall
euer R   15059 erthely] hertly L   15060 þe] *repeats* P, *om.* R   15061 heghe]
om. R

þat es our Lorde Godde alane—
On whilk þe grete citee standes
Of Paradyse oboun alle landes
And Halykirke, þat gode cyte— 15065
þat es Ihesu Cryst blissed be he—
On whilk thurgh trowthe es sette fast
þe strange castels þat ay sal last.
þat er þe haly hertes to fele
Of gode men þat lifs wele. 15070
   Of þis heghe roche comes þe welle
Of parfyte luf in þe herte to dwelle
þat es clensed and clene made
Of þe luf of þis werlde brade.
   þis welle es so clere and bryght 15075
þat þe hert may se thurgh gastly sight
In it, þat es so clere of colour,
And knawe hymself and his creatour,
Right als a man sees thurgh þe ayre
Hymself in a welle clere and fayre. 15080
   On þis welle þe hert it restes
þat after þe luf of Godde thristes
After þe trauaylle of gode werkes.
Als in boke wryten fyndes þis clerkes
þat Ihesu Cryst, Godde almyghty, 15085
When he had gane þat he was wery,

De Sobrietate et Temperancia

He sette hym doun a while to dwelle   fo. 90rb
And rested hym opon a welle,
Opon þe whilk þe nobell hert
þat wille hym kepe in gastly quert 15090
Settes itself and takes his rest

15063 On] Of þe L   þe] om. L   citee] sydes L   15065 þat] þe P   sidenote: Nota E
15066 be he] moght he be L   15067 thurgh] om. R   fast] stedfaste L
15068 castels] castell LRW   15070 Of] þat W   15074 of²] of god in L
15076 thurgh] be R   15077 In it þat es] And yitt þat L   15078 and²] in W
15079 Right] om. R   15080 a] om. L   15081 it] hym L   15082 þat] And L
Godde] adds itt P   15083 of gode] o godes S   15084 boke] a boke þus L, a boke R,
bokes S   wryten] om. LSR   þis] þis grete S, om. PR   15087 sidenote: Nota E
15088 opon a] besyde þe L   15089 þe¹] om. L   15090 hym kepe] trs. R
15091 it-] hym- EL   his] om. R, hyt P

In þe luf of Godde þat es best.
   þis welle es so swete and sauory
þat whaso drynkes þareof blethely
Alle othir swetenes he forgetes   15095
And alle sauours þat þat luf lettes.
   þis welle feles on na manere
Nouthir erthe ne mudde of þis werlde here,
And þarefore it es swete to drynk
And sauory, als þis gode men think.   15100
For euer þe lesse þat a kynde welle
Has of þe erthe sauour and smelle,
þe mare haalsom it es to a man
And wele þe better to drynk þan.
   þis es þe siker welle of Witte   15105
And of Wisdome, als clerkes calles it.
For he þat wil drynk of it wele,
He may knawe and thurgh skille fele
þe sauour and þe swetenes
þat in Godde almyghty es.   15110
And þis es þe souerayne Wytte
Of man here, als þis clerkes proues it:
To knawe his creature and fele
And with alle his hert to luf him wele.
For withouten þis philosophy,   15115
Alle othir witte es noght bot foly.
   þis Witte settes þe Haly Gaste
In þe herte God for to taste,
When he þe Gift of Wisdom bedes
þat þe hert with gastly ioy fedes.   15120
   þis gastly witte, þat comes anely
Of parfyte luf of Godde almyghty,
Maas þe hert so attempree
And so sobre, als it falles to be,

15093 and] and sa L   15096 þat¹] 3hyte E, `yit´ S, om. PW   þat²] þe L
15097 feles] foles R   na] a L   15098 of] on L   15099 And] om. R   es] om. S
15100 gode] om. R   15101 For] om. R   15102 þe] om. L   15103 it] om. W to]
vnto L   a] om. SR   15104 þe] om. LSW   15105-6 couplet om. W
15106 clerkes] mene E   15107 For] om. R   it] þat P   15109 þe²] om. W
15111 And] om. R þe] om. W   15112 Of] Of a L þis] om. L   15114 And] om. R
hert] om. L   15116 Alle] As W noght] om. P   15119-20 couplet om. W
15123 so] to R   15124 als] at W

And specially so wele it brynges   15125
To ryght Mesure in alle thinges,
So þat þe hert, als þis clerkes wate,

Donum Sapiencie   De Sobrietate et
Temperancia   Sanctificetur nomen tuum

þat es broght rightly in þat state   fo. 90ᵛᵃ
Es in rest and pees withouten stryf,
Als pees may be in þis dedely lyf.   15130
    Forwhy in þis werlde na man may
Lif in pees, nyght ne day,
Withouten + turment and fightyng,
Ne withouten bataylle of fondyng
þat Godde sendes thurgh grete luf   15135
His awen knyghtes here to pruf
And forþi þat þai suld cun vse right
þe armes of vertu and cun fight.
For elles may þai noght be talde
Goddis knyghtes, dughty and balde.   15140
    Wharefore men þat to armes tentes
In tyme of pees maas turnamentes.
Bot when þe gode knyght venquid has
þe turnament, away he gaas
And turnes hame and fightes na mare   15145
And at his eese restes hym þare.
    Right so þe gode hert als dose þe knyght.
When it has foghten and venquyd right
þe sharp turnamentes of fondynges
þat men assaylles and to synne brynges,   15150

15125 And] And so S   wele] om. R   brynges] brynge P   15126 in] om. ES
thinges] thynge P   15127 þis] om. R   15128 rightly] ryght W   þat²] þaire L
15129 and] om. R   15130 be] om. R   15131 na man] nane R   sidenote: Nota E
*15133 turment] turnament A, tourmentes W   15134 of] and ELPS
15135 thurgh] for R   15136 here] om. LR   15137-40 lines om. W
15137 And forþi] For R   cun vse] kenne hym L, vse SR   15138 and] and to LR
cun] om. R   15139 For] om. R   15141 Whare-] om. R   þat] þar R
15142 turnamentes] tormentes P   15143 Bot] om. R   venquid] vencude P, venqui'st'
(over eras.) S   15144 turnament] tourment P   away he] and oway L   15145 And¹]
om. R   and²] he R   15147 Right] om. R   als dose þe] of a gode L   sidenote: Nota E
15148 and] om. R   venquyd] vencused P, venquist S   15149 sharp] om. R
turnamentes] tourmentes EPS, turnement R   of] o L, of þe W   fondynges] fandyng S
15150 synne] þe ende L   brynges] bryng S

He comes after to hymself agayne
And hym restes in Godde mast certayne,
þat for nathynge wille hym faylle
Bot comfortes hym after þat trauaylle
So þat he forgetes þare sone   15155
Alle þe trauaylles þat he has done
And thinkes on Godde þat he laytes,
þare fyndes he þat he mast couaytes.

þis es þe fruyt þat es defautles
þat þe tree beres of Sobrenes,   15160
þe whilk, als I haf talde, may com
Anely of þe Gift of Wisdom.

Sobrenes and Attemperaunce
Maas þe hert of clene cuntynaunce,
And es noght elles, when it springes,   15165
Bot kepyng of Mesure in alle thinges.
Bot specially in thinges seuen
Men suld kepe Mesure euen,
þat er seuen degrees and na lesse

Donum Sapiencie   De Sobrietate et
Temperancia   Sanctificetur nomen tuum

fo. 90ᵛᵇ   Of Attemperaunce and Sobrenes.   15170
vij. sunt gradus Sobrietatis   þa er seuen maners of mesures
et Temperancie   þat falles to Crysten creatures,
And namely in seuen thinges to loke,
Als here es wryten in þis boke.

Ane es Mesure in Vndirstandyng   15175
Of þe trouthe bifore alle othir thinge;
Anothir es in Yhernyng and Wille
And in þe appetyte to fulfille,
þat thurgh þe flesshe and þe werld bathe

15152 mast] om. R   15153 hym] om. R   15154 Bot] And W   þat] om. R
15156 -uaylles] -uayll LPRW   15157-8 couplet om. W   15157 laytes] lattes R
15158 þare, he¹] trs. R   he²] om. E   mast] om. R   15159 þis] þat L   es¹] om. R
defautles] fautles RW   15161 þe] om. R   15163 at-] om. LPR   15165 And] It R
elles] om. P   15169 þat] þare L   15170 at-] om. LPRW   15171 þa] þat P
maners] maner P   sidenote om. LP   15173-4 couplet om. (at page boundary) W
15173 in] om. R   seuen thinges] trs. R   15174 es] er L   15175 sidenote: jᵘˢ. gradus
ES, 1. W (and so throughout the next fifteen lines to vijᵘˢ. gradus and 7.)   15176 þe] om. R
15177 es] om. W   in] om. L   15178 in] om. L   15179 þe¹] om. R

Vnto þe saul may oft do skathe.   15180
  þe thridde es in Speche of tung fre
And in wordes whatso þai be;
þe ferthe es in Listenyng with eres
Of othir mens wordes þat charge beres;
þe fift es in Clethyng of sere gyse   15185
And in othir apparaylle of pryse.
  þe sext es Mesure in þe manere
Of Cuntynaunce, of sight and chere,
And in hauyng and in berynge,
Namely of body in alle thinge.   15190
þe seuent es for Hele of þe body
In etynge and drynkynge namely.
  þe first degre þat Mesure es called   *j*^{us}. *gradus*
Es þat a man suld Mesure hald
In þe Vnderstandyng sympilly   15195
Of þe trouthe thurgh symple study
And in alle þe articles of it
Withouten any musyng of Wytte.
Forwhy Mesure he passes þat wille
Thurgh musyng seke any kynde skille   15200
In þat þat es so heghe a thinge
Oboun mans skille and vndirstandynge—
Als mystrowand men dose namely
þat þe trouthe mesures in som party
After þair vndirstandyng mast,   15205
And þat trauaylle of Witte þai wast.
  Bot þai suld mesure after Goddis wille
þair Vnderstandyng and þaire Skille
To þe Mesure of þe trouthe verray,
Als gode Crysten men dose ay.   15210

15180 Vnto] To RW   oft] *om.* R   15181 es] *om.* R   15182 And] *om.* R   in
wordes] ill worde W   15183 in] *om.* R   with] of E   15184 othir] *om.* R   mens]
man P   15185 clethyng] clethynges S   of] on R   15186 apparaylle] parayle L
15187 þe²] *om.* P   15188 and] of R   15189–90 *couplet trs.* L, *couplet om.* W
15189 And¹] *om.* R   15190 of, in] *trs.* S   15191 es] *om.* P   of þe] o L
15193 þat] *om.* W   *sidenote: om.* S, Mensura W   15194 Es þat] *trs.* W   suld mesure]
trs. LS   15195 sympilly] of symply W   15196 symple] *om.* L   15197 þe] *om.* L
15198 musyng] mouyng LR   15199 he] *om.* R   15200 musyng] moueyng LR
seke] sekes S   any] of R, and W   kynde] -kyne EP   15201–2 *couplet om.* W
15201 es] *om.* R   15203 dose] *om.* LR   *sidenote:* Nota E   15207 mesure] *om.* R
Goddis] gode S   wille] *partly in gutter* A   15209 þe¹] *om.* R   þe²] *om.* L

De Sobrietate et Temperancia

fo. 91ʳᵃ Als Saynt Paul says þus by skille,
Paulus 'Be na man mare wys þan right trouthe wille',
Bot lede his Witte thurgh Sobrenes
After þat þe Mesure of þe trouth es
þat Godde has gyuen vs to kepe   15215
To our hele and his worshepe.
Salamon And Salamon to his sone says yhete,
'Swete sone,' he says 'Mesure þi witte'.
þat es to say, als clerkes can se,
þat þou noght of swa self-wytte be   15220
Ne so fitched in þi Surquydry
þat þou ne be bouxsom þarby
For to trowe to al gode counsaylle
þat bathe to lyf and saul may auaylle.
And þat þou leue þi self-wytte and bowe   15225
To þam þat er mare wys þan þow.
And specially thurgh gastly myght
In þe Articles of þe Trouthe right,
Men suld leue þair self-wytte and -wille
And þair self-vnderstandyng and -skille   15230
And putte þam in þe seruage
Of þe Trouthe for mast auauntage,
Paulus Als says Saynt Paul, and noght yhern to se
Resoun kyndely þar nane may be,
Als þis cury`o´us men oft dose   15235
þat of þe Trouthe ouermykill wil muse.
Bot whaso wille his saul saue
And þe blisse of heuen wille haue,

15211 Als] And LSW   þus] *om.* R   *sidenote: om.* E; *add* Non plus sapere quam oportet sapere set sapere ad sobrietatem ELS   15212 na man] nane R   right] *om.* LR   15213 thurgh] with P   15214 þat] *om.* LP   þe¹] *om.* SR   þe²] *om.* SW   15215-16 *couplet om.* W   15216 To] Vnto L   15217 Salamon] *adds* says L   sone] *om.* P   *sidenote: om.* P   15220 swa] *om.* R   swa . . . wytte] twa wittes P   15221 so] *om.* R   þi] *om.* L, þe W   15222 ne] *om.* LS   15223 For] *om.* R   15224 bathe] *om.* R   lyf] body ELS   and] and to R   auaylle] vayle W   15225 þat þou] *om.* R   15228 þe²] *om.* SR   15229 wytte and] *om.* R   15230 þair] *om.* R   self-] *om.* L   15231 þe] *om.* W   15233 and] *om.* R   noght] *om.* ELS   yhern] gernes L, þe hert S   15235 Als] And W   þis] *om.* P   curyous] o *int. later* A   15236 þe] *om.* R   ouermykill wil] *trs.* S   muse] oise R   15237 -so] *om.* R   15238 wille] *om.* W

Hym bihoues after right Trouthe wirke
And trowe als trowes Halykirke.   15240
þe secund degree of Sobrenes   *ij^{us}. gradus*
þat þe secund manere of Mesure es
Es when men right Mesure settes
þat alle manere of outrage lettes
In þe Wille namely of Yhernynge   15245
And in þe appetyte of Likynge.
Wharethurgh men may so ordayne
A bridell to halde þe Wille agayne,
þat es to say þe brydell of Skille,
With whilk men suld lede þe Wille   15250
þat it may noght rynne ouertyte

De Sobrietate et Temperancia

To flesshely yhernynges ne to delyte,   fo. 91rb
Ne to vanytees ne Couatyse
Of þe werlde, þar mast perille lyse.
    Wharefore þe wyse man of grete witte   15255 *Sapiens*
Says þus openly in Haly Writte:
'It es noght inoghe', says he,
'þe couatyse of vanyte
Ne þe yhernyng of þi hert light
Bot þat þou restreyne þi wille right   15260
So þat þou nane wyse it fulfille.'
And þareto gifs he a gode skille.
    Forwhy if þou to þi herte wil do
Al þat it wille and assent þarto,
þou mas grete ioy to þine enemyse   15265
þat er þe fendes þat þe ay spyes.
Als a man dose on þe same manere
þat mas ioy to his aduersere

15239 after] *adds* þe L   right] *om.* R   15240 trowes] does P, trouth W
15241 secund] seuend R   *sidenote: om.* L, 2. W   15245 wille] whylk L   15246 in]
om. W   of] of þai ere S   15247 men] me R   15250 With] *om.* R   lede] wyth L
15252 flesshely] *om.* R   yhernynges] gernyng LR   15253-4 *couplet om.* W
15253 vanytees] vanite P   ne] ne to PR   15254 lyse] es L   15255 Wharefore] *om.* S
15258 þe] In L   15259 Ne] In W   þe] of R   þi] þe LRW   15260 wille] hert R,
hert and þi will W   15261-2 *couplet om.* W   15261 So] *om.* R   þou] þou on ELS
nane] nanekynne L   it] *om.* P   15262 And] *om.* R   15263 to] *om.* L, *after* P   wil]
after þou P   15264 wille] askes L   assent þar-] assentes P   15265 ioy to] vnto L,
ioy S   15266 ay spyes] aspyse LS   15268 -sere] -sary L

Agayne wham he suld fight in felde,
When he to hym wille hym yhelde.   15270
   þat man yheldes hym to þe fende right
Als he þat es ouercommen in fight
þat assentes to flesshely lykynges
Or to any wicked yhernynges.
   þarefore Saynt Petir þat Godde wele luued   15275
Petrus Says þus, als þis clerkes has proued:
'I bidde yhow', he says 'in Goddis name
þat yhe þat er here fer fra hame
Als vncouthe men and pilgrymes,
Kepe yhow wele here als Goddis lymes   15280
Fra yhernynges of flesshe þat ay fightes
Agayne þe saul, bathe days and nyghtes.'
   He þat es pilgryme, als yhe may se,
And commes in a straunge cuntre,
þar many theues and robbours bene,   15285
Als es in many cuntrees sene,
þat pilgrymes þat passes by þe strete
Spyes, and waytes with þam to mete
To robbe þam and fra þam reue
Al þat þai haue and noght þam leue.   15290
He may hym kepe fra þa theues alle
þat he noght in þair handes falle

Donum Sapiencie   **De Sobrietate et**
Temperancia   **Sanctificetur nomen tuum**

fo. 91va þat thinkes and castes with grete study
How he may passe mast sikerly.
   Alle þe gode men of þis werlde here   15295
Er straunge men to proue on þis manere,
For þai er out of þair cuntre.

15270 he] *after* wille R   15273–4 *couplet om.* W   15273 lykynges] lyking S
15274 yhernynges] yerning S   15275 wele] *om.* R   15276 *sidenote: om.* S, *in* W
add Obsecro vos tanquam aduenas et peregrinos abstinere vos a carnalibus desiderijs que
militant aduersus animam (carnem S) ES   15277 he says] *om.* L, he sayd W
15278 þat¹] *om.* R   here] *om.* ELS   15280 wele] *om.* R   15282 days] day R
15283 es] es a E   15285 þar] þat R   many] *om.* L   theues] schrewes W
15286 es] er L   cuntrees] cuntre R   15287 þat¹] *om.* P   15289 þam] þai me to L
15291–4 *lines om.* W   15291 fra] *om.* R   15293 grete] *om.* R   15295 þis] þe
ELS, ys R   15296 men] *om.* R   proue] reproue L

þat es Paradyse þar þai wald be;
þat es þe lande and þe herytage
Of gode men þat flees outrage.   15300
  þai er gode pylgryms, als þe boke telles,
Forwhy þai think here nathing elles
Bot make þair iournes, day and nyght,
Til þai com to þair cuntre right
þar þair right herytage lys.   15305
þat es þe citee of Paradys,
þe whilk Goddis pilgrymes by right ways
Sekes ay here, als Saynt Paul says,   *Paulus*
þat wille noght for werldely auauntage
In þis werlde here haue herytage.   15310
  Swilk pilgrymes þat wille passe sikerly
Puttes þam in gode cumpany
þat ledes þam right, als men may proue,
And sikerly in Trouthe and Luf.
Trouthe to pilgrymes shewes þe way,   15315
And Luf þam beres, nyght and day,
Til þai be broght to þat cuntre
þar þair right herytage suld be,
On whilk þai sette so fast þair thoght
þat þe way þider deres þam noght.   15320
  He þat hym to swilk company gifs
Thar noght drede robbours ne theues
þat waytes þe stretes þar men wendes;
Als I haf tolde, þa er þe fendes
þat robbes and taas alle þa namely   15325
þat has noght with þam gode cumpany,
Als þaas þat thurgh sere fandynges
Fulfilles here þair wicked yhernynges
þat puttes þam in þe fendes handes

15302 -why] *om.* R   nathing] noght L   15303 Bot] Bot to L   make] makes S
iournes] ioys R   day] dais P   15304 to] *om.* R   cuntre] countres L   15305 lys] es P
15307 þe] *om.* R   by] *om.* R   15308 ay] *om.* R   *sidenote: om.* L   *add* Non habemus
hic manentem ciuitatem set futuram inquirimus ES   15309 werldely] *om.* W
15311 sikerly] surly R   15313 men] I R, me W   15314 And¹] *om.* R   15315 þe]
om. R   15318 right herytage] *trs.* ER   15319 sette] caste sett L   so] *om.* R
15320 þat] *om.* R   15321 hym] *after* company L, *om.* R   to] *om.* R   gifs] todrawes R
15322 Thar] Hym thar L   15324 *line om.* R   þa] þat ES   þe] *om.* W   15325 taas]
om. ELS   15326 has] gase R   with þam gode] in grete R   15327 fandynges]
fandyng S   15328 yhernynges] yernyng S   15329 puttes] promptes W

And in his snares and in his bandes.   15330
  Trouthe and Luf of Godde almyghty
Withhaldes þe hert stedfastly
And withdrawes it fra alle wicked thoght
And fra fole wille þat it assent noght

Donum Sapiencie   De Sobrietate et
Temperancia   Sanctificetur nomen tuum

fo. 91ᵛᵇ To na synne þat comes ouerthwert.   15335
  þus Trouthe and Luf withhaldes þe hert.
    Right als men dose with þe faukoun
þat to fleghe es oft boun:
With þe iesse[s] men haldes hym stille
þat he fleghe noght after his wille.   15340
þe hert es als þe faukoun to flight,
þat fayne wald fleghe if þat it myght,
þat men may halde, als men may proue,
With þe iesses of Trouthe and Luf.
    þe hert oft fleghes perillously   15345
So þat it perisshes itself þarby
And falles sone, als I yhou telle,
In þe foghelers gilders of helle.
þat es þe fende þat waytes ay
To take þat foghell if he may.   15350
þarefore þe gode men þat er wys
Restreynes þair willes fra folys
And þair yhernynges fra al þat ille es
Thurgh Attemperaunce and Sobrenes.
    Wharefore Senek þat was a wyse man   15355
Says þus, als I shewe yhow can:
Seneca 'If þou lufs wele', says he,

15330 And aukes hym in snares and bandes L   And¹] *om.* R   in¹] *om.* P
15333 And] *om.* R   it] *om.* L   alle] *om.* ELSR, a (? *altered from* all) P   wicked] ilk ? P
15334 And] *om.* R   fole] foule LSW, fule P, foly R   15335 To] Vnto L
15336 trouthe and luf] *trs. nouns* E   15337 Right] *om.* R   with] *om.* L   þe] a P
15338 to] vnto L   fleghe] flyght LPRW   15339 *iesses] iesse A   hym] *adds* oft L
15342 þat²] *om.* PRW   15343 men²] we P, I R   15344 iesses] iesse L, s³ *int.* P
15346 perisshes] perich R   15348 In] Into L   foghelers] foule P, fologhers S   gilders]
kyllders S   15350 þat] þe LR   if] if þat ELS   15351 men þat er] mane þat es ELS
15352 Restreynes] Strenys R   þair willes] his wille ELS   15353 þair yhernynges] his
ʒhernyng (-ges L) ELS   15354 at-] *om.* P   15355 Wharefore] Foreþi ES, Forwhy L
þat was a] þe R   a] þe W   15356 þus] *om.* R   shewe yhow] *trs.* P   yhow] *om.* L
15357 lufs] luf LP   *sidenote om.* P

'To be sobre and attempre,
Restreyne þi yhernynges fra folys
And putte a bridell to þi Couatyse.'   15360
For als men haldes þe hors agayne
With a bridell þat wald rynne fayne
þat he ne ga noght at his wille,
Right swa men may hald þe hert stille
With þe bridell of Sobrenes   15365
And of Attemperaunce þat siker es,
þat it ne may on nane wyse
Gif it to werldely Couatyse
Ne til nane othir vanyte.
Swa suld þe hert restreyned be.   15370
  þe thridde degree þat men suld halde   *iij^{us}. gradus*
Es Mesure in Wordes and Speche called.
For Salamon says þat þe wyse man   *Salamon*
And þe wele-lered þat Wisdom can
Mesures alle his wordes right   15375
And tempres his speche with al his myght.

De Sobrietate et Temperancia

  And Saynt Ierom says, þe gode techer,   fo. 92ra
þus, als þe boke may wittenes bere,   *Ieronimus*
þat bi þe weght of wordes to neuen
Es common lyf attempred euen.   15380
þat es to say and to vnderstande
After þe wordes of þe tung stirande,
Men may knawe, whaso can,
þe witte or þe foly of þe man,
Als men may knawe a swyne and se   15385
By þe tung if þat it hale be.
  And þarefore þe wyse man of wytte   *Sapiens*

15359 Restreyne] Caste L   15360 And] *om*. L   þi] þe W   15361 þe] a S
15362 rynne] *at the head of the following line* R   15363 ne] *om*. LPSR   15364 Right]
om. R   15366 at-] *om*. LPSRW   15367 ne] *om*. LSR   on] of LS, not on R   nane]
nanekyn L   15371 *sidenote: om*. L, 3. W   15372 in] of ELS   wordes] word R   wordes
and] *om*. ES   15373 þat] *om*. P   *sidenote om*. LP   15374 -lered] *adds* mane E, rered R
þat] þat þe R   15376 speche] speches S, wordes R   al] *om*. R   15377 gode] wyse L
15378 þus] *om*. R   may] kanne L   15379 þat] þir R   bi] *om*. L, be R   þe] *int*. P, *om*. W
weght of wordes] wordes of weght R   15380 at-] *om*. P   15381 to²] *om*. LR
15382 þe¹] *om*. R   þe²] þi L   15384 þe witte or] Wyte of R   þe²] a L
15385-6 *couplet om*. W   15386 þat] *om*. LPSR   15387 And] *om*. PR   *sidenote om*. LS

Spekes þus and says in Haly Wrytte
þat þe wordes þat wyse men neuen
In balaunce er weghed ful euen.   15390
þat es to say þat he þat es wise
His wordes weghe withouten fayntyse
In þe balaunce of Resoun and Skille
And of Discrescioun, and noght of Wille,
Swa þat þe wordes in shewynge   15395
Hald right Mesure in alle thinge.
  It bene som men of swilk wille
þat can noght halde þair tung stille
Bot lates þe tung ga whyle it may
And gifs na kepe what þai say.   15400
Be it gode, be it ille þat þai speck
Or sothe or leghe, noght þai reck.
  þa men may wele lickened be
Vntill a milne, als men may se,
þat es withouten flode-yhate.   15405
þar þe water to þe millne has gate—
þat þe clowes of þe milne es called
þat þe water fra þe whele may hald—
þat turnes about and noght blynnes
Ay als þe cours of þe water rynnes.   15410
Right so commes `to´ þair tunges by vse
Ille wordes als water to þe milne duse.
  Bot þe wyse man of gode condycioun
Settes þe clowes of Discrescioun
To kepe and halde þe water agayne   15415
Of fole wordes and speche in vayne
þat þai passe noght by na party

15388 þus and] as R   in] om. R   15389 wyse men] þe wyse man R
15390 weghed] wowen L   ful] int. P, om. R   15391 to] at E   þat²] om. ELR
15392 weghe] weyghes LP, weth R   withouten] adds any S   15394 And¹] om. R
15395 þe wordes] trs. E   shewynge] weghyng W   15397 It] Yit ESR   15398 tung]
tonnges LP   15399 lates] lat W   ga] say P   15400 þai] it L   15401 be it²] or
RW   15402 leghe] fals P   15403 þa men] Bot þai L   15404 Vntill] To PRW
als] þat L   15405 es] int. PS   withouten] adds þe P, blank W   15406 þe¹] om. R
15407 clowes] clothers L   15408 may] sulde L   15409 and] om. R   15410 þe²]
om. R   15411 Right] om. R   to] int. A, om. R   þair] þe L   tunges] tunge ELW   by
vse] at head of next line L   15412 als] as þe R   15413 Bot] om. R   15414 clowes]
clothers L   15416 fole] foule LW, foly PR   speche] spekh P, speches W
15417-18 couplet om. W

Thurgh þe milne of þe tung namely.

De Sobrietate et Temperancia

And þarefore says þe wyse man þus   fo. 92ʳᵇ
In Haly Wrytte, als þe boke shewes vs: 15420 *Sapiens*
'Lat noght þe water ga', he says;
þat es to say, withhalde always
þi wordes of ille entencioun
At þe clowes of Discrescioun.
   Forwhy Salamon says alswa,   15425 *Salamon*
'He þat lates þat water ga
Ouerhastyly agayne Skille,
He es oft cause of mykill ille,
Of motes, of stryfs, and othir thinges'
þat of þe Wicked Tung oft springes,   15430
Als I sayd ar, þar I mast talde
Of þe Wicked Tung þat es so balde.
   And þarefore says þe wyse man wele,   *Sapiens*
In Haly Wrytte, als men may fele,
'Sette þi wordes', he says, 'In balaunce   15435
And weghe þam euen for alle chaunce',
And in þi mouthe a brydell withalle,
And take gode kepe þat þou noght falle
Thurgh þi tung bifore þi faas
þat spyes þe whareso þou gaas.   15440
   Whaso wille noght when he may
Weghe his wordes ar he þam say
In þe balaunce of Discrescyoun,
Als þis boke þareof makes mencioun,
Ne his tung halde with þe brydell of Skille   15445
þat suld kepe þe tung fra ille,
He falles in þe handes of his enemys

15418 namely] anely P   15419 And] *om.* P   15420 þe] *om.* R shewes] teches L *sidenote om.* S   15421 ga] gang L   15423 þi] þe LP, þat R   15424 At] And ES, Wyth L clowes] clothers L   15425 alswa] swa L   15426 þat] þe LPRW 15428 He es] Beys R oft] oft þe P   15429 of²] and L, *om.* R and] of W 15430 *line om., added later at page foot* P wicked] ill P oft] *om.* P   15431-2 *couplet reversed, marked for corr.* P, *couplet after* 15434 R, *couplet om.* W   15432 Of] þat of P 15433 And] *om.* R *sidenote om.* ELPS   15436 And] To RW euen] well P 15437 And] *om.* R in] *om.* W   15438 gode] *om.* LPRW   15441 -so] *om.* E when] *adds* þat L   15443 þe] *om.* P   15444 þareof] *om.* LPR, *before* S 15445-6 *couplet om.* W   15445 þe] *om.* R

þat er þe fendes þat hym ay spyes.
　　When þe enemys þat wille dwelle
On were til þai haf tane þe castelle　　　　　　15450
Fyndes þe yhates open wyde,
þai entre lightly on þat syde.
Right swa þe fendes þat waytes to wynne
þe castell of þe herte withinne
When þai fynde open þe mayster yhate,　　　　　15455
þat es þe mouthe, þar þai haf gate.
þai entre þan into þe castelle
þat þai wil halde while þai þare dwelle.

Dauid　　þarefore says þe prophete Davy
In þe sauter þus openly,　　　　　　　　　　　15460

Donum Sapiencie　　De Sobrietate et
Temperancia　　　Sanctificetur nomen tuum

fo. 92ᵛᵃ　'I haf sette', he says, 'als I couthe
Posui custodiam ori meo　Gode kepynge vnto my mouthe
et hostium circumstancie　Agayne myne enemy þat es agayne me',
labijs meis　þat es þe fende þat I may noght se.
　　þe kepyng of þe mouthe es þis　　　　　　　15465
Als Dauid sayd þat was of his:
Discrescioun and Skille to fele
þat examynes þe wordes wele
Byfore þai passe, als þe boke telles,
Out of þe mouthe þar þe tung dwelles.　　　　　15470
　　þis es þe balaunce to mesure dight
Of whilk þe wyse man spekes right,
þar þe wordes suld be euen layde
And weghed bifore ar þai war sayde.
Men suld knawe þat Sothfastnes　　　　　　　15475

15450 til] when L　　þai] *om.* S　　15451 open] opyns R　　15452 entre lightly] þan
enters lyghly L　　　15453 Right swa] To R　　fendes] fende L　　þat] þat ay P
15454 with-] to com L　　15455 mayster] water P　　15456 þar] whare L, þat R　　haf]
haue in LS　　15457-8 *couplet at page foot later* P, *couplet om.* W　　15457 þan] *om.* PR
þe] þat L　　15458 þare] may L, *om.* R　　15459 *sidenote: om.* P　　15461 he says]
om. P　　15462 vnto] to PR　　*sidenote: om.* P　　custodiam] *after* meo LS　　et . . . meis]
cum S　　labijs meis] mee L　　15463 myne] þe L　　enemy] enmys RW　　es] er R　　es
agayne] strifes with P　　15464 þat I may] I may hym R　　15465 þe¹] *om.* R
15466 sayd] says W　　þat] *om.* S　　15467 *sidenote:* Nota E　　15469-70 *couplet om.* W
15469 þai] þe E　　15471 þis es] þir er R　　to] of W　　15472 Of] þe L　　spekes] *adds*
of L　　15473 wordes] worde P　　layde] sayde layde L　　15474 weghed] woieghen L
bifore] *om.* R　　war] be R

Haldes þa balaunce þat so euen es,
For Sothfastnes accorde may
þe entencioun of þe hert ay
And þe wordes of þe mouthe fre
Alletogider, als falles to be,   15480
So þat þe mouthe + say noght elles
Bot Sothfastnes als þe herte telles.

   þise balaunce suld ay euen hynge
Withouten any wrange heldynge
Vnto þe left syde or to þe right;   15485
þan hynges it wele to Goddis sight.
For men suld for na mans luf
Ne for werldely gode þat men may pruf
Ne for fauour ne for hatred
Ne yhete for na drede of dede,   15490
Leue to folwe Sothfastnes
And to say sothe when myster es.
Ne men suld say na lesyng þan
Ne falsed in worde for na man.

   þe ferthe degree, als þe boke says,   15495   *iiij^{us}. gradus*
Of Sobrenes þat es to prays
Es a maner of Mesure called
In heryng þat men suld halde.
For als men suld Mesure kepe
In spekyng to Goddis worshepe,   15500
Right so men suld kepe Mesure right
In heryng with alle þair myght.

Donum Sapiencie   De Sobrietate et
Temperancia   Sanctificetur nomen tuum

   For als men may synne in Ille Spekyng,   fo. 92vb
So men may synne in ille heryng.
Wharefore he þat wille blethely here   15505
Ille of othir es partenere

15476 þa] þe W   15479 And] Als L   15480 als] as þai W   15481 So] *om.* R
*say] ne say A   15483–6 *lines om.* W   15483 ay] *om.* R   15485 Vnto] To PR
to] vnto L   15487 *sidenote:* Nota bene E, Nota S   15488 for] for na L
15492 sothe] *om.* P   15494 for] of W   15495 *sidenote: om.* L, *in* RW   *adds* de
audit⟨u⟩ W   15500 spekyng] *possibly* -nges W   to] of W   15501 Right . . . suld] So
sulde men (*trs.* R) PR   15503 For] *om.* R   15505 Whare-] *om.* R   15506 es]
men is P   partenere] parcynere LSR, parcayuere W

And felaw, whareso he dwelles,
Of þe synne of hym þat it telles.
Forwhy na man wald say blethely
Ille of othir ne vilany   15510
þat þair gode loos myght abate,
Namely bifore a man of state,
If he ne wened þat he myght pay
To hym þat heres hym vilany say.

Sapiens   Wharefore þus says þe haly man   15515
And so says þis clerkes þat clergy can
þat na man suld be ille speker,
Warne he fande som ille herer.
And if na herar war of ille,
Nane ille speker suld be by skille.   15520
   þise men of grete state, if þai war wys,
Suld take gode kepe and þam avyse
What þai suld here and what þai suld tro⟨we⟩,
Als I sal afterwarde shewe yhow.
Bot Flateryng, Leghes, and Losengery   15525
Er grete chepe in þair courtes namely.
þe mast derthe of anything þat es
Obout þam þare es Sothfastnes.
And þarefore þai er comonly
Deceyued thurgh swilk Losengery,   15530
For þai here blethely þat men þam says
And trowes lightly þat þat þam pays.

Seneca   Senek says, 'Nathing þat charge beres
To grete men faylles bot sothesayers,
For it er grete chepe of leghers,   15535
Of losengers, and of flateres'.

15508 þe] *om.* R   15509 For what man þat walde noght blethly L -why] *om.* R
15510 ne] here na L   15513 ne] noght R   15514 vilany] vylansly W
15515 Whare-] *om.* R   *sidenote*: Ieronimus quia non esset detractor nisi non esset auditor R
15516 so says] *om.* R þis] *om.* PW   15518 Warne] Ne R he] þai L   15519 And]
om. R of] *om.* L   15520 be] speke ES   15521 þise] *om.* R grete] *om.* P if]
and L   15522 gode] *om.* R þam] *adds* wele L   15523 What¹·²] *adds* þat E and]
om. P þai suld²] *om.* R trowe] *in gutter* A   15525 Bot] *om.* R *sidenote*: Nota E
15526 in . . . courtes] with þam R courtes] court W   15527 þe] *om.* W derthe]
dergh P, derk W anything] tonge R   15528 þare] þat LS, *om.* PR   15529 And]
om. R   15530 Deceyued] Receyued W   15531 For] *om.* PR þam] *om.* R
15532 þat¹] þase L þat²] *om.* PW   15533 says] says þat E nathing] not R *sidenote*:
om. L, Senek R   15535 For] *om.* R   15536 flateres] flatereres ELPRW

Men suld þair eres haf open ay
To here blethely, þat es to say
Gode wordes of gode men and leele
þat mykell auaylles to saul-hele.   15540
And þair eres þai suld ay sper
Agayne fole wordes þat may der.
    Wharefore þe wyse man says þus   *Sapiens*

De Sobrietate et Temperancia

In Haly Writte, als þe boke shewes vs: fo. 93ra
'Stoppe', he says, 'þine eres wele   15545
With thornes þat er sharp to fele,
And þe ille tung listen þou noght';
þat brynges a man in ille thoght.
    þe Ille Tung es, als I yhow telle,
þe tung of þe nedder of helle   15550
þat þai bere about þat spekes ille;
þat venyms þam þat listen þam wille.
    Agayne swilk tunges þat gretly deres
Men suld fille and stoppe þair eres
With sharpe thornes specially   15555
Of þe Drede of Godde almyghty,
Or with þe thornes thurgh whilk God was
Corowned anely for mans trespas.
þat es Mynde of Crystes Passyoun
þat vs broght fra þe fendes bandoun.   15560
    For whaso wild haue parfytely
Drede of our Lorde, Godde almyghty,
And 'of' his Passyoun right Mynde—
Als he suld haue if he war kynde—
He suld noght here blethely by skille   15565
þis flateres ne spekers of ille,
Ne fole wordes ne vnhonest,

15540 to] *om.* P   15541–2 *couplet om. at page boundary* W   15541 And] *om.* R
15542 fole] foule LR   15543 *sidenote om.* LP   15544 þe] *om.* LR   boke] bokes L
15547 And] *om.* R   tung] *adds* na L   15548 in] to R   15549 es] *om.* R   yhow] owe W
15551 þai bere] he beres W   about] *om.* R   15552 þam] *int.* P, *om.* R, hym W
15553 swilk tunges] þe tonng L   gretly] *om.* R   15554 fille and] *om.* R, stilland W
15556 þe] *om.* R   15557 þe] *om.* L   thornes] thorn R   thurgh] *om.* L   15559 es] es þe W
15560 vs] es S   15562 our Lorde] *om.* R   15563–4 *couplet om.* W   15563 of] *int.* A
15564 if] and LS   15565 by skille] be still W   15566 flateres] flaterers ELPR   ne] na
þir L   15567–8 *couplet om.* W   15567 fole] foule LP, fell R   vn-] *om.* R

Bot som men er þa[t] charges þam lest.
  Also men may in othir manere
Vnderstande, als yhe may here,   15570
þis worde þat grete charge beres,
'Stoppe wele with thornes þine eres'.
Thornes þat er sharpe semande
Bytokens sharpe wordes and prickande
Thurgh whilk þa þat spekes oft ille   15575
Men suld snybbe and make þam be stille
And shewe þam swilk semblaunt and chere
Als men wald noght þam blethely here.

De natura aspidis   Men has a manere of nedder sene
þat es ful venemous and kene   15580
þat es in Latyne called *aspis*;
þe kynde of þat nedder es þis.
Als-tyte als sho may se a man
þat sho wenes charme hir can

De Sobrietate et Temperancia

fo. 93ʳᵇ Scho stoppes hir ane ere with erthe fast   15585
And þe tothir with hir taylle at þe last
þat sho þe charmer may noght here
Ne þe charme, be he neuer so nere.
  þe nedder þat can hir eres þus ditte
Vs teches to stoppe our eres thurgh wytte   15590
þat we ne listen noght þis charmers
þat er flaterers and leghers
þat fals Flateryng mykill hauntes
And charmes þe ryche men and enchauntes.
  Bot whaso stoppes his eres ay   15595
Als dose þe nedder, þat es to say
þe tane with erthe þat it noght faylle

15568 men] *om.* ELS   er] *om.* P   *þat] þam AP   þam] *om.* P, þa R   15569 in] on PW   15571 þis] þe W   worde] wordes PW   15575 whilk] whaes L   þa] *om.* LP   15576 þam] *om.* R   be] *om.* PRW   15577 semblaunt] semblance R   15579 *sidenote: om.* P   De] *om.* ELS   15581–2 *couplet trs.* W   15582 þat] þe ES   þis] *om.* S   15583 may se] seys R   15584 charme hir] *trs.* L, charmer S   15585 hir ane] þe ta R   15586 þe¹] *om.* R   hir] þe LP   þe²] *om.* LR   15587 charmer] charme P   15588 he] it L   15589 hir] *om.* L   eres] ere W   þus] so R, *om.* W   *sidenote:* Nota contra adulatores E   15590 thurgh] with R   15591 ne] *om.* LPRW   15593–4 *couplet om.* W   15594 þe] þir L, *om.* S   men] *om.* R   en-] *om.* E   15595 -so] *om.* P   15596 to] for to L   15597 it] is W

And þe tothir ere with his taylle,
Hym thar haue na warde ne drede,
If he his Witte wil right lede,   15600
Of na charmes whareso he wendes
Of wicked tunges ne of þe fendes.

He stoppes right þe tane of his eres
With erthe, als þe boke wyttenes beres,
þat bithinkes hym þat he es noght   15605
Bot erthe and to erthe sal be broght
And thinkes alswa of his wrechednes,
How pouer, how vyle, how feble he es.
Wharefore he suld hym meke þarby
And halde hym noght worth of body.   15610

þe tothir ere he suld stoppe fast
With his taylle þat byhynde commes last,
þat es to say by vnderstandyng
He suld ay think on his endynge
And on þe dede þat he sal drye   15615
And wate neuer when he sal dye
Ne how, ne whare, ne in what stede,
Ne whider he sal when he es dede.
He þat couthe stoppe on þis manere
His eres, he suld noght blethely here   15620
Nathing be spoken to him ne sayde
Of whilk our Lorde suld be myspayde.
And on þis wyse a man may be
Right mesured and attempere.

        þe fift degree als men may fele   15625 v^{us}. gradus
Of Sobernes es to kepe wele

Donum Sapiencie   De Sobrietate et
Temperancia   Sanctificetur nomen tuum

Right Mesure withouten fayllyng   fo. 93va
In ryche apparaylle and in clethyng.

15598 his] hir W   15601 na] þase LS   charmes] charmers L   -so] *om.* R
15602 þe] *om.* PR   15603 right] *om.* R   15605 bi-] vmbe- L, *om.* R   hym] *om.* R
15607–8 *couplet om.* W   15607 And] Als E   alswa] *om.* R   his] *om.* R   15608 feble]
adds þat P   15609 Wharefore] *om.* R   hym] *om.* W   hym meke] *trs.* LR   15610 worth]
worthy W   15612 commes] come L   15615 on] of L   sal] sulde P   15616 neuer]
not R   15618 sal] sall ga L, sall wende S   15625 *sidenote: om.* L, *in* R, 5. gradus W
15627 withouten] *adds* any L   15628 in²] *om.* PRW   *sidenote*: De apparatu vestium R

þar men passes oft Mesure right
And maas grete outrage in mens sight.   15630
    And forþi þat swilk outrage
Of curiouste and grete costage
þat men maas obout þe body
Es halden grete synne and foly,
And enchesouns of synne may be   15635
In othir men, als men may se,
Men suld ay right Mesure kepe
In swilk thinges to Goddis worshepe.
For if swilk apparaylle ryche and gay
War noght swilk synne als I now say,   15640
Godde had noght spoken so sharply þan
In þe godspell agayne þe riche man
þat in riche purpur cledde hym oft
And in bys þat was so soft,
Of whase lyuyng God was noght payd,   15645
Als I haf herebifore sayde.
    A grete fole es a man or a womman,
And als a chylde es þat na wytte can
Ne Skille has ne Vnderstandynge,
þat enprydes hym of his clethynge.   15650
I suld wele a man a fole halde,
And a fole he may right be called
þat enprydes hym here gretly
Of þe garment opon his body.
þat suld be nane othir thinge   15655
Bot a token and a menynge
Of þe shame þat was wyde knawen
Of his first fader and of his awen.
    þis vsage þat we vse of clethyng

15629 þar] þase LS   oft] om. LP   15630 grete] om. R   15631 -þi] om. LSR
swilk] ilk S, skill R   15632 grete] of L   15634 and] and grete L   15635 -souns]
-son PRW (erasure follows P)   15636 men] ʒe P   15637 ay] after mesure S   right]
om. R   15638 thinges] etynge P   to] of R   Goddis] god S   15639 For if] Of L
15640 synne] om. LS   now] you LRW   15643 purpur] purpill R   cledde] glede E
15645 was noght] mys- R   15646 sayde] payde E   15647 a¹,²] om. PSR
15648 And als] þat es L   es] om. LW, int. P   wytte] gode W   15650 hym] adds here
E, þai me L   his] þaire L   15651 A full grete fole I hym halde L   I] Men S   wele]
after man R   a fole] om. W   15652 right] om. LR   right be] trs. S   15653 here]
adds ryght E   15654 opon] of LRW, on P   his] þe L   15557 was wyde] trs. W
15559 of] in R

Was funden first for þis thinge: 15660
For our formast fader synne
þat dampned hymself and al his kyn,
To couer his shame and ours to hyde.
Why suld we þan in þat haf Pryde?
When men sees a beer fayr dight   15665
And couerd with fayr clathes of sight,
þat es a token to knaw þarby

Donum Sapiencie   De Sobrietate et
Temperancia   Sanctificetur nomen tuum

þat withinne lyse a dede body.   fo. 93ᵛᵇ
   If þe pacok of his fayre taylle
Enpryde hym, it es na meruaylle,   15670
Ne if þe cok þat crawes loude
Of his creste in hert be proude.
For kynde mas hym swa to be,
And als his kynde wille, so dose he.
Sen he has nouthir Witte ne Skille,   15675
After his kynde he dose his wille.
   Bot man or womman, whethir so it be,
þat has Witte and Skille and Wille Fre
And wate wele withouten faylle
þat kynde hym gifs na ryche apparaylle,   15680
He suld noght enpryde hym namely
Of þe apparaylle on his body
Ne of þe quayntyse on þe hede,
For swilk Pryde makes þe saul dede.
   þarefore says þus þe wyse man   15685 *Sapiens*
In Haly Wrytte, als I fynde can:
'In fayre robes,' he says, 'enpryde þe noght,
Ne of þam haf na ioye in thoght.'
And Saynt Paul alsswa says þus right   *Paulus*

15660 for] of W   15661 formast] furst R   15662 al] *om.* R   *sidenote*: Nota E
15663 to²] *om.* R   15664 þan] *om.* R   15667 a token] þe tokʻenʻynge P
15669 If] Of E   15670 it] þat L   15671 if] of L   15674 *line om.* L, Als in þe
kynde of foules rede may 3e *supplied later at page foot* And] *om.* R   15675 Sen] Sone E
15677 so] *om.* PSR   15678 fre] se P   15679 And] þat RW   15680 ap-] *om.*
LPRW   15681 hym] *om.* R   15682 on] of LPSR   15683 of] on R   þe] *om.* LS
on] of LPSW   15684 makes] *om.* S   15685 þus] *om.* R   *sidenote: om.* S, *in* R
15687 he says] *om.* SR   says] sayde W   15688 Ne] þe S   15689 And] *om.* R
alsswa] *om.* L   alsswa says] *trs.* R   *sidenote: om.* L, *in* W

þat þis wymmen suld þam dight   15690
And þam apparaylle in Sobrenes,
And namely after þair state es,
þat es to say in mesure mast
Withouten outrage done in wast,
After þat þat þe state wille   15695
Of þe persone and after skille.
    Certes, methink þis may noght be
Withouten grete outrage to se
þat a persone sal haue anely
For þe vse of his awen body   15700
So many robes in a yhere
Of riche clathe of colour sere
Thurgh whilk many pouer men myght be
Sustayned, and so wald Charyte.
And al es done obout a body;   15705
þat es grete outrage and foly.
    And if þa robes and þat clethyng
War gyuen at his last endyng
For Goddes luf anely, yhete suld þat

De Sobrietate et Temperancia

fo. 94ra Vnto his saul helpe somwhat.   15710
Bot þai er gyuen specyally
Til herlotes for þair herlotry
And til mynstra`i′lles for þair dyn,
And þis es, als I proue, grete syn.
For he þat any gode gifs   15715
Til þa men þat synfully lifs
þat vses iapes and herlotrys,
Vnto þe fende he mas sacrafyse.
Forþi men suld kepe in swilk thinges
Mesure þat of Sobrenes springes,   15720

15690 wymmen] wyse men L   15692 after] *after* state R   es] it is R
15695 þat²] *om.* LW   15696 after] þat is P   15702 clathe] clothes W   of²]
and ELSR   colour] colours ELPSW   15703 men] *om.* R   15704 and] *om.* R
15705 And] *om.* R   es] *om.* W   a] þe LW   15710 Vnto] To R   -what] whar P
15713 mynstrailles] i *int., perhaps later* A   15714 And . . . als] þat L, þis sall R
proue] *adds* es L   15715 gode] godes LP   15716 þa men] þam R
15717 herlotrys] harlotry W   15718 Vnto] To PR   he] *om.* L, þai R   sacrafyse]
sacrafy W

After þat þat þe state wald
Of þe persone, als I haf talde.
   þe sext degree of Sobrenes   *vj^{us}. gradus*
And of Temperaunce namely þis es:
þat ilk man after his powere   15725
Suld Mesure kepe on gode manere
In beryng and in cuntynaunce
After þe wyse mans ordynaunce.
   Wharefore Senek says, 'If þou be
Rightly sobre and attempre,   15730
Take gode kepe and be war þarby
þat þe stirynges of þi body
And of þi hert be noght vnclene
Ne vnconable in beryng sene'.
For of disordynaunce of þe hert,   15735
When þe saul es noght in quert,
Comes, als es sene comonly,
þe disordynaunce of þe body.
   It er som þat er chyldisshe and nyce
And knawes noght þair awen vyce   15740
þat mas men thurgh þair folys
Halde þam foles and noght wys.
It falles wele til a man of valu
þat he be ledde thurgh þe vertu
Of Attemperaunce and Sobrenes   15745
þat tholes nane outrage þar it es
And mesured wele, als teches þis clerkes,
In alle his wordes and in alle his werkes,
And of so fayre contynaunce be
Byfore alle men þa[t] may hym se,   15750

15721 þat²] *om.* RW   15723 *sidenote: om.* L, *in* RW   15724 namely] anely P, *om.* R   15726 on] in P   15729 Whare-] *om.* R   if] if þat L   *sidenote:* Senek (*later*) E, Senecka LP   15730 Rightly] Ryght L   15731 gode] *om.* R   15732 -rynges] -ryng ELPS   þi] þe EP   15733 þi] þe E   15734 beryng] heryng EPS, *adds* be L 15735 disord-] discord- S   þe] *om.* ELR   15736 When] When þat L 15738 disord-] discord- SR   15739 It] Als S, ȝit R   som] *adds* mene E chyldisshe] chylderlyke L, childes PS   *sidenote:* Nota E   15740 And] þat L 15744 þe] *om.* L   15745 at-] *om.* LR   and] and of LR   15746 tholes] thole R þar] whare L   15747 mesured] mesure P   wele] *adds* 'kepes' P   þis] *om.* R 15748 in] *om.* PRW   alle] *om.* PR   15749 so] a ES, *om.* L   15750 men] *om.* ES *þat] þai A, þat þai W

De Sobrietate et Temperancia

fo. 94rb Swa þat na man may of his beryng
Take ille ensaumple or of his lyuynge
Ne þat he be noght halden vnwys,
Als a chylde or fole þat shewes folys.
Forwhy a philosophre þus shewes   15755
þat a chylde of elde and chylde of thewes
And chylde of wytte er alle ane;
þus may þe name of chylde be tane.
    And Haly Wrytte also says þus,
Als þis clerkes has oft shewed vs,   15760
þat a chylde of ane hundreth yhere
Maledictus puer C. Es weryed, als yhe may here.
annorum   þat es to say þat he or sho
þat has elde and na gode wil do
Bot lifs als a chylde in foly,   15765
He es weryed of Godde almyghty.
Paulus   Wherefore Saynt Paul says þus
Of hymself, als þe boke shewes vs,
'When I was,' he says, 'a chylde,
Als chylde I wroght and was ful wylde.   15770
Bot when I come to elde of man,
I left al my childehede þan'.
For whaso haldes a man of elde
A chylde þat na wytte can welde,
He haldes hym als þe manere es   15775
A fole þan þat es witteles.
þarefore I rede, als teches Haly Wrytte,
þat nane of yhow be chylde of wytte,
Bot bese in beryng meke and mylde
And lytell in malyce als a chylde.   15780

15751 Swa] *om.* R   15752 or] *om.* LR   15753 noght] *om.* L   15754 or] or a LP
(*the phrase int.* P)   15755 -why] *om.* R   15757 wytte] *adds* and L   15758 name]
man L   15759 also] *om.* R   *sidenote:* Sacra scriptura L   15760 þis] *om.* R   has . . .
shewed] oft shewes P   15762 *sidenote:* Ysayas lxv°. capitulo Puer centum annorum moriet
et peccator centum annorum maledictus erit R   puer] puer sit L   15763 þat²] *om.* ELS
15764 wil] can R   15767 *sidenote:* Cum essem paruulus sapiebam vt paruulus R
15768 shewes] says L   15769 says] sayd W   15770 Als] *add* a ELS   and was ful] þat
was EL, and was PRW   15771 Bot] *om.* R   to] to þe P   15777 þare-] Whar- W
teches] toches S, says R   15779 meke] good R

Now es þis a fayre thyng þan
And worshepefull to man and womman,
And namely til men of worshepe,
To halde sikerly and to kepe
Certayne Mesure withouten fayllyng   15785
In cuntynaunce and in berynge.
   þe seuent degre and þe last   *vij^{us}. gradus*
Es to kepe wele with hert stedfast
Mesure þat men skillefull calles
In etyng and drynkyng, als 'vs' falles.   15790
For outrage þat we se men vse

Donum Sapiencie   De Sobrietate et
Temperancia   Sanctificetur nomen tuum

In mete and drynk grete harme duse,   *fo. 94va*
Bathe to þe saul and to þe body,
Als I haf talde bifore openly.
   þarefore says Godde in þe godspelle   15795   *Dominus dicit in*
þus, als men heres þis clerkes telle,   *euangelio*
'Takes kepe, I bidde yhow', says he,
'þat yhour hertes noght greued be
Ne ouercharged with Glotony
Ne of drunkennes of body'.   15800
þat es to say and to vndirstande
þus, als es to our witte semande,
þat yhe ne do for nathinge
Outrage in etyng ne in drynkyng.
   Sobrenes kepes Mesure clene   15805
In etyng and drynkyng als es sene,
þat men do here nane outrage,
Forwhy it turnes to nane auauntage.
Of outrage obout þe bely,
In etynge and drynkyng namely,   15810

15781 Now es þis] þis is R   15782 And] And a S   -full] *om.* L   15783 And]
om. R   15784 to²] *om.* E   15787 *sidenote: om.* LS, *in* RW   15788 wele] *om.* R
15790 vs] *int. later* A, *om.* ELPSRW   15791 For] *om.* R   we se] many L
15792 mete and drynk] etyng and drynking L   grete] *om.* R   15793 Bathe] *om.* R
þe¹] *om.* L   to þe²] *om.* L   15794 bifore] *adds* here R   15795 *sidenote: in* R,
Euangelium ELS   15796 þis] *om.* L   15800 drunkennes] drynkes R
15801-4 *lines om.* W   15801 to²] *om.* R   15802 witte] wittes P   15803 ne] *om.*
L, noght S   15804 ne] and LS   in²] *om.* R   15806 and] and in E, *om.* R   es] ofte
es L   15808 -why] *om.* R   to] vnto L   15809 Of] *om.* L

þat stirs a man oft vnto vyce
Inoghe es spoken in þis tretyce
þare I haf spoken openly
Of þe synne of Glotony,
To whilk þe vertu of Sobrenes   15815
þat I of spake contraryous es.
þarefore I wille speke na mare now
Of þat synne þat I haf shewed yhowe.
  Now haf yhe herde me here neuen
Openly þe degrees seuen   15820
Of þe tree of Sobrenes
þat shewes alle fruyt þat gode es.
And if yhe blethely wil se
And knawe þe braunches of þis tre,
Byhalde alle othir vertus and loke   15825
þat er contened in þis boke.
Swa sal yhe fynde, als may falle,
þis vertu commonly ouer-alle;
Forwhy als I haf byfore talde
And shewed to þam þat me here wald,   15830
þis vertu þat alle vyces lettes

Donum Sapiencie   De Sobrietate et
Temperancia   Sanctificetur nomen tuum

fo. 94vb In alle vertus right Mesure settes.
  Wharefore I say þat alle vertus
Er braunches of þis þar men wele duse,
For þis vertu hym right shewes   15835
In alle othir vertus and thewes.
Wharefore I wil noght here sette
Nane othir braunche þat vyce may lette,
Bot alle þe vertus þat men may loke
And fynde wryten in þis boke   15840
I halde þam alle, mare and lesse,

15811 vnto] to ELPSRW   15816 -ryous] -ry L   15817 þare-] om. R
15819 Now] Now þan L here] om. LR   15822 alle] all þe L, om. R   15824 þe]
om. SR þis] þe ELSW   15827 falle] befalle L   15828 vertu] vertuz L
15829 -why] om. R   15830 to þam] om. R   15831 þis] þe L   15832 right]
good R right mesure] trs. P   15833 Whare-] om. R   15834 of þis] om. R þar] þat
PR   15835-8 lines om. W   15837 Whare-] om. R   15839 Bot] om. R
15840 And] I R fynde] funden L   15841 alle] om. E

Braunches of þe tree of Sobrenes.

  þis tree beres mykill faire fruyte
þat es speciall saul-bote
þat es pees of hert thurgh gastly mygh⟨t⟩,   15845
Als I byfore haf talde yhow right.
For he þat has þis vertu wele,
He has þe herte, als he may fele,
So twynned fra luf þat es werldely
And swa knytted to Godde almyghty   15850
Thurgh Charyte, als men may rede,
þat es parfyte luf and anehede.
And so fast in hym his luf he settes
þat he alle othir thinges forgettes,
Namely þat er noght ordayned right   15855
To Godde þat es ful of myght.
And on þis wyse, als I yhow say,
þe hert it restes in Godde ay,
þar he may alle comfort fele
And delyte and ioy þat hym lykes wele,   15860
þe whilk may passe, als I wene,
Alle othir delytes þat here er sene.
  þis comfort and þis ioy to tast
And þis delyte settes þe Haly Gast
In þe hert þat parfyte es   15865
In þe vertu of Sobrenes
þat men may fele specially com
Of þe haly Gift of Wisdom.
  Certes, whaso mȝght fele best
Swilk pees of hert, þat wald hym rest   15870

De Sobrietate et Temperancia

In Godde, of wham alle gode springes;   fo. 95ra
þat es fulfillyng of his yhernynges.

15844 speciall] specialy W   saul-] to saule- L   15845 of . . . thurgh] be R   myght]
partly in gutter A   15846 yhow] *om.* SRW   15847 For] *om.* R   15849 twynned]
twynand R   15851 may] *om.* R   15852 luf] *om.* R   15853 And] *om.* R   in] on R
in . . . luf] *trs. phrs.* ESR   he] *om.* ER   15855-6 *couplet om.* W   15855 Namely]
om. R   er noght] es L   15857 And] *om.* R   wyse] *om.* L   15860 *line after* 15862 P
And¹] And all þe L, *om.* R   and²] *om.* R   hym] *om.* L   15861 þe] *om.* R
15862 delytes] delyces ELS   15863 comfort . . . ioy] *trs. nouns* S   15864 delyte]
delytes (delices L) ELS   15866 In] þurgh S   15868 gift] gaste ELPS
15871 gode] godenes L   15872 ful-] *om.* L   fulfillyng] fulfilled W

He suld be blissed in þis werlde here
And in `þe´ tothir þat es mare clere,
For he suld wynne þat blissedhede   15875
þat Godde, als we in þe godspell rede,
Hight to þam ouer alle othir thinge
þat pees wille kepe withouten brekyng,
When he says þus: 'Blissed be þai
þat payseble er in hert ay,   15880
For þai sal be called Goddis sonnes'
And wonne with hym þar he wonnes.
   þise er þe paysebles to prayse,
Als Saynt Austyne openly says,
þat ordaynes and settes, day and nyght,   15885
Alle þe stirynges of þair hertes right
Vnder þe lordeshepe of right Skille
And of þe Gaste, als Resoun wille.
   þise er bi right Goddis sonnes called,
For pees þai kepe wele and halde.   15890
Forwhy þai bere þe right lickenes
Of þair fader þat Godde es
And Lorde of pees and of luf,
Als Saynt Paul says; þis may men proue.
   Wharefore Pees and Luf parfyte   15895
Es a thinge of gastly delyte
þat mas a man mast kyndely
Lyke to our Lorde Godde almyghty
And contrary to þe fende of helle,
Goddis enemy þat es fals and felle.   15900
   Also þai may Goddis sonnes be called
Thurgh anothir skille to halde.
For þai folwe þair fader ay nerre
þan othir þat er fra hym ferre.
For Pees and Luf þat es hym dere   15905

15874 þe] *int. later* A   clere] dere W   15877 othir] *om.* LS   15879 þus] *om.* R *sidenote*: Beati pacifici quoniam filij Dei vocabuntur ELS   15880 er] *after* hert S 15881 Goddis] god LR   15882 wonne] dwell (*followed by eras.*) P   15884 *sidenote*: Augustinus ELSRW   15886 þair] þe PR   hertes] hert LRW   15887 right] *after* þe S   15889 þise] þai R   Goddis] god LRW   15891 -why] *om.* R   þe] *om.* R 15892 þair] þe R   Godde] gode R   15894 þis] þus þis E, þus LP, þat I R   *sidenote*: Paulus ELS   15898 our Lorde] *om.* R   15901 Goddis] god LSW   15903 ay] *after* folwe W   nerre] nere RW   15904 ferre] fere RW

Hym folwes and haldes mare nere
þan any othir vertu þat es,
Als Haly Writte beres wyttenes.
    Also þai wirke þair Faders werkes
After his wille, als says þis clerkes.   15910

De Sobrietate et Temperancia

For Godde come noght at þe bigynnyng   fo. 95rb
Into þis werlde for nane othir thing
Bot for to make here Pees and Luf
Bytwene Godde and man for mans bihuf
And bitwene man and aungell bright   15915
And bitwene man and hymself right.
    Wharefore when Godde was borne als man,
þe aungels sang for þe pees þan
þat Godde hadde into erthe broght
Amange mankynde þat he had wroght.   15920
þan þai sange, als þam felle to do,
'Gloria in excelsis deo
Et in terra pax hominibus';
þat es 'Blisse to Godde and Pees to vs',
Als to men þat in erthe dwelles   15925
þat er of gode wille, and to nane elles.
    And forþi þat thurgh na yhernynge
þe paisebles sekes nane othir thing
Bot Pees, and Pees purchaces ay
Onence Godde in al þat þai may   15930
And onence þair neghpur here
And in þamself on gode manere,
þai may be called specially
þe childer of Godde almyghty.
For þair faders werk þai wirk,   15935
And of his werkes þai er noght irke.

    15906 nere] `t'here P   15909–10 *couplet om.* W   15911 noght] *om.* L
15915–16 *couplet trs.* W   15915 aungell] angels PW   15917 Whare-] *om.* R
15918 aungels] angell RW   þe²] *om.* LR   15921 þan] And þan W   15922 *sidenote:*
Gloria in excelsis Deo S   15923 *on same line as the previous* LR, *etc.* *at end of previous*
line S   15924 *sidenote:* Pax W   15926 wille] *om.* R   15927 And forþi] For R
thurgh] *om.* L   15928 nane] and nan R   15929 purchaces] purchase þai P
15930 in] *om.* E, *int.* P   þat] *om.* R   þai] he L   15931 þair] þi R   neghpur]
neghboures L   15932 in] to L   15933 þai] þis L, þat P   may] *om.* R
15935 For] *om.* R   15936 werkes] werke SW

And forþi þat men calles þam ay
'Goddis childer', blissed er þai
In þis werlde thurgh special grace
When þai Pees of Hert purchace.   15940
   Bot þis blissedhede sal be parfyte
When þai sal be with grete delyte,
Als þe boke mas here mencyoun,
In right paiseble possessyoun
Of þair Faders herytage fre   15945
þat passes alle thing þat may be
þat men can in þis werlde neuen;
þe whilk es þe kyngedom of heuen.
þare þai sal be in siker pees
And parfyte ioy þat neuer sal sees;   15950
þar alle þair willes and þair yhernynges

Donum Sapiencie   De Sobrietate et
Temperancia   Sanctificetur nomen tuum

fo. 95ᵛᵃ Sal be fulfilled in alle thinges;
þare na ma[ne]re of ille may be,
Ne dole, ne defaute, ne aduersyte,
Bot plente of alle thing þat gode es   15955
And ioy and blisse þat es endeles.
   þis sal be Pees mast profytable,
Pees mast honurable and delytable,
Pees mast siker and mast stedfast,
Pees mast parfyte þat ay sal last,   15960
Pees þat sal surmount and passe
Alle mens witte þat euer was,
Or sal be in alle mens lyf-dayse,
Als Saynt Paull þe apostell says.
   And sen it passes alle wytte of man,   15965
Al[le] wordes of man it passes þan.

15937 -þi] *om.* R   þat] *om.* S   calles] calle E   15941 Bot] *om.* R   be] *om.* L
15943–4 *couplet om.* W   15944 paiseble] passyble LS   15945 fre] sa fre L
15947–8 *couplet om.* W   15948 þe¹] *om.* R   15950 And] And in L   15951 alle]
om. R   willes] will P, willynges W   and] and all L   *15953 manere] mare AEP
15955 thing] *om.* R   15956 *line om.* R   15957 þis] þat L, Pees W   pees] *after* þis P
15958 mast] *adds* parfite S   15959 Pees] *adds* is P   mast²] *om.* ELPSR   15960 ay]
euer L   15961 sur-] ouer- L   surmount and] all thynges S   15962 Alle] Als E
15963 lyf-] *om.* R   15964 *sidenote*: Paulus ES   15965 And] *om.* R   wytte] wittes P
*15966 Alle] Als AEPS

Forwhy na hert of man think it may,
Ne ere yhete here, ne tung say,
Ne eghe myght neuer se thurgh sight,
War it neuer so clere and bright   15970
What ioy it es þat neuer endes,
þis Pees þat God has hight his frendes.
    þis es þe blissedhede for to take
Of paysebilnes þat I of spake,
To whilk þe vertu of Sobrenes   15975
Brynges a man þat sobre es
And to þe mede þat anely falles
To þam þat men paysebill calles.
þat es to be called Goddis sonnes
And wonne with hym þar he wonnes,   15980
Als men may here þis clerkes telle
How Godde says in þe godspelle.
'Blissed be þai', þus says he,
'þat er paysebill als þai suld be,
For þai sal be called thurgh right   15985
Goddis childer þat es ful of myght'.
    Now may yhe se here openly
And lightly knawe thurgh short study
What gode þe Gift dose of Wisdome
In þe herte þar it may com,   15990
What vice it outdrawes and what synne,
And what vertu it settes withinne.

Dominus dicit in euangelio.
Beati pacifici, quoniam ipsi
filij Dei vocabuntur

Donum Sapiencie   De Sobrietate et
Temperancia   Sanctificetur nomen tuum

Alle may men fynde in þis boke redy   fo. 95ᵛᵇ
And by many skilles proued appertly.

15967 For-] *om.* R   it] *om.* P   15968 yhete] *om.* R   say] it say L   15969 myght
neuer] *om.* R   neuer] euer W   se . . . sight] so clere and bryght E   15970 and] ne L,
so R   and bright] se 'itt' thurgh syght E   15972 God] *om.* P   his] to hys L
15973 for] *om.* R   15974 paysebilnes] pees P   of] before of P   15977 anely] þerto P
15978 paysebill] passyble L   15979–80 *couplet om.* W   15979 Goddis] god LSR
15980 wonne] dwell P   15981 þis] *om.* R   15983 *sidenote: in* R   Dominus . . .
euangelio] *om.* ES   dicit] *om.* LR   quoniam . . . vocabuntur] *om.* L   ipsi] *om.* ES   filij
Dei vocabuntur] Deum videbunt P   15984 paysebill] passyble L   15985 For] *om.* R
15987 se] se and W   15988 short] *om.* R   15989 þe . . . dose] it duse þe gyft R
15990 þar] whare L   15991 out-] *om.* S   outdrawes] draws out R   what²] *om.* R
15992 And] *om.* R   15993 Alle] Als L   men] me W   in . . . boke] here R
And] *om.* R   proued] proue ES

þe whilk gift withouten fayllyng 15995
Men may wynne thurgh þe first askyng
Sanctificetur nomen tuum Of þe Pater Noster þat we bidde.
For it es mast and heghest kidde,
It es þe first þat we craue.
Bot it es þe last to wynne and haue, 16000
For we most first at þe lawest bigynne,
Ar we may to þe heghest wynne.
þe lawest es Dredde of Godde of heuen
And Wisdom es þe heghest of þe seuen,
And bot we first bigynne at Drede, 16005
We may noght wele of Wisdom spede.
Forwhy Drede of Godde, when it wil com,
It es þe bigynnyng of Wisdom,
Als þe wyse man in boke shewes vs
And als I first talde, þat says þus: 16010
Inicium sapiencie est timor Domini.
þise twa giftes haldes þe tothir fast;
Godde sende vs bathe þe first and þe last.
þan er we siker, whareso we ga,
Of alle þe tothir bitwene þa twa;
þan may we of grace haue grete plente. 16015
Godde graunt vs þat it so mot be.
Amen

Here es þe ende of þis tretyce
þat spekes of many maner of vyce
And of vertus many and sere
And of alle þat nedefull war to lere 16020
And to knawe what es Goddis wille

15995 þe] om. R   15996 thurgh] be R   15997 Of] In S   þat we] when we
it R   *sidenote om.* L   15998 es] es þe LP (*int.* P)   and] and þe LS   16000 þe]
om. EL   and] and to S   16001 For] *om.* R   we . . . first] vs behoues L, we buse
furst R   most] mott L   þe] *om.* R   lawest] leiste P   16003 of¹] *om.* R   of heuen]
to neuen L   16004 And] *om.* R   þe¹] *om.* R   16005 And bot we] Bot if vs R
at] to P   16006 wele] *om.* R   16007 Forwhy] *om.* R   16008 þe] *om.* EL, a R
16009 in] in þe P   in boke] *om.* R   boke] bokes S   16010 And] *om.* PR
16010a *marg.* ELS, *in* R   est] *om.* ELPSR   16011 þe tothir] þase other L
16012 sende] sente R   þe¹] *om.* LR   16013 -so] *om.* R   16014 alle] *om.* R   þe]
þase L   tothir] oþer R   þa] þe W   16015 grete] *om.* R   16016 vs] *om.* SR
þat] *om.* R   so mot] *trs.* S   mot] *om.* L, may PR   16016a *marg.* EW, *om.* LP
16020 þat] *om.* R   lere] here W

And what es gode and what es ille,
What Godde greues and what hym payse,
Als þis boke here openly says.
    First to shewe I had delyte   16025
þe dignyte and þe grete profyte
Of þe Pater Noster specially
And þe vnderstandynge þarby.
    þareafter I tolde for lewed men mast
þe seuen Giftes of þe Haly Gast   16030
And what es mast þair offyce

And what es vertu and what es vyce.   fo. 96ra
    Alswa men myght here me neuen
þe heued Dedely Synnes Seuen,
With þair braunches and þair rotes   16035
þat in þe hert of man oft shotes,
And seuen special vertus
þat alle þa seuen synnes forduse
And þair braunches and þair degrees
þat lettes alle vyces and vanytees,   16040
And of þe seuen blissedhedes
I haf touched and of þair medes.
Alle es wryten here on þis boke.
    Whaso wil rede it ouer and loke,
It es na vertu vnnethes ne synne   16045
þat he ne sal fynde it wryten þarinne.
þan may he knawe and se þarby
Of what synne he es mast gilty
And what remedy es þareagayne
Or vertu þat es mast certayne.   16050
    Swa may a man knawe and se
What he es and what he suld be.

16022 And¹] om. R   16023 and] om. R   16024 here] om. LR   says] schewes L
16025 had] hald R   16026 grete] om. PRW   profyte] delite profitt L   16028 þe
vnderstandynge] of þe dignite L   16029 for] om. W   lewed men] þe lewed R
16031 es] it is R   mast þair] trs. R   16032 And¹,²] om. R   16033 Alswa] And swa L
16034 heued] om. R   16035 and] and with W   16036 þe] om. R   men] man LPSW
16038 alle] om. L   þa] þe E   16039 And¹] om. R   16040 þat] And P   alle] om. R
and] and all L   16041 of] om. LPS   16042 of] int. P, om. R   16043 Alle] Als L
here on] here in LW, in PR   16044 ouer] om. R   16045 ne] þe R   16046 þat]
Bot R   ne] om. LSR   wryten] om. R   þar-] here P, with- R   16048 he es mast] þai
er R   16049 And] om. R   16050 Or] Of LP   16052 and] om. R?   suld] sall LR

For a man may noght him wele shryue
Ne fra synne hym kepe in þis lyue,
Bot if he can knawe what es synne   16055
And what perille it es to dwelle þarinne.
   Ne a man may noght kepe Goddis lawe
Bot he can right vertus knawe.
For it es noght inoghe to a man
To kepe hym fra synne, al-if he can,   16060
Bot if he vse, als teches þis clerkes,
Gode vertus and do gode werkes.
   þarefore lewed men has grete nede
þis boke oft to here or rede
þat *Mirour* may be called bi skille,   16065
þar men may se bathe gode and ille.
For he þat has hym þareinne sene
May wyte whethir he be foul or clene.
   Now haf I þus to ende broght
Alle þe maters þat I haf soght,   16070
þe whilk men suld oft here and loke,
Als here es wryten in þis boke.

fo. 96rb   For whaso wille oft þam here or rede,
He sal noght faylle þat he ne sal spede
Of speciall grace þat hym sal wisse   16075
þe redy way to heuen blisse.
   At þis tyme wille I na mare say,
Bot yhe þat haf herde þis, I yhow pray
þat yhe pray for hym, bathe alde and yhung,
þat turned þis boke to Inglisshe tung,   16080

16053 For] *om.* R   may] þat canne L   noght him] *trs.* R   him wele] *trs.* LW   shryue]
serue R   16054 hym kepe] *trs.* LS   kepe] *adds* wele R   þis] his ESR   16055 if]
om. E   can] *om.* R   16056 And] *om.* R   16057 Ne a] Na LR   man] he R   noght]
wele L   16060 al-] *int.* P, *om.* R   16061 þis] *om.* R   16062 do] *om.* R
16064 or] and LPSW   16065 þat] A S   16066 þar] þat R   se] *om.* L, here R
bathe] *om.* R   16067 For] *om.* R   16068 whethir] if R   16069 Now . . . þus] þus
I haue R   16071 þe] *om.* R   oft] ofter S, *om.* R   16072 here] *om.* R
16073 For] *om.* R   oft þam] it oft L, þam R, *trs.* W   or] and R   16074 þat . . . sal]
wele to R   ne] *om.* LS   16077 At þis tyme] Now R   wille I] *trs.* S   16078 Bot]
om. R   þis] *om.* R   16079–86 *instead, R reads:* þat 3e wald pray specially/For freer Iohn
saule of Waldby/þat fast studyd day and nyght/And made þis tale in Latyn right/And
preched it with full good chere/To lered ʽandʼ lewed þat hym wold here/þer Ihesu Crist
graunt hym mede/In hewen for his good dede/Prays also with deuocion/For William saule
of Nassyngton/þat gaf hym als full besyly/Night and day to grete study/And made þis tale

Whareso he be and in what stede,
Whethir he lif or he be dede,
þat Godde almyghty graunt hym mede
In heuen-blisse for þis dede.
And yhe sal noght tyne yhour trauaylle;   16085
Of mede þarefore sal yhe noght faylle.
Forwhy þe boke appertely says   *Qui pro alijs orat pro*
þat whaso here for othir prayse,   *seipso laborat*
For hymself þan trauaylles he,
For þat es a token of Charyte.   16090
    Bot Godde þat alle gode may gif,
Graunt yhow grace so here to lif
þat yhe may com when yhe hethen wende
To þe blisse þat es withouten ende.
To whilk blisse he vs alle brynge   16095
þat on þe croyce for vs wald hynge.
Amen

---

in Ynglys tonge/Prays for hym old and ȝonge/þat Ihesu Crist kynge of blys/Graunte hym
ioy þat neuer sall mys/If ȝe pray ȝe sall noght faill/Of mede of Gode for your trauaill
16079 bathe] *om.* L, *int.* P   16080 to] in L   16082 he²] *om.* L   16083-4 *couplet*
om. ES   16084 þis] hys LP   dede] godedede L   16087 -why] *om.* R   þe] þis S
sidenote: om. L, *in* R   16088 þat] *om.* R   16089 þan] *om.* R   16090 token]
poynt R   16091 gode] godes L, *om.* R   16092 yhow] vs L   grace so] *trs.* S   so
here] *trs.* R   16093 yhe¹,²] we L   16094 þat es] *om.* LPR   16095 alle] *om.* LR
16096 þe] *om.* W   vs] vs all L   16096a *marg.* E, *om.* L, *at head of scribal colophon* R

COMMENTARY ON THE TEXT

This commentary will serve a variety of functions. First, it elucidates the text as printed by offering guidance to the poet's sometimes contorted grammar and pointing to the surprisingly small number of forms not attested in MED. It also attends to a variety of problems associated with constructing the text of *Speculum Vitae*, both explanations of emendations and some taste of the variety of attestation underlying various readings, both those printed and rejected. For this purpose, I frequently cite both the B-MSS and the readings of a narrow range of manuscripts of *Somme le roi* (primarily BSG and C). Allusions to the source and/or further French readings appear on a variety of occasions to illustrate the poet's handling, although I have made no effort at providing exhaustive illustration. Finally, I attempt to identify as many as possible of the poet's invocations of authority, virtually all of them inherited from *Somme le roi*. I have been exhaustive in identifying biblical citations; however, for patristic materials, I simply transmit Pamela Gradon's findings and have restricted myself to searching for those citations on which she offered no comment. Gradon's commentary, the most distinguished and detailed study of *Somme* transmission in any language, is replete with useful material and will repay extensive and careful study.

1–114 In succession to the three earlier Yorkshire poems of spiritual instruction, the poem begins with an extended prologue, designed to situate the entire endeavour. In particular, the poet is engaged here in revising the earlier prologue to *Cursor Mundi*. (That text, in turn, quotes from the earlier effort in *The Northern Homily Cycle* and is, in its turn, alluded to at the opening of *The Prick*.)

The first thirty-four lines, following the invocation, include a protracted modesty 'topos'. This material, perhaps conscious of the similar presentation near the start of Robert of Gretham's Anglo-Norman *Miroir* (see *Mirror* 4–5, 14–21), establishes the poet as a man of willing anonymity, a topic to which the conclusion of the whole returns. Lines 35–60 take up a theme conventional in thirteenth- and fourteenth-century prologues, the contrast between the vain poetry of romance and true spiritual edification (although the rhetoric of the poem is generally that of a romance disour). Lines 61–90, in keeping with earlier Northern precedents, discuss the decision to proceed in English; and the remainder announces the subject matter to be pursued here.

Attacks on romance entertainment, the subject of lines 35–60, feature in two exemplary Anglo-Norman precedents: Gretham (see *Mirror* 2–7) and the Yorkshire diocesan official William of Waddington's *Manuel des péches*.

For the ubiquity of such efforts, see Görlach, *Textual Tradition*, 7, 134, 221 n. 6, 263 n. 13; and the discussion in Hanna, *London Literature*, 148–53 (to the materials cited there, add *Genesis and Exodus* 1–34). But, particularly in its citation of texts specifically offensive, the poet here probably makes the first of a number of allusions to *Cursor Mundi*. The earlier poem offers a considerably more extensive list of texts. These include legitimate 'historical' narratives, perhaps Latinate ones (for example, Guido's account of the fall of Troy or Geoffrey of Monmouth's Arthur), *gesta* which contrast with those of Bible history.

Of the texts *Cursor* cites, *Speculum Vitae* shares only one, 'Ysumbras' (40). The poet's allusions extend to only four specifically romance items: 'Ysumbras' joined by 'Octavian', 'Beves of Hamtoun', and 'Guy of Warwick'. The first two certainly had a Northern circulation, although the earliest indication (s. xv$^{2/4}$) is their juxtaposition in Robert Thornton's anthology, Lincoln Cathedral, MS 91, fos. 98^v–114^v (*IMEV* 1918 + 1184). 'Beves' and 'Guy' are, of course, the great indigenous heroes of romance (*IMEV* 1993 and 3145, etc.); the earliest surviving extended example of Northern Middle English is a fragmentary copy of the latter (see *Fragments*).

The following lines (61–90) take up the decision to write in English. These sharply contrast with the *Cursor* poet's attack on French and his strenuously 'commune'-centred (community [of the realm], not a class-statement) opinions. In a less strident way, the poet here concurs in the 'commune' utility of English, its ubiquitous local usage, for an audience without access to clerical texts (lines 86–8, and compare 66, 69). But he equally acknowledges a fractured field of bi- and polylingual usage, while offering a fairly conventional placement of these behaviours (Latin and 'skole' 72, French and 'court' 74; but note the 'small', implicitly non-school Latin alluded to in 75).

11–14 Translate 'And also grant salvation to you who hear me and to all those who require . . . and grant me reward . . .'.

22 *Al-if*: The copytext's usual form for 'although'; see further 6367 n.

42 *whan þai cum to festes*: Compare the later evocation of the feast as a poetic site at the opening of *The Wars of Alexander*: 'When folk ere festid and fed, fayne wald þai here | Sum farand þinge eftir fode to faynen þare hertis.'

74 *þat vsed has court*: 'who have frequented courts'; *dwelled* later in the line probably indicates that the noun refers to magnatial households, rather than simply law courts (the abiding centre of Anglo-Norman usage).

95 On the title 'mirror', see Bradley, 'Backgrounds of the Title'.

98 Translate the slightly redundant line: 'That comes of the Pater Noster'.

101 *þe seuen askynges*: An allusion to the system of septenary catechetics; the actual discussion in these terms begins only at 3357. Much of the intervening portion of the poem, lines 114–2276, only in origin reflects

Somme le roi (compare BSG 67^r–71^r, *BVV* 97–103, which the poem rejoins immediately thereafter). Here the poet derives the terms and order of argument primarily from a Latin summary of *La Somme* itself, the 'Tabula de vtilitate oracionis dominice', presented in the Appendix below. Into this, at appropriate points, he inserts other materials. In some cases, he supplements the outline-like argument of the 'Tabula' from parallel portions of *La Somme* (for example, at lines 511–94, 620–72, 695–820). But he also adds other materials, some displaced passages from *La Somme* (see 1229–1452 n.) and some not (see 959–1228 and n.).

127 The sidenote does not appear in P and is variously placed in other copies. In B-MSS here present and with annotation system, it appears in B^{1}B^{2}B^{5}B^6. But B^9, like P, has no annotation here.

131–2 At Matt. 6: 5–13 (the prayer at v. 9); compare Luke 11: 2–4.

144 *þe naked lettre*: That is, the simple words, here contrasted with *þe vnderstandynge*, any interpretative comprehension (compare the more pointed *sentence* 'the meaning' in line 183).

163 *made it*: The LR transposition is metrically preferable, and is attested in all six B-MSS here extant. This then represents an isolative error of the central group, probably the result of reversion to prose word-order.

206 *loude or stille*: A romance filler-phrase, utilized (as frequently in the poem) for the rhyme. Literally 'aloud or quietly', the phrase means, 'in any circumstances, in any condition'. Compare 230 n.

209–10 Translate 'We say "Et dimitte" in order to destroy immediately the sins we have committed' (and similarly for the subsequent petitions).

221 sidenote: Although customarily equipped with marginal guides, B^{1}B^{5}B^9 omit this one. (Compare the variants *Pro omni bono impetrando* B^2; with *Pro*] D, B^7).

230 *nyght and day*: Like the example cited in 206 n., another romance filler, 'at any time, at all times'. The similar locution *arly and late* occurs sporadically later (1099, 2186, 8907, etc.).

232 *Godde to serue*: The transposition evidenced in LR is metrically attractive, but equally appears a potentially scribal smoothing of a metrically difficult line. The B-MSS split, B^{3}B^{6}B^{7}B^9 sharing the reading of A+, B^{1}B^{2}B^5 attesting that of L+.

246–9 Translate '(depends) all the power of the seven petitions, by those four words, so that we may recognize . . . how we shall govern ourselves . . .'. The variant 247 *þat*] *þan* L, although perhaps more grammatically direct, appears constructed to evade a difficulty; it is attested in none of the B-MSS.

252 *askynges*: The word answers Latin *petita* 'things sought (in prayer)'; the singular variant seeks to generalize the meaning 'prayer'.

269 *Bernard*: Probably 'Sermones in Psalmum "Qui habitat"' 15. 6 (PL 183: 246).

288 *maked, destayned*: *shuld make, ordaned* RW, the first asserting a less problematic metrical pattern, are also widely attested in the B-MSS (rewriting, including *wold . . . make* B^6; *ordeyneþ* B^1, B^8 here absent).

294a–b The couplet is universally attested outside the five central MSS, in all relevant B-MSS, with variants, notably *For*] *Bot* B^{1}B^{3}B^6, *Forwhy* B^7; *destayned*] *destayneþ* B^1, *ordeyned* B^2, *constreyneþ* B^3; *anely þam*] trs. B^{1}B^{3}B^{6}B^9; *þam*] *þo* B^{1}B^{2}B^7, om. B^5 (B^{4}B^8 here absent). Notably, P shares a substantial unique error with the rest of the group, presumably the small skip of their archetype through anticipation of the paragraph break (and probable marginal paraph).

296 *Thre thynges*: The conventional attributes of the deity, Power, Wisdom, and Love. The triad recurs at 862 ff., there apportioned, as is equally conventional, among the three persons.

365 *On*: Not only the majority reading of the central five but virtually universal in the B-MSS (*And on* B^1, *Of* B^2). The error I remove has probably been produced by the attraction of the subsequent line-opening, perhaps by varying scribal expansions of archetypal *O*.

366 *wele*: The tradition at large shows about the same range of variation as the five-manuscript family: B^{2}B^{3}B^9 agree with AP, B^{1}B^6 with E, B^5 with LS (*þat wele*] *als he* B^7). In any event, readings of the E- and R-type confirm the archetypal status of the adverb, and other scribes respond to a (metrical) line they find heavy and awkward (R presumably registers uncertainty as to what word was intended).

375–8 See Matt. 22: 36–8 (a citation of Deut. 6: 5).

386–9 Translate 'If we wish to demonstrate our love, we should more readily suffer our souls to be separated from our bodies than to be separated from God'.

405–28 A ME clarification, offering a definition of *Carles drede*, which, as the sidenote indicates, translates a technical term familiar in Latin handbook discussions, 'timor servilis' (essentially reverence enforced out of fear of punishment).

436, 446 *fynde . . . in þis boke*: Cross-references to the specific discussions below, at 959 ff. (the Decalogue) and 7321 ff. (the Works of Mercy; a perfunctory foretaste at 2168 ff.). Such self-citation, which occurs fairly frequently, presumably speaks to the reading practice the translator imagines for his work. The whole, with the aid of running titles and marginal sidenotes, is presumed susceptible to something like encyclopedic use on a dip-in basis by topic.

453 *in*[2]: Like RW, all B-MSS omit the word, perhaps because they find it extrametrical (although capable of elision to *n'in*).

455 *acount to*: Among B-MSS, B[2]B[6]B[7]B[8]B[9] agree with LPW, but note *acountes ȝiue* B[1]B[3], *acowntys to ȝeus* B[5].

459–66 This material, original to the poem, addresses a concern to which the author returns on several occasions; see 7248 n. The appropriate use of time and of one's intellectual faculties is inherent in most prologue accounts of the vacuity of romance; see 1–114 n. above.

472 *here*: While arguably the general 'in this life' seen elsewhere, perhaps a reference to in-church devotional reading?

473–4 *in stedes withoute | þar his body es borne about*: Probably a fairly early reference to the procession with the host on Corpus Christi Day, for which see Rubin, *Corpus Christi*, 243–71. The celebration was enjoined in York province by archbishop Melton in 1322 (p. 200), and there is a reference indicating the existence of a procession in York by 1366 (p. 255).

495–7 The variant reading of R is isolated, and all eight B-MSS here present agree with A etc.

522 *þe*: Universal agreement induces me to emend A, which is supported by only B[3]B[6] among the comparison manuscripts (*oure* B[8]).

527 *be*: Among B-MSS, only B[5] shares the LSRW reading *to be*.

541–6 *in som lande | Swilk a lawe*: The poet, here in the midst of a seventy-line passage taken from *La Somme*, suppresses its specific reference: 'par grace e par adopcion. Adopcion si est uns mos de lois, car selom les lois del empereor, quant vns haus hons n'a nul enfant, il puet eslire . . .' (SG 69[r]/11–13, *BVV* 100/5–7, clarifying the reference to Roman civil law).

544 *his*: The specifying *of hys* LPSRW also appears in B[1]B[3]B[5]B[8].

548 *Paul*: A congeries of Pauline ideas, for example Rom. 8: 14–7, Eph. 3: 26, Gal. 4: 28; for 'filii ire', Eph. 2: 3; for 'filii tenebrarum', Eph. 5: 8 and 1 Thes. 5: 5.

560–4 Translate 'the courtesy of God, who gives living men more readily plenty than little and gives more quickly to many of his faithful than to one'.

565 *Gregor*: Probably *Comm. in librum 1 Regum* 5.27 (on 1 Reg. [1 Sam] 10: 12) (PL 79: 302–3).

566 *right*: *rightwys* RW is isolated and unparalleled in any of the B-MSS, whose scribes understood that the second syllable of *prayere*, as customarily, bears stress.

569 *Als a candell*: Compare Matt. 5: 15–16.

581 *þis: his* LR is attested elsewhere, in B[1]B[3]B[5].

589 *wede*: 'Pledge', the universal reading of B-MSS as well; the ELS variants show a homeographic partial synonym. The Pauline reference is to Eph. 1: 14, and, as Gradon points out (158, 102/14–17 n.) Paul mentions 'the spirit of adoption' at Rom. 8: 15–17.

610 *And*: The text does not appear sensible without following SR and all B-MSS; the erring scribes have been attracted, perhaps utterly independently, to the succeeding line-opening, as at 365 above.

611 *othir suld*: The RW transposition also occurs in B^6B^7.

620 *Iame*: James 5: 16.

632 *thynges*: The reading, rare outside the five-text group (B^8 only), is confirmed by 635 *þe thridde thynge*; its disappearance from the tradition is predicated upon the obvious, that these are indeed sins, as line 633 indicates.

644, 645 *vnto, for*: Like PRW, all B-MSS read *to, thurgh*. The first variant, in one form or another, occurs ubiquitously across the MSS of the poem and provides one major strand of the variation distinguishing the general tradition from the five central copies. This indicates something of the triviality of much variation in the sample I have investigated; *to/vnto* alternation was favoured by the scribes for the resolution of metrical difficulties. Further examples from the first half of the poem (at which point I cease noting the variation) occur in the notes to 2062, 3370, 3528, 5114, 6381, 6838, 7408, 7990, and 8214.

667 *and þe . . . and þe*: Both uses of the article look suspiciously like they might be scribal, although equally, both appear fairly widely in the tradition ($þe^2$] om. $B^2B^3B^5B^6B^7$; $þe^3$] om. $B^3B^5B^7$). Similarly, at 833 the article *þe* appears only in B^7 among B-MSS. Lines concerning the Trinity appear to allow variation among the number of unstressed syllables in different copies.

672 *Ione*: John 14: 21.

693–4 Compare, most famously, Augustine's refutation of the Manichees, described in *Confessions* 7. The claim that this is a view expressed in Scripture relies upon such passages as the statement of the beneficence of Creation at 1 Tim. 4: 4 and the varying accounts of the genesis of sin at 1 John 3: 8–9, Rom. 5: 12, Ecclus. 25: 33.

696–712 *Godde apered*: See Exod. 3–4, esp. 3: 13–14.

698 *and*: Only B^1 and B^8 agree with LP in this omission.

707–8 E and P display difficulties with the couplet. The transposed version of P also appears in B^3B^9 (of the eight B-MSS here present), in both with *þan sayde he*] om. in their second line. The truncated form of the lines in E may reflect a similar effort to reduce apparent repetition.

724 ff. Compare *The Book of Privy Counseling*, 143/19–26, cited and discussed Gillespie, 'Postcards from the Edge', 146 (perhaps originally Bernard, 'Sermo 15 in Cantica'?).

741 *we*: ELRW are joined in the reading by B³B⁵B⁶B⁷ (*he* APS+ B²B⁸, B¹B⁹ out here); since the uses in 731–6 and 743–5 are uncontested, the minority scribes here have momentarily slipped into following the more adjacent pronoun *men* (= *me* '[some]one, people').

742 *whatso*: The unmetrical *what* (which R recognized as such) appears in all B-MSS present (B¹B⁹ still out).

745 *fynde we*: Transposition might be metrically preferable, but there are no variants in the B-MSS either.

752 The French ascribes the opinion to Job (BSG 70ᵛ/36, *BVV* 102/22), referring to Job 14: 4 (compare 23: 13).

759–60 *thing . . . þa þat er*: Translate 'He made those things that are (his creations)'; the scribes tend to ignore syntactic units larger than the single line.

762 *War . . . bot*: Translate 'Were otherwise nothing except'. As the punctuation indicates, the statement is continued in 764 'but only so in comparison with God'.

763 *Salamon*: Eccl. 1: 2, etc., 3: 19.

772 *lousynge*: With the variants cited in the collations, compare *losyng* B¹, *lesyng* B³B⁵.

775 *Iame*: Probably James 1: 17.

784 *stirynge*: Presumably reads metrically as *stir[y]ynge*, with retention of the medial syllable of OE styrian.

809 Compare 1 Cor. 13: 12.

824 *drede*: Given the lengthy exposition of the Decalogue and Creed, this discussion begins only at 1454.

825 The sidenote also appears in B¹B²B⁵B⁷.

828 *hinges*: The extraneous *here* also appears in B¹B²B⁷B⁹.

841–88 *In þe sonne*: Probably derived (the explanation does not appear in the Latin exposition) from the similar comparison at *Cursor Mundi* 287–322. Compare Langland's similar trinitarian explanations, as hand and candle, at *Piers* B.17: 134–253 (and *Roland and Vernagu* 713–18).

843 *als*: PRW *als of* appears in all B-MSS.

sidenote: A is apparently marked for an addition, but none appears, and, although the distinction is incomplete as regards the opening triad, it does reflect the development of the text, which is only two-, not threefold.

871–90 This triad—Memory, Reason, and Love—reflects ancient psychological theory, in which 'the inner wits' are reduced to three, in accord with the three cerebral ventricles identified in Galenic medicine. Gradon cites (160, 105/23–6 n.) Augustine's discussion, *De Trinitate* 4. 6 (PL 42: 1042).

897 *þe apostell*: See, for example, Eph. 4: 5 and the ensuing discussion, esp. verses 15–25; and such loci as 2 Tim. 1: 13, Gal. 2: 20.

900 *broght*: Although EP *wroght* is attractive, it is probably a scribal product, and all B-MSS agree with A.

901–4 *castell*: The castle metaphor as an image of self-custody or custody of the senses recurs through the poem, most particularly in the concluding discussions of self-restraint; see further 1933–40 (and n.), 4811–14, 5457–8, 9660–88, 11465–74, 11783–804, 12545–60, 14903–18, 14933–8, 15067–70, 15449–58. While the metaphor is clearly commonplace, it has extensive and distinguished ME analogues, for example *Ancrene Riwle*, the thirteenth-century homily 'Sawles warde', or *Piers* B.1: 12–26 and its reprise 5: 585–608; 9: 1–24; 19: 317–34 (and the ensuing action at the end of the poem).

919 *we suld*: The transposition of PRW occurs in all B-MSS.

925 ff. Halykirk is here assimilated to a traditional figure of the virtue Caritas, still available to Spenser; compare *Faerie Queene* 1. 10. 29–31. The association of the breasts of God's spouse, the Church, with sound doctrine is derived from standard glosses to the opening verse of the Canticle; compare Renevey, *Language, Self and Love*, e.g. 173–4 nn. 37–9.

934 *Haly Writte*: Although developed further at 951–8 as indicating the concord of the two testaments, the statement is, of course, not thoroughly accurate. While the Decalogue does come from Exod. 20, the Creed is non-biblical.

959–1228 Although *Somme* begins (BSG 13ʳ–17ʳ, *BVV* 1–9) with a tract on the Decalogue, followed, as here, by one on the Creed, the author has not relied exclusively on the French text for either. The presentation of the Ten Commandments differs radically from that of *Somme*, and I have not found any near source (not *Cursor*, nor the tract of BodL, MS Ashmole 751). There are some intriguing near parallels with the considerably more extensive Middle English 'standard Decalogue tract' (*IPMEP* 48). This has, for example, the disposition of ten into the two tablets Moses received, and, implicitly, the assignment of each of the first three commandments to the different persons (compare 985–8, 1010–1, etc. with *BVV* 317, 321 *passim*). The standard tract also has near parallels to the discussion of the fifth commandment, 'Thou shalt not kill' here (compare 1065–1104 with *BVV* 326 *passim*).

960 *byndes*: In spite of the profusion of variants among the central manuscripts, all B-MSS read as A.

978 *for*: Compare to B⁷B⁹ (much as R), ther 'by'fore B⁶ (much as W, but by correction in the main hand).

992 *ane*: Only B⁷B⁹ concur with the central copies; compare *only* B¹B⁵, *ay* B⁶ (like RW), om. B²B³B⁸.

994 *alle*: PRW's *all oþer* appears in all B-MSS except B²B⁵.

1018 *I am sothfastnes*: John 14: 6.

1027–30 The punctuation attempts to indicate the construction *clene . . . Fra*.

1030 *werk*: Although LSRW have the support of all B-MSS, the singular/plural contrast appears an indifferent reading, and one likely to have been attracted to plural *werkes* in the following lines. The problem is recurrent, at least in part because Northern copies do not always clearly distinguish the mark of abbreviation from the finishing stroke conventional on -*k* in anglicana; see 1766 n., 1807 n. below.

1040 *Acordande*: Confusion of Northern pr.p. and the adjective in -*a(u)nt* recorded in SR appears widely in the tradition, where only B⁷B⁹ retain the former. The poet shares such final unvoicing and often rhymes -*a(u)nt* with -*and(e)*; see e.g. 6305, 6331, 6518, 10217.

1047 *þam þat gastly bene*: That is, one's godparents and the parish priest.

1059–60 Translate 'People should grant honour to them through whom they have their life'.

1064 Translate '(Should long be) manifestly here that which he has been created' (emphatically answering 1062 *thurgh wham he es*). LP seem to have found this either so vacuous or so cryptic as to adjust the line, paralleled only in B³ *Longe on lyue here to seo*.

1094 *he es*: Translate 'He is reasonably (called) a murderer'. Although all the central copies read *he þat es*, the B-MSS support the printed reading in the variant *þat es*] *is a* B³B⁵B⁶B⁸B⁹. Other copies may have been influenced by the opening of line 1092.

1096 *þus*: RW are supported in their omission by none of the B-MSS.

1100–3 Translate 'Or slanders him with poisonous words, in order to reduce his praise; or withholds the food that should preserve the lives of those in need'.

1102 *þa*: Substitution of *þaim*, as in EPS, also occurs in B¹B²B⁷B⁹.

1106 *with*: ELPS *with na* has considerable support elsewhere in the tradition (only B⁷B⁹ concur with ARW), but the reading may represent a metrical adjustment on the assumption that the stress of *womman* falls on the stem, rather than the shift to an un- or only secondarily stressed syllable customary in rhyming position.

1127 *als*: All three variants can be parallelled elsewhere in the tradition (only B¹B⁷ agree with the text printed): B⁵B⁹ concur with L (in B⁹, *alle* added later in the line); B³, with P; B²B⁶B⁸, with S.

1132 *hidynges*: Compare *huydyng* B³B⁸, *wynnynges* B⁷ (as R), *biddynges* B⁹.

1176 *man*: ELP *nane* might either be correct or imported from the preceding line. In the first instance, ASRW would represent an over-specification of a sort that may have occurred any number of times independently (compare *nane* B¹, *men* B⁵B⁹). But finally, the governing construction appears the forward-looking (rather than retrospective) contrast 1175–8 'Ne . . . Suld man couayte . . . Ne a womman . . .'.

1184 *siluer ne gold*: The L transposition *Golde na syluer* would probably be metrically preferable, but is another of that copy's independent transpositions. B¹ tries to reduce the metrical difficulty by repeating *Neiþer* at the head. And at the line's end, P's difficulty with the rhyme-word 'jewel' appears elsewhere in B-MSS; cf. *metel* B³B⁸, *oþer metele* B².

1193 *þat haally may noght lifted be*: Essentially construing the last two commandments as partly complementary. The preceding enjoins the removal of *na moble*, portable property, while this takes up immovable assets.

1220 *þe*: arguably dittography in those MSS where present (including B⁷B⁹; compare *the* [*over eras.*] ?*first thre* B¹, *the whiche* B⁶).

1224 *þe Newe Lawe*: Because Jesus cites them, in response to inquiries at Matt. 19: 17–19.

1225 *thurgh*: RW are not supported in their omission in any of the B-MSS.

1229–1452 The discussion of the Apostles' Creed is, in its detailed language, generally a close rendition of the second tract of *Somme le roi* (BSG 15ᵛ–17ʳ, *BVV* 6/18–9/31). However, the tract has received a number of structural adjustments to bring it into conformity with norms of Yorkshire spiritual instruction, here exemplified by the Creed tract transmitted at BodL, MSS Ashmole 751, fo. 85ᵛ, and Hatton 12, fol. 211ᵛᵃᵇ. The division of the articles follows the local Creed tract, not that of *Somme le roi*, and the assignment of individual articles to specific apostles generally, although not exactly, accords with this English use, not that of the French. See further Gordon, 'The Articles of the Creed'.

1231 *þe twelf*: The LP transposition gives attractive sense; it is, however, isolated, found in no B-MSS.

1269 *myght*: LPR *myghtes* has significant support elsewhere (B¹B³B⁶B⁹, B⁸ absent). But it is probably filling out and making explicit a syllable implicitly present as -*e* of dative *myght[e]*.

1351 *godes of*: LP *godnes of* agrees with B³ and has reflexes elsewhere among B-MSS: *gode* B¹, *godnesse of* B⁵, *goodnes and of* B⁶, *godes and* B⁸. But BSG 16ᵛ/47 'tuit li bien de grace' (compare *BVV* 8/30) confirms the reading of A+. The variation is recurrent; see further 2698 n., 3221 n., etc.

1354 *seuen Giftes*: The fundamental 'seven' by which the poem is structured, not to be explicitly introduced until line 2321.

1359–60 Translate 'but that we consider and designate it different in person than the persons of the . . .'.

1377–1420 *Somme* only mentions and lists the sacraments (*BVV* 9/7–11). They appear there in a different order, and there is no parallel to the additional detailed information the author here provides.

1380 *nowe*: Compare *on a row* B^5, *nowe on rowe* B^9.

1381 *halde I*: $B^2B^3B^5B^8$ agree with PW *halden*.

1385 *mare or lesse*: Translate 'whether for a graver or less serious sin'; compare *Bathe dedely synne and venyele* 1400.

1386 *auter es*: The ELS reading *messe* is isolated, in none of the B-MSS. It has probably been generated from dissatisfaction with the number of syllables in the line and the rather unemphatic rhyme.

1394 *has*: Probably to be construed as representing contracted *h'as* 'he has'. Given the possible reading *grac-ë*, the line would be metrical with or without the expressed subject.

1395 *of*: The R variant *of þe* also appears in $B^1B^2B^6B^8$, but W's intruded gloss, *seruyng of*, unlike other examples below (see 1933–40 n.), has no parallel in the B-MSS.

1414–6 Translate 'Absolves a man and woman, if their intent accords with right reason, from mortal sin in the (sexual) act'.

1422 *in*: $B^3B^5B^6B^8B^9$ agree with PR in adding *it*.

1429 *Symonis*: As well as the majority reading of the collated MSS, also that of all seven B-MSS with a sidenote here (B^7 out, no sidenote B^3).

1434 *sal*: The EL omission is quite attractive (A may simply be grammatically finicky here) and has the support of $B^3B^5B^8$ (B^7 out).

1442 *þan sal*: A variety of variants attests to uncertainty about the metre: *þan sal þai* ERB^1, *sall þai* LSB^8, *þei schul* B^3. But *Endeles* is probably trisyllabic here and bears two of the stresses.

1469–1665 Most of the passage appears original to the poem and without parallel in either 'Tabula' or *La Somme*. The poet appears to have produced the discussion by consultation of other portions of the source or his poem: materials here from about line 1490 appear inspired by the discussion of Contemplation in the pure in heart who will see God from the discussion of 'Abstinence', and the eighty lines from 1583 on by portions of the discussion of 'Lechery' (and possibly reminiscences of book 2 of *The Prick*).

1476 *þar²*: The dissimilating variants are attested elsewhere: P's *os* in B^3, R's *whar* in B^1, and compare *þat* $B^5B^6B^8$ (B^7 out).

1484 *ay*: The omission in LSW is widespread, indeed the majority reading, also in B¹B²B³B⁸B⁹ (*se ay*] om. B⁵, B⁷ out). But *a* 'a single' must receive emphasis here, in contrast to 'ilka pece' in the preceding line.

1498 *ne*: The omission is absolutely ubiquitous among B-MSS and reflects those scribes' sense that the extra syllable, and thus the emphatic negative, is otiose following *thynge* pl., i.e. disyllabic *thynges*.

1510 *mast . . . hym*: Independent transpositions are rife throughout the tradition, for example, hym most wele B¹B⁹, most wold hym B⁵, although B⁸ (as W, B⁷ out).

1526 *a steghe*; Eventually described at 14689 ff.; cf. 2145 n.

1534 *of*: The RW omission only appears elsewhere in B⁵B⁹, although in the rewritten line of B¹ *of* is supplied by interlineation (B⁷ out).

1543 *Godde says*: Matt. 23: 12.

1557 *heght*: hegh EPSW is indifferent, if not facilior, and universal in the B-MSS here extant.

1560 *pise*: The suppression of the metrically otiose syllable in EL also occurs in B²B⁸.

1575 B-MSS include the variants *noght*] after *lat* B¹B³; *passe*] out passe B¹B⁹.

1582 Traces of the scribal line in L, unlike the similar effort at 1589 (nowhere else attested), appear in B-MSS; compare *him meke and*] make hym B⁶, meke him and B⁸.

1610 *him has*: ELPS adjust the variation in word-order to accord with the previous line; their transposition also occurs in B¹B⁵B⁶, while B³B⁸ omit *has* (and presumably sound the -*ë* of *dede*).

1633 Translate 'And gave him intelligence and reason to know'.

1641 Translate 'He suffered meekly every thing that might do harm (in order to give)'.

1644 *dose*: The R addition *bath*, a metrical smoothing, also appears in B³.

1650 *fendes*: LR *defendes*, which provides more emphatic metrical patterning, appears in all B-MSS except B².

1672 *lightens*: The easier LSW *lyghtes* 'alights' is widespread, in B¹B³B⁵B⁸B⁹ (*lustenyth* B⁶, a reading that confirms the suffixed form).

1676 *sharpe*: Like W, B¹B⁹ read *hard*, a variation that recurs at 5310.

1688 *now*: Compare ȝow B¹B⁸ (*ꝉ* om. B²).

1693 The sidenote, in much the same form as A, appears in all B-MSS with annotational programmes (similarly 1751, 1759).

1720 *it*: L's omission also appears in B⁵B⁶.

1734 (cf. 1740, 1742, 1752, as well as 1766 n. below) *werk*: The variant *hert* appears sporadically in a variety of copies; here in B^2 (and as a cancelled correction in B^8) and in 1752 in B^5. It, of course, shows the scribes as varyingly attentive to the change from the similarly worded earlier topic.

1745 *to*: ERW's omission (the syllable is both metrically and grammatically otiose) also occurs in $B^2B^3B^5B^8B^9$. Similarly, 1796 *and¹* is lacking in $B^1B^3B^5B^6B^8$.

1764 *yhernes*: *lufes* ELS is isolated, the only B-MSS variants more proximate synonymous substitutions, *coueytyth* B^5, *desirith* B^6.

1766 *werkes*: $B^2B^5B^7B^8$ have the singular, as W, but $B^1B^6B^9$ have *hert*, as LPR. See 1030 n.

1777 *with*: PRW's *by* is universal in B-MSS.

1787–2158 The discussion of the 'three + four virtues' here has been adapted from their later appearance in *La Somme* (see BSG 83^r–85^v, *BVV* 121–5). The discussion of the Theological Virtues includes all the materials of the French, but a good deal more, while that of the Cardinal Virtues represents close translation of materials in the source.

1791 *Meth-*: W *Meke-* also appears in $B^1B^8B^9$; cf. *Temperaunce* B^2B^5, *Meth* B^3.

1793 *thre*: A has a clarifying marginal addition *first*, mainly generated by contrast with *after* in the following line. Although the word is also present in RB^1B^9, it is a scribal clarification, and I have removed it. A, the copy here used as base text, has a small number of such later corrections, most similarly unconvincing, from a manuscript of the general transmissional tradition; see, for example, 6253–4, 13602, 15790.

1799 *Austyn*: Perhaps a general reference to the *Enchiridion* (PL 40: 231 ff.), as below at 1833; certainly, the most famous passage of this stripe, although relatively distant, is *De doctrina cristiana* 1. 37–9 (PL 34: 35–6). Gradon cites (167, 123/14–15 n.) 'De agone Christiano' 13 (PL 40: 299).

1805 *als says þis clerkes*: Following James 2: 17–26.

1807 *werk*: *werkes*, also in $B^2B^3B^5B^6$ (and corrected out later in B^1) is a product of any variety of mechanisms, for example dittography before *es*, assimilation to the biblical quotation of the Latin sidenote, confusion of otiose termination on -*k* with the similar abbreviation for -*es*. On the recurrence of this variation, compare 1030 n.; at 1880, $B^1B^2B^9$ read plural.

1817–32 See the further discussions at 4331–2, 4341–78, 5249–56.

1833 *Austyn*: See 1799 n.

1851 *Ione*: 1 John 4: 21.

1852 *for*: Also omitted in $B^2B^3B^5B^6B^8$, but metrically necessary.

1858 *wham he*: The stress clash at the caesura has produced smoothing variants beyond those attested in LR: *may*] *may here* B^1, *may ilk day* B^7.

1863 *Paul*: Probably a glossed version of a passage like Rom. 5: 1–5, 1 Cor. 13: 13, or 1 Thes. 1: 3.

1869 *for*: Metrically necessary, it has been removed as dittography by a range of scribes, including B¹B³B⁸.

1875 *had*: LSR *herde* has been contaminated from 1872; the reading also occurs in B²B⁶.

1878 *thre first*: Scribes elsewhere in the tradition also find the construction difficult: B²B⁵ (in the latter corrected in the original hand) omit *first* (as R), B³B⁸ transpose *first vertus* (as ES).

1882 *baytes*: 'Tastes', presumably correct, after *sauour* and anticipating *tastes* 1884. The commoner *laytes* 'seeks' is nearly universal in B-MSS (B² rewrites, so as to avoid the verb).

1891 *Salamon*: Solomon never quite says this. But note Wis. 18: 24, potentially alignable with Bede's important readings of the Cardinal Virtues as inherent in the descriptions of the ark and priestly garments. Compare also Prov. 8: 14, 24: 3 (the last with allusion to Wisdom's house), Prov. 9: 1 (a description underlying 1931 ff.).

1902 *gyen*: It is a little unclear why this verb should be so problematic, but the profuse variation of the copies collated is mirrored throughout the B-MSS: *kepe* B¹B⁹ (as W), *gouerne* B²B³B⁵, *geyn* B⁶, *gyle* B⁷, *noȝt* (*canc.*) *gouerne* B⁸. At 1963, the variation is less lush, *kepes* B¹B³B⁹ (as SW), *gyfes* B² (as L).

1913 *sundre*: Compare *depart* B²B⁶, *parten atwynne* B³, *dysundre* B⁵.

1915 *to*: *forto*, an echo of *forsake*, also appears in B⁶B⁸.

1933–40 W has inserted as English textual readings part of a sequence of glosses, perhaps originally Latin, and presumably authorial, since they elucidate a passage that, while clear enough in its general sense, relies on symbolic referents. Compare the series of explanations offered in the B-MSS:

  1933 *hous*] *hert* WB¹B⁹, `hert´ RB⁷B⁸, `id est herte´ B⁵

  1934 *hous*] *hert* WB¹B⁹, `hert´ RB⁷B⁸

  1936 *þe soule*] W, marg. *Anima* B¹, marg. *þe soule* `B²´B⁹, `id est sowle´ B⁵B⁷

  1937 *flesch*] W, marg. *Caro* B¹, marg. *þe flesche* B⁹, `þe flesshe´ B², `id est flesch´ B⁵B⁷

  1938 *lustes*] W, `B²B⁵B⁷B⁸´, `id est lustes´ B⁵B⁷

  1939 *þe fende*] W, marg. *Diabolus* B¹, marg. *þo fende* `B²´B⁹, `id est fende´ B⁵B⁷, `fend´ B⁸

  1940 *hatred and enuye*] WB⁶ (before *coldes* B⁶), marg. *odium et inuidia* B¹, marg. *hatereden and enuye* B⁹, int. (*id est h.* B⁷) B²B⁷, `id est elmye?´ B⁵, *envye* after *lette* and `hatred´ B⁸

1941 *westward*] marg. *Mundus* B¹, marg. *þo world* B⁹, `þe worlde´ B²B⁸, `id est werd´ B⁵, `id est þe werld´ B⁷

1942 *shours*] marg. *Cupiditas* B¹, marg. *Couetyse* B⁹, `couetice´ B²B⁸, `id est couetise´ B⁷, *couetise* after *shours* B⁶

1943, 1949, 1965 *offyces*: Following a stem ending in a sibilant, the plural inflection is susceptible to apocope. Overt plural forms appear in the first two examples in B²B³B⁵ (in the first, *vertues* B¹B⁹). At 1965, B¹B²B³B⁵ have the ambiguous *s*-less form that might represent either singular or plural.

1944 *sere*: W *diuers* also appears in B²B³B⁶ (here B⁵).

1946 *Placius*: As Gradon points out (168, 124/32 n.), the reference is probably not to Plato, but to Cicero's *De officiis*. He is probably also *þe (wis) philosophre* invoked at lines 2023 and 2034. The 'three offices' of Prudentia roughly follow Cicero's division of the virtue (in 'De inventione') into *memoria, intelligentia*, and *providentia*.

1948 *sayd*: The present of ELS also appears in B²B⁶ (corr. out in the original hand B⁵).

1949 The sidenote of ES also appears in B²B⁵B⁶B⁸ but is lacking in the other three B-MSS with annotational systems.

1950 *hym*: The neuter 'it' is universal in B-MSS.

1968 *hym may*: The transposition also occurs in B¹B⁵B⁸.

1972 *settes*: sittes LP, as also B¹B³B⁹, but translate, 'He constrains (cf. *betes* W?) under the guidance of reason (all the covetousness . . .), and he fears it'.

1979 *Ion*: 1 John 2: 16. The sidenote identification is virtually limited to ELS, which typically share extensive marking not found elsewhere. Among the B-MSS, only B⁵ shares their annotation here.

1981 *lust*: LPS *luf* is surely wrong, on the basis of the text cited, but the reading also appears in B²B³B⁵B⁸.

1997 *stifly*: Compare *stilleliche* B³, *stille* B⁸.

2003 *talde*: PS *cald* also appears in all B-MSS except B⁷B⁹ (hold B⁶), but the variation between the two graphic and lexical similars is endemic in the text.

2017 *strengthe²*: B³B⁸ try to dissimilate the readings and have *herte* instead.

2019 *wille*: PRW *wele* also appears in B²B³B⁵B⁶.

2025 *do*: EL *to do* is also attested in all B-MSS except B³.

2029 *lufrede(n)*: The metrically necessary suffix is a distinctive reading of the five central MSS; B¹B²B⁸B⁹ read *loue* (as RW), and other variants include: *loue* (*louen* B³) also B³B⁶B⁷, *to louyn* B⁵.

2034 *þe wys philosophre*: See 1946 n.

2045 *se*: The LR provision of the extra syllable *may* is isolated, but compare *riȝt se* B².

2049 *And*: RW's A also appears in B⁵B⁶B⁷.

2062 *To*: Vnto LPR appears elsewhere only in B⁷, which also uniquely agrees with LR in reading 2077 *þai sal*.

2073 *Paul*: Rom. 2: 13–16; Gradon (169, 126/18–21 n.) directs attention to a later point in the discussion, verses 26–7.

2093 *Austyn*: 'De moribus ecclesie' 15. 25 (PL 32: 1322); compare Gösta Hök, 'Augustine und die antike Tugendlehre', *Kerygma und Dogma*, 6 (1960), 104–30. The sidenote appears in all B-MSS with annotation except B⁶.

2145 *Iacob*: Gen. 28: 10–22; *þe Boke of Wisdom*, as Gradon points out (169–70, 127/15–16 n.), directs one to the analysis of the event at Wis. 10: 10. Jacob's vision of the ladder to heaven in Bethel is here implicitly identified with the 'trace' or way up God's mountain; the figure (there a *steghe*) recurs emphatically in the poet's discussion of Contemplation, at 14692–712, etc.

2156 *lifynge*: W *likynge* also occurs in B¹B⁵B⁹.

2163–4 The poem outlines the traditional distinction. The Active Life, expected of all Christians, requires knowledge of the virtues and enacting them in charitable works towards one's neighbour (here the 'Works of Mercy'). In contrast, the Contemplative Life is one totally devoted to the love of God, and customarily involves specifically speculative or intellectual devotions (not necessarily the pursuit of mystical unity). Compare Rolle's discussion, *Form of Living*, lines 836–93 (edn. 24–5). One might note the gesture towards a commonplace late medieval 'third way', the Mixed Life, at 2227–30 (although more usually conceived as blending contemplation into a life primarily 'active').

2168 ff. A very brief introduction to the seven Works of Mercy. The two sets of these, the 'Corporal' and 'Spiritual' works, are separated by a semicolon in the text at 2176. For discussion, see the poem's vastly extensive treatment, at 7539–8526 below.

2169 *ye*¹, ²: A substantial number of B-MSS, B¹B³B⁸B⁹, follow W in omitting both articles; B², like R, omits only the second.

2195–8 ES share a common homeoteleuthon, returning to copy at the second line with *bisy* in rhyme, rather than the first.

2196 *A lyf of rest*: Compare Rolle's applause for the contemplative life in *The Form of Living*: 'A gret doctour seith þai ben Goddis trone þat dwellen stille in a stid, and ben nat about rennynge, bot in swetnesse of Cristis loue ben stabled. And I haue loued for to sit' (EETS 293, 23/827–9).

2199–2200 A standard early evocation of the triad 'lectio', 'oracio', 'meditacio' appears in the tract 'De quadripartito exercitio cellae' of the Carthusian Adam of Dryburgh (d. 1212); see Gillespie, '*Lukynge in haly bukes*'.

2202–3 *Of . . . And of:* Follow from *redynge* 2201.

2220 *of:* In spite of overwhelming *on* elsewhere among the five central MSS (as well as in B¹B³B⁸B⁹), the reading is an indifferent. A (and other B-MSS) may have anticipated the prepositions in the following line, but equally, ELPS+ may adopt a reading dissimilating from them. And both sets may be responding to the ambiguous archetypal form *o* (see 365 n.).

2224 *bifore:* Most specifically in the discussion at 1571–1664.

2239 On the Three Foes of Mankind, see Howard, *The Three Temptations*, ch. 1.

2241 *aythir syde:* With the two sides, compare the castle metaphor earlier invoked with the Cardinal Virtues and the more general application at 2130. The distinction is ancient, perhaps earliest in Julius Pomerius and widespread; for discussion, see Harris, *Skelton's* Magnificence *and the Cardinal Virtue Tradition. The sidenote is present in all B-MSS with annotational systems (Primus inimicus mundus B⁷).*

2247–8 The transposition found in W also occurs in B¹B⁹, both of which also agree with W in omitting 2247 *Bot.*

2256 *and:* Although A here derives support from PW, the construction forces one to read either an awkward appositive or an otherwise unrecorded compound 'lust-liking'. It is more expeditious to follow the remaining copies and virtually all B-MSS (only the probably secondary error *lust and lykyng*] *lustyng* B³B⁸).

2277 At this point, the author segues to join the exposition of the Pater Noster in *La Somme* (*BVV* 103/20, BSG 71ʳ/10). Initially, in the summary of the 'four words', he expands a bit on that source, but replaces the musical metaphor under which *Somme* discusses the 'prologue' to the Pater Noster (2313–20).

2280–2 At this point, the poet is offering the French source's summary of the preceding argument. Here he invokes again the terms of the earlier lengthy discussion, 369–512, and the summary continues through 2398 with further allusions to earlier materials (for example, 2396 recalling the detailed discussion of Humility at 1535–1777).

2284 *Goddis,* **2293** *worde:* P's *his* and *vs* indicate that manuscript's passing conflation from the general tradition represented by RW+B-MSS (where the only variant is 2284 *Goddis*] om. B⁵).

2311 *fast fest:* Compare the haplographic *fastne* B²B³B⁸.

2318 *ane entre of way*: Alluding to John 10: 1–2 and its conventional evocation/exegesis in anti-mendicant rhetoric. The variant *of*] *of a*, in LP+RW, is also widely dispersed among B-MSS, in B²B³B⁵B⁸.

2321 The passage introduces the structure of the remainder, eventually to be a standard septenary analysis; see Tuve, *Allegorical Imagery*, supplemented by Aarts, 'The Pater Noster in Medieval English Literature', Henry, ' "The Pater Noster in a table ypeynted" ', Hussey, 'The Petitions of the Paternoster'.

2327–8 Translate 'implants in their stead seven virtues people should practise'.

2331 ff. Compare the discussions above, in first exposition: the petitions at 195–242, and the mental triad at 867–94.

2335–43 The centre of the rather sprawling (and not quite grammatically coordinated) sentence is provided by the first and the last lines. Three things make a man holy, in accord with the image of trinitarian powers in the human soul.

2336 *shewe vs*: W *schewen* also appears in B²; elsewhere in the B-MSS the only variant is the transposition of the two words in B⁵.

2345 *allekyns*: The LP reading *alle* also occurs in B¹B² (*eche a* B⁵B⁶).

2353 *come*: LSR *comes* is probably preferable, both grammatically and metrically; it also appears in B¹B⁵B⁹.

2377 *þis*: R *þus* also appears in all B-MSS except B²B⁷.

2396 *and fele*: Parallel to *tast wele*.

    licour: Neutrally 'liquor/liquid, drink', replacing *Somme* 'vin' (*BVV* 105/2, BSG 72ʳ/8). The English author similarly tones down references here to drunkenness or fervent love at 2363 and 2476 (compare BSG 'yure' 72ᵛ/35, 'de feruent amour' 72ᵛ/40–1).

2399 *þat¹*: The pleonastic use after the conjunction is suppressed in B²B³B⁸B⁹, as in LRW.

2411 *thre wyse*: Compare *Somme* 'v. manieres' (BSG 72ʳ/13; *BVV* 105/8 'sixe maneres'); the fourth and fifth of the intended series are introduced at 2435 and 2453, in the source by simple 'Apres' (BSG 72ʳ/23, 72ᵛ/29).

2430 *Godde*: PRW *hym* is universal in B-MSS.

2435 *þe*: W *þat* also occurs in B¹B⁹.

2444 *on*: The extrametrical *on þe* also appears in B¹B²B⁶B⁸.

2448 *litted*: Nearly all the manuscripts collated have preceding *es*, intruded from the uses in the preceding line. However, virtually all B-MSS read as R (*Hyt ys . . . dyhed* B¹, *litith* B⁶), and I here follow the majority transmission. The French offers no evidence.

2466 *bitter*: The erroneous PSW *better* also appears in B^{1}B^{6}B^{7}B^8.

2473 *renoueld*: The B-MSS show a range of forms comparable to those in the MSS collated: *rewled* B^5 (as L), *renewed* B^1 (as S), *releued* B^{3}B^8.

2506 *to*: EW *itt to* also appears in B^{1}B^9.

2507 *þe godespell*: Luke 17: 21.

2516–17 *mirk-*: The only full agreement with W appears in B^3, although B^2 reads 'derkenes' in the first line.

2523 *he^2*: The majority *þat he* appears elsewhere only in B^{1}B^8.

2525–6 *poudre . . . Of synne*: Compare BSG 73^r/14–15: 'tant de defautes e de pouties e de poudre sanz nombre' (*BVV* 106/27–8). The sun's direct light reveals motes one could not otherwise see and thus reveals the house one thought was clean actually to be dirty.

2549 *þan tase he a picke*: In conjunction with the later 15071–116, this reference provides the metaphor underlying the derivative sermon-cycle *Jacob's Well*. In the source, the metaphor continues through the parallels to 2565, 'o la pele de uraie confession' (BSG 73^v/34–5, *BVV* 107/14).

2561 *þan*: The translator simplifies the French, ignoring 'e prent un mautalent a soi meismes si qu'il comence le cuer a nectoier a certes' (BSG 73^v/31–3, *BVV* 107/10–2).

filth: B variants include *filt(h)es* B^{1}B^9 (as W), *filþe þu* (with more extensive rewriting) B^2. B^3 offers no evidence, having skipped from 2524 to 2571.

2572 *helle*: The French is more circumspect: 'vns enfers' (BSG 73^v/38, cf. *BVV* 107/18).

2583 *And þat*: This reading, an assertion of parallelism with 2579, appears universally in B-MSS, while the construction elsewhere is *Fader of pyte* | *Graunt* (2577–8) *And þou vouche saue. Somme*, where this is all a single complicated sentence, probably supports including *þat*; compare BSG 73^v/44–5 'e qu'il daigne uenir e manoir' (*BVV* 107/23).

2593–4 *þe gospell*: Matt. 13: 44.

2609 *here*: Taken as extrametrical and omitted, like LS, in B^{1}B^2.

2624 *so to do*: The same range of suppression of syllables deemed extraneous occurs in the B-MSS: so] *om.* B^1 (as R), do] *om.* B^{6}B^7 (as PW).

2633 *þat*: *And* AES mistakenly asserts parallelism with 2631. *þat* is universal in B-MSS, and answers *Somme* 'en sains angles du ciel qui font' (BSG 74^r/13–14, *BVV* 108/10–11).

2654 *gift*: The erroneous ELPR *gaste* also appears in B^{1}B^9.

2659–60 *in þat . . . þat*: Apparently pleonastic (and the second *þat* perhaps to be removed); translate '(our desires) that are or should be so that (these three petitions were) immediately (perfected in us)'.

2684, 2688 *For þe day*: Simplifying *Somme* 'por le/au iour passer' (BSG 74^v/37, 40; *BVV* 108/33, 35–6).

2695 'The person intends to ask for', *Somme* 'on requiert' (BSG 74^v/43).

2698 *þe godes*: *þe gode dedes* appears universally in the copies collated, but 2703 *godes* implies that the poet here also followed *Somme* 'tous les biens' (BSG 74^v/45, *BVV* 109/4). This is about the most venturesome of my emendations of the text; the poet's reading survives only in B^{1}B^5, where it may simply be a guess. Compare 1351 n.

2705 *blisseful*: All B-MSS follow R or W: blyssed B^{1}B^{5}B^7 (bissed B^2), blessed B^{3}B^{6}B^{8}B^9.

2708 *delitable*: Only B^1 agrees with PR *delectable*.

2713 The English poet here skips over a brief citation in *Somme*, an allusion to the protracted treatment in John 6 that animates the discussion: 'dont verite dit en l'euangile Ie sui li pains de uie qui descendi de (du C 87^v) ciel Qui mangera de cest pain il uiura touz iors sanz morir' (BSG 74^v/51–75^r/2, *BVV* 109/10–12).

2720 *In*: In spite of a different preposition in the five central copies, RW *In (þe)*, universal in B-MSS (In B^6 only), is probably the correct reading. The central MSS read the line in isolation and take the opening phrase as dependent on *dight* ('that bread prepared for the sacrament . . .'). But the word is the translator's rhyming supply, and the sense 'that consecrated bread [*dight* modifies the subject *brede*] men receive at/in the sacrament'. Compare BSG 75^r/6 'que tu prens ou sacrement del autel' (*BVV* 109/16).

2721 *Hastyly*: Gradon suggests (162, 111/1–2 n.) that the discussion may refer to Exod. 12: 11. But it seems concerned with contemporary fastidiousness about the eucharist, perhaps especially worries over lost crumbs (compare *þe gode morsels þat er smale* 2725). See Rubin, *Corpus Christi*, 43—and notice also her discussion at 336–41 (the more sinister possibility that communicants might retain hosts in their mouths to smuggle out of the church for their own purposes).

    ay: Omitted only in B^{2}B^8 (euere B^{3}B^5).

2723 *þe gredy man*: Although there are no variants, the adjective may have been attracted to surrounding uses of this stem; cf. *Somme* 'li lecheres' (BSG 75^r/8, *BVV* 109/18).

2734 *of his*: More accurate would be 'and þe'; cf. *Somme* 'e la deite' (BSG 75^r/13, *BVV* 109/25). Perhaps the scribes have confused *saul* (*Somme* 'e l'alme') with a derivative of OE *sufol* 'food'.

2747 *oft*: I emend A *of*. The variant occurs sporadically, yet frequently enough, for one to think *of* a legitimate form for 'oft(en)'; see 332 (W), 634 (R, as also 1693, 3998), 4863 (S), 4905 (L), and 1329 *of*] *aftyr* P.

2753 *And conceyues*: Compare *Somme* 'e recoit' (BSG 75^r/21; *BVV* 109/33 'renneþ' is presumably a scribalism).

2763 *it*: ER *he* seeks a human subject, not the heart; the reading is paralleled in he hit B^3, it be B^8.

2779 *Somme* has an extra sentence: 'Beneoite soit la prodefeme que du sien i mist la flour Ce fu la vierge Marie' (BSG 75^v/36–7, *BVV* 110/13–15).

2783 *blode*: Like the translator of *BVV* (110/18), the poet read BSG 75^v/39 'en son propre saim' as if it read 'sanc'; see Gradon's note (162, 111/33–4 n.).

2805 *our*: The less emphatic *oures* is surprisingly weakly attested in B-MSS, only in B^{1}B^{7}B^9 (good B^6).

2806 *vs it*: The PRW transposition is universal in B-MSS.

2809 *his chanouns*: Compare 2693 ff.; the eucharist has made the beggar one of God's own.

2812 *werkes*: The poet has read *Somme* 'hores' (canonical hours) (BSG 76^r/1, *BVV* 110/32) as 'oeures'.

2816 *þe*: The PRW omission occurs in all B-MSS except B^6.

2819 *Somme* has additional material: 'Le gros de la prouende nous prenons en nostre aoust ou ci`e'l quant nous le uerrons a descouert en sa biaute si com il est' (BSG 76^r/3–6, *BVV* 110/35–7).

2832 *þe Boke . . . of Wisdome*: Wis. 16: 20 (of the manna as angels' food).

2834 *hors*: *Somme* 'chienaille' (riff-raff) (BSG 76^r/15, *BVV* 111/8). Probably read by the poet as 'chieuaille', since his usual locution is 'common woman', rather than 'whore'.

2840 *pryue*: An exigency of rhyme; cf. *Somme* 'uerraie' (BSG 76^r/18, *BVV* 111/11).

2842 *Ione*: John 6: 31–5, 48–52. But the ascription in *Somme* is to 'saint Mahius l'euangelistes' (BSG 76^r/19, *BVV* 111/12), as Gradon suggests (162, 112/29–30 n.) to the word 'superstantialem' in the version of the Pater Noster at Matt. 6: 11.

2854 *mayne*: 'strength, vigour'. Compare *Somme* 'assez de sustance e de norissement' (BSG 76^r/24–5, *BVV* 111/18–19).

2870 *gladly*: (P)RW have the support of all B-MSS and answer *Somme* 'plus liement' (BSG 76^v/35, *BVV* 111/28).

2872–3 *his werkemen*: In reference to the parable of Matt. 20: 1–16.

2883–92 A ME addition, unparalleled in *La Somme*.

2893 *na gode worthy*: 'deserving of no good'.

2910–12 *frest*: *Somme* reads 'auoms acreu sor nos almes' (we have gathered up in our souls) (BSG 76ᵛ/44–5, *BVV* 112/1–2). The English says 'that we have here taken as a loan and pledged our souls . . .', an anticipatory translation in the main ignoring the French statement. Line 2912, 'the best pledge of the house' (that is, sin is a debt incurred to be paid off in hell), modifies *saules* 2911, the singular verb *es* probably to be understood as assimilated to the following predicate noun. Compare BSG 76ᵛ/45 'cest le meillor gage del hostel dont . . .' (*BVV* 112/1–3).

2953–4 *þe godspelle*: For example, Mark 11: 25, Luke 6: 37.

2957–8 The L reading at least stems from a perception of *in hert . . . or hatred* as possibly repetitious; B³B⁸ also omit *in hert*.

2975 *he*: *hym*, the older impersonal usage widely attested here, also appears in B²B⁷B⁹ (*þe* B³B⁸).

2981 *hym did*: The transposition, which attractively places *did* under stress, is also widespread in B-MSS, absent only from B¹B⁷.

2991 About 200 lines of the text, beginning at this point, are repeated in R. Presumably the scribe, after some hiatus, took up copying the poem at too early a point.

3007 *Godde vs commandes*: For example, at Luke 6: 27–35.

3018 *þe apostell*: Most notably, 1 Cor. 12: 12–27, but compare also Rom. 12: 5, Eph. 4: 4 and 16.

3019 *here luf*: The transposition of LPW, perhaps metrically preferable, also appears in B²B⁹.

3024 *Haly Writte*: 1 John 3: 15; compare the earlier discussion of the fifth commandment at 1065–1104.

3033–54 A ME addition, unparalleled at BSG 77ᵛ/52, *BVV* 113/25.

3041 *do*: LS routinely (the former with regularity) supply the Northern equivalent *ger*. Its avoidance (there is no evidence for the reading elsewhere here, only make B³) may be the poet's concession to a more general audience.

3055 *þat we charge mast*: *Somme* 'que nous fesons a Dieu' (BSG 77ᵛ/52, *BVV* 113/25).
      we: PRW *I* occurs in all B-MSS except B⁶.

3085 *vse*: Confused by ES with *duse*.

3090 *shewynge*: On the basis of the French, 'l'a si enlumine' (BSG 78ʳ/16–17, *BVV* 114/7), the form appears an English archetypal error, perhaps for *lyghtynge*. All the B-MSS agree with the printed reading.

3094 *cast*: The intrusive EPLS *to*, also in B¹B⁶B⁹, may be multiply motivated, from failure to acknowledge disyllabic *hert-ë* or as inadvertent dittography after *her-te*. The underlying construction is *mas . . . cast*.

3107–20 Basically original material, replacing that of *Somme* (BSG 78^{rv}/24–31, *BVV* 114/16–25). The implicit reference to 'Man's Three Foes' (also 3123–4) supplements that of *La Somme* to the devil alone.

3118 *ledde*: The word is confirmed by the biblical text, but all B-MSS, like PRW, have a form of 'felled' (fall B^6, P 'defiled'?), an intensification of the sense.

3126 *flesshe-*: Among the B-MSS, only B^9 fails to agree with EPRW in providing the easier adjective, rather than compound noun.

3135 *Bernard*: Perhaps in allusion to 'Parabola' 3, PL 183: 765–7, which also discusses the Gifts as antidotes to the Seven Deadly Sins. Bernard is offering a commonplace reading of Ps. 128: 3.

3147 *Paul*: Perhaps Eph. 3: 17 (more distantly Col. 1: 23), a usage founded on the parable of Matt. 7: 24–7, a suggestion followed in W's later scribal supply.

3157 *fresshes*: Compare BSG 78^v/47 'aronce' (*BVV* 115/2 bedeweþ).

3166 *sarzynays*: The majority MSS here (as all B-MSS except B^{3}B^{6}B^7) have taken the unfamiliar word as a proper noun, rather than the (postposited) adjective it is.

3178 *gift*: The variation with *gast* (see 2674 and endemic to the transmission) reflects a theological double usage: Isa. 11: 2–3 describes seven 'spiritus', but conventional moral teaching identifies these as 'dona sancti spiriti'.

3205 *Salamon*: Most succinctly Prov. 27: 21, but see also Wis. 3: 1–8 (and more distantly, Ecclus. 2: 1–5). Gradon suggests (164, 117/8–9 n.) Ecclus. 34: 9, 11.

3211 *noght*: A negative has dropped out completely in AEW. I follow the LS reading, in which these two MSS are only supported by B^2; all other B-MSS read as PR (perhaps a preferable reading, as implying haplography after *he*). *Somme* confirms a negative here; compare 'car il ne puet soi mesmes conoistre' (BSG 79^r/18, *BVV* 115/24–5).

3212 *feblesce*: Probably confirmed by W *feblest*, as well as agreement with A in B^{3}B^{6}B^{7}B^9; the remaining B-MSS read as the majority collated.

3221 *godenes*: Although there are no variants among the collated copies or in the B-MSS, perhaps an English error; compare BSG 79^r/23 'de ses biens' (*BVV* 115/30). See 1351 n., 3254 n.

3229 *La Somme*'s statement is more emphatic; cf. BSG 79^v/1 (*BVV* 115/33) 'une hore' (for a single hour).

3232 *We falle*: Cf. BSG 79ᵛ/2 'nous i entrons' (*BVV* 115/35 'we fallen yn aswiþe').

3251 *Austyn*: Gradon (164, 117/28–32 n.) identifies the source as 'De natura et gratia' 27. 31 (PL 44: 262).

3254 *gode*: Shared with B¹B³B⁵B⁷; compare gode dedes B⁹ (as W), the remaining B-MSS as R.

3262 *sex*: Surely correct, against BSG 79ᵛ/40 'vij.' (*BVV* 116/9).

3266 *rerewarde*: The small haplographic error *rewarde* is widespread, in all B-MSS except B²D⁶B⁷.

3280 *say*: The possibly original *to say* occurs widely in B-MSS, everywhere but in B²B⁶B⁷.

3284 *þe gospell*: John 14: 13–14, 15: 16, 16: 23–4.

3288–3356 Excepting lines 3299–3302, which correspond to BSG 79ᵛ/52–80ʳ/3 (*BVV* 116/21–5), all a ME addition, largely a generalized anticipation of a later discussion, that of devotion in prayer at lines 10151–324.

3317 *Paul*: 1 Cor. 14: 19 (slightly misapplied, since Paul is debunking glossolalia).

3327 sidenote: Walther 6476.

3345 sidenote: Matt. 6: 33.

3356 *þareinne*: *þarto* PR 'in addition', apparently responds to later *mare*; the reading also appears in all B-MSS except B¹B⁹.

3357 At this point, *Somme* provides its explanation of the Seven Gifts of the Holy Spirit (BSG 80ʳ/4–83ʳ/13, *BVV* 116–21). *Speculum Vitae*, however, returns to the 'Tabula' and reproduces its succinct, if complicated, explanation of the septenary scheme that underlies the remainder of the poem. Compare for example, the sidenotes to 3415 and 3417 to the 'Tabula' 174–5 in the edition of the Appendix. The poem rejoins the French at 3510, when it moves to take up the sin of Pride and its antidote, the Dread of God.

þus: *vs* A is utterly isolated among the MSS surveyed.

3365 *braunches*: The metaphor ultimately depends upon on the good and bad trees of the gospels (again at lines 3851–2); see Matt. 7: 16–20, 12: 33. Illustrations of such diagrammes occur frequently in late medieval manuscripts; for a salient example, with Northern circulation (BL, MS Arundel 507), see Sandler, *The Psalter of Robert de Lisle*, 50–3. For further discussion, see Robertson and Huppé, *Piers Plowman and Scriptural Tradition*, 191–8 (discussing *Piers* B.16: 1–89; compare 13: 409–20). See further 3479 n.

3370 *Vnto*: *To* PW appears in all B-MSS except B⁷, as again in 3417. In 3416, all B-MSS have *to*. See further 644 n.

3370–1 *þe Seuen Blissedhedes* | *And . . . Seuen Medes*: Just as recurrent in the poem (and as integral to developed septenary instruction) as the petitions of the Pater Noster. Ceaselessly cited through the text, the Beatitudes and their heavenly 'praemia' are drawn from Matt. 5: 3–9. See Augustine's discussion, cited Introduction n. 44, for the logic of excluding the eighth beatitude (Matt. 5:10) from the count.

3402 *sight*: Like PW, B^{1}B^{2}B^{6}B^9 supply the article.

3411, 3415 *And*: *þat* is universal in the B-MSS. Given the parallelism with other petitions, one might well emend.

3420 *here, ere*: Only a single B-MS, B^1, agrees with the ELS transposition, but the independent misunderstandings that underlie it are well attested elsewhere: *here*] *ere* B^{1}B^{3}B^8, *er*] *here* B^{1}B^{5}B^6, *euere and* B^{3}B^8.

3438 *þai*: All B-MSS support the majority reading save *he* B^6.

3479 *plants and settes*: The language of extirpation (ripping out vicious weeds) and insertion (planting virtuous growths) depends upon the vegetative metaphors mentioned in 3365 n. In *Somme*, these follow naturally from Lorens's discussion of the garden of virtue (from Cant. 4: 12) as a metaphor for the growth of grace, a passage not transmitted in *Speculum Vitae*.

3488 *pouer*: Although the reading is palpably wrong, all B-MSS except B^6 support *meke* PRW.

3493–3510 The poet here follows the 'Tabula', Appendix lines 191–8. In an important chapter, Lottin outlines (*Psychologie et morale*, vi. 445–77) the development of such argumentation. This begins with Anselm of Laon's explanation, included in the ordinary gloss, to Matt. 5: 3: 'His septem gradibus [beatitudinum] congruit septiformis operatio Spiritus Sancti quam Isaias describit, sed ille a summo, hec a imo; quia ibi docetur filius Dei descensurus ad ima, hic homo ad similitudinem Dei accensurus' (cited 446). Such explanation recurs at 3603–18 and again at the poem's end, 15987–16016.

3496 *order*: All B-MSS except B^{3}B^7 agree with LPW in supplying an article.

3503–6 *Dauid*: Ps. 110: 10 (compare Prov. 1: 7, 9: 10; Ecclus. 1: 16).

3525–8 A ME addition, not paralleled at BSG 18^r/24 (*BVV* 11/21).

3528 *into*: *in* PW also appears in B^{1}B^{5}B^{6}B^{7}B^9.

3573 *parte*: Although there are no variants, *maste parte* would better accord with the source (and the *eldest* daughter); compare BSG 18^v/41 'a grant part' (*BVV* 12/9).

3581 *quene*, **3583** *lyonesce*: Both are male in the source; compare BSG 18^v/43–4 'li roys . . . li lions' (*BVV* 12/12–13).

3599–628 Excepting 3623–5, all this material forms a ME addition, its centre at 3603–18 recapitulating the septenary system described at 3493–510.

3602 *þe*: Just as PRW, B¹B³B⁸B⁹ omit the article; the same four agree with RW's omission of 3642 *out*.

3629 The poem follows the *Somme* discussion carefully in outline, but (as in all earlier portions) abbreviates it considerably. For example, lines 3643–54 correspond to the far more extensive discussion, BSG 19ʳ/10–20ʳ/5 (*BVV* 13/3–14/21). The text concentrates heavily on definition, not on the homiletics and examples of the source. See further 3785 n.

3646 *Vilany* (in the sidenote *Rusticitas*): The word fairly specifically indicates 'peasant behaviour', an indifference to civilized niceties, or 'discourtesy'. Here the term largely conveys the failure to acknowledge a benefit in the only polite way, with thanks; note BSG 19ʳ/19, *BVV* 13/11 specifically glossing *vnkyndenesse* 'en clergois ingratitude'). The core of the dependent clause in the next sentence is 'a man forgets to thank God for . . .'.

3654 *And wate*: 'And yet he knows that', that is, his madness is in making no provision for repaying the loan of God's gifts he knows he owes.

3688 *ne he it*: This does reflect *Somme* 'e ia soit ce que nus pecchiez mortiex soit sanz despit de dieu' (BSG 20ᵛ/28–9, *BVV* 15/15–16). The problem appears to be the poet's conversion to a human subject, coupled with the poetic inversion of normal order 'þat he ne bigynnes it'; in these terms, R provides the logical grammatical placement of *ne*. But the profuse variation—*ne he*] trs. in all B-MSS except B²B⁷; *it*] om. B²B³B⁷B⁸ (as LS)—indicates that the awkward placement is archetypal.

3696 *or othir als wys*: 'Or think (falsely that) they are as wise as others'.

3704 *spredde*: It is just possible that *kyde* ELPS could rhyme with *thridde* (they have OE -*ydde* pl. and -*idda*, respectively), and if so, would be harder. The reading also occurs in B¹B⁵. But more normally, 'third' has short *e*, a consideration favouring the majority reading of the tradition, although *spredde* might be considered a reasonably obvious substitution following *wyde*.

3720 *falles*: The uninflected *falle* appears only in A and B⁹ of the MSS here surveyed.

3721–2 *Salamon*: Prov. 13: 10; Gradon (120, 22/1–2 n.) suggests Prov. 25: 8.

3725 *avaunte*: Only AE confuse *c* and *t* here, and all B-MSS have the reading printed. Although L here reads correctly (its -*t*- may, however, have been altered from -*c*-), it repeats the erroneous AE form nine times in the course of the later discussion 13682–740 (and at 13591).

3728 *or*[2]: Although the added *of* occurs in all B-MSS, it has probably been imported from the preceding line to re-enforce the parallellism.

3730 'And causes men to think that such (a marvel) is true of him.'

3738 The sense continues from *hethynge* | *Of othir men* 3736–7: 'scorns other men because they don't have his virtues and good men because'.

3745 *did hym*: I follow the majority in this small transposition, although perhaps indifferent, to prose order and not effecting the metre (both syllables are unstressed). This form of the line appears in all B-MSS except B[7] (*doþ hym* B[1]).

3775 *rightly*: *lyghtly* LR also appears in B[3]B[5]B[8].

3785 *felled*: 'felled', not an incongruous south-eastern form for 'filled'. The ME translator has, in the main, suppressed one of *Somme*'s two figures here; compare BSG 22[v]/31–4 (*BVV* 19/10–12): 'est li grans vens qui abate les granz tours e ces grans clochiers [a doublet that generates the statement at 3784; the French explains Vainglory's victims as 'li haut home e li plus uaillant'] e ces granz fous es forez met a terre e ces granz montaignes fait toutes crouler'. The second example, 'li denir au diable' (BSG 22[v]/35), is more fully presented, but the poet suppresses the subsequent extensive discussion of the three kinds of goods (cf. *godes* 3800), those of Nature, Fortune, and Grace (BSG 22[v]/38–23[v]/33, *BVV* 19/20–20/35). At 3802–16, the poem rejoins the source and gives the conclusion of the French discussion.

3801 *Forthy*: *For* PRW is the reading of all B-MSS except B[1]B[9].

3818 *som men*: Besides W, the extrametrical noun is also omitted in B[1]B[9]; a form where the two words have been run together (understood as *samen?*), like that in R, may underlie the error.

3825 One should note the poem's trilingualism. The English here directly translates the source language (BSG 23[v]/49–50, *BVV* 21/16–18): 'E ceste se deuise en iij. Car il este vne ypocrisie orde, vne sote, vne soutiue.' But the marginal finding notes effect a different translation of the same material into Latin. A similar example would be 3853, which answers BSG 24[r]/13–14 'fole paour e fole vergoigne' (*BVV* 22/3 has confused *peur* 'fear' and *paour* 'shame', in part under the influence of statements like 3856). See further 4275–6, where *Speculum Vitae* reverts to Latin identification of the basilisk, in contrast to *Somme* 'basilicor' (BSG 25[r]/13, *BVV* 23/29).

3853–72 The discussion of Foolish Shame, unusually, is more expansive than that of the source (BSG 24[r]/13–19, *BVV* 22/3–11), and includes an original discussion of *Folehardynes* 3871.

3863 *þat*: The word looks suspiciously like dittography, essentially meaning the same as *hym*. On that basis, it is omitted in PR, as well as B[3]B[6]B[7]B[8].

3864 *leues*: The synonymous *lettes* ELR also appears in B[1]B[2]B[8]B[9].

3865 *haf*: The printed reading is also found in B⁷; all other B-MSS read *to haue* except for B⁵, which omits (as PR).

3881 With the discussion of Humility, the ME poet returns to *La Somme*'s tract on virtues, abandoned to introduce Pride at 3510. This integration of or alternation between *Somme*'s early descriptions of sin and climactic presentation of virtues persists through the remainder of the text. The presentation of Humility, as customarily in these early portions, reduces the argument in the source; there are no parallels to several long sections, BSG 86ʳ/1–88ᵛ/28, 89ʳᵛ/18–43 (*BVV* 126/1–130/14, 131/23–32/16), and the materials noted in 4019–38 n. (Hereafter, I do not generally note such excisions.)

3889 *Bernard*: 'De gradibus humilitatis' 1. 2 (*PL* 182: 942B). The initial presentation of 'degrees' as a linked sequence (3881–934) derives from Bernard's presentation (in descending order) through the metaphor of Jacob's ladder (see 2145 n.). But, like a good modern self-help programme, he has twelve steps, not the seven here.

3891 *it*: The omission of LPW appears in all B-MSS.

3899 *within*: The unmetrical *in* ELS is supported by B³B⁵B⁸.

3913 *Bernard*: Compare 'De gradibus' 4. 14, 5. 18 (*PL* 182: 949C, 951C respectively).

3921 *Dauid*: 2 Kings 16: 5–13.

3923 *at him*: There are no variants, either in the copies customarily collated or in the B-MSS. But while an absolute use of *casten* 'reproach, revile' is plausible enough, the prepositional complement does appear problematic. It may either have replaced or subsumed by haplography the poet's reading *stan(e)s*; compare BSG 89ʳ/12–13 (*BVV* 131/16–17), rendering a detail of the biblical account, 'il le rechoioit de pierres e le laidengoit'.

3924 *suffird he*: The LPRW transposition, probably of minimal metrical effect (although stressing *al* is perhaps attractive), appears in all B-MSS except B³.

3933 *myght*: The LPSR plural occurs in all B-MSS except B⁹.

3952 *als þe boke vs leres*: Simply an awkward reference to the source. My silence about further references of this sort indicates that in those loci the poet simply uses *þe boke* as his marker for an allusion to his customary authority, Lorens.

3992 *thre*: The emendation seems almost required by the parallelisms of the argument here (three divisions each of thought, word, and deed). The reading indeed follows the *Somme*; compare 'en iij. manieres' (BSG 91ʳ/24, *BVV* 134/27). Among B-MSS, only B¹B⁹ support AEL(P)S.

4001–4 In *La Somme*, the exact wording of this material forms the introduction to the third point (here 4015); compare BSG 91ᵛ/40–3 (*BVV* 135/11–15). The metaphor is at least biblical in inspiration (compare Ecclus. 21: 18, Isa. 38: 17), but probably achieved prominence through the famous anecdote, 'Verba seniorum' 9. 9 (PL 73: 911).

4018 *dispyse*: See also 4025 *wickednes*, both apocopated forms with *-es* endings absorbed with the preceding consonant. For further examples, see 4805 and 4806 below, but the variation is widespread.

4019–38 Collapsing a considerably richer discussion in the source, BSG 92ʳᵛ/8–41 (*BVV* 135/35–136/32).

4032 *mysdede*; The marked plural *myssededes* appears, in addition to all MSS here collated, in all B-MSS except B⁷. I retain my copytext, since *dede pl.* (< OE dǣda, dǣde) is well exemplified elsewhere (for example 1648, 2946, 3967), and the 'modernized' plural is metrically equivalent here.

4034 *awes*: *awe* also appears in B²B⁷B⁹ (as EPSRW), all retaining the form of the OE pt.-present.

4061–2 Translate 'It is very dear to him to help all . . .'.

4066 *When he wesshe his disciples fete*: At the Last Supper, unique to John 13: 4–17.

4070 *aght maners*: Presented in the source as 'Les *aornemenz de Obedience* sont vij.' (BSG 94ʳ/6–7, *BVV* 138/31–5). The poet suppresses one of these, 'liement' (involving the difficult example of the obedient assassin, 94ʳ/13–18), altogether, and two others are divided in the English poem ('purement' at 4095–104 and 'vigerusement' at 4105–14).

4085 *withouten stryue*: 'without (verbal) contention, back-talk'; compare BSG 94ʳ/22–3 (*BVV* 139/14–15), which provides the sheep with a question that implicitly rejects the herd's commands.

4086 *hym wil*: The ELRW transposition also occurs in all B-MSS here present (B⁷ out).

4097 *blethely*: ELS *gladly* appears elsewhere only in BL, MS Harley 435, a copy Nelson implied ('The *Speculum Vitae*', 49, 65) might have spot-collated into its text readings out of the five-manuscript tradition.

4098 *gase*: The ELSR transposition to follow *fast* appears elsewhere only in B⁶B⁹.

4102 *semy*: Compare *Somme* (BSG 94ᵛ/30–1, *BVV* 139/22–3): 'tres uistes e tres ignaus'. This at least implies that the word, not in MED, functions as a doublet with *light* earlier in the line, although the French offers little help in explaining the form or etymology.

4123 *Als God did*: Matt. 14: 23.

4131 *in hir flours*: 'in her prime'; compare BSG 95^v/38 'come vne damoisele' (*BVV* 141/14 has '3ong').

4217 *A fals*: The article, omitted in P, appears in all B-MSS present (B^7 out), and is apt to be correct, on the basis of reasserted parallelism. *Somme* is not helpfully parallel; compare 'en faus iugemenz, en maloite leesce, en pesme doleurs' (BSG 24^v/50-1, *BVV* 23/9-10).

4256 *oft*: The reading is unique to the four MSS here, and the PRW omission appears in all B-MSS present (B^7 out). But the word appears necessary for a metrical line.

4257 *be þis*: The LPRW transposition, found in the majority of B-MSS (be thus B^6), may well be correct. The reading printed appears elsewhere only in B^5 and one further MS (B^7 out).

4268 *man*: PRW *mannes hert* also appears in most B-MSS (*om.* B^{3}B^8; B^7 out).

4276 *basiliscus*: For the basilisk's poisonous aura (although no mention of harming grain), see *Bestiary*, fo. 79^r. The grain in its three states as a metaphor for the advancement of virtue depends upon Mark 4: 26-9 and a famous piece of Gregorian exegesis, *Moralia* 22. 20. 46 (PL 76: 240-1).

4284 *kynde of þe ayre*: As 4283 *spyres* shows, the ME poet recognized the correct reading of the gospel passage he here suppressed, 'spicam' (Mark 4: 28), reproduced appropriately twice in BSG 25^r/17, 21 as 'en espi'. Thus, the spelling *ayre* must represent modern 'ear (of corn)', that is 'the plant's grain-bearing head' (OE ēar, eher), not the apparent 'air'.

4292 *þat growes*: *to growe* ELS appears in only three other copies (including B^2); most B-MSS agree with APRW (B^7 out).

4306 *þe envious may*: The PRW transposition appears virtually universally, in all B-MSS (B^7 out); only Harley 435 (see 4097 n.) and one other MS agree with the printed reading. But the inversion may well represent an effort at metrical smoothing.

4314 *Godde says* (and the sidenote): Compare Matt. 12: 32.

4321 *sauely*: The poet presumably read BSG 25^v/32 'sainement' (*BVV* 24/16) as 'sauuement'. I doubt very much that W *anly* offers any support for believing a harder reading has been lost, particularly in the context of unanimous B-MSS agreement with the reading printed.

4325 *hym wil*: The LPSRW transposition, not especially pointed, appears also in B^{1}B^{5}B^{6}B^9 (B^7 out).

4346-54, 4363-78 ME clarifications/elaborations of the French. In 4337-8, the subsequent discussion (at 4389) shows the construction is 'The fifth sin to recognize is Warring against Grace, as it appears in other men'.

4372 sidenote: Matt. 7: 21.

4379 *thridde*: With E's effort at avoiding 'thredde' in rhyme here, compare 3704 n.

sidenote: From BSG 25ᵛ/44 'obstinacions c'est durres du cuer' (*BVV* 24/31 'obduracion').

4422 *hym*: *wele* is limited to the five central manuscripts and is surely otiose.

4436–7 Embroidering upon *Somme* 'de cui nous tenons' (from whom we obtain our fief) (BSG 97ᵛ/33–4, *BVV* 144/12).

4448 *ayre*: the common sense, *Somme* 'aire' (BSG 97ᵛ/46, *BVV* 144/22).

4456 *blode*: The reading *his blode*, in B¹B²B³B⁶, as well as ELSRW, is probably dittographic.

4457–66 *Somme*, although also promising seven divisions, is not especially clearly divided (a series of statements introduced by 'Apres', rather than numbers). It could be construed (and was in the marginal marking of BSG 98ʳ–99ᵛ) as having eight members. This ambiguity the English poet eliminates by suppressing the apparent seventh member ('desport'); compare BSG 99ᵛ/30–40, *BVV* 147/7–17.

4460 *springes*: The inflected form appears in all B-MSS except B⁷.

4498 *stiryng*: P *thyng* also appears in B³B⁶B⁸ (*stirred* B²).

4524 *grete*: This reading is distinctly limited in the tradition, to the five central MSS, B³, and three other copies; competing readings include *clere* RB⁷ (*clene* B⁶), and omission of the word (W and the remaining B-MSS), a reading that appears metrically deficient. But W and the rest correspond to *Somme* 'la uertu' (BSG 98ᵛ/37, *BVV* 145/33). It is just possible that this was originally a headless line, with stress on introductory *þe*, and that many scribes have filled in independently this direct translation of the French because the line appears a stress short.

4537–46 Largely a ME addition (cf. BSG 99ʳ/1, *BVV* 146/13).

4595 *we*: the addition of *may*, in all B-MSS (*we may wel* B⁸, B⁷ out), probably is metrical suppletion following the failure to recognize the disyllabic plural *lym[e]s*.

4621–32 A ME addition.

4635–60 The English reverses the first two points of the source; see BSG 26ʳ/1–18, *BVV* 25/16–30.

4647 *greefly*: One of those readings that customarily generates profuse variation among the manuscripts (see 9207 n). Here one has the alternatives *gretely* EP+B² and *greuously* LSW+B¹B³B⁵B⁶B⁸B⁹.

4691–5 The ME specifies a number of further effects only alluded to in the French; see BSG 26ᵛ/37–8, *BVV* 26/16–17.

4713 *be*: LPR *to be* also occurs in B³B⁵B⁶B⁸; W *bifore* in B¹B⁹.

4716–17 Translating 'de remembrer e de moustrer ce qu'ele entent par parole' (BSG 101ʳ/22–3, *BVV* 150/9–10).

4729–36 The entire discussion of Evenhede has been severely truncated. Here the ME poet collapses a much more extensive treatment of each of the four points in turn. The material the poet chooses to reproduce here comes from the third point. In the French, it concludes with a sentence not here translated, 'e ces sont les iij. parties de la uertu de prudence selon le filosophe' (BSG 102ʳ/12–13, *BVV* 151/21–2). See further 4757–78 n.

4740 *wordes*: The ELS reading *worde* is paralleled in but a single copy elsewhere in the tradition.

4749–56 A not especially pointed ME expansion, integrating the classical 'quatuor adfectus' (compare BSG 102ᵛ/27–9, *BVV* 152/2–4).

4750 *saule*: The reading *awen*, corrected out in A, perhaps later, is isolated, and all B-MSS sensibly agree with PRW.

4757–78 The ME translator cuts this material so thoroughly that the tenor of the discussion only alludes, often without any particularly clear explanation, to the French source. At the start, the French is clear that Evenhede has seven degrees and seven branches (subsidiary virtues). But as well as degrees (4759, 4761), the first set are in the source also presented as 'sights', following upon portions of a lengthy discussion untranslated after line 4710. There (BSG 100ᵛ/39–50, *BVV* 149/4–16) Lorens associates the virtue with discretion in vision, the capacity to identify and to make appropriately moderate decisions. This follows allusions to the 'quatuor animalia plena oculis ante et retro' of Apoc. 4: 6 (their eyes also look 'intus' in 4: 8) and to the vision 'super lapidem unum septem oculi sunt' of Zach. 3: 9. See the further discussions in 4794 n. and 4825–52 n.

4767 *sal*: Although ELS *sulde* (also in B¹B²B³B⁶B⁸) is attractive, and may be confirmed by 4789, the ARW reading printed has the support of the other B-MSS. ELS+ may be accommodating the diction to the preceding line.

4768 *him*, **4771** *glyde*, **4776** *loke*: The provision of *to* before all three of these readings is unique to the group of three ELS and occurs in no B-MSS.

4792 *þe*: The AW article is certainly grammatically otiose, and its omission (also in B¹B², but compare *beþencking* B⁸) attractive.

4794 *þe lyne of Euenhede*: The translator scatters references to the figure through the discussion, even while he has suppressed the source material that explains it, a continuation of the materials discussed in 4757–78 n. At this point (BSG 100ᵛ/50–101ʳ/11, *BVV* 149/16–31) Lorens describes 'the Gyft of Knawyng' as 'li mestres des oeures', a mastermason who executes his building with a plumbline to insure the work is level, even, straight, and smooth. Although not explicit in the French, the figure extends that mentioned in the previous note; it relies upon Zachariah's prophecy of

Zorobabel building the temple. See especially 4: 10, where the plummet and seven-eyed stone (the cornerstone of the work) appear in conjunction.

4800 *oftner*: Compare ofter EPSR+B²B³B⁷B⁹, after LW+B⁶B⁸, *o3ter* B¹. Compare 5557 n.

4805–6 *offyce, vyce*: I have simply adjusted the rhyme, somewhat under-handedly; the variation and manuscript spellings reflect confusion over whether singulars or apocopated plurals are intended. The AELS plural forms appear elsewhere only in B⁶, and *Somme* confirms at least that *offyce* should be singular: 'si que chascun serue de son office sanz pecchie e sanz mesprisure' (BSG 103ʳ/23–4, *BVV* 153/17–18).

4815 *ded*: 'death'; compare *Somme* 'la mort' (BSG 103ᵛ/29–30, *BVV* 153/23).

4825–52 Severely truncating a sequence of relatively detailed discussions (BSG 103ᵛ/48–106ʳ/18, *BVV* 154/9–158/5). The poem's treatment, while it certainly presents Evenhede as rational restraint, largely suppresses (in a manner thoroughly consonant with the excision described in 4757–78 n.) Lorens's more complicated point. The full discussion describes Evenhede, as the plumbline metaphor would imply, as a straight and undeviating course between various extremes, for example, 'il prent garde que sa tour ne pende ne encline, ne a destre par prosperite ne a senestre par aduersite' (BSG 101ʳ/9–11; compare the earlier discussion at 2241–54). This quasi-Aristotelian view, after all, explains the unique nature of the virtue, 'Equitas' (equ[anim]ity, moderation, measure). One touch of such treatment does get through at lines 4861–4 (BSG 106ᵛ/31–3, *BVV* 158/20–2).

4858–61 The common archetypal scribe behind ELS seems to have remembered his next rhyme was 'entencioun', but returned to copy at the wrong usage. L appears to have restored part of the omitted materials in the wrong place through consultation of a second copy. In *Somme* (BSG 106ʳ/21–4, *BVV* 158/9–12), lines 4859–60 are presented explicitly as biblical citation, Matt. 6: 22–3.

4871 *haues*: The reading, in A's usual spelling *has(e)*, is unique to the five central copies, B⁷, and three other copies (*is* B¹).

4889–90 *Somme* presents the Sins in their conventional order, in which this couplet should follow 4884 (BSG 106ᵛ/45, *BVV* 159/5).

4906 *par*: Both sense and metre seem to have been obscure to the scribes; in addition to the collated variants, compare *whar* B¹ (as R), *pat* B²B³B⁵, *as* B¹B⁶B⁹ (as P), and *pare par*] *When* B⁷. But *Somme* 'la ou [there where] il deuroient tenir e trouer equite' (BSG 107ʳ/25, *BVV* 160/4–5) implies that the ES reading is correct.

4932 *hauntes*: The inflected form appears in all B-MSS. The line specifies the 'que li mauuais font' of the source (BSG 107ᵛ/42–3, *BVV* 160/26).

4934 *angers*: The singular, probably inspired by the parallel noun, appears widely, in all B-MSS except B⁷B⁸.

4937–40 A deliberatedly trinitarian specification of the source; compare 'e de grant plente de ioie de la presence (C 122ᵛ, BSG presente) Ihesu Crist' (BSG 107ᵛ/45–6, *BVV* 160/29).

4975 *þe hert*: Only B³B⁶ agree with EL in omitting the article.

4980 *ap-*: The alternation with *en-* is limited to the five MSS collated and a single other copy; cf. *al en-* B¹, *al ap-* B⁸.

4991 *Dasednes of Hert*: In *Somme* 'tenuites' (BSG 26ᵛ/50, *BVV* 26/30 'tendernesse').

4995–5002 A ME elaboration.

5003 *Tendernes of Flessh*: *Somme* 'tenretes, c'est moleste de cuer' (BSG 26ᵛ/ 53–4, *BVV* 26/33–4).

5006 *to*: The PSRW omission is general in the B-MSS, and *to* appears only in B⁵.

5044–52 A ME elaboration.

5049 *a swete*: *Somme* 'une suor' (BSG 27ʳ/15, *BVV* 27/16), that is, a hot bath. Compare the similar reading at 13058.

5051 *noght*: ELS *nouther* is unique, and R's omission shared only with B¹.

5052 *esement*: PRW *ese* is the reading of all B-MSS except B⁸.

5075 *hym war*: Follows, somewhat at the expense of logical grammar, from *leuer* 5073. Translate as if 'That had (found it) more preferable to lie . . . than it would be for him to endure . . .'.

5092–3 Compare *Somme* 'qui n'ose entrer ou sentier pur le limace' (BSG 27ʳᵛ/27–8, *BVV* 27/29).

5114 *vntil*: Limited to AES alone; all B-MSS agree with LPRW *to*. The variation is not easily resolved, since the majority may simply have opted for a single-syllable dip, not necessary in the metre. See 644 n.

5138 *may*: ELS *wille* is unique in the tradition.

5144 *a*¹, ²: While the P omission of the first article is nearly unique, in a single other copy, ELPS are joined in their omission of the second by B¹B⁶B⁷ and six other copies.

5152 *sal*: The reading, a present following on *think*, is unique to the four central copies and to Harley 435 (see 4097 n.); the remainder all read *sulde*.

5171 *so*: ELS *to* appears elsewhere in the tradition only in B⁵B⁶.

5186 *messes*: ELPS *messe* occurs elsewhere only in Harley 435, B³B⁵B⁸, and a single other MS. Within a cluster of plural forms, it is surely wrong, if an intended singular, but may simply represent another apocopated form.

5196 *oft in seruauntes se*: In *Somme*, the entire discussion of 'worse amending' is largely (though usually implicitly) cast within this figure. Compare, at a point analogous to the juncture of lines 5102–3, the introduction, 'Ce sont tecches de mauuais seriauns qui font que nul prodome ne les doit receuoir en son seruice' (BSG 27ᵛ/32–4, *BVV* 28/1–2). The evocation of the figure here corresponds to BSG 28ʳ/13 ff. (*BVV* 29/5 ff.).

5208 *to*: Following EL and six other copies; AS *for to* appears in only a single other MS, and all B-MSS omit as PRW, probably seeking to tighten the metre.

5252 *ne*: Limited to AEL and B⁷; the remainder, with all remaining B-MSS, omit.

5275 In *Somme*, the enumeration of parts is preceded (BSG 109ᵛ/32–42, *BVV* 164/1–15) by a lengthy explanatory statement. The 'philosophers', Lorens says, are responsible for dividing the virtue into six parts, to which Jesus added the seventh. Fortitude, as lines 1790–8 and 1885–908 have outlined, was one of the classical Cardinal Virtues, with a long history of pre-Christian discussions. Following Cicero's treatment at *De inventione* 2. 54. 163, the virtue was often divided into constituent 'parts' with different functions; that offered here has most in common with Macrobius', in his commentary on Cicero's *Somnium Scipionis*. See Tuve, *Allegorical Imagery*, 62–6, 443.

5278 *Lastandnes*: In Lorens's original statement 'Magnificence' (BSG 109ᵛ/39, *BVV* 164/10). But this identification is qualified at the equivalent to *Speculum* line 5367: 'Ceste uertu notre grant philosophe Ihesu Crist apele perseuuerance' (BSG 112ʳᵛ/26–7, *BVV* 169/1–3).

5283–4 *and fle . . . vanyte*: The French offers a more complicated explanation, 'grans choses d'espire' (BSG 109ᵛ/45, *BVV* 164/19–20), to disdain fear of endeavour or adversity. But the English poet, who telescopes the lengthy discussion of this virtue a great deal, has in mind Lorens's restatement at BSG 110ʳ/18 ff. (*BVV* 165/8 ff.).

5285 *Austyn*: Gradon identifies (191, 164/19–21 n.) as 'De libero arbitrio' 1. 13. 27 (PL 32: 1235).

5290 *mawgre hisse*: 'in spite of everything he can do'.

5299 *þe wys philosofre says*: Probably Cicero, a possibility also suggested by the allusion to 'agere et pati' in 5352, integral to his division of the virtue into four parts, two active and two passive.

5310 *sharpe*: The LPSR variant *harde* appears elsewhere only in Harley 435 and one other copy. The French here reads 'e la vie que tant apert aspre e espoentable elire' (BSG 110ʳ/22–3, *BVV* 165/12–13).

5331–2 On the showing of the French, A renders both contested variants here correctly. Compare 'une grant ardeur et un grant desirer de pursuir et grant fiance del acheuer' (BSG 111^r/17–19, cf. *BVV* 166/33–4). The variation has been at least partially generated by the syntax, the sequence of three actions (here marked off by commas) partially obscured by inversion of the parallel structure in 5331. The already rich trove of variants in the collations can be supplemented by the following: 5331 a] *ay* WB^{3}B^8, *ay with* B^{1}B^9, *neuere* B^5, *he yeuyth* B^6, *euery* Harley 435; 5332 *trouthe*] *trowe* ELWB^5, *in treuþe* B^2, *trewly* B^{3}B^8.

5334 *als a gode knyght*: *Somme* 'come lion' (BSG 111^r/19, *BVV* 167/1).

5335 *noght*: The LPS variant *nother* appears elsewhere only in B^{1}B^2 and Harley 435 (om. B^6).

5347 The line is a relative clause modifying *man* 5346.

5351 *ne maystry*: Coordinated with *victory* in the preceding line.

5364 *it*: i.e. his heart (5362).

5378 *at*: In B^7 alone of the B-MSS; the remainder agree with LPW (and Harley 435) in omitting the word (B^9 out).

5385 *to*: All B-MSS (B^9 out) agree with *in* PRW; translate *puttes . . . to* 'ascribes'.

5391 The sidenote is, of course, Matt. 5: 6; the text takes the verbs here as equivalent to *yhernes*, God's rewarding of desire, not necessarily achievement.

5392 *ay*: The RW omission also occurs in B^5 (*euere* B^{2}B^3 + Harley 435).

5402 *seuen corounnes of blisse*: The French makes it clear that these refer to Apoc. 12: 3 (BSG 113^r/13–14, *BVV* 170/12–13). There the crowns are on the head of 'the beast from the sea', taken in *Somme* as a type of the Sins; by battling against and conquering the beast, one will gain the promised crown(s) of life (compare Apoc. 3: 11).

5416 The proverb is Whiting F 141.

5442 *Murtherer*: The haplographic form *Murthere* I correct in A also occurs in B^{3}B^8.

5448 *acount yhelde*: Presumably with reference to 'Redde rationem villicationis tuae' (Luke 16: 2), in the parable of the unjust steward, customarily treated as a discussion of the Last Judgement.

5461 *sex condiciouns*: The formulation agrees with the French (BSG 114^v/41, *BVV* 173/5–6). However, at 5519, the poet divides the third condition, 'il se doit confesser apertement' (BSG 116^r/18, *BVV* 176/11–12), into two. As a result, the English text cites seven conditions (compare line 5847).

5522–6 An allusion to the 'circumstances' of sin, discussed at length in 5540–68 (cf. 5549 ff. n.), with cross-reference to this passage. Compare the discussion of Chaucer's Parson, I 960–81.

5539 *hym may*: The ELPS transposition occurs elsewhere only in B⁶ and Harley 435, the simpler transposition *may hym* in B⁸.

5549 ff. The poem states standard views on the imposition of penance according to the circumstances of sin, e.g. *a person . . . mare* 5549, that sex with a nun is worse than with a virgin, in turn worse than with an unmarried woman; *some stede mare* 5552, that a sin in a church is worse than one elsewhere; or *mare . . . in a heghe tyme* 5553, that sins are worse during prescribed vigils or holy days than at other times.

5557 *oftner*: Although only parallelled in B⁵, I retain; compare 4800 n.

5575–6 The opening of a major interpolation, continuing to 5834, that replaces extensive parallel materials in *Somme* (BSG 117ᵛ–118ʳ, *BVV* 179–80). This has been derived from a prominent local text, the discussion of sin in Richard Rolle's *Form of Living*. Translate 'Each of these three involves all the seven sins'. The triad, in this instance derived from Rolle's *Form*, is basically that of sins of thought, word, and deed, to which, again following Rolle, are added 'sins of omission' (*synnes of leuynge of gode vndone* 5592). With such a division, compare the discussion of Envy at 4213–72—but also the analysis of the virtue Humility at 1559–776.

5585 *on conscience hynges*: Translate 'adhere (or stick to) Conscience'.

5590 *has*: The A reading is unique and may require emendation to the majority's *haf*, as later in the line.

5600 *werst*: RW *wers* only occurs in B⁷ of the B-MSS (om. Harley 435).

5632–4 *thre maners of gode*: For the goods of Nature, Fortune, and Grace, discussed in *Somme* but omitted by the poet, see 3785 n.

5652 *vp-*: PW *vm-* is virtually unique in the entire tradition, in only a single further MS.

5660 *Wreghynge*: 'Disclosing (secrets that set people at odds)'; the easier substitution *Wrethynge* LP appears elsewhere only in B³ among B-MSS.

5680 *enchesoun*: The reading may be dittographic (*-outen en-*); the haplographic form *chesoun* PRW also occurs in B¹B²B⁵B⁶B⁷.

5709–10 The transposition of the lines in ERW also appears in B¹B⁹ and Harley 435.

5713 *reuerys*: Probably not, on the basis of other uses in the poem, 'dreams' but rather 'obliviousness'. For dreams, often seen in instructional literature as inspiring divination and magic (compare line 5722), see Owst, '*Sortilegium* in English Homiletic Literature'.

5763 Still controlled by the phrase *To trespas* 5753.

5765 *þe circumstaunce of synne*: As 5769–70 indicate, discussed above more fully at 5540–68. The first noun has, of course, an apocopated plural.

5788 *þat*: Probably for *þat þat*, i.e. 'the grace that'.

5816 *in nede*: That is, to relieve his own need; compare Langland's Sloth, *Piers* B.5: 385–441, a panoply of behaviours also described here.

5818 *þe Werkes of Mercy*: Unlike Langland's Sloth, who ignores the Corporal Works (see *Piers* B.5: 405, 429–35). The following lines outline the Spiritual Works of Mercy, to be much more fully discussed at 7539 ff.

5840 *awne ere*: Compare 'li confessers n'est que le oreille dieu (C 134ʳ, BSG *die*)' (BSG 118ʳ/24, *BVV* 180/26). The misunderstanding is unique to the five central copies; like RW, all B-MSS agree in adjective and noun (*owen berer* B¹, *owyn fere* B⁵).

5847 *þis*: The PRW omission also occurs in B¹B⁵B⁷B⁹ (thus B⁶).

5869–72 A ME addition.

5896 *armure*: Taking up the metaphor from 5426.

5917–20 The French is explicitly citing 'l'euangile' (BSG 120ᵛ/32, *BVV* 184/24), apparently Luke 8: 12–14, to which the weathercock forms a concluding figure. Part of the text, as paraphrased in the French, appears in the second couplet here.

5934–8 A ME addition.

5935 *and²*: All B-MSS agree with RW in omitting the following *alle*, a case of haplography.

5939 *after I can*: Simply provided for the rhyme; as the subsequent lines make clear, the poet is following his source in citing Solomon.

5942 *Salamon*: Might allude to any number of passages in the wisdom books, but perhaps most spectacularly to Ecclus. 25: 17–36 (especially verses 32–4). For the story of Sampson and Dalilah, see Judges 16. See further 9673 n.

5955–64 A ME addition.

5964 *he*: The omission is A's error in isolation, and the pronoun occurs in all B-MSS.

5967 *þe whyte robe of his lyuere*: As the French indicates (BSG 121ʳ/6, *BVV* 185/19–20), an allusion to the vestments of the bride, Apoc. 19: 8. The figure recurs in the discussion of the white robe of virginity at 11537.

5969 *þe ferth and þe fifi bataylle*: For this contrast of Fortitude in both prosperity and adversity, see also 2241 n., 4825 n., 5299 n.

5997 *Iohan*: Apoc. 3: 21.

6011–16 The French here adds brief materials connecting Antichrist with 'the beast from the sea' (Apoc. 13: 1), used as a symbol of the Seven Sins, in a passage suppressed in the English. Compare 'Ce est la beste qui sein Iohanz vit qui guerroiet li (querreoit les C 137ᵛ) seinz dont nus auons pieca parle' (BSG 121ᵛ/33–5, *BVV* 186/19–20).

6023–4 Identified in *Somme* as an allusion to Apoc., probably to 2: 26, 13: 10, or 14:12 (BSG 121^v/44, *BVV* 186/29–30).

6028 *ay*: The ELPW omission is shared by B^{1}B^{3}B^{6}B^{8}B^9, but appears a response to an unduly heavy line. If there is an otiose syllable, it is likely (as L perceives) that *a man* in fact reproduces the indefinite *me* 'a person'. In any event, stresses fall on *-sayl-*, *ay*, *last*, and *end*.

6030 *he*: LRW, along with B^{1}B^{2}B^{3}B^{5}B^{8}B^9, fail to see that the form could be elided as *h'as*.

6040–5 A ME addition.

6085 As Gradon says (198, 183/16–18 n.), Apoc. 2: 7. All B-MSS (except *ʒeue hem* B^2) agree with PRW in omitting *þe*.

6100–1 *hungre . . . thristes*: Generally, the scribes try to accommodate the verb forms to a single pattern, without recognizing that *hungre* follows the Northern pronoun rule but that the nonadjacent *thristes* (in all B-MSS except B^7) need not do so.

6102 ff. The text almost resists disambiguating punctuation. Translate 'with endless joy to which Fortitude brings a man—it only comes from the Gift of Strength'. Similarly, at 6106 ff., translate 'what the Gift may do; the fourth petition, where we explicitly pray for this Gift, may gain it for us'.

6122 *Bisy wynnynge*: Translating 'aquestier ardamment' (BSG 28^v/48, *BVV* 30/14).

6126 *be*: ELPS have support in their omission from B^{1}B^{6}B^{8}B^9. Although the word might be dittographic, it appears metrically necessary. The discussion 6125–42 represents a ME expansion of the *Somme*'s argument.

6141 *in*: All B-MSS follow PRW in this reading, except B^{3}B^8, which agree with ES *at*.

6143–4 Of course, as *Somme* explicitly indicates (BSG 28^v/42, *BVV* 30/7), translating 1 Tim. 6: 10, Chaucer's Pardoner's text.

6156 *braunche*: All B-MSS agree with RW in the omission.

6159–60 *Somme* has simply 'mauuais mestiers' (BSG 29^r/3, *BVV* 30/22). *Fole Play* 6162 corresponds to 'mauuais geus' in the source, but see 7238 n.

6173 In the discussion of Avarice, the *Speculum* poet shows a greater involvement in crafting the text than elsewhere. Lorens explicitly presents Okir/Usury as having seven parts (BSG 29^r/6, *BVV* 30/25). In contrast, the poem has twelve divisions, two of them, the ninth and tenth (6263–94) completely, it would appear, the poet's invention (perhaps intended as specifically local abuses?). Here, at 6173, *Speculum Vitae* divides Lorens's first point into two; the text distinguishes usurers 'withouten curtaysy' from ones 'curtays' (i.e. not harshly enforcing a written contract); compare BSG 29^r/14–16, *BVV* 30/35–6. The English poet's other interventions appear at

6229–62, where his seventh and eighth points are generated out of bits of Lorens's fifth (the sixth here); see BSG 29ᵛ/40–3, 29ᵛ/48–30ʳ/5; *BVV* 31/25–8, 32/2–11, respectively. See further 6343 n., 6375 n., 6425–54 n., 6475–98 n., 6501–12 n., etc.

6201–2 That is, those who profit from loans made by others; translate 'When a man has a usurious servant and takes the profit for his own use'. In the French, this material is followed by an attack on great lords who support, in return for a consideration, Jews and 'les caorsins' as lenders; see BSG 29ᵛ/31–4, *BVV* 31/14–19.

6215 *He*: Although there are no variants, the pronoun is probably otiose and to be suppressed; were one so to emend, the preceding line should end with a comma and this one with a full stop. Compare 'Cil sont vsurier deciple (so SJ; petit BSG and C) qui aprenent cel (tel C 33ᵛ) ord mestier' (BSG 29ᵛ/37–8, *BVV* 31/22–3).

6222 *for frest of þe pay*: 'because of having loaned that amount'. In the abuse described, one loans goods bought cheaply with a contract requiring repayment at market value at a future date when the the goods will be more expensive.

6248 *La Somme* offers a more circumstantial explanation, buying goods cheaply before they are ready for market and then insisting on the cut-rate price at the time of delivery; see BSG 30ʳ/2–5, *BVV* 32/9–11.

6253–6 A major crux, since the lines seem to have been absent from the archetype of the five central MSS (and thus, presumably supplied by conflation in L). The problem is amplified by A's obvious further conflation in 6255. Generally, all B-MSS share the RW readings. I have chosen to follow A in the couplet, ELPS for the line A has substituted from elsewhere and for the head of 6256. At the centre of 6253, I make one small excision; in the sequence *þat ne þe*, the scribes seem to have been confused by subordinating *ne* 'that . . . not'. Among the B-MSS, B²B⁶B⁷ agree with A, B¹B³B⁵B⁸ with LRW, *ne* B⁹. It remains possible, because the couplet 6253–4 has no parallel in *La Somme*, that the central manuscripts, in their lacking it, actually reproduce the archetypal text. Were that the case, the couplet has been intruded as additional clarification in other branches of the textual tradition. And further, if that were the case, line 6255 might well have originally had the form recorded in A.

6271 *to prys sette*: 'add the profit to the value', slightly confusing, since the lender is to deduct this amount from the principal he is owed.

6282 *if*: LPRW have support from all B-MSS (*ȝif þat* B¹, *þat* B³).

6343 *fyue maners*: In *La Somme*, only 'iiij. manieres' (BSG 30ʳ/21, *BVV* 32/30). The poet has given independent status to the discussion of 'Lytell Theft', in the original a subsidiary part of 'Covert Theft' (6419, BSG 30ᵛ/

45, *BVV* 33/24). In addition, he reverses the source's assignment of the categories 'priuee' and 'couert' (cf. BSG 30ʳ/23–4, *BVV* 32/35 and 33/3, etc.).

6367 A's normal form for '(al)though' is *al-if* (33×), but this introduces a small patch of variants for the usual form:

  þoghe 6367 (as B³B⁶): *alle* ELS, *if* RB¹B²B⁸B⁹ (*þof?* P, a form foreign to A; compare *of* B⁷, *alþow* B⁵)

  þohe 6568 (as B³B⁵B⁷): *If* ESRB¹B²B⁶B⁸B⁹, *To* L (*þof* P)

  þogh 6599 (as the rest): *If alle* ES, *If þat all* L, If RB²B⁵ (*þof* P)

Similar variation occurs sporadically later; see 7871, 11268 (and further the variants 25, 743, 1455, 1653, 3142, 3493).

6375 *grayfe*: With the description, compare Chaucer's Reeve, 'General Prologue' A 587–622. 6379–92 form a ME addition.

6381 *vntill*: Emendation to the majority form *till*, in all B-MSS except B⁷, is attractive but not metrically necessary.

6425–54 A ME elaboration.

6436 Translate 'For he steals everything that he takes above (what he has deserved)'.

6457 The line, as received, appears to say: 'and does not wish, even if he recognizes the object', and corresponds to BSG 30ᵛ/50–1 (*BVV* 33/29) 'e seuent bien a cui (qui C 34ᵛ) eles sont e ne les uuelent rendre'. This would suggest supplying after *noght* an implicit infinitive phrase 'to return it', which strikes me as unduly elliptical. Rather, I construe *be* as representing more usual *by(e)* 'buy' and translate 'and does not wish to pay for the thing, (although) having recognized it/its owner'. The simpler solution, reading *be* with *oknawen* ('doesn't wish the thing to be recognized'), does not explain the word-order.

6460 *þat it*: If *it* represents the pronoun, one of the two words is extraneous to the sense (although not the metre). But possibly *it* is a form for *yhete*.

6461 *theefes*: Perhaps too tiny an anomaly to attract attention, but the genitive termination might arguably have been omitted by attraction to the following *f-*, and RW are supported by only B⁷ among the B-MSS.

6472 Proverbial (Whiting F 112); compare *Siege of Jerusalem* 991–2.

6475–98 Largely ME expansion, only 6477–8 very closely approximating *La Somme* (BSG 31ʳ/5–8, *BVV* 34/3–6).

6501–12 The same six-part division appears in the source, but the translator has reordered the discussion (compare BSG 31ʳᵛ, *BVV* 34–5). The English poem is relatively free and expansive in its handling, perhaps most notably with the final group (6563–88), where Lorens considers secular officials, not rural deans (compare BSG 31ᵛ/29–30, *BVV* 34/34–35/2).

6535–6 Like Langland's Sloth at *Piers* B.5: 422–7.

6549 *tase*: Compare a similar variant involving verbs with and without adjacent pronouns at 6100. Here the variation may have been supported by possible confusion of *s* and *k*. B²B⁵B⁶ agree with the rejected A reading.

6553 *so fre*: I take the rather vapid *to se* of the five central copies as a replacement for this PRW reading, supported by all the B-MSS. It approximates the identification in *La Somme* 'ces granz prelaz' (BSG 31ʳ/ 36, *BVV* 34/31), and is simply a class-marker '(men) of such high status'. The archetype of the central MSS apparently (and plausibly) construed the phrase as an incongruous bit of moral approbation 'so noble/generous'.

6605 The *aght maner of men* here corresponds to *Somme*'s 'vij. maneres de genz' (BSG 31ᵛ/40, *BVV* 35/17; this translation has dropped the false assesour 6727/'mauuais assesseur' BSG 32ʳ/15 at 36/17). The *Speculum* translator has divided Lorens's fourth group into two sets of attorney-figures and is elsewhere engaged in similar doublings of the original account (for example, the false *clerk of fee* at 6701–12).

6624 *dispens*: The majority reading printed here appears in all B-MSS.

6629–38 A ME addition; in *La Somme* (BSG 31ᵛ/45–7, *BVV* 35/25–8), these are simply those who flee the jurisdiction of the court.

6646 *par²*: Other dissimilating readings, resembling those of LR and PW, occur widely in the B-MSS: *þat* B³B⁵B⁶B⁸, om. B¹B²B⁹. The specific application of this abuse to matrimonial cases seizes on a single detail of the original ('cil font les faus mariages', BSG 31ᵛ/48, not at *BVV* 35/30). However, such behaviours, while they may not have interested Lorens, appear prominently in English sentences of excommunication, for example Archbishop Pecham's at *Councils* 906, or the York *Manuale*, Surtees Society 63 (1875), *88–*89. See 6769 n.

6647 *for*: LRW's anticipatory *of* also appears in B¹B⁹.

6678 *auoket*: A has been 'corrected' from a MS in the broader common tradition; among B-MSS, only B³B⁸ support the original A reading, which agrees with the remainder of its group ELPS.

6684 *þus he*: The reading is unique to the five core MSS; B⁷ supports R *he swa*, and the remaining B-MSS PW *he*.

6702 *court baroun*: A court of manorial tenants, usually with the lord's steward sitting as judge.

6714 *þat . . .*: The first of a series of small grammatical niggles extending through the subsequent discussion. This line, of course, forms a relative clause modifying *domesman*. In 6722 ff., *haue* presumably is the principal verb of both clauses (although the second expresses a possibility, rather than, as the first, a fact). The two *yhete*s at the opening of the following paragraph are presumably coordinate in force. In 6746, the antecedent of *þai* is *men* (the good judge pays no attention to social status). Compare 'Erkenwald' 225–45, 265–72, the latter passage analogous to the claim of lines 6753–4 that proper justice demonstrates a perfection equivalent to that of religious 'order'.

6727 *assesour*: As line 6616, the definition in the following two lines, and the spelling of the Latin sidenote show, the poet does not here discuss an *assysour* 'juror', but a judge's aide. Forms in *e* and *i* regularly interchange in Anglo-Latin, and I suspect they might have done in ME as well. The correct reading appears only in four B-MSS, B¹B²B⁵ (sesoure B⁸), perhaps an indication that the scribes independently inserted the more familiar office.

6731 *taas*: With the cited variants, compare *haþ* B¹B⁹. The readings probably only by accident correspond to *Somme* 'por les seruises que il en ont' (BSG 32ʳ/17, not in *BVV*).

6737–54 This lengthy apology is a ME addition.

6750 *lyne*: In spite of its isolation (and the possibility that the scribe remembers an earlier locution, for example 4794, 4803, 4823, 4852), A's reading should probably be retained. B⁷ supports it, while all other B-MSS follow RW *lyfe* (*way* B⁵). The majority variant is well attested in the four previous uses of the phrase.

6769 *grete cursynge* (cf. 6790 *þe sentence of cursynge*): The usual late medieval 'sentences of cursing', i.e. sentences of excommunicaton, familiar because read in churches four times a year, routinely begin by anathematizing catalogues of such behaviours contemptuous of the Church or its rights. See, for example, archbishop Pecham's 1281 provisions, *Councils* 905–6; or the version in the York *Manuale*, Surtees Society, 63 (1875), *87–*88. See further 6646 n., 6831–44 n., 6859 n.

6792 *þat²*: While the demonstrative may have been generated by *þat¹*, the majority omission (for W is joined by all B-MSS except B⁶B⁷) may rest on a different interpretation of the metre.

6809–24 Some churches, for example Ripon Minster, claimed extensive rights of sanctuary—always a potential flashpoint between ecclesiastical and secular jurisdictions. Two of the articles in the complaint of Canterbury provincial clergy to Edward I in 1300 deal with perceived abuses; see *Councils* 1212.

6831–44 A ME addition, comparable to the added emphasis upon marriage mentioned 6646 n.

6838 *vnto*: LPW *to* is supported by all B-MSS except B⁷.

6840 For the distinction between solemn and privy vows, see the more explicit discussion at 11301–32.

6859 *wirke*: That is, the learned bishop, identified in the following line as the church's steward/patron, will 'work' (appoint) only after receiving a payment. The entire discussion through line 6906 is a litany of abuses specifically mentioned in 'sentences of cursing', for example Pecham at *Councils* 906.

6861 *þai*: W's *þa* also appears in virtually all the B-MSS (*he* B[7]). But the two readings are at best indifferents, if not actually just variant spellings of one another.

6891 *leste*: Although the locution is not grammatically logical, the A reading (also in B[2]B[8]) is confirmed by best B[5] (with others). The numerous copies reporting 'proper' *lesse* (including the remaining five B-MSS) either respond to a perceived grammatical problem or echo 6888, rather than transmit an anterior reading.

6906 *nere*: The LPRW variant *nerehand* is scantly attested, only in B[7] among the B-MSS.

6915–26 A ME addition. *Speculum Vitae* follows the source in dividing Simony into six parts, although it rearranges their order and provides considerable extra detail.

6922 *at*: The Northern form has been removed by substitution in all B-MSS, as in LPRW.

6927–34 Wisdom is given by God for communal purposes, not personal profit, a point Langland makes most forcefully about lawyers; compare *Piers* B.7: 40–60. There is extensive canonical discussion of the point, in the main predicated on Jesus' injunction at Matt. 10: 8; see Post et al., 'The Medieval Heritage of a Humanistic Ideal'.

6928 *Goddis borde*: The altar, where the host is consecrated.

6934 *erthly*: The PRW *werldly* appears in seven B-MSS (and the similar *worldes* in B[6]); it probably assimilates the anterior reading to *worde* earlier in the line.

6935–42 A ME addition.

6946 *þat*: 'Whatever', a sense vitiated by LRW's second *þat* ('that which'), a reading nonetheless transmitted in all B-MSS except B[3]B[5].

6948 *sex thinges*: In the French, these are not enumerated here, although the discussion has five marked parts (see BSG 33[v]–34[r], *BVV* 39–40). The ME poet has divided the first part, which in the source includes Witchcraft.

6996 *it*: the LRW omission occurs in seven B-MSS (B[2] reads as A).

7016 *in fyue maners*: Revamping *Somme*'s 'en 7. manieres' (BSG 34[v]/33, *BVV* 40/16). The English suppresses the fourth and fifth divisions of the source (BSG 34[v]/47–53, *BVV* 40/30–41/2), while 7023–54 expand upon Lorens's pair of one-sentence descriptions (BSG 34[v]/33–7, *BVV* 40/17–19).

7065 *he can*: Transposed, like RW, in all B-MSS except B¹.

7094 *Offyce or Craft of Foly*: This discussion represents a distinctive feature of *La Somme* and its derivatives, that some professions are, of their nature, sinful. The quite lengthy discussion here (it ends only at 7236) is almost entirely original. In *La Somme*, these 'mauuais mestiers' get short shrift, with simple exemplary naming of 'ces foles femmes . . . cil hiriaus e cil champions' (BSG 35ʳ/7–14, *BVV* 41/10–18). Langland, who is fascinated by such liminality, offers (as Skeat recognized long ago) the most extensive analogues for this treatment. Compare 7112 n., 7123 n., 7133 n., 7248 n.

7095 *seuen*: But nine are listed, a fact not lost on B³B⁵B⁶, who give that figure. Presumably, this largely original portion proved expansive (the sixth and seventh figures correspond to the last two mentioned in the source) and was not carefully revised.

7112 Langland on four occasions takes up a favourite issue of canon lawyers, whether, given the source of her income, a prostitute should be required to pay tithes. See *Piers* C.3: 301–2, 6: 305–6, 13: 73–5, 16: 259–61, and Brundage, 'Prostitution in the Medieval Canon Law', esp. 91–3.

7121 *leges*: That is, *leghes* 'lies' (see the similar form *Argnes* for usual *Arghnes* 5628 and, further, 12525 n.). Compare the Orleans magician of Chaucer's Franklin's Tale, F 1123–1208 (and the further condemnation of his skills, 1261–96). See again Owst, '*Sortilegium* in English Homiletic Literature'.

7123 *Faytours*: Langland's interest in fake poverty marks *Piers* from first (B.Prol: 42 'Faiteden') to last (the wheedling friars of B.20). The detail here resonates most closely with the description of false begging at B.7: 90–9; on the general fourteenth-century interest in discriminating between 'true' and 'false' poverty, see Aers, *Community, Gender, and Individual Identity*, ch. 1.

7126 *or*: The dissimilating reading *and*, in the majority of MSS collated, also occurs in all B-MSS except B⁶.

7133–4 *Sneckedrawers . . . Robertmen*: Langland, of course, refers to both, although never with such specifying detail as is offered here. Compare his 'lachedraweres' at C.8: 286 and 9: 193 (in a more extensive reprise of materials cited 7123 n.) and 'Roberdes knaues' (B.Prol: 44) and 'Roberd þe Robbere' (5: 461–76). On the latter group, see Takamiya, 'Richard and Robert as False Executors', esp. 49–51.

7145 *armour*: Only B⁷ concurs with RW in reporting a plural (attracted by a sequence of nouns in -s).

7169 The construction is impersonal: 'It is appropriate to "harlots" to display themselves publically (*on þe flore* = in the open part of a hall).'

7173–6 Translate 'And they can't argue about (rebel against?) that, when people request them to perform, because they are professed by rule to that sort of action'. 'To perform' in this translation is deliberately evasive. There is something wrong with line 7174 in all copies; I would suspect the archetypal rhyme-word was *gle*.

7178 *licken*: Although there are no variants, possibly an error for *lacken* 'deride, satirise'.

7181 Translate 'that do tumbling tricks and amuse the onlookers'.

7210 *ful*: Virtually all B-MSS follow PW in omitting the word; it only appears in B⁷ (*pus* B²). It is, however, necessary to the metre.

7212 *estresce*: LSR *destresse* is simply a guess, not a bad one, and widely reproduced in B-MSS, in B¹B³B⁶B⁷B⁸B⁹. As Nelson saw ('The Middle English *Speculum Vitae*', 616), the sense probably requires interpreting the spelling *escresce* as a an approximative homograph for an unrecorded French loan, from *estrece* 'rigour, tyranny, oppression'. Just possibly, *estresce* represents the plural *estretz* 'fines' (conceived as 'extracts' entered on a roll).

7217 *wryten in boke*: Compare Luke 5: 27, Mark 2: 14.

7224 *Hynge*: The intruded *To* of the majority of MSS also appears in B¹B²B⁵B⁷B⁹.

7231 *pat of*: 'who, through (their job description)'. The easier LPRW *For pat* appears in all B-MSS.

7235 *pis*: Common to the central group and only two other MSS in the entire tradition; B-MSS universally follow PRW *It*.

7238 *Fole Play*: In the French, simply 'mauuais geus' (BSG 35ʳ/15–16, *BVV* 41/20), but as the sidenote indicates, the ME poet wishes to insist on the rashness of these behaviours. Lorens enumerates only five parts, again subject to considerable supplementation in the poem. *Rauyn* is a portion of the first point in the French (BSG 35ʳ/22, *BVV* 41/27–8), *Sclaunder* a part of the third (BSG 35ʳᵛ/26–35, *BVV* 41/32–42/9), and the final two divisions are original to the English.

7248 *spendynge of tyme in wast*: The full discussion, generally lines 7269–96, is one of an extensive set of such treatments in the poem. Indeed, it is inherent in the decision, announced by the poet in his prologue, to turn from *vayne carpynge* (see the discussion 1–114 n.). For other examples, see at least 447–68, 3651–4, 5039–60, 6445–50, 7610–18, 8557–90, 9621–30, 9882–94, 10357–64, 10421–72, 13171–204, and 15199–206. The topic, of course, equally intrigues Langland; compare for example, his framing of the C version 'biographical passage' at 5.27–8 and 92–101 (and B.1: 138–41); or, Study's diatribe, replaying a number of *Speculum Vitae* concerns (including the last discussion cited above), at B.10: 30–80.

7256 *ne*: In AS and B⁷ only of the MSS here surveyed; the remainder, apparently ignoring the elision 'n'es', omit.

7266 *anely*: In AELS only and omitted in all B-MSS, as in PRW. The reading of the majority is quite attractive, but may simply respond to an unusually heavy line (and perhaps the metrical subordination of *houre* to *anely*).

7287 *willes*: The plural also appears in B⁶B⁷B⁸ (cf. *þam* B²).

7293 *to-*: Compare *the* B¹B²B³B⁹, *þer* B⁵B⁸, *þat* B⁶.

7306 *to²*: The SRW omission also appears in B¹B²B³B⁹.

7331–2 The *þat*-clause of the first line depends on the phrases of the second.

7342 *a lickenes*: Alluding to Gen. 1: 26–7.

7343 *In kynde*: The exigencies of English metre have truncated the reference: 'si come dist le liure que parle de la nature de bestes' (BSG 124ʳ/1–2, *BVV* 190/32). However, I find none of the three examples cited in *Bestiary*.

7347–8 Translate 'a mare . . . will allow . . . to suckle (from) her (teats) . . .'.

7349 *als we fynde in iestes*: The most prominent historical example would be, of course, the story of Romulus and Remus. The motif also occurs in the ME romance *William of Palerne*, and similar stories occur with some frequency as medieval exempla, for example Tubach, *Index Exemplorum*, nos. 1448, 3028, 5340, and especially 5350.

7358 *Of a bodi*: Modifying *lyms* 7357.

7370 *we*: I remain dubious about this reading, peculiar to AE and in no B-MS. But it is easier to explain its omission—scribes found it grammatically unnecessary and extrametrical—than it is to explain its appearance.

7377–90 The discussion follows from the citation in the French (BSG 124ᵛ/30–2, *BVV* 191/28–9) of Solomon, Eccl. 9: 8. 7384 only by accident echoes Rollean *incendium*; compare 2727 ff.

7392 *mast Godde*: The transposition of LSRW appears in all B-MSS except B¹B⁷. In 7394, ELS are joined in their reversal of *mast him* by only B¹B³B⁵B⁸ of the B-MSS.

7399–7400 The English builds upon explicit biblical citations in the French (BSG 124ᵛ/45–51, *BVV* 192/11–16): Tob. 4: 7 and Matt. 19: 21.

7405–6 Again, a marked citation in the source (BSG 125ᵛ/42–3, *BVV* 193/24–5), Solomon at Prov. 14: 31.

7408 *vnto*: PRW *to* is nearly ubiquitous in the B-MSS (only *vnto* B⁷), and many copies (B¹B²B³B⁶B⁹) also omit *it*.

7410 *þe godspelle*: Matt. 25: 40, within the lengthy passage (vv. 35–45) that conventionally defines the Corporal Works of Mercy, explicitly invoked at 7985.

7412 *it*: All B-MSS agree with RW in omitting the word.

7421–8 *Saynt Martyne*: See *Legenda* 152 (ii. 1134–6). The poet alludes to the legend again at 8070.

7432 Translate 'in accord with His (divine) courtesy'. The French (BSG 125ᵛ/28–30, *BVV* 193/10–11) explicitly presents this as a citation of James 1: 5.

7435 *Godde biddes vs*: Luke 6: 36.

7439 *þe wyse man*: Ecclus. 4: 10 (the French is more explicit than the English poet).

7447 *þe haly man*: In Lorens's French, explicitly referring to James 2: 13. Lines 7451–2 glance again at Matt. 25.

7458–64 *þe godspelle*: Luke 16: 19–25, more extensively discussed at 8015–36 (and a further reference at 15639–46).

7467–70 *Godde . . . At þe bridale*: Matt. 25: 1–13, extensively discussed in the later treatment of Chastity (see 10783 n.).

7478 *hert*: Although widespread (in all B-MSS, as well as ELPSW), the dittographic addition of *to* overlooks the possibility of reading disyllabic *hert-ë*.

7489 *þe gode marchande*: Probably in allusion to the parable of the talents, Luke 19: 12–26 (compare, more distantly, the pearl of great price, Matt. 13: 45).

7491 *Paul*: Perhaps Col. 3: 12 or Titus 3: 5.

7500 *Salamon*: Prov. 3: 9–10.

7516 *it yhelde agayne*: An efficacious confession of sins requires, for absolution, the restitution of all ill-got gains. Compare Langland's presentation of Avarice, particularly B.5: 230–6, 260–95, and the repeated command '*Redde*' (give it back) at 5: 461; 19: 187, 259, 300; 20: 308.

7531–4 *ensaumples*: Simply translating *La Somme*'s general reference.

7537–8 In the French, alleged to paraphrase a Psalter verse, but perhaps Prov. 21: 3 and 21 (not in BSG at 127ᵛ/47, *BVV* 198/22–5). BSG (and C) lack the discussion of the Works of Mercy, and I have drawn French citations from this point to line 8526 from SJ.

7547 Unlike the Corporal Works of Mercy, the spiritual set does not reflect an authoritative biblical locus. This devotional group appears to have developed by analogy with the biblical set in thirteenth-century commentaries on Peter Lombard's *Sentences*. The relationship between physical and spiritual works was certainly a topic already well worn when Aquinas took it up at *Summa* 2ᵃ 2ᵃᵉ Q. 32. 2, where he cites the widely circulating mnemonic distich (compare Walther 33805):

> Visito, poto, cibo, redimo, tego, colligo, condo;
> Consule, castiga, solare, remitte, fer, ora.

7557 *es*: The line is clearly short, and I insert the word found in PRW and all B-MSS (B^8 out, *ys also* B^5).

7591–7618 A ME elaboration, creating discussions of a length comparable to the following one about parents, which has come mostly from the French. Further small ME elaborations occur at lines 7635–42, 7725–30, and 7757–66 (*BVV* 200/7, 201/14, 201/28 respectively).

7639 *tetches*: *thewes* ELS is isolated, with no parallels among the B-MSS (*werkes* B^5).

7664 The proverb is Whiting L 455.

7674 *fole*: The use of the word routinely attracts a wide yet predictable scatter of variants. Here *folye* EP also appears in B^{2}B^{3}B^5, *foule* RW also in B^{8}B^9. Such variation frequently recurs in the poem; see also 9123 n., 9748 n., 11298 n., 11610 n. Although I collate *fole* and *foule* as if distinct words, at least one other interpretation is plausible. The poem shows frequent evidence for coalescence of earlier long *o* with earlier (long) *u* in certain phonetic environments. In such a context, *fole* may represent both 'words', and *foule* represent a back-spelling, a situation in which the historical representation of one form has become used for another with which it has subsequently become homonymous.

  fole condiciounes answers simple 'les pechiez' in the French (SJ, *BVV* 200/25–6); it probably represents the poet's rhyming elaboration.

7685 Alluding to Matt. 25: 44–5.

7695 *Paul*: 1 Thes. 5: 14.

7697 *Salamon*: Perhaps Ecclus. 25: 17–21 or 38: 19–23.

7701–4 The French indicates that the lines are a second biblical citation, also from Solomon: 'quar si comme il meismes le dit' (SJ, *BVV* 201/6), clarifying the citation of Prov. 27: 9. In conjunction with the LPRW omission of *þat*, this may imply that the received text errs.

7740 *Austyne*: 'Sermones de sanctis' 336. 5 (PL 38: 1474).

7751 *Godde says*: Heb. 12: 6.

7761 *Austyne*: Peter Lombard, *Collectanea in epistolas S. Pauli*, on Phil. 4: 4 (PL 192: 252–3), ascribes these views to Augustine. The passage does not appear at *BVV* 201/28.

7770 *His awen coppe*: That is, Jesus is the king who has already drunk the cup and wishes others to share his pain, more explicitly signalled in the French: 'li henas notre seignor a quoi il but sont les tribulacions de cest monde' (SJ, *BVV* 201/31–2). The passage alludes to the *calix* of persecution the sons of Zebedee wish to share at Matt. 20: 22–3 (explicitly invoked

9983 ff.) and that Jesus wishes to pass from him in Gethsemane, Matt. 26: 39.

7776 *sour*: On the basis of the French and of *sauour* 7780, probably an archetypal error for *s[au]our[y]*; the only variant is *our* B⁸. The full couplet is an anticipatory translation of materials fully rendered in 7779–82: 'c'est vne sause de vinaigre qui tost la sauor dou vin des deliz dou monde' (SJ, *BVV* 202/2–3).

7777–8 Translate 'a (dinner-table) course of memory of the pain . . .'.

7789–802 A ME elaboration, as is also 7812–32.

7806 *Gregor*: Like the further citations at 7885 and 7943, probably referring to the famous discussion of *Homeliae in Evangelia* 35. 4–5, 9 (PL 76: 1261–2, 1264–5).

7823 *Ieremye*: Lam. 1: 12.

7833–44 A common figure, derived from Exodus 15: 23–4.

7865 *Paul*: Probably alluding to Rom. 5: 3–5 (compare 2 Cor. 12: 9).

7867 *þe aungell*: Tob. 12: 13.

7871 *þogh*: ELS *yf* is a legitimate Yorkshire dialect variant for the A reading; compare also *of* B⁸, *þof* B⁹. See 6367 n.

7873–6 Conventional images of the 'work' done by tribulation, all biblically derived. For the gold in the furnace, see Ecclus. 2: 5 (as well as Prov. 17: 3, Wis. 3: 6); for the iron and file, compare Ecclus. 10: 10; for the flail and the chaff, Matt. 3: 12. A nearly proverbial triad in the Middle Ages, they ultimately reflect discussions like Gregory, *Moralia* 16. 32. 39 (PL 75: 1141), 20. 39. 76 (PL 76: 183–4).

7877 *Gregor*: A commonplace, but compare *Moralia* 34. 8. 17 (PL 76: 726).

7881 *þe boke*: Ecclus. 31: 2. 7884 *couerd* represents the poet's translation of 'environe' (surrounded), but the French was continuing the figure introduced by *sobre* in the preceding line: 'fet l'ame sobre que pechiez *enyure souent*' (SJ, *BVV* 202/35).

7885 *Gregor*: See 7806 n.

7891–4 *Iame*: James 1: 12; compare the crowns at Apoc. 2: 10, 4: 4–10.

7905–6 *es*: LSRW's positioning of the verb at the head of the second line certainly smoothes out the metre. But that is probably why it occurs, and the majority of the B-MSS scribes were content with the perhaps overweighted first line. Only B¹B⁹ have the L+ reading (B³ out with a lost leaf to 8199); B⁷ omits the verb.

7907 *Gregor*: Compare *Moralia* 12. 51. 57, 19. 23. 38 (PL 75: 1013; 76: 122–3).

7917–22 *þe godspelle*: Matt. 6: 15.

7925–30 See the extensive discussion 2947–3032.

7940 *sekenes*: A has intruded (and corrected) the RW reading, also in B¹B⁷B⁹ (B³ out).

7941 *Paul*: Perhaps 1 Cor. 9: 22.

7943 *Gregor*: See 7806 n.

7944 *boke*: LSRW's added *þat* also appears in all extant B-MSS.

7946 *suffres . . . despyte*: The poet translates 'il souffrit dolors', and may have had a defective exemplar here; compare 'il sent plus en soi les autrui dolors' (SJ, *BVV* 203/33).

7952–6 *þe godspell*: Matt. 5: 44–5.

7985 Compare 7410 n. Tobit is described as fulfilling works like these at Tob. 1: 19–20, but his great act, which leads to his suffering, is burying the dead, Tob. 1: 21 and 2: 3–9, on the basis of the collocation added to the acts of Matt. 25 to bring them up to the seven.

7990 *vnto*: Although probably metrically less preferable, majority *to* is virtually ubiquitous in the B-MSS as well (cf. *þat arn* B⁵, B³ out).

7993 *Thoby*: Tob. 4: 17.

7997 *Salamon*: Prov. 25: 21.

8005–8 *þe gospell*: Luke 14: 13–14. Compare the evocation of the verse at *Piers* B.13: 436–53 and comments on its fourteenth-century use to distinguish licit and illicit forms of poverty, Scase, *'Piers Plowman' and the New Articlericalism*, 63–4.

8015–36 See 7458–64 n.

8036 *nanekyns*: The variation of the collated copies also appears in the B-MSS, where only B⁷ shares the reading of AP (although compare *no maner* B⁶); *nakyns* ERW also occurs in B⁵B⁸, and *na* LS in B¹B²B⁹ (B³ out).

slecken: The text alternates between this form and its doublet, also from ON sloekkva, *slocken*. Here B²B⁷B⁹ read *slecken*, and B¹ *sloken*, but remaining B-MSS offer indications that they found the form difficult: *sclekene* (following *fol scke* expunged and cancelled) B⁵, *sclakyn* B⁶, *aslekene* B⁸ (B³ out).

8041 *þe gospelle*: Matt. 25: 34–5, 40.

8042 *þus*: Also absent, as in LSW, in B¹B⁵B⁹ (B³ out).

8057 *Thoby*: Tob. 4: 17; the following reference is to Isa. 58: 7.

8063–8 *Petir*: For Peter and Tabitha/Dorcas, see Acts 9: 36–41.

8072 *Als I tolde bifore*: At 7421–8; a ME addition with no parallel in the French (*BVV* 205/20).

8075–8 Translate 'may be a great reminder to the poor man, whenever he looks on (the clothes he was given), to pray that his benefactor be rewarded'.

8079 The poet follows *La Somme* in slightly revamping the received set of Corporal Works. Traditionally, discussions follow the distinction outlined in Matt. 25: 35–6; in this schema, the first two works are signalled by 'esurivi enim, et dedistis mihi manducare; sitivi, et dedistis mihi bibere'. These here have appeared (7989–90 et seq.) together as the 'first work'. Lorens apparently made this adjustment in order to free up one of the seven categories of 'work' for an original development. There is no reference in Matt. 25 to loaning money, but this is a similarly charitable act and one quite overtly opposed to (and thus 'remediating') Avarice. The contrast of virtuous and vicious act is particularly striking in the light of the extensively subdivided and meticulously described first 'branch' of the vice, Usury/ Okir. See further 6173 n.

8080 *þat er trew men*: The ES variant *and trewe men bene* is unparalleled in B-MSS, but its probable origins are signalled by *þat er*] *and are* B¹B⁵B⁹, *and were* B⁶ (B³ out).

8091 *þe Alde Lawe*: Deut. 15: 7–8.

8099 *þe godspell*: Matt. 5: 42.

8120 *þe godspell*: Matt. 6: 15, already cited at 7917–22; but compare also Matt. 18: 35, at the conclusion of the example next cited.

8125–6 *ensaumple . . . of þe ille seruand*: Matt. 18: 23–35. In spite of large-scale truncation of the sidenote in the MSS here collated, there is substantial support for the AE reading among B-MSS: the same reading in B⁸, Exemplum in euangelio B⁶B⁷. B⁹, like LPSRW, omits 'Euangelium', and B¹B²B⁵ offer no annotation at all (B³ out).

8145 *In Vitis patrum*: See 'Verba seniorum' 19. 1 (PL 73: 1040–1). Although here directly from the French source (*BVV* 206/17), the only Middle English uses of this text are virtually all Northern, anecdotes used for sermon exempla in *The Northern Homily Cycle* and a sequence of specifically heremitic prose translations, perhaps inspired by the career of Richard Rolle, edited EETS 329, 103–30.

8167 *Iob*: Perhaps Job 5: 11.

8177 *Iame*: James 1: 27 (also providing the incipit of *Ancrene Riwle*).

8181–8200 For the anecdote, see Tubach, *Index Exemplorum*, no. 5210 (from Étienne de Bourbon, a variant of Caesarius of Heisterbach, *Dialogus* 7. 45).

8181 *to þat*: An awkward translation of French 'Dont' (SJ, *BVV* 206/33).

8187 The profuse variation in the second half of the line, perhaps surprisingly, finds little confirmation in B-MSS; B⁵B⁷ concur with R (and compare L) in reading *to wasshe* (B³ out).

8190 *had*: ELSR *had a* appears widely in B-MSS (not in B²B⁶, B³ out). But, if a syllable is necessary here, it would have been provided by the final *-e* of *hadd-ë*.

8193 *drank*: Only B⁷ among the B-MSS supports LR in adding *it* (B³ out).

8203 *þe wyse man*: Perhaps Ecclus. 7: 39.

8210 *þe godspelle*: Simply a general reference to the Matt. 25 description of salvation through practice of the Works of Mercy.

8211–26 *Mary Torgan/Torkan*: The French, 'Marie d'Orgines' (SJ, *BVV* 207/15) clarifies the reference, to Mary d'Oignies (d. 1213). She is invoked as a model in Margery Kempe's *Book*, ch. 62, and a Middle English version of her life, derived from the standard hagiography of Jacques de Vitry, appears in BodL, MS Douce 114 (*IPMEP* 853). An unwilling bride, she persuaded her husband to live chastely, and the two occupied themselves in serving lepers. For further materials, see Mulder-Bakker, *Mary of Oignies*. ELPSRW *Torgayn* also appears in B³B⁵B⁷ (*Toragayn* B⁸); B²B³B⁵ report the Christian name as *Marion*.

8214 *vnto*: With the exception of B⁷, all B-MSS follow LPRW in reading *to* (and thus stressing disyllabic dative *god-ë*). See further 644 n.

8223–4 Translate this mixed construction 'your husband, who wished to be so meek that he has joined you in serving'.

8228 *þe godspelle*: Matt. 8: 2–3 (and its parallels, Mark 1: 40–2, Luke 5: 12–13), with a single leper; compare the appearance of ten (but no touch) at Luke 17: 12–14 and the inclusion of healing lepers in the statement of apostolic power at Matt. 10: 8.

  witteneses: All MSS except A show a more neatly metrical form, the apocope of *-esses* to *-ess*, widely attested in the poem; A has simply written the word in full.

8238 *Paul*: Phil. 2: 6–8.

8249 *Abraham*: See Gen. 18: 1–15; the child Isaac is, of course, the son who represents heavenly promise, as Paul explains at Gal. 4: 21–31. The subsequent Lot materials also follow immediately in the biblical account, at Gen. 19: 1–22.

8265 *Paul*: Heb. 13: 2.

8268 *eesed*: ELS *sesede* is isolated, with no confirmation in the B-MSS, and while potentially 'harder', is not entirely sensible ('gave a place to'? 'took in'?). The French might offer some support for such a reading, however; it essentially translates the Vulgate 'angelis . . . receptis', 'il receuoient les anges' (SJ, *BVV* 208/7).

8272 *þe godspelle*: Simply a further reference to Matt. 25: 40.

8277 *Of Saynt Gregor ensaumple*: The poet corrects a misattribution in the French; see *Legenda* 46 (i. 293). Contrast 'Dont sainz Gregoires raconte que' (SJ, *BVV* 208/12).

8292 *him²*: The LPR omission, which requires *sayd*-ë, also appears widely in B-MSS (B²B³B⁵B⁶B⁸; B⁴ is present through 8365). But the reading is arguably a haplographic response to the form of the line elsewhere.

8300–24 See 'Verba seniorum' 13. 9 (PL 73: 945).

8315 *yhone*: The specific Northern sense as general demonstrative 'that', not necessarily a directional indicator, is lost in PW and most B-MSS: *þe 3onde* B³, *3ond* B⁴B⁶, *3onder* B⁵B⁹, *3end* B⁸.

8334 *if þat*: The disyllabic extended form, necessary for the metre, has been reduced to simple *þat* in all B-MSS except B⁷, just as it has been in PRW. B¹ shows further variation, *if . . . may] of 3e way*; and B² agrees with E in reading *þai*.

8336 *Petir*: 1 Pet. 3: 19, although *La Somme* ascribes the citation to Paul (SJ, *BVV* 209/5).

8346, 8349 *comforte, comforted*: The variation between tenses in both lines depends to some degree on various scribes having copied each in relative isolation from the grammatical surround. In the first example, here emended, A (joined by B²B⁵B⁷B⁹) has been misled by the inserted clause 8345 *if . . . þare* and has missed the verb's dependence on *wald*, 'just as you should wish people to comfort you'. In the second example, where LSRW are supported only by B¹B⁹ (*comford* B⁴), variation reflects uncertainty over whether the parallelism is with past *was boun* or the more proximate *To visite*. The variation may have been further stimulated by the fact that *comfort* could stand as the apocopated past tense of the verb, as perhaps in B⁴'s reading in 8349.

8347 *Thoby*: Compare Tob. 1: 15.

8351 *Salamon*: Prov. 24: 11.

8353 *Danyell*: For his release of Susanna, see (the apocryphal) Daniel 13 (and the Middle English alliterative account, 'A Pistel of Susan').

8356 ff. For Jesus and the woman taken in adultery, see John 8: 3–11. The reading to which Lorens has subjected the account has largely been inspired by the ordinary gloss, which offers a variety of instructions on exercising justice.

8363 *Of*: Perhaps a misexpansion of archetypal *o* 'on', but all copies, including all B-MSS, read as the printed text.

8375 *Iob*; Job 29: 16.

8376 *bisily*: PR are isolated, without further support among the B-MSS.

8387 *fletchand*: The verb inspired considerable variation in B-MSS: *chidand* B¹, *changeande* B², *flyttande* (*hem flyttand* B⁵) B⁵B⁸, as LPSW. But the poet has simply imported the lexical form of the source; compare 'flechisse' (SJ, *BVV* 209/30).

8398 *þe godspelle*: Matt. 7: 1–2.

8401 *Paul*: Rom. 2: 1–2. Translate 8406 *Wharefore* 'for which'.

8414 *þat*: The rather fussy *what* ELPS also occurs in B¹B⁶B⁷. The line has no parallel at *BVV* 210/10.

8423 *of his mankynde*: 'coming from his humane/fellow feeling'. Compare the French 'par humanite' (SJ, 210/13–14).

8433 *Haly Wrytte*: James 2: 13; compare also the repeated refrains of Pss. 117 and 135.

8437 *Iohan*: Unfound, but probably in Chrysostom's *Opus imperfectum*; the text, in *Patrologia Graeca* 56, includes no homily for the most obvious reference, to the parable of the talents (Matt. 18).

8443 *Iame*: James 2: 13.

8454 Translate '(and) to appear (to him) in great awe'.

8463 *he went to helle*: Described, not in the Bible, but the apocryphal Gospel of Nicodemus; compare the most bravura ME treatment in *Piers* B.18.

8470–82 For the three examples, see Tobit 2: 1–7; Matt. 26: 6–13 (the identification with Mary Magdalene from John 11: 2 and 12: 1–8); and Matt. 27: 57–60, respectively.

8473 *Godde*: The RW addition *oft* appears in all B-MSS except B²B⁶ (B³ adds *muche*).

8476 *tokened*: B¹B⁹, on a variety of grounds those B-MSS closest to W, agree with it in reading *takenyng was* here; they also share the omission of 8491–5. Similarly, B⁹ alone among B-MSS agrees in reading *on* 8536, and B¹ alone in omitting *gode* 8544.

8491 *Iacob sayde*: Gen. 49: 29–31 (to all his sons, and not just Joseph).

8494 *fader*: Probably the historical plural, as French 'mes peres' implies (SJ, *BVV* 211/16).

8503 *a maner of fisshes*: Identified explicitly in *La Somme* as 'þe dolfyn' (*BVV* 211/20). *Bestiary*, however, has no such account, although a lengthy discussion of fishes (68ʳᵛ) insists upon theirs as a model of charitable behaviour that humans should emulate, mainly with regard to caring for their young. The full forms of the rhymes at 8503–4 (also in B³B⁵B⁷B⁸) probably represent graphemic fastidiousness, and they might well be represented and pronounced with the apocopated forms in other copies.

8513 *kynde*: While *kynde* 'natural affection' might be thoroughly appropriate for the non-Christians described in the preceding line, it seems less so here. This first noun may well reflect a substitution, motivated by repeated use of *kynde* in the preceding lines, for some other noun, as the more pointed French implies, 'pitie enformee de foi crestiene' (SJ, *BVV* 211/25).

8516 *saulles*: The singular attested in LPW also occurs in B¹B³B⁵B⁸B⁹.

8553 *Haly Writte*: Lev. 22: 19–21 and (8559ff.) Ecclus. 34: 24.

8565 *Austyn*: 'Sermones de scripturis' 80. 7 (PL 38: 497).

8573 *Haly Writte*: Ecclus. 12: 5.

8577 The question of discriminating alms also arises pregnantly in *Piers*; see 7123 n., 8005–8 n. Here the identification of *þe verray pouer* 8601 identifies them as the apostolic *pauperes spiritu* (Matt. 5: 3), alternatively as the *perfecti* who follow the counsel of Matt. 19: 21. But the subsequent discussion of licit giving is far from so limited.

8615, 8620, 8634–6 The injunction to look after father and mother in destitution follows from the discussion of the fourth commandment (Exod. 20: 12) at 1049–58. Jesus routinely refers to this among his various restatements of the commandments, for example Matt. 19: 17–19; see also Matt. 15: 4–6.

8622 *a manere of foull*: The French specifies the stork (BSG 128ᵛ/44 'cigoingne'; compare *BVV* 213/16). See *Bestiary* 61ʳ.

8630 *gode*: The AES intrusion of *a* does seem erroneous; in addition to its absence in LPRW, the B-MSS, without exception, lack it.

8641 Perhaps the outstanding biblical example of filial impiety would be Absalom's revolt against David, 2 Kings 15–18.

8649 The sidenote attested in ELS arguably should be added to the text of A.

8650 *gode²*: Although the word looks potentially echoic of the earlier usage, and the line is certainly metrical without it, AELS receive support from B¹B⁶B⁷B⁹.

8658 *þe boke says*: Probably a proleptic reference to Paul's 2 Cor. 9: 7 (cited both in the text and the Latin sidenote at 8687).

8661 *Gregor*: Gradon identifies (201, 193/26–8 n.) as 'In septem psalmos paenitentiales' 4 (PL 79: 595).

8668 *þe godspell*: Luke 21: 1–4.

8683 *þe wyse man*: Ecclus. 35: 11, followed by 2 Cor. 9: 7.

8693 *For*: The causal explanation of the preceding sentence seems preferable to the empty *Full* RW, perhaps partially generated by dissimilation from *For* 8691. Nonetheless, the RW reading appears in all B-MSS except B⁷ (*So* cancelled before *ful* B², B⁸ out).

8701 *þe wyse man*: Ecclus. 4: 8.

8709 *Salamon*: Prov. 3: 28, followed by Ecclus. 4: 3.

8731 *Senek*: Gradon compares (202, 194/23–4 n.) *De beneficiis* 2. 4.

8735 *commonly þis worde*: Whiting B 636, closely echoed at 8985; all the examples there cited are from *Somme*-derivatives.

8739 *þe wyse man*: Although the second citation mentions *anothir stede*, a consecutive quotation, Ecclus. 14: 11–13.

8761–2 Translate 'what people do for the benefit of poor men they do for God'.

8771 *Paul*: Following Gradon (292, 185/6–7 n.), Gal. 6: 10.

8791 *to*: There is little evidence supporting ELPR *þe*, elsewhere only in B⁶ (*to a* B³, *to þe* B⁵, *om.* B¹).

8793 *þe wyse man*: Prov. 19: 17, Ecclus. 35: 12.

8797 *Tobye*: Tob. 4: 7–9.

8806 *þat þai haue*: Follows from *vouched saue* in the previous line.

8807 *We rede*: Gradon cites the second of these examples (202, 195/26–30 n.) from Seneca, *De beneficiis* 2. 16. 1–2 (compare also Tubach, *Index Exemplorum*, no. 100).

8810 *gift*: The variants of the manuscripts collated occur widely elsewhere: ES *gyuene* in B³B⁸ (cf. *þe gift*] *biyeue* B⁹), LRW *þe gyft* in B¹B⁵B⁷B⁹. The latter is certainly echoic of preceding *þe*.

8829 *It*: This form plainly stands for the explicit reading of R, *yhit(te)*; compare *Yhete er som* 7003.

8831 *þe wyse man*: Ecclus. 29: 15.

8835 *Gregory*: Compare *Moralia* 19. 21. 33 (PL 76: 118–19).

8838 *haf*: EPR *haf þi* also occurs in B¹B⁷.

8839 *þe godspell*: Matt. 6: 3–4.

8847 *it*: The RW omission also occurs in B¹B³B⁵B⁶B⁹ (B⁸ out); B² omits *þe* as well.

8864 *smelle*: Translate 'produce/emit a (good) odour'. P *snelle* registers the difficulty, but is not especially germane to the discussion; the reading also appears in B³B⁶ (B¹B⁶B⁷B⁹ share W's omission of 8849–82, and B⁸ lacks a leaf). *La Somme* reads 'que nous facons nos bones oeures . . . luire' (BSG 130ᵛ/46–7; compare 'schyne' *BVV* 217/1). Thus 8863 *þe godspelle* probably refers to Matt. 5: 16.

8874 *þe godspell*: Luke 9: 26.

8883 *Gregory*: Gradon identifies (203, 196/18–20 n.) with *Moralia* 8. 48 (PL 75: 853).

8891 *þe prophete*: Isa. 58: 7.

8906 *Iobe*: Job 31: 19. He is the *haly man of clene lyfyng* cited, for comparative purposes, at the head of the next verse paragraph.

8930 *counsaylles*: The singular of LPRW is universal in the B-MSS (B⁷ torn).

8939 *payne*: All B-MSS support A's singular, against the plural of the other central manuscripts.

8945 *Haly Wrytte*: Ecclus. 30: 24 (also cited in the sidenote E 8969).

8953 *Austyn*: Gradon cites (203, 197/18–22 n.) *Enchiridion* 76 (PL 40: 268).

8962 Alludes to Exod. 20: 12, as glossed at 1049–58, but compare also Prov. 15: 20.

8967 *ne na*: The RW reduction of the negatives is universal in the B-MSS. Similarly, the PW omission of *awen* in the following line is widespread; only B⁷ retains the reading of A+; cf. *awen saul] oonule* B².

8978 *Dauid*: Ps. 40: 2, the discussion continued at 8993.

8985 See 8735 n.

9004 *Ane hidous worde*: Matt. 25: 41–3.

9014 *noght yhe*: Only B⁷ among the B-MSS reads as the printed text. R's transposition also occurs in B² and W *ȝe ne* in B¹B⁹. But there is a rich harvest of other variation: *ȝe me nouȝt* B³B⁸, *no met ye me* (all over eras.) B⁶, and *noght . . . soght] ȝe come nouth* B⁵.

9030 *þe godspell*: Matt. 25: 34, 40.

9035 *Fra*: ELSW's added *þe* receives virtually unanimous support from the B-MSS (only B⁷ reads as A). But the reading is predicated on a misunderstanding of the metre; *first*, with final *-ë*, and *tyme* are stressed, not *Fra*.

9046 *says Godde*: Matt. 5: 7, again at 9070.

9064 *sal*: That AL are wrong in intruding *he* is confirmed by *Somme*: 'ou misericorde les conduira e les herbergera' (BSG 132ᵛ/35–6, *BVV* 220/4–5).

9100 *thurgh gastly eghe*: The phrase depends on *may it knawe* 9098.

9120–8 The French, which has 'v. manieres' (BSG 35ᵛ/52, *BVV* 43/6), considers *þe dede* the fifth. It ascribes the distinction to Gregory, perhaps in reference to *Commentaria in librum I Regum* 5. 1. 13 (PL 79: 323).

9123 *fole*: Compare 7674 n, 9748 n; here the B-MSS variation includes foul B¹, foly B²B³B⁵B⁸. Compare *Somme* 'fol regard' (and 'fous atouchemens' in the parallel to 9125) (BSG 35ᵛ/53–4, *BVV* 43/7–8).

9129–40 A ME addition.

9129 *right als þe fisshe with þe hoke*: Proverbial, in Latin as well as English, Whiting F 230; but 9130 *þe boke* implies a biblical source, perhaps the description of the vengeful Chaldean in Hab. 1: 14–17 (and compare Eccl. 9: 12, Job 40: 20). The sidenote, with its neat rhetorical play between the non-parallel *hamo* and *homo*, recalls Andreas's famous etymology of 'amor' as derived from 'hamus' (*De amore* 1. 3). Andreas argues that the man in love tries to 'hook' his object.

9137 *bi it*: i.e. by the bait.

9140 *he*: This ELSRW reading receives remarkably little support elsewhere in the tradition, in only B¹B³B⁸. But the neuter pronoun has probably been supplied by attraction to uses in the preceding lines.

9141 *latches*: A unique usage in the poem, which appears to have strangely befuddled some scribes; the only B-MSS variants offer only a further gloss, *caccheþ* B¹B³B⁵.

9155–62 A ME addition. For *þe prophete*, see Ps. 118: 37.

9175 *þe wicked gast*; The French, 'li esperit de fornicacion' (BSG 36ʳ/7, *BVV* 43/17–18), implies that this alludes to Apoc. 17: 4–5.

9177 *whareso*: RW *whare* appears in all B-MSS as well.

9180, 9194–6 ME additions to fill out the argument in the source. The passage (9179–218) appears, as a prose derimage, interpolated as the conclusion of Rolle's tract on the decalogue at BodL, MS Hatton 12, fo. 211ʳᵇ⁻ᵛᵃ; see EETS 329, 139–40.

9181 *done it think on*: 'caused it to consider', usually accurately rendered through the B-MSS. The only variants, resembling those of LP, are the product of scribes who apparently have confused 'think' with the impersonal 'seem'; cf. *don hit* (repeats B⁸) *þenkeþ hou* (*on* B⁵, *him no* B⁸) B³B⁵B⁸.

9198–9 Compare *Somme* 'font plus de xx. pecchiez le ior' (BSG 36ʳ/19, *BVV* 43/30–1).

9207–19 Compare the presentation of Bathsheba in *Ancrene Wisse*, EETS 325, 22–5, a passage that also refers to Dina (see 11813).

9207 *greefly*: *greuosly* ELSRW+B¹B²B⁶B⁷B⁸B⁹, *gretly* P+B³B⁵. Compare 4647 n. In 9286, *greuously* is the virtually universal reading of the B-MSS (*gretliche* B³). The latter usage has no parallel in the source, but here Lorens twice wrote 'griefment' (BSG 36ʳ/23, 25; *BVV* 43/35, where 'gret' may be an error, 44/2).

9208 *wyse*: The ELS variant *grete*, probably contaminated from the preceding line, appears unique, in none of the B-MSS.

9219 *Salamon*: Eccl. 7: 27 (compare Ecclus. 9: 3).

9246, etc. *braunches*: The RW reading *degrese* occurs in all B-MSS, both here and throughout the subsequent discussion (9259, 9287, etc.). It depends on prioritizing, not the tree/branch metaphor of the source (BSG 36ᵛ/41–2 'en mult de branches', *BVV* 44/20), but the ascendant model of 9249–50.

9268 On wayward nuns, see Daichman, *Wayward Nuns*.

9278 *a wydow*: Lorens is more general: 'femme' (BSG 36ᵛ/51, *BVV* 44/30).

9286 *wele*: The PLW omission also appears in B²B⁵B⁷.

9294 *lifs*: ELS *lygges* is certainly overemphatic, but may reflect difficulty with an unfamiliar archetypal spelling like *leues*; in A, this has been interpreted as 'live', with Northern long *e* for earlier short *i*, confirmed by rhyme as an authorial form. But sporadic evidence might suggest that A has hypercorrected, and that the author intended *leue* 'remain'; cf. *dwelleþ* B¹, *leuyn* B⁶B⁸. The couplet has no parallel in *La Somme*.

9299 *fayth so*: Only B⁶B⁹ agree with W in omitting *so* (B⁶ reads *wordes* over an erasure); B¹B⁷ have *faiþes*, as R. *La Somme* provides only 'foi' (BSG 36ᵛ/ 54, *BVV* 44/34).

9310 *ful*: Only in B⁶B⁷B⁹ of the B-MSS.

9313 *fole*: Lorens wrote 'faus' (BSG 37ʳ/3), presumably read or interpreted by the English poet as 'fous'.

9315 *combraunce*: The prefixed form of EPSR receives no support from the B-MSS. 9315–18 form a ME elaboration on the French.

9336 *with his awen knyf*: The Merchant's January misinterprets the proverb at *Canterbury Tales* E 1839–40.

9337 *lust*: The reading of all B-MSS.

9356 *comere*: The scribes generally experienced little difficulty with this unusual word, not in MED but taken directly from the French, 'godmother, spiritual mother' (BSG 37ʳ/15–16, generalized at *BVV* 45/16). In the B-MSS, the only variants are *cowchere* B¹, *gomere* B⁵, *comehere* B⁹.

9365–70 A ME addition.

9391–9402 This exact canonical information on the degrees of affinity has been provided by the poet. The relaxation to prohibit marriage only within the fifth (rather than the conventional seventh) degree reflects canon 50 of the fourth Lateran Council.

9420 *of*: RW are certainly correct and supported by most B-MSS; B³B⁸ concur with P's uncorrected reading *þat*. The French does not offer comparable information: 'selom les ordres e les dignetez' (BSG 37ᵛ/30–1, cf. *BVV* 45/31–2).

9421–2 Although *þe haly order* 9417 refers to the sacrament 'ordo', ordination to the priesthood, this state includes within it *degre[s] and . . . order[s]*, traditionally seven of them. The poet here cites only the three 'higher orders' of priesthood, canonically those with expectations of celibacy. The couplet is a ME addition, as are lines 9436–8.

9443 *othir thre*: 'the last three', all of which involve sexual acts with those professed.

9444 *þe²*: A range of B-MSS, B¹B⁵B⁶B⁸, agree with the majority of those collated in omitting the article. But three B-MSS, B¹B⁸B⁹, like LW, omit *þe¹*, and the variation appears to represent selective haplography.

9451 *Godde had vengeaunce tane*: Gen. 19: 24–5. PRW's present tense also occurs in B¹B²B⁶B⁹.

9457–8 A brief ME addition.

9493 *fole*: see 9748 n.

9501 *þar it es soght*; Compare *Somme* 'requiert q'on gart le cuer' (BSG 134ᵛ/ 41–2, *BVV* 223/24–5), perhaps slightly misunderstood by the English poet.

9523 *þe godspelle*: John 15: 3.

9531 At this point, B⁴ becomes a continuous text, although its first folio is fragmentary and full readings only become available from 9588 (and actually, given a lost folio, from 9960).

9535 *lauour*: The commonplace penitential metaphors of the passage also appear in *Piers*. For the laundry of Conscience, see B.14: 16–28 and 15: 186– 94. The second of these passages alludes to the river of penitential tears (9557), a topic that recurs at *Piers* B.19: 360–80.

9537 *In þe Boke of Kynges*: 4 Kings 5: 1–14.

9558 *þe²*: PRW *his* is ubiquitous in the B-MSS (*om.* B⁵, as in E). Similarly, in 9564, RW's *Thurghe* occurs universally (the couplet *om.* B⁷).

9565 *Bernard*: Gradon identifies (205, 203/1–3 n) as epistola 113 (PL 182: 258).

9578 *Ensaumple*: Num. 21: 6–9, presumably an 'ensaumple' because not a literal scriptural reference, but one subjected to a commonplace figural or typological reading.

9581 *whilk*: Apparently to be taken as if a demonstrative—'swilk' or 'whilkso'—and not subordinating.

9596 *treacle*: Compare *Piers* B.1: 148–9.

9598 *tange* (and compare the analogous 13888): The substitution of 'tonge' occurs frequently (as it does in all uses of the word in ME): here only B⁴B⁷B⁹ among B-MSS read 'tange', at 13888 only B⁷. For similar variation, see *Cursor* 693 and Rolle, *Lessouns of Dirige* 365. But the real difficulty is whether the word is a derivative of the more or less synonymous *stang* 'sting' (compare 9582, 9599) or from a form in initial *t*-. The latter seems more likely, given the existence of a parallel verb, MED *tangen*, and the modern Shetland noun *tang* 'a pointed piece of metal'. In any event, the sense 'puncture, sting' is confirmed by *Somme* 'pointures' (BSG 135^v/29, *BVV* 225/1 'þe tonges'; compare in the source of the Rolle passage cited above, Latin 'aculeo').

9615 *Haly Writte*: Ecclus. 9: 11.

9619 *Paul*: 1 Cor. 15: 33, cited again at 11655.

9637 sidenote: Matt. 12: 34, explicitly a gospel quotation in the original (BSG 135^v/46–7, *BVV* 225/21).

9666 *þe prophete*: Jer. 9: 21.

9673 *Samson*, etc.: A conventional series (compare *Gawain and the Green Knight* 2414–26, or the sequence of examples early in Walter Map's 'Dissuasio Valerii'). The group were fixed in a widely disseminated Latin distich, 'Adam, Sampsonem, sic David, sic Salamonem | Feminas decipit; quis modo tutus erit?' See 5942 n.

9683 *Ierom*: For example, at *Commentaria in Isaiam* 3: 26 (PL 24: 72).

9690 *alde philosophres*: It's a little unclear to what Lorens was referring here. 'Philosophical' withdrawal to the wilderness might refer to the behaviour of some Cynics (for example, Diogenes in his tub *outside* the city), but the discussion resonates more strongly with the behaviour of explicitly Christian hermits (compare *Piers* B.15: 269–97). The report that 'philosophers' blinded themselves to preserve chastity sounds like a garbled account of the blinding of the prophet (not philosopher) Tiresias. (Of course, in Christian tradition, Origen took even more extreme measures to become 'a eunuch for the kingdom of heaven'.)

9706 *Fares als a horse*: Compare Ps. 32: 17. The horse of the passions being restrained by the reasonable rider is a commonplace; compare Spenser's off-the-cuff allusion at *Faerie Queene* 1. 1. 1.

9716 *Paul*: Gal. 5: 17, earlier evoked at 9164.

9725 *Bernard*: Compare *De moribus et officiis episcoporum* 3. 8 (PL 182: 816–17), cited again at 11395. The rather snappy citation sounds as if a proverbial quotation version.

9734 *Haly Wrytte*: For their regimen, see Dan. 1: 5–16, and for the fiery furnace Dan. 3: 13 ff. Their song of praise (Dan. 3: 52 ff.), 'Benedictus', was one of the seven Old Testament canticles regularly used in church services.

9748 *fole*: Although the usage is consistent through this section (compare 9493), the use of 'prav[us]' in the preceding sidenote indicates that RW, which routinely provide *foule*, are probably universally correct. Equally, the French gives 'mauuaise' in the full set of lections (9752, 9761, 9805, 9816); see BSG 136^v/43, 45, 48; 137^r/20 (translated twice; *BVV* 227/6, 7, 10; 228/

1). The B-MSS all have consistent forms through all five uses, B²B⁶B⁷B⁹ *fole*, the remainder *foul(e)*.

9763 *þe sauter*: Ps. 17: 26–7 (compare *Piers* B.5: 278).

9775 *nedely*: W *nedly to* also appears in B³B⁵ (*nede þan* B²).

9777 *þe wyse man*: This may simply be a second reference to David's Ps. 17: 27, although there are certainly parallels in any number of the Proverbs, perhaps most pointedly 15: 14, but see also 13: 20, 14: 24, 16: 2; Eccl. 1: 15, 7: 5–6. Gradon suggests (206, 205/31–2 n.) Ecclus. 8: 20.

9785 *in þe Boke of Kynges*: The story of Amnon and Tamar appears at 2 Kings 13: 1–29; that of Joseph and Potiphar's wife at Gen. 39: 6–20.

9797 *Paul*: 1 Cor. 6: 18.

9807 *þe aungell*: Gen. 19: 15–17.

9811 *may we*: The PRW transposition occurs universally in the B-MSS, like the omission of *to* in 9818 (present in B¹) and the reading *thurgh* in 9822 (B⁷ torn).

9820 *a comon worde*: Whiting P 723 followed by B 623.

9842 The devil's bridle is original to the English.

9849 *Idelnes*: Perhaps compare Prov. 19: 15.

9853 *Paul*: Eph. 4: 27.

9863 *rowme*: The doublet-translation of BSG 137ᵛ/37 'il done leu' (*BVV* 228/22 assimilated to earlier examples of 'tyme and stede').

9866 *Ierom*: Gradon compares (207, 206/30–2 n.) *Regula monachorum* 38 (PL 30: 422).

9874 *þe prophete*: Ezech. 16: 49; the point of the moralization is provided by the uncited 'et manum egeno et pauperi non porrigebant'.

9885 *outrage*: A's plural is supported by only B⁶B⁷ among the B-MSS.

9895 *Iob*: Compare Job 21: 7–13.

9905 *hert*: All B-MSS (B⁸ out) support the majority of those collated in omitting the preceding *þe*.

9908 *Ambros*: Gradon cites (207, 207/13–15 n.) 'De obitu Valentiani imperatoris' 32 (PL 16: 1369).

9911 *siker*: Specifying *Somme* 'bons' (BSG 138ʳ/2, *BVV* 229/12).

9912 *Agayne*: I follow LPR and all B-MSS present except B⁶ in dropping as intrusive *And* at the line opening. Compare BSG 138ʳ/2 'contre' (*BVV* 229/12).

9913 *Isider*: *Sententiae* 7. 1. 3 (PL 83: 671–2).

9926 *þe godspelle*: Mark 11: 24.

9931 *Iame*: James 1: 6–7.

9947 *þe sauter*: First Ps. 36: 5, then Ps. 56: 2.

9957 *þe godspelle*: Matt. 7: 8.

9975 *Iame*: James 4: 3.

9982 *Iohans moder*: Matt. 20: 20–4. The English poet is scrupulous, as the source is not; there (BSG 138^v/35–6, *BVV* 230/16–17) the presumptuous prayer is attributed to the apostles themselves.

9988 *Bot*: Although LS *for*, also the reading of B^{3}B^8, might appear preferable, the poet follows *Somme* 'ancois' (BSG 138^v/39, *BVV* 230/20). Thus *Bot* means 'rather' (as does the French), and introduces an alternative reading the poet feels requires a two-line gloss.

9997 *þe Pharysene*: Luke 18: 10–12.

10023 *large*: A's preceding *so*, in addition to being absent from all the copies collated, appears in none of the B-MSS.

10043–62 *Austyn*: Gradon identifies (208, 209/1–9 n.), together with subsequent materials here assigned to 'Ambrose', as *Enarrationes in Psalmos* 62: 6 (PL 36: 755–6).

10065 *thinges*: Like those copies collated, all B-MSS omit the subsequent *he says* in A.

10072 *þe godspelle*: John 14: 13–14 (compare 15: 16, 16: 23).

10076 *yhow . . . skille*: 'He will reasonably grant it to you', taken by most scribes, not as a divine quality, but as a condition of efficacious prayer. Among the B-MSS, only B^{4}B^{6}B^7 support A; B^{3}B^8 read as P, while B^{2}B^5 omit *it*, and B^{1}B^9 transpose *yhow it*.

10084 (and **10115**) *þe godspell*: Matt. 6: 33.

10089–90 Compare Whiting N 53, N 57.

10126 *defaylle*: The LPSRW reading *fayle* appears universally in the B-MSS (B^6 om. 10121–6), but may be unmetrical without additions like those common to ELS. *La Somme* offers no aid in resolving the difficulty; see 'rien ne faut' (BSG 139^v/50, *BVV* 232/22).

10128 *Haly Wrytte*: Ps. 33: 10.

10137 *Ierom*: Gradon identifies (208, 210/7–8 n.) as 'epistola 53' (PL 22: 549).

10157 *Godde says*: Matt. 6: 6. 10159 *hous* is presumably a misunderstanding (the Vulgate reading 'cubiculum' appears in the sidenote); compare *Somme* 'entre tes denz' (BSG 140^r/9, *BVV* 233/5).

10167 *Cipriane*: Gradon identifies (209, 210/20–5 n.) as 'Liber de oratione dominica' 31 (PL 4: 557).

10175 *Isider*: Gradon identifies (209, 210/26–7 n.) as *Sententiae* 3. 8 (PL 83: 673).

10179 *Austyn*: Gradon compares (209, 210/27–9 n.) *In Iohannem Evangelium Tractatus cxxiv* 9 (PL 35: 1464). In addition to the Latin, 10180 *lippes* has the support of *Somme* 'les leures' (BSG 140^r/20, *BVV* 233/15).

10191 *hare*: Misunderstanding *Somme* 'chieure' (BSG 140^r/24, *BVV* 233/21 'gote'), a reading the poet appears to have misconstrued as 'lieure'.

10193 *Godde weryed þe tree*: Matt. 21: 19. The explanation here, unlike that at 13576, is analogous to that of the ordinary gloss; compare 'quis habens folia, id est verba iusticie sine fructu operum, mereatur excidi'.

10205 Perhaps a reference to oral communications analogous to the macaronic writing (in all three languages) frequent from the thirteenth to fifteenth centuries. The passage reproduces *Somme* directly: 'il parle a Dieu patroillart com cil que parle moitie Englois moitie Francois' (BSG 140^v/29–30, *BVV* 233/27–30).

10216 *þat*: Unlike the usage in the previous line, has *he* 10214 as an antecedent. The man convinces the mute that he is speaking by miming speech only.

10223 *þe godspelle*: John 4: 24.

10229 *þe prophete*: Ps. 140: 2.

10236 ff. *flayres*: The B-MSS show a similar range of variant readings as those collated: *smelleþ* B²B⁴B⁶B⁷ (as SR), *saureþ* B³ (as L), *blasyth* B⁵ (B¹B⁸ read as A; B⁹ lacks 10149–252). MED knows only flair n., but the English poet follows Lorens closely; see 'flaire soef . . . flaire mout soef' (BSG 140^v/43–5, *BVV* 234/10, 12).

10258 *nedes*: This PRW reading appears virtually universally in the B-MSS (only B⁷ agrees with A+). It is confirmed by *La Somme* 'bosoigne' (BSG 140^v/53, *BVV* 234/19), and the *erand* in the central copies is probably a synonymous substitution.

10260 Compare Whiting F 392, more distantly F 410.

10268 *þe sauter*: Ps. 26: 7.

10270 *brynnand luf*: The phrase, redolent, of course, of Richard Rolle, appears in only three contexts in the poem—here, to describe a/effective prayer; on three occasions to describe the proper spirit in which to take the Eucharist (2727, 2754, 2786); and in one general reference to Rolle's primary subject, the fulfilment that comes from contemplation (14620).

10272 *Austyn*: Gradon identifies (209, 211/32–3 n.) as *Enarrationes in Psalmos* 37: 10 (PL 36: 404).

10277 *Gregor*: Gradon identifies (158, 99/18–21 n.) as *Moralia* 33. 22 (PL 76: 701).

10305 *Dauid*: Ps. 68: 2 (the Vulgate provides the sidenote); the following gospel reference is to Matt. 8: 23–5.

10324 *corrupcions*: Perhaps an error, but not clearly identifiable as the ME translator's misperception of the French or as a transmissional misunderstanding of his English archetype. Lorens wrote 'temptacions' (BSG 141ʳ/27, *BVV* 235/17). The only variant among the B-MSS is *corupcyon* B⁴.

10332 *owhare*: Except for its infrequency here (the unique usage in the poem), it's unclear why the word (OE āhwǣr 'anywhere') has attracted such variation. Certainly, the archetypal scribe behind the central MSS inserted an otiose mark of abbreviation after *ou-*, and the scribes of AELPS carefully followed what they found. But the reading caused less difficulty elsewhere; five B-MSS have some form of the printed reading, but compare *ouperqware* B², *ourewhere* B⁴, *onywher* B⁵, *ouerwhare* B⁷. The French offers no useful evidence; this phrase and the next two couplets form a ME addition.

10343 *werldely*, **10345** *for al þe woke*: The translator appears to have had some difficulty with the French here. First, the source describes the works, not as *werldely*, but 'corporels' (BSG 141ᵛ/32, *BVV* 235/24); perhaps the poet read this as 'temporels'. Line 10345 corresponds to the French continuation 'de la semeine', that is the labours eschewed on the holy day (C 159ʳ; '"ouerir tute' la semeine' BSG 141ᵛ/32, in a passage heavily corrected; *BVV* 235/25–6). There are no significant variants in either instance in the B-MSS.

10350 *In þe Alde Lawe*: As the third commandment (Exod. 20: 8–11), discussed at 1025–36 above. The parenthetical line 10352 qualifies *Sabate* 10351; as the earlier discussion indicates, Jewish sabbatical regulation has been converted in Christian discussions into a general injunction about behaviour on 'holy days' (compare 10365–70). 10353–6 allude to the punishment of an unnamed man at Num. 15: 32–6.

10383 *þat comes and gase*: If not simply a tag providing the rhyme, the clause may be designed to indicate that Easter is a movable feast.

10396 *þair*: That is, the saints', referring to *halughs* 10393 (similarly *in þam* 10399, *þair* 10401, etc.).

10422 *Shortly*: In *La Somme* 'legierement' (BSG 142ʳ/10–11, *BVV* 236/27).

10425–6 The couplet slightly reformulates *Somme* 'en vanitez e en besoignes que ne sont pas ordenees a Dieu' (BSG 142ʳ/12–13, *BVV* 236/28–9, where 'dedes' is scribal for 'nedes').

10425–6, 10437–8 The actual rhyme, *vanites:les*, appears only in the B¹B⁵B⁸ rendition of 10425–6. (The latter is an apocopated form of the second or third person present *leses* 'loses' reported in most MSS.) Elsewhere, B²B⁷ read as A, and the remainder report the reading printed (B³B⁸ offer no evidence in the second example, having collapsed 10435 and 10437 into a single couplet). As the Introduction, p. lxxvi, indicates, the graphemic systems of the MSS inadequately represent any phonic reproduction of the text. I here adopt a somewhat inconsistent presentation, merely removing A's isolated double plural *vaniteses*. Compare the correct rendition of the rhyme at 13603–4.

10432 In the French signalling a citation: 'ce dist vns saint' (BSG 142^r/15, *BVV* 236/32), perhaps in reference to the texts here cited in the Latin sidenotes. That opposite 10429 is non-biblical (and not in Walther), and the second probably a proverbial encapsulation of a discussion like Augustine, 'De fide et operibus' 6. 9 (PL 40: 202–3, there explicitly of instructing the newly baptized).

10439 *Senek*: Compare *De ira* 3. 28. 2–3.

10451 *Anselyne*: Gradon identifies (210, 214/11–12 n.) as 'Meditatio 2' (PL 158: 722).

Although A's form *Anselyne* certainly appears peculiar, and might be construed the product of confusing the minims of Latin 'Anselmus', I rather suspect it is a legitimate ME form. Certainly, it occurs in *BVV* as well (for example, 237/5), as well as later in A at 12855. The poet will have seen something like 'sains Ansiaumes' in his source text (for example, 88^v/29, *BVV* 130/14).

10456 *þe boke*: Job 14: 1 and 5.

10483 *Godde says*: Isa. 56: 7, cited by Jesus at Matt. 21: 13, the source of the sidenote, alluded to at 10333 and 10502–4.

10488 *Austyn*: Gradon compares (210, 214/25–215/2 n.) *In Iohannem Evangelium* 7 (PL 35: 1442).

10489 *come*: Present subjunctive. In the following line, *of Ingelande* is naturally the poet's supply (not at BSG 142^v/40, *BVV* 237/24), and 10497–504 are a ME addition.

10501 *priue*: The RW variant *fre* occurs only in B^{4}B^7 among the B-MSS (B^6 out).

10509 *alle þa dryue walde*: When he drove out the money-changers at Matt. 21: 12–13 (with another reference to the verse 'Domus meus').

10520 *idell*: Specifying the 'mauuaises' of the source (BSG 142^v/53, *BVV* 238/7).

10525 *done*: The added *hym* of PR also appears in B^{4}B^{5}B^{6}B^7. It may well be authorial; compare *Somme* 'li a fetes' (BSG 142^r/54–143^r/1, *BVV* 238/9).

10529 *oft*: PRW's omission is certainly haplographic and probably produces an unmetrical line; it is universal in the B-MSS.

10554 *Of*: Perhaps haplography for *Or (Na?) of*, as L *Na for* would suggest; compare *Somme* 'ne de lor bel atour' (BSG 143ʳ/12–13, *BVV* 238/24).

10556 *Dauid*: Compare his penance at 2 Kings 12, or such rhetoric as at Pss. 4: 1, 38: 13, 54: 2; for the citation in 10561–2, see Ps. 21: 7. Compare Langland's description of the earthy worm, *Piers* B.14. 41.

10563 *feblesce*: The A reading also appears in B³B⁴B⁷B⁹; the remaining B-MSS agree with the majority here collated. But the metre probably requires a word that can receive stress on the second syllable.

10564 *vanyte*: Although there are no variants either in the copies usually collated or in the B-MSS, the rhyme-word probably reflects English archetypal error. See *Somme* 'sa pacience, sa pouerte, e sa vielte' (BSG 143ʳ/17, *BVV* 238/30–1, translating as if 'nudite'). The poet probably wrote something like *vylyte*, assimilated to the commoner form.

10571–6 Alluding more or less directly to Job 1: 21.

10577 *Bernard*: The citation in the sidenote is derived from 'sermones in Psalmum "Qui habitat"' 12.4 (PL 183: 233); it also occurs at *Prick* 556–68 (with a very different translation). *sais* PRW also occurs in B¹B⁶B⁸B⁹.

10596 *Hester*: Compare the narrative at 5: 16 and the apocryphal prayer reported in ch. 14, especially verses 2 and 15–16. Lines 10603–6 are largely ME elaboration.

10608 *For it may make mens hertes vnstable*: Also given as the cause for withdrawal to a hermitage in the exemplum Rolle translated from Heraclitus' account of the Desert Fathers, ed. EETS 329, 14.

10621 *Paul*: The succession of three citations reflects the single discussion at 1 Tim. 2: 9–11 (compare 1 Cor. 11: 5–6, Titus 2:3).

10624 *our*: RW's omission receives no support from any of the B-MSS. The phrase is a ME elaboration.

10642 Probably with reference to the injunctions at 1 Cor. 11: 5–7. See BSG 143ᵛ/50 'non mie effrontees ne esbauleurees' (*BVV* 240/3–4).

10645 *als þe hert*: Not from *Bestiary*, but probably alluding to the common folk-belief that harts pause in their flight to look back at their pursuers (and thus resemble the proud horse of the next line). Both are interested in gauging the effects their activities produce on onlookers, not in any sober activity.

10659 *Ambros*: De sacramentis 6. 5. 20–1 (PL 16: 458–9).

10683 *þe aungel*: Tob. 12: 8. In 10685 *siker*, the poet intensifies Vulgate 'Bona' (reproduced in *Somme*).

10689 *an haly man*: Signalling the continuation of the preceding quotation from Ambrose.

10694 *agayne it drawes*: 'Pulls it back'.

10696 *Isidere*: *Sententiae* 7. 12–13 (PL 83: 674).

10699 *for drede*: The phrase, which doesn't seem to follow in the argument, is probably just an addition for rhyme. There is no parallel in *La Somme*, and Isidore says only 'adhuc mala committit'. Perhaps an archetypal error.

10700 *cese*: This PRW reading also appears universally in the B-MSS (the couplet *om.* B⁹) and corresponds to the French 'cesse' (BSG 144ʳ/24, *BVV* 241/4). *lette* in the central copies is probably a synonymous substitution.

10711 *þe prophete*: As Gradon points out (211, 217/31–2 n.), Lam. 3: 41.

10719 *þe apostoyll*: 1 Tim. 2: 8. Lines 10723–4 vaguely correspond to the reading of the ordinary gloss, which explains *levantes* as 'ad eterna non deprimentes ad terrena' and *manus* as 'affectum cordis qui Deum amplectitur'.

10730 *þe prophete*: Isa. 1: 15.

10749 *Haly Writte*: Perhaps Apoc. 16: 6, 19: 2.

10755 Translate 'Whoever wishes to take anything wrongfully'.

10768 Corresponding to *Somme* 'ne en teche de desloiaute' (BSG 144ᵛ/54, *BVV* 242/2–3).

10771 *Haly Wrytte*: Exod. 34: 20, the verse cited in the sidenote.

10783 *ensaumple*: The parable of the wise and foolish virgins, Matt. 25: 1–13, with further citations and allusions at 10455–60, 11832–48, 11909–22, 12054. It has appeared earlier at 7467–70, and many of Lorens's interpretations are derived from a discussion like that following the Bernardine passage cited at 9725.

10811 *Iame*: James 5: 15–16, extending to the allusion in 10819 *Godde says*.

10820 *hert clene*: Probably provided for rhyme; the French follows James's 'oratio fidei' and reads 'qui vient de foi' (SJ, clause skipped BSG and C; *BVV* 242/27).

10823 *þe Alde Lawe*: See Exod. 17, but the specific point relies on the interpretation at Judith 4: 13.

10829 *an haly man*: Perhaps Prov. 16: 32.

10832 *ten*: But *Somme* 'moult de' (BSG 145ᵛ/28, *BVV* 242/32).

10833 *Breuis oracio* . . . : Not biblical, nor (surprisingly) in Walther. The Pater Noster, as the poem earlier argues, is the ultimate prayer of brief efficaciousness; see 165–84. Langland's Will probably overstates the point at B.10: 465–74.

10837 *gode man*: But *Somme* 'bone vielle' (BSG 145ᵛ/30–1, *BVV* 243/3).

10853 *þe haly man*: Perhaps compare Ps. 33: 17–20 or 1 Pet. 3: 12.

10857–64 A ME addition.

10867 *abbot*: Surely an archetypal English error—the reading appears universally in the B-MSS as well—for original *abbay*; see *Somme* 'couent' (BSG 145ᵛ/41–2, *BVV* 243/15).

10873 *þe godspelle*: Matt. 18: 19.

10908 The English here suppresses a very long passage about the necessity of parents' educating young people in virtue (BSG 146ʳ, *BVV* 243–4). The topic has been the subject of extended treatment at 7619–42.

10929, 10943 *To saue*: Translate 'except that, excepting', the same as *Saue þat* 10969. Certainly, that is the implication of French 'sauue (SJ, sanz BSG and C) ce qu'il', 'sauue' (BSG 146ᵛ/34, 40; *BVV* 245/3–4).

10956 *Haly Writte*: The French makes clear that the reference is to the preceding lines and their allusion to Gen. 2: 23–4.

10965 *Haly Wrytte*: Matt. 19: 6, the source of the sidenote.

10971 *Paul*: Compare Eph. 5: 22–4, 33 or Titus 2: 3–5.

10979 *als þe boke shewes*: Added by the ME poet, presumably in allusion to such biblical incidents as Lot and his daughters, Gen. 19: 31–8 (compare Langland's reference, *Piers* B.1: 27–35).

10998 *in Paradyse*: Alluding to Gen. 2: 15, 18, and 24.

11013 *bifore þe heghe message*: The angelic Annunciation to Mary in Luke 1: 26 ff. The subsequent discussion of the 'mantle of marriage' and its value as an occult device to outwit the devil draws upon popular presentations of the Incarnation. One might compare the 'guile' that defeats Satan in *Piers* B.18, or depictions of Pilate's wife in the mystery plays.

11025 *to*: The PRW omission is widespread in the B-MSS (only B¹B⁸ read as A+). But although metrically awkward, the particle appears grammatically necessary, 'to which the church pays great attention'.

11027 *bytokens þe sposaylle*: Drawing upon Paul's discussion at Eph. 5: 22–5 and upon commonplace allegorizations of the Canticle.

11056 *his dette*: The idea that marriage incurs a 'debt', as the Wife of Bath well understands, comes from Paul, 1 Cor. 7: 3–5.

11143 *Raguell doghter*: For the story, see Tob. 6–8; the conversation reported at 11151–64 occurs at 6: 14–17.

11151–3 The poem's discussion is characterized by a variety of small additions on the etiquette of marital sex; other examples occur at 11200–4, 11209–12, 11237–40. In addition, the ME poet also offers more precise classification of the degree of sin involved in impermissible actions; 11192 *dedely* and 11259 *dedely syn* correspond to more pallid 'griefment' and 'on puet griefment pechier' in the source (BSG 148ᵛ/34, 149ʳ/7–8; *BVV* 248/ 24, 249/19).

11152 *case*: With W's omission, compare *at* B¹, *þat* B⁹; all the other B-MSS follow the text printed here.

11165 *vouches*: The RW variant *vouched* is widely disseminated in the B-MSS (only B¹B⁴B⁷ have the text printed). It reflects confusion over where the angel Raphael's speech ends; the past seems appropriate, if one believes Raphael to continue to explain the fate of Sara's previous husbands.

In the following line, the RW omission of *men* is without support in any of the B-MSS, although they show a rich range of variation for *engendrure* comparable to that in the MSS collated: *genderure* B¹B⁹ (as PS), *engendering* B⁴ (as W), *genderyng* B⁵, *engendre* B⁸.

11187 The prohibition reflects Lev. 15: 19–33. With the subsequent discussion, compare Langland's Wit on untimely sex as deviantly evil (*Piers* B.9: 121–58, 187–201) and the descent of Cain's kin, *Beowulf* 104–14.

11199 *For*: Possibly another example of an error unique to the central copies. The French reads 'si com dist' (BSG 148ᵛ/37, *BVV* 248/26), corresponding to PRW *For als*, ubiquitous in the B-MSS (As B⁵). But PRW+ may simply resort to the usual in an effort at making the grammar of the sentence more explicit. In the form of the central copies, one is supposed to understand 'That' at the head of the following line.

Ierom: *Commentaria in Ezechielem* 6 on 18: 5–6 (PL 25: 173). In the French, the view is assigned to Gregory.

11217 *þa tymes*: The fossilized OE dative of time, 'at those times'. RW, followed by all the B-MSS except *þat tyme* B⁵, uses a more explicit prepositional phrase.

11226 *Austyn*: 'Sermones de tempore' 207. 2 (PL 38: 1043).

11239 *For*: I take the PRW reading, supported by all B-MSS, as more pointed than that of the central group. Their archetypal scribe has probably tried to vary the line-openings and dissimilate the connective at the head of this line from that of the preceding.

11241–2 *a boke | Of kynde of bestes*: See *Bestiary* 15ᵛ, 16ʳ for discussion of the elephant's sexual abstemiousness.

11275–8 The syntax is difficult. The *þat*-clause of 11278 parallels *þat is fre* 11275 and, like it, modifies *þe werk* in the earlier line ('the deed . . . that doesn't harm on most occasions'). The central two lines of the four are basically parallel, 'may be a great sin when it is performed in a holy place or in a holy time'.

11288 *Paul*: 1 Cor. 7: 8–9.

11298 *fole*: Compare 9748 n., 11610 n. Here the B-MSS offer *foule* B¹B³B⁴B⁵B⁸ (as R), *foly* B⁶ (as W).

11300 *ledde*: Given the absence of variants either in the copies usually collated or the B-MSS, the reading looks suspiciously like an archetypal error, perhaps for *stedde*; compare 'embraser' (BSG 149^r/23, *BVV* 250/5 'besette al aboute').

11302 *Als yhe haf herde*: Apparently at 9277–80.

11310–12 As in the preceding treatment of marriage, the ME translator adds a great deal of incidental detail through his discussion of widowhood. In addition to these lines, 11346, 11348, 11357–8, 11366–8, 11387–90, 11424, and 11438–42 have no parallel in the source.

11331 *als says þe boke*: Not in the French, and presumably a reference to a canonist's manual.

11335 *a boke of bestes kynde*: The 'true turtle' appears at *Bestiary* 43^v (and is, of course, proverbial). 11336 resists punctuation; a relative clause modifying *ensaumple*, it disrupts the ongoing grammar of the sentence.

11350 *Iudith*: See Judith 8: 4–5 and compare the continuation of the discussion at 11414 (11423 ff. translate Judith 8: 6–8).

11359 *Paul*: 1 Tim. 5:11–13.

11368 *sightes*: The PW singular (implying the abstract 'looking at, interest in', rather than particular events) appears in all B-MSS except B^7. The couplet is a ME elaboration.

11376 *Luke*: Luke 2: 36–7.

11391 *Paul*: 1 Tim. 5: 6.

11395 *Bernarde*: See 9725 n.

11400 *drunken*: The specifically Northern usage 'to drown' has inspired a vast amount of variation, mostly synonymous substitutions like R *droune* (so also B^{4}B^9) and W *drenchen* (so B^{1}B^{3}B^8) (*dronkned* B^2, *drenchyd* B^5, *drynke* B^6). Notice also: *so*] *sone* B^{1}B^9, om. B^4. (B^7 lacks 11395–12108, owing to missing leaves.)

11406 *he ne sal*: The negative follows from *na* 11401 'no man may do so . . . without losing his life'.

11407–8 Alluding to Rom. 6: 23, the text animating the late fourteenth-century Yorkshire devotional tract *Gracia Dei*.

11408 *lyf*: But BSG 150^r/13 'l'ame' (*BVV* 251/18).

11414 *Iudith*: Compare 11350 n.

11429 *ryche*: LSRW *ryght* also appears in B^{2}B^{4}B^8 (B^{5}B^7 out), but the reading printed answers Judith 8: 7, as well as BSG 150^r/22 (*BVV* 251/28).

11458 *þe haly man in boke*: Jesus at Luke 20: 35–6, a specification of BSG 150^v/34 'dient li saint' (*BVV* 252/3–4).

11460 *has²*: The LSPR omission occurs in only B^8 of the B-MSS.

11467 *febell*: The added *a* of most MSS collated also appears in B^{1}B^{3}B^{5}B^8.

11476 *þe godspell*: Matt. 13: 44. Langland similarly invokes the parable at the end of 'the biographical passage'; but there (*Piers* C.5: 98a), it alludes to his (equally penitential) paragon of virtue, Piers the Plowman. Spenser also alludes to penitential ploughing of the flesh in naming his hero Red Cross Knight 'George' 'ge-orgos'; compare *Faerie Queene* 1. 10. 25–8.

11486 *trauaylle*: The singular of LPSRW is nearly universal in the B-MSS, only B³ having the plural. The majority accords with *Somme* 'labour' (BSG 150ᵛ/47, *BVV* 252/14–15), and AE have been attracted to the surrounding plural forms.

11493 *þe godspelle*: Matt. 22: 30.

11502 *als bright als*: RW *bryghter þan* is the universal reading of the B-MSS. The couplet is a ME addition.

11507 *Salamon*: Wis. 4: 1.

11515 *lyf*: AES add *and*, but all B-MSS concur with LPRW in omitting it and answer the French 'quant ele est clere par bone vie e honeste' (BSG 151ʳ/5–6, *BVV* 252/25–6).

11523 *Ierom*: Gradon (214, 228/9–12 n.) identifies as resembling statements in the 'epistola ad Eustochium' (PL 22: 394–425).

11532 *als a graue*: Alluding to the whited sepulchre of Matt. 23: 27–8.

11540 *robe*: The following *þat es* AELSR is pretty clearly a clarifying gloss. All B-MSS follow the PW omission except B¹. The robe itself reflects Apoc. variously (for example 3: 5, 15: 6, 19: 8), but reappears later, in the company of a linen belt (12179–242), associated specifically with clerical chastity; see 12191 n.

11544 *do skathe and gode*: This is surely a non sequitur, in the context, and the line has no parallel in *La Somme* (see BSG 151ʳ/17, *BVV* 253/2). Only one of the scribes surveyed, that of B⁶, made any effort at repair: *and*] *and no*. This is probably an archetypal error, and one without any particularly clear solution: 'may do skathe to þe gode'? 'skathe may do þe gode' (suggested by *may . . . skathe*] *scathe may do* B⁴)?

11551–2 Alluding to Luke 16: 13.

11554 *Ierom*: The French ascribes the citation to Gregory (BSG 151ʳ/22, *BVV* 253/7), but it probably refers (as does that at 11634) to 'Adversus Iovinianum' 1. 13 (PL 23: 231).

11558 *Ione*: 1 John 2: 15–16 (compare also 4: 2–6).

11561 *Paul*: Gal. 1: 10.

11581 *Bernard*: The citation, which extends to the reference at 11607, comes from *Epistolae* 113. 3 (PL 182: 257).

11590 *shenshipe*: Translating Bernard's standard etymology of Babylon as 'confusio' (cf. BSG 151ᵛ/36–7, *BVV* 253/25).

11607 *Bernarde*: Marking the end of the extended quotation that begins at 11581.

11610 *fole*: But RW *foule* probably more closely approximates BSG 151ᵛ/45 'mauuaise' (*BVV* 253/33). Similar examples occur at 11717 (BSG 152ᵛ/39, *BVV* 255/17 'mauuais') and 11758 (in an English addition). Among the B-MSS, only B²B⁶B⁹ support the central copies in these lections.

11611–12 A ME addition, as is 11614–18.

11619 *withouten þis*: I find the phrase impenetrable and suspect that the text has not been transmitted here (the phrase has no parallel in *La Somme*, at BSG 151ᵛ/46, *BVV* 254/2). 'Withouten þis' looks as if it may be involved in some contrast with 11621 'wythinne'. The biblical locus to which the poet here alludes (see the next note) emphasizes the daughter 'in vestitu deaurato, circumdata varietate' (verse 10), and the point may be that, unlike the tarted-up women attacked in the preceding lines, her rich clothing does not distract her from appropriately devout thoughts and action.

11621 *Dauid*: Ps. 44: 9–16, especially verse 14. Verse 11 is, of course, the proof-text underlying the homily 'Hali Meithhad'.

11626 *plese*: An infinitive dependent on *es* 11624.

11631 *ille*: But *Somme* 'charnels' (BSG 151ᵛ/52, *BVV* 254/9).

11634 *Ierom*: See 11554 n.

11655 *Paul*: 1 Cor. 15: 33; *herebifore* 11656 refers to the citation at 9619–20. There is no support in the B-MSS for the PR transposition of elements in the word, but W's simplified reading *byfore* also appears in B¹B⁵B⁹.

11659 *Senek*: *Ad Lucillium* 123. 9–10.

11679–82, 11686 ME elaborations.

11686 *heght*: RW *heghe* also appears in B³B⁴B⁶.

11688 *Salamon*: Cant. 2: 1–2. In spite of the clear reference to the *sponsa* as 'lief' in the next line, the widely distributed reading *lyfe* also occurs in B⁴B⁶.

11697 *Ione þe wangelist*: John traditionally is the 'discipulus quem diligebat Jesus' mentioned at John 13: 23 and 19: 25–7 as leaning on Jesus' breast at the Last Supper and receiving the Virgin into his custody. The reference of 11705–6 glances at other Last Supper materials; see John 13: 12–17 (more pointedly, Luke 22: 24–30). Jerome, for example, refers to John's great virtue as virginity (*Epistolae* 55. 5, PL 22: 564); this view appears to depend on seeing John as the groom of the wedding at Cana (John 2), who left his intended to follow Jesus.

11717 *fole*: See 11610.

11739 *Saynt Lucy*: See *Legenda* 4 (i. 51).

11747 *Ierom*: 'Adversus Iovinianum' 1. 33 (PL 23: 256).

11758 *fole*: See 11610.

11763, 11772 *Bernard*: Gradon identifies as 'Sermones de laudibus virginis matris' 1. 5 (PL 183: 58–9). With the second citation (and the discussion at 11785 ff.), compare the discussion of the Annunciation in the Rollean tract 'Of Three Workings in Man's Soul', ed. EETS 329, 84–8.

11767–8 The sense is difficult, hence the PR efforts at reading *gifs* as a form of '(be)gin' (cf. *gyues/gynes* B², *biginneþ* B³, *gynneth* B⁵). But the French shows that one should translate, 'God loves those whose Humility gives praise to their pure Virginity' (BSG 153^r/7–8: 'mout forment plest a Dieu cele ame a cui humilite done los a uirginite', compare *BVV* 256/3–4). The following statement provides reciprocal information, and has *Maydenhede* as its subject, granting beauty to Humility.

11813 *Dyna*: Gen. 34: 1–2 (the remainder of the chapter outlines her brothers' revenge).

18555–60 A ME elaboration.

11863 *þe yharde of þe hert*: In allusion to the Marian 'hortus conclusus' of Cant. 4: 12.

11875 *laumpe of glasse*: In the French, it is merely 'la lampe' (BSG 154^r/1, *BVV* 257/20), but the poet may be thinking of biblical passages like Ecclus. 21: 17, Wis. 15: 13.

11883 *Austyn*: Gradon identifies (216, 232/27 n.) as *De sancta virginitate* (PL 40: 412). *Wharefore* has the universal support of the B-MSS, but *La Somme* reads 'dont' (BSG 154^r/3, *BVV* 257/22).

11892 *nane*: The rejected *þe name* is restricted to the central manuscripts; *mone* B⁴, the only B-MSS variant, appears closely related to their extra minim and smoothing supply of *þe*. The French has a different construction; compare 'ne perisse en vous' (BSG 154^r/8, *BVV* 257/27–8).

11897 *Bernard*: Gradon identifies (216, 232/35–6 n.) as *Epistolae* 322 (PL 182: 527); Bernard, of course, alludes to Matt. 10: 22.

11913 *þat*: Extraneous and probably to be dropped, although the word appears in both those copies collated and all the B-MSS.

11927 *Austyne*: Gradon identifies (216, 233/11–15 n.) as *De diligendo Deo* 2 (PL 40: 849).

11939–40 The phrase *thurgh skill* is adverbial and modifies *say*. In the central manuscripts, the form of this line has influenced that of the next. PRW provide the correct connective in 11940, in accord with Lorens's 'e volente' (BSG 154^v/28, *BVV* 258/15).

11951 *Bernarde*: Gradon identifies (216, 233/23 ff. n.) as *Sermones super Cantica* 20. 3 (PL 183: 468).

11960 *vanyte*: There are no variants in the B-MSS, and this is uncertainly either the poet's misunderstanding of the French or an archetypal error. The French reads 'nicete' (SJ, a skip omitting equivalents to 11958–61 BSG 154^v/36 and C; *BVV* 258/26).

11981 *Haly Wrytte*: Perhaps Ps. 50: 12, or Ecclus. 3: 32 or 38: 10, or 1 Tim. 1: 5. Compare the similar statement, not restricted to chastity, at *Piers* B.13: 193.

11992 *fruyt*: This type of discussion is predicated on the gospel parable of the sower (cited in 12202). The conventional analysis in these terms (compare Langland's Tree of Charity, *Piers* B.16: 67–72; Chaucer, 'Parson's Tale' I 867–9) depends upon Jerome; see 'Adversus Iovinianum' 1. 3 (PL 23: 213) (and Jerome's non-retraction, *Epistolae* 48. 2, PL 22: 495). The numerical calculations here are not Jerome's, however.

11994 *fra*: The extended AES reading *fra alle* has no support in the B-MSS. The line forms a ME elaboration on the source.

12202 *In þe godspelle*: Matt. 13: 23.

12028, 12040 *sex*: LP (and the first line only, S) fail to follow the mathematical argument and adopt the conventional number. But for this symbolic calculation, the argument takes into account only those Works mentioned in the gospel (see 7984–8, 8467–72).

12030 *þat*: The grammar would run more smoothly with the connective excised, but *Then* B^6 is the only variant (B^5 has dropped 12000–73 at a folio boundary; B^7 out). A similar example appears, however, in 12055, again with minimal, although here attractive, variation (ȝitte B^{4}B^6).

12033–40 A ME addition, whose mathematics depends on multiplying the ten by the trinitarian three plus six/seven Works (note LS *seuen*, which appears to provide the appropriate calculation).

12061 *many*: *may* is an error common to AELS; the B-MSS universally agree with PRW (*may many* B^8, B^{5}B^7 still out). The reading printed is confirmed by *La Somme*: 'mout de' (BSG 155^r/22, *BVV* 260/4).

12075 *þe Lambes pase*: The discussion, which extends over the next thirty lines, draws primarily upon Apoc. 14: 1–5, with the *riche apparaylle* 12083 that of the lamb's bride at Apoc. 19: 8; compare the extensive presentation and discussion of *Pearl*.

12097 *delytable*: The majority reading throughout the tradition, although B^{1}B^5 read as R and B^{4}B^9 as P. The couplet is a ME addition.

12117 *halynes*: But *Somme* 'saintee' (C 175^r; BSG 156^v/36 'sainte't'e'; *BVV* 260/31), taken by the poet, perhaps following a reading like that of BSG, as 'sanctity', rather than 'cleanliness'.

12119 *þe sacrament*: That is, 'holy orders'; compare the brief notice at 1411–12.

12141 *Godde says*: Lev. 11: 44 (compare also 19: 2).

12151 *I haf sene wryten*: Probably in Jerome, 'Adversus Iovinianum' 1. 49 (PL 23: 282).

12173 *Paul*: 1 Tim. 3: 1–4.

12180 *þe New Lawe*: Luke 12: 35–8. However, *La Somme* reads 'la vielle loi' (BSG 156^r/13, *BVV* 261/33), and the adjective is probably an archetypal error. Lorens was alluding to passages like Lev. 8: 31, 11: 12–15 (compare Deut. 18: 1). Among the B-MSS, only B^6 reads *old*, and its scribe has probably recognized the reference and emended independently.

12191 *our Lorde Aaron badde*: The actual command to Moses appears at Exod. 28: 4 ff. (compare 29: 4–9, 31: 10) and Moses invests Aaron and his sons with the garments at Lev. 8: 7–9, 13. The subsequent moralization of the Vulgate's 'linea stricta' relies on explanations of the ordinary gloss, in this case the association of the colours of the priest's 'superhumerale' (Exod. 28: 6) with chastity and bodily cleanliness.

12203–4 A ME addition.

12207 Throughout the tradition, scribes have made various efforts to specify the object (implicitly *lynne-webbe* 12205). Thus B^{2}B^{3}B^5 provide an *it* before *bete* (as LPW) and B^7 one before *oft* (as S).

12219 *obout*, **12231** *oboun*: There are no variants, either in the copies usually collated or the B-MSS. But the two words should be the same, probably both *oboun*; compare 'par desore' and 'par desus' (BSG 156^v/30, 35; *BVV* 262/19, 22). Another example of possible archetypal error.

12241 *within*: Virtually all the B-MSS read as RW, with the word following *suld* (*be wiȝt and chast* B^8).

12247 *þe eghe bright*: Gradon points out (217, 237/3–4 n.) that the identification depends on allegorical readings of Ezech. 1: 18 (and its echo in Apoc. 4: 6).

12267 *men*: Arguably an unnecessary specification, mainly limited to the central copies (but also in B^{1}B^{3}B^8). BSG 156^v/52 reads 'laie'.

12279–92 A ME elaboration.

12283 *foul and*: The RW omission finds no support in the B-MSS.

12288 *þe boke*: Probably only referring to the proverb, Whiting E 198.

12291 *thurgh skille*: Modifies *worthy* in the preceding line.

12296 *Take*: The following PRW specification *godde* is nearly universal in the B-MSS (B^{1}B^2 alone concur with the printed text). But the word is surely otiose, both to sense and metre.

12305–18 The passage explicitly denies what would become an identifying tenet of later Lollardy; for a parallel example in an earlier fourteenth-century non-heterodox context, see Hanna, *London Literature*, 195–7. The discussion cannot be used to argue for a late date (one potentially Lollard-engaged), since the materials have been inherited from the source (BSG 157^r/13–20, *BVV* 263/19–27).

12310 *lesse*: ELS have simply imported the adverb of the previous line; their reading is isolated, without support in the B-MSS.

12323–32 A ME addition.

12327–8 One should probably construe: 'The evil priest who has that duty consecrates the sacrament (and)'.

12333 *þat*: RW *of* appears nearly universally in the B-MSS (B^5 agrees with the central group, B^7 is illegible). But it is, at best, indifferent.

12363 *es*: My punctuation seeks to preserve this awkward reading; one should probably understand the following line as headed by a suppressed *þat*. Only B^8 omits the word.

12374 *To*: Dropped in B^2?B^{3}B^{7}B^8, which intend to take the verb as an infinitive following *may* in the preceding line. But the parallelism with the subsequent *þan to winne* implies that *when he may* is largely parenthetical in force. Translate 'He has more joy to win one, whenever he's able, than to win . . .'.

12391–2 *a boke of Vitis Patrum*: See *Verba seniorum* 15. 39 (PL 73: 885–6). There are a good many small embellishments, most of them only a line or so, to the narrative received from *Somme*. For example, the French has no equivalent to line 12426, and line 12437 expands upon simple 'Le mestre' in the source (BSG 158^r/14, 19; *BVV* 265/12, 17).

12392 *þat*: LP *wha(sa)* takes the line as a separable unit; in the form I print, *þat* introduces a relative clause defining the *Men* of the preceding line.

12409–10 *he þat | þat*: Presumably '(spoke) he, the one who . . . what follows'.

12488 *hym bi*: The overwhelming evidence (all B-MSS read as W) implies that the archetype of the central copies dropped a phrase (haplography). The recorded readings seek to generate a further stressed syllable, largely through substitution for the now awkwardly isolated element *-seluen*. At this point, B^4 is absent; the MS lacks lines 12458–916, owing to missing leaves. Compare *Somme* 'e le fist seoir iouste lui' (BSG 158^v/37, *BVV* 266/6).

12511–28, 12561–70 This passage inspired the poet of the poem 'The Desert of Religion', transmitted in three closely related and hyperillustrated books from south-west Yorkshire. Indeed, much of 'The Desert' is simply citation of *Speculum Vitae*; for example, lines 11–34 reproduce 12505–28 here. See further Allen, 'The Desert of Religion: Addendum'. The *godspelle* account appears, of course, at Matt. 4: 1.

12525 *thorne-heghe*: The different compounds of ELS stem from confusion over an ambiguous archetypal spelling. *heghe* here represents *hegge* 'hedge', not 'high' (compare 7121 n.). Similar readings appear only in B², which agrees with ES. Compare *Somme* 'vne fort haie' (BSG 158ᵛ/52, *BVV* 266/22). *wapen* in 12529 corresponds to *La Somme*'s 'armoure' (BSG 158ᵛ/53, *BVV* 266/23).

12555 *body*: But *Somme* 'uentre' (BSG 159ʳ/9, *BVV* 267/4). There are no variants, either in the collated copies or the B-MSS. This is conceivably an archetypal error, since scattered *bely/body* variation marks the recorded variant sample, for example 12970 (R), 13012 (LPS), 13242 (PW), 14886 (PSRW).

12571 *Paul*: The main purport of the allusion, the reformation of the senses, alludes to Rom. 12: 1-2. This material is joined with more general Pauline injunctions to die to the world, for example Rom. 6: 3-12.

12574 *body-wittes*: I have allowed the unusual compound ('physical senses') of the central MSS to stand. The B-MSS universally read *bodely* (B⁴ out). *body-*, arguably, could represent a small example of haplography (bodyly), but, equally, the majority manuscripts may assimilate a difficult form to the usage of the previous line. The French is not very helpful: 'touz ses sens corporels' (BSG 159ʳ/16, *BVV* 267/11).

12581 *be*: I hope this member is to be grammatically parallel with 12579: 'so that he feel . . . but (that) he be . . .'. But the long sentence is filled with repetitions (compare 12578) that might have provoked scribes into dissimilar readings. Among the B-MSS, only B²B⁶ read *he* as AE; B³B⁷B⁸ have the reading printed (cf. ys B⁵; B³B⁸ also omit *als*), whilst B¹B⁹ omit the reading altogether. The poet here provides a second translation of materials from the French equivalent to 12578, where the source reads 'estre . . . si mort quant au monde' (BSG 159ʳ/17-18, *BVV* 267/13-14).

12584 *Paul*: Gal. 6: 14; the Vulgate's 'crucifixus est' corresponds to the *es vylly hynged* of the English.

12596 Qualifying *he* in the preceding line.

12605 *Paul*: Phil. 3: 20.

12615 *al*: Just as in PR, all B-MSS present omit the metrically necessary adjective.

12617 *Ione*: Matt. 19: 21, with parallels in the other synoptic gospels, but *not* in John.

12627-8 *þe haly man . . . In Vitis Patrum*: See *Verba seniorum* 6. 14 (PL 73: 891). *mone* represents 'money'; compare the source's formulation, 'Thesaurus monachi est voluntaria paupertas'.

12631 *Godde says*: Matt. 5: 3.

12636 The French reads 'qui est poure d'espirit, c'est de uolente' (BSG 159^v/43–4, *BVV* 268/6). Given the additions the poet has made, one has to translate rather cumbersomely: 'that is, who has received through grace the experience of voluntary poverty'.

12643–700 The lengthy allegorization refers to events of Genesis 19 (the angel's instructions at verse 17, Lot's wife at verse 26). Lorens has taken most of his materials from the ordinary gloss to the passage, which, although not linking the example so closely to the religious life, offers the proof-texts cited at 12701 and 12715. Compare, for example, lines 12683–96 with the explanation of *statuam salis*: 'ad condimentum fidelium; pena impii, eruditio iusti'.

12665 *Loth . . . bitaken*: Nearly all copies have the form *By Loth . . . be taken*, and A is isolated in clearly reading 'betoken' (only B^2 certainly agrees with A; cf. taken B^5). However, it is clear, on the evidence of the French, that A is at least correct about the verb; see 'La femme Loth senefie ceus que' (BSG 160^r/4, 268/21). But the French further implies that the prefix *bi-* (or majority verb *be*) has generated an ungrammatical echo at the line head. The introductory preposition *By*, present in all copies, those normally collated and B-MSS alike, is an archetypal error I have removed.

12667 The line presumably implies the condition 'and who look back to worldly things'.

12701 *þe godspelle*: Luke 17: 32.

12714 *first*: Like PRW, all B-MSS present (B^4 still out) omit the adverb.

12715 *þe godspelle*: Luke 9: 62.

12735 *þa*: The central MSS have assimilated the form to the lengthy succession of line-opening uses of *þat*. RW are supported by the great majority of B-MSS (*þes* B^{1}B^3, *þat* B^6, B^4 out). The line is part of a small ME elaboration; 12732, 12735–9 are the poet's reformulations of the source.

12740 *Paul*: Phil. 3: 13–14, the discussion drawing, as the allusion of 12746 indicates, on the earlier verse 8.

12751 *bathe heghe and laghe*; Presumably rather vapid filler ('in every case') and not literal.

12755 *als dose þe blynde*: Whiting B 218 (compare P 276).

12765 sidenote: Walter 10534a; 12764–6 form a ME elaboration.

12777 The mountain, a persistent image in the discussion, is now seen as Contemplation (Jerusalem 'visio pacis' in this world).

12785 *þam ledes to*: The transposition of PRW to place the verb at the line head intends to simplify the syntax by juxtaposing the verb as closely as possible with its subject, *gift* 12784. This form is ubiquitous in the B-MSS (B³ lacks *þam*; B²B³B⁵B⁸ lack *to*, as does P).

12789 *Godde says*: Matt. 5: 8, invoked again at 12919.

12794–6 Compare *Somme* 'il sont purge des tenebres d'errour quant a l'entendement e des taches de pecchie quant a la volente' (BSG 161ʳ/6–8, *BVV* 270/8–11). Thus, *Of* 12794 and *of*² 12796 are in parallel. But the latter line probably has archetypal haplography at the head; it should have begun 'And [als] . . .' ('and of the filth of sin so far as concerns the will'). There are no variants in the collated copies or the B-MSS.

12798 A confusing translation of Lorens's 'par foi enluminee de la clarte' (BSG 161ʳ/8–10, *BVV* 270/11–12).

12814 *Clere*: W *Fere* (cf. *Feyr* B¹B⁹) is probably an inspired guess at the sense.

12819 *our Lorde sayde*: John 20: 24–9.

12820 *To*: Universally supported by the B-MSS (L probably an independent substitution, replacing the archetypal reading underlying the central copies). Compare *Somme* 'a Saint Thomas' (BSG 161ʳ/19, *BVV* 270/23).

12830 I punctuate the line to indicate the implied relative *þat*; the line should be a subordinate clause, following French 'qui ci le uerront par foi' (BSG 161ʳ/23–4, *BVV* 270/27–8).

12834 *Paul*: 1 Cor. 13: 12.

12849 *Haly Writte*: Isa. 64: 4, cited by Paul at 1 Cor. 2: 9.

12852 *eres*: All B-MSS present share PW's singular *ere*. The reading is relatively indifferent, although *Somme* has singular 'oreille' (BSG 161ᵛ/35, but note the plural *BVV* 271/5).

12855 *Anselyne*: Gradon identifies (219, 244/22–34 n.) as *Proslogion* 24–5 (PL 158: 239–41).

12870 *a*: 'a single'. EPW *ay* also appears in B¹B⁷B⁹ (*thi* B⁶, *on* B⁸).

12879 *Austyn*: Compare *Confessions* 12. 13. 16 (PL 32: 831–2) and *De trinitate* 12. 14. 22 (PL 42: 1009–10).

12881 *sal*: The PRW reading, universal in the B-MSS, is confirmed by the French; compare 'uerra' (BSG 161ᵛ/50, *BVV* 271/20).

12889 *þe haly man*: The French indicates that this is a quotation from 'Hue de Saint Victor' (BSG 161ᵛ/54, *BVV* 271/26); compare *De sacramentis* 10. 4 (PL 176: 333).

12893 *For*: The B-MSS show the same diversity as those fully collated: *And* B¹ (as L), *om.* B²B³B⁵B⁸ (as EPSR), *For* B⁶B⁷B⁹ (as AW). The conjunction, although potentially echoic, follows the French: 'Car por ce uolt diex deuenir homs' (SJ, a skip in BSG at the boundary of fos. 161ᵛ/162ʳ, similarly C; *BVV* 271/27). See further Gradon's lengthy discussion (219–20, 245/4–5 n.).

12897 Compare BSG 162^r/1 'Pur ce que home le ueist' (*BVV* 271/29). The first use of *þat* gives the extended form of the conjunction, while the second use is simply a clumsy literalism. Moreover, the poet has misconstrued the French tense, which he should have translated 'sulde se'.

12940 *yhete*: Potentially intrusive (and yet necessary in at least one metrical reading of the line, not necessarily the most persuasive). The simple *ne* LRW agrees with most B-MSS (and B^{1}B^{2}B^5, reading as P; *n'* [*ner?*] B^8). The poet here is engaged in his customary summary introduction, materials translated more fully and directly at 14633 ff.

12960 *right*: Only a few B-MSS (B^{1}B^{8}B^9) agree with LSRW in suppressing the adverb.

12980–98 A ME addition.

13005 *þe godspelle*: Matt. 8: 30–2.

13032 *and*: PRW *hir and* are nearly universal in the B-MSS here extant (the line omitted in independent eyeskips B^{4}B^5, a lost page B^8); only B^2 has the reading printed (*and hit* B^1).

13034 *To Adam and Eue*: In Gen. 3.

13058 *and take a swete*: The French says simply: 'ieo fui trop plains; dormir m'estuet' (BSG 38^r/25–6, *BVV* 47/23). The poet rendered this accurately enough in the preceding line and the first half of this one. But he seems to have wondered if Lorens's verb might have been *estuver* 'to take a "stew", a hot bath' and to have offered alternate translations. See 5049 and the note, where similar behaviours are described.

13075 *so*: The reading, from ELPSR, may actually be a second-generation scribalism; *Somme* 'trop fu fort le vin' (BSG 38^v/32–3, 47/32) implies 'too strong'. All B-MSS read *ful*, as A.

13083 *tauernere*: Directly translating the French, the word means 'tavern-goer', not 'publican' (compare *BVV* 47/34).

13085 *bycomes*: The added *a* is considerably less well attested in B-MSS than in those collated, only *an* B^5, *a* B^8.

13095 *Gregor*: *Moralia* 30. 18. 60 (PL 76: 556–7). Gradon (131, 51/18–19 n.) cites rather *Moralia* 31. 45 (PL 76: 621) and *In Primum Regum Expositiones* 2. 3 (PL 79: 110).

13108 From this point (to the end of the poem, the last example at line 15918) R provides a sequence of rather inconsistently placed in-column headings to divide the argument. All these have been derived from the three-part running titles exemplified by the versos of A; the scribe imports one of the three pieces, in no very regular rotation, at intervals when it occurs to him. There are considerable variations in the number of lines set off in this way (from 29 up to 77 lines, once 100 and once 134 lines), but the scribe seems to be reproducing the running titles, either folio by folio or page by page, from a single-column exemplar with something like 37 lines to the page, from about 14450 perhaps 33 or 34 lines, in the last thousand lines 30–2 lines.

13110 *has elde*: Translate 'is of mature years'.

13118 *elles*: All B-MSS agree with PRW in omitting the word.

13146 *maystresce*: The French implies a different interpretation than the universal (in all B-MSS as well) reading of the word as 'mistress'. See BSG 39ʳ/8 'vne pecchie qui est proprement mestiers de (est . . . de follows SJ, est au BSG and C) diable' (*BVV* 48/27–8 'þe deueles owne craft'). I thus take the word to represent MED *maistrice* 'power, domination', rhyming either through substitution of suffixes or with shortened vowel in the suffix. The form in *BVV* might, however, suggest a different interpretation, and the reading could represent *myst(e)res* 'craft-trades', a half-rhyme. Compare the similar 13253 n.

13155 *luf*: The B-MSS (and PRW) unanimously support the reading printed. The ELS substitution *do* accidentally corresponds to *La Somme*: 'come il font' (BSG 39ʳ/11, *BVV* 48/33). In 13160, PRW's *wald do for* appears widely in B-MSS (only B³B⁸ read as the text I print); there is no close parallel in *Somme*.

13184 *þe prophete*: Presumably Jer. 33: 20, but Gradon (131, 52/23–4 n.) more plausibly suggests Isa. 5: 20.

13241–6 In the French (BSG 39ᵛ/46, *BVV* 50/11), ascribed to Paul, that is, the same citation as at line 14890, Phil. 3: 18–19.

13236 Translate '(In penance,) according to the demands of their sins', as the subsequent discussion (13415–18) explains.

13253 *maysters*: The unanimous reading of all manuscripts collated, including all B-MSS—but, alas, another archetypal error. Compare *Somme* 'martir au diable' (BSG 39ᵛ/52–3, *BVV* 50/17). This error must originally have occurred in an English hand, in which anglicana *r* has been confused with *y* and has provoked a more obvious substitution. Compare the similar 13146 n.

13294 Corresponds to *Somme* 'ij. mesures fait par pais faisant' (BSG 40ʳ/15–16, *BVV* 51/1), apparently read by the poet as if 'pois failant'.

13301 *þe mesure of Ipocrase*: Hippocrates' three long works were, of course, basic medical school texts. The first and most basic of these, *The Aphorisms*, begins with a book largely devoted to instructions on moderation in regimen (1. 4–20). However, to associate this with a diet *lytyll and strayte* misrepresents, since the Greek physician persistently balances his dietary recommendations with consideration of a range of other factors (for example, age, season, crisis in illness).

13347–52 A ME addition.

13359 *spare*: 'For you may save with such firmness that you may just as quickly destroy your body'. *fast* is the adverb.

13362 *To*: The B-MSS offer some support to those copies that insert a verb at the line head, *Do to* B³, *To fynd* B⁶B⁷ (as R) (a missing leaf in B¹, torn B⁴, an eyeskip B⁵). But the source implies that these copies all have failed to understand the construction, '*þou awe . . . to þi body*'; compare *Somme* 'tu dois' (BSG 40ᵛ/42, although note *BVV* 51/31 'þou schalt ȝyue').

13371–2 The wily devil in the French, who can quote Scripture, ascribes this final appeal to David (BSG 40ᵛ/46, *BVV* 51/34), perhaps alluding to Ps. 67: 36. Gradon, more plausibly, suggests (133, 54/34–5 n.) that the allusion is to Ps. 58: 10.

13425–6 The syntax has been slightly obscured to fit the shape of the couplet; *and fede* parallels *fille* in the preceding line, and the antecedent of *þat has nede* is the object *pouer men*.

13430 *grete²*: Among the B-MSS, only B² supports the RW omission of the word.

13457 *als felle þarto*: 'as would be appropriate (for so much effort)'.

13460 Translate 'with its proper taste'; in the next line, *a* means 'a single thing'. The entire discussion here bears comparison with that of Chaucer's Pardoner, C 485–588, who is largely drawing upon Jerome's 'Adversus Iovinianum' 2.

13488 *In tauerne*: The discussion of the locale as the devil's church (or school) continues the glutton's parody of appropriate devotions at 13049–70. The technique is certainly widespread; see, for example, Chaucer's Pardoner considering 'som honest thyng' in a tavern, C 321–8; Langland's treatment of his sin Glutton, with its extensive parody of penitential behaviour at *Piers* B.5: 296–363, or his identification of the alehouse as a demonic church at C.9: 98; or Fr John Lacy of Newcastle's tavern of sins (*IPMEP* 650). See further Owst, *Literature and Pulpit*, 434–41.

13498 *his awen*: The reading *þe fende* is not restricted to the central manuscripts; compare *þe fendes* B²B⁵.

13535–9 A ME elaboration.

13576 *þe tre*: The fig-tree of Matt. 21: 19–22. See 10193 n., where the leaves are differently interpreted, following the ordinary gloss, not the tree metaphor that guides this discussion.

13602 *or suld*: Confirmed by 'e deussent faire' (BSG 42ᵛ/42, *BVV* 55/17).

13615 *þe godspelle*: Matt. 12: 36.

13630 *balde*: The French reads only 'uolentiers' (BSG 43^r/3, *BVV* 55/33–4) and does not resolve the variation. But the 'good cheer' of the central copies seeks to extend the idea evoked by 'blithly' in 13631, and there is a greater likelihood 'bold cheer', the universal reading of the B-MSS, is correct.

13633 *fals*: The poet has probably misread 'fous' (BSG 43^r/6, *BVV* 55/36) as 'faus'. *fals* appears in all the B-MSS, as well as those collated here.

13673 Referring to the discussion of the same vice as a part of Pride at 3723–34.

13727–8 Translate 'Just as if they were able to do or say things much better than those (whom they are disparaging) could do'.

13739 *Bernarde*: Gradon identifies (135, 59/34–5 n.) as 'sermones in Psalmum "Qui habitat"' 11. 3–4 (PL 183: 226–7).

13758 A relative clause modifying *losengers* in the preceding line.

13760 Translate 'And feeds them (parallel with *at souke gifs* and *mas þam . . . ly*) with false/misleading interpretations (of their words and acts) which harm (them)'. *mas þam . . . ly* 13761 a bit too generally renders *La Somme*'s '(laitent) e endorment en leur pecchies par lor biau chanter' (BSG 44^r/8–9, *BVV* 57/29) and loses the connection with a nurse lullabying the baby to sleep.

13767 *þe beere*: *Bestiary* 21^v describes bears' predilection for honey, but contains no material on using it to lure them.

13768–78 A ME elaboration.

13784 *flaters*: The form, a reflex of ANF *flatour* not in MED, recurs in rhyme at 15536 and within the line at 15566 (while *flaterers* rhymes 13836). The poet follows his source, 'ces flateors' (BSG 44^r/13, *BVV* 57/33 'flaterers').

13795–8 Translate 'They increase it and add to it twice as much as he can actually say or do, and thus they construct more lies than truthful words, indeed exactly twice as many'.

13799 *Haly Writte*: Probably a general reference to the prohibition of the Decalogue (Exod. 20: 16, restated Matt. 19: 18).

13800 *þat spekes of it*: Modifies *Haly Writte* in the preceding line.

13807 *Haly Writte*: Perhaps Ps. 57: 5–6.

13815–6 *so wele | þan*: 'So much better than', apparently for the sake of the rhyme.

13818 *Placebo*: Compare the court-flatterer of this name in Chaucer's 'Merchant's Tale', E 1477–1518.

13826 *Haly Writte*: Wis. 17: 18.

13842 *Haly Writte*: The reference isn't particularly clear. However, Augustine's reading of the asp at Ps. 57: 5–6 (compare 15579 n.; *Enarrationes in Psalmos* 57. 10, PL 36: 681) is provocative. There, Augustine identifies the snake's tail with a willingness to delight in past sins. The association of flatterers with foxes' tails appears to me a subsidiary moralization, only by accident corresponding to the only comparable reference in Scripture, Judges 15: 4–5.

13844 Translate 'that rich men practice'.

13854 Translate '(although separate branches,) products of a single school, the scholars taught by the devil'.

13855–9 Much of this material is original, since the ME poet has been defeated by an untranslatable pun of his source: 'Ces sont les ij. seraines dont nus trouoms ou liure' (BSG 44ᵛ/41–2, *BVV* 58/31–2). The adder is identified in the source of line 13876 as that species 'qui ont a non seraines' (BSG 44ᵛ/45, *BVV* 59/7).

13859–60 *a boke* | *Of kynde of bestes*: In *Bestiary*, the mermaid appears at 65ᵛ and this adder at 82ᵛ.

13865 *eren*: The *i*-spellings of the central manuscripts AELS are thoroughly isolated in the tradition. Only B¹, among all the manuscripts consulted, reproduces the spelling. The word (OE earn) is further confirmed by *Somme* 'ongles d'aigle' (BSG 44ᵛ/44, omitted at *BVV* 59/1). *Bestiary* states that the lower half of a mermaid resembles a bird.

13877 *bi kynde*: The reading is virtually universal in the B-MSS (*þorow kende* B¹B⁵); only B² reads as AEL.

13879 A ME addition.

13887 *Salamon*: Probably Eccl. 10: 11.

13888 *tange*: See 9598 n. All the B-MSS, excepting B¹B³B⁴, follow PRW in lacking the *þai* interlined in A.

13894 Rather unusually for later portions of the poem, the translator here chooses to omit a rich sequence of figures (BSG 45ʳ/1–10, *BVV* 59/14–27).

13922 *says a 'botte'*: Compare *Somme* 'touz iors i trueue e i met i. mes' (BSG 45ʳ/22–3, *BVV* 60/7). As the citation shows, the source offers no support for PRW *mase*, the reading of all B-MSS as well.

13934 *in boke*: The scorpion does not appear in this form in *Bestiary*, but the figure is certainly proverbial, Whiting S 96 (compare Chaucer, 'Book of the Duchess' 635–41).

13938 Qualifying *anything* two lines before.

13952 *bere*: 'endure', weakened considerably in PRW *hafe*, the reading also of all B-MSS.

13955 Parenthetically modifies *a man* 13953. For a discussion of the tradition underlying the image, see Goldsmith, *The Figure of Piers Plowman*.

13963–4 Compare the cockles in the wheat at Matt. 13: 24–30.

13967 *þe godspelle*: John 8: 44.

13981 *gamalyon*: All the copies surveyed, both those usually collated and the B-MSS, show the initial *g-*, as does *Ayenbite* 62/31. (*BVV* 60/29 had no idea what Lorens meant by 'li chamelos' BSG 45ᵛ/42.) *Bestiary* includes no account, but the detail probably comes from the same variety of orientalia well known in English through *Mandeville's Travels*; see the edition, ii. 396. Compare 14268 n.

13991, 14000 *brynnande*: The translator misread *Somme* 'aidans' as 'ardans' (BSG 45ᵛ/46, 51; *BVV* 60/33, 61/2).

13995 *Austyne*: Gradon cites (136, 63/1–5 n.) 'De Mendacio' 11 (PL 40: 501), with further references to Augustine on helpful lies.

14001 Although the translator does not signal it, this paragraph is his discussion of 'plesande' lies; compare *Somme* 'les menconges plaisans' (BSG 45ᵛ/52–3, *BVV* 61/3).

14024 *our Lorde*: The three consecutive citations of divine prohibition here—*Godde* 14040 and *þe commandementes* 14046 are the others—probably all refer to the same texts: Exod. 20: 7, 16; and/or Matt. 5: 33–7 (see 14067 n.). In the materials parallel to 14046, Lorens explicitly had in mind only the first of these; compare 'ou secont comandement' (BSG 46ʳ/22–3, *BVV* 61/27).

14036 *hertly*: The universal reading of the copies consulted except P, including all B-MSS. But the reading is arguably another archetypal English error; compare *Somme* 'ardanment' (BSG 46ʳ/17–18, *BVV* 61/21 'wiþ grete hete'). If the poet directly sought to reproduce the French as transmitted here, he probably wrote something like *hete(d)ly*. But he may well have read his source, as Dan Michel did, '(h)ardiement', a reading that might explain the P variant, as well as suggest a different underlying authorial form. Compare Gradon's discussion (136, 63/22–3 n.).

14039 *Iame*: James 5: 12.

14056 *þam*: Probably a simple archetypal error for *þai*, stimulated by the inversion of word-order; compare *Somme* 'Cist ont Dieu' (BSG 46ʳ/26, *BVV* 61/31–2).

14065–70 A ME addition.

14067 *þe godspelle*: Matt. 5: 33–7, the same passage referred to at 14100 and 14107 (as *Goddis lawe*).

14106 *þat made alle thing*: But *Somme* 'qui tout set' (BSG 46ᵛ/43–4, *BVV* 62/15); the translator read his copy as 'fet'.

14109 *Poure*: Here 'pure', on the basis of the French.

14118 *wryten*: The added phrase in ELS has no support among the B-MSS (B⁴ has now broken off).

14125 Just as he provides extensive parallels for the discussion of Gluttony here (see 13460 n.), Chaucer's Pardoner gives a resonant diatribe against swearing, at C 629–60. Lines 14129–42 are an exuberant ME elaboration.

14138 *leste*: I drop A's following word *athe* as an extra-metrical gloss. However, evidence for its omission is somewhat fitful outside the central manuscripts; in addition to RW, B⁶B⁷B⁸ retain the word.

14159 Modifies *sweryng* in the preceding line.

14166 *es*: Implies the suppressed past participle *brettenet*. The reference to Jesus' intact body refers to John 19: 31–3; compare Langland's comments, *Piers* B.18: 71–7.

14177–8 The core of the sentence, broken up by parenthetical materials, is 'Such men act against reason and (consequently) do ill'. That is, both adverb(ial phrase)s modify *dose*, and *Howso* introduces subordinate materials exemplified in the following couplet.

14181 *Haly Writte*: Ps. 83: 12. Gradon connects the discussion in the following lines (137, 65/3–8 n.) with Gratian's comment at *Decretum* 2. 22. 5. 13 (*Corpus Iuris Canonici* 1: 886).

14193–4 The couplet concludes the central thread of the sentence, left in suspense after 14188; 'God is so courteous that (He does not permit) the devil . . .'.

14210 *trouthe*: Here 'a personal pledge, one's personal integrity'. *Somme* perhaps more clearly explains the point of the couplet, a double failure of faith and word: 'ce q'on a promis e grante ou par sa foi ou par son sairement' (BSG 47ʳ/22–4, *BVV* 63/13–15).

14215–18 A ME addition.

14219 *Austyn*: *De vera religione* 54. 104 (PL 34: 168).

14220 *Payse mare*: This is clearly wrong, since the next couplet appears to draw a conclusion—which is fundamentally the same point. The reading appears universally in the manuscripts consulted. But compare *Somme* 'semble tant au fait au diable' (BSG 47ʳ/26–7, *BVV* 63/17). The poet, if he was translating literally here, probably would have written something like *Lickens mare* 'more resembles'. But if an archetypal error, the received reading would have involved complicated scribal behaviour—first reproduction as *Lykes mare* 'is more pleasing to' and only that secondary reading then assimilated to the following couplet.

14223 *synne*: Only B¹B⁹ join RW in omitting the word.

14239–40 The verbs expand upon *Somme* 'commence . . . embraser' (BSG 47^v/36–7, *BVV* 63/29–30).

14258 A ME addition.

14266 *elsyne*: The word translates the French directly; compare 'alesnes', the same translated *pynnes* in 14270 and 14274 (respectively 'alesnes poignanz', 'alesnes', BSG 47^v/46–9, *BVV* 64/4–7).

14268 *lyke to a beste*: The porcupine does not occur in *Bestiary* (its hedgehog uses its spines only for protection and collecting apples, 36^r). As the association with India indicates, like the chameleon (see 13981 n.), the porcupine has probably been derived from oriental travel accounts; compare the reference at *Mandeville's Travels*, ii. 396–7. (The comment there on the beast's size accurately reflects its difference from the common European hedgehog.)

14270 *hornen*: The description of the hedgehog in *Bestiary* describes its quills as 'spin[e]'; this might support S *thornen* adj. 'thornlike', paralleled only in B^6.

14283 *Haly Wrytte*: Perhaps Luke 6: 28; compare Ecclus. 21: 30. Gradon compares (138, 66/21–2 n.) rather Ps. 100: 5.

14287 *Paul*: Perhaps Rom. 3: 14.

14289 *Salamon*: Compare Job 41: 11.

14305–6 A ME addition.

14318 *Haly Wrytte*: Perhaps 1 Tim. 6: 3–4.

14335 *First Godde*: For the revolt of Chore, and his colleagues Abiron and Dathan, see Num. 16. The subsequent materials, 14345 ff., describe earlier murmuring among the Hebrews, at Num. 14; for the curse (and the exclusion from it of Caleb and Joshua, 14355–7), see 14: 22–3, 29–38. Gradon points out (138, 67/15–22 n.) that the figure 600,000 follows Num. 26: 51. The poet refers to the scriptural passage again at 14565–8.

14346 *God þaim*: PRW, joined by all B-MSS present (*god haþ hem* B^1, out in an eyeskip B^6), transmit the reading of the French: 'que Dieu lor auoit promise' (BSG 48^r/25, *BVV* 65/6).

14353 *mete of heuen*: The manna, described in Exod. 16. Although probably unexceptionable, and recorded in all manuscripts consulted, including the B-MSS, the word *mete* is just conceivably an archetypal error, for *La Somme*'s explicit 'manne' (BSG 48^r/27, *BVV* 65/8).

14362 *graynes*: The term, repeated at 14466, again in rhyme, is troubling, because these are, through the account, twigs or leaves on the branches. Compare *Somme* 'branches' (BSG 48^v/30, 49^r/18). Perhaps the poet had an otherwise unattested derivative of Latin *ramus*, *raynes*.

14367 In *Somme*, the material on murmuring against God rather illogically follows that on murmuring against men (BSG 48ᵛ/44, *BVV* 65/28). The poet adjusts the order to move from greater insubordination to lesser.

14376 Suppressing *La Somme*'s detail, 'e chaunte la pater nostre' (BSG 48ᵛ/48, *BVV* 65/32–3). The devil's song is a parody Pater Noster because he inverts the petition 'Fiat voluntas tua'; in contrast, the next verse-paragraph alludes to the response at the end of mass, thanks to God for the gift of the Eucharist.

14393 *in herte*: A slightly maladept addition, forced by the rhyme. In *Somme*, the *angre* is, as usually in the poem, 'aduersitez' (BSG 49ʳ/4, *BVV* 66/7).

14406 *If*: May indicate 'although' (*BVV* 66/11), although *Somme* reads 'se' (BSG 49ʳ/7).

14459 *Salamon*: Wis. 1: 11–12.

14536 *Austyn*: *De moribus ecclesiae* 2. 11. 20 (PL 32: 1354).

14539–41 An added linguistic comment, answering the commentary in the prologue. That earlier locus associates Latin with 'skole' (71–2), and 'clergy' hear may carry that general sense of learnedness (as in Langland's personification of that name) rather than the more specific 'religious discourse'.

14557 *þis swerers*: *Somme* 'cil iuor' (BSG 49ᵛ/53, cil iuieur SJ; *BVV* 67/31), probably misunderstood by the poet.

14565–8 See 14335 n.

14569 *þe godspell*: Matt. 12: 31–2. The sin against the Holy Spirit (malice) is discussed extensively 4307–410; compare Langland's treatment, *Piers* B.17: 274–302. Lines 14574–90 are a ME elaboration.

14613 Unusually, the poet, who has suppressed Lorens's earlier discussions, provides a full account of the highest gift, Wisdom.

14628 *byfore*: At 2509–608, 3389–406.

14632 *fele and tast*: The locution draws upon the connection between *sapientia* 'wisdom' (*fele*, as quite usually here, means 'understand') and its related verb *sapere*, etymologically 'to taste'. For discussion, see Gillespie, 'Strange Images of Death'.

14641 Langland also has a version of the philosophers' sight, a vision of Nature basically through Reason alone; see *Piers* B.11: 320–404 and the further analysis at 12: 57–71, 128–58.

14664 *englaymed*: A colourful translation of *Somme* 'desordenee' (BSG 162ᵛ/36, *BVV* 272/31).

14675 Compare *Somme* 'par vne glu d'amour' (BSG 162ᵛ/41–2, *BVV* 273/6).

14691 *Iacob sawe*: Gen. 28: 12–22.

14713-4 Compare the opening chapters of Bernard's *De gradibus humilitatis* (PL 182:941ff.); Bernard's arguments underlie much of the discussion here.

14718 Surprisingly, not cited in Whiting.

14720 *a tree þat es grene*: Answering the gospel account of the fig-tree cursed for its barrenness at 13576; similar comparative views are implicitly evoked in the subsequent description of heavenly bliss, for example the paps of heaven (not of the devil's nurses) at 14743 or the tavern of heaven (not the devil's worldly one) at 14787.

14740 *com doun*: Only answered by *Vntill* 17748.

14749 *spoken bifore*: At 2165–88.

14772 *contraryus*: The poet perhaps misread or mistranslated his source manuscript. Compare *Somme* 'dont le contrepois de la char est si pesant' (BSG 163^v/33–4, *BVV* 274/22).

14789 *er ful*: 'est abandone' (BSG 163^v/41, *BVV* 274/30).

14799 *þe sauter boke*: Ps. 35: 9.

14800 *wryten*: PR are isolated in their omission, not found in any of the B-MSS.

14803 *þe prophete*: Isa. 66: 10–14, a vision of the exalted Jerusalem, including detail answering the *pappes* of 14743.

14811 *Dauid*: Ps. 35: 8–10, including the 'fons vitae', also resonant with the description of Apoc. 21: 6, 22: 1–5, with the tree of life (compare 14851).

14816 More pointed would be 'And þou þam fille sal'; compare *Somme* 'e les abeueres du flueue' (BSG 163^v/49, *BVV* 275/5–6), an accurate rendering of the Vulgate. Perhaps archetypal error.

14824 *ne dieghe*: The ELS reading receives no confirmation from the B-MSS. The French would tend to confirm A+ as a simple doublet: 'e faillir ne puet' (BSG 163^v/52, *BVV* 275/8).

14840 *Austyn*: De civitate Dei 20. 21. 1 (PL 41: 690).

14850 *Salamon*: Wis. 8: 7 (slightly misconstrued).

14855 *Haly Writte*: Perhaps in reference to the parable of the mustard seed, Matt. 13: 31–2.

14890 *Paull*: Phil. 3: 18–19.

14892 *reuyles*: The translator has misunderstood or misread Lorens's 'mult sauille' (he greatly soils himself) (BSG 164^r/27, *BVV* 276/10).

14918 Compare *La Somme* 'qui ne retient sa langue' (BSG 164^v/38, *BVV* 276/21–2); in the battle, the vices will not restrain the sinner's tongue but give it free reign.

14925 *þe first batayle*: That is, fights in the vanguard.

14930 *First tempted*: Matt. 4: 2–4.

14933 *assaylled also*: Gen. 3: 1–6.

14953 The line, an elaboration of the source, isn't entirely clear or sensible. Although there are no variants in any MS consulted, I suspect that material has dropped out after *has*, either *bene* (in which case, *he* means 'man') or the prefix *bi-* (in which case *He* would mean 'God'). Translate '(two eyes) that direct the (other) senses that man has been given' (or, 'that God has given [man]'). Since *he has* might elide to *h'as*, such a line would not have been overweighted, and a simple word in initial *b(e)-* might have appeared to the archetypal scribe echoic of *he*.

14957–8 The French says 'car nature est de petit soustenne e par trop de viande est souent abatue' (BSG 164ᵛ/53–4, *BVV* 277/1–3). The translator appears to have missed the sense of 'est . . . soustenne'—'is sustained by little food', rather than 'has little power to support itself'.

14964 *lyues*: The singular of ELSW also appears in B²B⁵B⁷. The French reads 'la vie des sainz' (BSG 165ʳ/3–4, *BVV* 277/5 'lyues'), but the translator may not have been scrupulous about number.

14968 *Salomon*: Probably a decontextualized reference to Prov. 20: 10, but a variety of statements in 'wisdom literature' might be adduced, for example Eccl. 7: 30, Wis. 7: 28.

14970 *right*: None of the B-MSS support RW in omitting this word (B⁹ breaks off soon, at 14992), and these copies have reduced the technical theological sense of the French ('droite mesure' BSG 165ʳ/7, *BVV* 277/9), comparable to *resoun right* 15005.

14999 *Bernard*: Gradon compares (222, 250/6–7 n.) the discussion at *De consideratione* 1. 8 (PL 182: 737–8).

15025 *Austyn*: Gradon compares (222, 250/20–3 n.) 'De musica' 6. 15. 50 (PL 22: 1189).

15032 *here doun*: 'Here beneath', viz. of lower things.

15036 *vayne bisynes*: *Somme* reads simply 'mesese' (BSG 165ᵛ/35, *BVV* 278/4).

15048 *alderhede*: A nonce usage, not in MED, within a ME elaboration. The word is a grammatically unusual compound; such forms typically involve adjectives or adverbs, for example 'alderbest'. The poet here apparently joins a reflex of OE ealra with the noun 'head' (conceivably, but far less likely, the suffix 'hede'), literally 'the ruler of us all'. Compare 2583–6.

15052 *þe haly godspelle*: John 16: 33.

15055 *Austyn*: Gradon cites (222, 250/34–5 n.) *Confessiones* I. 1 (PL 32: 661).

15073–4 The couplet modifies *þe herte* in the preceding line. Similarly, the parenthetical 15082 modifies *þe hert*, and the sense runs directly from *restes* at the end of 15081 to the prepositional phrase introduced by *After* at the head of 15083.

15084 *in boke wryten*: John 4. The well in Samaria is the 'fons Iacob', and it is from the metaphors of this passage (with an assist from 2549) that the author of *Jacob's Well* took the inspiration for the organizational metaphor for his sermon cycle, heavily dependent upon the poem.

15133 *turment*: A *turnament* is isolated; among B-MSS, only B² shares the reading (*tormentes* B¹ [as W], a lost folio B⁷). Just as the rendition 'werre and bataile' *BVV* 279/21, the scribe has been attracted to the surrounding discussion. The majority reading is confirmed by *La Somme* 'sanz torment e sanz aucune bataille de temptacion' (C 187ʳ; 'sanz temptacion' BSG 166ᵛ/31).

15147 *dose*: In spite of its placement, the verb of the main clause.

15156 *trauaylles*: The singular of LPRW appears only in B²B³ of the B-MSS (lost folio B⁷). The French has the plural (BSG 166ᵛ/41, *BVV* 279/32).

15159 *defautles*: Among the B-MSS, only B⁶ supports the prefixed form printed (fayntles B¹, lost folio B⁷).

15211 *Paul*: Rom. 12: 3, presumably also the source of the allusion at 15233.

15217 *Salamon*: Prov. 19: 27.

15237–40 A ME addition.

15255 *þe wyse man*: Ecclus. 18: 30–1.

15259 *light*: Lorens wrote a direct command 'Ne suie pas' (BSG 167ʳ/21, *BVV* 281/2). The ME poet seems to have read this as a form of 'luire', and his (mis)translation apparently means '(It is not enough) to alleviate'.

15275 *Petir*: 1 Pet. 2: 11.

15283–4 Apparently to be construed, 'He is a pilgrim who . . .', but the construction generally follows the source. *þat* 15287 confusingly has a different antecedent, the *theues and robbours* of 15285.

15308 *Paul*: Heb. 11: 13–16.

15341–2 In spite of difficulties in transmitting this couplet, among the B-MSS only B¹, which omits it (as does W), shows major variation here.

15355 *Senek*: Compare *Ad Lucillium* 88. 2–3.

15373 *Salamon*: Prov. 17: 27 (compare Eccl. 5: 1).

15377 *Ierom*: *Commentaria in Ezechielem* 45: 10 (PL 25: 450).

15387 *þe wyse man*: Ecclus. 21: 28, alluded to again at 15433.

15392 *weghe*: The absence of termination indicates the verb is subjunctive 'might/should weigh'; compare BSG 168^r/26 'doit si peser' (*BVV* 282/32).

15406–10 The passage fairly directly reproduces the source (BSG 168^v/29–31, *BVV* 282/37–283/1). Its difficulties arise from the author's intrusive explanation (things would be clearer, had 15407–8 followed 15405) that a floodgate or sluice is also known as a *clouse*. This Latinism, from its distribution in legal documents and names, may surprisingly have been a colloquial term. (The L variant probably attempts to reproduce the related form *cloure*.) Translate 'In that situation (*þar* 15406), the water has free passage to the mill, which then turns about incessantly . . .'.

15419 *þe wyse man*: Prov. 17: 14.

15425 *Salamon*: If not a reference to the preceding, probably Ecclus. 28: 28–30, as Gradon points out (225, 253/23–8 nn.).

15441 Combining Whiting W 275 and W 622 (compare W 576, W 605).

15459 *Dauy*: Ps. 38: 2; the Psalm 'Dixi custodiam' stands at the head of a 'nocturn', one of the conventional liturgical divisions of the Psalter, and is thus customarily illustrated—with an image of David pointing to his mouth.

15515 *þe haly man*: Compare R's ascription to Jerome; Gradon suggests (225, 256/24–7 n.) an allusion to Prov. 25: 23.

15521–36 Compare the extended treatment, a search for a truth-teller in the later *Mum and the Sothsegger* (and that poem's roots in the council scenes that occupy much of *Piers Plowman* B.3–4).

15533 *Senek*: For example, at *De beneficiis* 6. 33. 1–2.

15543 *þe wyse man*: Ecclus. 28: 28.

15579 *a manere of nedder*: The asp that stops its ear is actually biblical, from Ps. 57: 5–6 (compare *þe boke* 15604); it is also described at *Bestiary* 80^v.

15615–18 A small ME elaboration of the French, which says simply 'qui le doit mout espoenter' (BSG 170^r/15, *BVV* 285/25).

15641 *Godde*: A further allusion (see 8015–36) to Dives and Lazarus, Luke 16: 19 ff.; in the bibilical account, the actual rebuke comes from Abraham.

15651 *wele*: Perhaps an archetypal error for *swilk*? The French offers no parallel statement.

15660 *funden first*: Gen. 3: 7–11.

15684 The line provides a moralization for the richly dressed dead body described in 15665–8; in the French, the information is provided at that point (BSG 170^v/37–40, *BVV* 286/13–15).

15685 *þe wyse man*: Ecclus. 11: 14.

15689 *Paul*: 1 Tim. 2: 9–11, as earlier at 10621.

15715–18 A small ME addition.

15729 *Senek*: Probably too general a statement to be identified with any single passage.

15755 *a philosophre*: I have not found the source of the reference.

15759 *Haly Wrytte*: As R's sidenote indicates, Isa. 65: 20.

15767 *Paul*: 1 Cor. 13: 11.

15790 A's insertion is dubious, and nearly all B-MSS here read as the majority collated (*yt* B⁵; B⁸ has broken off at 15558). Without A's assertion, the end of the line makes good sense, 'as is appropriate'. But the metre, which led A to insert 'vs', remains dodgy. Possibly a second use of *in* has been lost by haplography before *drynkyng*.

15787 *Haly Wrytte*: 1 Cor. 14: 20.

15795 *þe godspelle*: Luke 21: 34.

15846 Referring to the discussion at 2507–92.

15851 *as . . . rede*: Probably to be construed within the following line and clause.

15876 *þe godspell*: Matt. 5: 9 (again at 15982).

15883 *paysebles*: A plural adjective from French; the usage is confirmed once in the poem in rhyme, at 9070.

15884 *Austyne*: Gradon compares (226, 261/6–8 n.) *De Genesi contra Manichaeos* 1. 20 (PL 34: 188).

15894 *Paul*: Rom. 8: 13–23, 2 Cor. 13: 11.

15908 *Haly Writte*: An addition to the French, perhaps a convenience for the rhyme; compare Wis. 3: 9, Zach. 8: 19. The subsequent verse paragraph alludes to Eph. 2: 13–17.

15918 *þe aungels sang*: Luke 2: 13–14. The reference in 15910 to clerical assertions is probably nothing more than general homiletics (although compare 2 Cor. 13: 11).

15953 *manere*: Excepting *mon* B⁶, all the B-MSS support this reading of LSRW, which is probably metrically preferable. The source offers no direction: 'la ou ne porra estre mal' (BSG 172ᵛ/41–2, *BVV* 289/34–5).

15959 *mast²*: In spite of the overwhelming omission of the word among the manuscripts collated, only B³ among the B-MSS extant at this point lacks it.

15964 *Paull*: Phil. 4: 7.

15966 *Alle*: The LRW reading printed here and supported in virtually all the B-MSS (*þe* B⁵) is confirmed by *Somme* 'toute parole' (BSG 172ᵛ/46, *BVV* 290/1).

15969–16016 An extensive ME addition, comparable to, but considerably more extended than, the summary paragraphs at the end of the discussion of each gift throughout the poem. Most of the material restates, with different emphasis, materials discussed earlier at 3493–3510 (see the n.).

16009 *þe wyse man*: Ecclus. 1: 16 (et alibi).

16026 *grete*: Most B-MSS, all except B⁵B⁷, omit the word.

16087 *þe boke*: But simply proverbial, Walther 24550.

APPENDIX: THE LATIN TRACT

Hope E. Allen long ago (1917) pointed out that opening portions of *Speculum Vitae* had not been derived from the poet's usual source, Lorens's *Somme*, but from early portions of a Latin septenary tract derived from *La Somme*. Allen's findings have been affirmed by subsequent scholars; see Doyle, 'A Survey of the Origins and Circulation', i. 77; *A Myrour to lewde men and wymmen*, ed. Nelson, 11 n. 9.

So far as I know, this text (Bloomfield no. 8834) survives in six copies:

A BL, MS Additional 15237, fos. 78^v–88^r (fos. 9–94 produced as a unit, s. xv$^{3/4}$). Folio 2^r has the opening of a receipt, dated 6 March 1529, in which J.W., priest of the chantry within the manor of Marewell, acknowledges payment of his wages from the Treasurer of Wolnesay. The places are perhaps Mare Fen and Welney on the border of Norfolk and Ely; this location would be consonant with *LALME*'s report (iv. 100) of the English in *Speculum Christiani* (fos. 9–57) as 'language of extreme S Lincs or NE Rutland'.

B BL, MS Burney 356, fos. 8^r–20^r (s. xv in.). The earliest recoverable provenance for the book is provided by the s. xvii stamped binding, with 'Dominus Edoardvs Dering miles et baronettus'. He was from Surrenden Dering, Kent; the English at fos. 43^v–55^v (within part 5 of the volume), is reported as *LALME* LP 5670 (iii. 501), language of extreme west-central Sussex.

H BL, MS Harley 1022, fos. 82^r–97^v (part 4 of the book, s. xiv^2 or xiv ex.). The tract is bound with a central Northern Rolle MS, mapped as *LALME* LP 115 (parts 1 and 3) and LP 4 (part 2), near Huddersfield and Keighley, respectively. See the description EETS 329, pp. xxx–xxxiii.

H^1 BL, MS Harley 1648, fos. 1^r–7^r (s. xv$^{2/4}$ or med.). This is a large format (*c*.425 mm × 290 mm) single quire of instructional tables, with no indication of provenance.

M Oxford, Merton College, MS 13, fos. 42^v–50^r (fos. 26–197 a unit, s. xv^1 or xv$^{2/4}$ [dated 1428]). Although the initial provenance is uncertain, the book was donated to Merton 1466/8 by Henry Sever, the Warden 1458–71.

R BodL, MS Rawlinson C.72, fos. 137ʳ–54ᵛ (s. xv in.). The volume breaks off with one of Oliger's rules for hermits, and the lyric in Edmund Rich's *Speculum ecclesie* (fo. 134ʳ) includes the Northern forms 'gase' and 'rewes'. The medieval binding includes raised pastedowns at each end cut down from letters: that at the front is from Stephen O.Carm. to William, with added date 1469; at the rear, one (? of confraternity) addressed to Beatrice Ros, mentioning '⟨cut off⟩ Clare sancti Damiani ac Minorissarum beneficia', and dated London, 20 April *s.a.* This recipient is probably Beatrice, a younger daughter of William, 6th lord Roos of Hamlake (Helmsley, North Yorkshire) and Belvoir (d. 1414), born after 1397. In the fifteenth-century family pedigree, Beatrice is described as 'monialis inter le Mynores', i.e. the house of Franciscan nuns near the Tower of London; see *Visitations of the North—Part III*, ed. C. H. Hunter-Blair, Surtees Society, 144 (Durham, 1930), 162–3.

This Latin text is called 'tabula de vtilitate oracionis dominice', probably an indication of its original form, as a 'table', rather than a consecutive prose treatise. **H¹**, laid out as elaborate series of *distinctiones* (a presentation more informally followed in **M**), seems to reflect this original form of the text. As a result of this presentation, the scribes vary a good deal in how fully they choose to present the various headings and divisions of the argument. **H** is similar in form to these two copies, but agrees textually with **R**, rather than the remainder, in its relative fullness of exposition. Both include materials available to the poet, yet not in other copies. For example, at lines 99–100 of the edition below, all of **ABH¹M** omit *inclinando . . . humiliter*, translated at *SV* 483–6 and present in **HR**. Instructively, **HR** are relatively early and inferentially Yorkshire copies, the remainder later and dispersed. Only **R** follows a rigorously continuous prose form and is here printed. I offer selected variants from **H**.

fo. 137ʳ
SV 97–114
Hic incipit tabula de vtilitate oracionis dominice in qua breuiter tractatur de 7. peticionibus eiusdem, videlicet Pater noster qui es in celis, Sanctificetur . . . 2° de 7. donis Spiritus Sancti, videlicet Sapiencie, Intellectus . . . 3° de 7. peccatis mortalibus, videlicet Gula, Luxuria . . . 4° de 7. virtutibus principalibus, videlicet Sobrietatis, Castitatis . . . 5° de 7. beatitudinibus et 5

earum meritis, videlicet Mundicie cordis, cuius meritum est visio diuina;
Pacificacionis, cuius premium est deificacio . . .

Pater noster tanquam caput omnium oracionum euidenter appro- SV 115–52
batur, quia ex sui virtute, quoniam ad omnia nobis necessaria pro vita
10 presenti et futura petenda sufficere videtur, quam quidem oracionem
vnusquisque Cristianus tam ex precepto quam ex consilio ecclesie
scire et intelligere tenetur. Nam qui illam oracionem scire necligit,
doctrinam Dei manifeste contempnit. Idcirco paruulus quando de
nouo ad librum apponitur, primo addiscit Pater noster. Nam istam
15 leccionem Dominus noster Ihesus Cristus docuit discipulos suos; ideo
merito dicitur oracio dominica. Vnde qui istam doctrinam scire et
intelligere volueri[n]t, erunt humiles vt paruulus; tales enim sunt veri
scolares sapientissimi magistri nostri Ihesu Cristi, quos de sua
doctrina instruit et informat. Multi tamen nudam literam istius
20 oracionis tantummodo sciunt set eius sentenciam totaliter nesciunt;
illi vero in ea modicam senciunt | saporem quasi nullam deuocionis fo. 137ᵛ
dulcedinem. Set qui bene et recte intelligant oracionem predictam
ipsam vt mel in ore senciunt dulcissimam.

Ista vero oracio est pre omnibus aliis priuilegiata ex dignitate, quia SV 153–70
25 ab ore Cristi primo fuerat prolata. Ex breuitate, quia sub paucissimis
verbis fuerat composita. Ex vtilitate, quia continet omnia nobis
necessaria quantum ad hanc vitam et futuram petenda.

Item est in verbis breuissima, vt facilius addiscatur et memorie SV 171–90
commendetur. Item est in sentencia longa vt maior deuocio in eadem
30 habeatur, quia nuda verba eiusdem oretenus debent dici, et tota eius
sentencia in corde intelligi et retineri. Item est facilis dicenda, vt
frequencius absque tedio eam recitemus. Item est subtilis intelligenda
vt magis et diligencius circa intellectum et sentenciam eiusdem
studere affectemus.

35 Item ista oracio ammouet omnia mala que sunt, aut preterita pro SV 205–20
quibus ammouendis dicimus, *Et dimitte nobis debita nostra sicut et nos*
dimittimus debitoribus nostris, petendo indulgenciam de preteritis. Aut
futura pro quibus ammouendis dicimus, *Et ne nos inducas in*
temptacionem, petendo cautelam de futuris. Aut presencia pro
40 quibus ammouendis dicimus, *Set libera nos a malo,* petendo abstinenciam de presentibus.

Item ista oracio impetrat omnia bona que sunt: aut temporalia, pro SV 221–40
quibus assequendis dicimus, *Panem nostrum cotidianum da nobis hodie,*
petendo rectum modum in carne viuendi. Aut spiritualia pro quibus
45 assequendis dicimus, *Fiat voluntas tua sicut in celo et in terra,* petendo

continuam voluntatem Deo complacendi. Aut eternalia pro quibus assequendis dicimus, *Adueniat regnum tuum*, petendo graciam merendi. Item ista oracio confirmat in nobis omne bonum, pro quo confirmando dicimus, *Sanctificetur nomen tuum*, petendo propositum firmum in bono perseuerandi.   50

SV 241–62   Set sciendum est quod in principio istius oracionis notantur
fo. 138ʳ   quatuor verba, | super quibus omnes 7. peticiones fundantur, que nos oportet necessario intelligere et corda nostra iuxta eorum sentenciam discrete et ordinate regulare antequam a Deo Patre mereamur audiri et petita optinere. Hec sunt 4. verba in principio 55 dicte oracionis, videlicet *Pater Noster Qui es In celis*.

SV 279–94   *Pater.* Hoc verbum ostendit nobis longitudinem diuine eternitatis, quia Deus Pater est eternus sine principio et fine, principium sine principio et finis sine fine, qui filios suos cum eo viuere in eternum predistinauit.   60

SV 295–   Item inducit nos ad congnoscendum in Deo Patre et in filiis suis, in
302   Deo Patre per potenciam, sapienciam, et bonitatem.

SV 303–10   Primo per potenciam, quia Deus est omnipotens, Pater, magister, et Dominus celi et terre, creator omnium creaturarum ac fons et origo omnium bonorum. Sicque congnoscitur eius potencia.   65

SV 311–18   2°. per sapienciam, quia Deus Pater totam familiam suam, et precipue filios suos quos creauit, sapienter regit et gubernat. Et sic congnoscitur eius sapiencia.

SV 319–34   3°. per bonitatem, quia Deus Pater filios suos diligit et eos, quando deliquerint, verberat et castigat et quando ad se redierint, eos benigne 70 admittit. Et sic eius bonitas congnoscitur.

SV 335–46   Item in filiis suis per nobilitatem, diuicias, pulcritudinem. Per nobilitatem, quia filii Dei Patris sunt filii excellentissimi imperatoris et regis omnium regum. Maior vero nobilitas esse non potest.

SV 347–54   2°. per diuicias, quia filii sui sunt heredes regni celestis, in quo 75 omnimode delicie et diuicie existunt. Maiores vero diuicie possideri non possunt.

SV 355–68   3°. per pulcritudinem, quia filii sui sunt creati ad ymaginem suam et similitudinem. Nam tantam pulcritudinem nulla mens cogitare nec sensus ymaginare potest.   80

SV 375–84   Item hoc verbum requirit specialiter nobis amorem, vt Deum Patrem amemus ex toto corde, scilicet vt magis ad dileccionem |
fo. 138ᵛ   Dei quam alicuius rei inclinemus et magis in eo quam in aliqua re delectemur.

85 Item ex tota anima, scilicet vt mallemus cicius vitam nostram a *SV* 385–92
corporibus nostris separare quam a Deo separari.

Item tota mente, scilicet vt sapienciam, intellectum, et cogitacio- *SV* 393–8
nem nostram magis in Deo quam in alia re occupemus.

Item requirit a nobis t[i]morem, vt Deum Patrem timeamus timore *SV* 399–
90 filiali, non seruili. 404

Item obedienciam, vt mandata Dei Patris custodiamus et eius *SV* 429–36
voluntatem perficiamus.

Item seruicium, vt Deo Patri debita obsequia seruitutis nostre *SV* 437–46
impendamus et eidem cum omni diligencia intendamus.

95 Item honorem, vt Deum Patrem pro beneficiis suis semper *SV* 447–59
laudemus et eidem gracias agamus ac omnia bona nobis collata ad
eius laudem tantummodo ex[p]endamus.

Item reuerenciam, vt semper quando aliquid a Deo petimus eidem *SV* 469–
omnimodam reuerenciam, cum deuocione inclinando et genuflec- 71, 483–6
100 tendo capitibus discoopertis, humiliter exhibeamus.

Noster. Hoc verbum ostendit nobis largitatem diuine caritatis, quia *SV* 559–64
Deus Pater noster dat libencius et largius pluribus quam vni soli,
cicius satis quam modicum. Ideo plus valet oracio pro omnibus in
communi quam pro vno solo in speciali.

105 Item requirit a nobis fratern[u]m amorem et firmam spem. *SV* 595–
Fraternum amorem, vt diligamus ad inuicem tanquam veri fratres 620
et filii vnius patris, qui est Deus, et vnius matris, que est Sancta
Ecclesia, et tanquam vera membra vnius corporis, quod est ecclesia,
cuius caput est Cristus. Et vt quilibet nostrum alteri succurrat et oret
110 pro alio tanquam veri socii in vna comitiua sancta inter quos omnia
bona sunt comunia.

Firmam spem, vt firmiter speremus obtinere quod a Deo Patre *SV* 673–84
iuste petimus, quia pater noster est et eius filii sumus.

Qui es. Hoc verbum ostendit nobis profunditatem sue veritatis, quia *SV* 685–92
115 Pater noster est verus Deus et verus homo. Et nullus alius deus est
preter ipsum per quem omnia facta sunt | et sine quo factum est nichil. fo. 139ʳ

Item requirit a nobis veram fidem et timorem. *SV* 821–30

Veram fidem, vt vere credamus in veritate Dei qui est Pater et *SV* 831–6,
Filius et Spiritus Sanctus, vnus deus in Trinitate et trinus in vnitate, 799–806,
813–20,
120 qui vbique est in celo et in terra et spiritualiter in mundis cordibus 867–72
quoruncumque filiorum suorum, cuius ymaginem in nobis videre
possimus per 3., scilicet per memoriam, per intelligenciam, et per
voluntatem que consistunt in anima.

SV 915–
50, 1377–
90

SV 1453–
68

SV 1519–
24, 1535·
70, 1665–
1776

SV 1777–
86, 2159–
2230

fo. 139ᵛ
SV 2231–
68

SV 2221–
30, 3361–
88

2°. vt vere credamus in virtute Ecclesie que est mater nostra et
sponsa Dei. Nam sicut mater infantem suum ex lacte vberum suorum 125
naturaliter nutrit, sic Sancta Ecclesia, mater nostra, nos nutrit et
instruit ex dulcedine Sacre Scripture pro nostra doctrina collecte, tam
ex Veteri Testamento a quo 10. precepta Decalogi extrahuntur, quam
ex Nouo Testamento per quod 12. Articuli Fidei declarantur et vij.
sacramenta intelliguntur.   130
    Item requirit a nobis timorem, quia licet Deus sit pater noster, est
tamen verax et iustus et reddet vnicuique iuxta opera sua, prout in
fine seculi manifeste patebit.
    In celis. Hoc verbum ostendit nobis altitudinem sue maiestatis, quia
sub Deo Patre omnia subiecta sunt et supra se nichil esse potest. Item 135
requirit a nobis humilitatem, vigorem, et probitatem. Primo humilitatem, quia tanta est altitudo celorum quod illuc ascendere non
valemus sine vera humilitate, que se ostendit in corde, ore, et
opere. In corde per frequentem meditacionem, per veram contricio-
nem, per bonam pacienciam, et per sanctam delectacionem. In ore per 140
integram confessionem, per continuam laudacionem, per deuotam
oracionem, et per bone doctrine demonstracionem. In opere per
debitam satisfaccionem, per humilem obedienciam, per bonorum
operum operacionem, et per vite asperitatem.
    2°. vigorem, quia via que ducit ad celos est ita arta, quod per eam 145
transire non possumus nisi roboremur virtutibus sacris. Que emanant
ex Vita Actiua, que consistit in Operibus Misericordie, in ieiunio, et
penitencia; et ex Vita Contemplatiua, que consistit in leccione,
oracione, et meditacione. |
    3°. probitatem, quia in regno celorum tanta est diuine maiestatis 150
magnitudo ac angelorum et aliorum sanctorum multitudo quod ibi
non valemus ingredi ad gloriam nisi per probitatem. Hoc meremur et
victoriam, et precipue mundi, carnis, et diaboli. Mundi qui nos
impugnat ex vna parte per prosperitatem, et vincitur per paupertatem
voluntariam; ex alia parte per aduersitatem, et vincitur per pacien- 155
ciam. Carnis que nos impugnat per delectationem, et vincitur per
abstinenciam. Diaboli qui nos impugnat per superbiam et vanam
gloriam, et vincitur per humilitatem.
    Per istas 7. peticiones impetrantur 7. dona Spiritus Sancti, que
extrahunt a corde 7. mortalia peccata et plantant in corde 7. virtutes 160
principales, que nos perducunt ad 7. beatitudines et ad earum merita.
Quarum quidem peticionum prima, scilicet *Sanctificetur nomen tuum*,
impetrat Donum Sapiencie, per quod extrahitur a corde peccatum

Gule et plantatur in corde virtus Sobrietatis et Temperancie, que nos
165 perducit ad beatitudinem [Pacificacionis], cuius meritum est [Deifi-
cacio].

2ª., scilicet *Adueniat etc.*, impetrat Donum Intellectus, per quod *SV* 3389-
extrahitur a corde peccatum Luxurie et plantatur in corde virtus 3406
Castitatis, que nos perducit ad beatitudinem Mundicie +, cuius
170 meritum est [Visio Dei].

3ª., scilicet *Fiat etc.*, impetrat Donum Consilii, per quod extrahitur *SV* 3407-
a corde peccatum Auaricie et plantatur in corde virtus Misericordie, 22
que nos perducit ad beatitudinem Misericordie actiue, cuius meritum
est Misericordia passiua.

175 4ª., scilicet *Panem nostrum etc.*, impetrat Donum Fortitudinis, per *SV* 3423-
quod extrahitur a corde peccatum Accidie et plantatur in corde virtus 40
Probitatis, que nos perducit ad beatitudinem Esuriei iusticie, cuius
meritum est Saturacio.

5ª., scilicet *Et dimitte etc.*, impetrat Donum Sciencie, per quod *SV* 3441-
180 extrahitur a corde peccatum Ire et plantatur in corde virtus Equitatis, 56
que nos perducit ad beatitudinem Luctus, cuius meritum est Con-
solacio.

6ª., scilicet *Et ne nos etc.*, impetrat Donum Pietatis, per quod *SV* 3457-
extrahitur a corde peccatum Inuidie et plantatur in corde virtus 72
185 Amicicie, que nos perducit ad beatitudinem Suauitatis, cuius meritum
est Possessio terre in habundancia. |

7ª., scilicet *Set libera etc.*, impetrat Donum Timoris Dei, per quod fo. 140ʳ
extrahitur a corde peccatum Superbie et plantatur in corde virtus *SV* 3473-
Humilitatis, que nos perducit ad beatitudinem Paupertatis spiritus, 90
190 cuius meritum est Regnum celorum.

Et licet 7. dona Sancti Spiritus in oracione dominica sint petita, *SV* 3493-
videlicet quodlibet secundum ordinem dignitatis sue descendendo, 3510
sicut 7. peticiones secundum ordinem dignitatis sue in dicta oracione
ponuntur, oportet nos tamen illas gracias impetrare secundum
195 ordinem dignitatis virtutum ascendendo, et incipere ad Donum
Timoris Dei quod impetratur per 7ᵃᵐ. peticionem oracionis predicte.
Nam inicium sapiencie timor domini. Per septimam peticionem, *Set
libera etc.*, impetratur Donum Timoris Dei . . . .

Selected variants of H

*17 voluerint] voluerit R
21 quasi] et quasi H
22 intelligant] intelligunt H

55–6 Hec . . . celis] *om.* H
61–3 et in . . . per] *om.* H
72 Item] *adds* inducit nos ad cognoscendum H   per] *om.* H
73 filii²] *adds* nobilissimi et H
74 vero] *om.* H
76 possideri] haberi H
78 suam] *after* similitudinem H
83 rei] alius rei corda nostra H   in eo . . . re] *om.* H
84 delectemur] delectemus H
*89 timorem] tremorem HR
*97 expendamus] extendamus R
*105 fraternum] fraternam R
117 *whole line om.* H
123 que . . . anima] *om.* H
124 virtute] vᵢtute R, virtutem H
129 et] *om.* H
137 altitudo celorum] *trs.* H
153 carnis . . . Mundi] *om.* H
155 alia] altera H
159 H *adds a paragraph of short, linked expositions of each petition, om.* R
*165 Pacificacionis, Deificacio] H, mundicie cordis, visio diuina R
*169 Mundicie] H, mundicie cordis R
*170 Visio Dei] H, pacificacionis deificacio R
192 videlicet] scilicet H
192–3 descendendo . . . sue] *om.* H
196 oracionis predicte] *om.* H
197 Per] quod de dono timoris dei impetratur per H (*and om. this material at* 208)

GLOSSARY

Given the length of the text, this glossary is selective. It intends to explain 'difficult forms', primarily all obsolete items and all words that have undergone substantial changes of form or meaning since the fourteenth century. (On a selective basis, it also cites a few unusual or opaque instances of words otherwise non-problematic.) For each item, I list the first five occurrences only.

Because my presentation is selective, I count upon a certain 'Northern literacy' in my reader. Thus I generally ignore obvious examples of regular *a/o* alternation (for OE *ā*), make no effort to mark such common variation as *i/y* or *-e/zero*, and I assume a reader's ability to recognize Northern byforms of common words. I avoid full records of inflectional forms for nouns and most weak verbs, unless scribal usage seems to me unduly confusing.

A

a, see ane

abate *v.* to strike down, reduce, lower 1100, 3059, 3580, 4269, 9718

aduersere *n.* adversary, enemy (the devil) 12554, 15268

affinyte *n.* kinship 9380

after, aftir *prep.* after (in its various senses), but esp. according to, in accord with, in proportion to 357, 608, 658, 890, 891

agayne-crokynge *n.* bending back on itself 12043

agaynesay *v.* to reject, refute 5670, 9795

agaynesayinge *n.* opposition, rebellion 5654; see also **gaynsayinge**

agaynestande *v. pr. subj. pl.* resist 3196

agaynestandynge *n.* resistance 2634, 14938

aght *num.* eight 4070, 6606

aghtene *num.* eighteen 4976, 4977, 5259

agh(t)ned *ord. num.* eighth 970, 1345, 6157, 6245, 6616

ay *adv.* ever, always 153, 192, 232, 280, 303

ay-lastand(e)(ly) *adj., adv.* eternal(ly) 310, 3401, 5371, 10051, 12733; *adv.* 753, 785

ay-lastyng *n.* eternality, everlastingness 2278

ayre *n.* the grain-bearing head of a plant 4284 n.

ay-whare *adv.* anywhere, everywhere 802

al, see **al-if**

alane *adv.* alone, uniquely, solely 1146, 9792, 13805, 14359, 14930

alanely *adv.* only, solely 4867

alday *adv.* continually, constantly 10412

alde *adj.* old 79, 940, 4611; *þe Alde Lawe* the Mosaic Law, law of the Old Testament 952, 955, 976; *þe secund boke of þe Alde Lawe* the biblical book Exodus 696

alderhede *n.* single leader or authority 15048 n.

al-if *conj.* although 22, 25, 46, 743, 806, 1455; al 3048, 7603, 7800, 11317; see also **if**

al(l)egge *v.* to alleviate, allay 1419, 7808

almusdede *n. (pl.)* act(s) of charity 1534, 4037, 4863, 7514, 7912

als *adv.* also 1127, 6562, 7867

als *conj.* as 4, 38, 70 (2×), 71, 100

als-tyte *adv.* immediately, quickly 8192, 8384, 8715, 8738, 9605; see also **tyte**

alswa *adv.* also 11, 120, 399, 573, 915 (only three examples not in rhyme, e.g. 14523); elsewhere usually also 185, 199, 347, 369, 1073 (three examples in rhyme, e.g. 4651)

al-weldande *pr. p., adj.* omnipotent, governing all things 752, 2737, 3174, 3402, 8447

amange *adv.* mixed in, intermixed 3230, 4907, 6663, 6731, 7037

a(ne) *adj., art.* a(n), one, a single 4, 18, 44, 94, 117

anehede *n.* unity 836, 1842, 3294, 15852

anelepy *adj. (and as n.)* single, solitary 10889, 10913

anely *adj., adv.* only, uniquely, alone 2, 144, 182, 303, 312

angre, anger *n.* hardship, adversity,

tribulation 1598, 1676, 1990, 1992, 2130

anguyse *n.* anguish, hardship, tribulation 7690, 7733

anothir *pron., ord. num.* another, the second (used to the exclusion of **othir**) 600, 1070, 1088, 1538, 1614

appayre *v.* to injure, damage, harm 3010, 6289, 6292, 9620, 10980; see also **enpayre**

appayrement *n.* injury, damage 4980

appert *adj.* open, plain 5430, 6349, 6353, 6804, 7268

ap(p)ertly *adv.* openly, blatantly 980, 1750, 2006, 2236, 3405

ap(p)ropr(i)ed *v. p.p.* specially devoted 6766, 12125, 12161

ar *conj., prep.* before 392, 1608, 3347, 3500, 4722, 5048

are *adv.* first, previously 391, 5047, 5541, 6262, 11174

arely *adj., adv.* early 1099, 2186, 8907, 10548, 10924 (the *adj.* only at 13169); *arely and/ne late* at any/no time

aresouned *v. p.p.* called to account, chastised 6243, 13612

argh(e) *adj.* timid, slow, unwilling, fearful 5096, 9521

arg(h)nes *n.* slackness, timidity 4990, 5079

askynge *n.* petition (of the Pater Noster) 101, 104, 195, 199, 203

assay *v.* to test, try, make trial of 4045, 5466

assent *n.* consent, agreement, those agreeing 6689, 6734, 6898; *of his* ~ *of* his opinion or his party 3523; *of ane* ~ in accord 10866

assesour *n.* legal adviser, adviser to a judge 6616, 6727

asseth(e) *n.* satisfaction; always in *make* ~ to repay a debt, offer (penitential) reparation 1739, 2920, 6194

assoynes *n. pl.* (legal) excuses for delay or non-performance 14493

assotynge *n.* behaving foolishly 5603

attachen *v.* to seize, arrest 6475

attaynt *v. p.p.* convicted of a crime 6699, 6710

attemperaunce *n.* the virtue Temperance or Sobriety 14607, 14983, 15028, 15163, 15170

attemp(e)re(e) *adj.* moderate(d),

temperate 11248, 15123, 15358, 15624, 15730

attempred *v. p.p.* moderated 15380

attry *adj.* poisonous, vicious 1101

aube *n.* the clerical vestment 'alba', alb 12236

auctorite *n.* power, authority 6554, 10992, 10995

auauntage advantage, benefit, profit 3779, 6250, 6265, 6308, 6315

auyse *n.* opinion 1884

avyse *v.* to advise, consider 4820, 13559, 15522

auysement *n.* consideration, forethought 8374, 8383, 14112, 14547

auoket *n.* advocate, one who speaks on another's behalf, lawyer 6610, 6661, 6667, 7567, 13751

avoutry, auouctery *n.* adultery 6408, 8358, 8410, 9292, 9308

awe *n.* fear, subjection 405, 6348, 6607, 7356, 7660; *standes nane* ~ *of* have no fear of 6607

awe(s) *v. pr. 3 sg.* (often impers.) owes, is obligated, ought, should, owns 368, 1736, 2025, 2923, 3066; *aght pa. t.* 1001, 2050, 3801, 6392, 6807

B

babils *n. pl.* scourges, whips 12426

bachilere *n.* knight in training, knightly retainer 2004

badde, see **bidde**

baylly *n.* a charge or office 3757

bayl(l)if *n.* bailiff, steward or reeve 3838, 6375, 6475, 6511, 6589

baytes *v. pr. 3 sg.* tastes, grazes on 1882

balde *adj.* ready, bold, (over)confident, brash 2004, 2766, 3121, 3548, 3652

baldely *adv.* confidently 427

bale *n.* hardship, trouble, affliction 4567, 7691, 12450

band(e) *n.* bond, union, chain 6647, 6649, 9254, 9399, 9401; *Goddes bandes* tribulation, illness 7978, 8170; see also **snare-bande**

bandoun *n.* subjection 12560; *to brynge vnto* ~ to subject someone, to bring them under one's control 12466

bane *n.* killer, destroyer 14864

banne *v.* to curse 4664, 14285

bannynge *n.* cursing 5651, 14294

barette *n.* strife 13538

barnage *n.* barons, court 13620

barne-gammen *n.* a child's game 4172

barnes *n. pl.* children 4663, 8593

barnhede *n.* youth, childhood 7640

be *v.* 8, 47, 49, 95; *subj.* 16, 22, 25; es *pr.
3 sg.* 51, 65, 68, 69, 90 (is only at
1063); er *pr. pl.* 2, 4, 26, 53, 139; ere
3696, 7737 (alt. with bene 339, 539,
577, 871, 986, but the latter the regular
form in rhyme 241, 342, 538, 557,
812); was *pa. t.* 44, 208, 645, 647;
wasse 9584; war(e) *pa. t. pl.* 85, 285,
387, 488, 495 (*pa. t. subj.* would be
746); warne *pa. t. subj. conj.* were it
not that 766, 3222, 6489, 8932, 9754;
bene *p.p.* 209, 1272, 1280, 1379, 5013

bede, beede *n.* prayer(s) 191, 4964, 5828,
10328, 10869

bede *v.* to command, offer 464, 3798,
4594, 5217, 7563; bedde *pa. t.* 9011,
11097; see also bidde

bedel(le)s *n. pl.* beadles, minor parish
disciplinary officials 6510, 6585, 6997

bene *n.* a game of some sort 7171
(elsewhere only the derivative use in
Jacob's Well)

benefyce *n.* a living attached to an office
(usually ecclesiastical) 3837, 6861, 6876,
6877, 6887

benysoun *n.* blessing 34

bere *v.* to bear (in its various senses,
incl.) to carry, bear (fruit, a child),
support, hold, endure, deport (oneself)
498, 779, 928, 970, 1149; bare *pa. t.*
11914, 12427; borne *p.p. adj.* 68, 474,
920, 1270, 8025

bery *v.* to thresh 4286

by and by *adv. phrs.* in turn 1233

bidde *v.* to command (senses of OE
bēodan, see also bede) 572, 701, 5112,
7373, 7435, 7439; bad(de) *pa. t.*
commanded 3148, 7841, 8135, 8216,
8264; to ask, pray (senses of OE
biddan) 6117, 7174, 7930, 13125, 15997;
bedes *pr. 3 sg.* 15119

byde *v.* to (a)wait, endure, endure to
win/see 1873, 5347, 5990, 8207, 8981;
bade *pa. t.* 8320

bidene *adv.* in a troop, completely,
immediately 8043, 9563

bidynge *n.* commandment 2500, 5637,
11384, 13329

bye *v.* to buy, pay for, atone for, redeem
6216, 6232, 6234; be 6457 n.; boght
pa. t. p.p. 880, 908, 1307, 1635, 1675

bigge *v.* to build 8942, 8943

byhoue *n.* profit, benefit, need 367, 2095,
2728, 5983, 8111, 8670; bihof 4750

bihoues *v. pr. 3s g.* (impers.) it is
necessary to/for, (with dative object as
subject) must, is/are obliged 250, 312,
455, 520, 608

bilets *n. pl.* some variety of headdress
10643 (elsewhere only *Cursor Mundi*
28016–18)

bynde *v.* to join, link, unite, constrain,
commit (by a vow) 261, 960, 1405,
5170, 6334; bounden *p.p.* 10915,
11306, 11439; bunden 4433, 9254

bys *n.* expensive cloth or a garment made
from it 15644

byte *v.* to bite, pierce 3899, 9138, 9607;
bote *v. pa. t.* bit 13036; biten *p.p.*
9597

bithink *v.* to consider, meditate on 1573,
1576, 1621, 1668, 13363

bithinkynge *n.* thought, meditation 1567,
1571, 2200, 2219, 4716

bytyde *v.* to befall, happen 1996, 6719,
10259; bitidde *pa. t.* 12704

bytyme *adv.* quickly 5113

bytrayst *v. pa. t.* betrayed 10862

blerynge *n.* making a moue or face,
mockery 5686

blethely *adv.* happily, willingly, with
pleasure 3898, 3912, 4021, 4037, 4068
(the parallel blithe *adj.* 8688 only)

blynnes *v. pr. 3 sg.* stops, ceases 14918,
15409

blissedhede *n.* beatitude, blessing 109,
112, 2330, 3370, 3381

boghe, bowe *v.* to bow, submit 3676,
4070, 4071, 4111, 5798; boghed *pa. t.*
8321, 8323; bowed 8449

bone *n.* boon, prayer, request 10170,
10776, 10799

borde *n.* board, table, a meal at table
6928, 9404, 12166

bordell *n.* whorehouse 7098, 9261

bordelry *n.* prostitution 9272

bost(e) *n.* boast, outcry, disturbance
5678, 7160

bote *n.* compensation, money payment
6891

bote, see also byte

642 GLOSSARY

bothe *n.* trading stall 10508

bouche *n.* sustenance; *bouche of court* provisions extended to support a courtly retinue 7204

boun *adj.* ready, prepared, prompt, eager 1080, 1666, 2207, 3116, 4295

boundes *n. pl.* boundaries, limits 11120, 11136, 11485

bounte *n.* goodness (not plenty) 319, 334, 722, 1866, 2091

bour *n.* bower, bedchamber, living quarters (as opposed to public parts of a dwelling) 7158

bourde *v.* to jest 10419, 10480

bourdes *n. pl.* jests 13470, 13643, 14003

bou(x)som(e) *adj.* obedient 431, 515, 1542, 1572, 1744

bouxsomly *adv.* obediently 2500, 3675, 4964

bouxsomnes *n.* obedience 430, 1061, 1730, 1741, 2281

brathe *adj.* angry, fierce 4653

brede *n.* breadth, width 2011, 5760, 5950, 7324

brest *v.* to burst 13018, 13476, 13479, 14244

bretens, see britten

brightes *v. pr. 3 sg.* brightens, illuminates 12840

brynne, brenne *v.* to burn 2438, 2727, 2754, 2786, 4998; **brynned** *pa. t.* 8030, 12662, 14341; **brent, brende, brenned, brynde** *p.p.* 4689, 7138, 9454, 9733, 9830, 11682

brynnynge, brennyng *n.* burning 9728, 9832

britten *v.* destroy, cut up, butcher 7741; **bretens** *pr. pl.* 14165

burdouns *n. pl.* staffs 7164

C

caffe *n.* chaff, the outer husk of the grain, bran 7876, 10184, 13963

caytyf *n.* wretch 13290, 13472

can *v.* can, know (how to), understand (an idea or a language) 67, 71, 73, 75, 76; **cun** 15137, 15138; **couth(e)** *pa. t.* 1707, 2054, 6346, 7636, 7730; *subj.?* 5700; *p.p.* 9489; *p.p. adj.* (well-)known 4234, 5460, 5756, 12957

can *v. pr.* 'do(es)', an untranslatable auxiliary used for purposes of metre

and rhyme 305, 687, 695, 1053, 1265; see also **gun**

cantell *n.* piece, bit 7424

carayne *n.* carcass, decaying corpse 11536; **caryoun** 13387

carl(e)s *n. pl.* servants 404, 405, 5606; *carles drede* 'timor servilis', non-virtuous respect out of fear of punishment

carols *n. pl.* round dances 5729

carp *v.* to speak 50

carpynge *n.* speech 36, 47, 49

case *n.* chance, situation, circumstance(s), peril 6276, 6340, 6435; *in ~ for* example 5341, 6373, 9822, 10859

catell *n.* livestock, chattels, property 6247, 6311, 6313, 6317, 7028

catte *n.* cat, a game (in the seventeenth century played with a bat, like cricket) 7171, 11675, 11677

cause *n.* cause (in its various senses), esp. legal case 5523, 5561, 5680, 6645, 6662

cautele *n.* subtlety, trick, device 6633, 6665, 14190

celers *n. pl.* storerooms 7504

certayne *n.* certain, s(ec)ure; *for ~* certainly 325, 8254, 8713, 11873

certes *adv.* certainly 9207, 9679, 10437, 10609, 12879

chace *v.* to drive (away), impel 4206, 5873, 6580, 10285, 14240

chalange *v.* to claim, assert one's title to 2267

chalenge *n.* claim, suit, detraction 6153, 6605

chaumbre *n.* private quarters or room, bedroom 496, 9789, 9792, 10491, 10496; *~ priue* 10501

chanoun *n.* canon, clergy serving a church 2809, 2813, 14426

chapiters *n. pl.* clerical assemblies, (ecclesiastical court) sessions 6565

charge *n.* load, weight, responsibility 5870, 13316, 13835, 14071, 15184; *bere ~ to* impose heavy responsibility

charge *v.* to weight down, account, stress, emphasize, blame, or rebuke 3055, 3774, 4346, 6230, 6673; **chargeande** *pr. p. adj.* weighty 6199, 9354

chasty *v.* to chastise, discipline (esp. the flesh), punish 324, 1732, 1765, 2179, 3568; **chastyde** *p.p.* 6495, 7308 chastying(e) *n.* chastisement 3566, 7744, 14476

chaufes *v. pr. 3 sg.* rouses, provokes, reprimands 2547

chaunce *n.* event, situation, occasion, accident, outcome, chance, luck 1936, 3720, 4228, 5275, 5363; *for alle ~* whatever befalls 12723, 15436

chepe *n.* bargain; *grete chepe* in great supply 15526, 15535

chere, chiere *n.* manner, behaviour, mien 2540, 4641, 5012, 6003, 8650; *mas ille ~* etc. behaves badly or unpleasantly

chese *v.* to choose 59, 293, 545, 1917, 2103; chees 4492; chese *pa. t.* 978; chosen *p.p.* 1370, 4449, 6903

chesyng *n.* choice 540, 587

chesouns *n. pl.* reasons 13617

cheuissaunce *n.* business, trade, pursuit of goods 7116, 8626

childer-getynge *n.* progeny, begetting of children 11049

chyldynge *n.* childbirth 11232

clayme *v.* to declare (oneself to be) 6016

clathe, see clethe

clatheles *adj.* without clothes, naked 8074

clene *adj.* pure, virtuous, chaste, free from 521, 558, 656, 816, 1027

clene *adv.* completely 2216, 2907, 4631, 5510, 5879

clennes *n.* purity, freedom from sin, chastity 2598, 3400, 9344, 9570, 9804

cleren *v.* to purify 211

clerenes *n.* brightness, purity, chastity 2521, 2573, 11510, 11512, 11517

clergy *n.* learning, learnedness, learned language (Latin) 84, 11508, 12267, 14540, 15516

clethe, clathe *v.* to clothe 2171, 7982, 8910; cledde *p.p.* 817, 5043, 7426, 7428; cladde 12194

cleuand *v. pr. p.* adhering, sticky 11438

clym, clymb(e) *v.* to climb 1526, 1530, 2126, 2129, 3615; climned *pa. t.* climbed 2057; clom(m)en *p.p.* 6033, 6040, 14709, 14729

cloose *n.* enclosed place, enclosure, cloister 11357, 11366

clowes *n.* floodgate, sluice of a mill 15407, 15414, 15424

combraunce *n.* trouble, difficulty,

destructive influence 5256, 6062, 8640, 9315

combred *v. p.p.* encumbered, loaded with 12436

com(e), cum *v.* to come 42, 98, 160, 312, 559; come (in long close o) *pa. t.* 1577, 2353, 3063, 4628, 5470; came 1587

comere *n.* godmother 9356 n.

com(m)onyng *n.* communion, congregation 625, 1365

comon *v.* to commune, consort with 657, 1376

comouns *n. pl.* 'commons', food 2810

compasment *n.* plotting 5125

conande *adj.* appropriate, competent 5475

condicioun *n.* state, social status, custom or behaviour, the logical sense 'precondition', esp. of sins or of confession 3050, 4857, 5461, 5481, 5511

conferme *v.* to strengthen, make fixed or firm, affirm 2347, 2410, 2661, 10400, 14102

confermynge *n.* the sacrament 'confirmation' (first communion) 9370

confounde *v.* to defeat, annihilate, beset 1980, 9317, 13032

conyng *n.* knowledge 1056

conteke, cunteck *n.* strife, quarrelling 5746, 12417, 12451, 13543, 14246

continaunce (cun-) *n.* countenance, appearance, mien 3672, 11064, 11068, 11618; *fole ~* vain sportiveness 5730, 9887

controue *v.* to contrive 13539, 13898

controuyng *n.* contriving 13972

conuersacioun *n.* habitual behaviour, social intercourse 12603, 12607, 12650

corne *n.* grain 4280, 4281, 4285, 4299, 5869

corporals *n. pl.* communion cloths 12129

corrump(n) *v.* to corrupt 2016, 11528, 11530, 11568, 11736

cosyn(n)e *n.* kinsperson 9275, 9390, 9406

cosours *n. pl.* coursers, horse-traders 7085

costage *n.* expenditure 3702, 3716, 6307, 6319, 6556

counterpayse *v.* to weigh 13561

cours(e) *n.* course (in its various senses, incl.) way, current, process, procedure, course at dinner 1769, 5575, 6561,

12049, 12052; *out of* ~ unduly,
abnormally

coustomabilly *adv.* habitually 14050,
14057

couth(e), see **can**

couayte *v.* to desire (generally, sexual as
well as financial; occasionally, e.g.
15158, non-pejorative) 971, 973, 1172,
1176, 1179

couaytynge *n.* desire 3636

couatyse *n.* desire, covetousness, the sin
Avarice 1197, 1705, 1973, 1982, 4522

couent *n.* convent, religious house 2696,
2705, 6897, 6913, 10865

couer *v.* to recover, regain strength
13026

craft *n.* skill, art, profession 5741, 6145,
6747; ~ *of foly* a profession corrupt in
its nature, a sinful trade 6159, 7094

craftyly *adv.* skilfully 1250

crased *v. p.p.* cracked 1482

craue *v.* to ask, demand 226, 235, 510,
677, 1660

crepes *v. pr. 3 sg.* crawls, moves slowly
5093, 5860, 10562, 10567

cry(e) *n.* outcry 3945, 7191, 10273,
10285, 14242

cry(e) *v.* to call out, plead, announce
2937, 3072, 7194, 8724, 10720

croked *adj.* misshapen, crippled 7126,
8006, 11203, 13506

cukkuk *n.* cuckoo 13711

cun-, see **can-**

cun(n) *v.* to show, demonstrate 3220,
13659, 13660, 14512

curyous *adj.* curious, overly fastidious,
overly ingenious 11814, 11826, 13629,
15235

curyouste curiosity, fastidiousness, undue
ingenuity or subtleness 11569, 11572,
11805, 11807, 13440, 15630

cursed *v. p.p.* excommunicated 6780,
6808, 6823

cursynge *n.* excommunication 6578,
6769, 6790

curta(y)sy *n.* noble behaviour,
graciousness, kindness, good manners
560, 1876, 2222, 6170, 6178

custome, coustom(e) *n.* practice, habit,
predilection 1034, 1052, 5167, 5745,
6427; *of* ~ habitually, as a habit 6398,
7302, 8279, 9915, 10181

D

dar *v. pr.* dare 4177, 5084, 5092, 5096,
5347; **durst** *pa. t.* 13913

dares *v. pr. 3 sg.* hides, lies motionless
with fear 13298

dasedly *adv.* indifferently, without
conviction 4992

dasednes *n.* lethargy, indifference 4985,
4991; ~ *of hert* 'tepiditas',
lukewarmness towards God

daungere *n.* danger, fastidiousness,
standoffishness 4522, 6273

dauntes *v. pr. 3 sg.* tames, breaks 7632

debate *n.* strife, contention 2185, 4685,
6992, 7199, 14317

debonere *adj.* sweet, meek, gracious 138,
2539, 4480, 4492

debonerly *adv.* graciously 327, 8704

debonerte *n.* mildness, gentleness,
courtesy 4464, 4479, 4490, 4881

dede *n.* death 391, 1082, 1088, 1241,
1294

dedeyne *n.* disdain, contempt,
contemptible behaviour 3671, 5609,
8232, 14228, 14257

dedely *adv.* to deadly effect, mortally
1098, 2924, 9198, 11107, 11116

de(e)le *v.* to give, distribute, share, have
sex with 7313, 8083, 8644, 11195,
11208

defaylle *v.* to lack, be wanting 10126

defaute *n.* fault, sin, lack, failure 2522,
2552, 2556, 3092, 3553

defautles *adj.* faultless, perfect 15159

defende *v.* to defend, refuse, prohibit
3570, 4197, 4384, 6054, 6075

defense *n.* prohibition 7252

degre *n.* step (literally in a ladder), grade,
level, the 'grade' of a relationship
(measured by generational 'steps') 1868,
3616, 3618, 3881, 3883

deynes *v. pr. pl. (sometimes impers.)*
deign, condescend 2061, 8902

dele *n.* piece; *ilka* ~ completely 6224,
7088, 7292, 12536

delyces *n. pl.* delicacies, delights (not
entirely separate from **delit(s)**) 354,
2830, 5935, 5978, 6000

delytable *adj.* delightful 2708, 9695,
12097, 12860, 14379

delyuer *v.* to release, relieve, liberate,
free 701, 1301, 1306, 3248, 3264

deme *v.* to judge 1291, 1338, 1620, 1710, 2077

demynge *n.* judgement 4217, 4221, 4715, 5683, 9990

denes *n. pl.* rural deans, responsible for ecclesiastical courts 6510, 6563

depart *v.* to separate, divide, distinguish, depart 389, 846, 1867, 2095, 5531

departynge *n.* departure, loss 6135, 6140

dere *adj.* dear, precious, valuable, scarce 929, 1842, 2997, 2895, 4640

dere *adv.* dearly, expensively, at great cost 1670, 6216, 6222, 6417, 6451

der(e) *v.* to harm, injure 1083, 1152, 2949, 3025, 3763

derne *adj.* secret 11088

destayned *v. pa. t.* destined 289

dett(e) *n.* debts, what is due or what one owes, incl. penance for sin and the 'debt' of marriage 1729, 1733, 1736, 2906, 2907

deuys *n.* scheme; *at paire* ~ according to their pleasure 14401

deuotion *n.* devotion, devout behaviour, religious desire 149, 180, 482, 624, 2208

dight *v.* (also *p.p.*) to arrange, prepare, assign, adorn, consecrate (the eucharist), clothe 592, 1401, 2720, 2825, 5996

dightyng(e) *n.* preparation, adornment 9226, 13452

dynge *v.* to strike, beat 7875, 12209

dyn(ne) *n.* uproar, (noisy) disorder 3733, 5418, 5568, 5676, 8955

dynt *n.* blow(s), stroke(s) 10840, 12434, 12573

diseese *n.* discomfort 13632

disherite *v. p.p.* disinherited 4691, 6414

dishert, diserte, desert *n.* desert, wilderness, place of eremitic or strait life 12511, 12513, 12516, 12517, 12519

disy *adj.* befuddled 13076

disordynaunce *n.* poor regulation 15735, 15738

dispendes (des-) *v. pr. 3 sg.* spends, expends 10424, 13173

dispendynge *n.* expense, expenditure 3714

dispens(e) *n.* expense, expenditure 12996, 13430

dispoylle *v.* to plunder 11473

disputysoun *n.* disputation, argument 13280

distribucioun *n.* allotment, gift 2807

ditte *v.* to shut or stop up 15589

dyuyne *adj.* divine; ~ *vertu* theological virtue 1793, 1795

do *v.* to 'do', cause, perform, behave, show, put, place, affix, add 213, 217, 250, 278, 419; *pr. pl.* 323, 402, 454; **dose** *pr. 3 sg.* 38, 198, 205, 415, 466; **duse** 10363, 10644, 10745, 12172, 13491 (preponderantly in rhyme, but cf. 13564, etc.); **did(e)** *pa. t.* 547, 847, 849, 1656, 2059; **done** *p.p.* 209, 530, 576, 662, 1000; *do away/fra* remove 847 etc.; *doinge out of* expulsion from 6578; *dose parto* add to it 13795

dole *n.* sorrow, lament 1598, 2560, 4231, 5438, 5613

doleful *adj.* grievous 13740

dome *n.* judgement, Last Judgement (sometimes specifically *pe grete dome*, e.g. 8042) 1828, 2292, 6346, 6473, 6723

domesman *n.* judge 1290, 6713, 6728, 8371, 8394; **domesmen** *pl.* 8366

dosill *n.* spigot, tap 4234

dotes *v. pr. pl.* act foolishly 8583, 12868

dout *n.* fear, doubt 989, 2287, 4705, 6253, 9934

dout *v.* to fear 9810, 9935, 9940

draght *n.* drink 13078, 14786

drawe, draghe *v.* to draw, drag 639, 1118, 2325, 3145, 3377; **droghe** *v. pa. t.* drew 4125; **drawen** *p.p.* 956, 1452, 6707, 10765

drede *n.* dread, fear, doubt 373, 399, 401, 402, 403

dredeful(l) *adj.* fearful, wary 3201, 5302, 9521, 10543, 11780

dreghe, drye *v.* to endure, suffer 2130, 4509, 13879, 15615

dresce *v. (refl.)* to address, prepare 4143, 8458

dressynge *n.* preparation, plotting 4255, 4267

droupes *v. pr. 3 sg.* crouches, cowers, lies hidden 13298

drouy *adj.* troubled, disturbed 15040

drunken *v.* to drown 11400, 12435, 13010, 13016, 13020

drurys(e) *n. pl.* treasures 3795, 3797

dughty *adj.* brave, noble, heroic 3194, 3203, 12490, 13691, 15140

dures *v. pr. 3 sg.* endures, lasts 12863

dwellandely *adv.* persistently 9966

dwellandnes *n.* persistence 9969

dwelle *v.* to live in, stay, tarry, persist 62, 74, 202, 642, 785

dwellynge *n.* tarrying, delay, persistence, residence 1324, 4919, 5543, 5768

dwynes *v. pr. pl.* shrink, diminish, dwindle away 5060

E

edyfye *v.* to teach 8924

e(e)se *v.* to relieve, refresh, console 4521, 4570, 8268, 14678

eft *adv.* again, afterwards 2474, 5743, 7327, 8449

eftsons *adv.* again, repeatedly 2741

eghtels *v. pr. 3 sg.* attempts, intends 3258, 11867

egrely *adv.* sharply 2255

eke *v.* to increase 4245, 5541, 8140

ekynge *n.* increasing 5760

elde *n.* (old) age, maturity 3653, 5768, 8440, 8624, 13110

elles *adj., adv.* else, otherwise 255, 762, 922, 1140, 1147

elsyne *n.* an awl or other pointed instrument 14266

enbraces *v. pr. 3 sg.* influences, afflicts 14239

enchesoun *n.* reason, cause, occasion 4697, 4746, 5680, 6619, 7754

endored *v. p.p., adj.* gilded, golden 11727, 11906, 11946

enfamyse *v.* to starve 12550

engendrure *n.* procreation 11166, 11510

englaymed *v. p.p.* made slimy, clogged up 14664

enioynes *v. pr. 3 sg.* links, joins 1840

enoynt *v. pr. pl.* anoint, smear, grease 13763, 13768; enoynte *p.p.* 13765

enpayre *v.* to injure, damage 12321; see also appayre

enpryde *v. refl.* to take pride (in oneself), glorify (oneself), behave proudly 10556, 15650, 15653, 15670, 15681

entremees *n.* interval, space between two courses 13470

envye *n.* the sin Envy, rancour, hatred 1288, 1703, 2957, 3002, 3462

er, es, see be

eren *n.* eagle 13865

estresce *n.* oppression 7212n

euen *adj.* equal, appropriate, just 1259, 2030, 3519, 5885, 8225

euen *adv.* equally, appropriately, justly, directly, in order, often pleonastic 'indeed' 108, 295, 1011, 1222, 1772

euencristen *n. (pl.)* 'proximus', neighbour(s), fellow Christian(s) 1042, 1738, 1845, 1848, 1856

euenhed(e) *n.* equ(anim)ity, moderation 4709, 4711, 4744, 4757, 4794

euenly *adv.* equitably, with moderation or equanimity 1991

F

faculte *n.* a branch of knowledge 6747, 7608

fade *adj.* pale, dim, insipid 2421, 2423

faylle *v.* to fail (in its various senses) 1594, 1600, 1609, 1821, 2248; frequently to lack, be absent (including impersonal uses), e.g. 2155, 3099, 3231

fayl(l)yng ceasing 240, 534, 872, 1682, 2113

fayne *adj., adv.* joyous, eager 328, 3972, 4519, 6626, 7223, 12454; *adv.* preferably, eagerly 3900, 4393, 7008, 9136, 9860

fayntys(e) *n.* weakness, corruption, faintness, cessation, doubt 1431, 1997, 3927, 3991, 4168

fayre *adv.* beautifully 8316, 11588, 11770

fayred *n.* beauty, fairness 9468

fayth(e) *n.* fidelity, trust 4401, 6743, 9299, 10961, 12261 (the poet's usual term for 'the [Christian] faith' is trouth, and 4401 exceptional)

faytours *n. pl.* fake beggars 7100, 7123, 8695

fallace *n.* deceit, deception, (legal) trickery, sophistry 1168, 5694, 14012, 14180

falle *v.* to fall, befall, happen, pertain (to), belong (to), be proper (to) 110, 206, 208, 214, 347; fel(l)(e) *pa. t.* 2932, 3521, 3528, 3563, 3674; als *falles* as is appropriate 1904, 3670, 5818, 5821, 6307

falsen *v.* to misrepresent, falsify 6705, 13945, 13946, 13949, 13954

fals(h)ed(e) *n.* falsehood, duplicity 1154, 3762, 3766, 5721, 6153 famyste *v. p.p.* starved 12559

fande, see fynde

fande(n), fonde *v.* to test, tempt 652, 3208, 3222, 9859, 9864; see also fondynge

fare *v.* to travel, befall, behave, persist (in a behaviour) 382, 4540, 4666, 4668, 4670; ferde *pa. t.* fared, behaved 1872, 12492

fast *adj.* firm 2476, 3175, 11881, 15853

fast *adv.* firmly, continually, completely, quickly 769, 1396, 1884, 2040, 2311

fastly *adv.* firmly, continually 11958, 11963

fatte *adj.* fat, fertile 7522, 7754, 7760, 13260

fauorable *adj.* pleasant, kind, showing favour 8422

fauour *n.* grace, privilege, favouritism 2035, 6718, 6722, 6903, 7502

fauourlesse *adj.* lacking kindness 8425

feblesce, febillesce *n.* feebleness, frailty 3212, 5190, 10563

fe(e) *n.* livestock, property, payment 6247, 6313, 6614, 7174, 7224; *clerk of* ∼ official of a feudal court

fele *v.* to perceive, understand 148, 152, 247, 267, 420

felle *adj.* fierce 1101, 3121, 3744, 3845, 4264

felle *n.* skin 1433; *in flesshe and* ∼ physically complete, with intact bodies 1433

felly *adv.* fiercely 5671, 14273

felnes *n.* fierceness, sharpness, savagery 3059, 14265

fen *n.* mud, excrement 10579, 10586, 13044

fendes *v. pr. 3 sg.* defends 1650

fer *adv.* far (in its various senses) 1558, 1822, 1827, 6068, 7728; ferre 12563; ferre(r) *comp.* further 12367, 15904

ferde, see fare

ferdnes *n.* fear 417

fere *adj.* fit, healthy 4572, 13115

fere *n.* companion, mate 5441, 6468, 9404, 11075, 11166

feres *v. pr. pl.* frightens, terrifies 7394; ferde *p.p., adj.* afraid 5091; see also for-fered

ferly *n., adj.* marvel(ous), wonder(ous) 8269, 11466, 13258

ferre, ferrer, see fer

ferth(e) *num. ord.* fourth 437, 966, 1123, 1285, 1386; fierth 2764

fest *v.* to fasten, fix 1396, 1405, 2311, 2385, 2453

fest(e)nyng *n.* fixity, firmness, making firm 237, 771, 2482

festens *v. pr. 3 sg.* fixes 193, 202, 2410, 2478, 2481

fikell *adj.* false, deceitful 13762

fyle *v.* to defile, soil, pollute 220, 5855, 6795, 7294, 9266

fylyng *n.* defilement, pollution 2345, 11542

fynde *v.* to find (in its various senses), incl. provide for, invent 143, 197, 199, 262, 436; fande *pa. t.* 9791, 10194, 12901 (*subj.*), 15518; fonde 13579; funden *p.p.* 1135, 2176, 7981, 8364, 8376

fyndynge *n.* nurture, provision 6441

fynes *v. pr. 3 sg.* refines, purifies 2413, 2414, 2461

first *adj., adv.* first (in its various senses) 263, 341, 375; *adv.* 35, 115, 375; previously 7389

fysyke *n.* medicine, medical practice 13231, 13299, 13305, 13306

fitched *v. p.p.* fixed, set 15221

fitte *n.* occasion, bout 6285

flaas *v. pr. 3 sg.* flays, skins 6472, 10736

flayre *v. pr. subj.* be fragrant 10236 n., 10240, 10241

flateres *n. pl.* flatterers 13784 n., 15536, 15566

flemed *v. p.p.* put to flight 4691, 6369

flesshely *adj., adv.* carnal(ly), pertaining to the flesh 2419, 5610, 9120, 9152, 9257; *adv.* 9211, 9388, 9790

flesshe-lust *n.* carnal desire 3126

flesshe-wille *n.* carnal desire 11859

fletchand *v. pr. p.* wavering, diverted 8387

fletes *v. pr. 3 sg.* floats, bobs about 9936

flyte *v.* to contend verbally, insult, slander 7278, 13535, 14217, 14255

flytynge *n.* insult, slander 14227, 14242, 14254, 14257

flitte *v.* to pass 6286, 7598

flote *n.* wave, current 9936

flour *n.* flower, flour, the most excellent part or state 10186, 11685, 11709, 11719; *in hir flours* flourishing, in her prime or beauty 4131

flum(me) *n.* river 9542, 9549

fole *adj.* foolish 3639, 3702, 3703, 3705, 3713; but also potentially 'foul' (see 7674 n.)

foly *n.* folly, foolishness, foolish (esp. bodily, sexual or bibulous) behaviour, sin 453, 459, 520, 1032, 1177

foly *v.* to do something foolish, have sex 968, 1106, 9230

folyly *adv.* foolishly 14072

fonde, see fanden, fynde

fondynge, fandynge *n.* trial, tribulation, temptation 3118, 3131, 3176, 3195, 3197

fone *adj., n.* fcw 6894, 6909, 8244, 10356

forayers *n. pl.* foragers, foregoers (who seek board and/or lodging for their lord) 8777, 8779

forbarre *v.* to obstruct, deprive of (a right, etc.) 6636

forbede *v. pr. pl.* forbid 1009, 1107, 2643, 6849, 9522; **forboden** *p.p.* 1126, 1166, 1196, 9330; **forbedde** 9363, 9389

forbere *v.* to suffer, tolerate, allow, abstain 1021, 3014, 3190, 4470, 4472

forby *adv.* by, beyond (limits) 1967

fordo *v.* to destroy, pervert 210, 652, 1399, 1414, 2098; **fordose** *v. pr. 3 sg.* 1399, 1414, 3531, 3585, 4979; **forduse** 12993, 14874, 16038 (all in rhyme); **fordidde** *pa. t.* 9700; **fordone** *p.p.* 3602, 4684, 8505, 9454, 9576

fordoynge *n.* destruction 4254, 4263

forfare *v.* to destroy 13360

for-fered *adj.* extremely afraid, in great fear 10313; see also feres

forgeten *v. p.p.* forgotten 3020, 10557, 12741

forlorne *v. p.p., adj.* completely lost, damned 1272

formast *adj. super.* first 1393, 1637, 15661

forsake *v.* to refuse, reject, abandon 59, 325, 392, 423, 1531

forswer(e) *v.* to perjure oneself, swear a false oath 3665, 6644, 13533, 14020, 14029; **forsworne** *p.p.* 6820, 7045, 14211

forswerynge *n.* perjury, swearing of false oaths 1168, 5642, 7018, 13953, 14018

forte *adj.* strong 5846 (in the set-phrase *Sampson þe forte*)

forthy *conj., adv.* because, therefore 1871, 1873, 1875, 2079, 2501

forthinkes *v. pr. 3 sg.* (impers.) regrets 13928

forthinkynge *n.* repentance, regret 3070, 4219, 5618

forwarde *adv.* from this time forth, henceforth 3109, 10531, 10920, 11446, 13345; **fraward** 5198

forwhy *conj.* for the reason that, because 897, 982, 1779, 1869, 1899

forworthen *v. p.p., adj.* feeble, degenerate 5072

fra *conj.* from the time that 1304 (cf. 9035, 11238)

frayst *v.* to learn by trial, test, seek 1818, 3998, 4147, 4461

fraunchys(e) *n.* freedom, legal right or power, the dignity conferred by such a right 6822, 6853, 14872

fraward, see forwarde

frawarde *adj.* self-willed, stubborn 3744, 5220, 5456, 5944, 14431

frawardnes *n.* rebellion, self-will 3107, 3742, 13595, 14446, 14448

fre, free *adj.* free (in various senses), noble, generous, virtuous 292, 298, 577, 880, 1725

frende *n.* friend, kinsman 2184, 2204, 3216, 4048, 4140

fresshes *v. pr. 3 sg.* refreshes, revives 3157

frest *n.* a loan (at interest or in return for a pledge) 2910, 3065, 6222, 7974, 8108

frest, frist *v.* to lend (at interest or in return for a pledge) 2170, 6165, 6184, 6221, 6323

frestynge *n.* a loan 6166, 6177, 8102

fulfille *v.* to fulfil, fill fully 432, 682, 1003, 1113, 1319

funden, see fynde

fur *n.* furrow 12722

G

gaynsayinge *n.* contradiction, back-talk 11932, 13330

gamalyon *n.* chameleon 13981

gange *v.* to walk, go 5117, 6656, 8745, 10428, 13506; **gangande** *pr. p.* 6819

gastly *adj., adv.* spiritual(ly) 224, 229, 1047, 1496, 1782; *adv.* 813, 1096, 1506, 2143, 2735 gate *n.* way, manner, street, passage 7200, 14912, 15405, 15456

gaudes *n. pl.* tricks 7103

gentell *adj.* noble, wellbred 2836, 2838, 7151

gerners *n. pl.* granaries 7503

gers *v. pr. pl.* cause, 'make' 8931

gesce (gess-) *v.* guess, think, estimate, understand 340, 2243, 3211, 3429, 3584

geten *v. p.p.* got(ten), procured, won, begotten, born 5788, 8548, 10583, 11200; **goten** 11645

gyen *v.* to guide, rule, direct 1902, 1962

gilden *adj.* golden; *Saynt Iohan with þe gilden mouth* John Chrysostom (a literal translation of the Greek epithet) 8237

gilders *n. pl.* traps, snares 15348

gilry, gylery *n.* guile, deceitful practice 1129, 5721, 7048, 7512, 8550

gynne *n.* device, strategem 11471

gyse *n.* manner, style 13464, 13975, 15185

gisyne *n.* childbed 11230

glayue *n.* lance, spear 7745

glose *v.* to offer a (false or misleading) interpretation 13785, 13792

glosynge *n.* misrepresentation 13760

goten, see geten

grayne *n.* bright red dye or colour 2472; *litted in* ~ dyed thoroughly

graythe *adj.* ready, immediate 13509

graythely *adv.* eagerly, readily 5831

grayue *n.* reeve, agent 6375

grape *v. pr. subj.* touch, examine 5156

gre *n.* degree, honour or victory 7186

greef *adj.* grievous, serious 5764, 7871, 9263, 9276, 9280

greefly *adv.* grievously, seriously 4647, 9207, 9286, 9297, 9307

greses *v. pr. 3 sg.* grazes 14677

grete *v.* to weep 3071, 4915, 4943, 4948, 7829

gretynge *n.* weeping 3450, 4920, 4921

greue *v.* to offend, injure 653, 1010, 1058, 1152, 1155

grynnynge *n.* grimacing, making faces 5685

grith *n.* truce, sanctuary 6813, 6818

groche, grotche *v. pr. pl.* to grudge, complain, murmur, be recalcitrant 5233, 5933, 8204, 8682, 14237

grochers *n. pl.* murmurers, those resistant to God 14447

grochynge *n.* grudging (against God), murmuring, complaint, recalcitrance 1000, 1569, 5210, 5231, 5677

ground(e) *n.* the ground, the bottom, foundation, basis 686, 1194, 1241, 4292, 5001

grubbes *v. pr. 3 sg.* digs 2550, 2567

gun *v. pa. t.* 'did', began to 4913, 5948, 8023, 8415, 8813; see also **can**

H

habyde *v.* to endure, anticipate, wait for, stop 909, 2242, 2810, 3628, 4178; **habade** *pa. t.* 1232

habye *v.* to pay or atone for 6451

habyte *n.* clothing, outfit (esp. one appropriate to a specific station) 10626, 11419, 11420, 12680, 12762

hayre *n.* hairshirt, penitential garb 11426

hald(e) *v.* to hold (in its various senses) incl. preserve, consider 24, 48, 81, 89, 93; **helde** *pa. t.* 3030, 8257, 9583, 9998, 11357; **halden** *p.p.* 438, 1084, 1124, 1216, 3906

haldes *n. pl.* fortresses 9682

hale *adj., adv.* whole, complete, undamaged, healthy 2726, 4568, 4572, 4670, 5115; *adv.* completely 1484, 12385

haly *adj.* holy 3, 87, 103, 242, 421; *Haly Writte* Scripture, the Bible 87, 693, 779, 924, 934

haly (usually haally) *adv.* wholly, completely 89, 1121, 1138, 1193, 1913

hals *n.* neck 6709

halsynge *n.* embracing 5758

halt *adj.* lame 11203

halughs, hal(o)wes *n. pl.* saints, holy spirits 1513, 3683, 4642, 4648, 7276

halwe, halugh *v.* to bless, sanctify, consecrate 2372, 2378, 2402, 2407, 2412; **halwed** *p.p., adj.* holy, consecrated

hamely *adj.* intimate 11699

hamelynes *n.* intimacy 11700

happe *n.* (good) luck, f/Fortune 4546, 5633

hardy *adj.* bold, confident 1836, 2004, 3548, 3867, 4966

hardyly *adv.* boldly, (over)confidently 11889, 13754, 13765

hardynes *n.* boldness, (over)confidence 4152, 4175, 5627

harlote, see **herlote**

hast *v.* to hasten, come quickly, impel 104, 2324, 3309, 4063, 5789

hatt, see **hetes**

haunt *v.* to use, practise 118, 636, 1034, 2167, 2191

hauntyng(e) *n.* use, accustomed resort 5726, 5729, 7019, 7055

hauyng *n.* having, possession, bearing, behaviour 3610, 15189

hecke *n.* hatch, upper part of a two-part door 7136

hede, see **heued**

heghe *v.* to exalt, raise up 1544, 1545

helar *n.* saviour 10082

helde, see **halde**

helde *v. imper.* bend, incline 1593, 6718, 6730, 8541, 8703

heldynge *n.* vacillation, slanting to one side 15484

hele *n.* health, salvation 12, 701, 1428, 2881, 5490; see also **saul-hele**

hele *v.* to hide, conceal 709, 1204, 11207

hent *v.* to seize, take 2706, 7309, 13335, 13599; **hent(e)** *pa. t.* 11282, 12483, 13035; **hent** *p.p.* 3096, 11282

herber *n.* inn, shelter, resting place 1587, 8250, 9016

herber (-bar) *v.* to house, shelter 2173, 7979, 8242, 8250, 8252

herberles *adj.* without shelter, bereft 8242, 9015

heresy *n.* erroneous belief 4402, 14530

heritage *n.* inheritance, property 592, 2998, 3573, 6411, 7961

herlote-, harlote *n.* rascal, lewd entertainer, minstrel 7103, 7163, 7167, 7169, 8584

herlotry *n.* dirty talk, minstrelsy (dismissively as vain) 5689, 7168, 8582, 9626, 13179

herre *n.* hinge 1905

hert *n.* hart, deer 10645

hert-lykynge *n.* desire or enjoyment pleasing to the emotions 1842, 9885

heste *n.* promise; *þe lande of* ~ the promised land, Palestine 14346

hetes *v. pr. 3 sg.* is called, promises 5966, 5993, 6000, 6024, 9956; **hight** *pa. t.,* *p.p.* 1006, 3503, 8211, 8253, 8490; **ight** 1945, 3922, 8065, 11143; **hatt** 7320

hethen *adv.* hence, from here 1815, 4613, 6138, 6218, 6369

hethyng(e) *n.* scorn, scornful words 3736, 5695, 12455, 14488

hetynge *n.* promise, enforceable contract 6178

heued *n.* head 116, 486, 4591, 4778, 7227; **hede** (usual in rhyme) 489, 617, 1808, etc.; **hede-synnes** capital sins, the Seven Deadly Sins 1701, 2326; *on þair hede* of their own making, for which they are solely responsible 13904

heuen-ryke *n.* the kingdom of heaven, heaven 870, 2704, 4165, 4190, 11488

hewe *n.* colour, complexion 11351, 11410, 12366, 12845

hide *n.* skin 10187, 11351

hidels *n.* secret place 8844

hidous *adj.* horrible, horrifying 7227, 9004, 14385, 14562

hyes *v. pr. 3 sg.* hastens 13219

hyng(e) *v.* to hang (in various senses) incl. to depend, pertain, attend on, impose on, hang on a gallows 102, 245, 595, 1390, 1428; **hinged** *p.p.* 6709, 9593, 12589

hight, see **hetes**

hirde *n.* guardian, shepherd 4086

hire *n.* pay(ment) 2870, 6430, 6432, 6536

hirnes *n. pl.* nooks, corners 4138

hone *v.* to hang about idly 8721

honest *adj.* virtuous, chaste 3403, 8501, 9490, 10627

honeste(e) *n.* chastity 11235, 13233, 13308

honestly *adv.* virtuously, chastely 10476, 11022

hope *v. pr. pl.* think, hope, expect 681, 684, 1831, 3970, 4359

hornen *adj.* like or made of horn 14270

hose *n. (pl.)* stockings 8056

hostelle *n.* house 3129, 13278

housil(l) *n.* the eucharist 5711, 5800

housill *v.* to consecrate or administer the Eucharist 6938

houe *v. pa. t.* lifted up, raised (as a godparent, from the baptismal font) 9359

houes *v. pr. 3 sg.* waits, hovers, dwells 4028, 9137

huswyf *n.* mistress of the house 2627

I

if *conj.* although 3015, 6367 n.; see also **al-if**

ight, see **hetes**

ilyke *adv.* the same, similarly 5367

ilk, ilke *pron. demon.* each 17, 67, 82, 121, 289; **ilka** 217, 462, 604, 627, 799

ilkan(e) *pron.* each one 203, 460, 462, 602, 609

ille *adj.* evil 25, 30, 58, 191, 198

ille-willy *adj.* ill-disposed 14470

in-comynge *n.* entry, admission 6907

inmyddes *prep. adv.* amidst 6064, 10310, 11905

inne *n.* residence, dwelling place (often for an overnight stop) 8778, 8780, 8786, 11345, 13039

inoghe *adj., adv.* enough, sufficient(ly), aplenty 799, 2931, 3160, 8836, 9815

inoghe *n.* sufficiency, plenty 561, 5157, 15812

inwitte *n.* intellect, reason 4342

irk(e) *adj.* tired, weary, irritated, reluctant 906, 3948, 9866, 15936

irke *v. (impers.)* to tire, be(come) unwilling 1533, 1880, 4559, 5246, 10474

irkynge *n.* reluctance, unwillingness 5614

it *adv., conj.* yet 8689, 8829, 8933, 13223, 13623; see also **yhete**

J

iangelars *n. pl.* idle speakers, gossips 13598, 13633

iangelynge *n.* vain speech 5673

iangle *v.* to speak idly or vainly, to tell tales or gossip 10481, 11363

iapes *n. pl.* idle jests or entertainments, minstrelsy (dismissively as vain) 5727, 5732, 7120, 7179, 8587

iesses *n. pl.* gesses, straps for holding a falcon 15339, 15344

iestes *n. pl.* histories, romances 41, 7349

iewes *n.* justice, sentence, punishment 13952

iog(e)lours *n. pl.* minstrels 5731, 7099, 7119, 8584

iolyfnes *n.* revelry, selfindulgence 13226

iolyfte *n.* revelry, selfindulgence 13247

iourne *n.* day's work, journey 2869, 15203

K

kele *v.* to cool, make cool 8033

kene *adj.* fierce 3850, 4632, 5929, 5945, 11690

kenne *v.* to instruct, recognize, learn 85, 92, 569, 632, 719

kepe *n.* heed 20, 31, 451, 1049, 2947

kepe *v.* to guard, preserve, comport 32, 501, 584, 570, 946

kepyng *n.* guard (of), custody, preservation (in sinlessness) 4792, 6209, 6374, 9491, 9611

kidde, kydde *v., p.p., adj.* known (for, as), proven, revealed 2595, 5340, 5547, 5636, 5670

kynde *adj.* natural 65, 2352, 3128, 11172, 11934

kynde *n.* nature, 'kind', natural feeling 177, 533, 535, 778, 877; *godes of ~* beneficial powers or abilities that come from birth (e.g. strength or beauty) 5633; *boke of ~ of bestes* bestiary 8508, 11241–2, 13859–60 (cf. 11335)

kyndely *adj., adv.* natural(ly) 318, 614, 3014, 4421, 4472

kyng-ryke *n.* kingdom 14288

knaue *n.* servingman 1180, 2833, 10136

knawe *v.* to know (in its various senses), incl. recognize, acknowledge 58, 125, 295, 310, 317; **knewe** *pa. t.* 6736, 7685, 10563; **knawen** *p.p.* 543, 925, 955

knytt *v.* (also *p.p.*) to join, fix 184, 421, 1405, 2387, 4413

L

lack(e) *v.* to criticize 28, 3942, 4257, 7050, 12258; **lakkes** 7053

lackynge *n.* criticism 5653

layne *v.* to hide, conceal 3679, 5535, 5666, 7088, 11209

laynynge *n.* hiding, concealment 5635, 7022, 7079

layre *n.* earth, mud 11534

layte *v.* to seek, strive for 1779, 3600, 6070, 15157

layth, lathe *adj.* savage, hostile, hateful, disinclined 4402, 5044, 7075, 12262

lake *n.* blemish 3042, 3842

lange *adj., adv.* long (in its various senses) 62, 172, 179, 1063, 1208; **langer** *comp.* 642, 12553; **lengar** 1057, 1324, 5558, 8746

langely *adv.* for a long time 12717

langynge *n.* desire 1189, 14621

lare *n.* learning, knowledge, doctrine 1721, 1724

large *adj.* big, expansive, generous 3697, 3718, 7429, 10023, 13269

largely *adv.* generously 2349, 7432, 7433, 7434, 8653

largesce *n.* (act of) generosity, freedom in giving, gift or tip 560, 2284, 4889, 7194, 7334; *crye a* ~ ask for a gift

last *n.* last or form for a shoe 7628

lastandly *adv.* persistently, repeatedly 1683, 4109, 10145

lastandnes *n.* persistence, the virtue perseverence 5278, 5367, 11880, 11898

lat-, see **lette**

latches *v. pr. 3 sg.* seizes, takes 9141

latches(ce) *n.* weariness, 'remissio', lack of zeal 5105, 5189, 8430, 8788

lathe, see **layth**

launces *v. pr. 3 sg.* flings, casts 14263

lauedy *n.* lady 2627, 4092, 8211, 9791, 13277; **lady** 10636, 10637; **ladys** *pl.* 9201, 10537, 10589

lavour *n.* wash-basin 9535

lawed, see **lewed, lawe**

lawe *v. refl.* to abase, humiliate 1544, 1546, 1582, 4079, 4083

lazar, lazer *n.* leper 7460, 8021, 8025

lede *v.* to lead, guide, direct 110, 254, 313, 923, 1540

leef *adj.* dear, preferred, eager 6449, 7033, 9264

leeffull *adj.* permissible, licit 1113

leeffully *adv.* permissibly 6309, 10904, 11102, 11057

leel(l)(e), lele *adj.* just, proper, honest, prompt, loyal 1124, 1216, 1730, 3215, 3954

leelly *adv.* properly, justly, in accord with contract 997, 1746, 6431, 6524, 6526

le(e)s(e) *v.* to lose, loosen 5415, 6698, 7002, 7292, 9698; **lese** *pr. 3 sg.* 13603; **lorne** *p.p.* lost, damned 922, 9210, 13661, 14212

lendes *n. pl.* loins 12185

lengar, see **lange**

lengthe *n.* length; *on lengthe* afar, to a distance 4113, 14264

len(n)e *v.* to give, grant, lend 2170, 4534, 6213, 7499, 8079; **lent** *p.p.* 6268, 8774

lere *v.* to learn, teach, 54, 115, 123, 125, 139; **lered** *p.p., adj., n.* learned men 70, 79, 5545, 5565, 6618

lerynge *n.* learning, instruction, teaching 7611, 9566, 14478

lesynge *n.* lie, fable (often spec. of entertainment) 1167, 8586, 13199, 13642, 13797

lessynge *n.* lessening 5760

let(t)e, lat *v.¹* to let (in various senses incl.) to allow, leave (off), stop, fail, account or esteem, act or behave 1576, 3030, 3242, 4531, 4826; **lete** *pa. t.* 4065, 8021, 9016, 11787; **laten** *v. p.p.* 6312

lette *v.²* to hinder, stop, hesitate, prevent 1940, 2102, 2120, 2563, 3074

lettyng *n.* hinderance, prevention 1330, 2357, 5106, 5144, 5656

lettre *n.* the literal text (always the phrase *naked lettre*) 144n, 181, 3306; a letter or legal document 6694, 10245, 10250

leue, lief *adj.* dear, beloved 4061, 4474; as *n.* 11689; **leuer** *adv. comp.* preferably 3317, 5073

leue *v.* to leave (behind), abandon, leave off or undone, remain 1826, 2194, 2643, 2798, 3035

leues, see **lyue**

lewed *adj., n.* ignorant, unlearned 70, 83, 5565, 6944, 7618; **lawed** 79, 5545, 6618, 14660

lew(e)te *n.* justice 7077, 8952

ly *v.* to lie, follow, belong in, pertain 443, 2011, 2333, 2635, 2663; **ligges** *pr. 3 sg.* 523, 5062, 8170, 10704, 10706; **liggen** *pr. pl.* 7978; **liggand** *pr. p.* 3747

libelles *n. pl.* legal documents, usually formal petitions for redress of a wrong 6694

licken *v.* to liken, compare, imitate (derisively) 1603, 3164, 3529, 3541, 4273

lief, see **leue**

lyf-days(e) life, days of life 7739, 10455, 15963

lyflade *n.* 'livelihood', sustenance 1103, 7112, 10742

ligg-, see **ly**

liggynge *n.* lying; *harde* ~ sleeping without a mattress or on the floor (as penitential chastisement) 11856

light *adj.* easy, cheap, free, active, vain, frivolous 173, 184, 1773, 3320, 4076

light *adv.* brightly 7382, 9745

light *v.*¹ to illuminate 2579, 2615, 3040, 3413, 4958

light *v.*² to descend 34; to relieve, alleviate 15259

lightens *v. pr. 3 sg.* illuminates 1672, 2346, 2358, 9093, 15007

lightly *adv.* easily, readily 176, 2002, 2252, 2275, 3481

lyke *v.* to please, be pleasurable 46, 1072, 2048, 4166, 9650; **likande** *pr. p., adj.* pleasant, pleasurable 9650, 9812, 10274, 10674, 11653

likenyng *n.* imitation, mocking gestures 5685

lykynge *n.* pleasure, delight, desire 993, 1178, 1842, 2256, 2424

likour *n.* liquid, liquor 2396, 4248, 7378, 8195, 9632

lyne *n.* plumb-line 1954, 4794, 4823, 4853, 6750

lynne(n) *n., adj.* linen 12194, 12196, 12202, 12205, 12229

list *v. impers. pr. 3 sg.* it is pleasing to, it pleases 5042, 5045, 5058, 5132, 5172

lyther *adj.* depraved, wretched, evil 5072, 7017, 7023, 7125

lytherhede *n.* perversity, enmity 5605

lithernes *n.* perversity 4989, 5061, 5064, 5077, 7059

littelhede *n.* littleness, failure 5081

littes *v. 3 sg.* dyes, colours, stains 2409, 2435, 2448, 2472; *thurgh-litted* thoroughly dyed or suffused 2443

lyttynge *n.* staining, suffusion 2452

lyue *v.* to live 562, 1057, 2929, 7122, 7729; **leues** *pr. 3 sg.* 6018, 10818

lyuere *n.* livery, the habit given a member of a household 5967, 12217

loke *v.* to heed, search, inspect, understand 88, 127, 435, 446, 521

loos(e) *n.* praise, renown, repute 1100, 3141, 3194, 3732, 3734

lorde, louerd *n.* lord, the Lord, husband 305, 705, 1255, 1357, 1712

losenge(ou)rs *n. pl.* liars, flatterers, deceivers 3733, 13757, 13773, 13853, 13870

losengery *n.* lying, flattery, deceitful praise 1169, 3755, 5649, 8920, 13752

loue *v.* to praise 28, 449, 465, 574, 669

louyng *n.* praise 9, 1691, 1715, 3777, 3954

louse *v.* to loose(n), dissolve 2482, 2486, 6650, 10966

lousynge *n.* loosening, change 772

lout(e) *v.* to bow, kneel, honour 485, 990, 12408, 12419, 12428

lowe *n.* flame 14244

lufrede *n.* love, affection 2029

lurdan *n.* rascal, scoundrel 8696, 12590

M

mayne *n.* strength, power 2854

mayntenaunce *n.* maintaining another in his quarrel, intrusion into other people's litigation 3703, 3719

mayntene *v.* to support (both generally and at law), to keep up 5746, 6488, 6662, 7195, 11010

maystresce *n.* domination, power 13146 n.

maystry *n.* lordship, power, strength, overbearing behaviour 637, 2547, 3461, 3534, 3600; *make* ~ to behave in a lordly or overbearing fashion 6557

maystry *v.* to master, dominate 14923

make *n.* mate, partner 11070, 11244, 11337

malese *n.* discomfort, sickness 7698, 8142

manace *n.* threats 14230, 14301

manace *v.* to threaten 13538

manhede *n.* the Manhood, (Christ's) human form 1282, 12898, 12906

mankynde *n.* the human race, humanity, humane feelings 7850, 8423 n., 9604, 15920

manslaer(e) *n.* murderer 1084, 1094, 1104, 3022, 4660

marches *n. pl.* border-areas, surrounding territory 9809, 9813

mare *adj., n.* greater 180, 343, 349, 384, 503

mas(e) *v. pr. 3 sg.* makes (in its various senses) 39, 194, 351, 423, 424 (**makes** also occurs, e.g. 276, 1802, 6133)

mater *n.* material (physical and literary), significant substance, topic, incentive 261, 1554, 1585, 8898, 10452

maugre *n.* scorn, spite, contempt 14510, 14511

mawgre *prep.* in spite of (anything he might do) 5290

mawmetry *n.* idol(atry), image worship
6969, 12397

mawtalent (mau-) *n.* ill will, rancour
2970, 2976, 3095

mede *n.* reward, payment, value 14, 111,
417, 3006, 3074

medelesse *adj.* without value or reward
11641

medle *n.* brawling, quarreling, dispute
4680; see also melle

mees *n.* mess, dish or course at a meal
7777, 13480

meke *v. refl.* to abase (oneself), humble
(oneself), humiliate (oneself) 1582,
3898, 5844, 8961, 10528

mekenes *n.* the virtue Humility 1537,
1556, 1558, 1559, 1564

melle *n.* melee, fight 13543, 14303,
14305; see also medle

memor(e) *n.* memory 14202, 14750

men *pron. indef.* (for unstressed me)
(any)one, people 64, 100, 115, 176 (cf.
the fairly unambiguous 740)

mend *v. pr. pl.* amend, repent 6660

mendes *n. pl.* amends, compensation
4703

mene *v.*¹ to remember (among other uses
of the verb 'to mean') 5509, 8337,
12151

mene *v.*² to lament 5880

menyhe, meyne *n.* household, retinue
313, 4637, 4661, 4663, 7417

menynge *n.*¹ reminder 8075

menynge *n.*² indication 15656

menske *n.* manhood, honour 8870

mercyable *adj.* merciful 3420, 4176,
7351, 7435, 7440

merke *n.* mark, indication, target 1562,
5588

merkes *n. pl.* borders, edges 11485

mermayden *n.* siren 13861

mes-, see mys-

meselle *n.* leper 8188, 8218, 8229, 9540,
9560

mesure *n.* measure, the mean,
moderation, the virtue Measure, a
measure 3380, 4795, 4800, 5726, 7020;
ouer ~ immoderate 5177, 5242

mesure *v.* to moderate 15204, 15207,
15218, 15375, 15624

mete *adj.* appropriate, proper 7628

mete *n.* food (including 'the ghostly
food', the Eucharist), dinner 1610,

2723, 2728, 2732, 2739; ~ *of heuen* the
manna of the Exodus (also **aungels
fode**) 14354

methe *n.* moderation, the virtue
Temperance 1923, 1937, 1965, 2015,
2107

methfulnes *n.* moderation, the virtue
Temperance 1791

metyng *n.* measurement, measuring 7064

mette *n.* measure 7065, 7066

mychars *n. pl.* sneakthieves 8696

middynge *n.* midden, garbage-heap
11713

mykel(l), mykil *adj., adv.* much, great,
large 261, 536, 736, 751, 1026

milne, millne *n.* watermill 15404, 15406,
15407, 15412, 15418

milne-clappe *n.* the clapper of a mill
13627

mynde *n.* memory, mind 178, 871, 874,
878, 1253

mynes *v. pr. 3 sg.* digs 2550, 2553

myres *n. pl.* bogs, quagmires 15060

mirke *adj.* dark, murky 1597

mirkenes *n.* darkness 2516, 2520, 12793

mysays *n., adj.* hardship, lack of
comforts 4046; *adj.* injured, crippled
7127, 7129

mysbileue *n.* religious error, heresy
1009, 5639, 14530, 14549

myschaunce (mes-) *n.* mishap, accident
1646, 4682, 5021, 7483, 8639

myschief (mes-) *n.* mischance, ill
fortune, sin 4062, 4527, 7027, 7034,
7146

myslykynge *n.* displeasure 6136

myspays(e) *v. pr. 3 sg.* displeases 1980,
3329, 5707, 13001, 13041

myssay *v.* to slander, insult 13534, 14217

missayinge *n.* slander, insult, defamation
4239, 5651, 14280, 14293

mysse *adv.* amiss, wrong(ful)ly 4340,
5232, 6206, 10105, 13168

mys(se) *n.* misdeed, sin 1826, 2949,
3886, 3902, 4028

mysse *v.* miss out on, lack, lose, fail to
gain 684, 1518, 2265, 3472, 5290

myster *n.* need, 5774, 12972, 15492

mistere *n.* handicraft, (skilled) trade 7609

mystrowand *v. pr. p., adj.* with
misplaced or mistaken faith 15203

misturnes *v. pr. pl.* turn awry or amiss
13180

moble *n.* possession, furniture 1182

momels *v. pr. 3 sg.* mumbles 14328

mon *v.* may, have power to 4704, 6227, 6294, 6338, 6539; may *pr.* 8, 54, 93, 95, 96; myght *pa. t.* 46, 359, 502, 797, 1322

mone(e) *n.* money 3791, 3796, 3798, 3800, 3802

morgage *n.* property used as security for a loan 6266

morsel(l) *n.* a bite, mouthful, small bit of food 2725, 10746, 14866

mot *v.* is permitted to, may 34, 2378, 2403, 2458, 2478

mote *v.* to moot, engage in legal argument, bring a legal case against 5681, 6609, 6620, 6630, 6635

motes *n. pl.* legal cases 15429

motynge *n.* litigation, quarrelling 3704, 3720, 3721

mowe-makyng *n.* making moues or faces 5686

mure *adj.* demure, meek 4480

muse *v.* to ponder (? with implications of over-fastidiousness) 796, 9204, 15236

musyng *n.* (idle) thought 2736, 15198, 15200

N

naked *n.* bare, naked 144, 181, 550, 2170, 3306

namely *adv.* particularly, in particular 42, 83, 189, 315, 472

neclygence *n.* spiritual heedlessness, lack of due care 5795, 11000

nedder *n.* snake, serpent 9579, 9581, 9583, 9586, 9595

nede *adj., adv.* necessar(il)y 1023, 5626; *adv.* 251

nedely *adv.* necessarily 7231, 9775, 9826

neghen *num.* nine 7240, 7264, 9199

neghent *ord. num.* ninth 971, 1363, 6159, 6263, 7107

nere *adv.* nearly 6906, 7032, 13018, 13074 (the *adj.* 4125, 7728, 9137, etc.); ~ *half* nearly half 7032

nerehande *adv.* nearly, close to 6933, 13476

nerre *adj., adv. comp.* nearer 12066, 15903; see also neste

nese *n.* nose 4808, 9655

nesshe *adj.* soft 13240, 14760

nest(e) *adj., adv.* next, nearest 902, 1267, 3741, 4814, 6797

nete *n.* cow 2740, 13118

neuen *v.* to name 196, 259, 271, 383, 715

newe *v. pr. pl.* renew, make new 14152

nyce *adj.* fastidious, foolish 10206, 13281, 15739

nycete *n.* foolishness, folly, fastidiousness 3554, 3737, 7182, 13173

nobillesce *n.* nobility, noble status 339, 341, 343, 4170, 5725; noblesce 3725

noblay *n.* nobility, noble status 10538

noght *n.* nothing (more usually *adv.* not) 48, 692, 694, 762, 765

noye *n.* hardship, injury 4179, 4227, 5347, 7720, 13025

noy(e) *v.* to injure 4690, 6009, 11140, 13993, 14007

note *n.* business, occupation 13086, 13447

nouaylleryse *n. pl.* novelties 5748

nouthir *conj.* neither (usually coordinated with ne/na) 78, 1183, 1191, 1823, 1967

nurture *n.* (proper) breeding or training 8689, 13208

O

o-, the normal representation of the prefix a-

oblyst *v. pp.* obliged 12122 (but cf. obliged 12352)

oboun, obown *adv., prep.* above 640, 1522, 1987, 2028, 2846; abouen 12930; abowen 2123; obouen 12857; obowen 2533, 3518 (trisyllabic forms often metrically required)

occupy *v.* to fill one's time 397, 5029, 9843, 11369

office *n.* duty, special purpose 204, 438, 1949, 1965, 1984

oftsithe(s) *adv.* often, many times 364, 2494, 5135, 7884, 9198

oght *pron.* anything, something (shading into *adv.* at all) 3339, 3666, 3729, 4240, 4548

oyntyng *n.* anointing, salve 7735

oker, okir *n.* usury 1127, 2917, 5707, 6151, 6163

okerer(e) *n.* usurer 6163, 6204, 6215, 6274, 8105

okeryng *n.* usury 6190

oknawen *v. p.p.* recognized 6457

onence, onentes *prep.* with regard to,

pertaining to 986, 988, 1042, 1044, 1282

on-heued *adv.* ahead 9707

ordayne *v.* to establish, prepare, direct, dedicate, command, judge, appoint to an office (esp. priesthood) 285, 578, 881, 1011, 1016

ordaynely *adv.* ordinately, properly, appropriately 2020, 8954

order *n.* order (in its various senses), incl. a state, spec. the sacrament Holy Orders 1387, 1928, 3496, 3532, 5710

ordinaunce *n.* rule, custom 6579

orisoun *n.* prayer 524, 4127, 5185, 10198, 10247

othir *adj., pron.* (the) second, (the) other(s) 41, 199, 221, 579, 596

o(u)thir *adj., conj.* (usually co-ordinated with **or**) either 208, 223, 463, 1871, 3837

outrage *n.* excess, lack of moderation, wantonness, violence 1010, 2685, 3701, 3715, 3780; *at outrage* immoderately 10632

outrage(o)us *adj.* extravagant, excessive 3714, 9119, 12994

outrageusnes *n.* extravagant or undisciplined behaviour 13217

out-shotes *v. pr. 3 sg.* expels 3623

outwith *adv.* externally 10795

ouer-al(le) *adj., adv.* everywhere, universal(ly) 477, 759, 805, 10300, 15828

ouercharged *v. p.p.* overweighted, overburdened 2140, 15799

ouercuryous *adj.* over- or unduly ingenious 10649

ouerdaynteously *adv.* in an unduly fine or dainty way 13105, 13422

ouer-dere *adv.* too expensively 8698, 8736, 8986

ouer-felle *adj.* unduly harsh or savage 8425

ouerhippe *v.* skip over, omit 1344, 8301

ouerhope *n.* presumption 1828, 4332, 4341, 4362, 5599

ouer-large *adj.* too generous, immoderate, excessive 4345, 4351

ouer-lightly *adv.* too readily or frivilously 8900

ouer-mesure *n.* excess, immoderate behaviour 9244

ouersettes *v. pr. 3 sg.* 'oversits', delays past (a proper time) 13471

ouer-skars *adj.* unduly small, niggardly 4352

ouerthwert *adv.* crosswise, sidewise, in addition, wrongly, perversely 2174, 3244, 3315, 5907; *adj.* perverse 5577

ouertymely *adv.* at an inopportune time, over too extended a period of time 13102

owhare *adv.* anywhere 13332

P

pa(a)se *n.* pass, passage, way, step, gait 6514, 12075, 13514

paen *n.* heathen, pagan 2052, 2075, 12152, 12396

pay *n.* pleasure, principal, payment 8, 439, 998, 2430, 2875; *to ∼* at pleasure, satisfactorily

pay *v.* to please 8, 1810, 2108, 2816, 2926, 3913; *halde hym payde* be content or satisfied 6204

payne *v. refl.* to take pains, act carefully, make an effort 4242, 5773, 11381, 12720, 13698

paysebilnes *n.* mildness, tranquillity, calm 3382, 15974

payseble *adj.* mild, gentle, peace-loving 3386, 15880, 15944, 15978; **paysebles** *n. pl.* 15883, 15928

papillarde *n.* (hypocritically) sanctimonious person, someone too ostensibly given to devotion 5123, 13346

part(e) *v.* to separate, divide, distinguish, share 388, 659, 1948, 5570, 7423

partenere *n.* co-participant, partaker 7650, 8500, 15506

party *n.* part, division, segment (more strongly separable than **part**) 1234, 1482, 1773, 1914, 3668

partlesse *adj.* without a part, non-participant, excluded 6642

Paskes *n.* Easter 10383

past *n.* dough 2778

pelour, pelure *n.* fur-trimmed or -lined garments 11596, 11597

percheand *v., pr. p., adj.* piercing 14265

peris(sh)e *v.* to perish, destroy, 6063, 8022, 9726, 10304, 10318

perre *n.* precious stones 11600

pille *v. pr. pl.* pillage 6543, 10736

pynchynge *n.* grudgingness, undue fault-finding 5655

pyne *n.* pain, injury, torture 1158; *do* ~ torment, put to torture 6598, 13008; *helle-pyne* the torments of hell 11405

pynes *v. pr. pl.* torment, torture, cause pain 12544, 14144

pitance *n.* payment 6914

pyte *n.* pity, piety 390, 516, 2577, 2942, 3156

play *n.* recreation, a game 5759, 6160, 7172, 7238, 7239

play *v.* to recreate oneself, play a game 7170, 7254, 7258, 7272, 10419

pledours *n. pl.* lawyers, presenters of court cases 6612, 6669, 6678, 7567

pleyn *v.* to complain, bewail, lament, bring a legal complaint 3894, 5933, 6622

pleynynge *n.* a complaint at law 5657

pleuyne *n.* pledge; *in* ~ with pledges 13070

poynt *n.* instant, degree, item 113, 3948, 4904, 7177, 9899; *in þe same* ~ *of* to the same degree of 771; *in* ~ *to* at the moment of, in danger of 10312, 14212

polist *p.p., adj.* polished, polite, (rhetorically) refined 10284, 13574

porke-de-spyne *n.* porcupine 14269

poudre *n.* dust, earth, 2525, 2528, 2557

pouste *n.* power 3228, 4662, 11156

prelate *n.* clergyman, esp. one of rank (e.g. bishop or abbot) 4104, 6507, 6553, 6827, 6898

prest *adj.* ready, eager 6655

pricke *v.* to pierce (and incite) 11718, 14259, 15574

prys *n.* price, value, prize, honour 3202, 3695, 3791, 4350, 5267

pryue *adj.* private, one's own, hidden, retired, secret, intimate, domestic or household 2840, 3807, 4137, 4146, 4679; *lettre* ~ a close or sealed letter 10257 (cf. **lettre with seele** 10253)

priuely *adv.* secretly 12401, 14326

priuyleged *adj.* distinguished, having special status 155

priuite *n.* secret(s), mystery, privacy 3828, 5665, 5698, 6211; *þe boke of priuytees* the Apocalypse 6082

procuracyes *n. pl.* costs of maintaining a visiting prelate 6558

procuratour *n.* representative, advocate 6613, 6679, 6692

professioun *n.* religious vows or commitment 7176, 9255, 9270, 11323, 12346

propre *adj.* private, personal, one's own; thus apt to, befitting (this person) 718, 747, 12614, 13547

proprely *adv.* appropriately, specifically 729, 749, 780, 811, 2096

proue *v.* to experience, demonstrate, test, attempt, approve 322, 386, 1323, 1511, 1844; *to* ~ to tell the truth 7383

prouendre *n.* prebend, the stipend attached to such a living 6879

pru, prow *n.* benefit, advantage 768, 3197, 6921, 7519

pruesce *n.* strength, fortitude ('probitas') 1539, 2232, 2237, 2298, 3430

purchace *v.* to acquire, obtain, attain, effect, bring to pass 273, 1352, 2322, 3045, 3604

purpur *n.* expensive cloth treated with purple dye 15643

puruay *v.* to govern, plan one's course 1958, 4735

purueaunce *n.* foresight 1935, 13361

Q

quaynt *adj.* (overly) ingenious 9203, 11412, 13635

quaynt(e)ly *adv.* (over)ingeniously 9201, 9202, 9212, 9213, 10613

quayntys(e) *n.* ingenuity, cunning, contrivance (fancy headwear), wisdom 5924, 9678, 10642, 11794, 11830

queme *adj.* pleasing, agreeable 5457

quert *n.* health, equilibrium, strength 701, 2009, 2151, 4505, 4987

quest *n.* quaestor, juror 6479

quy(c)k(e) *adj.* living, live(ly), vivifying 1339, 2083, 2086, 9759, 11238

quyte *v.* to repay, owe nothing, be free 3068, 3097, 6534, 6540, 6552; **quyte, quitte** *p.p.* 2918, 6769

quytinge (qwyt-) *n.* repayment 1729, 1733

R

rage *v.* to sport (sexually) 7113

rayke *n.* (impetuous) movement or course 11135

rayme v. pr. pl. charge ransom for 4693, 6543

ransake v. to search carefully 4781, 5574, 5833

rauns(i)oun n. redemption, financial payment to redeem someone or something 1128, 6596, 11020

rauyn(e), rauynne n. theft, robbery, including various judicial forms of extortion 5705, 6152, 6499, 6501, 6584

rauyst v. p.p. raped, rapt, in an ecstatic meditative state 1500, 4155, 11818, 14737

rawe n. row; only in phrase on ~ in succession 336, 371, 975, 1563, 3457

real adj. royal, supreme 2829

rebelle adj. rebellious, insubordinate 9715, 14485

recettes v. pr. 3 sg. shelters, hides 6465

reck(e) pr. pl. care, heed 3829, 7225, 8901, 14052, 15402

reckelesnes n. heedlessness, negligence 5103, 5127, 5135, 5138, 5143

recorde v. to recall, remember 2747, 10016, 10377, 10527, 13456

recouerere n. recovery from sin, redemption 2944

reddure n. severity, harshness 2934, 6571, 8427, 8442

rede n. counsel, injunction 1081, 1292, 5065, 5248, 5827

rede v. to counsel, read, understand 22, 26, 86, 618, 1053

redeles adj. bereft of counsel 2177, 7550

regarde n. respect; to ~ of with respect to, comparison with 764, 2573, 4158, 4160, 4162 (the same word as rewarde)

reke n. smoke 14243, 14244

religyoun n. religion, bound by religious rule; man of ~, etc. person in a regular clerical status 3784, 6401, 6800, 6908, 6910

religyous adj., n. religious, a person bound by religious rule or in 'regular' status 2967, 6397, 6801, 6841, 6926

remu v. to move, stir 5364

renay v. to deny 6956, 13540; p.p., adj. outcast, exiled, cursed 3659

renayinge n. denial, apostasy 3655, 3662, 6949, 6955

renoueld v. p.p. renewed 2473

rerewarde n. rearguard 3266, 6057, 6061

resoune n. rational or proper behaviour, the faculty Reason, a reason or cause, reasonable behaviour, an account or statement of accounts 156, 1956, 1971, 2012, 2013; bi ~ properly, reasonably 5453, 9231, 13941; bi ~ of because of 8597, 11005, 12146

rest v. to rest, remain 1508, 2625, 3170, 14680, 15049

reue v. to seize, snatch from, steal from, deprive of 2420, 2806, 3539, 3776, 5364

reuerys n. pl. obliviousnesses, vain pursuits, visions 5713, 9889, 10425

reuyle v. to insult, abuse, debase oneself 3923, 3928, 14891

rewarde n. reward, regard 21, 29, 3336, 4786, 4840 (the same word as regarde)

rewe v. to have pity, regret (impers.) 2183, 4566, 6240, 6600, 6735

rew(i)the n. ruth, pity, compassion 7938, 10112

ryf adj. abundant, plentiful, prevalent 3722, 4599, 4977, 5099, 7771

right adj. direct, proper 92, 337, 550, 564, 566; ~ reson the capacity for upright judgement

right adv. correctly, properly, directly, precisely, truly 34, 133, 139, 167, 228

rightwys(e) adj. righteous, just 593, 1255, 1467, 2334, 2408

rightwisly adv. justly, with right 2268, 2288

rightwisnes n. righteousness, the virtue Justice 840, 912, 1263, 1791, 1896

rynne v. to run 1667, 2267, 2936, 4081, 6380

ryots n. pl. disorders, disorderly behaviour, revelry 453, 6446, 13143, 13178, 13179

ryotours n. pl. revellers, debauchees 13142

ritches(ce) n. richness, quality of having riches 339, 349, 352, 2244, 2248

ryue v. pr. pl. tear, break 14142; ryuen p.p. 12433

robertmen n. pl. robbers, sneakthieves 7134

rode n. cross, rood 2444, 2981, 7362, 7816, 14132 (always distinguished from rodde rod 9580, 9590)

rose n. boasting, pursuit of praise 3712, 4557

rose v. to boast, praise 2989, 3712, 4557, 7086, 8830; **ruse** 13724

rotefast adj. firmly placed (like a tree held by its roots) 2484, 5359, 8206, 12079, 12808

roun v. to whisper, confess 5867

S

sab(b)ate n., adj. sabbath, seventh day 10351, 10356, 10368, 10370

sacres v. pr. 3 sg. consecrates 12134

sadde adj. serious, sober 10283

sadly, saddely adv. firmly, stably, continually, fully, soberly, solemnly 1990, 3149, 5825, 13050

sal v. shall, be obligated to 47, 49, 55, 57, 59; **suld** pa. t. 27, 112, 123, 136, 137

sammen adv. together 1822, 3000, 4171, 7272

sare adj. painful, miserable 3979, 4570, 4694, 7813; **sarer** comp. 13368

sare adv. painfully, with pain, miserably 2051, 3015, 3070, 3903, 4486

sare n. pain, illness, injury 2172, 3897, 10009

sary adj. miserable, depressed 2180, 4564, 5826, 7988

sarzynays adj. 'Saracen' (a kind of cement) 3166

saul-bote n. spiritual health or remedy, aid for one's soul 4035, 5961, 15844

saul-fode n. spiritual food (of the eucharist) 954, 1404

saul-hele n. salvation, the health of one's soul 5085, 6070, 6575, 8643, 10033; cf. hele of saul 10149

saul-mede n. spiritual reward 4752

sautes n. pl. jumps, tumbling 7181

sauour n. taste, smell, desire/pleasure, the attractive portion of 1882, 2389, 2393, 2751, 2831

sauo(u)ry adj. tasty, sweet, pleasant to the taste 8195, 12940, 14634, 15093, 15100

sauourles adj. insipid, without delight 147

sawe n. saying, speech 1101, 1852, 13810, 13832, 14601

sawe v. to sow 11486

sawyng n. sowing, fostering 5660

se v. to see (in its various senses) 30, 86, 96, 100, 155; **sese** pr. 3 sg. pl. 323, 761, 7182, 12155, 13270; **saw(e)** pa. t. 8287, 8414, 10311, 11486, 12402; **sagh** 7476; **sene** p.p., adj., adv. seen, visible, visibly, manifest(ly) 242, 354, 359, 537, 811

seculere adj., n. in the world, someone in holy orders with cure of souls, a priest 6841, 9425, 9428

see n. seat 12468

seles v. pr. 3 sg. seals, seals up, hides away 6459, 7060

semand(e) pr. p., adj. seemly, befitting 488, 1469, 1734, 11364, 13645 (in addition to use as pr. p. 'seeming', e.g. 853)

sembla(u)nd (-aunt) n. face or semblance, token, behaviour 7749, 8567, 9383, 10217, 13804

seme v. to seem (in its various senses) 1472, 1709, 1714, 1725, 1749; to ~ ? as is fitting 8454

semy adj. quick, nimble, prompt 4102 n.

sen conj. since 683, 5119, 7255, 7268, 7369; see also **sithen**

sentence n. meaning, sense, opinion, judgement or condemnation 172, 179, 183, 189, 6790

sepulture n. burial 8478, 8484

sere adj. various 87, 203, 204, 1482, 1901

seruage n. bondage, slavery, service 703, 1030, 14350, 15231; werk of ~ servile work, labour and/or sinful occupations 1030

serue v. to serve, preserve, deserve 230, 439, 570, 571, 990

sesoun n. season; in ~ ripe, seasonable (-bly), appropriate(ly) 4299, 7753, 13310, 13324

sette v. to set (in its various senses), incl. to assign, direct, adjust, plant 108, 128, 188, 381, 993; ~ to to add 6271; ~ bi to assess, value 8900, 14716; ~ at noght to assess as valueless 13905

sewet n. suit, right to leave 6595

shameful adj. shamefast, filled with shame, shameful 3180, 8609, 10640, 11065, 11092

shamefulnes n. modesty 11778

shende v. to harm, destroy 2240, 3120, 3270, 5064, 5136; **shent** p.p. 4579, 5208, 5906, 6227, 6384 shen(d)ship *n.* shame, disgrace 10, 644, 3217, 10535, 11590

shew(e) *v.* to show, demonstrate, display (often reflexive ∼ *him/it*), reveal, tell 69, 82, 277, 279, 338; shewed *p.p.* visible, manifest 69

shewynge *n.* appearance, revelation, demonstration, discussion 1692, 1721, 2423, 3090, 4717

shille *adj.* loud, shrill 4119

shone *v.* to avoid, refuse 12395, 13689

sho(o) *n.* shoe 7627, 7630; shone *pl.* 8056

shrewe *n.* scoundrel, cursed person 7624, 10864

shryue *v.* to confess orally 3902, 3903, 4366, 5023, 5068; shryuen *p.p.* 5569, 5848, 5879

sibbe *adj.* related (to) 9361, 9382, 9384, 9391, 9392

sib(be)red *n.* consanguinity, (spiritual) relationship 9367, 9368, 9369, 9378, 9380

syde *adv.* widely 11416

siker *adj.* certain, secure, stable, confident 51, 81, 119, 591, 600

sikerly *adv.* certainly, s(ec)urely, firmly 2008, 2312, 5318, 11721, 11870

sikernes *n.* security 1475, 2709, 5276, 5321

symplesce *n.* simpleness, straightforwardness 14182

sis(s)our *n.* juryman 6611, 6655

sithe *n.* time(s) (often singular in plural sense) 9199, 9542, 9562, 12023, 12052

sithen *adv.*, *conj.* afterwards, after, since 326, 1584, 4283, 5198; sethen 9139, 10353, 13088, 13445

skars(e) *adj.*, *adv.* niggardly, mean 6133, 13267, 13281, 13298, 13349; *adv.* 7065

skathe *n.* harm, damage, injury 5135, 5992, 6564, 6653, 7282

skathe *v.* to harm, injure 14010

skiftes *v. pr. pl.* divide up, parcel out 5762

skill(e) *n.* reason, wisdom 136, 197, 249, 318, 467; *by/thurgh* ∼ reasonably, properly, appropriately

skil(le)ful(l) *adj.* reasonable, appropriate 510, 678, 1416, 2306, 5301

skippe *v.* to move quickly 4081

skomfyte *v.* to defeat, disconcert 4882, 5964, 6077, 9608; skonfyte 12531

skotte *n.* tavern-reckoning, bill, what one owes 13091

skrykyng *n.* shrieking, outcry 5676

skrythe *v.* to slip, slide 4589

skulk *v.* to slink, move furtively 8412, 9858

sla(a) *v.* to slay, kill 967, 1065, 1078, 1096, 5256; slayne *p.p.* 1092, 7755, 9317, 11146, 11153; slawe 5169, 5260

slaere *n.* killer 1090

slecken *v.* to slake, alleviate 5485, 8036, 9741, 10296, 12535

sleghe *adj.* clever, intelligent, sly 4769, 4845, 4855, 6739, 9124

sleghely *adv.* cleverly, wisely, slyly 1948, 2259, 3145, 3755, 4122

sleght *n.* skill, intelligence, the virtue Prudence, trick(ery), stratagem 215, 1790, 4730, 4777, 5725

slocken *v.* to slake, alleviate 7462, 9731

sloghes *n. pl.* mudholes 2072

smert *adj.* active, quick, vital, violent, painful 1069, 1836, 1982, 2254, 2549

smert *v.* to hurt, harm, damage, give pain 105, 2112, 4484, 7934, 12210

smertly *adv.* vigorously, violently 3445, 12460

snare-bande *n.* binding net 9217

snecke *n.* lock, latch 7135

sneckedrawers *n. pl.* sneakthieves, home-invaders 7101, 7133

snybbe *v.* to chastise, chide 3746, 4029, 5679, 5820, 14500

socour *n.* aid, help 7157

socour *v.* to aid, help 612, 1046, 1940

soght *v. p.p.* chosen, pursued 3323, 11745; but also (all uses in rhyme) *adj.* *(adv.?)* (very loosely) present, available, ?directly, at all, very 1162, 2123, 4143, 6229, 8735

solace *n.* joy, fulfilment, entertainment (often *pl.* and dismissive, e.g. 7181) 2489, 2570, 3452, 4145, 4545

solempnyte *n.* (public) ceremony 10380, 11314, 12082

somonours *n. pl.* ecclesiastical court officials responsible for the appearance of sinners 6585

somtyme, sumtyme *adv.* on (an) occasion, once, formerly 322, 2052, 5053, 5173, 5383

sone *adv.* immediately, at once 210, 265, 529, 563, 575

sone *n.* son; *sones drede* 'timor filialis', proper respect for God born of love 402

sothe *adj.*, *adv.* true, truly 1473, 5670, 7410, 10750, 13798; *adv.* 3909, 13127, 13747, 13819

sothe *n.* (the) truth, a factual situation (in law) 730, 1024, 1473, 3909, 4574

sothen *v. p.p.* boiled, cooked 2780, 2781

sothfast *adj.* true, firm 1457, 7705, 10109, 14060

sothfastly *adv.* truly, firmly 757, 769, 781, 1348, 2537

sothfastnes *n.* truth(fulness) 686, 720, 829, 831, 914

soune *n.* sound 13827

souerayne *adj.* surpassing, superlative, pre-eminent 1517, 1864, 1865, 1866, 2376

souerayne *n.* lord, master, superior 1747, 3680, 3684, 4503, 4506

soueraynely *adv.* primarily, pre-eminently 10149

spar(e) *v.* to spare (in its various senses), incl. desist from (an act or from harming a person), save, hoard, starve (and discipline) 1651, 5956, 6134, 6518, 7040

spede *n.* benefit 246; *ful gode* ~ very swiftly 1299

spede *v.* to profit, prosper, do well, give or have success 5, 252, 265, 314, 600

spense *n.* expenses, expenditure 3756, 6378

sper(re) *v.* to shut up or out 2276, 7468, 7472, 9641, 9669

spycery *n.* various spices 8196

spire *v.* to inquire 5697

spyres *v. pr. 3 sg.* sprouts, ears 4283

spitell *n.* hospital, hospice 8184

spore *n.* spur, a game 7170 (elsewhere only in *Jacob's Well*)

sposaylle *n.* marriage, wedlock 1110, 6833, 6838, 9296, 9396

spousebreke *n.* violation of bonds or laws concerning marriage 6832

sprentes *v. pr. pl.* spring up, bubble out 941, 14291

springe *v.* to well up, spring out, sprout 506, 935, 943, 2161, 2296

stable *v.* make stable, establish, guide 422, 3170, 9069, 10994, 10998

stadde, stedde *v. p.p.* placed, disposed, beset 4380, 7139, 7465

stalwarde *adj.* strong, firm, resolute, overpowering 1835, 2761, 2774, 4966, 5018

starande *pr. p.*, *adj.* shining, ? ostentatious 11411

state *n.* condition of life, order, place, (great) rank or status 652, 1928, 2122, 3010, 3599

stede *n.* place (incl. textual locus), farmstead 108, 473, 480, 490, 807; *stand in (mykel)* ~ to be of (great) value 7984, 8765, 8784, 10850; *in* ~ *(of)* in the place (of), as a substitute 3367, 3621

steghe *n.* ladder 1526, 1530, 1532, 1534, 3616

stey, steghe *v. pa. t.* ascended 1328, 10386

stycke *v.* to fix firmly 4268; stoken *p.p.* closed, shut up 9681

stifly *adv.* valiantly, firmly 1997

stille *adj.*, *adv.* quiet(ly), continually 18, 1133, 3030, 3247, 4739; *loude or* ~ in any (whatever the) condition 206 n., 1690, 2068, 2209, 6972

stir *v.* to stir, move, incite 229, 295, 777, 1454, 1519; stird(e) *p.p.* 3180, 11962

stiryng *n.* movement, change, impulse 774, 784, 4498, 11717, 15004

stirte *v. pa. t.* started (up), moved quickly 12481

stoken, see stycke

stoppe *v.* to obstruct, stop up, reduce (a debt) 6181, 6291, 15545, 15554, 15572

store *n.* items on hand, storage or storehouse, supply, plenty 2798, 6193, 6423, 7399, 7765

story *n.* (hi)story 10378

stound *n.* period of time 4291

stour(e) *n.* battle 5419, 5987, 7864, 7895

stout *adj.* harsh, overbearing 3478, 3845, 13292

strayte *adj.* narrow, confining, limited, difficult 1780, 2138, 4692, 6123, 11386

straytely *adv.* narrowly, closely, rigourously 6130, 9017, 10350, 10752, 12222

strandes *n. pl.* streams, brooks 12878

strang(e), stronge *adj.*[1] strong, in its various senses, incl. difficult 3150, 3166, 3168, 3749, 4106

strange *adj.*[2] foreign, outside one's household 8614

strekes *v. pr. pl.* stretches 10645

strengthe *n.* (spiritual) strength, the virtue Fortitude 227, 1538, 1649, 1778, 1782

stryke *v.* to beat, move 3136, 3139, 3142, 3154, 5350

strype *v.* to thresh, winnow 4286

sturdy *adj.* harsh, insubordinate 14469

sturdynes *n.* harshness, resistance, insubordination 5749

substancyele *adj.* (of the eucharist) pertaining to 'substance' or the inherent(ly divine) nature, filled with (divine) 'substance', sustaining 2844, 2852, 2853, 2858

suddeken *n.* subdeacon, the third highest state of clerical order 11326, 12111

suffraunce *n.* patience 1569, 1673, 2253, 5276, 5341

sumtyme, see **somtyme**

sundre *v.* to separate, distinguish 1913, 2457

surquid(e)ry *n.* presumption 3634, 3691, 13734, 15221

surquidrous *adj.* presumptuous 13716

swa *conj., adv.* so 16, 309, 1066, 1095, 2699; so routine, esp. in cmpds. **whaso/whareso** 62, 114, 119, 151, 203

swilk *adj.* such 7, 94, 139, 241, 367

swynk *v.* to labour 9877

swynke *n.* labour 8001

swythe *adv.* strongly, quickly, vigourously 4590, 9541, 12481

T

tables *n. pl.* boardlike surfaces, tablets, a board game like draughts or chess 982, 7239, 13197, 14048

ta(ke) *v.* to take, bestow, give 20, 21, 29, 31, 60; **tas(e)** *pr.* 1049, 1281, 1393, 2549, 3163; **tane** *p.p.* 72, 121, 564, 860, 958; **taken** 976, 11421

tale *n.* count, account, story 4669, 5139, 5490, 5732, 5767; *gifs neuer* ~ takes no account, thinks it unnecessary to render account

talent *n.* desire, will 449, 1967, 2641, 4326, 4507

tallyage *n.* giving tallies (rather than payment) for goods 6548

tange *n.* sting, bite of a serpent 9598 n., 13888

tary *v.* to delay, put off until later 4936, 5130, 5805, 6734, 8718

tast(e) *v.* to taste, perceive, experience (typically used metaphorically for spiritual perception of the ineffable) 668, 834, 857, 1244, 1345

tauernere *n.* tavern-goer, tavern-frequenter 13083

teendes *n. pl.* tithes 6787

telle *v.* to count, account, recount 61, 200, 305, 336, 530; **talde, tolde** *pa. t.* 447, 939, 1223, 2003, 2159, 3308

tempres *v. pr. 3 sg.* moderates 13168, 15376

tende *ord. num.* tenth 973, 1423, 6161, 6275, 7237

tenders *v. pr. 3 sg.* grows tender, becomes affected 1671

tene *n.* anger, vexation 2560, 5668

tenes *v. pr. 3 sg. refl.* becomes angry 14273

tent *n.* heed 712, 1007, 1020, 1185, 3163

tent *v.* to attend, heed, tend to 123, 1377, 1425, 2796, 4568

terme *n.* the end, a designated period with a termination date 5198, 6221, 10986

terme-day *n.* the day fixed as the end of an agreement (for payment) 5204, 6221

tetche *n.* habit 7631, 7634, 7639

þa *demon.* those 12, 72, 118, 125, 203

thar *v. pr. 3 sg.* is need for, needs 4851, 11682, 11720, 15322, 15599

tharne *v.* to lack, do without 6234, 7402, 7454, 8568, 8594

therf-daghe *n.* sourdough 9756

thewes *n. pl.* behaviours, virtues 1695, 7621, 7636, 9620, 10980

thigge *v.* to beg, receive food as a dole 7233

thynk *v.* to think, consider 47, 113, 362, 363, 873; *impersonal* it seems 147, 661, 5864, 6421, 6227 (e.g. methynk it seems to me 661); **thoght** *pa. t.* 8814, 8913

thirles *v. pr. 3 sg.* penetrates, pierces 10834

thole *v.* to suffer, endure, allow 387, 1092, 1286, 1639, 1641

thorne-heghe *n.* hedge of thorns 12525 (cf. **hegge** 11862) thral(le)dom *n.* servitude (to) 1033, 5958, 14421, 14886

threpe *v.* to rebuke 5669

threpying *n.* rebuking, strife, quarrelling 5645

thrungen *v. p.p.* pressed, beset 15053

tyce *v.* to entice, draw 5164

tyde *n.* time 4157, 4781, 5111, 6049, 12005

tyffyng *n.* self-beautification 9203

tillen *v.* to draw, entice, lure 7338, 9800, 13373, 13769

tyne *v.* to lose 1157, 3271, 4348, 4698, 4901; tynt *p.p.* 10431, 11821, 11872, 12418, 12574

tynyng *n.* loss 6304

tyte *adv.* (titter, tittar, tittest *comp.*, *super.*) readily, soon, quickly 178, 387, 561, 1536, 1680; see also **als-tyte**

tokenynge *n.* sign(s), symbol 8478, 10602, 10662, 11064, 11701

tome *adj.* empty 10766, 10774, 10787, 11914

tome-hande *adj.* empty-handed 10769, 10775, 10798

to-whyles *adv.* in the meantime 7293

trace *n.* track, path, model 540, 2132

trayst *n.* trust 1817, 1820, 1821, 5082, 6021

trayst *v.* to trust 1607, 1825, 1829, 3946, 3997

traystynge *n.* the virtue 'Fiducia' 5276, 5311

trantes *n. pl.* tricks, strategems 7162

trauaylle *n.* work, labour, hardship, anxiety 14, 1599, 2166, 5087, 6128

trauaylle *v.* to labour, to work upon, vex 5054, 8153, 11140, 11158, 12464

treacle *n.* 'theriac', a medicament especially powerful against snakebite 3564, 3750, 9596, 13882, 14519

tre(e) *n.* tree, piece of wood 3151, 3852, 5359, 6086, 6148

tregetry *n.* witchcraft 5722

tregettes *n. pl.* tricks, magic stunts 7120

tresoun *n.* trickery, deception, treason 2014, 3766, 5454, 5721

tressurs *n. pl.* hairnets, headdresses 10643

trewfles *n. pl.* idle or obscene talk, stories, or songs 5661, 13198; **trofles** 10482; **troefles** 13470, 13643

trye *v.* to test, prove 1024, 2779

trouth *n.*[1] trough, i.e. the baptismal font 558

trouth(e) *n.*[2] (the Christian) faith, one's pledged word, troth, fidelity, integrity 122, 550, 558, 564, 668; **trewith** 6742

trowans *n. pl.* beggars, vagrants, rogues 8695

trowe *v.* to believe, trust 4, 70, 277, 826, 831

trowyng *n.* belief, faith 3953, 3957, 14537

truffeurs *n. pl.* liars, deceivers 14002

tunne *n.* tun, barrel 4238, 9631, 14789

twynne *v.* to separate 1638, 2456, 9366, 11280, 12155

twynnyng *n.* separation, division 10963

U

vgly *adj.* horrible, horrifying 4161, 10320, 12406

vmlappe *v.* to enwrap, enclose 10297

vnbouxsom *adj.* disobedient 5220, 5471, 7303

vnbouxsomly *adv.* disobediently 3086

vnbouxsomnes *n.* disobedience 3677, 3679, 5212, 5215, 7251

vnclene *adj.* impure, given to sin, 'bodily' 2071, 2545, 9169, 9267, 9289

vnclennes *n.* impurity 1117, 2555

vnconable *adj.* inappropriate, improper 5611, 8557, 11605, 15734

vnconande *pr. p., adj.* ignorant 2178, 2399, 5823, 7552, 7584

vncouthe (vnk-) *adj.* unknown, ignorant, inexperienced 1938, 11816, 14496, 14865, 15279

vnderynge *n.* lowlyness, submissiveness 4468

vnderloute *v. p.p., adj.* subjected, subjugated 13291

vndertakyng *n.* (making a) promise or pledge 5758

vneses *v. pr. 3 sg.* breaks his ease, bestirs/disturbs himself 5051

vnhalwed *adj.* unconsecrated 6765

vnhoneste *adj.* lacking virtue, deceitful 7222, 15567

vnkeped *v. p.p.* unprotected, unpreserved 14213, 14914

vnkynde *adj.* unnatural, perverse 8632, 12994, 14143

vnkyndely *adj.*, *adv.* unnatural(ly) 8638, 9331, 9468, 13180

vnkyndenes *n.* unnaturalness, perversion 1669, 3644, 8642, 9331

vnknawyng *n.* ignorance 7677

vnleffull, vnleeffull *adj.* impermissible, illicit 1128, 1131, 6966

vnnethes *adv.* scarcely, hardly 3167, 4308, 4327, 4406, 5172

vnordaynely *adv.* inappropriately 9345

vnqwitte *p.p.*, *adj.* unpaid 3075

vnredy *adj.* unwise 5131

vnrewith *n.* lack of compassion 5638

vnskilful(le) *adj.* unreasonable, immoderate 1198, 7024

vnskilfully *adv.* unreasonably 7026

vnskilwyse *adj.* unreasonable 14552

vnsleghe *adj.* unintelligent, uninstructed 731

vnsuffraunce *n.* lack of patience 5612, 14437

vntholemode *adj.* impatient, unwilling to suffer 5212

vntholemodenes *n.* impatience, unwillingness to suffer 5225

vp(pe) *adv.* up 1526, 1558, 1906; ~ *and doun* up and down (the physical sense), everywhere, completely 1567, 1606, 2441, 8188, 14690; *(nouthir)* ~ *ne doun* in any way, at all 3154, 3180

vphald *v.* to hold up, support 9943, 10151, 12225

vphaldyng *n.* support 14957

vprysynge *n.* rising, the Ascension or Resurrection 11495

vsage *n.* (customary) use 66, 10207, 11498, 13227, 14858

vse *v.* to do or follow customarily, practice, use 64, 74, 2228, 2803, 2933

V

vaylle *v.* to avail, help, aid 2653, 4532, 5277, 7703, 14480

valu *n.* quality, excellence, usefulness, benefit 2091, 2758, 5272, 11948, 11978

vaunt *v.* to boast 13667, 13707, 13733

vaunters *n. pl.* boasters 13674

vauntyng(e) *n.* boasting 3705, 3723, 5674, 13591, 13664

venymes *v. pr. pl.* poison, fill with venom 9582, 9598, 13889, 13933, 15552

venquid *v. p.p.* conquered, overcome 15143, 15148

verray *adj.*, *adv.* true, truly 139, 532, 688 (2x), 758

verrayly *adv.* truly 4554

vertuous *adj.* powerful, capable 3038, 7494

vilayne *adj.* churlish, uncouth 9238, 9612, 9620, 9628, 11657

vilayn(e)s *adj.* villainous 8690, 9624, 13086, 13665, 14053, 14140

vilaynesly *adv.* villainously 8693, 14159, 14169, 14295, 14557

vilany(e) *n.* peasant behaviour, rudeness, sin, shame, ill usage, ingratitude 1287, 1989, 3646, 3745, 4643

vitaylles *n. pl.* victuals, food 12549

vitaylles *v. pr. 3 sg.* victuals, stocks with food 2790

W

wage *n.* payment, salary 2834, 7203, 14982

waghes *n. pl.* waves 1605

wayke *adj.* weak 5019

wayne *n.* wagon 7756

wayte *v.* to anticipate, watch for, lie in ambush for 1881, 4272, 4849, 5344, 5492

wake *v.* to wake, be vigilant or on a vigil, to watch 9937, 10935, 13172, 13189, 13473

wakynge *n.* vigil(s) 5176, 11855, 12543, 13195, 14987

wame, wambe *n.* belly, womb 1588, 2781

wan, see **wynne**

wande *n.* staff, rod 7744

wanhope *n.* despair 1824, 4333, 4355, 4361, 5214

wantes *v. pr. 3 sg.* (often impersonal) lacks, is lacking 7161, 9987, 13508, 13515, 13523

wapen *n.* weapon 1072, 12529

war *adj.* aware, wary 795, 1020, 1066, 1909, 5304

warde *n.* guardian 903; concern, dread 15599

war(e), see **be**

waryes *v. pr. 3 sg.* curses 13184; **weryed** *pa. t.* 10193, 13578; *p.p.* 9005, 14286, 15762

warysoun *n.* reward, payment 2808, 4443, 6864, 7795, 12054

warisshes *v. pr. 3 sg.* cures, heals 10815; **waryst** *p.p.* 9587, 9589

warly *adv.* circumspectly, carefully 4801

warne, see **be**

warne, werne *v.* to warn, deny, refuse 35, 4384, 6293, 6437, 7113

warnes *n.* wariness, P/prudence, consciousness 1893, 1909, 1919, 1935, 1949

warnystore *n.* storehouse, treasury 2788, 11798

wasshe *v.* to wash 8187, 8286, 9536, 9541, 12207; **wesshe** *pa. t.* 4066, 8189, 9545, 9562; **wasshen** *p.p.* 2472, 2474, 2840, 9546, 9564; **wasshed** 5856

wast *p.p., adj.* futile, vain 2082

wast(e) *v.* to use wastefully, dissipate, destroy, devastate 63, 2517, 2520, 3258, 3592

wate *adj.* wet 11535, 14395

wate, see **wyte** *v.*[1]

water *n.* water, pool 2423, 5860, 5863, 7462, 7837

wathes *n. pl.* perils 1910

webbe *n.* woven piece of cloth 12205

wedde (wede once) *n.* pledge, promise, item to be pledged 589, 2912, 6278, 6282, 6287

weddelayke *n.* marriage, marital sex 11055, 11103, 11136, 11160, 11172

wedde-sette *v. p.p.* pledged (to fulfill a debt) 7149

weghand *pr. p., adj.* of weight, grave 9324

welde *v.* to control, possess, preserve 4433, 5447, 6189, 15774

wele *n.* prosperity 1991, 5372

wellande *v. pr. p.* boiling 14290

welle *n.* spring, source 4310, 12847, 12878, 13489, 14818

weltre *v. pr. pl.* wallow 2071

wemme *n.* fault, blemish 8556, 11016, 11733

wemmeles *adj.* unblemished, immaculate 11023, 11730, 11977

wenche *n.* young person (not necessarily female, although so here) 9428

wende *v.* to travel, go 234, 1371, 1436, 1445, 1580

wene *v.* to think, suppose, believe (except in the common filler *als I* ~, usually

with connotations of mistaken belief) 340, 360, 655, 988, 1196; **wende** *pa. t.* 8285

wenyng *n.* (foolish) thought or expectation 5599, 9989

were *n.* war 4683, 4685, 7146, 10827, 12415

were *v. pr. subj.* protect, guard, preserve, keep 6288, 11723, 14910, 14927

wereyinge *n.* waging of war 4337, 4340, 4389, 4396

weryed, see **waryes**

werk(e) *n.* work (in its various senses) 446, 714, 948, 1030, 1031; *þe* ~ . . . *of sposaylle* the duties of marriage, esp. licit sex 10969–70

werked *v. p.p.* ached 13076

werne, see **warne**

werrays *v. pr. 3 sg.* wages war 3577, 3579

whese *v.* make a coughing noise, honk 5098

whethen *adv.* whence 1577, 3063, 4628, 4721, 12410

whethir *pron.* whichever (of the two) 294, 1992, 8155, 9358, 11069; whence **whethir** *conj.* 1436, 1615, 1999, 5545, 6363 (untranslatable 'May?' at head of questions 13065)

whilk *pron. demon.* which 96, 110, 196, 197, 313

whilk-so *pron.* whatever, of whatever status 10868

wycke *adj.* wicked, evil 4267, 9250, 14260 (usually **wicked,** e.g. 1208, 1445, 1922)

wydewhare *adv.* everywhere 4246

wight *adj.* active, vigorous, eager 1836, 3548, 7862

wight *n.* being, person 3363, 7449, 8286, 8798, 9005

wightly *adv.* actively, eagerly 4076, 4101

wyly *adj.* tricky, devious 4084, 6029, 11470

wild *v. pa. t.* (for usual **wald(e))** would, wished 5238, 15561

wille *n.* the will, desire, volition 58, 232, 239, 250, 292

willeful *adj.* voluntary 2250

willefully *adv.* voluntarily 967

wynne *v.* to win (in its various senses), incl. gain, obtain, earn, proceed, go, depart 192, 629, 660, 1555, 2236; **wan**

pa. t. 6190, 8546; **wonne(n)** *p.p.* 4254,
6196, 7002, 7518, 9685
wynnynge *n.* gain, profit 6122, 6139,
6299, 6301, 6303
wirgh *n.* throat 13335
wirghe *v.* 'worry', strangle, seize by the
throat 13032
wirk(e) *v.* to work, perform, make,
construct 608, 797, 829, 905, 948;
wroght *pa. t., p.p., adj.* 145, 171, 212,
315, 377
wisse *v.* to direct, instruct 718, 1909,
4866, 7591, 8769
wissynge *n.* direction, instruction 4510
wytand(e)ly *adv.* consciously,
deliberately 4399, 6465
wyte, wytte *v.*[1] to know, understand 837,
5832, 6109, 6968, 7179; **wate** *pr.* 1285,
1399, 1616, 3425, 3612; **wit** *pr. subj.*
1608; **wist** *pa. t.* 290, 3964, 6391, 8379
wyte *v.*[2] to blame 3685, 6530, 7278,
7614, 14055
wytes *v. pr. 3 sg.* passes, is transitory
8867, 12772
withhalde *v.* to hold back, retain,
restrain 1144, 6277, 6536, 6538;
withhalden *p.p.* 1133, 1146
withy *n.* the willow tree, a rope made of
willow, hence gallows 6484
wytynge *n.* knowledge, consciousness
1134, 14009, 14176
wytnes *n.* witness, the Paraclete 586,
6659, 11391
witte *n.* one of the senses, intellect, reason,
strategem (?) 188, 422, 584, 795, 856
wytty *adj.* wise, intelligent 263, 3206,
8598, 10229
wlatsom *adj.* disgusting, nauseating
1586, 1592, 9449, 9461, 14896
wode *adj.* mad, insane 3862, 4082, 4668,
6794, 6933
wodenes *n.* madness 3651, 4671
woke *n.* week 2687, 8152, 10345
wone *n.* customary behaviour, 'wont'
5170
wone, wonne *v.* to live, dwell, accustom
oneself 1350, 1658, 2370, 2584, 3383
wonynge *n.* dwelling-place 1316
wonne(n), see **wynne**
wors(c)hepe (-shipe) *v.* to worship,
honour, care for 669, 819, 966, 1050, 1062
worshepe *n.* honour, worship 452, 3141,
3682, 3777, 4014

worth *n.* value 6240, 8164, 10814
worth(e) *adj.* valuable, of value 568,
6238, 7492, 8164, 10814
wrange *adj.* wrongful, sinful, evil 1132,
5599 (2x), 5891, 6670
wrange, wronge *adv.* wrongfully,
sinfully, amiss 323, 797, 1139, 2962,
3085
wrangehope *n.* false expectation 5599,
5891
wrangewyse *adj.* wrongful, sinful 1198,
6616, 13536
wrangwisly *adv.* wrongfully, sinfully
6574, 6603
wrath(e) *adj.* angry 2548, 3745, 3910,
4647, 4654
wreghe *v.* to disclose, accuse 1698;
wreyes *pr. 3 sg.* 2566, 4031
wreghyng *n.*[1] uncovering or unveiling,
disclosure, accusation 1689, 1693, 6995
wreghyng *n.*[2] deceit 5660
wrenkes *n. pl.* tricks, strategems 6683
wreth(e) *n.* wrath, anger 552, 2971, 3446,
4483, 4496
wreth(e) *v.* to anger 408, 2924, 5436,
6653, 11830
wrye *v.* to cover, deceive 1081
wrying *n.* revelation, disclosure 6954
wrotes *v. pr. 3 sg.* roots about 12945

Y

yh-, the regular grapheme for y- (or the
letter 'yogh'), e.g. **yhates** 4811 =
yates or **ʒates** 'gates'
yhede *v. pa. t.* went, passed 10416,
11420, 11822, 12400
yhelde *v.* to yield, repay, surrender,
(pr)offer 1138, 1458, 2027, 3654, 4034;
yhelde *pa. t.* 7817; **yholden** *p.p.* 8136
yheme *n.* heed 9553
yheme *v.* to heed, guard, attend to 2078,
4692, 4723, 5458, 8367
yherne *v.* to yearn for, desire 637, 910,
1119, 1141, 1174
yhernynge *n.* desire 2211, 2368, 2376,
2657, 2755
yhete *adv., conj.* yet 201, 221, 295, 335,
582; **yhit(te)** 5397, 13714, 14252; see
also **it**
yhone *demon. adj.* that (without sense of
distance?) 8315

INDEX OF PERSONAL NAMES

I cite only 'stripped forms' without titles such as Sir or Saint and provide also the Latin by-forms, where they appear in sidenotes. I cite these notes occasionally, with a star, in situations where the English text lacks a specific reference. Thus, the list, in conjunction with the Commentary on the Text, may serve, in part, as an index of cited authorities. The remainder of the entries mainly refer to biblical figures and Christian saints whom the poet evokes for exemplary purposes.

Aaron the Jewish high-priest, brother of Moses 12191, 12197

Abiron one of those who revolted with Chore and was destroyed (Num. 16) 14337

Abraham the patriarch 8249

Adam the first man 13034

Alisaundre Alexander the Great 8811

Amalech attacker of the Hebrews in the desert (Exod. 17), who is destroyed 10826

Ambros, Ambrosius Ambrose, bishop of Milan 9909, 10063, 10659

Amon Amnon, David's son, who seduces his sister Tamar 9787

Andrewe, Andreas the apostle Andrew 1253*, 1266

Anne Anne, mother of the Virgin 11378

Anselyne, Anselmus Anselm of Bec, archbishop of Canterbury 10451, 12855

Antecryst the false prophet who will appear in the last days 6007, 6011

Austyn(e), Augustinus Augustine, bishop of Hippo 1799, 1833, 2093, 3251, 5285, 7740, 7761, 8565, 8953, 10043, 10062, 10179, 10272, 10433*, 10488, 11226, 11883, 11927, 11944, 12879, 13995, 14219, 14536, 14840, 15025, 15055, 15884

Bernard(e), Bernardus Bernard of Clairvaux 269, 3135, 3889, 3913, 9565, 9725, 10577, 11395, 11581, 11607, 11763, 11772, 11897, 11951, 13739, 14999

Berthelmewe, Bartholomeus the apostle Bartholomew 1345*, 1362

Beuis of Hamptoun the hero of a well-known romance 43

Caleph Caleb 14357

Cipriane, Ciprianus Cyprian, bishop of Carthage 10167

Danyell the prophet Daniel 8353

Dathan one of those who revolted with Chore and was destroyed (Num. 16) 14337

Dauid, Dauy (often þe prophete) David, the king and psalmist 3503, 3921, 8978, 8993, 9155*, 9675, 9763*, 9787, 9947*, 9953*, 10231*, 10267, 10305, 10556, 11621, 14811, 15459, 15466

Dyna daughter of Jacob, who wanders out and is raped by Sichem (Gen. 34) 11813

Dorcas Dorcas or Tabitha, resurrected by Peter 8065

Eue the first woman 13034, 13339

(Dame) Fortune Fortune, the bestower of temporal prosperity and need 5971

Gye of Warwyke the hero of a well-known romance 45

Gregor, Gregorius Pope Gregory the Great 565, 7806, 7877, 7885, 7907, 7943, 8277, 8661, 8835, 8883, 10277, 13095

Helyseus the prophet Elijah 9538

Hester Esther, the valiant woman hero of the biblical book 10596

Ipocrase the physician Hippocrates of Cos 13301

Iraell, Iraele Israel, properly the name of the patriarch Jacob (Gen. 32: 28); thus

the biblical 'wisdom books' 763, 1891,
3205, 3721, 5942, 7500, 7506, 7697,
7997, 8351, 8709, 8717*, 9219, 9674,
11507, 11688, 13887, 14289, 14458,
14850, 14968, 15217, 15373, 15425
Sampson (þe forte) Sampson the
Nazarene 5946, 9673
Sare Sarah, Tobit the younger's wife
11143
Sarre Sarah, wife of Abraham 8254
Sarzyne, Sarzyn(e)s follower(s) of Islam
538, 2992, 6958, 8511, 14156 (cf.
sarzynays *adj.* 3166)
Semay Shimei, who reviled David 3922
Senek, Seneca the Roman philosopher

and dramatist Seneca 8731, 10439,
11659, 15355, 15533, 15729
Simon the apostle Simon 1423*, 1427,
1429*, 1438
Sussan Susannah, saved from false
charges by Daniel 8355

T(h)oby Tobit the elder, the charitable
and suffering hero of the biblical book
7868, 7988, 7993, 8057, 8347, 8470,
8797, 10683; or, his son, also Tobit
11144, 11149, 11151
Thomas the apostle Thomas 1297*,
1326, 12820
Tullus the Roman statesman and author
M. Tullius Cicero 15006

BIBLICAL REFERENCES AND ALLUSIONS

These refer much more directly to the commentary than the text, which is often allusive and does not always mark its citations.

Genesis
1: 26–7 7342
2: 15, 18, 24 10998
2: 23–4 10956
3 13034
3: 1–6 14933
3: 7–11 15660
18: 1–15 8249
19: 1–22 8249
19: 15–17 9807
19: 17, 26 12643–700
19: 24–25 9451
19: 31–8 10979
28: 10–22 2145, 14691
34: 1–2 11813
39: 6–20 9785
49: 29–31 8491

Exodus
3: 13–14 696–712
12: 11 2721
15: 23–4 7833–44
16 14353
17 10823
20: 1–17 934, 959–1198
20: 7 14024
20: 8–11 10350
20: 12 8615 ff., 8962
20: 16 13799
28: 4 ff. (cf. 29: 4–9, 31: 10) 12191
34: 20 10771

Leviticus
8: 7–9, 13 12191
8: 31, 11: 12–15 12180
11: 44 (cf. 19: 2) 12141
15: 19–33 11187
22: 19–21 8553

Numbers
14, esp. 14: 22–3, 29–38 14335, 14565–8
15: 32–6 10350
16 14335
21: 6–9 9578
26: 51 14335

Deuteronomy
15: 7–8 8091
18: 1 12180

Judges
16 5942

2 Kings
12 10556
13: 1–29 9785
15–18 8641
16: 5–13 3921

4 Kings
5: 1–14 9537

Tobit
1: 15 8347
1: 19–21, 2: 3–9 7985
2: 1–7 8470–82
4: 7 7399–7400
4: 7–9 8797
4: 17 7993, 8057
6–8, esp. 6: 14–17 11143
12: 8 10683
12: 13 7867

Judith
4: 13 10823
8: 4–5 11350
8: 6–8 11414, 11429

Esther
5: 16, 14: 2, 15–16 10596

Job
1: 21 10571–6
5: 11 8167
14: 1, 5 10456
14: 4 (cf. Job 23: 13) 752
21: 7–13 9895
29: 16 8375
31: 19 8906
40: 20 9129
41: 11 14289

Psalms
4: 1 10556
17: 26–7 9763, 9777
21: 7 10561–2
26: 7 10268
32: 17 9706

6: 28 14283
6: 36 7435
6: 37 2953–4
8: 12–14 5917–20
9: 26 8874
9: 62 12715
11: 2–4 (the alternative version of the 'Pater Noster') 131–2
12: 35–8 12180
14: 13–14 8005–8
16: 2 5448
16: 13 11551–2
16: 19–25 7458–64, 8015–36, 15639–46
17: 12–14 8228
17: 21 2507
17: 32 12701
18: 10–12 9997
19: 12–26 7489
20: 35–6 11458
21: 1–4 8668
21: 34 15795
22: 24–30 11697

John
2 11697
4 15084
4: 24 10223
6, esp. 6: 31–5, 48–52 2713, 2842
8: 3–11 8356 ff.
8: 44 13967
10: 1–2 2318
11: 2, 12: 1–8 8470–82
13: 4–17 4066, 11697
13: 23 11697
14: 6 1018
14: 13–14 3284, 10072
14: 21 672
15: 3 9523
15: 16, 16: 23–4 3284, 10072
16: 33 15052
19: 25–7 11697
20: 24–9 12819

Acts
9: 36–41 8063–8

Romans
2: 1–2 8401
2: 13–16, 26–7 2073
3: 14 14287
5: 1–5 1863
5: 3–5 7865
5: 12 693–4
6: 3–12 12571
6: 23 11407–8

8: 13–23 15894
8: 14–17 548, 589
12: 1–2 12571
12: 3 15211, 15233
12: 5 3018

1 Corinthians
2: 9 12849
6: 18 9797
7: 3–5 11056
7: 8–9 11288
9: 22 7941
11: 5–6 10621, 15689
11: 5–7 10642
12: 12–27 3018
13: 11 15767
13: 12 809, 12834
13: 13 1863
14: 19 3317
14: 20 15787
15: 33 9619, 11655

2 Corinthians
9: 7 8658, 8687
12: 9 7865
13: 11 15894, 15918

Galatians
1: 10 11561
2: 20 897
4: 21–31 8249
4: 28 548
5: 17 9164, 9716
6: 10 8771
6: 14 12584

Ephesians
1: 14 589
2: 3 548
2: 13–17 15908
3: 17 3147
3: 26 548
4: 4 and 16 3018
4: 5 and 15–25 897
4: 27 9853
5: 8 548
5: 22–4, 33 10971
5: 22–5 11027

Philippians
2: 6–8 8238
3: 8, 13–14 12740
3: 18–19 13241–6, 14890
3: 20 12605
4: 7 15964

Colossians
1: 23 3147
3: 12 7491

Printed and bound by CPI Group (UK) Ltd, Croydon, CR0 4YY